21st-CENTURY OXFORD AUTHORS

GENERAL EDITOR

SEAMUS PERRY

This volume in the 21st-Century Oxford Authors series offers students and readers a comprehensive selection of the work of John Donne (1572–1631). Accompanied by full scholarly apparatus, this authoritative edition enables students to study Donne's work in the order in which it was written, and, wherever possible, using the text of the first published version.

The volume presents a wholly new edition of Donne's verse and prose, consisting of a selection of Donne's compositions that circulated in manuscript or in print form during his lifetime. Each text is paired with a generous complement of historical and textual annotation, which enables students to access and appreciate the excitement with which Donne's contemporaries— his first readers—discovered his famous and incomparable originality, audacity, ingenuity, and wit. The edition incorporates new directions and emphases in scholarly editing that equip students with a better understanding of the texts and the contexts in which they were produced, such as the history of readership and the history of texts as material objects.

Explanatory notes and commentary are included, to enhance the study, understanding, and enjoyment of these works, and the edition includes an Introduction to the life and works of Donne, and a Chronology.

Janel Mueller is the William Rainey Harper Distinguished Service Professor Emerita, Department of English and the College, The University of Chicago. She is the former editor of *Modern Philology* and the former dean of the Division of the Humanities at Chicago. She has published on a range of subjects in English Reformation and Renaissance literature, focusing particularly on the writings of Elizabeth I and Katherine Parr.

Seamus Perry is the General Editor of the 21st-Century Oxford Authors series. He is Professor of English Literature at the University of Oxford and a Fellow of Balliol College. His publications include *Coleridge and the Uses of Division* and *Coleridge's Notebooks: A Selection*, and, co-edited with Robert Douglas-Fairhurst, *Tennyson Among the Poets* (all OUP).

D1329888

21st-CENTURY OXFORD AUTHORS

John Donne

EDITED BY

JANEL MUELLER

UNIVERSITY PRESS

OXFORD
UNIVERSITY PRESS

Great Clarendon Street, Oxford, OX2 6DP,
United Kingdom

Oxford University Press is a department of the University of Oxford.
It furthers the University's objective of excellence in research, scholarship,
and education by publishing worldwide. Oxford is a registered trade mark of
Oxford University Press in the UK and in certain other countries

Published in the United States of America by Oxford University Press
198 Madison Avenue, New York, NY 10016, United States of America

British Library Cataloguing in Publication Data

Data available

Library of Congress Cataloging in Publication Data

Data available

ISBN 978–0–19–959656–0 (Hbk.)
ISBN 978–0–19–879764–7 (Pbk.)

Printed and bound by
CPI Group (UK) Ltd, Croydon, CRO 4YY

King James said Dr Donne's verses were like the peace of God they passed all understanding.

A jotting in the notebook of Archdeacon Thomas Plume (1630–1704), no. 8 in John Donne: The Critical Heritage, *ed. A. J. Smith (1975).*

ACKNOWLEDGEMENTS

Early modern advances in knowledge were sometimes represented as fortunate outcomes of the enhanced perspective gained by standing on the shoulders of one's predecessors. In editing Donne I have repeatedly found myself in just such a position, and I want to acknowledge preceding scholarship that has been particularly indispensable to me. First, the series of Oxford editions—R. C. Bald's *John Donne: A Life* (1970), completed by Wesley Milgate; Helen Gardner's *The Divine Poems* (1952, 1978) and *The Elegies and the Songs and Sonnets* (1965); Wesley Milgate's *The Satires, Epigrams and Verse Letters* (1967) and *The Epithalamions, Anniversaries and Epicedes* (1978); Helen Peters's *Paradoxes and Problems* (1989); and Evelyn M. Simpson's *Essays in Divinity* (1952)—as well as the Cambridge editions of Geoffrey Keynes's *A Bibliography of Dr. John Donne*, 4th edn (1973). Robin Robbins's two-volume *Complete Poems of John Donne* (2008) has yielded a wealth of contextual lore, rivalled on the bibliographical front by the ongoing monumental *Variorum Edition of the Poetry of John Donne* (1995–), under the general editorship of Gary A. Stringer. Critical and contextual overviews assembled in Achsah Guibbory, ed., *The Cambridge Companion to John Donne* (2006), and Jeanne Shami, Dennis Flynn, and M. Thomas Hester, eds, *The Oxford Handbook of John Donne* (2011) have also been invaluable resources for me.

Proceeding from books to persons, I have profited greatly from generous help and counsel provided by Peter Beal, Kenneth R. Johnston, Peter McCullough, Seamus Perry, Daniel Starza Smith, the members of the English Renaissance Workshop at the University of Chicago, and the staffs of the Bodleian Library, the British Library, Cambridge University Library, The National Archives, the Joseph Regenstein Library of the University of Chicago, and the Victoria and Albert Museum. Caroline Hawley, Ela Kotkowska, and Charles Lauder, Jr of Oxford University Press handled the manuscript and proofs of this edition with acute understanding and much professional expertise, for which I am deeply grateful. After this edition appeared in hard cover, a former PhD student of mine, Gregory Kneidel, generously undertook on his own initiative to compile a list of inconsistencies or inaccuracies in my transcriptions from the Westmoreland and Dowden manuscripts, for which he has my heartfelt thanks. The present paperback edition incorporates his corrections. At the most personal level, my late husband, Ian Mueller, advanced my understanding of relevant aspects of ancient Greek philosophy, astronomy, and geometry as well as scholastic philosophy and theology by sharing with me his own understanding of these subjects. I dedicate this edition to his memory.

CONTENTS

CONTENTS

LIST OF ILLUSTRATIONS

INTRODUCTION

By the time of his death in 1631, John Donne had become a notable figure among his London contemporaries. A supremely compelling preacher as dean of St Paul's, the cathedral at the city's heart, he also numbered among the select group of the king's chaplains-in-ordinary who were assigned to preach regularly at court and, on royal command, from the open-air pulpit at Paul's Cross.[1] Beyond his personal presence, Donne's literary reputation was gathering momentum. During the last decade of his life and continuing for three decades thereafter—from the later 1620s to the later 1650s—he reached unsurpassed prominence as an author in both manuscript and print transmission. Singly or in gatherings, his poems (and, to a lesser extent, his sermons) circulated ever more widely in handwritten copies made by avid readers or their scribes, which other readers or scribes copied in turn.[2] The first printed edition of Donne's *Poems* appeared in 1633, two years after his death, prefaced by an outpouring of versified tributes to his originality and genius. Two more editions of the poems followed in the next eight years, and three further editions in the following fifteen years. Donne's son John, who had also taken holy orders, saw 145 of his father's 160 extant sermons through the press in three major collections: *LXXX Sermons* (1640), *Fifty Sermons* (1649), and *XXVI Sermons* (1661). The son additionally undertook to burnish his father's aura of prestige by the then unusual expedient of publishing a sizeable portion of his private correspondence as *Letters to Several Persons of Honour: Written by John Donne Sometime Dean of St Pauls London* (1651).

Phenomenal although it was in its magnitude and lustre, Donne's posthumous reputation in the seventeenth century is not the concern that shapes the present volume. Rather, the guidelines formulated by general editor Seamus Perry for prospective editors of the *21st-Century Oxford Authors* series ask each 'to consider how his or her volume might convey something of the circumstances of the original appearances of the texts: the editions should be mindful not only of the chronology of composition but also that of publication'. These guidelines emphasize 'the merits of presenting texts in their initial order of appearance rather than by strict date of original composition' as well as the inclusion of evocative facsimiles to 'pay greater attention . . . to the

---

[1] See Peter E. McCullough, 'Donne as Preacher at Court: Precarious "Inthronization"', in David Colclough, ed., *John Donne's Professional Lives* (2003), 179–204.

[2] According to the editors of the *Donne Variorum* project, which will present an exhaustive record of the bibliographical specifics, about 5000 manuscripts containing works by Donne survive from the 17th century, as against 739 manuscripts for Ben Jonson and 822 manuscripts for Sir Walter Raleigh.

material history of the writings presented, conveying some sense of the ways in which they originally found their readership'.[3]

In Donne's case, such an edition must address a trio of interrelated questions: What did Donne have to say about his conception of himself as an author? What does his oeuvre look like as an output developing in time, alternating among kinds of verse and prose in the order in which he wrote and selectively allowed what he wrote to circulate, in manuscript or in print? What would be the emerging idea of Donne as author formed by contemporary readers during his lifetime, on the basis of what texts they encountered, and in what manuscripts or printed editions? At this initial juncture, some general observations are in order.

It was a standard view until quite recently that Donne could not have been widely known as an author in his own day. The scarcity of pre-1631 manuscripts of Donne's poetry and prose was taken to indicate that few people could have read any of his work during the greater part of his lifetime.[4] Moreover, we know the names of scarcely two dozen of his contemporary readers. These we know mainly from verse letters or prose correspondence that Donne addressed to them—and they have their place in the present edition. The early readers of his writings in manuscript included associates and friends from his law-student days at the Inns of Court; later, gatherings of literati and wits who clubbed together in their favoured London taverns as well as prospective patrons and patronesses among the nobility and gentry during the long years in which Donne hoped for a secular position at court or in diplomatic service abroad. Such evidence prompted the inference that a social and intellectual elite composed Donne's readership in his lifetime.

This was taken to be the whole picture until it was realized that access to Donne's work in manuscript was not limited to his friends and the elite. We now know that twenty-five of Donne's poems were published in their entirety, and another six in part, during his lifetime by a wider circle of readers, and that 60 volumes containing 154 printings and reprintings of these poems of his had appeared prior to Donne's death in 1631.[5] These findings establish that Donne's poetry had a substantially larger readership in his lifetime than had previously been thought, even though the identities of most of these readers remain unknown to us.

---

[3] Seamus Perry, general editor, '21st-Century Oxford Authors: Some Guidelines for Editors' (personal communication).

[4] Alan MacColl, 'The Circulation of Donne's Poems in Manuscript', in A. J. Smith, ed., *John Donne: Essays in Celebration* (1972), 28–46; 'Introduction', in *John Donne: The Critical Heritage*, ed. A. J. Smith (1975), 1–13; Deborah Aldrich Larson, 'Donne's Contemporary Reputation: Evidence from Some Commonplace Books and Manuscript Miscellanies', *John Donne Journal* (1995), 12: 115–30.

[5] Ernest W. Sullivan, II, *The Influence of John Donne: His Uncollected 17th-Century Printed Verse* (1993), 5–6, and Sullivan, 'John Donne's Seventeenth-Century Readers', in Jeanne Shami, Dennis Flynn, and M. Thomas Hester, eds, *The Oxford Handbook of John Donne* (2011), 29.

At the same time, however, the appearance of Donne's name (or even his initials) in conjunction with a work of his during his lifetime was a rare occurrence, whether in manuscript or in print. He is not identified as the author of either the Latin or the English edition of *Ignatius His Conclave* (1611); likewise, his poetic tributes to the deceased Elizabeth Drury in *A Funeral Elegy*, *First Anniversary* (1611), and *Second Anniversary* (1612) appeared in print without an attribution, although Donne's friends and some others knew he was the author. Exceptions to such anonymity in print include the two print publications that Donne dedicated to royalty—his *Pseudo-Martyr* (1610) to King James I, and his *Devotions upon Emergent Occasions* (1624) to Prince Charles—as well as five sermons he published in the 1620s; their title pages identify Donne as the doctor of divinity he became in 1615 and specify his ecclesiastical appointments. Otherwise, Donne's compositions generally remained unascribed, including the half-dozen lyrics on love themes that circulated as song texts in print or manuscript, as well as the single or scattered poems in the earliest manuscript miscellanies and the mostly generic groupings of his poems in their earliest manuscript collections. With very few exceptions, both the miscellanies and the collections containing his works are thought to date around 1620 at the earliest, when Donne was 48 years old.[6]

The first surviving evidence of Donne's readership attaches to his satires, a set of five highly circumstantial and tonally scathing critiques of contemporary abuses such as corruption at court and worldly motives in religion, composed between 1593 and 1598, during the height of the initial brief vogue of this genre.[7] But a decade elapses before the first evidence emerges as to who was reading Donne's satires, in an epigram sent by Ben Jonson to his and Donne's principal patron in and around 1608, 'To Lucy, Countesse of Bedford, with M. Donnes Satyres':

> ...these, desir'd by you, the makers ends
> Crowne with their owne. Rare poems aske rare friends.
> Yet, *Satyres*, since the most of mankind bee
> Their un-avoided subject, fewest see:...
> They, then, that living where the matter 'is bred,
> Dare for these poemes, yet, both ask, and read,
> And like them too, must needfully, though few,
> Be of the best: and 'mongst those, best are you.[8]

---

[6] Peter Beal, *Index of English Literary Manuscripts* (1980), 1.1: 250–61.

[7] For this dating which incorporates earlier scholars' work, see Annabel Patterson, 'Satirical Writing: Donne in Shadows', in Achsah Guibbory, ed., *The Cambridge Companion to John Donne* (2006), 118–20.

[8] 'To Lucy, Countesse of Bedford', ll. 5–14, in *Ben Jonson*, ed. C. H. Herford, Percy Simpson, and Evelyn Simpson (1925), 8:60–1.

Jonson writes of Donne and his verse in a familiar, admiring fashion that bespeaks the two poets' closeness in this period when Jonson was sending his epigrams to Donne and Donne contributed a commendatory Latin epigram to preface Jonson's satirical comedy *Volpone* when it was published in 1607.[9] Jonson further implies that Lady Bedford had requested him to obtain copies of Donne's satires for her. He has done this, and now puts himself forward as a connoisseur of these 'rare poems'—'rare' both in their quality and in their mode of circulation, in personalized copies by personalized means of transmission, to 'the best' of readers only. It was daring of her to 'ask' for 'these poemes' but, even more, to 'read, | And like them too' in their unsparing exposure of venality and folly. Lady Bedford's exalted virtue and intelligence qualify her as an ideal as well as a privileged reader. Donne's satires cannot offend in a quarter where no offence can be taken or given.[10]

Jonson comes to the fore again in or around 1608 as a likely source for Donne's satires and other earlier verse compositions. In drawing up a list of 'Manuscripts to gett', Francis Davison, author of *A Poetical Rhapsody*, itemized 'Satyres, Elegies, Epigrams &c. by John Don. quaere [seek] some from Eleaz[er] Hodgson, Ben: Johnson'.[11] Davison evidently knew (or thought he knew) that Jonson would have copies and could be asked, as a friend, for their temporary loan. This inference is strengthened by Davison's list, on the back of the same sheet, of manuscripts he had lent to others; one entry reads 'John Duns Satyres.—my br[other] Christopher'. Still further evidence comes from an epigram published by the minor poet Thomas Freeman in 1614. It indicates that Donne's five satires were circulating in some venues as a manuscript 'book', together with two verse letters, 'The Storme' and 'The Calme', written to a close friend Christopher Brooke, while Donne was serving as a member of the Cadiz expedition in 1596. Freeman addressed Donne in the guise of the Roman satirist Persius *redivivus*:

> The *Storme* describ'd, hath set thy name afloate,
> Thy *Calme*, a gale of famous winde hath got:
> Thy *Satyres* short, too soone we them o'erlooke,
> I pray thee Persius write a bigger booke.[12]

---

[9] Dennis Flynn has detected an emulation of Jonson's bravado in this, Donne's first decision to allow a work of his to be printed, as contrasted with Donne's previous misgivings about circulating his satires, communicated to Sir Henry Goodyere in a Latin letter of 1605. See Flynn, 'Donne's Travels and Earliest Publications', in Shami, Flynn, and Hester, eds, *The Oxford Handbook of John Donne*, 509–12.

[10] Jonson may be alluding as well to the formal order issued by the Court of High Commission in June 1599 prohibiting further printing and circulation of satires and epigrams without explicit permission, this to be sought presumably from the bishop of London. See *A Transcript of the Registers of the Company of Stationers of London*, ed. Edward Arber (1878–94), 3:316.

[11] British Library, Harley MS 298, 159ᵛ, cited in John Donne, *The Satires, Epigrams, and Verse Letters*, ed. Wesley Milgate (1967), lix.

[12] Thomas Freeman, *Rubbe, and a Great Cast* (1614), no. 84, in *Donne: The Critical Heritage*, ed. Smith, 72.

Christopher Brooke (*c*.1570–1628) shared a chamber with Donne at Lincoln's Inn while they were fellow students there; later the two would live opposite one another in Drury Lane. Both Christopher and his brother Samuel wrote verse, and Christopher in particular won recognition for his literary and dramatic activities at Lincoln's Inn during and after his student days.[13] Not only was he the recipient of Donne's verse epistles 'The Storme' and (very probably) 'The Calme' but, in all likelihood, of Donne's satires as well. Drummond of Hawthornden made a note that his copy of Satire 2 was 'After C. B. Coppy'.[14]

Little more than half a century ago, another of Donne's close friends, Rowland Woodward, came to prominence not merely as a reader but as the copyist of the most inclusive assemblage of Donne's compositions prior to 1600—satires, elegies, verse letters, epigrams, and prose paradoxes—that has survived to the present. The Westmoreland manuscript, now in the Henry W. and Albert A. Berg Collection of the New York Public Library, preserves generally and, in some cases, uniquely sound, early versions of the texts that it contains. Sometime between 1952 and 1965 Alan MacColl identified the handwriting of the Westmoreland manuscript as that of Woodward himself—one of the two most significant identifications among the few that have been made of scribal hands in the manuscripts of Donne's poems.[15] Because it undoubtedly stands in a very near relation to the original compositions in Donne's own papers, this manuscript possesses high textual authority.[16]

In the present edition, the contents of the Westmoreland manuscript are reproduced for the first time, in keeping with its two discrete gatherings: verse and prose composed by Donne before 1600 when he was in service as a secretary to Sir Thomas Egerton; and religious poetry composed by Donne between 1607 and (probably) 1620. The Westmoreland assemblage of Donne's pre-1600 writings composes the first unit of readings in the present edition. It is followed by a brief second unit consisting of the autograph letters Donne wrote in the late winter and spring of 1602, first cheekily informing his father-in-law, Sir George More, that he had secretly married More's daughter, Anne, some weeks before Christmas 1601, then rapidly gradating into urgent pleas to Sir George and to Donne's employer, Sir Thomas Egerton, for forgiveness of the rash act that resulted in Donne's dismissal as

---

[13] Brooke 'entered Lincoln's Inn on 15 March 1587, was called to the bar on 9 June 1594, and formally called to the bench on 11 June 1611' (Michelle O'Callaghan, 'Christopher Brooke', online entry in the *Oxford Dictionary of National Biography*).

[14] *The Poems of John Donne*, ed. Herbert J. C. Grierson (1912), 2:111.

[15] See John Donne, *The Elegies and the Songs and Sonnets*, ed. Helen Gardner (1965), lxxii.

[16] 'Bibliographical Description of the Westmoreland Manuscript of Donne's Poems', online posting by the New York Public Library, drawing on an unpublished paper by Ted-Larry Pebworth (April 1991).

Egerton's secretary.[17] Donne's marriage had the further effect of bringing to a close his earliest phase of authorship: the satires, elegies, verse letters to male friends, epigrams, and prose paradoxes that Rowland Woodward copied into the Westmoreland manuscript.

Born in 1573, Woodward was Donne's junior by one year; he entered Lincoln's Inn in January 1591. After preliminary studies at Thavies Inn, Donne himself entered Lincoln's Inn in May 1592. There, on the copious evidence of verse letters to male friends in the Westmoreland manuscript, Donne and Rowland Woodward associated with Rowland's younger brother, Thomas, Christopher Brooke and his brother Samuel, Everard Guilpin, and Beaupré Bell—law students melded by their shared literary interests and premium on wit into a companionable group that wrote verses to one another and encouraged each other's efforts. Such was the social context of the pre-1600 Donne materials in the Westmoreland manuscript.

At a later date, in the role of secretary to another of Donne's friends, Sir Henry Wotton, then English ambassador to Venice, Rowland Woodward would again be in direct contact with Donne, who visited Venice during travels on the continent with Sir Walter Chute for a few months in 1605–6. From 1608 Rowland Woodward worked for Thomas Ravis, Bishop of London.[18] Donne would give Woodward a copy of his controversial prose tract, *Pseudo-Martyr*, published in 1610, attesting to continuing contact between the two longtime friends.[19] Rowland Woodward's final appointment was as secretary to Francis Fane (1583/4–1629), first earl of Westmoreland, another alumnus of Lincoln's Inn, admitted in 1597.[20] It was for the earl that Woodward compiled the Westmoreland manuscript.

Fortunately, there is testimony from Donne in other letters that sheds light on his attitudes towards his various writings as well as his handling of the verses he wrote.[21] After his appointment as Egerton's secretary around 1598–9, Donne wrote to the friend who became closest to him, Sir Henry Goodyere, consenting to send some copies of his prose paradoxes while warning about their bravado and advising Goodyere to read warily. Aware of the risk of being

---

[17] For this collection, superbly reproduced in facsimile, with accompanying transcriptions and annotation, see *John Donne's Marriage Letters in the Folger Shakespeare Library*, ed. M. Thomas Hester, Robert Parker Sorlien, and Dennis Flynn (2005).

[18] M. C. Deas, 'A Note on Rowland Woodward, the Friend of Donne', *Review of English Studies* (1931), 7:454–7.

[19] R. C. Bald, *John Donne: A Life* (1970), 53, 74, 146, 150, 222 n.

[20] Material evidence linking Woodward and Westmoreland includes an alabaster monument to Woodward erected by his wife in the church at Apethorp, the earl's seat (Deas, 'A Note on Rowland Woodward', 457).

[21] The following discussion of the literary and textual ramifications of Donne's friendship with Goodyere is indebted to Daniel Starza Smith, who generously allowed me access to his DPhil thesis, *John Donne and the Conway Papers*, University College, London (2010).

misinterpreted, Donne also asked him not to circulate the prose paradoxes, satires, and elegies any further:

Sir, Only in obedience I send you some of my paradoxes; I love you and myself and them too well to send them willingly for they carry with them a confession of their lightnes, and your trouble and my shame...They are rather alarums to Truth to arme her, than enemies; and they have only this advantadg to scape from being called ill things that they are nothings:...Yet Sir though I know their low price, except I receave by your next letter an assurance upon the religion of your friendship that no coppy shal bee taken for any respect of these or any other my compositions sent to you, I shall sinn against my conscience if I send you any more. I speak that in plainness which becomes (methinks) our honesties; and therefore call not this a distrustful but a free spirit...To my satyrs there belongs some feare, and to some elegies and these [paradoxes] perhaps, shame...Therefore I am desirous to hyde them.[22]

Donne carefully distinguishes the grounds for dealing with his writings as limited commodities. His elegies and paradoxes might bring his social credit into question if they were to circulate beyond an envisaged audience of like-minded associates who would register and relish their complexities.[23] His satires, however, caused Donne 'some feare', for they might have been found seditious after the Court of High Commission order of June 1599 prohibited the further printing and circulation of satires and epigrams.[24]

Sir Henry Goodyere (1571–1628), Donne's elder by one year, matriculated from St John's College, Cambridge, in 1587 and entered the Middle Temple, which had close associations with Lincoln's Inn, in 1589. It is not known when Goodyere and Donne first met. In 1593 Goodyere married Frances, a daughter of his uncle, another Sir Henry Goodyere (1534–95), who settled on his nephew his estate at Polesworth—encumbered, however, with sizeable debts. The younger Sir Henry was knighted by the earl of Essex during his Irish campaign of 1599, and it was in that year, from Ireland, that he first made written contact with Donne.[25] From as early as 1600

---

[22] Leicestershire Record Office, DG. 7/Lit. 2, 308v. The Donne materials in this, the Burley MS, comprise four poems, eighteen epigrams, ten paradoxes, and copies of several letters in the hand of an unidentified scribe, which Peter Beal dates *c.*1620–33 in *Index of English Literary Manuscripts*, 1.1, 236. After Sir Herbert Grierson mistakenly reported in his *Life and Letters of John Donne* (1912), that the Burley MS had been destroyed, Donne scholars used a transcript of the MS as the source for quotations from this letter. Evelyn M. Simpson believed that it was written to Sir Henry Wotton (*A Study of the Prose Works of John Donne* (1948), 316).

[23] Achsah Guibbory, 'Erotic Poetry', in Guibbory, ed., *The Cambridge Companion to Donne*, 134.

[24] The severity of this order had its intended repressive effect; works by Joseph Hall, John Marston, Everard Guilpin, and Thomas Middleton were burned in 1599 (Patterson, 'Satirical Writing', 118).

[25] This discovery will be announced in the Oxford University Press edition of Donne's letters (in preparation). It has been determined that the letter numbered 25 in chap. 12 of Evelyn M. Simpson's *A Study of the Prose Works of Donne* was Goodyere's first letter to Donne, that letter 10 was Donne's reply, arriving after Goodyere had left Ireland, and letter 13 is Donne's explanation that his first letter had not reached Goodyere. I am grateful to Daniel Starza Smith for this

Goodyere and Donne began their largely successful efforts to maintain a weekly exchange of letters; Tuesday was Donne's day to write. Goodyere's prospects for advancement at court were severely hindered for a time by his association with Essex, who had been convicted of treason and executed in 1601. But Goodyere did enjoy the patronage of Edward Russell, earl of Bedford, and his wife Lucy (Harrington), countess of Bedford; her father had been a close friend of his uncle, the elder Sir Henry, and had witnessed his will.[26] What is more, Goodyere undertook to share the benefits of this patronage with Donne. He is credited with introducing Donne to Lady Bedford around 1607, and both men regularly transmitted each other's letters to her.

The character of Donne's and Goodyere's friendship, and specifically that of their literary interrelations, can be gathered from a number of letters in the collection, *Letters to Several Persons of Honour*, and from Donne's verse letters to Goodyere in the present edition. While Goodyere was the superior in social status and connections, Donne did not refrain from giving his friend frank advice regarding his financial extravagance and his religious doubts. More significantly in the context of this introduction, Donne's letters reveal that the two men were exchanging books: specific volumes are mentioned, and Donne reports that Goodyere's books make his own study 'a pretty library'—although this would have been no match for Goodyere's own imposing library at Polesworth.[27] Most significantly of all, Donne entrusted a number of his manuscript compositions to Goodyere for safekeeping. On one occasion Donne assumes that his friend will have 'laid my papers and books by', and asks that they be returned. At another point, when Goodyere was about to depart on a visit to Elizabeth Hastings, countess of Huntingdon, Donne writes: 'I pray send to my lodging my [hand]written Books: and if you may stay very long, I pray send that Letter in which I sent you certain heads which I purposed to enlarge, for I have them not in any other paper'.[28] Goodyere evidently had access to his friend's jottings as well as his finished drafts.

Donne's phrasing of his request that Goodyere return his manuscripts does not merely imply that his friend was safekeeping them, but that Goodyere's library had become Donne's chosen place for storing his work. He elsewhere says that the 'errand' of one verse problem he was sending to Goodyere 'is, to aske for his fellows . . . and such other of my papers as you will lend me till you return'.[29] Donne casts himself as a borrower of his own works

---

information, which he received from Dennis Flynn, one of the editors of this long-anticipated edition of Donne's letters begun by the late I. A. Shapiro. See further the fine-grained discussion of Donne, Goodyere, and manuscript circulation in Starza Smith, *John Donne and the Conway Papers* (2014), 175–307.

[26] Bald, *Donne: A Life*, 171.
[27] *Letters to Several Persons of Honour: Written by John Donne Sometime Dean of St Pauls London* (1651), hereafter cited as *Letters*, 60, 213, 235, 31.
[28] *Letters*, 69, 225–6.   [29] *Letters*, 99.

from Goodyere's library. Twice in subsequent years he would again ask Goodyere to keep manuscript copies of his poems because he had not retained copies for himself. And in a letter of 1605 Donne revealed that he was revising some of his writings, apparently with the intention of printing them. He asks Goodyere to gather together certain papers he had been sent, including Latin epigrams and a satirical catalogue of books. Donne says he will revise certain items and destroy others.[30] This intention to print some of his compositions in 1605 would not be realized; one crucial factor must have been Donne's own ambivalence. In a facetious but revealing turn of phrase, his mock Latin catalogue of books bears the subtitle 'non vendibilium'—'not for sale', with a play on the tense of the participle, 'not to be sold'.

In all of Donne's letters, Alan MacColl has observed, 'there is only one passage that refers to his actually writing out and distributing copies of a poem', and this occurs in a letter to Goodyere.[31] Regarding 'The Litanye', a moderately lengthy stanzaic poem composed probably in 1608, Donne explains to his friend that 'though a copy of it were due to you now, yet I am so unable to serve my self with writing it for you at this time, (being some 30 staves of 9 lines) that I must intreat you to take a promise that you shall have the first'.[32] Donne implies that his practice was to send Goodyere copies of his poems as soon as they were written and before he sent copies to anyone else.

Other passages in letters to Goodyere contain references to Donne's verse. In one, Donne responds to his friend's request that he write a poem about 'the Countesse'—in this context, evidently the countess of Huntingdon. Donne refuses at first, giving two reasons: to prevent her from thinking of him as a poet rather than one embarked on 'a graver course' in life, and to maintain his 'integrity to the other Countesse', Lady Bedford. Eventually reversing himself with the rationalization that Lady Huntingdon is Lady Bedford's 'Picture', an exact likeness of her virtues, Donne agrees to write, but only on the condition that he will not be 'traduced, nor esteemed light' in Lady Bedford's judgement. If Goodyere finds the verses unsuitable, he is to keep them for himself. Although Donne generally admonished his friends to prevent his compositions from coming to the notice of unintended readers, he was aware that Goodyere was circulating them. At one juncture he would

---

[30] This letter was first printed in *Poems, by J.D.* (1633), 351–2. Bald, *Donne: A Life*, 241, dated it to 1611, but as Dennis Flynn shows, drawing on I. A. Shapiro's still unpublished commentary, it was sent before Donne's travels on the Continent with Sir Walter Chute in 1605–6 (Flynn, 'Donne's Travels and Earliest Publications', 510–13). Donne's satirical book catalogue is *The Courtier's Library, or Catalogus Librorum Aulicorum*, ed. Evelyn M. Simpson (1930), which she (p. 13) dated to 1604–5.
[31] Alan MacColl, 'The Circulation of Donne's Poems in Manuscript', in Smith, ed., *John Donne: Essays in Celebration*, 32.
[32] *Letters*, 33.

administer a measured reproach: 'Some of my Pacquets have had more honour than I wished them: which is to be delivered into the hands of greater personages, than I addressed them unto.'[33]

A note of ambivalence can be detected nevertheless in this reproach of Donne's. After Goodyere introduced him to Lady Bedford, he had promptly set about cultivating her patronage by addressing verse letters of high-flown compliment to her as well as composing funeral elegies on the untimely deaths of two of Lady Bedford's intimate companions, Cecilia Bulstrode and Lady Markham. Donne had therefore been acquiring, at first hand, a sense of what advantages and prospects of advancement might follow from his verses being 'delivered into the hands of greater personages'. Within three years he made his boldest venture in this direction by writing 'A Funeral Elegy', lamenting the death of a 15-year-old heiress, Elizabeth Drury, whom he had never met, and by accepting the invitation of her appreciative parents, Sir Robert and Lady Drury, to travel with them in France, Germany, and the Low Countries. Donne further compounded his poetic and professional self-investment in the Drurys' patronage by composing and publishing his two hyperbolic, ingeniously elaborated *Anniversary* poems (1611, 1612). The *First Anniversary* equates the soul of Elizabeth Drury with the world soul and her death with the decay of the world; the *Second Anniversary* traces Elizabeth Drury's paradigmatic status and progression as a blessed soul taken up into heaven immediately after death. The present edition reproduces as its third unit of readings 'A Funeral Elegy' and the *Anniversaries* as they appeared in the first complete edition of 1612.

While the *Anniversaries* secured Donne the approbation and financial support of the Drurys, Lady Bedford's favour cooled upon reading the extravagant praises he had lavished on a mere girl. Ben Jonson also thought that Donne had committed an error of judgement in his *Anniversaries*, telling him that if they 'had been written of the Virgin Marie', they 'had been something', to which Donne 'answered that he described the Idea of a Woman and not as she was'.[34] Jonson's negative opinion must have been particularly wounding to Donne on two counts. He and Donne had formerly paid tribute to each other's work in the context of their familiarity with Lady Bedford. And now, in 1612, Jonson had become a leading figure in the so-called Mermaid Club (or Sirenaical Gentlemen)—a group of lawyers, members of Parliament, and

[33] *Letters*, 103–4, 126. The 1651 edition heads the latter letter 'To Sir H. Wootton.' [Henry Wotton], but the editors of the forthcoming Oxford edition of Donne's letters will reassign this letter to Goodyere as recipient. Daniel Starza Smith has additionally observed that, given the scale of the Donne–Goodyere correspondence, copies of Donne's letters preserved by Goodyere are likely to have furnished materials for the 1651 edition published by Donne's son John (*Donne and the Conway Papers*, 206).

[34] Jonson himself reported this exchange in his 'Conversations with William Drummond of Hawthornden', which took place during a trip to Scotland in 1619 (*Donne: The Critical Heritage*, ed. Smith, 69).

gentlemen, several of whom were also writers and wits, who patronized the Mermaid Tavern in Cheapside, off Bread Street, in London.[35]

Occasionally, Donne himself was of this company, as were Christopher Brooke, Sir Robert Cotton, George Garrard, John Hoskins, Inigo Jones, Richard Martin, Samuel Purchas, and others. Former Inns of Court men were represented: Brooke and Donne from Lincoln's Inn; Hoskins and Martin from the Middle Temple. What were London literati thinking and saying about the *Anniversaries*, which some knew Donne had authored? Print publication made for a potentially broad readership. Donne found out soon enough. In a letter of April 1612 to a close friend and fellow Mermaid Club member, George Garrard, Donne chastised himself for allowing his *Anniversaries* to appear in print (even anonymously, as already noted): 'Of my Anniversaries, the fault that I acknowledge in my self, is to have descended to print any thing in verse... I confess I wonder how I declined to it, and do not pardon my self'.[36]

Descended from a wealthy London mercantile family, George Garrard became friendly with Donne during 1607–11 when the two men rented lodgings from the same London landlord in a house in the Strand. Garrard and Donne were also affiliated as members of Lady Bedford's circle; Garrard solicited Donne to write his elegy on Cecelia Bulstrode. During his travels with the Drurys in 1611–12, Donne attempted to write to Garrard with the same regularity as he wrote to Goodyere, but several letters went astray.[37] One letter that did reach Garrard contained the passage quoted in the previous paragraph. Garrard's was an exceptionally sympathetic ear to be available to Donne in these circumstances. He reminisced in later years that he 'never had Patience in all my life to transcribe Poems, except they were very transcendent, such as Dean Donn writ in his younger days'.[38] How thoroughly Garrard

---

[35] See I. A. Shapiro, 'The "Mermaid Club"', *Modern Language Review* (1950), 45: 6–17; Michael Strachan, 'The Mermaid Club: A New Discovery', *History Today* (1967), 17: 533–8; Michelle O'Callaghan, 'Tavern Societies, the Inns of Court, and the Culture of Conviviality in Early 17th-Century London', in Adam Smyth, ed., *A Pleasing Sinne* (2004), 37–51; and Starza Smith, *Donne and the Conway Papers*, 108, 187–88.

[36] 'To my honoured friend G. G. Esquire', in *Letters*, 238. But there was a quotient of favourable reaction too: the dramatist John Webster echoed phrasing from the *Anniversaries* at several points in his writings in 1612–13 as did several of the writers who offered funeral tributes to Prince Henry, who died in 1612. See *Donne: The Critical Heritage*, ed. Smith, 36–8. On the association of attitudes hostile to print with 'the amateur poets of the Court' and the contrasting embrace of print publication by 'professional poets outside or only on the edge of Court circles', see J. W. Saunders, 'The Stigma of Print: A Note on the Social Bases of Tudor Poetry', *Essays in Criticism* (1951), 1:139–64. For Donne's further expression of misgivings to Garrard about addressing a poem in manuscript to the countess of Salisbury, see the headnote to 'To the Countess of Salisbury. August 1614', in the Notes section for 'From the Dowden Manuscript, Pre-1615 Compositions' in this volume.

[37] Bald, *Donne: A Life*, 158–9, 178, 247, 249, 251, 260–1, 277.

[38] George Garrard to Thomas Wentworth, 10 November 1634, in *The Earl of Strafforde's Letters and Dispatches*, ed. William Knowler (1739), 1.338.

had acted on his admiration for Donne's poems is evidenced by the Dowden manuscript, which Gary A. Stringer has identified as being entirely in Garrard's handwriting.[39]

This is the other of the two most significant identifications that have been made of scribal hands in earlier manuscripts of Donne's poems. The Dowden manuscript, now in the Bodleian Library of the University of Oxford, is a quarto volume of 142 leaves containing 99 poems by Donne. Even before it was known to be in Garrard's hand, it had been accorded pride of place among Group 1 manuscripts of Donne's poetry for the consistently high quality of its readings and the proximity of its inferred relation to Donne's original compositions.[40] All of the love poems in the present edition (those first captioned 'Songs and Sonnets' in the 1635 edition of *Poems, by J.D.*) have been transcribed from the Dowden manuscript, as have elegies, verse letters, religious verse, and epithalamia not contained in the Westmoreland manuscript. The unique contents from the Dowden manuscript compose the fourth unit of readings in the present edition, and the unique late items from the Westmoreland manuscript compose the fifth. These two collections in the handwriting of two of Donne's friends thus stand here in a mutually complementary relation, bearing material witness to the earliest recoverable stage of access to Donne's poetry by readers who were his contemporaries and friends, and became his copyists.

In the eyes of twentieth-century editors of Donne, the great significance of the Dowden manuscript lay in its being the closest extant witness to a collection that Donne was making of his poems with the intention of publishing them in late 1614, as his farewell to the world before taking holy orders. Donne's startling revival of interest in print publication a mere two years after berating himself for printing his *Anniversaries* indicates just how acute was the personal and professional dilemma confronting him at this date.[41] In a court that witnessed factional struggles after the deaths of the much admired heir to the throne, Prince Henry, and the king's chief minister, Robert Cecil, earl of Salisbury, in 1612, a new royal favourite, Robert Carr, catapulted to

[39] Gary Stringer made the claim that the entirety of the Dowden manuscript, Bodleian, MS Eng. poet. e. 99, is in George Garrard's handwriting as a respondent to a panel on 'Digitizing Donne' at the John Donne Society conference in February 2009. Daniel Starza Smith, who concurs in Stringer's identification, is the source of this information.

[40] Peter Beal classifies the Dowden manuscript as Delta 1, the lead item in his census of manuscript collections of poems by Donne, and dates it *c.*1620–33 (*Index of English Literary Manuscripts*, 1.1, 250). For characterizations of the contents and editorial significance of manuscript Groups 1, 2, and 3 of Donne's verse, see *The Divine Poems*, ed. Helen Gardner, rev. edn (1978), lvii–lxviii; and Donne, *The Satires, Epigrams and Verse Letters*, ed. Milgate, xli–liv. *The Poems of John Donne*, ed. Grierson, 2:cxi–cxii, originated these manuscript groupings.

[41] See Jeanne Shami, 'Donne's Decision to Take Orders', in Shami, Flynn, and Hester, eds, *The Oxford Handbook of John Donne*, 523–36.

prominence. In short order James I created Carr viscount Rochester, then earl of Somerset, as his seemingly boundless influence with the king became obvious to all eyes. Significantly, the earl took particular interest in the control of ecclesiastical appointments.

In the spring of 1613, Donne made definite his considered decision to seek ordination in the Church of England, which the king had wished him to do at least since 1610 when he published *Pseudo-Martyr*. The way forward to realizing this vocation, Donne clearly saw, lay in cultivating Somerset's patronage. In the course of 1614 the earl made repeated promises and gifts of money to Donne while also insisting, contrary to Donne's own resolution, that he propose himself for a series of secular appointments including a Privy Council clerkship, the secretaryship of the Virginia Company, and one of the six clerkships in Chancery. Nor was it only on these fronts that Somerset and Donne were at cross-purposes. Somerset also wanted Donne to publish his poems before seeking ordination.

Circumstantially constrained and financially obligated by his attachment to Somerset, Donne turned to Goodyere, asking in a letter dated 20 December 1614 'to borrow that old book of you' and explaining that he was gathering up his poetical 'rags' in order to print them, specifically requesting a poem he calls '*A nostre Countesse chez vous*'—lines presumably addressed to Lady Bedford. Donne ruefully admits the difficulty of collecting his poems; it 'cost me more diligence to seek them', he tells Goodyere, 'than it did to make them'. Donne has a further anxiety: Goodyere is at all costs to keep the knowledge of his intention to publish his poems from Lady Bedford, since the volume had to be dedicated to Somerset, and she belonged to a rival court faction. Donne emphasizes that he is 'under an unescapable necessity'. He is determined to see the volume through the press at once 'not for much publique view, but at mine own cost, a few Copies... for I must do this, as a valediction to the world, before I take Orders'.[42] The muddled reasoning is as untypical of Donne as it is obvious. How could he have supposed that his poems could be printed, even in 'a few Copies', and yet shielded from 'much publique view'? How could he have imagined that his sexually explicit, cynically outspoken elegies and love lyrics would comport with 'a valediction to the World' in the form of a printed collection of his poems, characterized as his last preparatory step before entering the ministry?

It is not known why Donne's intention of printing his poems in late 1614 went unrealized, but the Dowden manuscript in Garrard's hand very likely constitutes material evidence of timely scribal assistance given to Donne by this friend, who at this date was courting Somerset's favour himself. Whatever the actual circumstances were in their entirety, certain aspects of the ordering

---

[42] *Letters*, 196-7.

of the poems in the Dowden manuscript reveal the delicate balancing act with which Donne attempted both to placate Lady Bedford and to gratify Somerset. With its 99 poems, this is a comprehensive collection that proceeds sequentially by genre, then by chronological order, for the most part, within generic categories. The sequence runs as follows: satires; elegies; funeral elegies (Lady Markham, Mrs. Bulstrode); verse letters (sorted according to male and female addressees); religious poems (*La Corona*; Holy Sonnets; 'The Crosse', 'Annunciation [and Passion]', 'A Litanye', 'Goodfriday. 1613'), love lyrics ('Songs and Sonnets'); two epithalamia (the latter an elaborate composition marking the 1613 marriage of Somerset to Frances Howard, countess of Essex), followed by an extended tribute to Lady Bedford's brother who had died in February 1614. 'Obsequies to the Lord Harrington', written in the complex hyperbolic mode of the *Anniversaries*, is the final item in Dowden; the poem's last lines address the deceased young lord and, by extension, its readers: 'in thy grave I do interre my Muse, | Who, by my griefe,... | ... hath spoke, and spoke her last.'[43] On the threshold of being ordained as a minister, Donne solemnly forswears the writing of poetry.

Like this resolve, which fortunately was not strictly adhered to, Donne's attitude towards the circulation of his work in manuscript or print would continue to be shaped in subsequent years by his determination to put his literary talents to constructive use in his society. When he took holy orders in January 1615, Donne ended his life's drawn-out phase of suspended judgement and suspended animation regarding his course of action and his place in the world. Yet his vocational quest would persist and even intensify thereafter. David Colclough has finely formulated this as 'Donne's desire to have an intellectual identity in the world—to be publicly recognised as one who searches for knowledge—and . . . it is against this aim that all of his writing is measured.'[44] Measured, that is, first and foremost by Donne himself, whose ongoing critical reflection on his work yields self-judgements that mingle assurance of its worth with uncertainty about its reception.

In the latter connection, a particularly revealing episode occurred in the spring of 1619 when King James assigned Donne to serve as chaplain to James Hay, viscount Doncaster, during an embassy to Germany and Bohemia. Donne felt keen reluctance at the prospect of taking a leave from his readership in divinity at Lincoln's Inn, where he had a devoted congregation of fellow benchers, and of entrusting himself to the perils of travel through a Europe on the brink of religious war. Explicit phrases in his 'Sermon of Valediction' and his 'Hymn to Christ, at the Authors... going into Germany' register Donne's fear that he would die in the course of this assignment. To

---

[43] Helen Gardner first recognized the logic of this sequence (*The Divine Poems*, lx).
[44] 'Introduction', in Colclough, ed., *John Donne's Professional Lives*, 16.

prepare for such an eventuality he took the initiative of ensuring that the works he had most stringently withheld from circulation—his manuscript treatise on suicide, *Biathanatos*, and a 'book' of his 'poems' (presumably the 1614 gathering)—found safekeeping with two close friends.

Donne's letter to his younger friend and fellow poet Sir Edward Herbert accompanying a manuscript copy of *Biathanatos* displays a wit made edgy by the work's problematic subject and the tenseness of the moment. This book 'shall not...kill it self; that is, not bury it self...Since it is content to live, it cannot chuse a wholsomer aire than your Library, where Authors of all complexions are presented...I know your love to me will make in my favour and discharge'. Donne wrote on the same subject in the same circumstances to the well-placed courtier Sir Robert Ker, earl of Ancrum, a relative and confidant of the earl of Somerset, with whom Donne had become familiar in dealings over the intended publication of his poems in 1614. He took Ker into unusually full confidence:

Besides the Poems, of which you took a promise, I send you another Book...written by me many years since; and because it is upon a misinterpretable subject, I have always gone so near suppressing it, as that it is onely not burnt...: onely to some particular friends in both Universities, then when I writ it, I did communicate it...it is a Book written by *Jack Donne*, and not by D. *Donne*. Reserve it for me, if I live, and if I die, I only forbid it the Presse, and the Fire: publish it not, but yet burn it not; and between those, do what you will with it. Love me still.[45]

Interestingly, these 1619 reflections on *Biathanatos* are almost equally pertinent to the most sexually explicit and cynically outspoken of the lyrics we know as the elegies and 'songs and sonnets', a number of which were entrusted to the sophisticated courtier Ker at this time together with the rest of the manuscript collection of his poems to which Donne refers. After the death of his wife, Anne, in August 1617, Donne might have thought it feasible to relax somewhat the strictures he had placed on the circulation of his highly innovative, convention-defying love lyrics, since there was no longer any danger of exposing Anne to hurt or offence from possibly scandalized reactions of readers. Perhaps this is why he focuses his emphasis on *Biathanatos* and only mentions his poems in passing. Whatever the overall state of his thinking about what he had authored, Donne in the spring of 1619 showed himself principally concerned with the physical preservation of one problematic work. With the further passage of time, however, he would develop a distinctly positive recognition of the opportunities for self-realization and self-expression that could open up to him through select publication of what were now, almost

[45] 'To the Noblest Knight Sir *Edward Herbert* L. of Cherbury, sent to him with his Book *Biathanatos*', 'To Sir *Robert Carre* now Earle of Ancrum, with my Book *Biathanatos* at my going into Germany', in *Letters*, 20–2. The original of Donne's letter to Sir Edward Herbert is preserved in the Bodleian Library.

exclusively, his religious writings in prose, as befitted the dean of St Paul's.[46]
Donne was confirmed in that appointment, made at King James's behest, in
late November 1621.

Donne's first explicit recognition that some of his sermons might have a
future life in print is found in an autograph letter of 1 December 1622 written
to his friend Sir Thomas Roe, English ambassador to the imperial Ottoman
court at Istanbul. Donne thanks Roe for his interest in his recent preaching
on public concerns at the king's command. He says he is sending Roe his
Paul's Cross sermon of 15 September, an exposition and defence of the
recently issued royal *Directions to Preachers*, forbidding the treatment of con-
troversial matters in the pulpit. Donne also remarks that many Londoners
have been outraged by the proposed marriage of Prince Charles to the
Spanish Infanta, adding judiciously, 'I know to be sorry for some things that
are donne (that is, sorry that our tymes are overtaken with a necessity to do
them) proceeds of true zeale; but to conclude the worst upon the first degree
of ill, is a distilling with too hot a fire.'

Donne continues in some detail: 'One of these occurrences gave the occa-
sion to this sermon, which by commandement I preached and which I send to
your Lordship. Some few weekes after that, I preachd another at the same
place: upon the Gun-powder day' (the anniversary of the 5 November 1605
discovery of Guy Fawkes's Catholic conspiracy to blow up the chambers of
Parliament when the king was in attendance). 'Therein', says Donne, 'I was
left more to mine owne liberty; and therfore I would I could also send your
Lordship a Copy of that; but that one, which, also by commandement I did
write after the preachinge, is as yet in his Majesties hand, and, I know not
whether he will in it, as he did in the other, after his readinge thereof, com-
mand it to be printed; and, whilst it is in that suspence, I know your Lordship
would call it Indiscretion, to send out any copy thereof; neither truly, ame
I able to committ that fault, for I have no Copy.'

In the event, the king would not command this Gunpowder Plot sermon of
Donne's to be published. But Donne had another development of a similar
sort to report to Roe as well as a ringing affirmation to convey regarding his
vocation as a preacher. 'A few days after that, I preached, by invitation of the
Virginian Company, to an honorable auditory, and they recompenced me with
a new commandment, in their Service, to printe that: and that, I hope comes
[to you] with this: for, with papers of that kinde, I am the apter...in the
Exercise of my Ministery.... I beseech you let this have some waight..., that

---

[46] On the complex interrelations of authoring and publishing at this period, see Steven W.
May, 'Tudor Aristocrats and the Mythical "Stigma of Print"', *Renaissance Papers* (1980), 11–18;
Wendy Wall, *The Imprint of Gender: Authorship and Publication in the English Renaissance* (1993);
Arthur F. Marotti, *Manuscript, Print, and the English Renaissance Lyric* (1995); and Stephen
B. Dobranski, *Readers and Authorship in Early Modern England* (2005).

the assiduity of doing the churche of God that service, which, (in a poore measure) I am thought to be able to do, possesses me, and fills me.'[47]

Issued both singly and in groupings that saw successive printings, five of Donne's sermons commissioned for presentation at important public venues were published in his lifetime. Their typically descriptive period titles read as follows, all significantly identifying Donne by name and profession as preacher and dean of St Paul's:

(1) *A Sermon upon the XV. Verse of the XX. Chapter of the Booke of Judges, Wherein occasion was justly taken for the Publication of some Reasons, which his Sacred Majestie had beene pleased to give, of those Directions for Preachers, which he had formerly sent forth. Preached at the Crosse the 15th of September. 1622. By John Donne, Doctor of Divinitie and Deane of Saint Pauls, London, And now by commandement of his Majestie published, as it was then preached.* London, 1622.

(2) *A Sermon upon the VIII. Verse of the I. Chapter of the Acts of the Apostles. Preach'd To the Honourable Company of the Virginian Plantation. 13. November 1622. By John Donne Deane of St. Pauls, London.* London, 1622.

(3) *Encaenia. The Feast of Dedication Celebrated At Lincolnes Inne, in a Sermon there upon Ascension day, 1623. At the Dedication of a new Chappell there, Consecrated by the Right Reverend Father in God, the Bishop of London. Preached by John Donne, Deane of St. Pauls.* London, 1623.

(4) *The First Sermon Preached to King Charles, At Saint James: 3. April. 1625. By John Donne, Deane of Saint Pauls, London.* London, 1625.

(5) *A Sermon, Preached To The Kings Majestie At Whitehall, 24. February 1625. By John Donne, Deane of Saint Pauls, London. And now by his Majestes commandment Published.* London, 1626.[48]

While word-limit constraints prevent inclusion of any of Donne's sermons in the present volume, this omission is being amply offset by the publication of *The Oxford Edition of the Sermons of John Donne* under the general editorship of Peter McCullough; its first meticulously edited and annotated volumes have begun to be available. Yet even such meagre evidence as the wording of the sermon title pages quoted above suffices to register the contrast between the two media in which Donne's works typically circulated in his lifetime: his verse, in manuscript and for the most part unascribed; his prose, in print and for the most part attributed to him by name.

The last and longest of the works in the present volume, Donne's *Devotions upon Emergent Occasions* (1624), affords prime material for closing reflections

---

[47] Donne's letter to Roe is preserved in The National Archives, Kew, as State Papers Domestic, James I, 14/134/59.

[48] Sir Geoffrey Keynes, *A Bibliography of Dr. John Donne*, 4th edn (1973), 31–47.

on the questions addressed in this Introduction—how Donne's contemporaries encountered and regarded his authorship, in what medium and what circumstances; how his works circulated or were restricted in circulation; how Donne conceived of himself as an author, and to what criteria of judgement he held himself and his works accountable. The genesis of the *Devotions*, as Donne himself explains, lay in his own recent experience. An illness of unspecified character but graphically described symptoms and stages suddenly struck him in November and December of 1623, confining him to his sickbed and bringing him close to death. Contrary to his own expectation and the fears of his doctors, Donne would recover slowly in the early weeks of 1624, during which time he composed his *Devotions*. He was able to return to the pulpit of St Paul's at Easter of that year. With the exception of certain passages of his prose letters and verse letters to male friends, Donne is nowhere so autobiographical, so confessional about the condition of his body and the thoughts and emotions it elicits, than he is—at length and in detail—in this literary product of his illness in 1623–4.

Like his *Anniversary* poems, Donne's prose *Devotions* are profoundly original in their generic hybridity and richness. The latter work develops as a series of 23 stages or episodes in an illness, each addressed in an opening Meditation, an intermediate Expostulation (or debating with God), and a concluding Prayer. Meditations and prayers are standard components of the genre of formal devotion.[49] Donne innovates, however, in his Expostulations. These take shape in a barrage of biblical quotations from which the anguished and anxious speaker seeks to extract God's will and purpose for him in his illness. In their intense engagement with determining the meaning of various Scriptural texts and making immediate personal application of these meanings to the speaker's present state, Donne's Expostulations function, in effect, as mini-sermons to himself, compensating for the preaching from the pulpit that his illness has rendered him unable to perform. The effect of the Expostulations as mini-sermons is further heightened by Donne's frequent recourse to typology and metaphor in teasing meanings from his clusters of biblical quotations—as such and such was a sign of God's chastisement to the Psalmist David or to Job or to Moses or to King Hezekiah, so it may likewise be to the speaker (and the reader) of the *Devotions*. An acute mindfulness of his vocational responsibility to preach lies close to the surface of Donne's articulation in his Expostulations.[50]

After Donne had finished composing the *Devotions* early in 1624, he promptly set about exploring not only the possibility of their publication but of their publication with a dedication to the heir to the throne, Prince Charles.

---

[49] Kate Narveson, 'The Devotion', in Shami, Flynn, and Hester, eds, *The Oxford Handbook of John Donne*, 308.

[50] Janel Mueller, 'The Exegesis of Experience: Dean Donne's *Devotions upon Emergent Occasions*', *Journal of English and Germanic Philology* (1968), 67.1, 1–19.

Donne wrote with delicacy and deference to his most favourably positioned contact at court, his friend since the Somerset connection a decade earlier, Sir Robert Ker, earl of Ancrum, then in service to Prince Charles as a gentleman of the bedchamber:

Sir, Though I have left my bed, I have not left my bed-side; I sit there still…I have used this leisure, to put the meditations had in my sicknesse, into some such order, as may minister some holy delight. They arise to so many sheetes (perchance 20) as that without staying for that furniture of an Epistle,…my Friends importun'd me to Print them.…That, being in hand, through this long Trunke, that reaches from Saint *Pauls* to Saint *James* [the current residence of the king and court], I whisper into your eare this question, whether there be an uncomlinesse, or unseasonablenesse, in presenting matter of Devotion, or Mortification, to that Prince, whom I pray God nothing may ever Mortifie, but Holinesse. If you allow my purposes in generall, I pray cast your eye upon the Title and the Epistle, and rectifie me in them. I submit substance, and circumstance to you, and the poore Author of both,

Your very humble and very thankful Servant
in Christ Jesus,
J. Donne.[51]

Donne would receive Ker's positive judgement and encouragement. The first edition of *Devotions upon Emergent Occasions* appeared in February 1624, followed by a second edition in the same year, a third edition in 1626, a reissue of the third edition with a variant title page in the same year, and a fourth edition in 1627—to enumerate only the five printings that occurred in Donne's lifetime.[52]

After Donne sought print publication under the aegis of royal approval, readers' reactions to the *Devotions* were not slow in coming. The earliest of these registers recognition of a balance between Donne's extreme ingenuity and his no less strong pastoral intent. John Chamberlain, the inveterate London letter-writer of the time, wrote as follows to his equally inveterate recipient, Sir Dudley Carleton, the English ambassador to the States-General at The Hague, on 21 February 1624: 'I wold have sent…yf I had met with a convenient messenger…Dr Donnes Devotions in his sicknes, newly come abrode, wherin are many curious and daintie conceits, not for common capacities, but surely full of pietie and true feeling'.[53] The next reaction to be registered in writing was that of Sir Francis Bacon, himself a master of eloquence whose attention was caught by the opening of Donne's Meditation 17, 'No Man is an *Iland*, intire of it selfe; every man is a peece of the *Continent,* a part of the *maine*'. In his 1625 essay 'Of Goodnesse and Goodnesse of Nature', Bacon paid Donne the compliment of assimilating Donne's phrasing within

[51] *Letters*, 249–50.
[52] Keynes, *Bibliography of Donne*, 4th edn, 83–7.
[53] *The Letters of John Chamberlain*, ed. Norman Egbert McClure (1939), 2:545.

his own: 'If a Man be Gracious, and Curteous to Strangers, it shewes, he is a Citizen of the World, And that His Heart, is no Island, cut off from other Lands; but a Continent, that joynes to them'.[54] The last of the earliest known reactions of readers of Donne's *Devotions* is an anonymous inscription in a copy of the third edition (1627), written in a contemporary hand. Like Bacon, this anonymous reader pays Donne a compliment—this time, that of outright imitation—in a versified paradox asserting the impossibility that the *Devotions* will find an appropriately receptive readership:

On this witty and pious Book.

Here Wit and Piety together shine;
That, shows the Poet; This, the sound Divine.
Then why so few, or Good, or Witty, share
Wit with the Poett; with the Preacher, prayer?
The Reason's plain: The Good the Preacher quit
Lest they should be corrupted by the Witt,
And Witts deny to read the Poet's gist
For fear they be converted by the Priest.[55]

The pessimism of the anonymous versifier's paradox should be met with doubt and resistance; this is how to engage with paradoxes, as Donne himself had advised Goodyere. Concurrently, however, the glibness of this versifier's lines in imitation of Donne drives home a truth to be accepted without question or denial, then or now. Donne is quite simply inimitable.

[54] Sir Francis Bacon, *The Essayes or Counsels, Civill and Morall*, ed. Michael Kiernan (1985), 40. Keynes, *Bibliography of Donne*, 4th edn, 83, points out that this appropriation of Donne by Bacon was first noted in 1960 by John Crossett, 'Bacon and Donne', *Notes and Queries*, new series 7, 386–7.

[55] These lines were inscribed in a volume now in the library of the University of Sheffield, shelfmark 821.33 (*Donne: The Critical Heritage*, ed. Smith, 78).

A NOTE ON EDITORIAL PRACTICES

Seamus Perry's guidelines for editors of volumes in the 21st-Century Oxford Authors series highlight two general editorial principles: the 'accessibility', in most cases, 'of very lightly modernized texts' to present-day readers, and the presentation of texts 'in a way that is mindful of their early publication . . . so that the texts retain at least some sense of their original character in print'. I have implemented these principles straightforwardly with regard to the three printed volumes whose contents are reproduced in this edition: 'A Funeral Elegy' and the two *Anniversaries*, and the *Devotions upon Emergent Occasions*.

Perry's further specifications regarding editorial practice have guided my treatment of the rest of the contents of the present edition: manuscripts written in the hands of George Gerrard, Rowland Woodward, and Donne himself. In Perry's words, 'a minimum of modernizing will be normal', including

conventions such as the long 's'; archaic uses of ' ', 'j', 'u', and 'v'; the expansion of contractions such as 'wch' and '&'. And thereafter, editors will need to make decisions on an individual basis: the norm should be the retention of original spelling and punctuation, and the tactful modernization of italicisation and capitalisation; but there will be cases in which individual editors choose to deviate from these guidelines, due to the nature of the original texts. . . . In particular, editors, especially of early modern works, may feel that creating an acceptable level of legibility for the modern reader requires a slightly greater degree of modernisation.

True to the spirit of judicious flexibility that animates these guidelines, in transcribing texts from manuscript and print I have expanded all contracted word forms while retaining, with few exceptions, original punctuation and original spelling. Exceptions include removing or inserting punctuation at junctures where the sense of the passage is obscured in the original as well as modernizing the spelling of names of persons and places to make them readily recognizable (for example, 'Rouen' rather than 'Roan'). Original spelling has additionally been subjected to two other sorts of modification aimed at easing the comprehension of meaning by preventing the puzzlement or misunderstanding that homonyms and unfamiliar period spellings can produce.

Thus, for example, in transcribing homonyms I distinguish, as the original texts often do not, between 'bred' and 'bread', 'coarse' and 'course', 'currant' and 'current', 'dew' and 'due', 'discrete' and 'discreet', 'fayne' and 'feign', 'guilt' and 'gilt', 'heard' and 'herd', 'lest' and 'least', 'loose' and 'lose', 'loth' and 'loathe', 'ordnance' and 'ordinance', 'pray' and 'prey', 'soar' and 'sore', 'than' and 'then', 'the' and 'thee', 'there' and 'their', 'through' and 'thorough', 'to' and 'too', 'waight' and 'wait', 'wright' and 'write'.

In transcribing instances of unfamiliar and hence potentially misleading spelling, I have, for example, adjusted 'accoumpted' to 'accounted', 'adge' to 'age', 'burthen' to 'burden', 'cold' to 'could,' 'corse' to 'corpse', 'enow' to 'enough', 'furder' to 'further', 'geast' to 'jest', 'hair' to 'heir', 'leacher' to 'lecher', 'lien' to 'lain'; 'sallet' to 'salad', 'sone' to 'soone', 'sterve' to 'starve', 'tand' to 'tannd', 'toung' to 'tongue'; and, where applicable, 'breathe' to 'breath', 'chose' to 'choose', 'cloth' to 'clothe', 'nere' to 'ne'er', 'ore' to 'o'er', 'red' to 'read' (the past participle), 'robd' to 'robbd', 'stopd' to 'stoopd', 'straw' to 'strew', 'tell' to 'till', 'travel' to 'travail', 'weare' to 'were', 'whether' to 'whither', 'woo' to 'woe', 'wrong' to 'wrung'. But where end-rhymes would be negatively affected, I often retain the original spelling.

A third and final category of modification has aimed at making Donne's versecraft more readily accessible to modern ears and eyes. I have inserted a diaresis mark (umlaut) above vowels that must be separately voiced to render the rhythm of a line perceptible—e.g., 'My loneness is; But Spartanes fashiöne' (Westmoreland MS); 'Poysonous, or Purgative, or Cordyäll' (Dowden MS). In the far more frequent, complementary case, where the rhythm of a line requires two syllables to be elided, I have inserted an apostrophe at the site of elision if the original lacks one—e.g., 'To' out drinke the Sea: out sweare the Letanee' (Westmoreland MS); 'You, as you 'are Vertues Temple, not as Shee' (Dowden MS).

In the *Anniversaries* and the *Devotions*, both texts for which the existence of errata lists gives good grounds to suppose that Donne proofread the texts after they were set in type, I have reproduced what by present-day standards may seem an excess of capitalization, italics, and comma punctuation. But these typographical features served as vehicles for rhetorical emphasis in Donne's era, and readers recognized and responded to them as such. Finally, in the *Devotions*, where marginal references to biblical texts are incorrect or incomplete, these have been silently regularized, and references originally given in Latin are here given in English.

A NOTE ON THE CHRONOLOGY OF DONNE'S LIFE

Specific dates and the sequential ordering of significant occurrences in Donne's life during the period of compositions included in this volume (1590–1624) are registered at appropriate points in the commentary and notes that follow. A more detailed chronology of Donne's life may be found in R. C. Bald, *John Donne: A Life* (1970), 537–46, and one with a longer timeline and more inclusive entries in Achsah Guibbory, ed., *The Cambridge Companion to John Donne* (2006), xiv–xviii.

FROM THE WESTMORELAND
MANUSCRIPT, PRE-1600
COMPOSITIONS

Satyra 1.ᵃ

Away thou changeling motley humorist
Leave me, and in this standing wodden chest
Consorted with these few bookes, let me ly
In prison, and here be coffind, when I dy
Here are Gods conduits grave Divines, and here   5
Natures Secretary, the Philosopher.
And joly Statesmen, which teach how to ty
The Sinews of a Citties mystique body.
Here gathering Chroniclers, and by them stand
Giddy fantastique Poets of each Land.   10
Shall I leave all this constant companee
And follow headlong wild, uncertaine thee?
First sweare by thy best love in earnest
(If thou which Lovst all canst love any best)
Thou wilt not leave me in the middle street   15
Though some more spruce companion thou do meet.
Not though a Captane do come in thy way
Bright parcel-gilt with forty dead mens pay,
Nor though a briske perfumd pert Courtier
Deigne with a nod thy curtesy to answer.   )   20
Nor come a velvet Justice with a long
Great traine of blewcotes 12 or 14 strong,
Shallt thou grine and fawne on him, or prepare
A speach to court his bewteous sone and heire.
For better and worse take me, or leave mee   25
To take and leave me, is adulteree.
O monster, superstitious Puritane
Of refind manners, yet ceremonial man.
That when thou meetst one, with inquyring eyes
Dost search, and like a needy broker prize   30
The silke and gould he weares, and to that rate
So high or low dost vaile thy formall hatt.
That wilt consort none, untill thou have knowen
What Lands he hath in hope, or of his owne.
As though all thy companions should make thee   35
Joyntures and mary thy deare companee.

[p. 6]
Why shouldst thou, that dost not only approve
But in ranke itchy Lust desyre and love
The nakednesse and barenesse to injoy
Of thy plump muddy whore and prostitute boy,   40
Hate Vertu though she be naked and bare?
At birth, and death our bodyes naked are:
And till our Soules be unapparellëd
Of bodyes, they from blis are banishëd.
Mans first blest state was naked, when by sin   45
He lost that, yet he was clothd but in beasts skin:
And in this coarse attire which now I weare
With God and with the Muses I confer.
But since thou like a contrite penitent
Charitably warnd of thy sins dost repent   50
These Vanities and giddinesses, Lo
I shut my chamber dore and come let's go.
But sooner may a cheape whore that hath beene
Worne by as many severall men in sin
As are black feathers or muske color hose   55
Name her childs right trew father mongst all those,
Sooner may one guesse who shall beare away
Th' infant of London heire to an India,
And sooner may a gulling weather spy
By drawing forth heavens Scheame, tell certainly   60
What fashiond hatts, or ruffs, or suites next yeare
Our supple-witted antiek Youths will weare
Than thou when thou departst from hence canst show
Whether, why, when, or with whome thou wouldst go.
But how shall I be pardond my offence   65
That thus have sind against my conscience?
Now we are in the street: he first of all
Improvidently proud creepes to the wall
And so imprisond and hemm'd in by mee
Sells for a Little state his Libertee.   70
Yet though he cannot skip forth now to greet
Every fine silken painted foole we meet,
[p. 7]
He them to him with amerous smiles allures
And grins, smacks, shruggs, and such an itch indures
As Prentices or schooleboyes which do know   75
Of some gay sport abroade, yet dare not go.
And as fidlers stoop lowest at hiyest sound
So to the most brave stoopes he nighest ground.
But to a grave man he doth move no more

Than the wise politique horse would hertofore 80
Or thou O Elephant or Ape wilt do
When any names the king of Spayne to you.
Now leapes he upright, joggs me, 'and cryes do 'you see
Yonder well favord Youth? Which? Yea, t'is hee
That dances so divinely. Oh sayd I 85
Stand still, must you dance here for company?
He droopt: We went, till one which did excell
Th' Indians in drinking his Tabacco well
Mett us: they talkt: I whisperd Let us go:
May be you smell him not, trewly I do. 90
He heares not me: but on the other side
A many colerd peacock having spied
Leaves him and me: I for my lost sheepe stay,
He followes, overtakes, goes on the way
Saying, him; whom I last lefte, all repute 95
For his devise in handsomming a sute;
To judge of Lace, pink, panes, cutt, print, or pleight
Of all the Court to have the best conceit.
Our dull Comedians want him: Let him go
But Oh God strengthen thee why stoopst thou so? 100
Why: he hath travayld. Long? No: but to mee
Which understand none he doth seeme to bee
Perfect french and Italian: I replide
So is the pox: he answered not but spide
More men of Sort, of parts, and qualities. 105
At last his Love he in a window spies
And like Light dew exhald, he flings from mee,
Violently ravishd to his Lecheree.
Many were there: he could command no more:
He quarreld, fought, bled, and turnd out of dore 110
Directly came to me hanging the hed
And Constantly awhile must keepe his bed. /

Satyra 2.ᵃ [p. 8]

Sir, Though (I thanke God for it) I do hate
Perfectly all this towne, yet ther is one State
In all ill things so excellently best
That hate towards them breds pity towards the rest.
Though Poetry indeed be such a Sin 5

As I thinke that brings dearths and Spaniards in,
Though like the pestilence or old fashiond love
It ridlingly catch men, and doth remove
Never till it be starv'd out, yet their State
Is poore, disarm'd, like Papists not worth hate.   10
One like a wretch which at barr judgd as dead
Yet prompts him which stands next, and could not read
And saves his life, gives Ideot Actors means
Starving himselfe to live by his labord Sceanes.
As in some Organes puppets dance above   15
And bellows pant below which them do move.
One would move Love by rhimes, but witchcrafts charmes
Bring not now their old feares, nor their old harmes.
Ramms and Slings now are seely batteree
Pistolets are the best artilleree.   20
And they who write to Lords, rewards to gett
Are they not like boyes singing at dores for meat?
And they who write because all write have still
That 'scuse for writing and for writing ill.
But he is worst, who beggerly doth chaw   25
Others witts fruites, and in his ravenous maw
Rawly digested doth those things outspue
As his owne things, and they'are his owne: 'tis true.
For if one eate my meate, though it be knowne
The meat was myne, the excrement 'is his owne.   30
But these do me no harme. Nor they which use
To outswive dildos; and out usure Jewes:
To' out drinke the Sea: out sweare the Letanee:
Who with Sins all kinds as familiar bee
As Confessors: and for whose sinfull sake   35
Schoolemen new tenements in hell must make.
[p. 9]   Whose strange sins Canonists could hardly tell
In which Commandments large receite they dwell.
But these punish themselves: the insolence
Of Coscus only breeds my great offence.   40
Whome time which rotts all, and makes botches poxe
And plodding on must make a calfe an oxe
Hath made a Lawyer: which was alas of late
But a scarse Poet: Jolyer of this state
Than are new benefic'd Ministers, he throwes   45
[Like nets or lime twigs wheresoe'er he goes]
His title of Barrister on every wenche:
And woos in Language of the Pleas and Benche.

A motion Lady: Speake Coscus: I have beene
In love ere since tricesimo of the Queene: 50
Continuell Claimes I 'have made, Injunctions gott
To stay my Rivals suite, that he should not
Proceede: Spare me: In Hilary terme I went
You sayd if I returnd this Sise in Lent
I should be in remitter of your grace,   55
In th'interim my letters should take place
Of afidavits. Words words which would teare
The tender Labyrinth of a soft mayds eare
More, more, than ten Sclavonians scolding, more
Than when Winds in our ruynd Abbeys rore.   60
When sick of Poetry and possest with Muse
Thou wast, and mad, I hop'd: but men which chuse
Law practise for meere gayne, bold Soule, repute
Worse than imbrotheled Strumpets prostitute.
Now Like an owelike Watchman he must walke   65
His hand still at a bill: Now he must talke
Idely Like Prisoners, which whole months will sweare
That only Suretiship hath brought them there:
And to every Sutor Ly in every thing
Like a kings favorit, yea like a king.   70
Like a wedge in a blocke wring to the barr
Bearing Like Asses and more shameles farr
Than carted whores ly to the grave Judg: for
Bastardy abounds not in kings titles, nor
Simony and Sodomy in Churchmens Lives   75
As these things do in him, by these he thrives.
Shortly' (as the sea) he will compasse all our land   [p. 10]
From Scotts to Wight, from Mount to Dover strand,
And spying heires melting with gluttonee
Satan will not joy at their sins as hee.   80
For as a thrifty wench scrapes kitchin stuffe
And barrelling the drippings and the snuffe
Of wasting candels which in 30 yeare
Relique-like kept perchance buyes wedding geare
Piecemeale he getts Lands, and spends as much time   85
Wringing each acre as men pulling Prime.
In Parchments then large as his fields he drawes
Assurances; bigg as glossd civil Lawes:
So huge that men in our times forwardnesse
Are fathers of the Church for wryting lesse.   90
These he wrytes not: nor for these written payes,

Therfore spares no length: As in those first dayes
When Luther was profest, he did desyre
Short Pater nosters, saying as a fryer
Each day his beads, but having lefte those lawes   95
Adds to Christs prayer, the power and glory clause.
But when he sells or changes lands, he' impayres
His writings, and, unwatch'd, leaves out ses heires
As slily as any Commenter goes by
Hard words or sense: Or in divinity   100
As Controverters in vouchd texts leave out
Shrewd Words which might against them cleare the doubt.
Where are those spred woods which clothd hertofore
These bought lands? Not built, nor burnt within dore.
Where th' old landlords troopes and almes? In great halls   105
Carthusian fasts, and fulsome Bacchanalls
Equally' I hate: Meanes blesse: In rich mens homes
I bid kill some beasts, but not Hecatomes.
None starve, none surfet so: But oh we' allow
Good workes as good, but out of fashion now   110
Like old rich wardrobes. But my words none drawes
Within the vast reach of th' huge Statute Lawes. /

[p. 11]

Satyra 3.ª

Kind pity choakes my spleene; brave scorne forbids
These teares to issue which swell my eylids.
I must nor Laugh, nor Weepe sin, and be wise,
May rayling then ease these worne maladyes?
Is not our Mistres fayre Religiön   5
As worthy' of all our Soules devotiön
As vertu was to the first blind Age?
Are not heavens joyes as valiant to assuage
Lusts, as Earths honor was to them? Alas
As we do them in meanes, shall they surpas   10
Us in the end? And shall thy fathers spiritt
Meete blind Philosophers in heaven, whose meritt
Of strict Life may be' imputed fayth, and heare
Thee whome he tought wayes easy and neare
To follow, damn'd? Oh if thou darest, feare this   15
This feare great courage, and high valor is.
Darest thou ayd mutinous Dutch? darest thou lay

Thee in Shipps wooden Sepulchers, a prey
To Leaders rage, to stormes, to shott, to dearthe,
Darest thou dive Seas, and dungeons of the earthe? 20
Hast thou couragious fyer to thaw the yce
Of frozen North discoveryes, and thrice
Colder than Salamanders, Like divine
Children in th' oven, fires of Spayne 'and the Line:
Whose Cuntryes Limbecks to our bodyes bee? 25
Canst thou for gayne beare? and must every hee
Which cryes not Goddesse to thy Mistres, draw,
Or eate thy poysonous words? Courage of straw.
O desperate Coward, wilt thou seeme bold, and
To thy foes, and his who made thee, to stand 30
Soldier in his worlds garrison, thus yeild
And for forbid warrs, leave th' appointed field.
Know thy foes: the foule Devill, whom thou
Striv'st to please, for hate not love would allow
Thee fayne his whole Realme to be ridd: and as 35
The worlds all parts wither away and pas,
So the worlds selfe thy other lov'd foe is
In her decrepit wayne, and thou loving this
Dost Love a witherd and worne strumpet. Last   [p. 12]
Flesh (it selfes death) and joyes, which flesh can tast 40
Thou lov'st, and thy fayre goodly soule, which doth
Give this flesh power, to tast joy, thou dost lothe.
Seeke true Religion. Oh where? Myrius
Thinking her unhous'd here, and fled from us
Seekes her at Rome; There, because he doth know 45
That she was there a thousand yeares ago
He loves her raggs so, as we here obay
The State Cloth wher the Prince sate yesterday.
Crantz to such brave Loves will not be enthralld
But Loves her only, who at Geneva is calld 50
Religiön, playne, simple, sullen, young,
Contemptuous, yet unhandsome; as among
Lecherous humors, ther is one, which judges
No wenches wholesome, but coarse cuntry drudges.
Graius stayes still at home here: and because 55
Some Preachers, vile Ambitious bawds, and Lawes
Still new, like fashions, bidd him thinke, that shee
Which dwells with us, is only perfect, hee
Imbraceth her, whome his Godfathers will
Tender to him being tender; as wards still 60

Take such wifes as their Guardians offer, or
Pay values. Careles Phrygas doth abhor
All, because all cannot be good; as one
Knowing some women whores, dares mary none.
Graccus loves all as one, and thinkes that so   65
As women do in divers Cuntryes go
In divers habitts, yet are still one kind,
So doth, so is Religion; and this blind-
nes, too much light breeds. But unmoved thou
Of force Must one, and forc'd but one allow;   70
And the right; aske thy father which is shee;
Lett him aske his; Though Truthe and falshood bee
Neare twins, yet Truth a litle elder is.
Be busy to seeke her, beleeve me this
Hee' is not of none, nor worst which seekes the best.   75
To' adore, or scorne an Image, or protest,
[p. 13]   May all be bad; doubt wisely; In strange way
To stand inquyring right is not to stray.
To sleepe, or run wrong, is. On a high hill
Ragged and steepe Truthe dwels; and he that will   80
Reach it, about must, and about [must] go
And what th' hills sodainnes resists, win so.
Yet strive so, that before Age (Deaths twilight)
Thy mind rest; for none can worke in that night.
To will implyes delay: therfore now do.   85
Hard deedes the bodyes paynes, hard knowledg too
The minds endeavors reach; and Misteryes
Are as the Sun, dazeling, yet playne to' all eyes.
Keepe the truthe which thou hast found: men do not stand
In so ill case here, that God hath with his hand   90
Signd kings blanc charters, to kill whom they hate,
Nor are they Vicars, but hangmen to fate.
Foole and wretch wilt thou let thy soule be tyde
To Mens lawes, by which she shall not be tryed
At the last day? Oh will it then serve thee   95
To say a Philipp, or a Gregorie,
A Harry, or a Martin tought me this?
Is not this excuse for meere contrarys
Equally stronge? cannot both sides say so?
That thou mayst rightly obay power, her bounds know: 100
Those past, her nature, and name is chang'd, to be
Then, humble to her is Idolatree.

As streames are, power is: Those blest flowers which dwell
At the rough streames calm head thrive and prove well:
But having lefte their rootes, and themselves given   105
To the streames tyrannous rage, Alas, are driven
Through Mills, rocks, and woods, and at last allmost
Consum'd in going, in the Sea are lost.
So perish Soules, which more chuse, mens unjust
Power, from God claym'd, than God himselfe to trust. /   110

Satyra 4.ᵃ   [p. 14]

Well, I may now receave and dy; my Sin
Indeede is greate, but I have beene in
A Purgatory, such as feard hell is
A recreation, and scant mapp of this.
My mind nor with prides itche, nor yet hath beene   5
Poysoned with love to see, or to bee seene;
I had no suite there, nor new sute to show,
Yet went to Court; But as Glaze which did go
To' a Masse in jeast, catch'd, was fayne to disburse
The hundred Marks which is the Statuts curse   10
Before he scap'd, so it pleasd my destinee
(Guilty of my sin of going) to thinke mee
As prone to' all ill, and of good as forgett-
full, as proud, lustfull, and as much in debt,
As vayne, as wittlesse, and as false as they   15
Which dwell at Court, for once going that way.
Therfore I sufferd this. Towards me did run
A thing more strange, than on Niles slime, the sun
Ere bredd; or all which into Noahs Arke came;
A thing which would have pos'd Adam to name;   20
Stranger than seaven Antiquaries studyes,
Than Africks Monsters, Guyanas rarityes.
Stranger than strangers; one who for a Dane
In the Danes Massacre had sure beene slayne,
If he had livd then; And without helpe dyes   25
When next the Prentises gainst Strangers rise.
One whom the watch at noone lets scarse go by;
One to whom th' examining Justice sure would cry
Sir, by your Priesthood tell me what you are.

His clothes were strange, though coarse; and black though
 bare.   30
Sleevelesse his Jerkin was, and it had beene
Velvett; but t' was now (so much ground was seene)
Become tufftaffeta, And our Children shall
See it playne rash awhile, then nought at all.
[p. 15] This thing hath traveld, and sayth, speakes all tongs 35
And only knowes what to all states belongs.
Made of th' accents, and best phrases of all these
He speakes one Language. If strange meats displease
Art can deceave, or hunger force my tast.
But Pedants Motly tong, soldiers bumbast,   40
Montebancks drugg tong, nor the termes of Law
Are strong inough preparatives, to draw
Mee, to beare this; yet I must be content
With his tong: in his tong calld Complement.
In which he can win widows; and pay skores; 45
Make men speake treason; cosen subtilst whores;
Outflatter favorites, and outly either
Jovius, or Surius, or both together.
He names me,' and comes to me, I whisper, God,
How have I sin'd, that thy wraths furious rod, 50
This fellow, chuseth me? He sayth, Sir,
I love your judgment; whom do you prefer
For the best Linguist? And I selely
Sayd, that I thought, Calepines Dictionary.
Nay, but of Men, most sweete Sir; Beza then 55
Some Jesuits, and two reverent men
Of our two Academyes I nam'd; There
He stopd me; 'and sayd; Nay, your Apostles were
Good pretty Linguists; and so Panurge was,
Yet a poore gentleman all these may pas   60
By travaile. Then as yf he would have sold
His tong he praysd it, and such wonders told
That I was fayne to say; If you had livd, Sir,
Time inough to have beene Interpreter
To Babels bricklayers, sure that tower had stood. 65
He adds; If of Court life you knew the good
You would leave lonenes. I sayd, not alone
My loneness is; But Spartanes fashiöne
To teach by paynting Drunkards doth not last
Now; Aretines Pictures have made few chast. 70
[p. 16] No more can Princes Courts, though ther be few

Better pictures of Vice, teach me Vertu.
He like a too' high stretch'd Lute string squeakd, Oh Sir,
Tis sweete to talke of kings. At Westminster
Sayd I, the man that keepes the Abbey tombes   75
And for his price doth, with whoever comes
Of all our Harryes, and our Edwards talke
From king, to king, and all their kinne can walke,
Your eares shall heare nought but king; your eyes meet
Kings only; the way to it, is Kings Street.   80
He smackd, and cryed, He' is base, mechanique, coarse
So' are all your Englishmen in their discourse:
Are not your frenchmen neat? Myne? as you see,
I have but one frenchman, looke, he followes mee.
Certes, they are neatly clothd, I of this mind ame   85
Your only wearing is this Grogerame.
Not so, Sir, I have more; Under this pitche
He would not fly. I chafd him. But as itche
Scratchd into smart, and as blunt Iron ground
Into an edg, hurts worse, so, I foole, found   90
Crossing hurt me. To fitt my sullennesse
He to an other key his stile doth dresse.
And asks, what Newes? I tell him, of new playes.
He takes my hand, and as a Still which stays
A Sembriefe twixt each dropp, he niggardly   95
As loth to' inrich me so, tells many ly.
More than ten Holinsheds, and Halls, and Stowes
Of trivial household trashe he knowes; he knowes
When the Queene smild or frownd; and he knowes
    what
A subtile Statesman may gather of that.   100
He knowes who loves whome; and who by poyson
Hasts to' an Offices reversiön.
He knows who hath sold his Land, and now doth begg
A licence, old Iron, shoues, bootes, or egg-
shells to transport. Shortly boyes shall not play   105
At blowpoynt, or span counter, but they pay   [p. 17]
Toll to some Courtier; And wiser than all us
He knowes which Lady is not painted. Thus
He with home meats tryes me; I belch, spue, spitt,
Looke pale and sickly like a Patient, yett   110
He thrusts more; And as if he had undertooke
To say Gallobelgicus without booke
Speakes of all States and deeds which have been since

The Spanyards came, to' the losse of Amiens;
Like a bigg Wife at sight of lothd meat   115
Redy to travayle, so I belche and sweat
To heare his Maccaron talke; In vayne, for yet
Ether my humor, or his owne to fitt
He like a priviledg'd Spy, whome nothing can
Discredit, Libels now gainst each great man.   120
He names a price for every office payd,
He says our Warrs thrive ill, because delayd;
That offices are entayld; and that ther are
Perpetuityes of them, Lasting as farr
As the Last day; And that great officers   125
Do with the Pyrats share, and Dunkirkers.
Who wasts in meat, in Clothes, in horse he notes,
Who loves whores, who boyes, and who goates.
I more amas'd than Circes Prisoners, when
They felt themselves turne beasts, felt myselfe then   130
Becomming traytor; and mee thought I saw
One of our Gyant Statuts ope his jaw
To sucke me in for hearing him. I found
That as burnt venomd Lechers do grow sound
By giving others their sores, I might grow   135
Guilty and he free; Therfore I did show
All Signes of Lothing; But since I ame in
I must pay myne, and my forefathers sin
To the last farthing; Therfore to my powre
Toughly' and stubbornly,' I beare this crosse; but
    th' houre   140
Of mercy now was come, he tryes to bring
Me to pay 'a fine to scape his torturing;
[p. 18]   And says, Sir, can you spare me? I sayd Willingly;
Nay, Sir, can you spare me a crowne? Thankfully' I
Gave it as ransome; but as fidlers still   145
Though they be payd to be gone, yet needs will
Thrust one more Jigg upon you, so did hee
With his long complementall thanks vex mee.
But he is gone, thanks to his needy want
And the Prerogative of my Crowne; Skant   150
His thanks were ended; when I which did see
All the Court filld with more strange things than hee
Run from thence with such or more hast than one
Who feares more actions, doth make from prisone.
At home in holesome solitarines   155

My piteous soule began the wretchednes
Of suiters at Court to mourne. And a traunce
Like his who dream't he saw hell, did advaunce
It selfe on me: and such men as he saw there
I saw at Court, and worse, and more. Low feare 160
Becomes the guilty, not th' accuser; Then
Shall I, nones slave, of high-borne or raysd men
Fear frownes? and my Mistres Truth betray thee,
To th' huffing braggart pufte Nobilitee?
No, No. Thou which since yesterday hast beene 165
Allmost about the whole world, hast thou seene
O Sun, in all thy journey, Vanity
Such as swells the bladder of our Court? I
Thinke he which made yon waxen garden, and
Transplanted it from Italy to stand 170
With us at London, flouts our Court here, for
Just such gay paynted things, which no sapp, nor
Tast have in them, ours are, and natural
Some of the stocks are there, fruits bastard all.
T'is ten a clock and past: All whom the Mues 175
Balon, Tennys, Dyett, or the Stewes
Had all the morning held, now the second
Time Made ready that day, in flocks are found
In the Presence; and I, (God pardon mee.)
As fresh and sweete th' apparrells be, as bee 180 [p. 19]
The fields they sold to buy them; For a king
Those hose are, cryes his flatterers, and bring
Them next weeke to the Theatre to sell.
Wants reach all states; Me seemes they do as well
At Stage, as Court. All are Players; who ere lookes 185
(For themselves dare not go) o'er Cheapside bookes
Shall find their Wardrobes Inventory. Now
The Ladyes come; As Pyrats which did know
That ther came weake ships fraught with Cuchianel,
The men boord them; and prayse, as they thinke, wel 190
Ther bewtyes: they the mens witts; both are bought.
Why good witts ne'er weare scarlett gownes, I thought
This cause; These men, mens witts for speaches buy
And women buy all reddes which scarlett dy.
He calld her bewty Lymetwiggs, her haire nett, 195
She feares her druggs ill layd, her hayre loose sett.
Would not Heraclitus laugh to see Macrine
From hatt to shoo, himselfe at dore refine,

As the Presence were a Meschite? And lift
His skirts and hose, and call his clothes to shrift;   200
Making them confesse, not only mortal
Great staines and holes in them, but venial
Feathers or dust, with which they fornicate;
And then by Durers rules survays the state
Of his each limbe, and with strings th' odds tryes   205
Of his neck to his legg, and wast to thighs.
So in immaculate clothes, and symmetry
Perfect as Circles, with such nicety
As a young Preacher at his first time goes
To preach, he enters; and a Lady which ows   210
Him not so much as good will straight arrests
And unto her protests, protests, protests,
So much, as at Rome would serve to have throwne
Ten Cardinals into th' Inquisitiön.
And whisperd by Jhesu so' often, that a   215
Pursevant would have ravishd him away
[p. 20]   For saying Our Ladys Psalter. But t'is fitt
That they each other plague, they meritt it.
But here comes Glorius that will plague them both.
Who in the other extreame only doth   220
Call a rough carelesnesse good fashiöne.
Whose cloke his spurs teare, whom he spitts on
He cares not. His ill words do no harme
To him. He rusheth in; as if Arme Arme
He came to cry; and though his face be' as ill   225
As theirs which in old hangings whip Christ, still
He strives to looke worse; he keepes all in aw
Jeasts like a licensd foole, commands like law.
Tyr'd now Ile leave this Place; and but pleasd so
As men which from Jayles to' execution go,   230
Go through the great Chamber (why is it hung
With the 7 deadly sins?) beeing among
Those Ascaparts, men bigg inough to throw
Charing Crosse for a barr, men which do know
No token of worth, but Queenes man, and Fine   235
Living, barrells of beefe, flagons of wine.
I shooke Like a spyed spy. Preachers which are
Seas of witt and arts, you can, then dare
Drowne the sins of this Place, for for mee
Who ame a skant brooke, it inough shal bee   240
To wash their staines away; Though I yett

With Maccabees Modesty the meritt
Of my worke lessen; yet some wise men shall
(I hope) esteeme my writts canonicall. /

Satyra 5.ᵃ

Thou shalt not laugh in this leafe, Muse, nor they
Whome any pity warmes. He which did lay
Rules to make Courtiers (he beeing understood
May make good Courtiers, but who Courtiers good)
Frees from the stings of jeasts all, who' in extreame   5
Are wretched or wicked: Of these two a theame
Charity and Liberty give me. What is hee
Who Officers rage and Suters miseree
Can wright and jeast? If all things be in all
(As I thinke, since all which were are and shall   10
Bee, be made of the same Elements
Each thing, each thing implyes or represents)
Then man is a world, in which Officers
Are the vast ravishing seas, and Suters
Springs, now full, now shallow, now dry; which to   15
That which drownes them run. These selfe reasons do
Prove the world a man; in which Officers
Are the devowring Stomack, and Suters
Th' excrement which they voyd. All men are dust;
How much worse are Suters who to mens lust   20
Are made prayes? O worse than dust or wormes meat,
For they do eat you now, whose selves wormes shall eat.
They are the Mills which grind you, yet you are
The wind which drives them; And a wastfull warr
Is fought against you, and you fight it. They   25
Adulterate law, and you prepare ther way
Like wittols; The' issue your owne ruine is.
Greatest, and fayrest Empresse, know you this?
Alas, no more than Thames calme head doth know
Whose meades her armes drowne, or whose corne o'erflow.   30
You, Sir, whose righteousnesse she loves, whom I
By having leave to serve ame most richly
For service payd, authorizd now, begin
To know and weede out this enormous sin.
O age of rusty Iron, some better witt   35

Call it some worse name, yf aught equall itt.

[p. 22] The Iron Age that was, when Justice was sold, now
Injustice is sold deerer farr; Allow
All claym'd fees and dutyes, Gamesters, anone
The mony which you sweare and sweat for is gone   40
Into' other hands; So controverted lands
Like Angelica, scape the strivers hands.
If law be in the Judges hart, and he
Have no hart to resist letter or fee
Wher wilt thou appeal? Power of the Courts below   45
Flow from the first maine hedd: And these can throw
Thee, if they suck thee in, to misery
To fetters, halters; But if th' injury
Steele thee to dare complayne, alas, thou goest
Against the streame when upwards; when thou' art most   50
Heavy and most faynt. And in those labors, they
Gainst whome thou shouldst complayne, will in thy way
Become great seas, o'er which when thou shalt bee
Forc'd to make golden bridges, thou shalt see
That all thy gold was drownd in them before.   55
All things follow their likes; only who 'have, may have more.
Judges are Gods. He who made and sayd them so
Ment not men should be forc'd to them to go
By meanes of Angells. When supplications
We send to God; to Dominatiöns,   60
Powers, Cherubins, and all heavens Courts, if wee
Should pay fees, as here, dayly bread would bee
Scarse to kings; so t' is. Would it not anger
A Stoick, a Coward, yea a Martyr
To see a Pursevant come in, and call   65
All his Clothes, Copes; bookes, Primmers; and all
His Plate, Chalices; and mistake them away
And aske a fee for comming? Oh ne'er may
Fayre laws whight reverent name be strumpeted
To warrant thefts; she is established   70
Recorder to Destiny on Earth; and shee
Speakes fates words; and but tells us who must bee
[p. 23] Rich, who poore, who in chaynes, who in jayles;
She is all fayre, but yet hath foule long nayles;
With which she scratcheth Suters. In bodyes   75
Of men (so in law) nayles are th' extremityes
So' Officers stretch to more than law can do
As our nayles reach what no els part comes to.

Why bar'st thou to yon Officer foole? hath hee
Gott those goods for which earst men bar'd to thee?   80
Foole twise, thrise; Thou' hast bought wrong, and now
    hungerly
Begst right. But that dole comes not till these dy.
Thou' hast much; and laws Urim and Thummin try
Thou wouldst for more; and for all hast paper
Inough to clothe all the great Carriques pepper.   85
Sell that, and by that thou much more shalt leese
Than Hamman if he sold 'his antiquitees.
O wretch, that thy fortunes should moralize
AEsops fables; and make tales Prophesies.
Thou art that swimming dogg whom shadows cosenéd   90
And div'dst neere drowning for what vanishéd. /

[p. 24: blank]

Elegia 1.ª

[p. 25]

Not that in color it was like thy haire
For armelets of that thou maist let me weare;
Nor that thy hand it ofte embrac'd and kist,
For so it had that good which ofte I mist,
Nor for that silly old moralitee   5
That as those links are tyed our love should bee
Mourne I that I thy sevenfold chayne have lost
Nor for the lucke sake but the bitter cost.
Oh shall twelve righteous Angels which as yet
No leaven of vile sodder did admit;   10
Nor yet by any taint have stray'd or gone
From the first state of ther creatïon;
Angels which heaven commanded, to provide
All things to me, and be my faythfull guide
To gayne new frinds, to' appease great enemyes   15
To comfort my soule when I ly or rise;
Shall these twelve innocents, by thy severe
Sentence, dread Judge, my sins great burden beare?
Shall they be damn'd and in the furnace throwne
And punisht for offenses not their owne?   20
They save not me, they do not ease my paynes
When in that hell they' are burn'd and tyed in chaynes.
Were they but crownes of France, I caréd not
For most of theim their naturall cuntry rott

I thinke possesseth; they come here to us   25
So leane, so pale, so lame, so ruinous,
And howsoe'er french kings most Christian bee
Their crownes are circumcis'd most Jewishly.
Or were they Spanish stamps, still traveling
That are become as Catholique as their king   30
Those unlick'd beare whelps, unfild pistolets,
That more than canon shotts avayles or letts,
Which negligently left unrounded, looke
Like many angled figures in the booke

[p. 26]   Of some great Conjuror, which would enforce   35
Nature, as these do justice from her course.
Which, as the soule quickens head, feete and hart
As streames like vaynes, run through th' Earths every part
Visit all Cuntryes, and have slily made
Gorgious France ragged, ruynd and decayd;   40
Scotland which knew no state, proud in one day
And mangled seventene-headed Belgia;
Or were it such gold as that, wherwithall
Almighty Chimicks from each minerall
Having by subtile fyre a soule outpulld   45
Are durtely and desperatly gulld,
I would not spitt to quench the fyre they' were in
For they are guilty of much haynous sin.
But shall my harmelesse Angels perish? shall
I lose my guard, my ease, my food, my all?   50
Much hope which they should nourish wilbe dead
Much of my able youth and lustihead
Will vanish; if thou love, let them alone
For thou wilt love me lesse, when they are gone.
Oh be content that some loud squeaking Crier   55
Well pleased with one leane thredbare groat for hyer
May like a devill rore through every street
And gall the finders conscience if they meet.
Or let me creepe to some dread Conjurer
Which with fantastique scheames fulfills much paper,   60
Which hath devided heaven in tenements
And with whores, theves, and murderers stuffd his rents
So full, that though he passe them all in sin
He leaves himselfe no roome to enter in,
And if when all his art and time is spent   65
He say, t' will ne'er be found, oh be content.
Receave the doome from him ungrudgingly

Because he is the mouthe of destiny.
Thou sayst, alas the gold doth still remayne
Though it be changd and put into a Chayne.　70
So in those first falne Angels resteth still　　　　[p. 27]
Wisdom and knowledg; but t' is turnd to ill.
As these should do good works and should provide
Necessityes, but now must nource thy pride.
And they are still bad Angels, myne are none　75
For forme gives beeing, and their forme is gone.
Pity these Angels yet, their dignityes
Passe Vertues, Powers, and Principalityes.
But thou art resolute, thy will be donne.
Yet with such anguish, as her only sonne　　　80
The mother in the hungry grave doth lay
Unto the fyre these martyrs I betray.
Good soules, for you give life to every thing,
Good Angels, for good messages you bring,
Destin'd you might have been to such a one　85
As would have lov'd, and worshipd you alone.
One which would suffer hunger, nakednes,
Yea death ere he would make you numberles.
But I ame guilty of your sad decay;
May your few fellows longer with me stay.　　90
But oh thou wretched finder whom I hate
So much, as 'I allmost pity thy estate,
Gold beeing the heaviest metall amongst all
May my most heavy curse upon thee fall.
Here fetterd, manacled, and hangd in chaines　95
First maist thou be, then chaind to hellish paynes.
Or be with forraign gold bribd to betray
Thy Cuntry, and fayle both of that 'and thy pay.
May the next thing thou stoopst to reach, containe
Poyson, whose nimble fume rott thy moist braine:　100
Or libells, or some interdicted thing
Which negligently kept, thy ruyne bring.
Lust bred diseases rott thee 'and dwell with thee
Itchy desyre, and no abilitee.
May all the hurt which ever gold hath wrought,　105
[All mischiefes which all devills ever thought]
Want after plenty, poore and gowty age　　　　[p. 28]
The plagues of travelers, love and mariage
Afflict thee, and at thy lifes latest moment
May thy swolne sinnes themselves to thee present.　110

But I forgive; repent then honest man
Gold is restorative, restore it then
Or if with it thou beest loth to depart
Because t' is cordial, would 't were at thy hart. /

[p. 29]

Elegia 2.[a]

As the sweet sweate of roses in a still
As that which from chafd muscatts pores doth trill
As the allmighty balme of the' early East
Such are the sweat dropps on my Mistres brest:
And on her neck her skin such lustre setts   5
They seeme no sweat drops but pearle carcanetts.
Ranck sweaty froth thy Mistres brow defiles
Like spermatique issue of ripe menstrous biles.
Or like that scumm, which by needs lawles law
Enforc'd, Sancerres starvëd men did draw   10
From perboyld shoes and books and all the rest
Which were with any soveraigne fatnes blest.
And like vile lying stones in saffrond tinne
Or warts or wheales they hang upon her skinne.
Round, as the world 'is her head on every side   15
Like to that fatal ball which fell on Ide.
Or that wherof God had such jealousy
As for the raveshing therof we dy:
Thy head is like a roughewen statue of jeat
Where marks for eyes, nose, mouth, are yet scarse sett, 20
Like the first Chaos, or flat seeming face
Of Cinthia, when th' Earthes shadows her embrace.
Like Proserpines whigt bewty-keeping chest,
Or Joves best fortunes urne, is her faire brest.
Thyne like worme eaten truncks clothd in Celes skin   25
Or grave that's durt without, and stinck within.
And like the slender stalke at whose end stands
The woodbine quivering, are her armes, and hands.
Like rough-barkd Elmeboughs, or the russet skin
Of men late skourg'd for madnes or for sin,   30
Like sun-parch'd quarters on the city gate
Such is thy tann'd skins lamentable state.
And like a bunch of ragged carrets stand
The short swolne fingers of thy gowty hand.

Then like the Chimicks masculine equall fyre   35   [p. 30]
Which in the limbecks warme wombe doth inspyre
Into th' Earths worthlesse durt a soule of gold
Such chearishing heate her best lovd part doth hold.
Thyne 'is like the drad mouthe of a fired gun
Or like hott liquid metals newly run   40
Into clay molds, or like that Etna
Wher round about the gras is burnt away.
Are not your kissings then as filthy' and more
As a worme sucking an envenomd sore?
Doth not thy fearfull hand in feeling quake   45
As one which gathring flouers still feard a snake?
Is not your last act harsh and violent
As when a Plough a stony ground doth rent?
So kis good turtells, so devoutly nice
Are Priests in handling reverent sacrifice;   50
And such in searching wounds the surgeon is
As we when we embrace or touch or kis.
Leave her, and I will leave comparing thus:
She, and Comparisons are odious. /

Elegia 3.[a]   [p. 31]

Once and but once found in thy companee
All thy suppos'd escapes are layd on mee.
And as a thiefe at barr is questiond there
By all the men, that have beene robbd that yeare
So am I, (by this trayterous meanes surprizd)   5
By thy Hydroptique father catechiz'd.
Though he had wont to search with glazèd eyes
As though he came to kill a cocatrice,
Though he have ofte sworne that he would remove
Thy bewtyes bewty, and food of our love,   10
Hope of his goods, yf I with thee were seene
Yet close and secret as our soules we 'have beene.
Though thy immortall mother which doth ly
Still buried in her bed, yet will not dy,
Take this advantage to sleepe out daye light   15
And watch thy entryes and returnes all night,
And when she takes thy hand, and would seeme kind
Doth search what rings and armelets she can find,

And kissing notes the color of thy face
And fearing lest thou 'art swolne doth thee embrace,   20
And to try yf thou long doth name strange meates
And notes thy palenes, blushings, sighes, and sweates,
And politiquely will to thee confes
The sins of her owne youths ranke lustines,
Yet love these sorceryes did remove, and move   25
Thee to gull thyne owne mother for my love.
Thy little brethren which like faery sprights
Ofte skipt into our chamber those sweete nights
And kist and ingled on thy fathers knee
Were brib'd next day to tell what they did see.   30
The grimm eight foot high Ironbound serving man
That ofte names God in othes and only then
He that to barr the first gate doth as wide
As the great Rhodian Colossus stride,
Which if in hell no other paynes ther were
Makes me feare hell because he must be there,   35

[p. 32]   Though by thy father he were hyr'd for this
Could never witnes any touch or kis.
But oh too common ill, I brought with mee
That which betrai'd me to mine enemee: 40
A loud perfume, which at my entrance cryed
Even at thy fathers nose, so we were spyed.
When like a tyrant king, that in his bed
Smelt gunpowder, the pale wretch shiverëd.
Had it been some bad smell, he would have thought   45
That his owne feete or breath that smell had wrought.
But as we, in our Ile emprisonnëd
Where Cattell only and divers doggs are bred
The pretious Unicornes strange Monsters call
So thought he good strange that had none at all.   50
I tought my silkes their whistling to forbeare
Even my opprest shoes dumb and speachles were;
Only thou bitter sweet whom I had layd
Next me, me trayterously hast betrayd,
And unsuspected hast invisibly   55
At once fled unto him and stayd with mee.
Base excrement of earth, which dost confound
Sence, from distinguishing the sick from sound;
By thee the seely amorous sucks his death
By drawing in a leprous harlots breath: 60
By thee the greatest staine to mans estate

Falls on us, to be calld effeminate.
Though you be much lov'd in the Princes hall
There things that seeme exceed substantiall.
Gods when ye fum'd on Altars were pleasd well   65
Because you were burnt, not that they likd the smell.
You are lothsome all beeing taken simply alone;
Shall we love ill things joynd and hate each one?
If you were good, your good doth soon decay
And you are rare that takes the good away.   70
All my perfumes I give most willingly
To' embalme thy fathers corse; What, will he dy? /

Elegia 4.^a

Fond woman which wouldst have thy husband dy
And yet complaynst of his great jealosy.
If swolne with poyson he lay in 'his last bed
His body with a sere barke coverëd;
Drawing his breath as thick and short as can   5
The nimblest crocheting Musiciän,
Redy with lothsome vomiting to spue
His Soule out of one hell into a new,
Made deafe with his pure kindreds howling cryes
Begging with few faignd teares great legacies,   10
Thou wouldst not weepe, but joly' and frolick bee
As a slave which to morrow should be free.
Yet weepst thou when thou seest him hungerly
Swallow his owne death, hearts-bane jealosy.
Oh give him many thankes; hee 'is courteous   15
That in suspecting kindly warneth us.
We must not as we usd, flout openly
In scoffing riddles his deformity;
Nor at his boord together being sate
With words nor touche scarse lookes adulterate.   20
Nor when he swolne and pamperd with great fare
Sitts downe and snorts cag'd in his basket chaire
Must we usurpe his owne bed any more
Nor kis and play in 'his house as before.
Now I see many dangers, for that is   25
His Realme, his Castle, and his Diocis.
But if as envyous men which would revile

Their Prince, or coyne his gold, themselves exile
Into an other cuntry, and do it there,
We play' in an other house, what should we feare?   30
There we will skorn his houshould policyes,
His seely plotts and pensionary spyes,
As the inhabitants of Thames right side
Do Londons Maier or Germans the Popes pride. /

[p. 34]

Elegia 5.ᵃ

Oh let not me serve so, as those men serve
Whom honors smokes at once fatten and starve;
Poorely enrich't with great mens words or looks
Nor so write my name in thy loving books
As those idolaterous flatterers, which still   5
Their Princes stiles, with many Realmes fulfill
Whence they no tribute have, and where no sway:
Such services I offer, as shall pay
Themselves: I hate dead Names: O then let mee
Favorit in Ordinary, or no favorit bee.   10
When my soule was in her owne body sheathd
Nor yet by Othes betrothd, nor kisses breathd
Into my Purgatory, faythles thee,
Thy hart seemd waxe, and steele thy constancee.
So careles flowers strowd on the waters face   15
The curlëd whirlepooles suck, smack, and embrace,
Yet drowne them: So the tapers beamy ey
Amorously twinckling beckens the giddy fly
Yet burnes his wings: and such the Devil is
Scarse visiting them who are intyrely his.   20
When I behold a streame, which from the spring,
Doth with doutfull melodious murmuring,
Or in a speechles slumber calmely ride
Her wedded channels bosome, and then chide
And bend her browes, and swell yf any bow   25
Do but stoope downe to kisse her upmost brow;
Yet if her often gnawing kisses win
The trayterous banke to gape and let her in
She rusheth violently, and doth divorce
Her from her native and her long kept course   30
And rores and braves it, and in gallant skorne

In flattering eddyes promising retorne
She flouts the Channell, who thenceforth is dry:
Then say I That is shee, and this ame I.
Yet let not thy deepe bitternes begett   35
Careles despayre in me, for that will whett
My mind to skorne, And Oh love dulld with payne
Was ne'er so wise, nor well armd as disdayne.
Then with new eyes I shall survay thee, 'and spy
Death in thy cheekes, and darknesse in thine ey.   40
Though hope bred Fayth and love, thus tought I shall   [p. 35]
As Nations do from Rome, from thy love fall.
My hate shall outgrow thyne, and utterly
I will renounce thy dallyance: and when I
Ame the Recusant, in that resolute state   45
What hurts it me to be excommunicate? /

Elegia 6.ᵃ

Natures lay Ideott, I tought thee to love
And in that Sophistry, Oh thou dost prove
Too subtile: foole, thou didst not understand
The mistique language of the ey nor hand.
Nor couldst thou judg the difference of the aire   5
Of sighs, and say, This lyes, this sounds dispayre.
Nor by th' eyes water call a malady
Desperatly hott or changing feverously.
I had not tought thee then, the Alphabett
Of flowers, how they devisefully being sett   10
And bound up, might with speechlesse secresy
Deliver arrands mutely 'and mutually
Remember since all thy words usd to bee
To every Sutor, Aye, yf my frinds agree.
Since houshold charmes thy husbands name to teach   15
Were all the love-tricks that thy witt could reach,
And since an howers discourse could scarse have made
One answer in thee, and that ill arrayd
In broken Proverbs, and torne sentences.
Thou art not by so many dutyes his   20
That from the worlds Common having severd thee
Inlayd thee, neyther to bee seene nor see
As myne, which have with amorous delicacyes

Refind thee into a blisfull paradise;
Thy graces and good words my creatures bee,   25
I planted knowledg and lifes tree in thee
Which, oh, shall strangers tast? Must I alas
Frame and enamell plate, and drinke in glas?
Chafe waxe for others seals, breake a Colts force,
And leave him then, beeing made a redy horse? /   30

[p. 36]

Elegia 7.ª

Till I have peace with thee, warr other Men;
And when I have peace, can I leave thee then?
All other warrs are scrupulous; only thou
O fayr free City, mayst thy selfe allow
To any one: In Flanders, who can tell   5
Whether the Maister pres or men rebell?
Only we know, that which all Ideots say
They beare most blows which come to part the fray.
France in her Lunatique giddines did hate
Ever our Men, yea and our God of late.   10
Yet she relys upon our Angels well
Which ne'er returne; no more than they which fell.
Sick Ireland is with a strange warr posses't
Like to an Ague; now raging, now at rest;
Which time will cure: yet it must do her good   15
If she were purgd, and her head vayne let blood.
And Midas joyes our Spanish journeys give,
We touch all gold, but find no food to live.
And I should be in that hott parching clime
To dust and ashes turnd before my time.   20
To mew me in a Ship, is to enthrall
Me in a prison that were like to fall.
Or in a Cloyster, save that there men dwell
In a calme heaven, here in a swaggering hell.
Long voyages are long consumptiöns   25
And ships are carts for executiöns.
Yea they are deaths; is't not all one to fly
Into an other world, as 't is to dy?
Here let me warr; in these armes let me ly
Here let me parley, batter, bleede, and dy.   30
Thy armes imprison me, and myne armes thee,

Thy hart thy ransome is, take myne for mee.
Other men warr that they ther rest may gayne
But we will rest that we may fight agayne.
Those warrs the' ignorant, these th' experienc'd love;   35
There we are allways under, here above.
There Engines farr off breed a just trew feare;
Neere thrusts, pikes, stabs, yea bullets hurt not here.
There lyes are wrongs; here safe uprightly ly:
There men kill men, we 'will make one by and by.   40
Thou nothing; I not halfe so much shall do   [p. 37]
In these warrs, as they may which from us two
Shall spring. Thousands we see which travaile not
To warrs, but stay swords, armes and shott
To make at home; And shall not I do then   45
More glorious service staying to make men? /

Elegia 8.ᵃ

Come Madame, come, All rest my powers defy;
Untill I labor, I in labor ly.
The foe oft times having the foe in sight
Is tyrd with standing though they never fight.
Off with that girdle, like heavens zones glistering   5
But a farr fayrer world encompassing.
Unpin that spangled brestplate, which you weare
That th' eyes of busy fooles may be stopt there.
Unlace your selfe: for that harmonious chime
Tells me from you that now 't is your bed time.   10
Off with that happy buske whom I envy
That still can be, and still can stand so nigh.
Your gownes going off, such bewteous state reveales
As when from flowry meads th' hills shadow steales.
Off with your wiry coronet and show   15
The hairy Diademe which on you doth grow.
Now off with those shoes and then safely tredd
In this loves halowed temple; this soft bedd.
In such whight robes, heaven[s] Angels us'd to bee
Receavd by men: Thou, Angel bringst with thee   20
A heaven like Mahomets Paradise: And though
Ill spirights walke in whight, we easily know
By this these Angels from an evill spright

They sett our hairs, but these the flesh upright.
License my roving hands, and let them go   25
Behind, before, above, betweene, below.
Oh my America, my newfound land,
My kingdome, safelyest when with one man man'd.
My myne of pretious stones; my empiree
How blest ame I in this discovering thee!   30
[p. 38]   To enter in these bonds, is to be free
Then where my hand is sett, my seale shal bee.
Full Nakednes, all joyes are due to thee
As soules unbodied, bodyes uncloth'd must bee,
To tast whole joyes. Gems which you women use   35
Are as Atlantas balls cast in mens views
That when a fooles ey lighteth on a gem
His earthly soule may covet theirs, not them.
Like pictures, or like bookes gay coverings, made
For lay men, are all women thus arayd,   40
Themselves are mistique bookes, which only wee
Whom their imputed grace will dignify
Must see revealed. Then since I may know,
As liberally as to a midwife show
Thy selfe. Cast all, yea this whight linnen hence; 45
There is no penance, much lesse innocence.
To teach thee I ame naked first: why then
What needst thou have more covering then a man? /

[p. 39]   *Elegia 9.*ᵃ

Allthough thy hand, and fayth and good works too,
Have seald thy love which nothing should undoo,
Yea though thou fall back, that Apostasee
Confirme thy love; yet much much I feare thee.
Women are like the Arts: forc'd unto none   5
Open to all Searchers; unprized if unknowne.
If I have caught a bird, and let him fly
Another fowler using these meanes as I
May catch the same bird, 'and as these things bee
Women are made for men, not him nor mee.   10
Foxes and Gotes, All beasts change when they please:
Shall women more hott, wyly, wild than these
Be bound to one man, and did Nature then

Idly make them apter to' endure than men?
They are our cloggs, and their owne; if a man bee   15
Chayned to a Galley, yet this Galley is free.
Who hath a plowland casts all 'his seed corne there
And yet allows his ground more corne should beare.
Though Danubë into the sea must flow
The sea receives the Rhine, Volga, and Po.   20
By Nature which gave it, this libertee
Thou lov'st, but oh, canst thou love it and mee?
Likenes glues love: Then yf so thou do
To make us like and love, must I change too?
More than thy hate, I hate 'it: rather let me   25
Allow her change, than change as ofte as shee.
And so not teache, but force my opinione
To love not any one, nor every one.
To live in one land, is captivity,
To run all cuntryes a wild roguery.   30
Waters stinck soone yf in one place they bide
And in the vast sea are worse putrifide.
But when they kisse one banke and leaving this
Never looke backe but the next banke do kis
Then are they purest. Change is the nurcery   35
Of Musick, Joye, Life, and Eternity. /

Elegia 10.^a   [p. 40]

Marry and love thy Flavia for shee
Hath all things wherby others beuteous bee.
For though her eyes be smale, her mouth is great
Though they be Ivory, yet her teethe are Jeat:
Though they be dimme, yet she is light inough   5
And though her harsh haire fall, her skin is rough.
What though her cheekes be yellow, her hair 'is red,
Give her thyne; and she hath a Maydenhead.
These things are bewtyes Elements: where these
Meete in one, that one must as perfect please.   10
If red and whight, and each good quality
Bee in thy wench, ne'er aske, wher it doth ly.
In buying things perfumd, we aske if there
Be muske and amber in it, but not where.
Though all her parts be not in th' usuall place   15

She 'hath yet an Anagram of a good face.
If we might put the letters but one way
In the leane dearth of letters, what could we say?
When by the gamut some musitians make
A perfect song, others will undertake   20
By the same gamut chang'd, to equall itt
Things simply good can never be unfitt.
She is fayre as any' yf all be like her,
And if none be then she is singuler.
All love is wonder, yf we justly doo   25
Accoumpt her wonderful, why not lovely too?
Love built on bewty soone as bewty dyes;
Chuse this face changd by no deformityes.
Women are all like Angels: the fayre bee
Like those which fell to worse; but such as she,   30
Like to good Angels nothing can impayre:
'T is lesse griefe to be foule than to' have beene fayre.
For one nights revells silke and gold we chuse
But in long journeys cloth, and leather use.
Bewty is barren oft: best husbands say   35
There is best land wher ther is foulest way.
Oh what a soveraigne plaister will she bee
If thy past sins have tought thee jealousie?
Here needes no spyes nor eunuchs: her committ
Safe to thy foes, yea to a Marmositt.   40
When Belgiaes Cityes, the round cuntryes drowne
That durty foulnes guards, and armes the towne:
So doth her face guard her. And so for thee
Which, forc'd by business, absent oft must bee
She whose face like clouds turns the day to night   45
Who mightier than the sea makes moones seeme whight,
Who though seaven yeares she in the stews had layd
A Nunnery durst receive, and thinke a mayd,
And though in childbirths labor she did ly
Midwifes would sweare, 't weare but a timpany,   50
Whom, yf she 'accuse herself, I credit lesse
Than witches which impossibles confesse,
Whom dildoes, bedstaves, and her velvett glas
Would be as loth to touch as Joseph was.
One like none and likd of none fittest were,   55
For things in fashion every man will weare. /

[p. 41]

Elegia 11.^a

By our first strange and fatal interview
By all desyres which therof did insue:
By our long starving hopes, by that remorce
Which my words masculine persuasive force
Begott in thee, and by the memoree   5
Of hurts which spyes and rivalls threat'ned mee
I calmely begg: But by thy Parents wrath
By all paynes which want and Divorcement hath
I conjure thee: And all those othes which I
And thou have sworne to seale joynt constancy   10
Here I unsweare, and oversweare them thus
Thou shalt not love by meanes so dangerous.
Temper o fayre love, loves impetuous rage
Be my trew mistres still, not my faignd Page.
I'le go: and by thy kind leave leave behind   15
Thee, only worthy to nurce in my mind
Thirst to come backe: Oh yf thou dy before,
From other lands my soule towards thee shall soare:
Thy else allmighty bewty cannot move
Rage from the seas, nor thy love teache them love.   20
Nor tame wild Boreas' harshnes, thou hast read   [p. 42]
How roughly he in pieces shiverëd
Fayr Orithia whom he swore he lovd.
Fall ill or good, 't is madnes to have provd
Dangers unurg'd; feed on this flatteree,   25
That absent lovers one in th' other bee.
Dissemble nothing, not a boy; nor change
Thy bodyes habit, nor minds, be not strange
To thy selfe only, all will spy in thy face
A blushing womanly discovering grace.   30
Richly clothd Apes are calld Apes; and as soone
Eclips'd as bright, we call the moone the moone.
Men of France, changeable Cameleons
Spittles of diseases, shops of fashions
Loves fuellers and the rightest companee   35
Of Players which upon the worlds stage bee
Will quickly know thee, and know thee, and alas
Th' indifferent Italian as we pas
His warme land, well content to thinke thee Page,

Will haunt thee with such lust and hideous rage   40
As Lots fayre guests were vext; But none of these
Nor spungy' Hydroptique Dutche shall thee displease
If thou stay here: Oh stay here; for for thee
England is only a worthy gallerie
To walke in Expectation till from thence   45
Our great king call thee into his presence.
When I ame gone dreame me some happines
Nor let thy looks our long hid love confes.
Nor prayse nor disprayse mee: blesse nor curse
Openly loves force: Nor in bed fright thy nourse   50
With midnights startings, crying out Oh Oh
Nurse oh my love is slayne: I saw him go
Ore the whight Alpes alone, I saw him, I,
Assaild, fight, taken, stab'd, bleede, fall, and dy.
Augur me better chance; except dredd Jove   55
Thinke it inough for me, to' have had thy love. /

[p. 43] ## Elegia 12.ᵃ

Here take my picture, though I bid farwell;
Thyne in my hart, wher my soule dwells shall dwell.
'T is like me now, but I dead, 't wilbe more,
When we are shadows bothe, than 't was before.
When weatherbeaten I come back; my hand   5
Perchance with rude oares torne, or sunsbeams
    tann'd.
My face and breast of hayrecloth, and my head
With cares rash sodain hoarines o'erspred,
My body a sack of bones, broken within
And powders blew staines scatterd on my skin,   10
If rivall fooles taxe thee to' have lov'd a man
So foule and coarse, as oh I may seeme then
This shall say what I was; and thou shalt say,
Do his hurts reache mee? doth my worthe decay?
Or do they reach his judging mind, that hee   15
Should like 'and love les, what he did love to see?
That which in him was fayre or delicate
Was but the milke which in loves childish state
Did nourse it: who now 'is growne strong inough
To feede 'on that which to disusd tasts seems tough. /   20

Elegia 13.ᵃ

Sorrow, who to this house, scarse knew the way
Is, oh, heire of it; our all is his prey.
This strange chance claymes strange wonder; and to us
Nothing can be so strange, as to weepe thus.
Tis well his lifes loud speaking works deserve   5
And give prayse too, our cold tongues could not serve.
Tis well he kept teares from our eyes before
That to fitt this deepe il we might have store.
Oh yf a sweete bryer clymbe up by a tree
If to a Paradise that transplanted bee   10
Or felld and burnt for holy sacrifice
Yet that must wither which by it did rise;
As we for him dead: Though no family
Ere riggd a soule for heavens discovery
With whom more venturers more boldly dare   15
Venter their states with him in joy to share.
We lose what all frinds lovd, him; he gaines now   [p. 44]
But life by Deathe, which worst foes would allow;
If he could have foes, in whose practice grew
All vertues whose names subtile Schoolemen knew.   20
What ease, can hope that we 'shall see him, begett,
When we must dy first, and cannot dy yett?
His Children are his pictures, oh they bee
Pictures of him dead, senseles, cold as hee.
Here needes no marble tomb; since he is gone   25
He and about him, his, are turnd to stone. /

Epithalamium   [p. 45]

1.   The sun beames in the East are spred
     Leave leave, fayr bride, your solitary bed.
     No more shall you return to it alone.
     It nourseth sadnes, and your bodyes print
     Like to a grave the yielding Downe doth dint.   5
     You and your other you meete ther anone.
     Put forth, put forth that warme balme-breathing thigh
     Which when next time you in these sheetes will smother
     Ther it must meet an other

Which never was, but must be ofte more nigh;   10
Come glad from thence, go gladder then you came
To day put on perfection and a womans name.

2.   Daughters of London, you which bee
Our golden Mines and furnish'd Treasuree;
You which are Angels, yet still bring with you   15
Thousands of Angels on your mariage dayes,
Helpe with your presence and devise to prayse
These rites which also unto you grow due.
Conceitedly dres her, and be assignd
By you fitt place for every flower and Jewell,   20
Make her for love fitt fuell,
As gay as Flora, and as rich as Inde,
So may she fayre, rich, glad, 'and in nothing lame
To day put on perfection and a womans name.

3.   And you frolique Patriciäns,   25
Sonnes of these Senators, wealths deepe oceans,
Yee painted Courtiers, Barrells of others witts,
Yee Cuntrymen, who but your Beasts, love none,
Yee of those fellowships wherof he 'is one
Of study 'and play made strange Hermaphroditts   30
Here shine: This bridegrome to the Temple bring.
Lo, in yon path which store of strawd flowers graceth
The sober virgin paceth
Except my sight fayle: 't is no other thing.
Weepe not, nor blush; here is no griefe nor shame   35
To day put on perfection and a womans name.

[p. 46]   4.   Thy two-leavd gates, fayre Temple' unfold
And these two in thy sacred bosome hold
Till mistically joynd, but one they bee:
Then may thy leane amd hunger starvëd wombe   40
Long time expect their bodyes and ther tombe
Long after ther owne Parents fatten thee.
All elder claymes and all cold barrennes
All yielding to new loves, be farr for ever
Which might these two dissever.   45
All wayes, all th' other may each one possesse,
For the best bride, best worthy' of prayer and fame,
To day puts on perfection & a womans name.

5.   O, winter dayes bring much delight
Not for themselves but for they soone bring night.   50

Other sweetes wait thee than these divers meates,
Other disports than dauncing jolityes,
Other love tricks than glauncing with the eyes,
But that the Sun still in our halfe spheare sweates
He flyes in winter, but now he stands still.   55
Yet shadows turne: Noone point he hath attained
His steedes will be restrained
But gallop lively downe the westerne hill.
Thou shalt when he hath run the worlds half frame
To night put on perfection and a womans name.   60

6. The amorous evening star is rose.
    Why should not then our amorous star enclose
    Herselfe in her wish'd bed: release your strings,
    Musiciäns; and Dauncers take some truce
    With these your pleasing labors; for great use   65
    As much wearines as perfection brings.
    You, and not only you, but all toyld beasts
    Rest duly': at night; all ther toyles are dispenced,
    But in ther beds commenced
    Are other labors and more dainty feasts.   70
    Shee goes a mayd, who lest she turn the same,
To night puts on perfection and a womans name.

7. Thy virgins girdle now unty   [p. 47]
    And in thy nuptiall bed, loves Altar, ly
    A pleasing sacrifice: Now disposses   75
    Thee of these chaines and robes, which were put on
    To' adorne the day, not thee; for thou alone
    Like Vertu 'and Truth art best in nakednes,
    This bed is only to Virginitee
    A grave, but to a better state a cradle.   80
    Till now thou wast but able
    To bee, what now thou art: then that by thee
    No more be sayd, I may be, but I ame,
To night put on perfection and a womans name.

8. Even like a faythfull man content   85
    That this life for a better should be spent,
    So she a mothers riche stile doth prefer.
    And at the bridegromes wish'd approch doth ly
    Like an appointed lambe, when tenderly
    The Priest comes on his knees to' embowell her.   90
    Now sleepe or watche with more joye: and o light
    Of heav'n, to morrow rise thou hott and early:

This sun will love so dearly
Her rest, that long, long, we shall want her sight.
Wonders are wrought, for she which had no maime   95
To night puts on perfection and a womans name. /

[p. 48: blank]
[p. 49]
To Mr C. B.

Thou, which art I, (tis nothing to be so)
Thou which art still thy selfe, by these shalt know
Part of our passage, and a hand or eye
By Hilliard drawne, is worth a history
By a worse painter made; And without pryde   5
When by thy judgment they are dignifyde
My lines are such: tis the preheminence
Of frindship only to' impute excellence.
England to' whom we owe, what we be and have
Sad, that her sonnes did seeke a forreigne grave   10
(For Fates or Fortunes drifts none can soothsay,
Honor and Misery have one face and way)
From out her pregnant intrails sigh'd a wind
Which at th' aires middle marble roome did find
Such strong resistance, that it selfe it threw   15
Downward agayne; and so when it did view
How in the Port our fleete deare time did leese
Withering like prisoners which ly but for fees,
Mildly it kist our Sayles, and fresh and sweete
As to a stomack stervd, whose insides meete,   20
Meat comes, it came; and swole our Sayles, when wee
So joyd, as Sara' her swelling joyd to see.
But 't was but so kind as our Cuntrymen
Which bring frinds one days way, and leave
    them then.
Then, like two mighty kings, which dwelling farr   25
Asunder, meete against a third to warr
The South, and West winds joyn'd; and as they blew
Waves like a rolling trench before them threw.
Sooner than you read this line, did the gale
Like shott, not feard till felt, our Sayles assayle.   30
And what at first was calld a gust, the same
Hath now a Stormes, anon a Tempests name.

Jonah, I pitty thee, and curse those men
Who when the storme rag'd most, did wake thee then.
Sleep is paynes easiest salve, and doth fullfill   35
All Offices of death, except to kill.
But when I wakd, I saw that I saw not: [p. 50]
I, and the Sun which should teach me, 'had forgott
East, West, Day, Night: and I could but say
If the world 'had lasted, now it had beene day.   40
Thousands our noyses were, yet we mongst all
Could none by his right name, but Thunder call.
Lightning was all our Light; and it raind more
Than yf the Sun had drunke the Sea before.
Some coffind in ther cabbins ly, equally   45
Grievd that they are not dead, and yet must dy.
And as sin-burdned Soules, from graves will creepe
At the Last day, some forth ther cabbins peepe,
And tremblingly' aske, what newes; and do heare so
Like jealous husbands what they would not know.   50
Some sitting on the hatches would seeme there
With hideous gazinge to feare away feare.
There note they the Ships sicknesses, the Mast
Shak'd with this Ague, and the Hold and Wast
With a salt dropsy clog'd; and all our tacklings   55
Snapping like to high stretch'd treble strings.
And from our tatterd Sayles raggs dropp downe, so
As from one hang'd in chaines a yeare ago.
Even our Ordnance plac'd for our defence
Strive to breake loose, and scape away from thence.   60
Pumping hath tyr'd our men; and what's the gaine?
Seas into Seas throwne we suck in againe.
Hearing hath deafd our Saylers; and yf they
Knew how to heare, ther's none knew what to say.
Compar'd to these stormes, Deathe is but a qualme,   65
Hell somwhat lightsome, 'and the Bermuda calme.
Darknes, Lights elder brother, his birth right
Claymes ore this world, and to' heaven hath chas'd Light.
All things are one; and that one, none can bee,
Since all formes uniforme deformitee   70
Doth cover; so that we, except God say
Another Fiat, shall have no more Day.
So violent, yet long these Furies bee,
That, though thyne absence starve me' I wish not thee. /

[p. 51]

To Mr H.W.
20 July. 1598. At Court.

Here 'is no more newes than vertu: I may 'as well
Tell you Calais', or St Michaels tale for newes, as tell
That vice doth here habitually dwell.

/ Yet as to get stomacks we walke up and downe
And toyle to sweeten rest, so may God frowne   5
If but to lothe both, I haunt Court or towne.

/ For here no one, is, from th' extremitee
Of Vice by any other reason free,
But that the next to' him still is worse than hee.

/ In this worlds warrfare they whome rugged Fate   10
(Gods Commissary) doth so throughly hate
As' in the Courts squadron to marshall their state

/ If they stand arm'd with seely honestee
With wishing prayers, and neat integritee,
Like Indians 'gainst Spanish hostes they bee.   15

/ Suspitious boldnes to this place belongs;
And to' have as many eares as all have tongues:
Tender to know, tough to acknowledge wrongs.

/ Beleeve me, Sir, in my youths giddiest dayes,
When to be like the Court was a Playes prayse,   20
Playes were not so like Courts, as Courts 'are like playes.

/ Then let us at these Mimick Antiques jest
Whose deepest Projects, and egregious gests
Are but dull Morals of a game at Chests.

/ But now tis incongruity to smile.   25
Therfore I end: And bid farewell a while;
At Court; though, From Court, were the better stile. /

To Mr. H.W.

[p. 52]

Sir, More than kisses, letters mingle soules:
For thus, frinds absent speake. This ease controules
The tediousnes of my life: But for these
I could Ideate nothing which could please:

1. From the Westmoreland manuscript. 'To Mr H. W. 20 July 1598. At Court.' This gathering of Donne's pre-1600 compositions, entirely written in Rowland Woodward's handwriting, has diagonal slash lines to mark off individual stanzas of poems and to separate individual compositions. New York Public Library, Berg Collection. NYPL Digital Gallery Detail ID 1695916.

But I should wither in one day and pas   5
To' a bottle of hay, that am a locke of grasse.
Life is a voyage; and in our lifes ways
Cuntryes Courts, Towns, are Rocks or Remoraes.
They breake, or stop all ships, yet our state 'is such
That though than pitche they staine worse, we must touch. 10
If in the furnace of the even line
Or under th' adverse Icy Poles thou pine,
Thou knowest two temperate regions girded in,
Dwell there: But, oh, what refuge canst thou win
Parch'd in the Court, and in the Cuntry frozen?   15
Shall Cityes built of both extreames be chosen?
Can Dung and Garlick be 'a perfume? or can
A Scorpion and Torpedo cure a Man?
Cityes are worst of all three; Of all three
(O knotty riddle) each is worst equally.   20
Cityes are Sepulchers; They who dwell there
Are Carcases as if no such ther were.
And Courts are Theaters, where some men play
Princes; some slaves; all to' one end and 'of one Clay.
The Cuntry is a Desert, where no Good   25
Gaind, 'as Habitts, not borne, is understood.
There Men become Beasts, and prone to more Evills,
In Cityes, blocks, and in a lewd Court, Devills.
As in the first Chaos, confusedlie
Each Elements qualityes were in th' other three,   30
So Pride, Lust, Covetise, being severall
To these three places, yet all are in all.
And mingled thus, ther issue' incestuous.
Falshood 'is denizend; Vertu 'is barbarous.
[p. 53] Let no man say there, Vertues flinty wall   35
'Shall lock vice in me; I'le do none, but know all.
Men are Spunges, which to poure out receive;
Who know false play, rather then lose, deceive.
For in best understandings, sinne began
Angels sinn'd first, then Devills, and then Man.   40
Only perchance Beasts sinne not; wretched wee
Are Beasts in all, but whight integritee.
I thinke, yf Men, which in these places live
Durst looke for themselves, and themselves retrive,
They would like strangers greete themselves, seeing then   45
Utopian youth, growne old Italian.
Be then thyne owne home; And in thy selfe dwell;

Inne any where, Continuance maketh Hell.
And seeing the Snayle, which every where doth rome
Carying his own house still, still is at home,   50
Follow (for he is easy pac'd) this Snayle
Be thyne own Pallace, or the world 'is thy Jaile.
And in the worlds sea, do not like Corke sleepe
Upon the waters face; Nor in the Deepe
Sinck like a lead without a lyne; But as   55
Fishes glide leaving no print wher they pas,
Nor making sound, So closely thy Course go
Let Men dispute whether thou breathe or no.
Only' in this one thing be no Galenist. To' make
Courts hott Ambitions holesome, do not take   60
A Dram of Cuntryes dullnes, do not add
Correctives, but, as Chimicks, purge the badd.
But Sir, 'I advise not you; I rather do
Say o'er those lessons, which I learnd of you.
Whome, free from German Schismes, and lightnes   65
Of France, and fayre Italyes faythlesnes,
Having from these suckd, all they had of worthe: [p. 54]
And brought home that Faythe, which you caryed forthe
I throughly love. But if my self I 'have wonne
To know my Rules, I have, and you have   70

Donne. /

To Mr. R.W.

Like one who' in her third widowhed doth profes
Her selfe a Nun, tir'd to a retirednes
So' affects my Muse now a chast fallownes,

/ Since she to few, yet to too many 'hath showne
How love song weedes, 'and satirique thornes are growne   5
Wher seedes of better arts were early sowne.

/ Though to use and love poetry, to mee
Betroth'd to' no one art, be no adulteree,
Omissions of good, ill, as ill deedes bee.

/ For though to' us it seeme, and be light and thin,   10
Yet in those faythfull scales where God throwes in
Mens workes, vanity wayes as much as sin.

/ If our Soules have staind their first whight, yet wee
May clothe them with fayth and deare honestee,
Which God imputes as native puritee.   15

/ Ther is no vertu but Religiöne.
Wise, valiant, sober, just, are names which none
Wants which wants not vice-covering discretiöne.

/ Seeke we then our selves in our selves; for as
Men force the Sun with much more force to pas   20
By gathering his beams with a christall glas,

[p. 55]   / So we, if we into our selves will turne
Blowing our sparks of vertu, may out-burne
The straw which doth about our harts sojourne.

/ You know Phisitians when they would infuse   25
Into' any oyle the soule of simples: use
Places, wher they may ly still warme to chuse.

/ So works retirednesse in us; to roame
Giddily, 'and be every where but at home
Such freedome doth a banishment become.   30

/ We are but Farmers of our selves yet may,
If we can stock our selves and thrive, uplay
Much much dear treasure for the great rent day.

/ Manure thy selfe then, to thy selfe be' aprov'd
And with vayne outward things be no more movd,   35
But to' know that I love thee and would be lov'd. /

[p. 56]   ## To Mr. T.W.

All haile sweet Poet, more full of more strong fyre
Than hath or shall enkindle any spiritt.
I lovd what nature gave thee, but this meritt
    Of witt and art I love not, but admyre.
Who have before, or shall write after thee,   5
Ther works, though toughly labourëd, wilbee
    Like infancy or age, to mans firm stay,
    Or early and late twilights to midday.

Men say and truly, that they better be
   Which be envied than pitied, therfore I   10
   Because I wish thee best, do thee envy,
~~Oh wouldst thou by like reason pity mee.~~
   ~~But care not for mee~~: I that ever was
   In natures and in fortunes gifts alas,
~~Before thy grace got~~ in the Muses schoole,   15
A Monster and a begger, am now a foole.

   Oh how I grieve that lateborne Modesty
Hath got such roote in easy waxen harts
That men may not themselves ther owne good parts
   Extoll, without suspect of surquedry.   20
For but thy selfe no Subject can be found
Worthy thy quill, nor any quill resound
   Thy worth but thyne: how good it were to see
   A poeme in thy prayse and writt by thee.

Now if this song be too' harsh for ryme, yet as   25
   The Painters bad god made a good devill
   T' will be good prose, although the verse be evill,
If thou forget the ryme as thou dost pas.
   Then wryte, that I may follow, and so bee
   Thy debtor, thy' Eccho, thy foyle, thy Zanee.   30
I shall be thought, if myne like thyne I shape
All the worlds Lyon though I be thy Ape. /

To Mr J. D. [p. 57]

Thou sendst me prose and rimes; I send, for those,
Lynes, which beeing nether, seeme 'or verse or prose.
They' are lame and harsh, and have no heat at all
But what thy liberall beams on them let fall.
The nimble fyer which in thy braynes doth dwell: 5
Is it the fyre of heaven or that of hell?
It doth beget 'and conferr like hevens eye,
And like hells fyer it burnes eternally.
And thos whom in thy fury and judgment
Thy verse shall scourge, like hell it will torment.   10
Have mercy on me and my sinfull Muse

Which, rubb'd and tickled wth thyne, could not chuse
But spend some of her pithe, and yeild to bee
One in that chaste and mistique tribadree.
Bassaes adultery no fruit did leave,   15
Nor theirs which their swolne thighs did nimbly
    weave,
And with new armes and mouthes, embrace and kis;
Though they had issue, was not like to this.
Thy Muse, oh strange and holy lecheree,
Beeing a mayd still, gott this song on mee.   20

To Mr T.W.

Hast thee, harsh verse, as fast 'as thy lame measure
Will give thee leave, ~~to him my payne and pleasure~~.
I 'have given thee, and yet thou art too weake,
Feete, and a reasoning soul and tongue to speake.
~~Plead for mee, and so by thyne and my labour~~   5
~~I ame thy creator, thou my saviour.~~
Tell him all questions which men have defended,
Both of the place and paynes of hell, are ended.
~~And 't is decreed that hell is but privation~~
~~Of him, at least in this earths habitation,~~   10
And 'tis wher I ame, wher in every streete
Infections follow, overtake and meete,
Live I, or dy by you my love is sent
And you 'are my [pawnes] or els my testament.

[p. 58]

To L. of D.

See, Sir, how as the suns hott masculine flame
   Begetts strange creatures on Nile's durty slime
   In me your fatherly yet lusty rime
(For these songs are the fruit) have wroght the same.
But though th' engendring force from whence they came 5
   Be strong inough, and nature do admit
   Seaven to be borne at on[c]e, I send as yet
But six, they say the seventh hath still some maime.
I chose your judgment, which the same degree

Doth with her sister, your invention, hold   10
As fyer these drossy rimes to purifie
  Or as Elixar to change them to gold.
You are that Alchimist which allways had
Witt, whose one sparke could make good things of bad. /

To Mr T.W.

Pregnant again with th' old twins Hope and Feare,
Oft have I askt for thee, both how and where
Thou wert, and what my hopes of letters were.
As in the streets sly beggers narrowly
Marke motions of the givers hand and ey   5
And evermore conceave some hope therby.
And now thyne alms is given, thy letters read,
The body risen agayne, the which was dead
And thy poore starveling bountifully fed.
After this banquet my soule doth say grace,   10
And prayse thee for 'it, and zealously embrace
Thy love, though I thinke thy love in this case
  To be as gluttons', which say midst their meate
  They love that best of which they most do eate. /

To Mr T.W.   [p. 59]

At once from hence my lines and I depart
I to my soft still walks, ~~they to my hart:~~
I to the Nurse, they to the child of art.
Yet as a firm house, though the Carpenter
Perish, doth stand: As an Ambassador   5
Lyes safe howe'er his king be in danger,
So though I languish prest with melancholy
My verse, the strict map of my misery,
~~Shall live to see that for whose want I dy~~
Therfore I envy them and do repent   10
That from unhappy me, things happy' are sent.
Yet as a picture or bare sacrament
  Accept these lines, and if in them ther bee
  ~~Meritt of love, bestow that love on mee.~~ /

To Mr R.W.

Zealously my Muse doth salute all thee
Enquiring of that mistique trinitee
Whereof thou 'and all to' whom heavens do infuse
Like fyer, are made: thy body, mind, and Muse.
Dost thou recover sicknes, or prevent?   5
Or is thy mind travaild with discontent?
Or art thou parted from the world and mee
In a good skorn of the worlds vanitee?
Or is thy devout Muse retyrd to sing
Upon her tender Elegiaque string?   10
Our minds part not; joyne then thy Muse with myne
For myne is barren thus devorc'd from thyne. /

[p. 60]

To Mr R.W.

Muse not that by thy mind thy body 'is led:
For by thy mind, my mind's distemperëd.
So thy Care lives long, for I bearing part,
It eates not only thyne, but my swolne hart.
And when it gives us intermissiön   5
We take new harts for it to feede upon.
But as a lay mans Genius doth controule
Body 'and mind, the Muse beeing the Soules Soule
Of Poets, that methinks should ease our anguish,
Allthough our bodyes wither and minds languish.   10
Write then, that my griefes, which thyne got, may bee
Cur'd by thy charming soveraigne melodee. /

To Mr C.B.

Thy friend whom thy deserts to thee enchaine,
    Urg'd by this inexcusable' occasion,
    Thee and the Saint of his affectiön
Leaving behind, doth of both wants complaine.
And let the love I beare to both sustaine   5
    No blott nor maime by [this] divisiön:

Strong is this love which tyes our harts in one,
And strong that love pursued with anxious payne.
And though besides thy selfe I leave behind
    Heavens liberall and Earths thrice fairer sunne,   10
    Going to wher sterne winter ay doth wonne,
Yet loves hott fyres which martir my sad mind
    Do send forth scalding sighes, which have the art
    To melt all Ice but that which walls her hart. /

To Mr E.G.   [p. 61]

Even as lame things thirst their perfection, so
The slimy rimes bred in our vale below,
Bearing with them much of my love and hart
Fly unto that Parnassus, wher thou art.
There thou o'erseest London. Here I 'have been   5
By staing in London too much overseene.
Now pleasures dearth our City doth posses
Our Theaters are filld with emptines.
As lancke and thin is every street and way
As a Woman deliverd yesterday.   10
Nothing wherat to laugh my spleene espyes
But bearbaitings or law exercise.
Therfore Ile leave it, and in the Cuntry strive
Pleasure, now fled from London, to retrive.
Do thou so too: and fill not like a Bee   15
Thy thighs with hony, but as plenteously
'As Russian Merchants, thy selfes whole vessell load,
And then at winter retaile it here abroad.
Bless us with Suffolks Sweets; and as that is
Thy garden, make thy hive and warehouse this. /

To Mr R. W.   [p. 62]

If as myne is, thy life a slumber bee,
Seeme whom thou readst these lines to dreame of mee:
Never did Morpheus nor his brethren weare
Shapes so like those shapes whom they 'would appeare
As this my letter is like mee, for it   5

Hath my name, words, hand, feete, hart, mind, and witt,
It is my deede of gift of mee to thee,
It is my will, my selfe the legacee.
So thy retyrings I love, yea envy,
Bred in thee by a wise melancholy,   10
That I reioyce that unto wher thou art
Though I stay here, I can thus send my hart;
As kindly' as any' inamored Patïent
His Picture to his absent Love hath sent.
All news I thinke sooner reach thee than mee;   15
Havens are heavens, and ships wing'd Angels bee
The which both Gospel, and sterne threatnings bringe.
Guianas harvest is nipt in the springe,
I feare. And with us (me thinks) fate deales so
As with the Jewes Guide, God did: He did show   20
Him the riche land, but barr'd the entry in:
Ah slownes is our punishment and sin.
Perchance these Spanish busnesses beeing donne,
Which, as the Earth betweene the Moone and Sonne,
Eclips the light which Guiana would give   25
Our discontinued hopes we shall retrive.
But yf (as all th' All must) hopes smoke away,
Is not allmighty Vertu' an India?
If men be worlds, ther is in every one
Somthing to' answer in some proportïone   30
All the worlds riches: and in good men this
Vertu our formes forme, and our Souls Soule is. /

[p. 63]   *To Mr R.W.*

Kindly I envy thy songs perfection
    Built of all th' elements as our bodyes are:
    That litle of earth that 'is in it, is a faire
Delicious garden where all sweetes are sowne.
In it is cherishing fyer which dryes in mee   5
    Griefe which did drowne me: and halfe quench'd by it
    Are Satirique fyres which urg'd me to' have writt
In skorne of all: for now I admyre thee.
    And as Ayre doth fulfill the hollownes
    Of rotten walls; So it myne emptines.   10

Where tost and movd it did begett this sound
Which as a lame Eccho' of thyne doth rebound.
   O I was dead: but since thy song new life did give,
   I recreated even by thy creature live. /

To Mr S.B.

O thou which to search out the secret parts
   Of th' India, or rather Paradise
   Of knowledg, hast with courage and advise
Lately launchd into the vast sea of Arts;
Disdaigne not in thy constant travailing   5
   To do as other Voyagers, and make
   Some turnes into lesse creekes, and wisely take
Fresh water at th' Heliconian Spring.
I sing not Syren-like to tempt, for I
   Am harsh, nor as those Scismatiques with you   10
   Which draw all witts of good hope to ther crew:
But seene in you bright sparks of poetry
   I though I brought no fuell, had desyre
   With these articulate blasts to blow the fyre. /

To Mr J.L.   [p. 64]

Of that short roll of frinds, writt in my hart
Which with thy name begins, since their depart
Whether in th' English Provinces they bee,
Or drinke of Po, Sequane, or Danubee,
Ther 's none that somtimes greets us not; and yett   5
Your Trent is Lethe; that passed, us you forgett.
You do not dutyes of Societies
If from th' embrace of a lov'd wife you rise,
View your fatt beasts, stretchd barnes, and labord fields,
Eate, play, ride, take all joyes, which all day yields   10
And then agayne to your embracements go.
Some howers on us your frinds, and some bestow
Upon thy Muse; els both we shall repent
I, that my love, she that her gifts on thee are spent. /

To Mr B.B.

Is not thy sacred hunger of science
    Yet satisfied? Is not thy braines rich hive
    Fullfilld with hony which thou dost derive
From the Arts spirits and their Quintessence?
Then weane thy selfe at last, and thee withdraw   5
    From Cambridge thy old Nource, and as the rest
    Here toughly chew, and sturdily disgest
Th' immense vast volumes of our common law.
And begin soone, lest my griefe grieve thee too:
    Which is, that that which I should 'have begonne   10
    In my youths morning, now late must be donne.
And I, as giddy travailers, must do
    Which stay in sleepe all day, and having lost
    Light and strength, dark and tyr'd must then ride post.
If thou unto thy Muse be marriëd   15
    Embrace her well: encrease and multiply;
    Be farr from me that strange adultery
To tempt thee and procure her widowhed.
My Muse (for I had one) because I 'ame cold
    Divorc'd her selfe: the cause beeing in mee,   20
    That I can take no new in bigamee,
Not my will only but power doth withhold.
[p. 65]   Hence comes it that these rimes which never had
    Mother, want matter; and they only have
    A little forme the which their father gave;   25
They are prophane, imperfect, oh too bad
    To be counted children of Poetree
    Except confirmd and bishoppëd by thee. /

To Mr J.L.

Blest are your North parts, for all this long time
My Sun 'is with you: cold and darke is our clime.
Heavens Sun which stayd so long from us this yeare
Stayd in your North (I thinke) for she was there,
And hither by kind nature drawne from thence   5
Here rages, burnes, and threatens pestilence.
Yet I as long as she from hence doth stay

Thinke this no South, no sommer, nor no day.
With thee my kind and unkind hart is run,
There sacrifice it to that bewteous Sun.   10
And since thou 'art in Paradise and needst crave
No joyes addition, helpe thy frind to save.
So may thy pastures with their flowery feasts
As sodainly as lard, fatt thy leane beasts;
So may thy woods oft polld, yet ever weare   15
A greene and, when thou wilt, a golden haire.
So may all thy sheepe bring forth twins, and so
In chace and race may thy horse all outgo.
So may thy love and courage ne'er be cold:
Thy sonne ne'er ward, thy fair wife ne'er seeme old.   20
But may'st thou wish great things and them attaine,
As thou telst her, and none but her, my paine. /

. . . .

Paradox 1. [p. 81]
That all things kill themselves.

To affect, yea to effect their owne deaths, all living are impor-
tun'd. Not by nature only, which perfects them, but by Art and
education, which perfects her. Plants quickned and inhabited by
the most unworthy soule, which therfore nether will, nor worke,
affect an end, a perfection, a Death. This they spend their spir-
its to attain, this attain'd, they languish and wither. And by how
much the more by mans industry, they are warm'd, and cherisht,
and pamper'd, so much the more early they climbe to this per-
fection, this Deathe. And yf between men, not to defend, be to
kill, what a heinous selfe murder is it, not to defend it selfe? This
defence, because beasts neglect, they kill themselves: because
they excede us in number, in strength and in a lawles liberty. Yea,
of horses, and so of other beasts, they which inherit most courage
for beeing bred of galantest parents, and by artificiall nursing are
bettrd, will run to their own Deathes, neyther sollicited by spurrs,
which they neede not, nor by honor, which they apprehend not.
If then the valiant kill himselfe, who can excuse the coward? Or
how shall man be free from this, since the first man taught us
this? except we cannot kill our selves because he killd us all. Yet

lest some thing should repaire this common ruine, we kill dayly
our bodyes with surfeits, and our minds with anguishes. Of our
Powers, remembring kills our memory. Of affections, lusting our
lust. Of Vertues, giving kills liberality. And if these things kill
themselves, they do it in their best and supreme perfection, for
after perfection immediatly followes exces: which changes the
nature and names, and makes them not the same things. If then
the best things kill themselves soonest (for no perfection indures)
and all things labor to this perfection, all travaile to ther owne
Death: Yea the frame of the whole world (yf it were possible for
God to be idle) yet because it begun must dy: Then in this idlenes
imagind in God, what could kill the world, but it selfe? since out
of it, nothing is. /

[p. 82]
Paradox 2.
That women ought to paint themselves.

Foulnes is lothesome; can that be so which helpes it? Who forbids
his beloved to gird in her wast, to mend by shoeing her une-
ven lamenes, to burnish her teethe, or to perfume her breath?
Yet that the face be more precisely regarded, it concernes more.
For as open confessing sinners are allwayes punished, but the
wary and conceald, offending without witnes, do it allso without
punishment, so the secret parts needes les respect. But of the face
discoverd to all survayes and examinations ther is not too nice
a jealousy. Nor doth it only draw the busy ey, but allso is most
subject to the divinest touche of all, to kissing, the strange and
misticall union of soules. If she should prostitute her selfe to a
more worthy man than thy selfe, how earnestly and how justly
wouldst thou exclaime? Then for want of this easy repayring, to
betray her body to ruine and Deformity, the tiranous ravishers
and sodain deflowrers of all women, what a hainous adultery is it?
What thou most lov'st in her face is color, and this painting gives
that. But thou hat'st it not because it is, but because thou knowest
it: Foole, whom only ignorance makes happy. The starrs, the sun,
the skies, whom thou admirest, alas have no color, but are faire
because they seeme color'd; If this seeming will not satisfy thee in
her, thou hast good assurance of her color, when thou seest her lay
it on. If her face be painted upon a board or a wall, thou wilt love

it, and the board and the wall. Canst thou lothe it then, when it smiles, speakes, and kisses, because it is painted?

Are we not more delighted with seeing fruits, and birds, and beasts painted, than with the naturalls? And do we not with pleasure behold the painted shapes of Devills and Monsters, whom trew we durst not regard? We repayre the ruine of our houses, but first cold tempest warns us of it, and bites us through it: we mend the wracke and washe the staines of our apparell, but first our ey and body is offended. But by this providence of women this is prevented. If in kissing and breathing upon her, the painting fal off, thou art angry: wilt thou be so too, yf it stick on? Thou didst love her: if thou begins't to hate her then, it is because she is not painted. If thou wilt say now, thou didst hate before, thou didst hate and love together. Be constant in some thing; and love her who shewes great love to thee, by taking these paines to seeme lovely to thee. /

Paradox 3.   [p. 83]
That old Men are more fantastique than younge.

Who reads this Paradox but thinks me more fantastique than I was yesterday when I did not think this? And if one day makes this sensible change in me, what will the burden of many yeares? To be fantastique in young men, is a conceitfull distemperature, and a witty madnes: but in old men whose senses are withered, it becomes naturall, therfore more full and perfect. For as when we sleepe, our fansy is most strong, so is it in Age, which is a slumber of the deepe sleepe of Deathe. They taxe us of inconstancy, which in themselves yong they allow'd, so that reproving that which they did approve, their inconstancy exceeds ours, because they have changd once more then we. Yea, they are more idly busied in conceiting apparell than we, for we when we are melancolique, weare black; when lusty, greene; when forsaken, tawny; pleasing our owne only inward affections, leaving them to others indifferent. But they prescribe laws, and constraine, the Noble, the Scholler, the Merchant and all estates to certaine habits. The old men of our time have chang'd with patience ther own bodyes, much of ther laws, much of ther language, yea ther Religion, yet they accuse us. To be amorous is proper and naturall in a yong, but in an old man most fantastique. And that ridling humor of Jealousy, which seekes and would not find, which inquires and repents his knowledg, is in them most common yet most fantastique. Yea that which falls never in yong men, is in them both fantastique and naturall; that is Coveteousnes; even at their journeys end to make great provision. Is any habit of yong men so fantastique as in the hottest seasons to be double gownd and hooded, like our elders? Or seemes it so ridiculous to weare long haire as to weare none? Truly, as amongst Philosophers, the Sceptique which doubts all is more contentious then eyther the Dogmatique which affirmes or Academique which denyes all; so are these uncertaine elders, which both call them fantastique, which follow others inventions, and them allso which are led by ther owne humors suggestion, more fantastique then eyther. /

[p. 84]

Paradox 4.
That Nature is our worst Guide.

Shall she be guide to all creatures which is herselfe one? Or if she allso have a guide, shall any creature have a better guide than us? The affections of Lust and Anger, yea even to erre, is naturall: shall we follow these? Can she be a good guide to us, which hath corrupted not us only but her selfe? Was not the first man by desyre of knowledg corrupted, even in the whight integrity of Nature? And did not Nature, if Nature do any thing, infuse in him this desyre of knowledge, and so this corruption in him, in her selfe, in us? If by nature we shall understand our essence, our definition, our reasonablenes, then this, beeing alike common to all men (the ideot and wisard beeing equally reasonable) why shall not all men having one nature, follow one course? Or if we shall understand our inclinations, Alas, how unable a guide is that which followes the temperature of our slimy bodyes? for we cannot say that we derive our inclinations, our minds, our soules, from our parents by any way. To say it, as All from All, is error in reason, for then with the first, nothing remaynes; or as part from all, is error in experience, for then this part equally imparted to many children, would (like Gavelkind lands) in few generations become nothing. Or to say it by communication is error in Divinity, for to communicate the ability of communicating whole essense with any but God is utter blasphemy. And if thou hast thy fathers nature and inclination, he

allso had his fathers, and so climing up, all come of one man; all
have one nature, all shall embrace one course. But that cannot be.
Therfore our complexions and bodyes we inherit from parents,
our inclinations and minds follow that. For our mind is heavy in
our bodyes afflictions, and rejoyceth in our bodyes pleasures: How
then shall this nature governe us, which is governd by the worst
part of us? Nature though we chase it away will returne: 'tis true.
But these good motions and inspirations which be our guides,
must be wooed and courted, and wellcomed, or els they abandon
us. And that old *Tu nihil invita etc.* must not be sayd, thou shalt,
but thou wilt do nothing against nature: so unwilling, he notes
us, to curbe our naturall appetites. We call our bastards allways
our naturall issue, and we designe a foole by no name so ordinar-
ily, as by the name of naturall. And that poore knowledg wherby
we but conceive what raine is, what winds, what thunder, we call
Metaphisique, supernaturall. Such small things, such nothings,
do we allow to our plaine natures comprehension. Lastly by fol-
lowing her, we lose the pleasant and lawfull commodityes of this
life, for we shall drink water, and eat akornes and rootes, and those
not so sweete and delicate as now by mans art and industry they
are made. We shall lose allso the necessityes of Societyes, Lawes,
Arts, and Sciences, which are all the workmanship of man. Yea
we shall lack that last best refuge of Misery, Death: because no
deathe is naturall. For yf yee will not dare to call all Deathes vio-
lent (though I see not why sicknesses be not violences), yet confes
that all deaths proceede of this defect of that, which nature made
perfect and would preserve, and therfore are all against Nature. /

Paradox 5.
That only Cowards dare dy.

[p. 85]

Extreames are equally removed from the meane: So that head-
long desperatnes as much offends true valor, as backward cow-
ardise. Of which sort I reckon justly all unenforced deathes.
When will your valiant man dy? necessited? so cowards suffer
what cannot be avoyded. And to run to death unimportun'd, is
to run into the first condemn'd desperatnes. Will he dy when he
is riche and happy? Then by living he might do more good. And
in afflictions and misery death is the chosen refuge of cowards.
Fortiter ille facit qui miser esse potest. But it is tought and practisd

amongst our valiants, that rather than our reputation suffer any maime, or we any misery, we shall offer our brests to the canons mouth, yea to our swords points. And this seemes a brave, and a fiery [climbing] which is indeed a cowardly, an earthly, and a groveling Spiritt. Why do they chaine their slaves to the gallyes, but that they thirst their deathes, and would at every lashe leap into the sea? Why do they take weapons from condemned men, but to barr them of that ease which cowards affect, a speedy death? Truly this life is a tempest, and a warfare; and he that dares dy to escape the anguishes of it seemes to me but so valiant, as he which dares hange himselfe, lest he be prest to the warrs. I have seene one in that extremity of melancholy, which was then become madness, strive to make his owne breathe an instrument to stop his breathe, and labor to choke himself: but alas he was mad. And we knew another, that languished under the oppression of a poore disgrace so much, that he tooke more paines to dy, than would have servd to have nourish'd life and spirit inough to have outlivd his disgrace. What foole will call this cowardlines valor, or this basenes humility? And lastly of those men which dy that Allegoricall death of entring into Religion, how few are found fitt for any shew of valiancy, but only of soft and supple metall, made only for cowardly solitarynes? /

[p. 86]   # Paradox 6.

That the gifts of the body are better than those of the mind or of fortune.

I say agayne that the body makes the mind: not that it created it a mind, but formes it a good or bad mind. And this mind may be confounded with soule, without any violence or injustice to Reason or Philosophy, when our soule (me seemes) is enhabled by our body, not this by that. My body licenceth my soule to see the worlds bewtyes through myne eyes, to heare pleasant things through myne eares, and affords it apt organs for conveyance of all perceivable delights. But alas my mind cannot make any part, that is not of it selfe disposed, to see or heare: though without dout she be as able and as willing to see behind as before. Now yf my soule would say, that she enhables my parts to tast these pleasures, but is herselfe only delighted with those riche sweetnesses which her inward ey and senses apprehend, she should dissemble: for

I see her often solaced with bewtyes which she sees through myne eyes, and Musicke which through myne eares she heares. This perfection then my body hath, that it can impart to my mind all her pleasures, and my mind hath this maime, that she neyther teache my indisposed parts her facultyes, nor to the parts best disposd shew that bewty of Angels or Musicke of Spheares, wherof she boasts the contemplation. Are Chastity, Temperance, or fortitude gifts of the mind? I appeale to phisicians whether the cause of these be not in the body. Healthe is a gifte of the body, and patience in sickness, of the mind; then who will say this patience, is as good a happines as health, when we must be extreamly miserable to have this happines? And for nourishing of civil Societies and mutual love amongst men, which is one cheife end why we are men, I say the bewty, proportion, and presence of the body hath a more masculine force in begetting this love than the vertues of the mind: for it strikes us sodainly, and posses-seth us immediatly, when to know these vertues, requyres sound judgment in him which shall discerne, and a long triall and con-versation betweene them. And even at last, alas how much of our faythe and beleefe, shall we be driven to bestow, to assure our selves that these vertues are not counterfayted? For it is the same to be and to seeme vertuous, because he that hath no vertu can dissemble none, but he that hath a litle may gild, and enamell, yea transforme much vice into vertu. For, allow a man to be dis-creet and flexible to companies, which are great vertues and gifts of the mind, this discretion wilbe to him the soule and Elixar of all vertue. So that touch'd with this, even pride shalbe made civill humility, and cowardise, honorable and wise valor. But in things seene ther is not this danger. For the body which thou lovst and esteemst fayre, is fayre certainly, and yf it be not faire in perfec-tion, yet is it fayre in the same degree that thy judgment is good. [p. 87] And in a faire body I do seldome suspect a disproportiond mind, or expect a good in a deformed. As when I see a goodly house, I assure my self of a worthy possessor; and from ruinous wythered buildings I turne away, because it seemes eyther stuffd with var-lets as a prison, or handled by an unthrifty negligent tenant, that so suffreth the wast therof. And truly the gifts of fortune which are riches, are only handmayds yea pandars of the bodyes pleas-ure: with ther service we nourish health, we preserve bewty, and we buy delights. So that vertue which must be lovd for her selfe and respects no further end is indeed nothing; and riches whose end is the good of the body, cannot be so perfectly good, as the end wherto it levells. /

Paradox 7.

That a wise man is knowne by much Laughinge.

Ride si sapis o puella ride; yf thou beest wise laugh. For since the powers of discourse, and reason, and laughter, be equally proper to only man, why shall not he be most wise which hath most use of laughing, as well as he which hath most of reasoning and discoursing? I allwayes did and shall understand that Adage, *per risum multum possis cognoscere stultum*, that by such laughing thou mayst know ther is a foole: not that the laughers are fooles, but that amongst them ther is some foole at whome wise men laugh. Which mov'd Erasmus to put this as the first argument in the mouthe of his Folly, that she made beholders laughe. For fooles are the most laughed at, and laugh least themselves of any. And Nature saw this faculty to be so necessary in man, that she hath beene content that by more causes we should be importun'd to laughe than by the exercise of any other power. For things in themselves utterly contrary begett this effect; for we laugh both at witty and absurd things. At both which sorts I have seene men laugh so long and so ernestly, that at last they have wept that they could laugh no more. And therfore the poet, having describ'd the quietnes of a wise retired man, sayth in one what we had sayd before in many lines, *Quid facit Canius tuus? ridet.* We have receaved that even the extremity of laughing, yea of weeping allso, hath beene accounted wisdome: and *Democritus* and *Heraclitus* the lovers of these extremes have beene called lovers of wisdome. Now amongst our wise men, I dowbt not, but many would be found, who would laughe at *Heraclitus* his weepinge, none which would weepe at *Democritus* laughing. At the hearing of Comedies or other witty reports, I have noted some, which not understanding the jests, have yet chosen this as the best meanes to seeme wise and understanding, to laugh when their companions laughe; and I have presumd them ignorant whom I have seene unmovd. A foole, if he come into a Princes court and see a gay man leaning at the wall, so glistering and so painted in many colors that he is hardly discernd from one of the pictures in the Arras hangings, his body like an [p. 88] yronbound chest girt in, and thicke ribbd with broad gold laces, may and commonly doth envy him, but alas shall a wise man, which may not only not envy this fellow, but not pity him, do nothing at this monster? Yes: let him laugh. And if one of these hott colerique firebrands, which nourish themselves by quarreling and kindling others, spitt upon a foole but one sparke of disgrace, he like a thatchd house quickly burning, may be angry. But the wise man as cold as the Salamander, may not only not be angry with him, but not be sory for him. Therfore let him laughe. So shall he be known a man, because he can laughe: a wiseman, for he knowes what to laughe; and a valiant, that he dares laughe. For who laughs is justly reputed more wise than at whome it is laughed. And hence I thinke proceeds that which in the later formall times I have much noted, that now when our superstitious civility of manners is become but a mutuall tickling Flattery of one another, allmost every man affects an humor of jesting, and is content to deject, and to deforme him-selfe, yea to become foole, to none other end which I can spy, but to give his wise companions occasion to laughe, and show themselves wise. Which promptnes of laughing is so great in wise men, that I thinke all wise men (yf any wise men do read this paradox) will laugh both at it and me. /

Paradox 8.
That good is more common than evill.

I have not beene so pitifully tird with any vanity, as with silly old mens exclayming against our tymes and extolling ther owne; alas they betray themselves. For yf the tymes be chang'd, their manners have chang'd them, but their senses are to pleasure, as sick mens tasts to liquors. For indeed no new thing is done in the world. All things are what and as they were; and good is as ever it was, most plenteous, and must of necessity be more common than evill, because it hath this for nature and end, and perfection, to be common. It makes love to all creatures, and all affect it. So that in the worlds early infancy, ther was a tyme when nothing was evill; but if this world shall suf-fer dotage in the extremest crookednes therof, ther shalbe no time when nothing shalbe good. It dares appeare and spred and glister in the world, but evill buryes it selfe in Night and darknes; and is suppresst and chastis'd, when good is cherished and rewarded. And as Embroderers, Lapidaryes, and other Artisans can by all things adorne their works, for by adding better things they better them so much, by equall things they double ther goodnes, and by worse they encrease their show, and lustre, and eminency, So good doth not only prostitute her owne [amiablenes] to all, but refuseth no ayd, no, not of her utter contrary, evill, yf she may be more common to us; for evill manners are parents of good lawes. So for the fashions of habits, for our movings in gestures, for phrases in speech, we say they were good as long as they were usd, that is, as long as they were common: and we eate, we walke, we sleepe only when it is, or seems [p. 89] good to do so. All faire, all profitable, all vertuous is good. And these three things I thinke embrace all things but their utter contraryes, of which allso, foule may be riche and vertuous, poore may be vertuous and faire, vicious may be faire and riche. So that good hath this good meanes to be common, that some subjects she can possesse intyrely, and in subjects poysond with evill, she can humbly stoope to accompany the evill. And of indifferent, many things are become perfectly good only by beeing common, as customes by use are made binding laws. But I remember nothing that is therfore ill because it is common but women: of whom allso they which are most common are the best of the occupation which they profes. /

Paradox 9.
That by Discord things increase.

Nullos esse Deos, inane caelum
Affirmat Selius, probatque, quod se
Factum, dum negat haec, videt beatum.

So I assever this the more boldly, because while I mantaine it, and feele the contrary repugnancies and adverse fightings of the Elements in my body, my body increaseth; and whilst I differ from common opinions, by this discord the number of my *Paradoxes* increaseth. All the riche benefitts which we can feign in concord is but an even conservation of things, in which evennes we may expect no change nor motion; therfore no increase or augmentation, which is a member of motion. And yf this unity and peace can give increase to things, how mightily is Discord and warr to this purpose, which are indeed the only ordinary parents of peace. Discord is never so barren that it affords no fruites, for the fall of one state is at worst the increase of an other; because it is as impossible to find a discommodity without any advantage as corruption without generation. But it is the nature and office of Concord to preserve only: which property when it leaves, it differs from it selfe, which is the greatest Discord of all. All Victoryes and Emperyes gain'd by warr, and all judiciall decidings of doubts in peace, I claime chilldren of Discord. And who can deny that Controversies in religion are growne greater by Discord; and not the Controversies only but even Religion it selfe, for in a troubled misery men are allwayes

more religious than in a Secure peace. The number of good men [p. 90]
(the only charitable harborers of Concord) we see is thin, and dayly
melts and waynes, but of bad and discording men it is infinit and
growes hourely. We are acertaind of all disputable doubts, only by
arguing, and differing in opinion; and yf formal disputation, which
is but a painted, counterfait, and dissembled Discord, can worke
us this benefitt, what shall not a full and main discord accomplish?
Truly, methinks I ow a devotion, yea a sacrifice to Discord for cast-
ing that ball vpon Ida, and for all that busines of Troy: whom ruind
I admyre more then *Rome* or *Babylon* or *Quinzay*. Nor are removd
corners fulfilld only with her fame, but with Cityes and thrones
planted by her fugitives. Lastly betweene cowardise and dispayre,
valor is ingendred: and so the Discord of extreames begetts all ver-
tues. But of like things ther is no issue without miracle: *Uxor pes-
sima, pessimus maritus, Miror tam malè convenire vobis.* He wonders
that, betweene two so like, ther could be any discord, yet for all this
discord perchance ther was ne'er the lesse increase. /

Paradox 10.
*That it is possible to find some vertue
in some women.*

I ame not of that sear'd impudency that I dare defend women, or
pronounce them good: yet when we see phisitians allow some vertu
in every poyson, alas why should we except Women? Since, cer-
tainly they are good for phisick: at least so, as wine is good for a
fever. And though they be the occasioners of most sins, they are
allso the punishers and revengers of the same sins. For I haue sel-
dome seene one which consumes his substance or body upon them,
escape diseases or beggery. And this is their justice. And if *Suum
cuique dare* be the fulfilling of all civil justice, they are most just: for
they deny that which is theirs to no man. *Tanquam non liceat nulla
puella negat.* And who may doubt of great wisdome in them, that
doth but observe with how much labor and cunning our Justices
and other dispencers of the laws study to entrap them, and how
zealously our Preachers dehort men from them, only by urging
ther subteltyes amd policies, and wisdom which are in them, yea
in the worst and most prostitute sort of them. Or who can deny
them a good measure of fortitude, if he consider how many valiant
men they have overthrowne, and beeing them selves overthrowne, [p. 91]

how much and how patiently they beare? And though they be all most intemperat, I care not: for I undertooke to furnish them with some vertue, not all. Necessity which makes even bad things good, prevayles allso for them: and we must say of them as of sharpe punishing laws; If men were free from infirmityes, they were needlesse: but they are both good Scourges for bad men. These or none must serve for reasons: and it is my great happiness that Examples prove not rules, for to confirm this the World affords not one Example. /

....

Epigrams

[p. 93] *Hero and Leander.*	Both robbd of ayre, we both ly in one ground, Both whom one fyer had burnd, one water drownd.

Pyramus and Thisbe.   Two by themselves, each other, Love and Feare
                          Slayne, cruell frinds, by parting have joynd here.

Niobe.   By childrens birth, and death, I ame become
             So dry, that I am now made myne owne tombe.

Nave arsa.   Out of a fyred ship, which by no way
                 But drowning could be rescued from the flame,
                 Some men leapd forthe, and ever as they came
                 Neere the foes ships, did by their shott decay.
                 So all were lost, which in the ship were found:
                 They in the sea beeing burnt, they in the burnt
                     ship drowned.

Caso d' un muro.   Under an under-min'd, and shott-brusd wall
                       A too-bold Captaine perish'd by the fall;
                       Whose brave misfortune happiest men envyde
                       That had a towne for tombe his corpse to hyde.

Zoppo   I ame unable (yonder begger cryes)
            To stand or move; yf he say trew, he lyes.

Cadiz   If you from spoyle of th' old worlds farthest end
and   To the new world your kindled valors bend,
Guiana.   What brave Examples then do prove it trew
                That one things end doth still beginne a new.

———————

Il Cavaliere Beyond th' old Pillers many have travailed
Giovanni   Towards the Suns cradel, and his throne, and bed.
Wingefield   A fitter Piller our Earle did bestow
                In that late Iland; for he well did know
                Farther than Wingefield no man dares to go.

———————

                Your Mistres, that you follow whores, still taxeth you,
                Tis strange she should confes it, though 'it be true.

———————

                Thy sins and haires may no man equall call,
                For as thy sins increase, thy haires do fall.

———————

Antiquary.   If in his study Hammon hath such care   [p. 94]
                To' hang all old strange things, let his wife beware.

———————

                Thou call'st me effeminate, for I love womens joyes.
                I call not thee manly, though thou follow boyes.

———————

                Thy father all from thee by his last Will
                Gave to the poore; thou hast good title still.

———————

                Thou in the fields walkst out thy supping howres
                And yet thou swearst thou hast supp'd like a king;
                Like Nebuchadnezzar, perchance with gras and
                    flowres:
                A salad worse than Spanish dyeting.

———————

Mercurius   Like Aesops fellow slaves, O Mercury,
Gallo-   Which could do all things, thy fayth is; and I
Belgicus.   Like Aesops selfe, which nothing; I confesse
                I should have had more fayth if thou hadst less.
                Thy credit lost thy credit: 'tis sinne to doo
                In this case as thou wouldst be done unto,
                To believe all. Change thy name: thou art like
                Mercury in stealing, and lyest like a Greeke.

———————

Thy flattering picture, Phryne, is like thee
Only in this, that you both painted bee.

———————————

Philo with 12 yeares study hath beene griev'd
To be' understood, when will he be beleevd?

———————————

Klokius so deeply' hath vowd ne'er more to come
In bawdy house, that he dares not go home.

———————————

Martial   Why this man gelded Martiäl I muse;
castrato.   Except himselfe alone his tricks would use,
                 As Katherine, for the Courts sake put downe stews.

———————————

Compassion in the world agayne is bredd:
Ralphius is sick, the Broker keepes his bedd.

———————————

[p. 95] *To a Jet*   Thou art not so blacke as my hart
ring sent   Nor halfe so britle as her hart thou art.
to me.   What wouldst thou say, shall both our properties
                  by thee be spoke?
              Nothing more endless, nothing sooner broke.

Mariage rings are not of this stuffe: 5
Oh, why should aught lesse pretious, or lesse
   tough
Figure our loves? Except in thy name thou have
   bid it say:
I 'am cheape, and nought but fashion; flinge me
   away.

Yet stay with me since thou art come;
Circle this fingers top, which didst her thombe. 10
Be proud, and safe, that thou dost dwell with
   mee;
She that, Oh, broke her faythe, would soon
   breake thee. /

[pp. 96–105] Ten blank leaves follow, to conclude the vellum-bound
        volume.

———————————

FROM THE LOSELEY PAPERS,
LETTERS CONCERNING DONNE'S
SECRET MARRIAGE TO ANNE
MORE, FEBRUARY–MARCH 1602

Letter 1. John Donne to Sir George More, 2 February 1602.

[Addressed, with traces of seal] To the right worshipfull Sir George More knight.

Sir

If a very respective feare of your displeasure, and a doubt, that my Lord whom I know out of your worthiness to love you much, would be so compassionate with you, as to add his anger to yours, did not so much increase my sicknes, as that I cannot stir I had taken the boldnes, to have donne the Office of this letter by way- 5 ting upon you my self: To have given you truthe, and clearnes of this matter between your Daughter and me; and to show to you plainly the limits of our fault, by which I know your wisdome wyll proportion the punishment. So long since, as at her being at York House, this had foundacion: and so much then of promise and 10 Contract built upon yt, as without violence to Conscience might not be shaken. At her lyeng in town this last parliament, I found meanes to see her twice or thrice; we both knew the obligacions that lay upon us, and wee adventurd equally; and about three weeks before Christmas we married. And as at the doinge, there 15 were not usd above fyve persons, of which I protest to you by my salvation, there was not one that had any dependence or relation to you, so in all the passage of it, did I forbear to use any such person, who by furtheringe of yt might violate any trust or duty towards you. The reasons, why I did not fore-acquaint you with it, (to deal 20 with the same plainnes that I have usd) were these. I knew my present estate lesse than fitt for her; I knew, (yet I knew not why) that I stood not right in your Opinion; I knew that to have given any intimacion of yt, had been to impossibilitate the whole matter. And then having those honest purposes in our harts, and those 25 fetters in our Consciences, me thinks we should be pardoned, if our fault be but this, that wee did not by fore-revealinge of yt, con- sent to our hindrance and torment. Sir, I acknowledge my fault to be so great, as I dare scarse offer any other prayer to you in myne own behalf, than this, to beleeve this truthe, that I neyther had 30 dishonest end nor meanes. But for her, whom I tender much more, than my fortunes, or lyfe (els I would I might neyther joy in this lyfe, nor enjoy the next) I humbly beg of you, that she may not, to her danger, feele the terror of your sodaine anger. I know this

35 letter shall find you full of passion: but I know no passion can alter
your reason and wisdome; to which I adventure to commend these
perticulers; That yt ys irremediably donne; That if you incense
my Lord, you Destroy her and me; That yt is easye to give us
happines; And that my Endevors and industrie, if it please you to
40 prosper them, may soone make me somewhat worthyer of her. If
any take the advantage of your displeasure against me, and fill you
with ill thoughts of me, my Comfort is that you know, that fayth
and thanks are due them onely, that speak when theyr informa-
cions might do good: which now yt cannot work towards any
45 party. For my Excuse I can say nothing except I knew, what were
sayd to you. Sir, I have truly told you this matter; and I humbly
beseeche you, so to deale in yt, as the persuasions of Nature, rea-
son, wisdome, and Christianity shall informe you; And to accept
the vowes, of one whom you may now rayse or scatter, which are,
50 that as all my love ys directed unchangeably upon her, so all my
labors shall concur to her contentment, and to show my humble
obedience to your selfe.

From my lodginge by the Savoy. 2 February 1601[2]

Yours in all Duty and humblenes
J: Donne.

Letter 2. John Donne to Sir George More, *11 February 1602.*

[Addressed, with traces of seal] To the right worshipfull Sir
George More knight.

Sir

The inward accusacions in my Conscience, that I have offended
you, beyond any ability of redeeming yt by me, and the feeling of
my Lords heavy displeasure, following yt, forceth me to write
though I know my fault make my letters very ungracious to you.
5 Allmighty God whom I call to witnesse, that all my greife ys that
I have in this manner offended you, and him, direct you to beleeve,
that which out of an humble and afflicted hart I now write to you.
And since we have no meanes to move God, when he wyll not
hear our prayers, to hear them, but by praying, I humbly beseech
10 you, to allow, by his gracious example, my penitence so good
Entertainment, as yt may have a beliefe, and a pittie. Of nothinge

in this one fault, that I hear layd to me, can I disculpe my selfe, but of the contemptuous and despightfull purpose towards yow, which I hear ys surmised against me. But for my dutifull regard to my late lady, for my Religion, and for my lyfe, I refer my self to 15 them, that may have observd them. I humbly beseeche you, to take off these weights, and to put my fault into the balance alone, as yt was donne, without the addicion of these yll reports: And though then yt wyll be too heavy for me, yett then yt will less grieve you to pardon yt. How litle and how short the comfort and 20 pleasure of Destroyeng ys, I know your wisdome and Religion informs you. And though perchance you intend not utter Destruction, yett the way through which I fall towards yt, ys so headlong, that beeing thus pushd, I shall soone be at bottome. For yt pleaseth God, from whom I acknowledge the punishment to be 25 just, to accompany my other ylls, with so much sicknes as I have noe refuge, but that of Mercy, which I beg, of him, my Lord, and you. Which I hope you wyll not repent to have afforded me, since all my Endevors, and the whole course of my lyfe shall be bent to make my selfe worthy of your favor and her love, whose peace of 30 Conscience, and quiett, I know must be much wounded and vio-lenced, if your displeasure sever us. I can present nothing to your thoughts which you knew not before, but my submission, my repentance, and my harty desire, to do anything satisfactory to your just displeasure: of which I beseech you to make a charitable 35 use and Construction.

From the Fleete: 11 February 1601[2]

Yours in all faythfull duty and obedience
J: Donne.

Letter 3. John Donne to Lord Keeper Thomas Egerton, 12 February 1602.

[Addressed, with intact impression of Donne's personal seal, a sheaf of snakes] To the right honorable my very good Lord and Master, Sir Thomas Egerton knight; Lord keeper of the great Seale of England.

To excuse my Offence, or so much to resist the just punishment for ytt, as to move your Lordship to withdraw ytt, I thought till now, were to aggravate my fault. But since yt hath pleasd God, to joyne

with you in punishing therof, with increasing my sicknes, and that
5 he gives me now Audience by prayer, yt emboldneth me also to
address my humble request to your Lordship that you would admit
into your favorable Consideracion, how farr my intentions were
from doing dishonor to your Lordships house; and how unable
I ame to escape utter and present Destruction if your Lordship
10 judge only the Effect and Deede. My services never had so much
worthe in them, as to deserve the favors, wherewith they were payd:
But they had alwayes so much honesty, as that onely this, hath
staynd them. Your Justice hath been Mercifull, in making me know
my offence, and yt hath much profited me, that I ame dejected.
15 Since then I ame so intirely yours, that even your disfavors have
wrought good upon me, I humbly beseeche you that all my good
may proceed from your Lordship. And that, since Sir George
More, whom I leave no humble way unsought, to regaine, referrs all
to your Lordship, you would be pleasd to lessen that Correction,
20 which your just wisdome hath destind for me; and so to pitty my
sicknes, and other Misery, as shall best agree with your honorable
disposition. Allmighty god accompany all your Lordships pur-
poses, and bless you and yours with many good dayes.

Fleet. 12 February 1601[2]

> Your Lordships most dejected and poorest Servant
> J: Donne.

Letter 4. John Donne to Sir George More.
13 February 1602.

[Addressed, with remnants of seal] To the right worshipfull Sir
George More knight.

Sir

From you, to whom next to God, I shall owe my health, by
enjoyeng by your Mediacion this mild change of Imprisonment, I
desire to derive all my good fortune and Content in this world.
And therefore with my most unfeyned thanks, present to you my
5 humble peticion that you would be pleased to hope, that as that
fault which was layd to me, of having deceivd some gentlewomen
before, and that of loving a corrupt Religion are vanishd and
smokd away (as I assure my self, out of theyr weaknes they are),
And that as the Devyll in the Article of our Death takes the advan-
10 tadge of our weaknes and feare to aggravate our Sinns to our

Conscience, so some uncharitable Malice hath presented my
Debts doble at least, So, many of the Imputacions layd upon me,
would fall off, if I might but shake and purge my self in your pres-
ence. But if that were donne, of this Offence committed to you I
cannot acquit my self. Of which yet, I hope that God, to whom for 15
that I hartily direct many prayers, wyll informe you to make that
use, that as of Evyll Manners good lawes growe, so out of our dis-
obedience and boldnes, you wyll take Occasion to show Mercy and
tendernes. And when yt shall please god to soften your hart so
much towards us, as to pardon us, I beseech you allso to undertake 20
that charitable office of beeing my Mediator to my Lord whom as
upon your just Complaint you found full of justice, I doubt not but
you shall allso find full of Mercy: for so ys the Almighty pattern of
Justice and Mercy, equally full of both. My Conscience and such
Affection as in my Conscience becomes an honest man, embold- 25
neth me to make one request more, which ys that by some kind and
Comfortable message, you would be pleasd to give some ease of the
afflictions which I know your Daughter in her Mind suffers; and
that (if it be not against your other purposes) I may with your leave

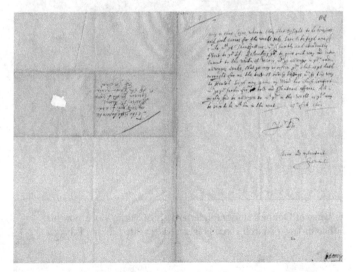

2. Verso and recto of Donne's autograph letter to Lord Keeper Thomas
Egerton, 13 February 1602, thanking him for securing Donne's release
from prison after his elopement with Anne More, and appealing for
pardon for his 'bold and presumtous offence'. Signed by Donne in a
show of submission and humility at the bottom right hand corner of the
sheet. Folger Shakespeare Library, L.b.530.

3. Verso of Donne's autograph letter to Sir George More, now his
father-in-law, 1 March 1602. Folger Shakespeare Library, L.b.532.

If I could fear, yt I am so much worthyns as ys in yor: there were no Mercy
or yf these waights oppresst onely my shoulders and my fortunes, and not my
conscience and her, whose good ys dearer to me by much then my lyfe, I
should not thus troble yor: at my Ll. But when I see that this storme
hath shakd me at roote in my Lords fauor; where I was well planted
and haue iust reason to fear, that these yll reports wch Malice hath
raysd of me, may haue trobled her, I can leaue no honest way untryed
to remedy these miseryes; nor find any way more honest then this wch
of an humble and repentant hart for the fault, come to yor: to beg
both yor pardon, and assistance in my sute to my L. I should wrong yor:
as much againe as I did, if I should think yor: sought to destroy me.
but though I be not hastuongly destroyd I languish and rust dangerously,
from seeking p'ferment abroad: my loue and conscience restrains
me, from hoping for them here. My Lords disgracings cut me off. My Em-
prisonment and theyrs whose loue to me brought them to yt hath already
cost me 40ll. And the loue of my frinds though yt be not utterly growne
ded vppon my fortunes, yet I shadw suffers somewhat in this long and
vncertain disgraces of myne. I therfore humbly beseech yor: to haue
so charitable a pitty, of what I haue, and do and must suffer, as to take
to yor selfe the comfort of hauing saved from such destruction as
yor iust anger might haue layd vpon him a sorrowfull and honest man.
I was bold in my last letter to beg leaue of yor: that I might wright
to yor daughter. Though I vnderstood therupon, that after the
thursday yor: were not displeasd that I should yet I haue not nor
wyll not wthout yor knowledge do yt. But now I beseech yor: that
I may: since I protest before god yt is the greatest of my afflic-
tions not to do yt. In all the world ys not more true sorrow
then in my hart, nor more vnderstanding of true repentance then
in yors. And therfore god whose pardon in such cases ys neuer denyed
giues me leaue to hope that yor: wyll fauorably consider my mi-
seryes. To his mercifull guiding and protection I comend yor:
and cease to troble yor. 1o Martij: 1601

yors in all humblenes
and dutifull obedience

J. Donne

4. Recto of Donne's autograph letter to Sir George More, now his
father-in-law, 1 March 1602, imploring More's pardon for the offense of
the marriage with Anne, asking his help in regaining employment with
Egerton, and requesting permission to write to Anne. Signed by Donne
at the bottom right-hand corner of the sheet, again showing submission
and humility. Folger Shakespeare Library, L.b.532.

30   write to her; for without your leave I wyll never attempt any thing
     concerning her. God so have mercy upon me, as I ame unchange-
     ably resolvd, to bend all my Courses to make me fitt for her; which
     if God, and my Lord and you be pleasd to strengthen I hope
35   neyther my Debts, which I can easily Order, nor any thing els shall
     interrupt. Allmighty god keep you in his favor, and restore me to
     his and yours. From my Chamber, whither by your favor I ame
     Come.

     13 February 1601[2].

                                        Yours in all dutifull Obedience
                                                           J: Donne.

Letter 5. John Donne to Lord Keeper Thomas
Egerton, 13 February 1602.

[Addressed, no remnant of seal] To the right honorable my very
good Lord and Master, Sir Thomas Egerton knight, Lord keeper
of the great Seale of England.

Onely in that Coyne, wherin they that Delight to do benefitts, and
good turnes for the works sake, love to be payd, ame I rich, which
ys Thankfullnes; which I humbly and abundantly present to your
Lordship. Beseeching you, to give such way and Entertainmemt to
5   this vertu of Mercy, which ys allways in you, and allwayes awake,
    that yt may so soften you, that as yt hath wrought for me the best
    of bodily blessings, which ys, this way to Health, So yt may gaine
    my Mind her Cheife Comfort, which ys your pardon for my bold
    and presumtuous offence. Allmighty god be allwayes so with you
10 in this world, as you may be sure to be with him in the next.

    13 February 1601[2].

                                              Your Lordships
                                              poore and repentant
                                              Servant
                                              J: Donne

Letter 6. John Donne to Sir George More, 1 March 1602.

[Addressed, with remnant of seal] To the right worshipfull Sir
George More knight.

Sir

    If I could fear, that in so much worthynes as ys in you, there were
no Mercy, or yf these weights opprest onely my shoulders, and my
fortunes, and not my conscience, and hers, whose good ys dearer to
me by much more than my lyfe, I should not thus troble you with my 5
letters. But when I see that this storme hath shakd me at roote, in my
Lords favor, wher I was well planted, and have just reason to fear,
that those yll reports which Malice hath raysd of me, may have trob-
led her, I can leave no honest way untryed to remedy these miseryes,
nor find any way more honest than this, out of an humble and 10
repentant hart, for the fault donne to you to beg both your pardon
and assistance in my suit to my Lord. I should wrong you as much
againe, as I did, if I should think you sought to destroy me. But
though I be not hedlongly destroyd, I languish and rust dangerously.
From seeking preferments abroad, my love and Conscience restrains 15
me. From hoping for them here, my Lords disgracings cut me off.
My Emprisonments, and theyrs whose love to me brought them to
yt, hath already cost me 40 pounds. And the love of my frinds,
though yt be not utterly grounded upon my fortunes, yet I know
suffers somewhat, in these long and uncertain disgraces of myne. I 20
therfore humbly beseech you, to have so charitable a pitty, of what I
have, and do, and must suffer, as to take to your selfe the Comfort, of
having saved from such destruction, as your just Anger might have
layd upon him a sorowfull and honest man. I was bold in my last
letter to beg leave of you, that I might write to your Daughter. 25
Though I understood therupon, that after the Thursday you were
not displeasd that I should, yet I have not nor wyll not without your
knowledge do yt. But now I beseech you that I may; since I protest
before God, yt is the greatest of my afflictions, not to do yt. In all the
world ys not more true sorrow, than in my hart, nor more under- 30
standing of true repentance than in yours; And therfore God, whose
pardon in such cases ys never denyed, gives me leave to hope, that
you wyll favorably consider my necessityes. To his mercifull guid-
ing, and protection I commend you, and cease to troble you.

1 March 1601[2].

                     Yours in all humblenes and dutifull obedience
                                     J: Donne.

Letter 7. John Donne to Lord Keeper Thomas Egerton, 1 March 1602.

[Addressed, with remnant of seal] To the right honorable my very good Lord and Master, Sir Thomas Egerton knight Lord keeper of the great Seal of England.

That offence which was to God in this Matter, his Mercy hath assurd my Conscience, ys pardoned. The Commissioners who minister his Anger and Mercy encline also to remitt yt. Sir George More, of whose learning and wisdome, I have good knowledge, and
5 therfore good hope of his Moderacion, hath sayd, before his last going, that he was so far from being any Cause or Mover of my punishment or disgrace, that if yt fitted his reputacion, he would be a sutor to your Lordship for my restoringe. All these Irons are knock'd off; yett I perish in as heavy fetters as ever, whilst I lan-
10 guish under your Lordships Anger. How soone my History is dis-patchd? I was carefully and honestly bred; enjoyed an indifferent fortune; I had, (and I had understandinge inough to value yt) the Sweetnes and security of a freedome and independency; without markinge out to my hopes, any place of profitt, I had a desire to be
15 your Lordships servant; by the favor which your good Sonns love to me, obteind, I was 4 years your Lordships Secretary, not dis-honest, nor greedy. The sicknes of which I dyed, ys, that I begonne in your Lordships house, this love. Wher I shalbe buried, I know not. It ys late now, for me (but that Necessity, as yt hath continually
20 an Autumne and a wytheringe, so yt hath ever a springe, and must put forthe,) to beginne that Course, which some years past, I pur-posd, to travaile; though I could now do yt, not much disadvan-tadgeably. But I have some bridle upon me now, more than then, by my Marriadge of this gentlewoman: in providing for whom, I
25 can and wyll show my self very honest, though not so fortunate. To seek preferment here, with any but your Lordship were a Madnes. Every great Man, to whom I shall address any such suit, wyll silently dispute the Case, and say, Would my Lord keeper so dis-graciously have imprisond him, and flung him away, if he had not
30 donne some other great fault, of which wee hear not? So that to the burden of my true weaknesses, I shall have this Addicion, of a very prejudiciall suspicion, that I ame worse than, I hope, your Lordship dothe think me, or would that the world should thinke. I have ther-fore no way before me; but must turn back to your Lordship, who
35 knowes that Redemtion was no less worke than Creation. I know

my fault so well and so well acknowledge yt, that I protest I have
not so much as inwardly grudged, nor startled at the punishment.
I know your Lordships disposicion so well, as though in course of
Justice, yt be of proofe against clamors of Offendors, yet yt ys not
strong inough to resist yt selfe, and I know yt self naturally enclines 40
yt to pitty. I know myne own Necessity, out of which I humbly beg;
that your Lordship wyll so much entender your hart towards me,
as to give me leave to come into your presence. Affliction, Misery,
and destruction are not there; and every where els, wher I ame,
they are.   45

1 March 1601[2].

              Your Lordships most poore and most penitent Servant
                                                         J: Donne.

THE ANNIVERSARIES, 1611, 1612[1]

[1] The source for the text of the *Anniversaries* here is the first complete printed edition of 1612 (*Short-Title Catalogue* 7023)—specifically, the copy in the collection of the Henry E. Huntington Library and Art Gallery, accessible on the Early English Books Online (EEBO) website.

The First Anniuersarie.

AN ANATOMIE of the VVorld.

Wherein,

BY OCCASION OF

the vntimely death of Mistris

ELIZABETH DRVRY,

the frailtie and the decay of
this whole World is
represented.

LONDON,

Printed by *M. Bradwood* for *S. Macham,* and are
to be sold at his shop in Pauls Church-yard at the
signe of the Bull-head. 1612.

5. Title-page of the *First Anniversary* in the first complete edition of
1612. Folger Shakespeare Library, STC 7023, sig. A1.

The First Anniversarie.

AN

ANATOMIE

of the World.

Wherein,

BY OCCASION OF

the untimely death of Mistris

ELIZABETH DRURY,

the frailtie and the decay of
this whole World is
represented.

LONDON,

Printed by *M. Bradwood* for *S. Macham*, and are
to be sold at his shop in Pauls Church-yard at the
signe of the Bull-head.   1612.

TO THE PRAISE
of the Dead, and the
ANATOMY.

Well dy'de the World, that we might live to see
This World of wit, in his Anatomee:
No evill wants his good: so wilder heires
Bedew their fathers Toombes with forcëd teares,
Whose state requites their losse; whiles thus we gaine   5

[A2v] Well may we walke in blacks, but not complaine.
Yet how can I consent the world is dead
While this Muse lives? which in his spirits stead
Seemes to informe a world: and bids it bee,
In spight of losse, or fraile mortalitee?   10
And thou the subject of this wel-borne thought,
Thrise noble maid, couldst not have found nor sought
A fitter time to yeeld to thy sad fate,
Than whiles this spirit lives; that can relate

[A3r] Thy worth so well to our last nephews eyne,   15
That they shall wonder both at his, and thine.
Admirëd match! where strives in mutuall grace
The cunning Pencil, and the comely face:
A taske, which thy faire goodnesse made too much
For the bold pride of vulgar pens to touch;   20
Enough is us to praise them that praise thee,
And say that but enough those praises bee,
Which had'st thou liv'd, had hid their fearefull head

[A3v] From th' angry checkings of thy modest red:
Death bars reward and shame: when envy's gone,   25
And gaine; 'tis safe to give the dead their owne.
As then the wise Egyptians wont to lay
More on their Tombes than houses: these of clay,
But those of brasse, or marble were, so wee
Give more unto thy Ghost than unto thee.   30
Yet what we give to thee, thou gav'st to us,
And maiest but thanke thy selfe, for being thus;

Yet what thou gav'st, and wert, O happy maid,   [A4r]
Thy grace profest all due, where 'tis repayd.
So these high songs that to thee suited beene,   35
Serve but to sound thy makers praise in thine,
Which thy deare soule as sweetly sings to him
Amid the Quire of Saints and Seraphim,
As any Angels tongue can sing of thee;
The subjects differ, tho the skill agree.   40
For as by infant-yeeres men judge of age,
Thy early love, thy vertues, did presage   [A4v]
What an hie part thou bear'st in those best songs
Whereto no burden, nor no ends belongs.
Sing on, thou Virgin soule, whose lossefull gaine   45
Thy love-sicke Parents have bewayl'd in vaine;
Ne'er may thy name be in our songs forgot
Till we shall sing thy ditty, and thy note.

The First Anniversary.

AN
ANATOMIE
of the World.

When that rich soule which to her heav'n is gone,
Whom all they celebrate, who know they' have one,
(For who is sure he hath a soule, unlesse
It see, and Judge, and follow worthinesse,
And by Deedes praise it? He who doth not this,   5

[2] May lodge an In-mate soule, but 'tis not his.)
When that Queene ended here her progresse time,
And as t' her standing house, to heav'n did clymbe,
Where, loth to make the Saints attend her long,
Shee's now a part both of the Choir, and Song,   10
This world in that great earthquake languishëd;
For in a common Bath of teares it bled,
Which drew the strongest vitall spirits out:

[3] But succour'd then with a perplexëd doubt,
Whether the world did lose or gaine in this,   15
(Because since now no other way there is
But goodnesse, to see her, whom all would see,
All must endevour to be good as shee),
This great consumption to a fever turn'd.
And so the world had fits; it joy'd, it mourned.   20
And, as men thinke that Agues physicke are,
And th' Ague being spent, give over care:
So thou, sicke world, mistak'st thy selfe to bee
Well, when alas, thou 'art in a Lethargee.
Her death did wound and tame thee then, and then   25
Thou mightst have better spar'd the Sunne, or Man;
That wound was deepe, but 'tis more misery,

[4] That thou hast lost thy sense and memory.
T'was heavy then to heare thy voyce of moan,
But this is worse, that thou art speechlesse growne.   30

Thou hast forgot thy name thou hadst; thou wast
Nothing but she, and her thou hast o'erpast.
For as a child kept from the Font, untill
A Prince, expected long, come to fulfill
The Ceremonies, thou unnam'd hadst laid,   35
Had not her comming, thee her Palace made:
Her name defin'd thee, gave thee forme and frame,
And thou forget'st to celebrate thy name.

[5] Some months she hath beene dead (but being dead,
Measures of times are all determinëd)   40
But long shee 'ath been away, long, long, yet none
Offers to tell us who it is that's gone.
But as in states doubtfull of future heyres,
When sicknesse without remedy impaires
The present Prince, they're loth it should be said,   45
The Prince doth languish, or the Prince is dead:
So mankind, feeling now a generall thaw,
A strong example gone, equall to law,
The Cyment which did faithfully compact

[6] And glue all vertues, now resolv'd and slack'd,   50
Thought it some blasphemy to say she 'was dead;
Or that our weaknesse was discoverëd
In that confession; therefore spoke no more
Than tongues, the soule being gone, the losse deplore.
But though it be too late to succour thee,   55
Sicke world, yea dead, yea putrified, since shee
Thy 'ntrinsique Balme, and thy preservative,
Can never be renew'd, thou never live:
I (since no man can make thee live) will trie
What we may gaine by thy Anatomy.   60

[7] Her death hath taught us dearely, that thou art
Corrupt and mortall in thy purest part.
Let no man say, the world it selfe being dead,
'Tis labour lost to have discoverëd
The worlds infirmities, since there is none   65
Alive to study this dissectiön.
For there's a kind of world remaining still,   *What life the*
Though shee which did inanimate and fill   *world hath still.*
The world, be gone, yet in this last long night
Her Ghost doth walk: that is, a glimmering light,   70
A faint weake love of vertue and of good

[8] Reflects from her, on them which understood
Her worth. And though she have shut in all day,

The twilight of her memory doth stay,
Which, from the carcasse of the old world free,   75
Creates a new world, and new creatures bee
Produc'd: The matter and the stuffe of this,
Her vertue; and the forme our practise is.
And though to be thus Elemented, arme
These Creatures from home-born intrinsique harme,   80
(For all assum'd unto this Dignitee
So many weedlesse Paradises bee,

[9]   Which of themselves produce no vene'mous sinne,
Except some forraine Serpent bring it in)
Yet, because outward stormes the strongest breake,   85
And strength it selfe by confidence growes weake,
This new world may be safer, being told

The sicknesses   The dangers and diseases of the old:
of the world.   For with due temper men do them forgoe,
Or covet things, when they their true worth know.   90

Impossibility   There is no health; Physitians say that wee
of health.   At best enjoy but a neutralitee.
And can there be worse sickness than to know

[10] That we are never well, nor can be so?
We are borne ruinous: poore mothers crie   95
That children come not right, nor orderly,
Except they headlong come, and fall upon
An ominous precipitatiön.
How witty's ruine! how importunate
Upon mankinde! It labour'd to frustrate   100
Even God's purpose; and made woman, sent
For mans reliefe, cause of his languishment.
They were to good ends, and they are so still,
But access'ory, and principall in ill.

[11] For tht first mariage was our funerall: 105
One woman at one blow then kill'd us all,
And singly, one by one, they kill us now.
We doe delightfully our selves allow
To that consumption; and profusely blinde,
We kill our selves to propagate our kinde.   110
And yet we doe not that; we are not men:
There is not now that mankinde, which was then,
Whenas the Sunne and man did seeme to strive

Shortnesse of   (Joynt tenants of the world) who should survive.
life.   When Stag, and Raven, and the long-liv'd tree,   115

[12] Compar'd with man, dy'de in minoritee;

When, if a slow-pac'd starre had stolne away
From the observers marking, he might stay
Two or three hundred yeeres to see 't againe,
And then make up his observation plaine;   120
When, as the age was long, the size was great.
Mans growth confess'd and recompenc'd the meat:
So spaciöus and large, that every soule
Did a faire Kingdome and large Realme controule;
And when the very stature, thus erect,   125
Did that soule a good way towards Heaven direct.
[13] Where is this mankind now? who lives to age
Fit to be made *Methuselah* his page?
Alas, we scarse live long enough to trie
Whether a new-made clocke runne right, or lie.   130
Old Grandsires talk of yesterday with sorrow,
And for our children we reserve to-morrow.
So short is life, that every peasant strives,
In a torne house, or field, to have three lives.
And as in lasting, so in length is man,   135
Contracted to an inch, who was a span.   *Shortnesse of*
For had a man at first, in Forrests stray'd,   *stature.*
[14] Or shipwrack'd in the Sea, one would have laid
A wager that an Elephant or Whale
That met him, would not hastily assaile   140
A thing so equal to him. Now alas,
The Fayries and the Pigmies well may passe
As credible; mankind decayes so soone,
We're scarse our Fathers shadowes cast at noone.
Onely death addes t' our length: nor are we growne   145
In stature to be men, till we are none.
But this were light, did our less volume hold
All the old Text; or had we chang'd to gold
Their silver; or dispos'd into lesse glas
[15] Spirits of vertue, which then scatterd was.   150
But 'tis not so: w' are not retir'd, but dampt;
And as our bodies, so our minds are crampt,
'Tis shrinking, not close-weaving, that hath thus
In minde and body both, bedwarfèd us.
We seeme ambitious, Gods whole worke t' undoe;   155
Of nothing he made us, and we strive too
To bring our selves to nothing backe; and we
Do what we can, to do 't so soone as he.
With new diseases on our selves we warre,

[16] And with new phisicke, a worse Engin farre.   160
      Thus man, this worlds Vice-Emperor, in whom
      All faculties, all graces are at home,
      And if in other Creatures they appeare,
      They're but mans ministers and Legates there
      To worke on their rebellions, and reduce   165
      Them to Civility, and to mans use:
      This man whom God did woo, and loth t' attend
      Till man came up, did downe to man descend,
      This man, so great, that all that is, is his,
      Oh what a trifle, and poore thing he is!   170

[17] If man were anything, he's nothing now:
      Helpe, or at least some time to wast, allow
      T' his other wants, yet when he did depart
      With her whom we lament, he lost his hart.
      She, of whom th' Ancients seem'd to prophesie   175
      When they called vertues by the name of shee;
      She in whom vertue was so much refin'd
      That for Alloy unto so pure a minde
      Shee tooke the weaker Sex; she that could drive
      The poys'onous tincture and the stayne of *Eve*   180
      Out of her thoughts and deeds, and purifie

[18] All, by a true religious Alchimy:
      Shee, she is dead; shee's dead: when thou know'st this,
      Thou know'st how poore a trifling thing man is;
      And learn'st thus much by our Anatomee,   185
      The heart being perish'd, no part can be free.
      And that, except thou feed (not banquet) on
      The supernaturall food, Religiön,
      Thy better Growth growes witheréd and scant;
      Be more than man, or thou 'rt lesse than an Ant.   190
      Then, as mankind, so is the worlds whole frame
      Quite out of joynt, almost created lame;

[19] For, before God had made up all the rest,
      Corruption entred, and deprav'd the best:
      It seiz'd the Angels and then, first of all   195
      The world did in her Cradle take a fall,
      And turn'd her brains, and tooke a gen'erall maime
      Wronging each joynt of th' universall frame.
      The noblest part, man, felt it first; and then
      Both beasts and plants, curst in the curse of man.   200

Decay of   So did the world from the first houre decay:
nature in other   That evening was beginning of the day,
parts.

And now the Springs and Sommers which we see
[20] Like sonnes of women after fifty bee.
And new Philosophy cals all in doubt: 205
The Element of fire is quite put out;
The Sunne is lost, and th' earth; and no mans wit
Can wel direct him where to looke for it.
And freely men confesse that this world's spent
When in the Planets, and the Firmament   210
They seeke so many new; they see that this
Is crumbled out againe t' his Atomies.
'Tis all in pieces, all coherence gone,
[21] All just supply and all Relation:
Prince, Subject, Father, Sonne are things forgot,   215
For every man alone thinkes he hath got
To be a Phoenix, and that then can bee
None of that kinde, of which he is, but hee.
This is the worlds condition now, and now
She that should all parts to reunion bow,   220
She that had all Magnetique force alone,
To draw and fasten sundred parts in one;
She whom wise nature had invented then
When she observ'd that every sort of men
Did in their voyage in this worlds Sea stray,   225
[22] And needed a new compasse for their way;
Shee that was best, and first originall
Of all faire copies, and the generall
Steward to Fate; shee whose rich eyes and brest
Gilt the West Indies and perfum'd the East,   230
Whose having breath'd in this world did bestow
Spice on those Isles and bade them still smell so,
And that rich Indie which doth gold interre
Is but as single money, coyn'd from her;
She, to' whom this world must it self refer   235
As Suburbs or the Microcosme of her,
[23] Shee, shee is dead; shee's dead: when thou know'st this,
Thou know'st how lame a cripple this world is,
And learn'st thus much by our Anatomy:
That this worlds gen'erall sickenesse doth not lie   240
In any humour, or one certaine part;
But as thou saw'st it rotten at the heart,
Thou seest a Hectique fever hath got hold
Of the whole substance, not to be contrould;
And that thou hast but one way, not t' admit   245

The worlds infection, to be none of it.
For the worlds subtlest immaterial parts
[24]   Feele this consuming wound and ages darts;
For the worlds beauty is decayd or gone:
Beauty, that's colour and proportiön.   250
Disformity   We thinke the heav'ns enjoy their Sphericall,
of parts.   Their round proportiön, embracing all.
But yet their various and perplexëd course
Observ'd in divers ages doth enforce
Men to finde out so many' Eccentrique parts,   255
Such divers downe-right lines, such overthwarts,
As disproportion that pure forme. It teares
The Firmament in eight and forty shares,
[25]   And in these constellations there arise
New starres, and old doe vanish from our eyes   260
As though heav'n suffred earthquakes, peace or war,
When new Towers rise, and old demolish'd are.
They have empaled within a Zodiake
The free-borne Sunne, and keep twelve signes awake
To watch his steps; the Goat and Crabbe controule   265
And fright him backe, who els to eyther Pole
(Did not these Tropiques fetter him) might runne,
For his course is not round. Nor can the Sunne
Perfect a Circle, or maintaine his way
[26]   One inche direct; but where he rose to-day   270
He comes no more, but with a cousening line
Steales by that point, and so is Serpentine;
And seeming weary with his reeling thus,
He meanes to sleepe, being now falne nearer us.
So, of the starres which boast that they doe runne   275
In Circle still, none ends where he begunne.
All their proportion's lame; it sinks, it swels.
For of Meridians and Parallels
Man hath weav'd out a net, and this net throwne
Upon the Heav'ns, and now they are his owne.   280
[27]   Loth to go up the hill, or labour thus
To go to heav'n, we make heav'n come to us.
We spur, we rein the stars, and in their race
They're díversly content t' obey our pace.
But keepes the earth her round proportion still?   285
Doth not a Teneriffe, or highest Hill,
Rise so high like a Rocke, that one might thinke
The floating Moone would shipwrack there and sinke?

Seas are so deepe that Whales, being strooke to-day,
Perchance to-morrow, scarse at middle way   290
Of their wish'd journeys end, the bottom, dye.
[28]   And men, to sound depths, so much line untie
As one might justly thinke that there would rise
At end thereof, one of th' Antipodes.
If under all, a Vault infernall be   295
(Which sure is spaciöus, except that we
Invent another torment, that there must
Millions into a strait hot roome be thrust),
Then solidnesse and roundnesse have no place.
Are these but warts and pock-holes in the face   300
Of th' earth? Thinke so. But yet confesse, in this
The worlds proportiön disfigured is,
[29]   That those two legges whereon it doth rely,
Reward and punishment, are bent awry.
And, Oh, it can no more be questionëd   305
That beauties best, proportiön, is dead,
Since even griefe it selfe, which now alone
Is left us, is without proportiön.
Shee, by whose lines proportiön should bee
Examin'd, measure of all Symmetree,   310
Whom, had that Ancient seene, who thought soules made
Of Harmony, he would at next have said
That Harmony was shee, and thence infer
[30]   That soules were but Resultances from her,
And did from her into our bodies go   315
As, to our eyes, the formes from objects flow.
Shee who, if those great Doctors truely said
That th' Arke to mans proportiöns was made,
Had beene a type for that, as that might be
A type of her in this, that contrary   320
Both Elements, and Passions liv'd at peace
In her, who caus'd all Civill war to cease.
Shee after whom, what forme soe'er we see
Is discord, and rude incongruitee:
[31]   Shee, shee is dead, shee's dead; when thou know'st this,   325
Thou know'st how ugly' a monster this world is,
And learn'st thus much by our Anatomee,
That here is nothing to enamor thee.
And that, not onely faults in inward parts,
Corruptions in our braines or in our harts,   330
Poys'oning the fountaines whence our actions spring,

Endanger us; but that, if every thing
Be not done fitly' and in proportiön
To satisfie wise and good lookers on,
(Since most men be such as most thinke they bee)   335
[32] They're lothsome too, by this Deformitee.
For good, and well, must in our actions meete;
Wicked is not much worse than indiscreet.
But beauties other, second Element,
Colour, and lustre now, is as neere spent.   340
And had the world his just proportiön,
Were it a ring still, yet the stone is gone:
As a compassionate Turcoyse which doth tell
By looking pale, the wearer is not well,
As Gold fals sicke, being stung with Mercury,   345
All the worlds parts, of such complexion bee.
[33] When nature was most busie, the first weeke,
Swadling the new-borne earth, God seem'd to like
That she should sport herselfe sometimes, and play,
To mingle 'and vary colours every day.   350
And then, as though she could not make inow,
Himselfe his various Rainbow did allow.
Sight is the noblest sense of any one,
Yet sight hath onely colour to feed on;
And colour is decayd: summers robe growes   355
Duskie, and like an oft dyed garment showes.
Our blushing redde, which us'd in cheekes to spred,
[34] Is inward sunke, and onely' our soules are redde.
Perchance the world might have recoverëd,
If she whom we lament had not beene dead: 360
But shee in whom all white, and red, and blew
(Beauties ingredients) voluntary grew
As in an unvext Paradise; from whom
Did all things verdure, and their lustre come,
Whose composition was miraculous,   365
Being all color, all Diaphanous
(For Ayre and Fire but thicke grosse bodies were,
And liveliest stones but drowsie' and pale to her),
[35] She, shee is dead; shee's dead: when thou know'st this,
Thou know'st how wan a Ghost this our world is: 370
And learn'st thus much by our Anatomee,
That it should more affright than pleasure thee.
And that, since all faire color then did sinke,
'Tis now but wicked vanity to thinke

To colour vitious deeds with good pretence, 375
Or with bought colors to illude mens sense.
Nor in aught more this worlds decay appeares,
Than that her influence the heav'n forbeares,
Or that the Elements doe not feele this:
[36] The father, or the mother barren is. 380
The clouds conceive not raine, or doe not powre,
In the due birth-time, downe the balmy showre.
Th' Ayre doth not motherly sit on the earth,
To hatch her seasons, and give all things birth.
Spring-times were common cradles, but are toombes; 385
And false-conceptions fill the generall wombs.
Th' Ayre showes such Meteörs, as none can see
Not onely what they meane, but what they bee;
Earth such new wormes, as would have troubled much
Th' Egyptian Magis to have made more such. 390
[37] What Artist now dares boast that he can bring
Heav'n hither, or constellate any thing
So as the influence of those starres may bee
Imprisoned in an Hearbe or Charme or Tree,
And doe by touch, all which those starres could doe? 395
The art is lost, and correspondence too.
For heav'n gives little, and the earth takes less,
And man least knowes their trade and purposes.
If this commerce twixt heaven and earth were not
Embarr'd, and all this traffique quite forgot, 400
Shee, for whose losse we have lamented thus
[38] Would work more fully' and powerf'ully on us.
Since herbes and roots by dying, lose not all,
But they, yea Ashes too, are med'cinall,
Death could not quench her vertue so, but that 405
It would be (if not follow'd) wondred at:
And all the world would be one dying Swan,
To sing her funerall praise, and vainish then.
But as some Serpents poison hurteth not
Except it be from the live Serpent shot, 410
So doth her vertue need her here, to fit
That unto us: she working more than it.
[39] But she, in whom, to such maturity
Vertue was grown past growth, that it must die;
Shee, from whose influence all Impression came, 415
But by Receivers impotencies, lame;
Who, though she could not transubstantiate

Weaknesse
in the want of
correspondence
of heaven and
earth.

All states to gold, yet gilded every state:
So that some Princes have some temperance;
Some Counsaylors some purpose to advance   420
The common profite; and some people have
Some stay, no more than Kings should give, to crave;
Some women have some taciturnity;
[40]   Some Nunneries, some graines of chastity.
She that did thus much, and much more could do,   425
But that our age was Iron, and rusty too,
Shee, shee is dead; shee's dead: when thou knowst this,
Thou know'st how drie a Cinder this world is;
And learn'st thus much by our Anatomy,
That 'tis in vaine to dew or mollifie   430
It with thy Teares or Sweat or Bloud: no thing
Is worth our travaile, griefe, or perishing,
But those rich joyes which did possesse her hart,
Of which shee's now partaker, and a part.
Conclusion. [41] But as in cutting up a man that's dead,   435
The body will not last out, to have read
On every part, and therefore men direct
Their speech to parts that are of most effect:
So the worlds carcasse would not last, if I
Were punctuall in this Anatomy.   440
Nor smels it well to hearers, if one tell
Them their disease, who faine would thinke they're well.
Here therefore be the end: And, blessèd maid,
Of whom is meant what ever hath been said
Or shall be spoken well by any tongue,   445
[42]   Whose name refines coarse lines, and makes prose song,
Accept this tribute and his first yeeres rent,
Who till his dark short tapers end be spent,
As oft as thy feast sees this widowed earth,
Will yearely celebrate thy second birth,   450
That is, thy death. For though the soule of man
Be got when man is made, 'tis borne but then
When man doth die. Our body's as the wombe,
And as a mid-wife death directs it home.
And you her creatures, whom she workes upon,   455
And have your last and best concoctiön
[43]   From her example and her vertue, 'if you
In reverence to her doe thinke it due,
That no one should her prayses thus reherse,
As matter fit for Chronicle, not verse: 460

Vouchsafe to call to minde, that God did make
A last, and lasting'st peece, a song. He spake
To *Moses*, to deliver unto all,
That song: because he knew they would let fall
The Law, the Prophets, and the History,   465
But keepe the song still in their memory.
Such an opinion (in due measure) made
[44]   Me this great Office boldly to invade.
Nor could incomprehensiblenesse deterre
Me, from thus trying to imprison her.   470
Which, when I saw that a strict grave could doe,
I saw not why verse might not doe so too.
Verse hath a middle nature: Heav'n keeps soules,
The Grave keepes bodies, Verse the Fame enroules.

[45]

A FUNERALL
ELEGIE.

'Tis lost, to trust a Tombe with such a guest,
Or to confine her in a Marble chest.
Alas, what's Marble, Jet, or Porphiry,
Priz'd with the Chrysolite of either eye,
Or with those Pearles and Rubies which shee was?　　5
Joyne the two Indies in one Tombe, 'tis glas;
And so is all to her materials,

[46] Though every inche were ten Escorials.
Yet shee's demolish'd: Can we keepe her then
In workes of hands, or of the wits of men?　　10
Can these memorials, ragges of paper, give
Life to that name, by which name they must live?
Sickly, alas, short-liv'd, aborted bee
Those Carkas verses, whose soule is not shee.
And can shee, who no longer would be shee,　　15
Being such a Tabernacle, stoope to bee
In paper wrapt; Or, when she would not lie
In such a house, dwell in an Elegie?

[47] But 'tis no matter; we may well allow
Verse to live so long as the world will now.　　20
For her death wounded it. The world containes
Princes for armes, and Counsaylors for braines,
Lawyers for tongues, Divines for hearts, and more,
The Rich for stomachs, and for backes the Pore;
The Officers for hands, Merchants for feet　　25
By which remote and distant Countries meet.
But those fine spirits, which doe tune and set
This Organ, are those peeces which beget
Wonder and love: And these were shee; and shee

[48] Being spent, the world must needes decrepit bee.　　30
For since death will proceed to triumph still,
He can find nothing, after her, to kill,
Except the world it selfe, so great as shee.

Thus brave and confident may Nature bee,
Death cannot give her such another blow, 35
Because shee cannot such another show.
But must we say shee's dead? May't not be said
That as a sundred Clocke is peece-meale laid,
Not to be lost, but by the makers hand
Repolish'd, without error then to stand; 40
[49] Or as the Afrique Niger streame enwombs
It selfe into the earth, and after comes
(Having first made a naturall bridge, to passe
For many leagues), farre greater than it was,
May't not be said, that her grave shall restore 45
Her, greater, purer, firmer than before?
Heav'n may say this, and joy in't; but can wee
Who live, and lack her here, this vantage see?
What is't to us, alas, if there have beene
An Angell made a Throne, or Cherubin? 50
[50] We lose by't: And as agëd men are glad,
Being tastless growne, to joy in joyes they had,
So now the sicke, starv'd world must feed upon
This joy, that we had here, who now is gone.
Rejoyce then Nature, and this world, that you 55
Fearing the last fires hastning to subdue
Your force and vigor, ere it were neere gone,
Wisely bestow'd, and layd it all on one.
One, whose cleare body was so pure and thin,
Because it need disguise no thought within. 60
'Twas but a through-light scarfe, her minde t'enroule,
Or exhalation breath'd out from her soule.
[51] One whom all men who durst no more, admir'd,
And whom, who e'er had worth enough, desir'd;
As when a Temple's built, Saints emulate 65
To which of them it shall be consecrate.
But as when Heav'n lookes on us with new eyes,
Those new starres ev'ry Artist exercise,
What place they should assigne to them, they doubt,
Argue' and agree not, till those starres go out: 70
So the world studied whose this peece should be,
Till she can be nobodies else, nor shee;
But like a Lampe of Balsamum, desir'd
[52] Rather t' adorne than last, shee soone expir'd,
Cloath'd in her Virgin white integrity; 75
For mariage, though it doe not staine, doth dye.

To scape th' infirmities which wait upon
Woman, shee went away, before she 'was one.
And the worlds busie noyse to overcome,
Tooke so much death as serv'd for opium.   80
For though she could not, nor could chuse to die,
Shee 'hath yeelded to too long an Extasie.
He which not knowing her sad History,
Should come to reade the booke of Destinie,

[53]   How faire and chast, humble and high shee 'had beene,   85
Much promis'd, much perform'd, at not fifteene,
And meas'ring future things by things before,
Should turne the leafe to read, and reade no more,
Would thinke that either destinie mistooke,
Or that some leaves were torne out of the booke.   90
But 'tis not so: Fate did but usher her
To yeares of Reasons use, and then infer
Her dest'ny to her selfe; which liberty
She tooke but for thus much, thus much to die.
Her modesty not suff'ring her to bee   95

[54]   Fellow-Commissioner with Destinee,
Shee did no more but die; if after her
Any shall live, which dare true good prefer,
Ev'ry such person is her delegate,
T' accomplish that which should have beene her fate.   100
They shall make up that booke, and shall have thankes
Of Fate and her, for filling up their blanks.
For future vertuous deeds are Legacies,
Which from the gift of her example rise.
And 'tis in heaven part of spir'tuall mirth,   105
To see how well, the good play her, on earth.

FINIS

The Second Anniuerſarie.

OF
THE PROGRES
of the Soule.

Wherein :
BY OCCASION OF THE
Religious Death of Miſtris
ELIZABETH DRVRY,
the incommodities of the Soule
in this life and her exaltation in
the next, are Contem-
plated.

LONDON,
Printed by *M. Bradwood* for *S. Macham,* and are
to beſould at his ſhop in Pauls Church-yard at
the ſigne of the Bull-head,
1612.

6. Title-page of the *Second Anniversary* in the first complete edition of
1612. Folger Shakespeare Library, STC 7023, sig. E1.

The Second Anniversarie.

OF

THE PROGRES

of the Soule.

Wherein:

BY OCCASION OF THE

Religious Death of Mistris

ELIZABETH DRURY,

the incommodities of the Soule
in this life and her exaltation in
the next, are Contem-
plated.

LONDON,

Printed by *M. Bradwood* for *S. Macham*, and are
to be sould at his shop in Pauls Church-yard at
the signe of the Bull-head.

1612.

THE HARBINGER
to the Progres.

Two soules move here, and mine (a third) must move
Paces of admiration, and of love.
Thy soule (Deare Virgin) whose this tribute is,
Mov'd from this mortall sphere to lovely blisse,
And yet moves still, and still aspires to see   5
The worlds last day, thy glories full degree:

Like as those starres which thou o'er-lookest farre,
Are in their place, and yet still movëd are,
No soule (whiles with the luggage of this clay
It cloggëd is) can follow thee halfe way,   10
Or see thy sight, which doth our thoughts outgoe
So fast, that now the lightning moves but slow.
But now thou art as high in heaven flowne
As heav'ns from us; what soule besides thine owne
Can tell thy joyes, or say he can relate   15

Thy glorious Journals in that blessed state?
I envie thee (Rich soule) I envie thee,
Although I cannot yet thy glory see.
And thou (Great spirit) which hers follow'd hast
So fast, as none can follow thine so fast,   20
So farre as none can follow thine so farre
(And if this flesh did not the passage barre
Had'st raught her), let me wonder at thy flight
Which long agone had'st lost the vulgar sight

And now mak'st proud the better eyes, that they   25
Can see thee less'ned in thine aery way;
So while thou mak'st her soules hy progresse knowne
Thou mak'st a noble progresse of thine owne.
From this worlds carcasse having mounted hie
To that pure life of Immortalitie;   30
Since thine aspiring thoughts themselves so raise
That more may not beseeme a creatures praise,
Yet still thou vow'st her more; and every yeare

Mak'st a new progresse, while thou wandrest here;   [E4r]
Still upwards mount, and let thy makers praise   35
Honor thy Laura, and adorne thy laies.
And since thy Muse her head in heaven shrouds
Oh let her never stoope below the clouds:
And if those glorious sainted soules may know
Or what we doe, or what we sing below,   40
Those acts, those songs shall still content them best
Which praise those awfull powers that make them blest.

The Second Anniversarie.

OF

THE PROGRES

of the Soule.

<table>
<tr><td>*The entrance.*</td><td>Nothing could make mee sooner to confesse</td><td></td></tr>
<tr><td></td><td>That this world had an everlastingnesse</td><td></td></tr>
<tr><td></td><td>Than to consider, that a yeare is runne</td><td></td></tr>
<tr><td></td><td>Since both this lower worlds and the Sunnes Sunne,</td><td></td></tr>
<tr><td></td><td>The Lustre, and the vigor of this All</td><td>5</td></tr>
<tr><td>[2]</td><td>Did set; 't were Blasphemy to say, did fall.</td><td></td></tr>
</table>

[1]

The entrance. Nothing could make mee sooner to confesse
That this world had an everlastingnesse
Than to consider, that a yeare is runne
Since both this lower worlds and the Sunnes Sunne,
The Lustre, and the vigor of this All   5
[2] Did set; 't were Blasphemy to say, did fall.
But as a ship which hath strooke saile, doth runne
By force of that force which before, it wonne,
Or as sometimes in a beheaded man,
Though at those two Red seas which freely ran,   10
One from the Trunke, another from the Head,
His soule be sail'd to her eternall bed,
His eies will twinckle, and his tongue will roll,
As though he beckned and cal'd back his Soul,
He graspes his hands, and he puls up his feet,   15
And seemes to reach, and to step forth to meet
[3] His soule: when all these motions which we saw
Are but as Ice, which crackles at a thaw;
Or as a Lute, which in moist weather rings
Her knell alone, by cracking of her strings: 20
So strugles this dead world, now shee is gone;
For there is motion in corruptiön.
As some Daies are at the Creation nam'd
Before the sunne, the which fram'd Daies, was fram'd:
So after this sunns set, some show appeares,   25
And orderly vicisitude of yeares.
Yet a new Deluge, and of Lethe flood,
[4] Hath drown'd us all, All have forgot all good,
Forgetting her, the maine Reserve of all;
Yet in this Deluge, grosse and generall,   30
Thou seest mee strive for life; my life shalbe

To bee hereafter prais'd, for praysing thee,
Immortal Mayd, who though thou wouldst refuse
The name of Mother, be unto my Muse
A Father, since her chaste Ambition is   35
Yearely to bring forth such a child as this.
These Hymnes may worke on future wits, and so
May great Grand-children of thy praises grow.
[5]   And so, though not Revive, embalme and spice
The world, which else would putrify with vice,   40
For thus Man may extend thy progeny,
Untill man doe but vanish, and not die.
These Hymns thy issue may encrease so long,
As till Gods great Venite change the song.
Thirst for that time, O my insatiate soule,   45   *A just disestimation*
And serve thy thirst with Gods safe-sealing Bowle.   *of this world.*
Bee thirsty still, and drink still, till thou goe:
'Tis th' onely Health, to be Hydropique so.
Forget this rotten world. And unto thee
[6]   Let thine owne times as an old story be;   50
Be not concern'd: study not why, nor when;
Do not so much as not beleeve a man.
For though to erre be worst, to try truths forth
Is far more busines than this world is worth.
The World is but a Carkas; thou art fed   55
By it, but as a worm that carkas bred;
And why shouldst thou, poor worme, consider more
When this world will grow better than before
Than those thy fellow-wormes doe think upon
That carkasses last resurrectiön.   60
[7]   Forget this world, and scarse thinke of it so,
As of old cloathes cast off a yeare agoe.
To be thus stupid is Alacrity;
Men thus lethargique have best Memory.
Looke upward; that's towards her, whose happy state   65
We now lament not, but congratulate.
Shee, to whom all this world was but a stage,
Where all sat harkning how her youthfull age
Should be emploid, because in all she did,
Some Figure of the Golden times was hid.   70
Who could not lacke, what e'er this world could give,
[8]   Because shee was the forme that made it live;
Nor could complaine, that this world was unfit
To be stayd in, then when shee was in it.

Shee that first tried indifferent desires 75
By vertue,' and vertue by religious fires;
Shee to whose person Paradise adher'd
As Courts to Princes; shee whose eies enspheard
Star-light inough, t' have made the South controll
(Had shee beene there) the Star-full Northern Pole; 80
Shee, shee is gone; shee's gone: when thou know'st this,
What fragmentary rubbidge this world is

[9] Thou know'st, and that it is not worth a thought;
He honors it too much that thinks it naught.

Contemplation
of our state in
our death-bed.

Thinke then, my soule, that death is but a Groome, 85
Which brings a Taper to the outward roome,
Whence thou spiest first a little glimm'ring light,
And after, brings it nearer to thy sight:
For such approaches doth Heav'n make in death.
Thinke thy selfe laboring now with broken breath, 90
And thinke those broken and lost Notes to bee
Division, and thy happiest Harmonee.

[10] Thinke thee laid on thy death bed, loose and slacke;
And thinke that but unbinding of a packe
To take one precious thing, thy soule, from thence. 95
Thinke thy selfe parch'd with fevers violence:
Anger thine Ague more, by calling it
Thy Physicke; chide the slacknesse of the fit.
Thinke that thou hear'st thy knell, and thinke no more,
But that, as Bels cal'd thee to Church before, 100
So this, to the Triumphant Church cals thee.
Thinke Satans Sergeants round about thee bee,
And thinke that but for Legacies they thrust;
Give one thy Pride, t' another give thy Lust;

[11] Give them those sinnes which they gave thee before, 105
And trust th' immac'late blood to wash thy score.
Thinke thy friends weeping round, and thinke that they
Weepe but because they goe not yet thy way.
Thinke that they close thine eyes, and thinke in this,
That they confesse much in the world, amisse, 110
Who dare not trust a dead mans eye with that
Which they from God and Angels cover not.
Thinke that they shroud thee up, and thinke from thence
They reinvest thee in white innocence.
Thinke that thy body rots, and (if so lowe, 115

[12] Thy soule exalted so, thy thoughts can goe)
Thinke thee a Prince, who of themselves create

Wormes which insensibly devoure their state.
Thinke that they bury thee, and thinke that rite
Laies thee to sleepe but a saint Lucies night.   120
Thinke these things cheerefully; and if thou bee
Drowsie or slacke, remember then that shee,
Shee whose Complexion was so even made,
That which of her Ingredients should invade
The other three, no Feare, no art could guesse: 125
So far were all remov'd from more or lesse.

[13] But as in Mithridate, or just perfumes,
Where all good things being met, no one presumes
To governe or to triumph on the rest,
Onely because all were, no part was best.   130
And as, though all doe know, that quantities
Are made of lines, and lines from Points arise,
None can these lines or quantities unjoynt
And say this is a line, or this a point:
So though the Elements and Humors were   135
In her, one could not say, This governes there.
Whose even constitution might have wonne

[14] Any disease to venture on the Sunne
Rather than her; and make a spirit feare
That he to disuniting, subject were;   140
To whose proportions, if we would compare
Cubes, they're unstable; Circles, Angulare.
She who was such a Chaine, as Fate emploies
To bring mankind all Fortunes it enjoies:
So fast, so even wrought, as one would thinke   145
No Accident could threaten any linke;
Shee, shee embrac'd a sicknesse, gave it meat,
The purest Blood, and Breath, that ere it eat.

[15] And hath taught us, that though a good man hath
Title to Heav'n, and plead it by his Faith,   150
And though he may pretend a conquest, since
Heav'n was content to suffer violence;
Yea, though he plead a long possession too
(For they're in Heav'n on Earth, who Heav'ns workes do),
Though he had right, and power, and Place before,   155
Yet Death must usher, and unlocke the doore.
Thinke further on thy selfe, my soule, and thinke   *Incommodities of the*
How thou at first wast made but in a sinke;   *Soule in the Body.*
Thinke that it argued some infirmitee,
[16] That those two soules, which then thou foundst in mee,   160

Thou fed'st upon, and drew'st into thee, both
My second soule of sense, and first of growth.
Thinke but how poore thou 'wast, how obnoxioüs,
Whom a small lump of flesh could poison thus.
This curded milke, this poore unlittered whelpe,   165
My body, could beyond escape or helpe
Infect thee with orig'nall sinne, and thou
Couldst neither then refuse, nor leave it now.
Thinke that no stubborne sullen Anchorit,
Which fixt to' a Pillar, or a Grave doth sit   170
[17]   Bedded and Bath'd in all his Ordures, dwels
So fowly' as our soules in their first-built Cels.
Thinke in how poore a prison thou didst lie;
After, enabled but to sucke and crie.
Thinke, when 't was growne to most, 't was a poore Inne,   175
A Province pack'd up in two yards of skinne,
And that usurp'd, or threatned with the rage
Of sicknesses, or their true mother, Age.

Her liberty   But thinke that Death hath now enfranchis'd thee,
by death.   Thou hast thy' expansion now and libertee;   180
Thinke that a rusty Peece, discharg'd, is flowne
[18]   In peeces, and the bullet is his owne,
And freely flies: This to thy soule allow,
Thinke thy shell broke, thinke thy Soule hatch'd but now.
And thinke this slow-pac'd soule, which late did cleave   185
To' a body,' and went but by the bodies leave
Twenty, perchance, or thirty mile a day,
Dispatches in a minute all the way
Twixt Heav'n and Earth. Shee staies not in the Ayre
To looke what Meteors there themselves prepare;   190
She carries no desire to know, nor sense,
Whether th' Ayres middle Region be intense,
[19]   For th' Element of fire, shee doth not know
Whether shee past by such a place or no;
She bates not at the Moone, nor cares to trie   195
Whether in that new world, men live, and die.
Venus retards her not, to' enquire how shee
Can (being one Star) Hesper 'and Vesper bee;
Hee that charm'd Argus' eies, sweet Mercury
Workes not on her, who now is growne all Ey;   200
Who, if shee meete the body of the Sunne,
Goes through, not staying till his course be runne;
Who finds in Mars his Campe, no corps of Guard;

[20] Nor is by Jove, nor by his father barrd;
     But ere shee can consider how she went,   205
     At once is at, and through the Firmament.
     And as these stars were but so many beades
     Strunge on one string, speed undistinguish'd leades
     Her through those spheares as through the beades, a string,
     Whose quicke succession makes it still one thing,   210
     As doth the Pith which, lest our Bodies slacke,
     Strings fast the little bones of necke, and backe:
     So by the soule doth death string Heav'n and Earth.
     For when our soule enjoyes this, her third birth
[21] (Creation gave her one; a second, grace),   215
     Heav'n is as neare, and present to her face,
     As colours are, and objects in a roome
     Where darknesse was before, when Tapers come.
     This must, my soule, thy long-short Progresse bee,
     To' advance these thoughts: remember then, that shee,   220
     Shee whose fair body no such prison was,
     But that a soule might well be pleas'd to passe
     An Age in her; shee whose rich beauty lent
     Mintage to others beauties, for they went
     But for so much, as they were like to her;   225
[22] Shee, in whose body (if wee dare prefer
     This low world, to so high a mark as shee)
     The Westerne treasure, Easterne spiceree,
     Europe, and Afrique, and the unknowne rest
     Were easily found, or what in them was best,   230
     And when we 'have made this large Discoveree
     Of all in her, some one part then will bee
     Twenty such parts, whose plenty' and riches is
     Inough to make twenty such worlds as this.
     Shee, whom had they knowne, who did first betrothe   235
[23] The Tute'lar Angels, and assigned one, both
     To Nations, Cities, and to Companies,
     To Functions, Offices, and Dignities,
     And to each severall man, to him and him,
     They would have giv'n her one for ev'ry limbe.   240
     Shee, of whose soule, if we may say, 'twas Gold,
     Her body was th' Electrum, and did hold
     Many degrees of that; we understood
     Her by her sight; her pure and elo'quent blood
     Spoke in her cheekes, and so distinctly wrought   245
     That one might almost say, her bodie thought,

Shee, shee, thus richly' and largely hous'd, is gone;

[24] And chides us slow-pac'd snailes, who crawle upon
Our prisons prison, earth, nor thinke us well
Longer, than whilst we beare our brittle shell.   250

Her ignorance in this
life and knowledge
in the next.

But 'twere but little to have chang'd our roome,
If, as we were in this our living Tombe
Oppress'd with ignorance, we still were so:
Poore soule, in this thy flesh what dost thou know?
Thou know'st thy self so little,' as thou know'st not,   255
How thou did'st die, nor how thou wast begot.
Thou neither know'st how thou at first cam'st in,
Nor how thou took'st the poyson of mans sin.

[25] Nor dost thou (though thou know'st, that thou art so)
By what way thou art made immortall, know.   260
Thou art too narrow, wretch, to comprehend
Even thy selfe: yea, though thou wouldst but bend
To know thy body. Have not all soules thought
For many ages, that our body' is wrought
Of Ayre, and Fire, and other Elements?   265
And now they think of new ingredients.
And one soule thinkes one, and another way;
Another thinkes, and 'tis an even lay.
Knowst thou but how the stone doth enter in

[26] The bladders Cave, and never breake the skin?   270
Knowst thou how blood, which to the hart doth flow,
Doth from one ventricle to th' other go?
And for the putrid stuffe, which thou dost spit,
Knowst thou how thy lungs have attracted it?
There are no passages, so that there is   275
(For aught thou knowst) piercing of substances.
And of those many' opinions which men raise
Of Nailes and Haires, dost thou know which to praise?
What hope have we to know our selves, when wee
Know not the least things, which for our use bee?   280

[27] We see in Authors, too stiffe to recant,
A hundred controversies of an Ant.
And yet one watches, starves, freeses, and sweats
To know but Catechismes and Alphabets
Of unconcerning things, matters of fact: 285
How others on our stage their parts did Act,
What Caesar did, yea, and what Cicero said;
Why grasse is greene, or why our blood is red,
Are mysteries which none have reach'd unto.

In this low forme, poore soule, what wilt thou doe?   290
When wilt thou shake off this Pedantery,
[28]   Of being taught by sense, and Fantasy?
Thou look'st through spectacles; small things seeme great
Below; But up unto the watch-towre get,
And see all things despoyled of fallacies;   295
Thou shalt not peepe through lattices of eies,
Nor heare through Laberinths of eares, nor learne
By circuit, or collections to discerne.
In Heav'n thou strait know'st all, concerning it,
And what concerns it not shall strait forget.   300
There thou (but in no other schoole) maist bee
Perchance as learned, and as full, as shee:
[29]   Shee who all Libraries had throughly read
At home, in her owne thoughts, and practisëd
So much good as would make as many more;   305
Shee whose example they must all implore,
Who would or doe or thinke well, and confesse
That aye the vertuous Actions they expresse
Are but a new, and worse editiön
Of her some one thought, or one actiön;   310
Shee who in th' Art of knowing Heav'n, was growne
Here upon Earth, to such perfectiön
That shee hath, e'er since to Heav'n shee came,
[30]   (In a far fairer print) but read the same;
Shee, shee, not satisfied with all this weight,   315
(For so much knowledge as would over-freight
Another, did but Ballast her) is gone,
As well t' enjoy as get perfectiöne;
And cals us after her, in that shee tooke
(Taking herselfe) our best, and worthiest booke.   320
Returne not, my soule, from this extasee,
And meditation of what thou shalt bee,
To earthly thoughts, till it to thee appeare,
With whom thy conversation must be there.
[31]   With whom wilt thou Converse? what statiön   325
Canst thou choose out, free from infectiön,
That will not give thee theirs, nor drink in thine?
Shalt thou not finde a spungy slack Divine
Drinke and sucke in, th' Instructions of Great men,
And, for the word of God, vent them again?   330
Are there not some Courts (And then, no things bee
So like as Courts), which in this let us see,

*Of our company in this
life and in the next.*

That wits and tongues of Libellars are weake,
Because they doe more ill, than these can speake?
The poyson 'is gone through all; poysons affect   335
[32]   Chiefly the cheefest parts, but some effect
In Nailes, and Haires, yea excrements, will show:
So will the poyson' of sinne, in the most low.
Up, up, my drowsie soule, where thy new eare
Shall in the Angels songs no discord heare: 340
Where thou shalt see the blessëd Mother-maid
Joy in not being that, which men have said;
Where shee' is exalted more for being good
Than for her interest, of motherhood;
Up to those Patriarckes, which did longer sit   345
Expecting Christ, than they 'have enjoyed him yet;
[33]   Up to those Prophets, which now gladly see
Their Prophecies growne to be Historee;
Up to th' Apostles, who did bravely runne
All the Sunnes course, with more light than the Sunne; 350
Up to those Martyrs, who did calmely bleed
Oyle to th' Apostles lamps, dew to their seed;
Up to those Virgins, who thought that almost
They made joynt-tenants with the Holy Ghost,
If they to any should his Temple give.   355
Up, up, for in that squadron there doth live
Shee, who hath carried thither, new degrees
[34]   (As to their number) to their dignitees.
Shee, who being to herselfe a state, enjoyd
All royalties which any state employd,   360
For shee made wars, and triumph'd; reason still
Did not o'erthrow, but rectifie her will;
And shee made peace, for no peace is like this,
That beauty' and chastity together kisse.
She did high justice, for shee crucified   365
Ev'ry first motion of rebellious pride;
And shee gave pardons, and was liberall,
For, onely' her selfe except, shee pardond all.
[35]   Shee coynd in this, that her impressions gave
To all our actions all the worth they have.   370
Shee gave protections; the thoughts of her brest
Satans rude Officers could ne'er arrest.
As these prerogatives, being met in one,
Made her a soveraigne state, religiön
Made her a Church; and these two made her all.   375

Shee who was all this All, and could not fall
To worse, by company (for shee was still
More Antidote than all the world was ill)
Shee, shee doth leave it, and by Death, survive

[36] All this, in Heav'n: whither, who doth not strive 380
The more, because shee 'is there, he doth not know
That accidentall joyes in Heav'n doe grow.
But pause, My soule, and study, ere thou fall
On accidentall joyes, th' essentiall.

Still, before Accessories doe abide 385
A triall, must the principall be tried.
And what essentiall joy canst thou expect
Here upon earth? what permanent effect
Of transitory causes? Dost thou love
Beauty? (And Beauty worthy'est is to move) 390

[37] Poore cous'ned cous'nor, that she, and that thou,
Which did begin to love, are neither now.
You are both fluid, chang'd since yesterday;
Next day repaires (but ill) last daies decay.
Nor are (although the river keep the name) 395
Yesterdaies waters, and to-daies the same.
So flowes her face, and thine eies; neither now
That saint, nor Pilgrime, which your loving vow
Concernd, remaines; but whil'st you thinke you bee
Constant, you' are hourly in inconstancee. 400

Honour may have pretence unto our love
[38] Because that, God did live so long above
Without this Honour, and then lov'd it so,
That he at last made Creatures to bestow
Honour on him: not that he needed it, 405
But that, to his hands, man might grow more fit.
But since all honors from inferiors flow,
(For they doe give it; Princes doe but show
Whom they would have so honor'd) and that this
On such opinions, and capacities 410
Is built, as rise and fall, to more and lesse:
Alas, 'tis but a casuall happinesse.

[39] Hath ever any man to' himselfe assigned
This or that happinesse, to' arrest his minde,
But that another man, which takes a worse, 415
Thinke him a foole for having tane that course?
They who did labour Babels tower t' erect,
Might have considered, that for that effect,

Of essentiall joy in this
life and in the next.

All this whole solid Earth could not allow
Nor furnish forth Materials enow;   420
And that this Center, to raise such a place
Was far too little, to have beene the Base:
No more affords this world, foundatiöne
[40]   T' erect true joye, were all the meanes in one.
But as the Heathen made them sev'rall gods,   425
Of all Gods Benefits, and all his Rods
(For as the Wine, and Corne, and Onions are
Gods unto them, so Agues bee, and war),
And as by changing that whole precious Gold
To such small copper coynes, they lost the old,   430
And lost their onely God, who ever must
Be sought alone, and not in such a thrust:
So much mankind true happinesse mistakes;
No Joye enjoyes that man, that many makes.
[41]   Then, soule, to thy first pitch worke up againe: 435
Know that all lines which circles doe containe,
For once that they the center touch, do touch
Twice the circumference; and be thou such.
Double on Heav'n thy thoughts on Earth employd:
All will not serve; Onely who have enjoyd   440
The sight of God, in fulnesse, can thinke it,
For it is both the object, and the wit.
This is essentiall joye, where neither hee
Can suffer Diminutiön, nor wee;
'Tis such a full, and such a filling good;   445
[42]   Had th' Angels once look'd on them, they had stood.
To fill the place of one of them, or more,
Shee whom we celebrate, is gone before;
Shee, who had here so much essential joye
As no chance could distract, much lesse destroy,   450
Who with Gods presence was acquainted so
(Hearing, and speaking to him) as to know
His face, in any natu'rall Stone, or Tree,
Better than when in Images they bee;
Who kept, by diligent devotiön,   455
Gods Image in such reparatiön
[43]   Within her heart, that what decay was growne,
Was her first Parents fault, and not her own;
Who being solicited to any Act,
Still heard God pleading his safe precontract;   460
Who by a faithful confidence, was here

Betrothed to God, and now is married there;
Whose twilights were more cleare than our midday,
Who dreamt devoutlier than most use to pray;
Who being here fill'd with grace, yet strove to bee   465
Both where more grace, and more capacitee
At once is given: shee to Heav'n is gone,
[44] Who made this world in some proportiön
A heav'n, and here, became unto us all,
Joye (as our joyes admit) essentiäll.   470
But could this low world joyes essentiall touch,   *Of accidentall joyes*
Heav'ns accidentall joyes would pass them much.   *in both places.*
How poore and lame, must then our casuall bee?
If thy Prince will his subjects to call thee
My Lord, and this doe swell thee, thou art then   475
By being a greater, growne to be less Man.
When no Physician of Redresse can speake,
A joyfull casuall violence may breake
[45] A dangerous Apostem in thy brest;
And whilst thou joy'st in this, the dange'rous rest,   480
The bag may rise up, and so strangle thee.
What aye was casuäll, may ever bee.
What should the Nature change? Or make the same
Certaine, which was but casuall, when it came?
All casuall joy doth loud and plainly say,   485
Onely by comming, that it can away.
Onely in Heav'n joies strength is never spent;
And accidentall things are permanent.
Joy of a soules arrivall ne'er decaies;
[46] For that soule ever joyes, and ever staies.   490
Joy that their last great Consummatiön
Approches in the resurrectiön:
When earthly bodies more celestiall
Shalbe, than Angels were, for they could fall;
This kind of joy doth every day admit   495
Degrees of growth, but none of losing it.
In this fresh joy, 'tis no small part, that shee,
Shee, in whose goodnesse, he that names degree
Doth injure her ('Tis losse to be cal'd best,
There where the stuffe is not such as the rest);   500
[47] Shee, who left such a body 'as even shee
Onely in Heav'n could learne, how it can bee
Made better; for shee rather was two soules,
Or like to full, on-both-sides-written Rolls,

Where eies might read upon the outward skin 505
As strong Records for God, as mind's within.
Shee, who by making full perfection grow,
Peeces a Circle, and still keepes it so,
Long'd for, and longing for 'it, to heav'n is gone,
Where shee receives, and gives additiön. 510

Conclusion.

[48] Here in a place, where mis-devotion frames
A thousand praiers to saints, whose very names
The ancient Church knew not, Heav'n knowes not yet,
And where, what lawes of poetry admit,
Lawes of religion have at least the same, 515
Immortal Maid, I might invoque thy name.
Could any Saint provoke that appetite,
Thou here shouldst make mee a French convertite.
But thou wouldst not; nor wouldst thou be content,
To take this for my second yeeres true Rent, 520
Did this coine beare any' other stampe than his,
That gave thee power to doe; me, to say this.

[49] Since his will is, that to posteritee,
Thou should'st for life, and death, a patterne bee;
And that the world should notice have of this, 525
The purpose, and th' Autority is his.
Thou art the Proclamation; and I am
The Trumpet, at whose voice the people came.

FINIS

FROM THE DOWDEN MANUSCRIPT, PRE-1615 COMPOSITIONS

Elegye. On Loves Progresse.

Who ever Loves, yf he doe not propose
  The right true end of Love, He 'ys One which goes
To Sea, for Nothing, but to make him sicke;
  And Love 'ys a Bearewhelpe borne, Yf wee o'erlicke
Our Love, and force yt new strange shapes to take,   5
  Wee Erre, and of a Lumpe, a Monster make.   [23r]
Were not a Calfe a Monster, that were growne
  Fac'd like a Man, though better than hys owne?
Perfection is in Unitye; Prefer
  One woman first, and then one thinge in her.   10
I, when I value Gold may thincke upon
  The Ductillnes, the Applicatiöne,
The wholsomenes, the Ingenuitye
  From Rust, from Soyle, from fyre ever free;
But if I love yt, 't is because 't is made   15
  By our new Nature, Use, the soule of trade.
All these, in woemen, wee might thincke upon
  (Yf woemen had them) but yett Love but one.
Can men more injure woemen, than to say,
  They Love them for that, by which they 'are not they?   20
Makes Vertue woeman? Must I coole my blood
  Till I both bee, and finde One wise and good?
May barren Angells Love soe: But if wee
  Make Love to woman, Vertue is not Shee,
As Beauty 'is not, nor wealth: He that strayes thus   25
  From Her, to hers, ys more adulterous
Than if he tooke her Mayde. Search every Spheare
  And Firmament, our Cupid is not there;
He 'is an Infernall God, and under Ground,
  With Pluto dwells, where Gold and Fyre abound.   30
Men to such Gods, theyre sacrificing coales
  Did not in Altars lay, but Pitts and holes.   [23v]
Although wee see Celestiall Bodyes move
  Above the Earth, The Earth wee tyll and Love;

So wee her Ayres contemplate, words and Hart   35
   And Vertues; But wee Love the Centrique Part.
Nor is the soule more worthy, or more fitt
   For Love than thys, as Infinite, as ytt.
But in attayning thys desired Place,
   How much they stray, that sett out at the face.   40
The Hayre a Forest is of Ambushes,
   Of Springës, Snares, Fetters, and Manacles.
The browe becalmes Us, when 't is smooth, and playne;
   And when 't is wrinckled, shipwracks us agayne.
Smooth, 't is a Paradise, where wee would have   45
   Immortall stay, and wrinckled 't is our Grave.
The Nose like to the first Meridian runns,
   Not twixt an East, and West, but twixt two Sunns.
It leaves a Cheeke, a rosye Hemispheare
   On eyther Side, and then directs us, where   50
Upon the Ilands fortunate wee fall,
   (Not faynte Canarye, but Ambrosyall)
Her swelling Lips: To which when wee are come,
   Wee Anchor there, and thincke ourselves at home;
For they seeme all; There Syrens Songes, and there   55
   Wise Delphique oracles doe fill the Eare.
[24r]   There in a Creeke, where chosen Pearles doe swell,
   The Remora, her cleaving tongue doth dwell.
These, and the Glorious Promont'ry her Chinne
   O'er past: And the streight Hellespont betweene   60
The Sestos, and Abydos of her brests,
   Not of two Lovers, but two Loves, the Nests,
Succeedes a boundles Sea, but that thyne Eye
   Some Iland Moles may scattred there descrye.
And sailing towards her India, in that way   65
   Shall at her fayre Atlantique Navell stay;
Though thence the Current bee thy Pilott made,
   Yett ere thou bee, where thou wouldst be, embayde,
Thou shalt upon another Forrest sett,
   Where some doe shipwracke, and no further gett.   70
When thou art there, consider what thys Chace
   Mispent, by thy beginning at the face.
Rather sett out belowe; Practise my Art.
   Some Symmetrye, the Foote hath, with that Part
Which thou dost seeke, and ys thy Map for that,   75
   Lovelye enough to stop, but not stay att.

Least Subject to disguise, and change it is
   Men say, the Devill never can change hys.
It is the Embleam which hath figur'd
   Firmnes; Tis the first Part that comes to Bed.   80
Civilitye, wee see, refin'd the Kisse
   Which, at the face begonne, transplanted is   [24v]
Since to the hand, since to th' Imperiall knee,
   Now at the Papall foote delights to bee;
If Kings thincke that the nearer waye, and doe   85
   Rise from the Foote, Lovers may doe so too.
For as free Sphears move faster farr than can
   Birds, whom the Ayre resists, so may that Man
Which goes this Emptye, and Ethereall way,
   Than if at Beautyes Elements he stay;   90
Rich Nature hath in woman wisely made
   Two Purses, and theyre mouths aversely Layd.
They then, which to the Lower, Tribute owe,
   That way, which that Exchequer Lookes, must goe.
Hee which doth not, hys Error ys as Greate,   95
   As who by Clyster gave the Stomacke meate.

Elegye. On the Lady Marckham.

Man is the worlde, and death the' Oceän
   To which God gives the Lower parts of Man.
The sea invirons all, and though as yett
   God have sett marks, and boundes twixt Us and ytt,
Yett doth it roare, and gnawe, and still pretend,   5
   And breakes our banckes, when e'er yt takes a frend.
Then our Land waters (Teares of Passion) vent   [25r]
   Our waters there, above our Firmament,
(Teares which our Soule doth for her Sinn lett fall)
   Take all a brackish tast, and funerall.   10
And even these Teares, which should wash Sin, are Sin,
   Wee, after Gods Noah,' drowne our worlde agayne.
Nothing but Man of all invenom'd thinges
   Doth worke upon ytselfe, with Inborne stinges;
Teares are false Spectacles, wee cannot see   15
   Through Passions mist, what they are, or what wee.

In her thys Sea of Death hath made no breach,
  But as the Tyde doth wash the slimye beach
And leaves embroydered workes upon the Sand,
  So ys her flesh refin'd, by Deaths cold hand.   20
As men of China, after an Ages stay,
  Doe take up [Porcelane] where they buryed Clay,
So at thys Grave, her Lymbecke which refynes,
  The Dyamonds, Rubyes, Saphyres, Pearles, and Mynes
Of which thys flesh was, her Soule shall inspyre   25
  Flesh of such stuffe, as God when his Last fyer
Annulls thys world, to recompence yt, shall
  Make and name them, th' Elixar of thys All.
They say the Sea, when it gaynes, loseth too.
  Yf Carnall Death (the yonger brother) doe   30
Usurpe the body, our Soule which subject is
[25v]   To th' Elder death by Sin, is freed by thys.
They perish both, [when they] attempt the just,
  For Graves our Trophees are, and both dead Dust.
Soe, unobnoxious now, She 'hath buryed both,   35
  For none to death sinns, that to [sin] is loth.
Nor [do] they dye, which are not Loth to dye.
  Soe hath shee thys, and that Virginitye.
Grace was in her extreamelye diligent
  That kept her from Sin, yett made her repent.   40
Of what small Spotts, pure white complaynes; Alas
  How litle Poyson breakes a Christall glas?
She sinned, but just enough to lett us see
  That Gods word must be true; All Sinners bee.
So much did zeale her Conscience rectifye,   45
  That extreame truith lack'd litle of a lye,
Making Omissions Acts, laying the Touch
  Of Sinne, on thinges that sometimes may be such.
As Moses Cherubines, whose Natures doe
  Surpasse all Speede, by him are wingëd too: 50
So woulde her Soule, already' in Heaven, seeme then
  To Clyme by Teares, the Common stayres of Men.
How fitt she was for God, I am Content
  To speake, that Death his vaine hast may repent.
How fitt for Us, how eaven, and how sweete,   55
  How good in all her Titles, and how meete
[26r]   To have reformd thys forward Heresye,
  That women can no Parts of Frendship bee.

Howe Morall, how devine shall not be told
  Lest they that heare her Virtues, thincke her Old.   60
And lest wee take Deaths Part, and make him glad
  Of such a Prey, and to hys Tryumph adde.

Elegye on Mrs Boulstred.

Death, I recant, and say, Unsayd by mee,
  What e'er hath slipt, that might diminish Thee.
Spirituall Treason, Atheisme 't is to say,
  That any can thy Summons disobay.
Th' Earthes face ys but thy Table; There are sett   5
  Plants, Cattell, Men, Dishes for Death to eate.
In a rude hunger, now he millions draws
  Into' hys bloodye, or Plaguy, or starved jawes.
Nowe he will seeme to spare, and doth more wast
  Eatinge the best first, well preserv'd to last.   10
Now wantonly he spoyles, and eates us not
  But breakes off frindes, and letts us peecemeale rott.
Nor will thys Earth serve him; Hee sinckes the Deepe,
  Where harmelesse fish Monastique Silence keepe.
Who, (were Death dead) by Roes of living Sand   15
  Might spunge that Element, and make yt Land.
He roundes the Ayre, and breakes the Hymnique notes,   [26v]
  In Birdes, Heavens choristers, Organique throates:
Which (if they did not dye) might seeme to bee
  A tenth rancke in the Heav'nly Hier'archye.   20
O strong, and Long-liv'd Death, how camst thou In?
  And how without Creation didst beginne?
Thou hast, and shalt see dead, before thou Dyest
  All the foure Monarchyes, and Antichrist.
How could I thincke Thee nothing, that see now   25
  In all thys all, Nothinge else is, but Thou.
Our Birthes, and Lyfe, Vices, and Vertues bee
  Wastfull consumptions, and Degrees of Thee.
For wee, to live, our bellowes were, and breath,
  Nor are wee mortall, Dying, Dead, but Death.   30
And though thou beest, O mighty Bird of Preye,
  So much reclaym'd by God, that thou must lay

All that thou killst at hys feete, yett doth hee
   Reserve but fewe, and leaves the Most to Thee.
And of those fewe, now Thou hast overthrowne   35
   One whom thy blowe makes, not ours, nor thyne owne.
Shee was more Storyes high. Hopelesse to come
   To' her Soule, thou 'hast offred at her Lower roome.
Her Soule and body was a King and Court,
   But thou hast both of Captayne miss'd, and fort.   40
As houses fall not, though the King remove,
   Bodyes of Saints rest for theyre Soules above.

[27r]   Death getts twixt Soules and Bodyes, such a Place
   As Sinne insinuates twixt Just men and Grace.
Both workes a Separatione, no Divorce: 45
   Her Soule is gon to usher up her Corpse,
Which shall be 'almost another Soule; for there
   Bodyes are purer, than best Soules are here.
Because in her, her Virtues did outgoe
   Her yeares, wouldst Thou, O Em'ulous Death, doe so?   50
And kill her yonge to thy Losse? Must the Cost
   Of Beauty, 'and Witt, apt to doe harme, bee lost?
What though thou foundst her Proofe gainst Sinns
   of youth?
   Oh every Age a divers Sinne pursueth.
Thou shouldst have stayde, and taken better holde: 55
   Shortly ambitious, Covetous, when Olde
She might have prov'd. And such Devotiön
   Might once have stray'd to Superstitiön.
Yf all her Vertues must have growen, yett might
   Abundant Vertue 'have bred a proud delight.   60
Had she perseverd Just, there would have bin
   Some that would sinne, mis-thincking She did Sin:
Such as would Call her frendship, Love, and feigne
   To Socyablenes, a name profane;
Or Sinne, by tempting, or not daring that,   65
   By wishing, though they never told her what.
Thus mightest Thou 'have slayne more Soules, hadst thou
   not crost
   Thyselfe; and to Tryumph, thyne Armye lost.

[27v]   Yett though these wayes bee Lost, thou hast left One
   Which ys, Immoderate Griefe that She is gone.   70
But wee may scape that Sinne, yett weepe as much:
   Our Teares are due, because wee are not such.
Some Teares, that knott of frindes, her death must Cost
   Because the Chayne is broke, but no Lincke Lost.

An Elegye on Prince Henry.
....

The Calme.   [31v]

Our storme is past, and that Stormes tyrannous rage
A stupid Calme, but Nothing it, doth swage.
The Fable is inverted, and farr more
A Blocke afflictes now, than a Storke before,   [31v]
Stormes chafe, and soone weare out themselves, or Us;   5
In Calmes, Heaven laughes, to see us languish thus.
As steady,' as I can wish that my thoughts were,
Smooth as thy Mistres Glasse, or what shines there,
The Sea is now; And as these Isles which wee
Seeke, when wee can move, our Ships rooted bee.   10
As Water did in Stormes, now Pitch runns out,
As Lead when a fir'd Church becomes One Spout.
And all our beauty, and our Trimme decayes,
Like Courts removing, or like Ended Playes.
The fighting Place nowe Seamens raggs supplye,   15
And all the Tackling is a Fripperye.
No Use of Lanthornes, and in One Place laye
Feathers, and Dust, to day, and yesterday.
Earths Hollownesses, which the worlds Lungs are,
Have no more Wind than th' Upper Vault of Ayre;   20
Wee can nor left frindes, nor sought foes recover
But Meteorlike, save that wee move not, hover.
Only the Calenture together drawes
Deare frindes, which meete dead in greate fishes jawes.
And on the hatches, as on Altars Lyes   25
Each One, hys owne Priest, and 'hys owne Sacrifice:
Who live, that Miracle to multiplye
When Walkers in hott Ovens, doe not dye.
If in despyte of these, wee Swimme, that hath
No more refreshing than our brimstone Bath,   30
But from the Sea, into the Ship wee turne   [32v]
Like parboyld wretches, on the Coales to burne,
Like Bajazet encag'd, the Shepheards scoffe,
Or like slacke sinewed Samson, hys hayre off,
Languish our Ships. Now, as a Myriade   35
Of Antes, durst the Emperors Loved Snake invade,

The crawlinge Galleyes, Sea Jayles, finny Chips
Might brave our Venices, now bed ridde ships.
Whether a rotten State, and hope of gayne,
Or to disuse mee from the queasye payne   40
Of beeing belov'd, and Loving, or the thirst
Of honor, or fayre death, outpusht mee first,
I lose my End, for here as well as I
A Desperate may Live, 'and a Coward dye.
Stagg, Dogg, and all which from, or towards flyes   45
Is payd with lyfe, or prey, or doing dyes.
Fate grudges us all, and doth subtly lay
A Scourge, 'gainst which wee all forgett to pray.
He that at Sea prayes for more winde, as well
Under the Poles may beg Colde, heate in Hell.   50
What are wee then? how little more, Alas,
Is Man now, than before he was? he was
Nothing; for Us, wee are for Nothing fitt,
Chance, or Ourselves still disproportion itt.
Wee have noe Power, noe Will, noe Sense; I lye,   55
I should not then thus feele thys Miserye.

. . . .

To Sir Henry Goodyere.

Who makes the Past, a Patterne for next yeare,
    Turnes no new leafe, but still the same thinges reads,
Seene thinges he sees agayne, heard thinges doth heare
    And makes hys Life, but like a payre of beades.

A Pallace, when 'tis that, which yt should bee   5
[34v]   Leaves groweing, and stands such, or Else decayes,
But he which dwells there, is not soe; for hee
    Strives to urge upward, and hys fortune rayse.

So had your Body' her morning, hath her Noone,
    And shall not better, her next change is Night.   10
But her fayre Larger Guest, to' whom Sunne and Moone
    Are Sparkes, and short-lived, claymes another right.

The Noble soule by Age growes Lustyer,
    Her appetite, and her digestion mend,
Wee must not starve, nor hope to pamper her   15
    With woemens milke, and papp unto the End.

Provide you Manlyer Dyett, you have seene
  All Libraryes, which are Schooles, Camps, and Courts.
But aske your Garners, if you have not bin
  In harvests, too indulgent to your Sports.   20

Would you redeeme yt? then yourselfe transplant
  Awhyle from hence; perchance outlandish ground
Beares not more witt than Ours, but yett more skant
  Are those Diversions there, which here abound.

To be a Stranger, hath that benifitt,   25
  Wee can beginings, but not habitts choake.
Goe; whither? Hence; You gett, if you forgett.
  New faults, till they prescribe in Us, are Smoake.

Our Soule, whose Country 'is Heav'n, and God her father,
  Into thys world, Corruptions Sincke, is sent;   30 [35r]
Yett so much in her travayle she doth gather,
  That She retornes home wiser than she went.

It payes you all, yf it teach you to spare,
  And make you 'asham'd, to make your hawkes prayse,
    yours.
Which, when herselfe she lessens in the Ayre   35
  You then first say, that high enough she toures.

Howsoe'er keepe the lively tast you hold
  Of God, Love him as now, but feare him more,
And in your Afternoones, thincke what you told
  And promis'd him, at morning Prayer before.   40

Lett Falshood like a Discord anger you,
  Else bee not froward; But why doe I touch
Thinges of which none ys in your Practise newe?
  And Fables, or fruite trenchers teach as much.

But thus I make you keepe your Promise, Sir: 45
  Riding I had you, though you still stayd there,
And in these thoughts, allthough you never stirre,
  You came with mee to Mitcham, and are here.

To Sir Edward Herbert, at Juliers.

Man is a Lumpe, where all Beasts kneaded bee;
Wisedome makes him an Arke, where all agree.
The Foole in whom these Beasts doe live a-jarre;   [35v]

Is Sport to others, and a Theater.
No[r] scapes he soe, but is himselfe theyre Preye;   5
All which was Man in him, ys eate awaye.
And now hys Beasts on One Another feed
Yett couple 'in Anger, and new monsters breed.
How happy 'is hee, which hath due place assignd
To' hys Beasts, and disaforested hys Mind?   10
Empayld himselfe, to keepe them out, not In.
Can sowe, and dares trust Corne, where they have bin;
Can Use hys horse, Goate, Wolfe, and every Beast,
And is not Asse himselfe to all the rest.
Else, Man not only is the Herd of Swine,   15
But he 'ys those Devills too, which did inclyne
Them to a headlong rage, and made them worse.
For Man can adde weight to Heavens heavyest Curse.
As Soules (they say) by our first touch take in
The Poysonous tincture of Originall Sinne   20
So to the Punnishments which God doth flinge,
Our Apprehension contributes the stinge.
To Us, as to hys Chickens, he doth Cast
Hemlocke, and wee, as men, hys Hemlocke tast.
Wee doe infuse, to what he ment for meate,   25
Corrosivenes, or intense Cold, or heate.
For God no such Specifique Poyson hath
As kills, wee know not howe; Hys fiercest wrath
[36r]   Hath no Antipathye; But may be Good,
At least for Physick, if not for food.   30
Thus Man, that might be 'hys Pleasure, is hys Rod;
And is hys Devill, that might be hys God.
Since then our Busines ys to rectifye
Nature, to what She was, wee 'are led awrye
By them, who Man to Us, in litle, showe;   35
Greater than due, no forme wee can bestowe
On him: for Man into himselfe can drawe
All: All hys Faith can swallowe, or Reason chawe.
All that ys fill'd, and all that which doth fill
All the round world, to Man ys but a Pill.   40
In all it workes not, but yt is in All
Poysonous, or Purgative, or Cordyäll.
For knowledge kindles Calentures in some,
And ys to Others Icy Opium.
As brave, as true, ys that Profession then,   45

Which you doe use to make: That you know man.
Thys makes yt Credible; You 'have dwelt upone
All worthy bookes, and now are such a One.
Actions are Authors; And of those in you,
Your frindes find every day a Mart of Newe. 50

To the Countesse of Bedford.

Madame,
Reason ys our Soules left hand, Faythe her right,
By these we reach Divinitye, thats you; [36v]
Theyre Loves, who have the blessings of your Sight,
Grew from theyre reason, Mine from farr fayth grewe.

But as, Although a squint lefthandednes 5
Bee 'Ungratious; Yett wee cannot want that hand:
So would I, not to' increase, but to expresse
My Fayth, as I beleeve, So Understand.

Therfore I study you, first in your Saints,
Those frindes, whom your Election glorifyes, 10
Then in your Deeds, Accesses, and Restraints,
And what you read, and what yourselfe devise.

But soone the Reasons why you' are lov'd by All,
Growe Infinite, and so passe Reasons reach;
Then backe againe to' Implicite fayth I fall, 15
And rest on what the Catholique voice doth teach:

That you are Good; And not One Heretique
Denies ytt: Yf he did, yett you are soe.
For Rocks which high to Some, 'and deepe rooted sticke,
Waves wash, not undermyne, nor overthrowe. 20

In every thinge there naturally growes
A Balsamum to keepe yt fresh, and newe,
If 'twere not injurd by Extrinsique blowes,
Your Birth and Beauty are thys Balme in you.

But You of Learning and Religiöne 25
And Vertue, 'and such Ingredients, have made
A Methridate, whose Operatiöne
Keepes off, or Cures what can be done or sayde. [37r]

Yett thys is not your Physicke, but your foode,
A Dyett fitt for you: For you are here   30
The first good Angell, since the worlds frame stood,
That ever did in womans Shape appeare.

Since you are, then, Gods Master Peece, and so
Hys factor for our loves; Doe as you doe;
Make your retorne home gratious; And bestowe   35
Thys lyfe on that; So make One lyfe of two.
For so God helpe mee, I 'would not misse you there,
For all the Good which you can doe mee here.

To the Countesse of Bedford.

Madame,
You have refind mee; And to worthyest thinges
    Virtue, Art, Beauty, Fortune, now I see
Rarenes, or Use, Not Nature value brings,
    And such as they are circumstanc'd, they bee.
Two ills can ne'er perplexe us, Sinne to' Excuse   5
But of two Good thinges, wee may leave, and chuse.

Therfore at Court, Which ys not Vertues Clyme
    Where a transcendent height, (as Lowenes mee)
Makes her not bee, or not showe; All my Rime,
    Your Vertues challenge, which there rarest bee.   10
[37v] For as darke Texts needes Notes: There some must bee
To Usher Virtue, and say, Thys is Shee.

So in the Country' is Beauty; To thys Place
    You are the Season, Madame, you the Day;
Tis but a Grave of Spices, tyll your Face   15
    Exhale them, and a thicke close bud display.
Widow'd and reclus'd Else, her sweetes She' enshrines,
As China when the Sunne at Brazil dines.

Out from your Charyott, Morning breakes at Night
    And falsifyes both Computations soe,   20
Since a new worlde doth rise here from your Sight
    Wee your new Creatures, by new reckninges goe,
Thys showes that you from Nature lothly stray
That suffer not an Artificiall day.

In thys you 'have made the Court, the Antipodes,   25
   And will'd your Delegate, the Vulgar Sunne,
To doe profane Autumnall Offices,
   Whylst here to you, wee Sacrificers runne,
And whether Priestes, or Organes, you wee' obay,
Wee sound your Influence, and your Dictates say.   30

Yet to that Deitye which dwells in you,
   Your Virtuous Soule, I now not sacrifise,
These are Petitions, and not Hymns; They sue
   But that I may survay the Edifice.
In all Religions as much Care hath bin   35
Of Temples frames, and Beauty, as Rytes within.

As all which goe to Rome, doe not thereby   [38r]
   Esteeme Religions, and hold fast the best,
But serve Discourse, and Curiositye
   With that which doth religion but invest,   40
And shunne th' entanglinge Laborinths of Schooles,
And make yt witt, to thincke the wiser fooles.

So in thys Pilgrimage I would beholde
   You, as you 'are Vertues Temple, not as Shee:
What walls of tender Christall her Enfolde,   45
   What Eyes, Hands, Bosome, her pure Altars bee,
And after thys Survay, oppose to all
Bablers of Chappels, you th' Escorial.

Yett not as Consecrate, but meerely' as fayre
   On these I cast a lay, and country Eye.   50
Of past, and future storyes, which are rare,
   I find you all Record, all Prophecye;
Purge but the Booke of Fate, that yt admitte
No sad, nor guiltye Legends, you are ytt.

If Good, and Lovely were not One, of both   55
   You were the Transcript, and Originall.
The Elements, the Parent, and the Growth
   And every Peece of you, is both theyre All.
So' intyre are all your Deedes, and You, that You
Must doe the same thinge still; You cannot two.   60

But these (as nice thinne Schoole Devinitye
   Serves Heresye to further, or represse)
Tast of Poetique rage, or flatterye,   [38v]
   And need not, where all harts one truth profes.

7. Recto of the single sheet of the verse letter, 'To the Honorable Lady, the Lady Carey, and Mistress Riche from Amiens,' the only known poem of Donne's to survive in the presentation copy written entirely in his hand. His diagonal slash lines separate stanzas of the poem. Bodleian Library, MS Eng. poet. d.197.

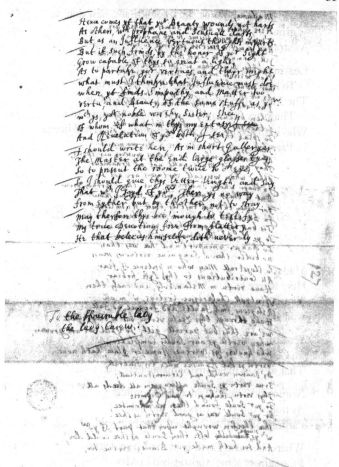

8. Verso of the single sheet of the verse letter, 'To the Honorable Lady, the Lady Carey, and Mistress Riche from Amiens.' His diagonal slash lines separate stanzas of the poem. Bodleian Library, MS Eng. poet. d.197.

Oft from new Proofes, and new Phrase, new doubts
   growe   65
As strange Attyre aliens the men wee knowe.

Leaving then busy Prayse, and All appeale
   To higher Courts, Senses Decree ys true;
The Myne, the Magazin, the Commonweale,
   The story of Beauty' in Twicknam ys, and You.   70
Who hath seene One, would both; As, who had beene
In Paradise, would seeke the Cherubine.

A Letter to the Lady Carey, and Mrs Essex Riche, from Amiens.

Madame,
Here where by All, All Saintes invokëd are,
'T were too much Schisme to bee Singulare,
And gainst a Practize generall to warr.

Yett, turning to' Saints, should my Humilitye
To Other Saint than you, directed bee,   5
That were to make my Schisme heresye.

Nor would I bee a Convertite so colde
As not to tell yt; If thys bee too bolde,
Pardons are in thys Markett cheapely sold.

Where, because Fayth is in too Lowe degree,   10
[39r]   I thought yt some Apostleship in Mee
To speake thinges, which by fayth alone I see:

That is of you, who are a firmament
Of Virtues, where no One ys growen, or spent,
They 'are your Materialls, not your Ornament.   15

Others, whom wee call Vertuous, are not soe
In theyre whole substance, but theyre Virtues growe
But in theyre humors, and at Seasons showe.

For when through tastlesse flatt humilitye
In dough-baked men, some harmlessnes wee see   20
Tis but hys flegme that's Vertuous, and not Hee.

So ys the blood sometimes: who ever ran
To danger unimportun'd, he was then
No better than a Sanguine Vertuous man.

So Cloysterall men who, in Pretence of feare,   25
All Contribution to thys lyfe forbeare,
Have Vertue' in Melancholye,' and only there.

Spirituall Cholerique Critiques, which in All
Religions find faults, and forgive no fall,
Have, through thys zeale, Virtue but in theyre Gall.   30

We 'are thus but Parcell-gilt, to Gold we 'are growne
When Vertue is our Soules Complexiön:
Who knowes hys Vertues Name, or Place, hath None.

Virtue 'is but Aguish, when tis severall,
By Occasion waked, and Circumstantiall,   35 [39v]
True Vertue 'ys Soule, alwayes in all deedes all.

Thys Vertue, thincking to give dignitye
To your Soule, found there no infirmitye,
For your Soule was as Good Vertue as Shee.

She therfore wrought upon that Part of you   40
Which is scarce lesse than Soule, as She could doe,
And so hath made your beautye vertue too.

Hence comes yt, that your beautye wounds not hartes,
As Others, with Prophane, and sensuall dartes,
But as an Influence, Virtuous thoughts imparts.   45

But yf such frindes by the' honor of your Sight
Grow Capable of thys so greate a Light
As to partake your Vertues, and theyre might,

What must I thincke that Influence must doe,
Where yt findes sympathy, and matter too,   50
Vertue; and Beauty' of the same stuffe, as you?

Which ys your Noble worthy Sister, Shee
Of whom, if what in thys my Extasye,
And revelation of you both, I see,

I should write here, as in short Galleryes,   55
The Master at the End Large Glasses tyes
So to present the roome twise to your Eyes:

So I should give thys Letter Length, and say
That which I sayd of you: There is no way
From Eyther, but by the' other not to stray.   60

[40r]   May therfore thys be' Enough to testifye
My true devotion, free from Flatterye;
Hee that beleaves himselfe, doth never lye.

To the Countesse of Salisbury. August 1614.

Fayre, Greate, and Good, since seeing You, wee see
What Heavn can doe, and what any' Earth can bee,
Since now your beauty shines, now when the Sunne
Growne stale, is to soe lowe a Value runne
That his dischevel'd beames, and scattred fyres   5
Serve but for Ladyes Periwiggs, and Tyres
In Lovers Sonnetts, you come to repayre
Gods booke of Creatures, teaching what is fayre.
Since now, when all is wither'd, shroncke, and dryde,
All Vertue ebbd out, to a dead lowe tyde,   10
All the worlds frame beeing crumbled into sand
Where ev'ry Man thincks by Himselfe to stand,
Integritye, frendship, and Confidence,
Cements of Greatenes, beeing vapor'd hence,
And narrowe Man, beeing fill'd with litle shares,   15
Court, City, Church, are all shops of small wares,
All having blowne to Sparks, theyre Noble fyre
And drawne theyre sound gold-Ingott into wyre,
All trying by a Love of Litleness
To make Abridgments, and to drawe to lesse   20
Even that Nothing, which at first wee were;
Since in these Times your Greatenes doth appeare
And that wee Learne by ytt, that Man to gett
Towards him that's infinite, must first be greate;
Since in an Age so ill, as none ys fitt   25
[40v]   So much as to accuse, much lesse mend yt;
(For who can judge, or wittnes of those Times
Where all alike are guiltye of the Crimes?)
Where he that would be Good, is thought by All
A Monster, or at best, fantasticall,   30

Since nowe you durst bee Good, and that I doe
Discerne, by daring to Contemplate you,
That there may be Degrees of Fayre, Greate, Good,
Through your Light, Largenes, Vertue, understood;
Yf in thys Sacrifice of myne, be shown   35
Any small sparcke of these, call yt your owne.
And if thinges like these, have bin sayd by mee
Of Others, Call nott that Idolatree.
For had God made man first, and Man had seene
The third dayes fruites, and flowers, and various
    Greene,   40
He might have sayd the best that he could say
Of those fayre Creatures, which were made that day;
And when next Day, he had admir'd the birth
Of Sunne, Moone, Starrs, fayrer than Late prays'd
    Earth,
Hee might have sayd the best that he could say,   45
And not be chidde for praysing yesterday.
So though some thinges are not together true
(As that Another' is worthyest, and that you)
Yett to say soe, doth nott Condemne a Man,
Yf when he spoke them, they were both true then.   50
How fayre a Proofe of thys, in our Soule growes!
Wee first have Soules of Growth, and Sence, and those
When our last Soule, our Soule Immortall came,
Were swallowd into yt, and have no Name.
Nor doth he injure those Soules, which doth Cast   55
The Power and Prayse of both them, on the Last.
No more doe I wrong Any; I adore   [41r]
The same thinges now, which I ador'd before,
The Subject chang'd, and Measure; The same thinge
In a lowe Constable, and in the King   60
I reverence, Hys Power to worke on Mee.
So did I humbly reverence each Degree
Of Fayre, Greate, Good, but more, now I am come
From having found theyre walkes, to find theyre home.
And as I owe my first Soules thanckes, that they   65
For my Last Soule did fitt and mould my Clay,
So am I Debtor unto them, whose worthe
Enabled mee to profitt, and take forthe
Thys new greate lesson, thus to study you,
Which none, not reading others first, could doe.   70

Nor Lacke I Light to read thys Booke, though I
In a darke Cave, yea in a Grave doe lye,
For as your fellow-Angells, soe you doe
Illustrate them who come to study you.
The first whom wee in Historyes doe find   75
To have profest all Artes, was One borne blind;
So though I 'am borne, without those Eyes to live
Which fortune, who hath none herselfe, doth give,
Which are fitt meanes to see bright Courts, and you,
Yett may I see you thus, as now I doe;   80
I shall by that All Goodnes have discern'd,
And though I burne my Librarye, be learnd.

Holy Sonnetts.
La Corona.

I.

Deigne at my handes thys Crowne of Prayer and Prayse,
Weav'd in my lowe devoute Melancholye,
Thou which of Good, hast, yea, art Treasurye,
All-changing unchang'd Antiënt of Dayes,
But doe not with a Vile Crowne of frayle Bayes   5
Reward my Muses whighte Sinceritye.
But what thy thorny Crowne gayn'd, that give mee,
A Crowne of Glorye which doth flowre alwayes,
The Ends crowne our workes, but thou crownst our Ends,
For att our End, beginns our Endles rest.   10
The first last End, now zealously possest,
With a stronge sober thirst my soule attends;
'Tis time that hart and voyce be lifted high,
Salvatiön to all that will is nighe.

2.

Salvatiön to all that will is nighe,
That all, which allwayes is all everywhere,
Which cannot Sin, and yett all Sinns must beare,
Which cannot Dye, yett cannot chuse but Dye;
Loe, faythfull virgin, yeildes himselfe to lye   5
In Prison, in thy [W]ombe; and though he there
Can take noe sinne, nor thou give, yett he 'will weare,

Taken from thence, flesh which Deaths force may trye.
Ere by the Spheares time was Created, thou
Wast in hys Mind, who ys thy Sonne, and brother.   10
Whom thou conceivst, Conceivd, yea thou art now   [42r]
Thy Makers Maker, and thy fathers Mother,
Thou 'hast Light in darke, and shuttst in litle roome,
Immensitye cloystred in thy deare wombe.

3.

Immensitye cloystred in thy deare wombe
Now leaves hys welbeloved Imprisonment,
Therfore he 'hath made himselfe to hys Intent
Weake enough now into' our world to come.
But oh, for Thee, for Him, hath the' Inn no roome?   5
Yett lay him in thys stall, and from the' Orient
Starrs, and wise men will travel to prevent
The' Effects of Herods jealous generall doome.
Seest thou, my Soule, with thy fayths Eyes, how Hee,
Which fills all Place, yett none holds him, doth lye?   10
Was not hys Pitty towards Thee, wondrous high,
That would have neede to bee Pityed by Thee?
Kisse him, and with him into Egypt goe
With hys kind mother, who partakes thy woe.

4.

With hys kind mother who partakes thy woe,
Joseph, turne backe: See where your child doth sitt,
Blowing, yea blowing out those sparkes of witt
Which himselfe on those Doctors did bestowe.
The word but latelye could not speake, and loe   5
It suddenly speakes wonders: whence comes ytt,
That all which was, and all which should bee writt
A shallowe seeming Childe should deeplye knowe?
Hys Godhead was not Soule to hys Manhood,
Nor hath Time mellowed him to thys ripenes   10 [42v]
But as, for One which hath 'a long taske, 'tis good
With the Sun to begin his busïnes,
Hee, in hys Ages Morning thus begann
By Miracles exceeding Power of Man.

5.

By Miracles exceeding Power of Man,
  He fayth in some; Envy in some begatt.
  For what weake Spirittes admire, ambitious hate;

In both Affections many to him ran.
But oh the worst are most; they will and can   5
   Alas, and doe, unto the' Immaculate,
   Whose Creature Fate ys, now prescribe a Fate,
Measuring selfe-lifes Infinitye to' [a] span,
Nay to an Inch. Loe, where condemnëd Hee
   Beares hys owne Crosse with Payne; yett by and by,   10
   When itt beares him, he must beare more and Dye.
Now Thou art lifted up, draw mee to Thee;
   And at thy Death giving such Liberall dole,
   Moyst with one drop of thy blood, my dry Soule.

6.

Moyst with one drop of thy blood, my dry Soule
   Shall, (though Shee now bee in Extreame degree
   Too stonye hard, and yett too fleshly) bee
Freed, by that drop, from beeing starv'd, hard, or foule,
And life by thys Death abled, shall controule   5
   Death, whom thy Death slew. Nor shall to Mee
   Feare of first, or last Death, bring Miserye
[43r]   If in thy litle Booke, my name thou' inroule;
Flesh in that [long] Sleepe is not putrifyed,
   But made that there, of which, and for which t' was;   10
   Nor Can by other meanes bee glorifyed.
May then Sinns sleepe, and Death soone from mee passe,
   That wakt from both, I agayne risen maye
   Salute the Last, and Everlasting Day.

7.

Salute the Last, and everlasting Day,
   Joye at th' uprising of thys Sunne, and S[o]nne
   Yea, whose just teares, or tribulatiöne
Have purelye washt, or burnt your drossy Claye.
Behold the Highest, parting hence away,   5
   Lightens the darke Clouds which he treds upon,
   Nor doth hee by Ascending, showe alone,
But first hee, and hee first enters the way.
Oh strong Ramm which hast battred heavn for Mee,
   Mild Lambe which with thy Blood, hast mark'd the Path,   10
   Bright Torche, which shinst, that I the way may see;
Oh with thy owne blood quenche thy owne just wrath,
    And if thy holy Spirritt my Muse did rayse,
    Deigne at my handes thys Crowne of Prayer and Prayse.

Sonnett.

1.

As due by many Titles, I resigne
  Myselfe to Thee, O God, first I was made
  By thee, and for Thee, 'and when I was decayd,   [43v]
Thy blood bought that, the which before was thyne,
I am thy Sonne, made with Thyselfe to shyne;   5
  Thy Servant, whose paynes thou hast still repayde,
  Thy Sheepe, thyne Image; and till I betrayde
Myselfe, A Temple of thy Spiritt devine.
Why doth the Devill then usurpe on mee?
  Why doth he steale, nay ravish that's thy right?   10
  Except thou rise, and for thyne owne workes fight,
Oh I shall soone despayre, when I doe see
  That thou lovst Mankind well, yett wilt not chuse mee,
  And Satan hates mee, yett is Loth to Lose mee.

2.

Oh my blacke Soule, now thou art summonëd,
  By Sicknes, Deaths Herald, and Champion,
  Thou 'art like a Pilgrim, which abroad hath donne
Treason, and durst not turne to whence he's fled,
Or like a Theefe, which till Deaths doome be read   5
  Wisheth himselfe delivered from Prison;
  But damnd, and haled to Executiön,
Wisheth that still he might be' emprisond;
Yett Grace, yf thou repent, thou canst not Lacke,
  But who shall give Thee that grace to beginne?   10
  Oh make thyselfe with holy Mourning blacke,
And red with blushing, as thou art with Sinne;
  Or wash Thee in Christs blood, which hath thys might
  That beeing redd, it dyes red Soules to whyght.

3.   [44r]

Thys is my Playes Last Sceane, here heavens appoynte
  My Pilgrimage' Last mile; and my race
  Idly, yett quickly runn, hath thys Last pace,
My Spanns Last Inch, my minutes Last pointe,
And glottonous death will instantly unjoynte   5
  My Body, 'and Soule, and I shall sleepe a space,
  Or presently, I knowe not, see that face,
Whose feare already shakes my every Jointe.

Then as my Soule, to' heaven her first seate, takes flight
  And Earth borne Body, in the Earth shall dwell,   10
So falls my Sinns, that All may have theyre right,
   To where they 'are bred, and would presse mee, to hell;
Impute Mee righteous, thus purged of Evill,
For thus I Leave the World, the flesh, and Devill.

4.

At the round Earths Imagind Corners, blowe
  Your Trumpetts, Angells, and Arise, arise
  From Death, you numberlesse Infynityes
Of Soules, and to your scattred Bodyes goe:
All whom the flood did, and Fyre shall o'erthrowe,   5
  All whom Warr, Dea[r]th, Age, Agues, Tirannies
  Despayre, Law, Chance, hath slayne, and you
      whose Eyes
Shall beholde God, and never taste Deaths woe.
But lett them sleepe Lord, and mee mourne a pace;
  For if above all these my Sinns abound,   10
Tis Late to aske abundance of thy Grace,
  When wee are there; Here, on thys lowly Ground

[44v] Teach mee how to repent; for that's as good
  As if thou 'hadst seald my Pardon, with thy Blood.

5.

If Poysonous Mineralls, and if that Tree
  Whose fruite threw death, On else immortall Us,
  Yf Lecherous Goates, yf serpents envious
Cannot be damn'd; Alas why shoulde I bee?
Why shoulde Intent, or reason, borne in Mee   5
  Make Sins, else equall, in mee more heynous?
  And Mercye beeing easye, 'and glorious
To God in hys sterne wrath, why threatens hee?
But who am I, that dare dispute with Thee?
  Oh God; Oh of thyne only worthy blood   10
  And my Teares make a heavenlye Lethean flood,
And drowne in it, my Sinnes blacke Memorie;
  That thou remember them, Some clayme as Debt,
  I thincke yt Mercy, if thou wilt forgett.

6.

Death bee not Proude, though some have called Thee
  Mightye, and dreadfull, for thou art not soe,
  For those whom thou thinckst thou dost o'erthrowe

Dye not, Poore Death, nor yett canst Thou kill mee.
From Rest, and Sleepe, which but thy Pictures bee 5
   Much Pleasure, then from Thee much more must flowe,
   And soonest our best men with Thee doe goe,
Rest of theyre bones, and Soules deliverye.
Thou 'art slave to Fate, Chance, Kings, and desperate
    Men,
   And dost with Poyson, Warr, and Sicknes dwell, 10
   And Poppy,' or Charmes can make us sleepe as well
    And better than thy Stroake; why swellst thou then?   [45r]
   One short Sleepe past, wee wake eternally,
   And Death shalbe no more, Death thou shalt Dye.

7.

Spitt in my face you Jewes, and pierce my Side,
   Buffett, and Scoffe, scourge, and crucifye mee,
   For I have sinn'd, and sinn'd, and only hee
Who could do none Iniquitye, hath Dyed;
Butt by my death cannot be satisfyed 5
   My Sinns, which passe the Jewes Iniquitye.
   They kill'd once an Inglorious Man, but I
Cruci'fye him daily, bee'ing now gloryfyed.
Oh lett mee then hys strange Love still admire;
   Kings Pardon, but he bore our Punnishment. 10
And Jacob came cloth'd in vile harsh attyre,
   But to supplant, and with gainfull intent;
God cloth'd himselfe in Vile Mans flesh, that so
Hee might bee weake enough to suffer woe.

8.

Why are wee by all Creatures wayted on?
   Why doe the Prodi'gall Elements supplye
   Lyfe, and Food to mee, Bee'ing more pure than I,
Simple, and farther from Corruptiön?
Why brookst thou, Ignorant Horse, Subjectiön? 5
   Why dost thou, Bull, and Boar, so seelily
   Dissemble weakenes, 'and by One Mans Stroake Dye,
Whose whole kind you might swallowe,' and feed upon?
Weaker I am, woe 'ys me, and worse than you.   [45v]
   You have not sinn'd, nor neede be timorous; 10
   But wonder' at a greater wonder, for to' us
Created Nature doth these thinges subdue,
   But theyre Creator, whom Sinne nor Nature tyed,
   For us, his Creatures, and hys Foes hath Dyed.

9.

What if thys Present were the worlds Last Night?
    Marke in my hart, O Soule, where thou dost dwell,
    The Picture of Christ crucifyed, and tell
Whether hys Countenance can Thee affright:
Teares in hys Eyes quenche the Amasing Light,   5
    Blood fills hys frownes, which from hys Pierced head fell,
    And can that Tongue adjudge Thee [un]to Hell,
Which Prayed forgivenes for hys foes fierce Spight?
No, no; But as in my Idolatrye,
    I sayd to all my Prophane Mistrisses,   10
    Beautye, of Pitty, foulenes only is
A signe of Rigor: So I say to Thee,
    To wicked Spiritts are horrid shapes assign'd,
    Thys beauteous forme assures a Piteous mind.

10.

Batter my hart, three Person'd God, for you
    As yett, but knocke, breathe, shine, and seeke to mend;
    That I may rise, and stand, o'erthrowe mee, 'and bend
Your force to breake, blowe, burne, and make mee newe.
[46r]   I, like an Usurpt towne, to' Another due,   5
    Labor to' admitt you, but oh to no End.
    Reason your Viceroy 'in Mee, mee should defend,
But is captiv'd and proves weake, or untrue.
Yett dearely' I Love you, and would be Loved fayne,
    But am betroth'd unto your Enemye;   10
Divorce mee,' Untye, or breake that knott agayne;
    Take Mee to you, Imprison mee, for I
Except you' inthrall mee, never shall be free,
Nor ever chast, except you ravish mee.

11.

Wilt thou Love God, as Hee Thee; then digest
    My Soule, thys wholesome Meditatiöne,
    How God the Spiritt, by Angells wayted on
In Heaven, doth make hys Temple in thy brest;
The Father' having begott a Sonne most blest,   5
    And still begetting (for he ne'er begonne)
    Hath deign'd to chuse Thee by Adoptiöne,
Co-heyre to' hys Glory,' and Sabbaths endles rest.
And as a robbd man, which by search doth find
    Hys stolne stuffe sold, must Lose, or buy' it agayne: 10
    The S[o]nne of Glory came downe, and was slayne,

Us, whom he' had made, and Satan stolne, to' unbinde.
   'T was much that Man was made like God before,
   But that God should be made like Man, much more.

12.

Father, Part of his doble Interest
   Unto thy kingdome, thy Sonne gives to Mee,
   Hys Jointure in the knottye Trinitye
He keepes, and gives me his Deaths Conquest.
Thys Lambe, whose Death, with lyfe the world hath blest,   5
   Was from the worlds beginning slayne; and hee   [46v]
   Hath made two wills, which with the Legacee
Of hys, 'and thy kingdome, doth thy Sonne invest,
Yett such are those Lawes, that men argue yett
   Whether a Man those Statutes can fulfill.   10
None doth; But all-healing grace, and Spiritt
   Revive agayne what Lawe and letter kill.
Thy Lawes abridgment, and thy Last Command
Is all but Love; Oh lett that Last Will stand.

The Crosse.

Since Christ embrac'd the Crosse itselfe, dare I
Hys Image, th' Image of the Crosse deny?
Would I have Proffitt by the Sacrifice,
And dare the chosen Altar to despise?
It bore all other Sinns; but is it fitt   5
That it should beare the Sin of scorning ytt?
Who from the Picture woulde averte hys Eye?
How woulde he fly hys Paines, who there did dye?
From Mee, no Pulpitt, nor misgrounded Lawe,
Nor Scandall taken shall thys Crosse withdrawe.   10
It shall not, for it cannot, For the Losse
Of thys Crosse were to mee Another Crosse;
Better were worse, for no Afflictiön,
No Crosse is soe extreame, as to have none.
Who can blott out that Crosse, which th' Instrument   15
Of God, dew'd on mee in the Sacrament?
Who can denye mee Power and Libertye   [47r]
To stretch myne Armes, and myne owne Crosse to bee?
Swimme, and at everye stroake, thou art thy Crosse.

The Mast, and Yard makes One, where Seas doe tosse.   20
Looke downe, thou spyest ou[t] Crosses in small thinges.
Looke up, thou seest Birdes rays'd on Crossèd winges.
All the Globes frame, and Spheares, is Nothing Else,
But the Meridians crossinge Parallells;
Materiall Crosses, then, Good Physicke bee,   25
And yett Spirituall have chiefe dignitye.
These for extracted Chimique medicine serve,
And Cure much better, and as well preserve;
Then are you your owne Phisicke, or need none,
When stilld, or purg'd by Tribulatiön.   30
For when that Crosse, ungrudg'd, unto you sticks,
Then are you to yourselfe, a Crucifixe.
As perchance, Carvers doe not faces make,
But that away, which hid them there, doe take.
Let Crosses soe, take what hid Christ in Thee,   35
And be hys Image, or not his, but Hee.
But as oft, Alchimists doe Coyners prove,
Soe may a Selfe-despising gett Selfe Love.
And then, as worst Surfetts, of best meates bee,
So ys Pride yssued from Humilitye,   40
For 'tis no Childe, but Monster. Therfore Crosse
Your Joy in Crosses, else, 'tis doble Losse;
And Crosse thy Senses; else both they and thou
Must perish soone, and to destruction bowe.
For yf th' Eye seeke good Objects, and will take   45
No Crosse from Bad, wee cannot scape a Snake.
[47v]   So with harsh, hard, soure, stinking, Crosse the Rest.
Make them Indifferent. Call Nothing best.
But most the Eye needes crossing; that can rome,
And move; To th' others th' Objects must come home.   50
And crosse thy Hart: for that in Man alone,
Pants downewards, and hath Palpitatiön;
Crosse those dejections, when it downeward tends,
And when it to forbidden heights pretends.
And as thy brayne, through bony walls doth vent   55
By Sutures, which a Crosses forme present:
So when thy brayne workes, ere thou utter yt,
Crosse, and Correct Concupiscence of Witt.
Be Covetous of Crosses, Lett none fall,
Crosse no Man else, but crosse thyselfe in all.   60
Then doth the Crosse of Christ worke fruitfully
Within our hartes, when wee love harmelessly

That Cross's Pictures much, and with more Care
That Cross's Children, which our Crosses are.

The Annuntiation.

Tamely' frayle Body, abstayne to day; to day
My soule eates twice, Christ hither, and away.
Shee sees him Man, so like God made in thys,
That of them both, a Circle, Embleame ys,
Whose first and Last Concurre; Thys doubtfull day   5
Of feast, or Fast, Christ came, and went away.
She sees him Nothing twice at Once, who 'ys all;
She sees a Cedar plant itselfe, and fall;
Her Maker put to making; And the head
Of lyfe, at Once not yett alive, and dead.   10 [48r]
Shee sees at once the Virgin Mother stay
Reclusd at home, Publique at Golgotha.
Sad and rejoyc'd Shee's seene at once, and seene
At almost fiftye, and at scarce fifteene.
At Once a Sonne is promisd her, and gone,   15
Gabriel gives Christ to her; Hee her to John.
Not fully' a Mother, Shees in Orbitye;
At once receaver; and the Legacye.
All thys, and all betweene, thys Day hath showne:
Th' Abridgment of Christs story, which makes One,   20
(As in playne Mapps, the farthest West is East)
Of th' Angells Ave,' and Consummatum est.
How well the Church, Gods Court of Facultyes,
Deales, in sometimes, and seldome joyning these!
As by the Selfe fixd Pole wee never doe   25
Direct our Course, but the next starr thereto,
Which showes where th' other is, and which wee say
(Because it strayes not farr) doth never stray:
So God, by 'hys Church, neerest to him, wee knowe,
And stand firme, if wee by her Motion goe;   30
His Spiritt, as hys fierye Pillar, doth
Lead, And 'hys Church as Cloude, to One Ende both.
This Churche, by letting these dayes joyne, hath showne
Death and Conception in Mankind ys One.
Or 'twas in him, the same Humilitye,   35

That he would be a Man, and leave to bee;
Or as Creation he hath made, as God
With the last Judgment, but one Periöd,
Hys imitating Spouse woulde joyne in One

[48v]   Manhoods Extreames: Hee shall come, Hee ys gone.   40
Or as, though One blood drop, which thence did fall,
Accepted woulde have servd, he yett shed All:
So though the Least of hys Paines, deedes, or wordes,
Would busy a lyfe, Shee All, this day affordes.
Thys Treasure then, in Grosse, my Soule uplay,   45
And in my lyfe retayle yt every Day. /

The Litanye.

The Father.

1. Father of Heavn, and Him, by whom
   Itt, and Us for ytt, and all else, for us,
      Thou madest, and Govern'st ever, Come
   And Re-create mee, now growen ruinous.
         My Hart ys by Dejection, Clay,   5
            And by Self-Murder, redd;
   From thys redd Earth, O Father, purge away
   All Vicious tinctures, that new fashionëd
   I may rise up from Death, before I 'am dead.

The Sonne.

2. O Sonne of God, who seeing two thinges,   10
   Sinne and Death, crept in, which were never made,
      By bearing One, tryedst with what stings
   [49r]   The other could thyne Heritage invade;
         O bee thou nayld unto my hart
            And crucifyed agayne,   15
   Part not from yt, though it from Thee would part,
   But lett yt bee, by 'applying so thy Payne,
   Drownd in thy blood, and in thy Passion slayne.

The Holy Ghost.

3. O holy Ghost, whose Temple I
Ame, But of mudd walls, and condensëd Dust,　　20
　　And beeing Sacrilegiously
Halfe wasted with youths fires, Of Pride, and Lust,
　　　　Must with new stormes bee weather-beate;
　　　　Double in my hart thy flame,
Which Lett devout sad teares intend, And lett　　25
(Though thys glasse Lanterrne, Flesh, do suffer Mayme)
Fyre, Sacrifice, Priest, Altar, bee the same.

The Trinitye.

4. O Blessed glorious Trinitye
Bones to Philosophye, but milke to Fayth,
　　Which, as wise Serpents, diversly　　30
Most Slipperines, yett most entanglings hath,
　　　　As you Distinguish'd undistinct
　　　　By Power, Love, Knowledge bee,
Give mee such a Selfe-different Instinct;
Of these, lett all mee elemented bee,　　35　[49v]
Of Power, to Love, to knowe, you' unnumbred Three.

The virgin Mary.

5. For that fayre blessed Mother mayd
Whose flesh redeem'd us, That shee-Cherubin
　　Which unlock'd Paradice, and made
One Clayme for Innocence, and disseis'd Sin;　　40
　　　　Whose wombe was a strange Heav'n, for there
　　　　God clothd himselfe, and grewe,
Our zealous thancks wee poure; As her Deeds were
Our helpes, so are her Prayers; Nor can Shee sue
In vayne, who hath such Titles unto you.　　45

The Angells.

6. And since thys life our Nonage ys,
And wee in Wardship to thyne Angells bee,
    Native in Heavns fayre Pallacys,
Where wee shall bee but Denizend by Thee;
        As the' Earth conceiving by the Sunne   50
        Yields fayre Diversitee,
Yett never knowes which Course that light doth runne,
Soe lett me study, that myne Actions bee
Worthy theyre Sight, though blind in how they see.

The Patriarchs.

7. And lett thy Patriarchs desire   55
(Those greate Grandfathers of thy Church, which sawe
[50r]   More in the Cloude, than wee in Fyre;
Whom Nature clear'd more, than Us Grace, and Lawe,
        And now in Heav'n still pray, that wee
        May use our newe helpes right)   60
Be satisfyed, and fructifye in mee,
Lett not my Minde be blinder by more light,
Nor Fayth, by reason added, Lose her Sight.

The Prophetts.

8. Thy Eagle-sighted Prophetts too,
Which were thy Churches Organs, and did sound   65
    That harmonye, which made of two
One Lawe, And did Unite, but not confound;
        Those heavenly Poets, which did see
        Thy will, and yt expresse
In Rithmique feete: In Common pray for mee,   70
That I by them excuse not my Excesse
In seeking Secretts or Poetiquenes.

The Apostles.

9. And thy Illustrious Zodiacke
Of twelve Apostles, which ingirt thys All,
   From whom, who ever doe not take   75
Theyre light, to darke deepe pitts, throw downe, and fall,
     As through theyre Prayers, thou 'hast lett me knowe
     That theyre bookes are Divine;
May they pray still, and bee heard: That I goe   [50v]
Th' old broade way in Applyinge; Oh decline   80
Mee, when my Comment would make thy word, myne.

The Martyres.

10. And since Thou soe Desirouslye
Did'st Long to Die, that Long before thou couldst,
   And Long since, thou no more couldst Die,
That in thy scattered Mistique Body, wouldst   85
     In Abel Die, and ever since
     In thyne, Lett theyre blood come
To begg for Us, a Discreete Patiënce
Of death, or [of] worse Lyfe; for, oh, to some,
Not to bee Martyres ys a Martyrdome.   90

The Confessors.

11. Therefore with Thee triumpheth there
A Virgin squadron of whyte Confessors
   Whose bloods Betroth'd, not marryed were,
Tendred, not taken by those Ravishers,
     They know, and pray that wee may knowe   95
     In every Christiän
Hourly tempestuous Persecutions growe.
Tentations Martyre us Alive; A man
Is to himselfe a Diocletiän.

The Virgines.

12. Thy Cold whyte Snowy Nunnerye   100

[51r]   Which, as thy mother, theyre high Abbesse, sent
        Theyre Bodyes backe agayne to Thee,
    As thou hadst lent them, cleane, and Innocent,
            Though they have not obtaind of Thee
                That, or thy Church, or I   105
    Should keepe, as they, our first Integritye;
    Divorce thou Sinne in Us, Or bid it Die,
    And call chast widowhead Virginitye.

The Doctors.

13. Thy Sacred Academy above,

    Of Doctors whose paines have unclasp'd, and taught   110
        Both Bookes of lyfe to Us (for Love
    To know Thy Scriptures, tells us wee are wrought
            In thy' other Booke) pray for us there
                That what they have mis-done
    Or mis-sayd, wee to that may not adhere.   115
    Theyre zeale may be our Sinne; Lord, Lett us runne
    Meane wayes, and call them Starrs, but not the Sunne.

14. And whylst this Universall Quire,

    That Church in Tryumph, thys in warrfare here,
        Warm'd with one all-partaking fyre   120
    Of Love, that none bee Lost, which cost Thee Deare,
            Pray ceaslesly; 'and thou Hearken too,
                (Since to be Gratiöus
    Our taske ys treble, To Praye, Beare, and Doe)
    Heare thys Prayer Lord, O Lord, deliver us,   125

[51v]   From trusting in those Prayers, though pour'd
        out thus.

    15. From beeing Anxious, or Secure;
    Dead clodds of Sadnes, or Light Squibbs of Mirth,
        From thincking that greate Courts immure
    All, or noe happines, or that thys Earth   130
            Is only for our Prison fram'd;
                Or that thou 'art Covetous
    To them thou Lov'st, Or that they are maimd

From reaching thys worlds sweete, who seeke Thee thus
With all theyre might, Good Lord, deliver us. 135

16. From needing danger to bee Good,
From oweing thee yesterdayes Tears to day,
     From trusting so much to thy blood
That, in that hope, wee wound our Soule away,
          From Bribing Thee with Almes, to' excuse 140
          Some Sinne more burdenous,
From light affecting in Religion newes,
From thinking us all Soule, neglecting thus
Our mutuall Dutyes, Lord, deliver Us.

17. From tempting Satan to tempt Us, 145
By our Connivence, or slacke Companie,
     From measuring Ill, by Vitiöus,
Neglectinge to choake Sinnes spawne, Vanitye,
          From Indiscreete Humilitye
          Which might be scandalous 150 [52r]
And cast reproach on Christianitye,
From beeing Spyes, or to Spyes pervious,
From Thirst, or Scorne of Fame, Deliver Us.

18. Deliver us for thy Descent
Into the Virgin; whose wombe was a Place 155
     Of midle kinde; And thou, beeing sent
To' ungratious Us, stayedst at her, full of Grace;
          And through thy poor Birth, where first Thou
          Glorifyest Povertie,
And yett soone after, Riches didst allowe, 160
By' accepting Kings gifts in the' Epiphanie,
Deliver, and make Us, to both wayes, free.

19. And through that bitter Agonie
Which is still th' Agonie of pious witts
     Disputing what distorted thee 165
And interrupted Evenness, with fitts;
          And through thy free Confessiöne,
          Though thereby they were then
Made blind, so that thou mightst from them have gone,
Good Lord, deliver Us: And teach us when 170
Wee may not, and wee may blinde unjust Men.

20. Through thy submitting All, To Blowes
Thy face, thy clothes to spoyle, Thy fame to Scorne;

All wayes, which Rage, or Justice knowes
         And by which thou couldst showe that thou wast borne;   175
            And through thy Gallant Humblenes
            Which thou in Death didst showe,
         Dying before thy Soule they could expresse:
         Deliver us from Death, by Dying soe
         To thys world, ere thys worlde doe bid us goe.   180

         21. When Senses, which thy Soldiors are,
         Wee arme against Thee, and they fight for Sin;
            When want, sent but to tame, doth warr,
         And worke Despayre a Breach to enter in;
               When Plenty, Gods Image, and Seale   185
               Makes us Idolatrous,
         And Love yt, not him whom yt should reveale;
         When wee are mov'd to seeme Religiöus
         Only to vent witt, Lord, deliver Us.

         22. In Churches where the' Infirmitye   190
         Of him that speakes, diminishes the Word;
            When Magistrates doe mis-applye
         To us, as wee judge, Lay, or Ghostly sword;
               When Plague, which ys thyne Angell, reignes,
               Or Warrs, thy Champions, swaye;   195
         When Heresye, thy second Deluge, gains
         In th' houre of Death, the' Eve of Last Judgment day,
         Deliver us from the Sinister way.

23. Heare us, O heare us, Lord; To Thee
         A Sinner is more Musique, when he prayes,   200
            Than Spheares, or Angells prayses bee,
         In Panegyrique Alleluiäes;
            Heare us, for tyll thou heare us, Lord,
         Wee knowe not what to say;
         Thyne Eare, to' our Sighs, Teares, Thoughts, gives
            Voice and word;   205
         O Thou, who Satan heardst in Jobs sicke Day,
         Heare Thyselfe now; for thou in Us dost pray.

         24. That wee may Change to Evenness
         Thys intermitting Aguish Pietye,
            That snatching Cramps of Wickednes,
         And Apoplexyes of fast Sinne, may Dye,   210
            That Musique of thy Promises

Not threates in Thunder, may
Awaken us, to our just Offices;
What in thy Booke, thou dost, or Creatures say,   215
That wee may heare, Lord, heare Us, when wee pray.

25. That our Ears Sicknes wee may Cure   [53v]
And rectifye those Labyrinths aright;
    That wee, by Hearkninge, not procure
Our Prayse, nor others Disprayse so invite;   220
        That wee gett not a Slipperines
        And Senselesly declyne
From hearing bold witts jest at Kings Excesse
To' admitt the Like of Majestye Divine:
That wee may Locke our Eares, Lord, open thyne.   225

26. That Livinge Lawe, the Magistrate,
Which to give Us, and make us Physicke, doth
    Our Vices often aggravate;
That Preachers taxing Sinne, before her growth,
        That Satan, and invenom'd Men   230
        Which well, if we starve, dine,
When they doe most accuse Us, may see then,
Us to amendment heare them, Thee decline:
That wee may open our Eares; Lord, Locke thyne.

27. That Learning, thyne Embassador,   235
From thyne Allegiänce wee never tempt;
    That Beauty, Paradises flower
For Physicke made, from Poyson bee exempt;
        That Witt, borne apt, high good to doe,
        By dwelling Lazily   240
On Natures Nothing, bee not Nothing too;
That our affections kill us not, nor Dye:
Heare Us, weake Ecchoes, O thou Eare, and Crye.

28. Sonne of God, heare Us, And since Thou
By taking our blood, owest yt us agayne,   245
    Gayne to thy Selfe, or us allowe,
And lett not both us and thyselfe bee slayne;   [54r]
        O Lambe of God, which tookst our Sin,
        Which coulde not sticke to Thee:
O Lett yt not retorne to Us again,   250
But Patient, and Physitian beeing free,
As sinne is Nothinge, Lett yt No where bee.

Goodfriday. 1613. Riding towards Wales.

Lett Mans Soule be a Spheare, and then, in thys
The' Intelligence that moves, Devotion ys,
And as the other Spheares, by beeing growne
Subject to forrayne Motions, Lose theyre owne,
And beeing by Others hurryed ev'ry day, 5
Scarce in a yeare, theyre naturall forme obay:
Pleasure, or busines soe, our Soules admitt
For theyre first mover, and are whirld by itt.
Hence is 't, that I am caryed towards the West
Thys Day, when my Soules forme bends towards the East. 10
There I should see a Sunne, by rising sett,
And by that setting endles day begett.
But that Christ on thys Crosse, did rise and fall,
Sinne had eternally benighted all.
Yett dare I 'almost be glad, I doe not see 15
That Spectacle of too much weight for mee.

[54v] Who sees Gods face, that ys Selfe-lyfe, must dye:
What a Death were yt then to see God dye?
It made his owne Lieutenant, Nature, Shrincke,
It made hys foote stoolle cracke; And the Sunne wincke. 20
Could I beholde those hands, which span the Poles,
And tune all Spheares at once, peirc'd with those holes?
Could I behold that Endlesse Heighth, which ys
[Zenith to us, and to' our Antipodes,
Humbled belowe us? Or that blood, which ys] 25
The Seate of all our soules, if not of his,
Make Durt of Dust? Or that Flesh which was worne
By God, for hys Apparrell, raggd and torne?
If on these thinges I durst not Looke, durst I
Upon hys miserable Mother cast myne Eye, 30
Who was Gods [Partner] here, and furnish'd thus
Halfe of that Sacrifice, which ransomnd Us?
Though these thinges, as I ride, bee from myne Eye,
They 'are Present yett unto my Memorye,
For that Lookes towards them: And thou Lookst
    towards Mee, 35
O Savior, as thou hangst upon the Tree;
I turne my backe to Thee, but to receave
Corrections, tyll thy Mercyes bid Thee Leave;
O thincke mee worth thyne Anger; Punish mee;

Burne off my Rusts, and my Deformitye.   40
Restore thyne Image, so much by thy Grace,
That thou mayest know mee, and Ile turne my Face. /

....

Song.   [100r]

Send home my Long stray'd Eyes to mee
Which, oh, too long have dwelt on Thee,
Yett since there they 'have learnd such Ill,
   Such forc'd fashions
   And false Passions   5
   That They be
   Made by Thee,
Fitt for no good sight, keepe them still.

Send home my harmlesse hart agayne,
Which no unworthy thought could stayne;   10
Which if it be taught by thyne
   To make Jestings
   Of Protestings
   And crosse both
   Word and Oath,   15
Keepe it, for then 'tis none of myne.

Yett send mee backe my Hart and Eyes
That I may knowe, and see thy lyes
And may Laugh, when that Thou
   Art in Anguish   20
   And dost Languish
   For some One
   That will none,
Or prove as false as thou art nowe. /

Song.   [100v]

Come live with mee, and be my Love,
And we will some newe pleasures prove,
Of Golden sandes, and christall brookes
With silken lines, and silver hookes.

There will the river whispering runne   5
Warm'd by thy Eyes more than the sunne,
And there the' inamor'd fish will stay,
Begging themselves they may betray;

When thou wilt swimme in that live bath,
Each fish, which every channell hath,   10
Will amorously to Thee swimme,
Gladder to catch Thee, than Thou him.

Yf Thou to bee so seene, beest loth
By Sun, or Moone, thou darknest both,
And if myselfe have leave to see,   15
I need not theyre light, having Thee.

Lett others freeze with angling reedes,
And cutt theyre Legges with Shelles, and weedes,
Or trecherously, poore fish besett
With strangling snare, or windowy nett;   20

Lett coarse bold handes, from slimy nest
The bedded fish in bankes outwrest,
Or curious Traytors, Sleave–silke flyes
Bewitch poore fishes wandring Eyes.

[101r]   For the[e] there needes no such deceyte,   25
For thou thyselfe art thyne owne bayte;
That fish that is not catch'd thereby,
Alas, is wiser farr than I. /

The Apparition.

When by thy skorne, O Murdress, I am dead,
    And that thou thinckst Thee free
From all sollicitatiön from mee,
Then shall my Ghost come to thy bed,
And Thee, feign'd Vestall, in worse Armes shall see;   5
Then thy sicke Taper will beginne to wincke,
And he whose Thou art then, Beeing tyred before
Will, if thou stirre, or pinch to wake him, thincke
    Thou callst for more,
And in false Sleepe will from Thee shrincke.   10
Thou, poore Aspen wretch, neglected then

[Bathd] in a Cold quicksilver sweate wilt lye,
   A Veryer Ghost than I.
What I will say, I will not tell Thee nowe
Lest that preserve Thee; 'And since my Love is spent,   15
I 'had rather Thou shouldst painefully repent
Than by my threatnings rest still Innocent. /

Song.

Hee is starke madd, who ever sayes
That he hath bin in Love an houre,
Yett not that Love so soone decayes,
But that it can ten in Lesse space devoure;
Who will beleave mee, Yf I sweare   5
That I have had the Plague a yeare?
Who would not laughe at mee, if I should say,
I sawe a flask of Powder burne a day?

Ah what a Trifle is a Hart,
Yf once into Loves handes yt come?   10
All other Griefes allowe a Part
To other Griefes, and aske themselves but some.
They come to Us, but Us Love drawes;
He swallowes Us, and never chawes.
By him, as by chaynd shott, whole ranckes doe dye;   15
Hee is the Tyran Pike, our Harts the frye.

Yf 'twere not soe, what did become
Of my hart, when I first sawe Thee?
I brought a Hart into the Roome,
But from the roome I carryed none with mee.   20
Yf it had gone to Thee, I knowe
Myne would have taught thy hart to showe
More Pitty [un]to mee; But Love, Alas,
At one first blowe, did shiver yt as Glas.

Yett nothing can to nothing fall,   25
Nor any Place bee empty quite;
Therfore, I thincke my brest hath all   [102r]
Those Peeces still, though they bee not unite.
And now, as broken glasses showe
A hundred lesser faces, so   30

My Ragges of hart can like, wish, and adore,
But after one such Love, can love noe more. /

Stand still, and I will reade to Thee
A Lecture, Love, in Loves Philosophye,
   Those three houres, which wee 'have spent
In walking here, two Shadowes went
   Along with us, which wee ourselves produc'd.   5
But, now the Sunne is just above our heads,
   Wee doe those shadowes tread,
And to brave clearenes all thinges are reduc'd.
   So whyles our infant Love did growe,
Disguises did, and shadowes flowe   10
   From us, and our Care; But now 'tis not soe.
That Love hath not attaind the Least degree,
   Which ys still dilligent, lest others see.

Except our Love at this Noone stay,
Wee shall newe shadowes make the other way: 15
   As the first were made to blind
Others, these which come behind
   Will worke upon our selves, and blind our Eyes.
If once Love fainte, and westwardly decline,
   To mee, Thou falsely thyne,   20
And I to Thee, myne Actions shall disguise.
   The morning shadowes weare away,
But these growe Longer all the day;
   But oh, Loves day ys short, if Love decay.
Love is a Growinge or full constant light,   25
And hys First Minute after Noone ys Night. /

[102v]

A Valediction.

As Vertuous men passe mildly away,
   And whisper to theyre soules to goe,
And some of theyre sad friendes doe say
   The breath goes now, and some say noe:

So lett us melt, and make no noyse,   5
   No teare flouds, nor sigh tempests move,

'T were Prophanation of our Joyes
   To tell the Layetye our Love;

Moving of th' Earth brings harmes and feares,
   Men recken what it did, and ment,   10
But trepidations of the Sphears,
   Though greater farr, is innocent.

Dull Sublunarye Lovers Love   [103r]
   (Whose Soule is Sense) cannot admitt
Absence, because it doth remove   15
   Those thinges which elemented yt.

But wee by 'a Love so much refind
   That ourselves know not what it is,
Inter-assurëd of the mind,
   Care lesse, Eyes, Lipps, and hands to misse.   20

Our two Soules, therefore, which are One
   (Though I must goe) endure not yett
A breach, but an Expansiön
   Like Gold to Ayerie thinness beate.

If they bee two, they are two soe   25
   As stiffe twin Compasses are two.
Thy Soule, the fixt Foote, makes no showe
   To move, but doth if the' other doe.

And though yt in the Center sitt,
   Yett when the Other far doth roame,   30
It leanes, and hearkens after yt
   And growes erect, as it comes home.

Such wilt Thou bee to mee, who must
   Like th' other Foote obliquelye runne;
Thy firmnes makes my Circle Just,   35
   And makes mee End, where I begunne. /

I wonder, by my trothe, what Thou, and I   [103v]
Did, tyll wee Lov'd, were wee not weand, tyll then?
But suck'd on Countreys pleasures childishly?
Or snorted wee in 'the seven Sleepers den?
'T was so; but thys, All Pleasures fancyes bee;   5
If ever Any Beauty I did see,
Which I desir'd and gott, 't was but a Dreame of Thee.

And now, Good morrowe to our waking Soules,
Which watch not one another out of feare,
For Love, all love of other sights controules,
And makes one little roome an every where.   10
Lett Sea-discoverers to new worlds have gon,
Lett mapps, to others, worlds on worlds have showne;
Lett us possesse one worlde, Each hath One, and is One.

My face in thyne Eye, thyne in myne appears,
And true playne harts doe in the faces rest;   15
Where can wee find two better Hemispheares,
Without sharpe North, without declining West?
What ever dyes, was not mixt equally.
If our two Loves bee One, or Thou and I   20
Love so alike that none doe slacken, none can dye. /

Song.

Goe, and catch a falling Starr,
    Gett with child a Mandrake roote,
Tell mee where all past years are,
    Or who cleft the Devills foote.
[104r]   Teach mee to heare Mermayds singing,   5
    Or to keepe off Envyes stinging,
        And find
        What wind
Serves to advance an honest minde.

Yf Thou beest borne to strange sights   10
    Thinges invisible [to] see,
Ride ten thousand dayes and nights
    Till Age snowe whyte hayres on Thee;
Thou, when thou retorn'st, wilt tell mee
    All strange wonders that befell thee,   15
        And sweare
        No wheare
Lives a woman true and fayre.

If thou findst One, lett mee knowe
    Such a Pilgrimage were sweete;   20
Yett doe not, I would not goe,
    Though at next dore wee might meete.
Though she were true when you mett her

And last, till you write your letter,
   Yett Shee   25
   Will bee
False, ere I come, to two, or three. /

Now Thou hast Lov'd mee one whole day,   [104v]
To morrow when Thou leav'st, what wilt thou say?
Wilt Thou then Antedate some newe made vowe?
   Or say that nowe
Wee are not just those persons, which wee were?   5
Or that Oathes made in reverentiall feare
Of Love, and hys wrath, any may forsweare?
Or as true deaths true Mariadges untye,
So Lovers Contracts, Images of those
Binde but tyll Sleepe, Deaths Image, them unloose?   10
   Or your owne End to justifye
For having purpos'd change and fa[ls]hood, you
Can have noe way but falshood to bee true?
Vayne Lunatique, against these scapes I coulde
   Dispute, and conquer, if I woulde,   15
    Which I abstayne to doe,
For by tomorrowe, I may thincke soe too. /

Image of her whom I love, more than Shee,
   Whose fayre Impression in my faythfull hart,
Makes mee her Medall, and makes her Love mee,
   As Kinges doe Coynes, to which theyre stampes impart
The Value: Goe, and take my hart from hence,   5
   Which now is growne too Great and good for mee.
Honors oppresse weake spirits, and our Sense   [105r]
   Stronge Objects dull: the more, the lesse wee see.
When you are gon, and Reason gon with you,
   Then Fantasye is Queene, and Soule, and All;   10
She can present joyes meaner than you doe,
   Convenïent, and more proportionall.
So, If I dreame I have you, I have you,
   For all our joyes are but fantasticall;
And soe I scape the Payne, for Payne is true,   15
   And Sleepe which Lockes up Sense, doth Locke out all.

After a Such fruition I shall wake,
  And, but the waking, nothing shall repent;
And shall to Love more thanckfull Sonnetts make
  Than if more Honor, Teares, and Paynes were spent.   20
But Dearest Hart, and dearer Image, stay;
  Alas, true Joyes at best are dreame ynough:
Though you stay here, you passe too fast away,
  For even at first, lyfes Taper is a Snuffe.
Filld with her Love, may I be rather growne   25
  Madd with much hart, than Ideott with none. /

Ad Solem.

Busy Old foole, unruly Sunne,
  Why dost Thou thus

[105v] Through Windowes, and through Curtaynes call on Us?
Must to thy motions, Lovers Seasons runne?
    Saucye Pedantique wretch, goe chide   5
    Late Schooleboyes, and soure Prentises.
  Goe tell Court huntsmen, that the King will ride;
  Call Countrey Ants, to Harvest offices.
Love, all alike, noe Season knowes, nor Clyme,
Nor houres, Dayes, Months, which are the raggs of Time.   10

    Thy beames so reverend and strong
    Why shouldst thou thincke?
I coulde ecclipse and cloude them with a wincke,
But that I would not lose her sight so Long;
    If her Eyes have not blynded thine,   15
    Looke, and to morrow late, tell mee
  Wheather both Indiës, of Spice, and Myne,
  Bee where thou leftst them, or lye here with mee.
Aske for those Kings, whom thou sawest yesterday,
And thou shalt heare, All here in One bed lay.   20

    She' is all states, And all Princes I,
    Nothing Else is.
Princes doe but play us. Compar'd to Thys,
All honor's Mimique; All wealth Alchimye.
    Thou, Sunne, art halfe as happye 'as wee   25
    In that the worlde's contracted thus;
  Thyne Age askes Ease, and since thy duetyes bee
  To warme the worlde, that's done in warming us.

Shyne here to Us, and thou art every where;   [106r]
Thys Bed thy Center ys, these walls thy Spheare. /   30

Song.

I can Love both fayre and browne,
Her whom abundance melts, and her whom want betrayes,
Her who Loves Loneness best, and her who Maskes and
    Playes;
Her whom the Country form'd, and whom the Towne.
Her who beleeves, and her who tryes,   5
Her who still weepes, with spungye Eyes,
And her who is dry Corke, and never Cryes.
I can Love her, and her, and you, and you;
I Can Love any, so Shee be not true.

Will no other Vice content you?   10
Will 'it not serve your turne to doe as did your Mothers?
Have you old vices spent, 'and now would find out Others?
Or doth a feare that men are true, torment you?
Oh, wee are not, be not you soe;
Lett mee, and doe you, twenty knowe;   15
Racke mee, but binde mee not, and lett me goe.
Must I, which came to travailë through you
Growe your fix'd Subject, because you are true?

Venus heard mee sigh this Song,
And by Loves sweetest Part, Varietye, She swore   20
She' heard not thys till now; And that 'it should be so no more.
She went, examin'd, and retorn'd ere Long,
And sayd, Alas, but two or three   [106v]
Poore Heretiques in Love there bee,
Which thincke to' establish dangerous Constancye.   25
But I have told them, since you will bee true,
You shall be true to them who 'were false to you. /

For every houre that thou wilt spare mee nowe,
    I will allowe,
Usurious God of Love, twentye to Thee
When with my browne, my gray hayres equall bee.
Till then, Love, Lett my body reigne, And lett   5

9. From the Dowden manuscript, poems written by Donne before the end of 1614, in a collection entirely in the handwriting of George Garrard. From the section of love lyrics: the closing lines of the Song 'I can Love both fayre and browne' [The Indifferent], the whole of 'For every houre that thou wilt spare mee nowe' [Love's Usury], and the opening lines 'For Godsake holde your Toungue, and lett mee love' [The Canonization]. Like Donne himself and like Woodward, Garrard employs diagonal slashes to separate stanzas of poems and to mark off individual poems. Bodleian Library, MS Eng. poet.3.99, fols. 206v–207r.

Mee travel, Sojorne, Snatche, Plott, Have, forgett,
Resume my Last yeares Relict, Thincke that yett
    Wee'had never mett.

Lett mee thincke any Rivalls letter myne,
    And at next nine 10
Keepe Midnightes promise; Mistake by the way
The mayd, and tell the Lady 'of that delaye.
Onely Lett me Love none; No, not the Sport,
From Country Grasse, to Comfitures of Court,
Or Cityes quelques choses, lett report 15
    My Mynde transport.

Thys bargayne 'is Good, if when I 'am Olde, I bee
    Inflamd by Thee.
[107r] If thyne owne honor, or my Shame, or Payne
    Thou covett, most at that Age thou shalt gayne; 20
    Doe thy will then, then Subject and Degree

And fruites of Love, Love, I submitt to Thee.
Spare mee till then; Ile beare yt, though Shee bee
   One that Loves Mee. /

The Canonization.

For Godsake holde your Toungue, and lett mee love,
  Or chyde my Palsye, or my Goute,
My five gray haires, or ruind fortune floute;
    With wealth your State, your mind with Arts improve.
      Take you a Course, gett you a Place,   5
      Observe hys honor, or hys Grace,
    And the Kings reall or hys stampëd face
      Contemplate; what you will, approve,
      So you will Lett mee Love.

Alas, alas, who 'is injurd by my Love?   10
  What Merchants Ships have my Sighs drownd?
Who sayes my Teares have overflow'd hys Ground?
    When did my Colds a forward Spring remove?
      When did the heates which my Veines fill
      Adde One Man to the Plaguy bill?   15
Soldyers find Warrs, and Lawyers find out still
    Litigious men, which quarrells move,   [107v]
      Though She and I doe love.

Call us what you will, wee' are made such by Love;
  Call her One, mee another flye;   20
Wee 'are Tapers too, and at [our] owne Cost dye,
    And wee in Us finde the 'Eagle, and the Dove.
      The Phenix ridle hath more witt
      By Us, wee two, beeing One, are ytt.
So to One Neutrall thinge both Sexes fitt: 25
    Wee dye, and rise the same, and prove
      Misterious by thys Love.

Wee can dye by it, yf not Live by Love.
  And yf unfitt for Tombes, and hearse
Our Legende bee, yt wilbe fitt for verse.   30
    And if no Peece of Chronicle wee prove,
      Wee'le build in Sonnetts pretty roome[s].

As well a well wrought Urne becomes
The greatest Ashes, as halfe Acre tombes.
     And by these hymns, all shall approve   35
       Us Canonized for Love.

And Thus Invoke us: You whom reverend Love
    Made One anothers Hermitage,

[108r]   You to whom Love was Peace, that now is Rage,
     Who did the whole worlds Soule extract, and drawe   40
      Into the Glasses of your Eyes
      So made such Mirrors, and Such Spyes
That they did all to you Epitomize.
     Countryes, Townes, Courts, beg from above
      A patterne of [y]our Love. /   45

Song.

I am two fooles, I knowe,
For Loving, and for saying so
   In whining Poetrye.
But where's that Wiseman, that would not be I
   If she would not denye?   5
Then, as th' Earths inward narrowe crooked lanes
Do purge Seawaters frettfull salt away,
   I thought, if I could draw my Paines
Through rimes Vexation, I should them allaye.
Griefe brought to numbers cannot be so fierce,   10
For he tames yt, that fetters yt in Verse.

   But when I have done soe,
Some man, hys Art and Voice to showe,
   Dothe sett and sing my Payne,

[108v]   And by delighting many, frees agayne   15
   Griefe, which Verse did restrayne.
To Love and Griefe tribute of Verse belongs,
But not of Such as pleases when tis redd;
   Both are increasëd by such songs,
For both theyre Tryumphes soe are publishëd;   20
And I, which was two Fooles, doe so growe three:
Who are a little wise, the best fooles bee. /

Yf yett I have not all your Love,
Deare, I shall never have yt all;
I cannot breathe one other sigh to move,
Nor can intreate One other Teare to fall.
All my Treasure, which should purchase Thee, 5
Sighes, Teares, and Oathes, and Letters, I have spent;
Yett no more can be due to mee
Than at the bargayne made was ment.
Yf then thy Gift of Love were Partiäll,
That some to mee, some should to others fall, 10
    Deare, I shall never have Thee all.

Or if then, thou gavest mee all,
All was but All, which thou hadst then,
But if in thy Hart since, there be, or shall
Newe Love created bee, by other men 15
Which have theyre Stockes Intyre, and can in Teares,
In Sighes, in Oathes, and Letters outbid mee:
Thys new Love may begett new feares, [109r]
For thys Love was not vowed by Thee,
And yett, it was: thy gift beeing Generall. 20
The Ground, thy Hart, is myne; what ever shall
    Growe there, Deare, I should have yt all.

Yett I would not have all yett,
Hee that All hath, can have no more,
And since my Love doth every day admit 25
New Growthe, Thou shouldst have new rewards in store;
Thou canst not every day give mee thy hart,
If thou canst give it then, thou never gavest yt.
Loves Ridles are, that though thy hart depart,
It stayes at home, and Thou with losing savest yt, 30
But wee will have a way more liberall
Than changing harts, to joyne The[m], so wee shall
Bee One, and One Anothers All. /

Song.

Sweetest Love I doe not goe, for wearines of Thee,
Nor in hope the world can showe, a fitter Love for mee.

But since that I
Must dye at Last, tis best, To use myselfe in Jest,
Thus by feign'd Deaths to Dye.   5

Yesternight the Sunne went hence; And yett is here to Day,
He hath no Desire nor Sence, nor halfe so short a way.
Then feare not mee,

[109v] But beleeve that I shall make, Speedyer jorneyes, since
I take
More winges, and Spurrs than Hee.   10

Ô how feble is Mans Power, that if Good fortune fall,
Cannot adde an other houre, Nor a lost houre recall;
But come bad chance,
And wee Joyne to yt our Strength, And wee teach yt Art
and length,
It selfe o'er Us to' advance.   15

When thou sighst, thou sighst not winde, but sighst
my Soule away,
When thou weepst, unkindly kind, my lifes blood doth
decay.
It cannot bee
That thou lov'st mee, as thou sayst, if in thyne my life
thou waste,
Thou art the best of Mee.   20

Lett not thy divining hart forethincke mee any ill,
Destinye may take thy Part, and may thy fears fullfill,
But thincke that wee
Are but turnd aside to sleepe; They who One Another
keepe
Alive, ne'er parted bee. /   25

Song.

When I dyed Last (And, Deare, I dye
As often as from Thee I goe,
Though it bee an houre agoe,
For Lovers houres be full Eternitye);
I can remember yett that I   5
Something did say, and something did bestowe,

Though I bee dead, which sent mee, I should bee   [110r]
Myne owne Executor and Legacee.

I heard mee say, tell her anone
That myselfe, that['s] you, not I,   10
Did kill mee, And when I felt me Dye,
I bid mee send my hart, when I was gone;
But I, alas, could there finde none.
When I had rippd mee, and searchd where hart did lye,
It killd me 'agayne, that I who still was true   15
In lyfe, in my Last will should cozen you.

Yett I found something like a Hart,
But Colors yt, and Corners had.
It was not good, it was not bad,
It was intyre to none, and fewe had Part;   20
As Good as could bee made by Art
It seemd; and therfore for our Losse [is] sad.
I ment to send thys hart in stead of myne,
But oh, no Man could hold yt, for 'twas thyne. /

A Feaver.

Oh doe not dye, for I shall hate
   All woemen soe, when thou art gone,
That Thee I shall not celebrate,
   When I remember, thou wast One.

But yet thou canst not dye, I knowe;   5
   To leave thys world behind ys Death.
But when thou from thys worlde will goe,   [110v]
   The whole worlde vapors with thy breath.

Or if when Thou, the worlds Soule, goest,
   It stay, 'tis but thy Carkas then;   10
The fairest woman, but thy Ghost,
   But Corrupt wormes, the worthyest men.

O wrangling Schooles, that searche what fyre
   Shall burne thys worlde: Had none the witt
Unto thys knowledge to aspire,   15
   That thys her feaver might be ytt?

And yett shee cannot wast by thys,
  Nor Long beare thys torturing wrong,
For much Corruption needfull ys
  To fuell such a feaver Long.   20

These burning fitts but Meteors bee,
  Whose matter in Thee is soone spent.
Thy beauty' and all Parts which are Thee
  Are Unchangeable Firmament.

Yett t'was of my mind, seising Thee,   25
  Though it in Thee cannot persever,
For I had rather Owner bee
  Of thee one houre, than all else for' ever. /

[111r]   *Ayre and Angells.*

Twice or thrice had I Loved Thee,
Before I knewe thy face, or name:
So in a Voice, soe in a shapeles flame
Angells affect us oft, and worship'd bee;
  Still when, to where thou wert, I came,   5
Some lovely glorious Nothing I did see.
  But since my Soule, whose childe Love ys,
Takes limbs of flesh, and else could nothing doe;
  More subtile than the Parent ys,
Love must not bee, but take a Body too.   10
  And therfore what thou wert; And who,
    I bid Love aske, and now
That it assumes thy body, I allowe,
And fixe itselfe in thy lippe, Eye, and browe.

Whyles thus to ballast Love, I thought,   15
And so more stedily to have gone
With wares which would sincke Admiratiön,
I sawe, I had Loves Pinnace overfraught.
  Ev'ry thy Hayre, for Love to worke upon,
Is much too much; Some fitter must be sought.   20
  For nor in Nothing, nor in thinges
Extreme and scattering bright can Love inhere,
  Then, as an Angell, face and winges
Of Ayre, not pure as yt, yett pure doth weare:

    So thy Love may bee my Loves Spheare.   25
      Just such Disparitee   [111v]
As ys twixt Ayre, and Angells Puritee,
Twixt womens Love, and mens, will ever bee. /

Tis true, tis day, what though it bee?
Ô wilt Thou [therefore] rise from mee?
Why should wee rise, because tis Light?
Did wee lye downe, because t'was Night?
Love, which in despight of Darknes brought us hither,   5
Should in despight of Light keepe us together.

[Lyght hath no Tongue, but is all Eye.]
Yf it could speak, as well as spye,
Thys were the worst, that it could say,
That beeing well, I fayne would stay,   10
And that I Lov'd my hart, and honor so,
That I would not from him which had them, goe.

Must busines Thee from hence remove?
Oh, that's the worst disease of Love;
The Poore, the Foule, the false, Love can   15
Admitt, but not the busyed man.
He which hath busines, and makes Love, doth doe
Such wrong, as when a marryed Man doth wooe. /

    Take heede of Loving Mee.   [112r]
At least remember I forbad yt Thee,
Not that I shall repayre my' unthrifty waste
Of breath and blood, upon thy Sighes, and Teares;
[By being to thee then what to' me thou wast;]   5
But so greate joy our lyfe at once outweares.
Then lest thy Love by my death frustrate bee,
If Thou love Mee, take heed of Loving mee.

    Take heed of hating mee,
Or too much triumph in the Victoree.   10
Not that I shall bee myne owne Officer,
And hate with hate agayne retalliate;
But thou wilt Lose the stile of Conquerer,

If I, thy Conquest, perish by thy hate.
Then lest my beeing nothing Lessen Thee,   15
Yf thou hate mee, take heede of hating mee.

  Yett Love, and hate me too,
So these Extreames shall neythers office doe.
Love mee, that I may dye the gentler way;
Hate mee, because thy Loves too greate for mee.   20
Or lett these two themselves, not Mee decay,
So shall I live: thy Sta[g]e, not Tryumph bee.
Then lest thy Love, hate, and Mee thou undoe,
Ô Lett me Live, O Love and hate me too. /

[112v]   All Kings, and all theyre favorites,
All Glory of honnors, Beautyes, Witts,
The Sunne itselfe, which makes Times as they passe,
Is elder by a yeare now than it was
When Thou and I first One another sawe.   5
All other thinges to theyre destruction drawe;
Only our Love hath no decay.
Thys no to Morrow hath, nor yesterday;
Running, it never runns from Us away,
But truly keepes the first, last, everlasting day.   10

Two Graves must hide thyne and my Corpse;
If one might, Death were no Divorce.
Alas, as well as other Princes, wee
(Who Prince enough in One another bee)
Must leave at last in Death, these Eyes and Eares,   15
Oft fed with true Oathes, and with sweete salt Teares.
But Soules where nothing dwells but Love,
(All other Thoughts beeing Inmates) then shall prove
This, or a Love encreasëd there above,
When Bodyes to theyre Graves, Soules from theyre
    Graves remove.   20

And then wee shall be throughly blest,
But wee no more than all the rest.
Here upon Earth, we are Kings; and but wee,
None are such Kings, and of such, Subjects bee.
Who is so safe as wee? where none can doe   25
Treason to us, except one of Us two.
True and false feares Lett us refrayne.

Lett us Love nobly, 'and Live, and adde agayne
Yeares and yeares, unto yeares, till wee attayne   [113r]
To write threescore; Thys is the Second of our Reigne. /   30

A Valediction. Of my name in the window.

1. My name engrav'd herein
Doth contribute my firmnes to thys Glasse,
   Which, ever since that charme, hath beene
   As hard, as that which grav'd yt, was.
Thyne eye will give yt Price inough, to mocke   5
   The Diamonds of eyther Rocke.

2. Tis much that Glasse should bee
As all confessing, and through-shine, as I,
   Tis more, that yt showes Thee to Thee,
   And cleare reflects thee to thyne Eye.   10
But all such Rules, Loves Magique can undoe;
   Here you see mee, and I ame you.

3. As noe one Pointe, nor Dash,
Which are but Accessary to thys Name,
   The Showers and Tempests can outwash: 15
   So shall all Times find mee the same.
You thys Intirenes better may fullfill,
   Who have the Patterne with you still.   [113v]

4. Or if too hard and deepe
Thys Learning bee, for a scratchd Name to teache,   20
   Ytt, as a given Deaths head keepe,
   Lovers Mortalitye to preach,
Or thincke thys ragged bony name to bee
   My ruinous Anatomee.

5. Then, as all my Soules bee   25
Emparadis'd in you, (in whom alone
   I understand, and Growe, and see)
   The Rafters of my body, Bone
Beeing still with you, the Muscle, Sinewe, 'and Vayne
   Which tyle thys house, will come agayne.   30

6. Till my retorne repayre
And recompact my Scattred body soe
   As all the Virtuous Powers which are

Fix'd in the Starrs, are sayd to flowe
Into such characters as gravëd bee   35
    When those Starrs have Supremacye.

7. Soe since thy[s] Name was Cutt
When Love and Griefe theyre Exaltation had,
    No dore agaynst thys Names Influence shutt,
    As much more Loving, as more sadd   40
'T will make Thee. And Thou shouldst, tyll I retorne,
    Since I dye daily, daily mourne.

[114r]   8. When thy' inconsiderate hand
Flings out thys Casement, with my trembling Name,
    To Looke [on] One whose witt or Land   45
    New battry to thy hart may frame,
Then thincke this Name alive, and that Thou thus
    In ytt, offend'st my Geniüs.

9. And when thy melted mayd,
Corrupted by thy Lovers Gold, and Page,   50
    His letter at thy Pillowe hath layd,
    Disputed yt, and tam'd thy rage,
And thou beginnst to thaw towards him, for thys,
    May my Name step in, and hyde hys.

10. And if thys Treason goe   55
To' an Overt Act, and that Thou write agayne:
    In Superscribing, thys Name flowe
    Into thy fancy, from the Pane,
So in forgetting, thou remembrest right,
    And unaware to mee shalt write.   60

11. But Glasse and lynes must bee
No meanes, our firme Substantiall Love to keepe,
    Neere Death inflicts thys Lethargye,
    And thys I murmure in my Sleepe.
Impute thys Idle talke, to that I goe,   65
    For Dying men talke often soe. /

[114v]   *Elegye. Autumnall.*

No Springe, nor Summer beauty hath such Grace
As I have seene in One Autumnall face.

Young beautyes force [y]our Love, and that's a Rape;
Thys doth but Counsayle, yett you cannott scape.
If 't were a Shame to Love, here 't were no Shame,   5
Affection here takes Reverences Name.
Were her first yeares the Golden Age? That's true,
But nowe Shee's Gold oft tryed, and ever newe.
That was her Torrid, and inflaming Time;
This is her Tolerable Tropique Clyme.   10
Fayre Eyes, who askes more heate than comes from hence,
Hee in a feaver wishes Pestilence.
Call not these wrinckles Graves; Yf Graves they were,
They were Loves Graves, for Else he ys noe where.
Yett lyes not Love dead here, but here doth sitt   15
Vowed to thys trench, like an Anachoritt;
And here till hers, which must be hys Death, come,
He doth not digg a Grave, but build a Tombe.
Here dwells he, though he sojorne every where
In Progresse, yett his standing house is here: 20
Here, where still Evening ys, not Noone, nor Night,
Where no Voluptuousnes, yett all Delight.
In all [her] wordes, unto all hearers fitt,
You may at Revells, you at Counsell sitt.
Thys is Loves Timber, youth hys underwood: 25
There hee as Wine in June bringes blood,
Which then comes Seasonablyest, when our Tast
And appetite to other thinges is Past.
Xerxes' strange Lydian Love, the Platane Tree   [115r]
Was lov'd for Age, none beeing so lardge as She.   30
Or else because beeing yonge, Nature did blesse
Her Youth with Ages Glory, Barrennes.
Yf wee Love thinges Long sought, Age is a Thinge
Which wee are fiftye yeares in Compassing;
If transitory thinges, which soone decay,   35
Age must bee Lovelyest at the Latest day.
But name not winter faces, whose Skinne's slacke,
Lanke as an Unthrifts Purse, but a Soules Sacke,
Whose Eyes seeke Lyght within; for all here 'ys Shade,
Whose mouthes are holes, rather worne out than made,   40
Whose everye Tooth to' a severall Place is gone,
To vexe theyre Soules at resurrectiön.
Name not these Living Deaths-heads unto me,
For these not Antiënt, but Antique bee.
I hate Extreames; Yett I had rather stay   45

With Tombes than Cradles to weare out a day.
Since Such Loves Naturall Lation ys, May still
My Love descend, and Jorney downe the Hill,
Not panting after groweing beautyes: So
I shall Ebb on with them, who homewards goe. /   50

Blasted with Sighes and surrounded with Teares,
    Hither I come to Seeke the Springe,
And at myne Eyes and at mine Eares,

[115v]   Receave such balmes, as else cure every thinge;
    But O Selfe Traytor, I doe bring   5
The Spyder Love, which transubstantiates all,
    And can convert Manna to Gall.
And that thys Place may thoroughly bee thought
    True Paradice, I have the Serpent brought.
'Twere wholsommer for mee, that Winter did   10
    Benight the Glory of thys Place,
And that a Grave frost did forbidde
These Trees to laughe and mocke me to my face;
    But that I may not thys disgrace indure,
    Love, lett mee Some Sencelesse peece of thys Place bee;   15
Make mee a Mandrake, so I may grone here,
Or a stone fountayne, weeping out my yeare.
    Hither with Christall Vyalls, Lovers come,
And take my Teares, which are Loves Wine,
And trye your mistres Teares at home,   20
For all are false, that tast not just like myne.
    Alas, hartes doe not in Eyes shine,
Nor can you more judge womans thoughts by Teares
    Than by her Shadowe, what she weares.
O Perverse Sex, where none is true but Shee   25
    Who's therfore true, because her Truth kills mee. /

Epitaph.

Madam,
That I might make your Cabinett my Tombe
    And for my Fame, which I Love next my Soule,

Next to my Soule provide the happyest roome,   [116r]
   Admitt to that Place thys Last farewell Scroule.
[Others] by Testament give Legacyes; But I,   5
   Dying, of you doe beg a Legacye.

Omnibus.

My fortune and my [ch]oyce thys Custome breake,
When wee are Speechles growne, to make Stones speake.
Though no stone tell Thee what I was, yett Thou
In my Graves Inside see, what thou art nowe.   10
Yett thou 'art not yett soe good; Tyll us death lay
To ripe and mellowe here, wee 'are stubborne Clay.
Parentes make us Earth; And soules dignifye
Us to be Glasse. Here to growe Gold, wee lye;
Whylst in our Soules, Sinne bred and pampred ys,   15
Our Soules become Wormeaten Carkases:
So wee Ourselves miraculously destroy.
Here bodyes with lesse Myracle injoye
Such Priviledges; Enabled here to scale
Heaven, when the Trumpetts Ayre shall them exhale.   20
Heare thys, and mend Thyselfe, and thou mendst mee,
By making mee, beeing dead, doe good to Thee.
And thincke mee well composd, that I could now
A last sicke houre to Syllables allowe.

Valediction of the Booke.

Ile Tell thee now (Deare Love) what thou sha[l]t doe
To anger Destinye, as She doth Us,
How I shall stay, though She Eloyne mee thus;   [116v]
And how Posteritye shall know yt too.
   How thyne may out-endure   5
   Sybills Glory, and obscure
Her who from Pindar could allure,
  And [her] through whose helpe Lucan ys not lame,
And her whose booke (they say) Homer did find and
   name.

Study our Manuscripts, those Myriades   10
Of Letters, which have passd twixt Thee and Mee;
Thence write our Annalls, and in them will bee
To All whom Loves Subliming fyre invades
    Rule and Example found;
      There, the fayth of any Ground   15
    No Scismatique will dare to wound
That sees, how Love thys Grace to us affords
To make, to keepe, to Use, to bee, these hys records.

This booke, as Long Liv'd as the Elements
Or as the worlds forme, thys all-gravëd Tome,   20
In Cyphar writte, or new made Idiome,
Wee for Loves Clergye only' are Instruments.
    When thys Booke is made thus,
      Should agayne the ravenous
    Vandalls, and Gothes inundate us,   25
    Learning were safe; In thys our Universe
Schooles might Learne Sciences, Spheares Musicke,
    Angells Verse.

[117r]   Here Loves Devines, (since all Devinitye
Is Love or wonder) may find all they seeke,
Whether abstract spirituall Love they Like,   30
Theyre Soules exhald with what they doe not see,
    Or loth so to amuze
    Fayths infirmitys, they chuse
    Something which they may see and Use;
For though Minde be the Heaven, where Love doth sitt,   35
Beauty' a Convenient Type may bee to fygure ytt.

Here more than in theyre bookes may Lawyers find
Both by what Titles, Mistresses are Ours,
And howe Prerogative those states devoures,
Transferd from Love himselfe, to womankind,   40
    Who though from hart and Eyes
    They Exact great Subsedyes,
    Forsake him, who on them relyes;
And for the Cause, Honor or Conscience give,
Chimeraes, vayne as they, or theyre Prerogative.   45

Here Statesmen (or of them, they which can read)
May of theyre Occupation find the Grounds:
Love and theyre Art alike yt deadly wounds,
Yf to Consider what tis, One proceede.
    In both they doe excell   50

Who the present governe well,
  Whose weakenes none doth, or dares tell;
In this thy Booke, such will theire Nothing see,
As in the Bible some can finde out Alchimye.

Thus vent thy Thoughts; Abroad Ile study Thee,   55 [117v]
As he removes farr off, that greate heighths takes;
Howe greate Love ys, Presence best tryall makes,
But Absence tryes how long thys Love wil bee.
    To take a Latitude
      Sunne or Starrs are fitlyest viewd   60
   At theyre brightest; but to conclude
Of Longitudes, what other way have wee
But to marke when and where the darke Ecclipses
    bee? /

Good wee must Love, and m[u]st hate ill,
For ill is ill, and good Good still;
   But there are thinges Indifferent
Which wee may neyther hate nor Love,
But One and then another prove   5
   As wee shall find our Fancy bent.

If then at first, wise Nature had
Made Woemen eyther good or bad
   Then some wee might hate, and some chuse:
But since She did them so create,
That wee may neyther Love nor hate,   10
   Only thys rests: All, all may use.

If they were good, it would bee seene,
Good is [as] Visible as Greene,
   And to all Eyes, itselfe betrayes.   15
If they were bad, they could not Last,   [118r]
Bad doth itselfe, and others wast,
   So they deserve nor blame, nor Prayse.

But They are Ours as fruites are Ours.
He that but tasts, he that devoures,   20
   And he which leaves all, doth as well;
Chang'd Loves are but chang'd sorts of meate,
And when he hath the Kernell eate,
   Who doth not fling away the shell? /

Spring.

I scarce beleave my Love to be so pure
   As I had thought ytt was,
   Because it doth endure
Vicissitude, and Season, as the Gras.
Mee thincks I lyed all winter, when I swore   5
My Love was Infi'nite, if Spring make yt more.
But yf thys Medicine, Love, which cures all Sorrowe
With more, Not only bee no quintessence,
But mixt of all stuffs, paining Soule or Sense,
And of the Sunne his working vigor borrowe,   10
Love's not so pure, and abstract, as they use
To say, which have no Mistres, but theyre Muse.
But as all [else], beeing Elemented too,
Love sometimes would contemplate, sometimes doe.

[118v]   And yett not greater, but more eminent   15
   Love by the Spring is growne.
   As in the Firmament,
Starrs by the Sunne are not enlardgd but showne:
Gentle Love Deedes, as blossomes on a bough,
From Loves awakened roote doe bud out nowe.   20
If as in Water stird, more Circles bee
Produc'd by One, Love Such Additions take,
Those, like to many Spheares, but one heaven make,
For they are all Concentrique unto Thee;
And though Each Spring doe adde to Love newe heate,   25
As Princes doe in time of Actions gett
New taxes, and remitte them not in Peace,
No Winter shall abate the Springes Encrease. /

Love, Any Devill else but you,
Would for a given Soule, give something too.
At Court your fellowes every Day
Give th' Art of Riming, Huntsmanship and Play
For them, who were theyre owne before;   5
Only' I have Nothing, which gave more,
But am, Alas, by beeing Lowly, Lower.

I aske not dispensation now
To falsifye a Teare or vowe;

I doe not sue from Thee to drawe   10
A *Non Obstante* 'in Natures Lawe.
These are Prerogatives; They inhere
In Thee and Thyne: None should forsweare,   [119r]
Except that he Loves Minion were.

Give mee thy weakenes, make mee blind   15
Both wayes, as thou and thyne, in Eyes and Minde;
Love, Lett mee never know that thys
Ys Love, or that Love childish is.
Lett mee not knowe that others knowe
That She knowes my Payne: Lest that so   20
A tender Shame make mee myne owne newe woe.

If thou give Nothing, yett th[ou]' art just,
Because I would not thy first Motions trust;
Small townes withstand stiffe tyll greate Shott
Enforce them; by warrs Lawe condition not.   25
Such in Loves warrfare is my Case,
I may not Article for grace,
Having put Love at last to shew this face.

This face, by which he could command
And change th' Idolatrye of any land;   30
This face, which wheresoe'er yt comes,
Can call vow'd men from Cloysters, dead from Tombes;
And melt both Poles at Once, and store
Desarts with Cittyes, and make more
Mynes in the Earth, than quarreyes were before.   35

For thys, Love is enrag'd with mee,
Yett kills not. If I must example bee
To future Rebells; if th' unborne
Must Learne, by my beeing cutt up, and torne: [119v]
Kill, and disect mee, Love; For thys   40
Torture agaynst thyne owne End ys.
Rackt Carkases make ill Anatomyes. /

Some man unworthy to bee Possessor
Of old or new Love, himselfe beeing false or weake,
Thought his Paine and Shame would be lesser
If on Womankind he might hys Anger wreake;
    And thence a Lawe did Growe: 5

One should but One man knowe.
But are other Creatures soe?

Are Sunne, Moone, or Starrs by Law forbidden
To' smile where they list, or lend away theyre light?
Are Birdes divorc'd, or are they chidden,   10
If they Leave theyre Mate,' or lye abroad a Night?
    Beasts did no Jointures lose
    Though they new Lovers chuse,
    But wee are made worse than those.

Who e'er riggd fayre Ship to lye in harbors,   15
And not to seeke new Lands, or not to deale with All?
Or build fayre houses, sett Trees and Arbors,
Only to locke up, or Else to lett them fall?
    Good is not Good unlesse
    A Thousand it possesse,   20
    But doth wast with greedynesse. /

[120r]

The Dreame.

Deare Love, for nothing lesse than Thee
Would I have broke thys happy Dreame.
    It was a Theame
For Reason, much too stronge for Fantasye,
Therfore thou wakdst mee wisely; yett   5
My Dreame thou brokest not, but continuedst ytt.
Thou art so Truth, that thoughts of Thee suffice
To make Dreames Truth, and fables Historyes.
Enter these Armes, for since thou thoughtst ytt best
Not to dreame all my Dreame, letts doe the rest.   10

As Lightnings, or a Tapers light,
Thyne Eyes, and not thys Noyse wakd me,
    Yett I thought Thee
(Thou Lovest Truith) but an Angell at first Sight.
But when I sawe thou sawest my hart,   15
And knewst my Thoughts, beyond an Angells art;
When thou knewst what I dremt, when thou knewest when
Excess of Joy would wake mee, and camst then,
I doe confesse, yt could not chuse but bee
Profanenes, to thincke Thee any Thinge but Thee.   20

Comming and staying shew'd Thee Thee,
But rising makes mee doubt yt now,
   Thou art not Thou.
That Love is weake, when feare's as strong as hee;
'Tis not all Spiritt, pure, and brave,   25 [120v]
Yf mixture yt of Feare, Shame, honor have.
Perchance, as Torches which must readye bee,
Men light, and put out: so Thou dealst with mee,
Thou Cam'st to kindle, goest to Come; Thus I
Will dreame that hope agayne, but Else will Dye. /   30

A Valediction.

   Lett me poure forth
My Teares, before thy face, whylst I stay here,
For thy face coynes them, and thy stampe they beare,
And by thys Mintage, they are something worth,
   For thus they bee   5
   Pregnant of Thee.
Fruites of much Griefe they are, Embleames of more,
When a Teare falls, that thou falls, which yt bore,
Soe Thou, and I are Nothing then, when on a diverse shore.

   On a round Ball   10
A workeman that hath Copyes by, can lay
An Europe, Afrique, and an Asiä,
And quickly make that which was nothing, all;
   Soe doth each Teare
   Which Thee doth weare,
A Globe, yea worlde by that Impression growe,   15
Till thy Teares mixte with myne doe overflowe
This worlde: by waters sent from Thee, my heaven dissolvëd so.

   Ô more than Moone,
Drawe not up seas, to drowne mee in thy spheare,   20 [121r]
Weepe mee not dead in thyne Armes, but forbeare
To teach the Sea, what it may doe too soone:
   Lett not the Winde
   Example finde
To doe mee more harme than yt purposeth;   25
Since thou and I sigh one Anothers breath,
Who e'er sighs most, ys cruellst, and hasts the others death. /

Mummye.

Some that have deeper digg'd Loves Myne than I
Say, where hys Centrique happines doth lye.
    I have lov'd, and gott, and tolde,
But should I love, gett, tell, tyll I were olde,
I should not finde that hidden Misterye;   5
        Oh 'tis Imposture all.
And as no Chymique yett th' Elixar gott
    But glorifyes his Pregnant Pott,
    If by the way to him befall
Some Odoriferous thinge or Medcynall: 10
    So Lovers dreame a ritch and Long delight,
    But gett a Winter-seeming Sommers Night.

Our Ease, our thrift, our honor, and our Day
Shall wee for thys vaine Bubbles shadowe pay?
    Ends Love in thys? that my Man   15
Can be as happye 'as I can: if he Can
Endure the Short scorne of a Bridgroomes Play?
        That Loving Wretch that sweares
    'Tis not the Bodyes marry, but the Mindes,
    Which he in her Angelique findes,   20
    Would sweare as justly that he heares
In that dayes rude hoarse Minstrallsey the Spheares.
    Hope not for Minde in woeman; Att theyre best,
    Sweetnes, and Witt; they 'are but Mummye possest. /

[121v]

The Flea.

Marke but thys flea, and marke in thys
How litle, that which thou denyest mee, ys.
    It suck't mee first, and now suckes Thee,
And in thys flea, our two blouds mingled bee.
Thou know'st that thys cannot bee sayd   5
A Sinne, nor Shame, nor Losse of Maydenhead.
    Yett this enjoyes before yt woo,
And pamperd swells with one blood made of two,
And thys, alas, is more than wee would doe.

Oh stay, three lives in One flea spare,   10
Where wee allmost, yea more than marryed are.

Thys Flea is you, and I, and thys
Our Maryadge bedd, and marryage Temple ys.
    Though Parents grudge, and you, we 'are mett
And Cloystred in these Living walls of Jett.   15
    Though Use make you apt to kill mee,
Lett not to that, Selfe Murder added bee,
And Sacriledge; Three Sinns in killing Three.

Cruell and sodayne, hast thou since   [122r]
Purpled thy Nayle, in blood of Innocence?   20
    Wherein Could thys Flea guiltye bee,
Except in that drop which it suckt from Thee?
Yett thou tryumphst, and sayst that Thou
Findst not thyselfe nor mee the weaker now.
    'Tis true; Then learne howe false feares bee.   25
Just so much honor, when thou yieldst to mee
Will wast, as thys Fleas death tooke lyfe from Thee. /

The Curse.

Who ever guesses, thinckes, or dreames he knowes
Who is my Mistres, wither by thys Curse:
    His only,' and only' hys Purse
    May some dull hart to Love dispose,
And she yield then to All that are hys foes;   5
May he be scornd by One, whom all else scorne,
Forsweare to others, what to' her he hath sworne,
With feare of missing, shame of getting, torne;

Madnes hys Sorrowe, Goute hys Cramps, may hee
Make, by but thincking, who hath made him such;   10
    And may hee feele no touch
    Of Conscience, but of fame; And bee
Anguish'd, not [that] 't was Sinne, but that 't was Shee.
In Early and Long Scarcenes may hee rott
For Land, which had bin hys, if he had nott   15
Himselfe incestuously an heyre begott.   [122v]

May he dreame Treason, and beleave that Hee
Ment to performe yt, and confesse, and dye,
    And no Record tell why;
    Hys sonnes, which none of hys may bee,   20

Inherritt nothing, but hys infamye.
Or may [he] so Long Parasites have fed
That he would fayne be theyres, whom he hath bredd,
And at the Last be circumcis'd for bread.

The Venom of all Stepdames, Gamsters gall,   25
What Tyrants and theyre Subjects interwish,
   What Plants, Mynes, Beasts, Fowle, Fishe
   Can Contribute; All ill which All
Prophetts or Poetts spake; And All which shall
Be' annexed in Scedules unto this by mee,
Fall on that Man; for if it bee a Shee,   30
Nature before hand hath outcursëd Mee. /

The Extasye.

Where like a Pillowe on a Bed,
   A Pregnant bancke swel'd up, to rest
The Violetts reclyning head,
   Satt wee two, One Anothers best,

Our handes were firmely cimented   5
   With a fast balme, which thence did spring,
[123r]   Our Eyebeames twisted, and did thredd
   Our Eyes, upon one double string.

So to' intergraft our hands, as yett
   Was all the meanes to make us One,   10
And Pictures on our Eyes to gett
   Was all our Propagatiön.

As twixt two equall Armyes, Fate
   Suspends uncertayne Victorie,
Our Soules, which to advance theyre state   15
   Were gon out, hange twixt her, and Mee.

And whylst our Soules negotiate there,
   We like Sepulchrall Statues lay;
All day the same our Postures were,
   And wee sayd nothing all the day.   20

If any, so by Love refind,
   That he Soules Language understood,

And by good Love were growen all mind,
   Within Convenient distance stoode:

Hee (though he knowes not which Soule spake,   25
   Because both ment, both spake the same)
Might thence a new Concoction take,
   And part farr purer than he came.

This Extasye doth unperplexe
   (We sayd) and tell Us what wee Love.   30
Wee see by thys, yt was not Sexe;   [123v]
   Wee see, wee saw not what did move.

But as all severall Soules contayne
   Mixture of thinges, they know not what,
Love, these mixt Soules doth mixe agayne,   35
   And makes both One, Each thys, and that.

A Single Violett transplant,
   The Strength, the Color, and the Size,
All which before was poore and skant,
   Redobles still and multiplyes.   40

When Love, with one another so
   Interanimates two Soules:
That abler Soule which thence doth flowe,
   Defectes of Lonelines controules.

Wee then, who are thys new Soule, know   45
   Of what wee are composd, and made,
For th' Atomi of which wee growe
   Are Soules, whom no Change can invade.

But oh Alas, so long, so farr
   Our bodyes why doe wee forbeare?   50
They' are Ours, though they' are not wee; Wee are
   Th' Intelligences, they the Spheare.

Wee owe them thanckes, because they thus   [124r]
   Did us to Us at first convay,
Yeilded theyre forces, Sense, to Us   55
   Nor are drosse to Us, but Allay.

On Man, Heavens Influence workes not so,
   But that it first imprints the Ayre,
For Soule into the Soule may flowe,
   Though it to body first repayre.   60

As our blood labors to begett
   Spirites, as like Soules as yt can,
Because such fingers need to knitt
   That Subtile knott which makes Us man.

So must pure Lovers Soules descend   65
   T' Affections, and to Facultyes,
Which Sense may reach, and apprehend;
   Else, a Great Prince in Prison lyes.

To' our Bodyes turne wee then, that So
   Weake men, on Love reveald may looke;   70
Loves Misteryes in Soules doe growe,
   But yett the body is hys booke.

[124v]   And if some Lover, such as wee
   Have heard thys Dialogue of One,
Lett him still marke Us, he shall see   75
   Small Change, when wee 'are to Bodyes gon. /

I have done one braver thinge
   Than all the Worthyes did;
Yett a braver thence doth spring,
   Which is, to keepe that hyd.

It were but Madnes now to' impart   5
   The Skill of Specular Stone,
When he which can have learnt the Art
   To cutt yt, can find none.

So, if I now should utter thys,
   Others (because no more   10
Such stuffe to worke upon there ys)
   Would Love but as before;

But he who Lovelines within
   Hath found, All outward lothes;
For he who Color Loves, and skin   15
   Loves but theyre oldest Clothes.

Yf as I have, you also doe
   Vertu attyr'd in Woman see,
[125r]   And dare Love that, and say so too,
   And forgett the Hee, and Shee: 20

And if thys Love, though placëd soe,
   From Prophane men you hide,
Which will no fayth on thys bestowe,
   Or if they doe, deride:
Then you have done a braver thinge,   25
   Than all the worthyes did;
And a braver thence will springe,
   Which is, to keepe that hyd. /

Loves Deitye.

I Long to talke with some Old Lovers Ghost,
   Who dyed before the God of Love was borne.
I cannot thincke that he who then Lov'd most,
   Suncke so Lowe, as to Love One which did Scorne.
But since thys God produc'd a Destinee,   5
And that Vice-Nature, Custome, letts it bee,
   I must Love her, that Loves not mee.

Sure they which made him God, ment not so much,
   Nor he in his young Godhead practis'd it.
But when an Eaven flame two harts did touch,   10 [125v]
   His Office was indulgentlye to fitt
Actives to Passives; Correspondenc[i]e
Only hys Subject was: It cannot bee
   Love, Till I Love her, that Loves mee.

But every Moderne God will now extend   15
   Hys vast Prerogative as farr as Jove;
To rage, to lust, to write to, to Commend,
   All ys the Purlewe of the God of Love.
Oh, were wee wakened by thys Tyrannee
To' Ungod thys Child agayne, it could nott bee   20
   That I should Love, who Loves not mee.

Rebell and Atheist too, why murmure I,
   As thoughe I felt the worst that Love could doe?
Love might make mee leave Loving, or might trye
   A deeper Plague, to make her love mee too.   25
Which, since She Loves before, I am loth to see;
Falshood ys worse than Hate, and that must bee
   If shee whom I Love, should Love mee. /

Loves Dyett.

To what a Cumbersome unwieldines
And burdenous Corpulence my Love had growen,
[126r]   But that I did, to make ytt Lesse
        And keepe yt in Proportiön,
Give yt a Dyett, made yt feed upon   5
That, which Love worst indu[r]es, Discretiön.

Above One Sigh a Day, I 'allowd him not;
Of which, my fortune, and my falts had part.
        And if sometimes by stealth he gott
        A Shee-Sighe from my mistres hart,   10
And thought to feast on That, I lett him see,
'T was neyther very sound, nor ment to mee.

If he wrung from me a Teare, I brind yt too
With Scorne or Shame, that hym yt nourish'd not.
        If he suck'd hers, I lett him knowe   15
        'T was not a Teare which he had gott:
Hys drincke was Counterfayte, as was hys Meate,
For Eyes which roll towards all, weepe not, but sweate.

What ever he would Dictate, I writt that,
But burnt my Letters. When Shee writte to mee,   20
        And that that favor made him fatt,
        I sayd, If any Title bee
Convayde by this, Ah, what doth yt availe,
To be the fortieth Name in an Entayle?

Thus I reclaym'd my Bussard Love, to flye   25
At what, and when, and how, and where I chuse:
[126v]   Now negligent of sporte, I lye,
        And now, as other fawkners use,
I springe a Mistres, sweare, write, sigh, and weepe,
And the Game kill'd, or lost, goe talke, and Sleepe. /   30

The Will.

Before I sigh my Last gaspe, lett mee breathe
(Greate Love) some Legacyes. Here I bequeath
Myne Eyes to Argus, if myne Eyes can see;
If they be blynde, then, Love, I give them Thee,
My Tonge to Fame; To' Ambassadors myne Eares;   5

To Woemen, or the Sea, my Teares.
Thou, Love, hast taught mee heretofore,
By making mee Serve her who 'had twenty more,
That I should give to none but such as had too much before.

My Constancy I to the Planetts give,   10
My Truith to them who at the Court doe live;
Myne Ingenuitye and Opennesse
To Jesuits; To Buffones, my Pensivenes;
My Silence to' any, who abroad hath bin;
    My Money to a Capuchin.   15
      Thou, Love, taughtst mee, by 'appointing mee
    To Love there where no Love receav'd can bee,
Only to give to such, as have an Incapacitye.

I give my Reputatiön to those   [127r]
Which were my frindes; Myne Industrye to Foes.   20
To Schoolemen I bequeath my doubtfullnes;
My Sicknes to Physitions, or excesse;
To Nature, all that I in rime have writt;
    And to my Companye, my Witt.
      Thou, Love, by makinge me adore   25
    Her who begott thys Love in mee before,
Taughtst mee to make as though I gave, when I did but
    restore.

To him for whom the Passing Bell next tolls,
I give my Phisicke bookes; my written rolls
Of Morrall Counsayles, I to Bedlam give;   30
My brazen Medalls unto them which live
In want of bread; To them, which pass among
    All Forrayners, myne English tongue.
      Thou, Love, by making mee Love One
    Who thinckst her frendship a fitt Portiön   35
For yonger Lovers, dost my Gifts thus disproportiön.

Therefore Ile give no more; But Ile undoe
The world by Dyeing, because Love dyes too.
Then all your beautyes wilbe no more worth
Than Gold in Mynes, where none doth drawe yt forth;   40
And all your Graces no more Use shall have
    Than a Sun dyall in a Grave.
      Thou, Love, taughtst mee, by making mee   [127v]
    Love her who doth neglect both Mee and Thee,
To' Invent, and Practize thys One way, to' Annihilate
    all Three. /   45

The Funerall.

Who ever comes to shroude mee, doe not harme
　　　Nor question much
That Subtill wreath of Hayre, which crownes myne Arme,
The Misterye, the Signe, you must not touche,
　　　For 'tis my outward Soule,   5
Viceroy to that which, then to Heav'n beeing gone,
　　　Will leave thys to Controule
And keepe these limnes, her Provinces, from Dissolutiön.

For if the Sinewye thread my brayne letts fall
　　　Through every Part   10
Can tye those Parts, and make mee One of All;
These haires which upward grewe, and strength and Art
　　　Have from a better brayne,
Can better doe 'yt; Except shee ment that I
　　　By thys should know my Payne,   15
As Prisoners then are Manacled, when they 'are condemn'd
　　to Dye.

What e'er she ment by 'it, bury it with mee.
　　　For since I am
Loves Martyre, yt might breede Idolatree,
If into others hand these Reliques came.   20
　　　As 'twas humilitye
To' afford to yt all which a Soule can doe,
　　　Soe 'tys some braverye,
That since you would save none of mee, I bury some of you. /

[128r]

The Blossome.

Litle thinckst Thou, poore flowre,
　　　Whom I have watch'd six or seven dayes,
And seene thy birth, and seene what every houre
Gave to thy Growth, Thee to thys heighth to rayse,
And nowe dost Laugh, and tryumph on thys boughe;   5
　　　Litle thinckst Thou
That yt will freeze anon, and that I shall
To morrowe fynde Thee falne, or not at all.

Litle thinckst Thou, Poore Hart,
    That Laborst yett to nestle Thee,   10
And thinckst by hov'ringe here to gett a Part
In a forbidden, or forbidding Tree,
And hop'st her stiffnes by longe Siege to bowe;
    Litle thinckst Thou
That thou to morrowe, ere that Sunne doth wake,   15
Must with thys Sunne and Mee a jorney take.

    But Thou, which Lovst to bee   [128v]
    Subtile to plague thyselfe, wilt say,
Alas, if you must goe, what's that to mee?
Here Lyes my busines, and here I will stay.   20
You goe to frindes, whose Love and meanes present
    Various Content
To your Eyes, Eares, and Tongue, and ev'ry Part,
If then your Body goe, what neede you 'a Hart?

    Well then, stay here. But knowe,   25
    When Thou hast stayd, and done thy Most,
A naked thincking Hart that makes noe showe
Is to a Woman but a kind of Ghost.
How shall She knowe my Hart? Or having none,
    Know Thee for One?   30
Practize may make her know some other part;
But take my word, She doth not knowe a Hart.

    Meete mee at London then,
    Twenty dayes hence, and Thou shalt see
Mee fresher and more fatt, by beeing with men,   35
Than if I had stayd still with Her, and Thee.
For Godsake, if you can, bee you so too.
    I would give you
There, to another frend, whom wee shall finde
As Glad to have my body, as my Minde. /   40

The Primerose.   [129r]

    Upon thys Primerose hyll,
    Where, yf Heav'n would distill
A showre of rayne, each severall drop might goe
To hys owne Primerose, and growe Manna soe,
And where theyre forme, and theyre Infinitee   5

Make a terrestriall Galaxie
As the Small Starrs doe in the Skye,
I walke to find a True-Love; And I see
That 't ys not a mere woman that is Shee,
But must or more, or lesse, than woman bee.   10

Yett knowe I not which flower
I wish: A Sixe, or Foure.
For should my True-Love lesse than woman bee,
Shee were scarce any thinge. And then, should shee
Bee more than woman, Shee would gett above   15
All thought of Sexe, and thincke to move
My Hart to study' her, not to Love.
Bothe these were Monsters. Since there must reside
Falshood in woman, I coulde more abide
She were by Art, than Nature falsifyed.   20

Live, Primerose, then, and thrive
With thy true Number, five.
And women, whom thys flower doth represent,
With thys Mysterious Number bee Content.
[129v]   Ten is the furthest Number; if halfe Ten   25
Belonge unto each woman, then
Each woman may take halfe us men.
Or if thys will not serve theyre turne, since All
Numbers are odde or eaven, and they fall
First into' thys Five, woemen may take Us All. /   30

The Relique.

When my Grave is broke up agayne,
Some second Guest to Intertayne
(For Graves have learnt that woman-head
To be to more than One a bed)
And hee that diggs it spyes   5
A Bracelett of bright haire about the bone,
Will not he lett 'us alone?
And thincke that there a Loving Couple lyes,
Who hop'd that thys Device might be a way
To make theyre Soules, at the last busy day,   10
Meete at thys Grave, and make a little stay.

If thys fall in a Time, or Land,
Where Misse-Devotion doth Command,
Hee that doth digge yt up will bring
Us to the Bishop, and the King,   15
    To make Us Reliques; then
You shalbe 'a Mary Magdalen, and I   [130r]
    A Something Else thereby.
All woemen shall adore Us, and some Men.
And since at such time, Miracles are sought,   20
I would have that Age, by thys Paper, taught
What Miracles wee harmelesse Lovers wrought.

First wee Lov'd well, and faythfully
Yett knew not what wee Lov'd, nor why;
Difference of Sexe, wee never knewe   25
More than our guardian Angells doe.
    Comming and goeing, wee
Perchance might kisse, but not betwixt those meales;
    Our handes ne'er toucht the Seales
Which Nature, injurd by Late Lawe, setts free.   30
These Miracles wee did. But now, alas,
All Measure and all Languadge I should passe,
Should I tell what a Miracle Shee was. /

The Dampe.

When I am dead, and Doctors know not why,
    And my frendes Curiositye
Will have me Cutt up, to survay each Part;
When they shall find your Picture in my Hart,
    You thincke a Sodayne Dampe of Love   5
    Will through all theyre Senses move,
    And worke on them, as mee, and so preferre   [130v]
Your Murder, to the name of Massacre.

Poore Victoryes. But if you dare be brave,
    And pleasure in your Conquest have,   10
First kill th' enormous Gyant, your Disdayne;
And lett th' Enchantresse, Honor, next be slayne;
    And like a Goth and Vandall rise,
    Deface Records and Historyes

Of your owne Arts and Tryumphs over men;　　15
And without such Advantage kill mee then.

For I could muster up, as well as you,
　My Gyants and my Witches too,
Which are Vast Constancy and Secrettnes;
But these I neyther Looke for, nor professe.　　20
　Kill mee as Woman; Lett me Dye
　As a meere Man. Doe you but trye
Your Passive Valor; and you shall find then,
Naked, you 'have Odds enough of any Man. /

An Epithalamion or Maryage Song, on the Lady Elisabeth, and Frederick Count Palatine, beeing maryed on Saint Valentines day.

1. Hayle, Bishop Valentine, whose Day thys is,
　　All the Ayre ys thy Diocese,
　　And all the chirping Queristers
And other Birdes, are thy Parishioners.
　　Thou maryest every yeare　　5
The Lyrique Larke, and the grave whisp'ring Dove,
The Sparrowe that neglects his lyfe for Love,
The household Bird with the redd stomacher.
　　Thou makst the blacke bird speed as soone
As doth the Goldfinche, or the Halcyone.　　10
The Husband Cocke Lookes out, and streight is sped,
And meetes hys wife, which bringes her feather bedd.
Thys day more cheerefully than ever shyne,
Thys Day, which might enflame thyselfe, Old Valentyne.

2. Tyll now, Thou warmst with multiplying Loves　　15
　　Two Larkes, two Sparrowes, or two Doves.
　　All that is Nothing unto thys,
For thou thys day couplest two Phenixes.
　　Thou mak'st a Taper see
What the Sunne never sawe. And what the Arke　　20
(Which was of fowles and beasts, the Cage and Parke)
Did not contayne, one bed contaynes through Thee,
　　Two Phenixes, whose joynëd brests
Are unto One Another mutuall Nests

[1311]

Where Motion kindles such fyres as shall give 25
Young Phenixes, and yett the Old shall live.
Whose Love and Corage never shall declyne, [131v]
But make the whole yeare through, thy day, O Valentine.

3. Up then, fayre Phenix Bride, frustrate the Sunne;
    Thyselfe from thyne affectiön 30
    Tak'st warmth enough. And from thyne Eye
All lesser birdes will take theyre Jollitye.
    Up, Up, Fayre Bride, and call
Thy Starrs from out theyre severall boxes. Take
Thy Rubyes, Pearles, and Dyamonds forth, and make 35
Thyselfe a Constellation of them All;
    And by theyre blazing signifye
That a Greate Princesse falls, but doth not Dye.
Bee Thou a new Starr that to Us portends
Ends of much wonder; And be Thou those Ends. 40
Since Thou dost thys day in new Glory shyne,
May All men date Records, from thys thy Valentyne.

4. Come forth, come forth; And as One glorious flame
    Meeting Another growes the same,
    So meete thy Fredericke; and so 45
To an unseperable Union growe.
    Since Separatiön
Falls not on such thinges as are infinite,
Nor thinges which are but One can disunite,
You 'are twice inseparable: Greate, and One. 50
    Goe then to where the Bishop stayes
    To make You One his way, which divers wayes [132r]
Must be effected. And when All is past,
And that you 'are One, by harts and hands made fast,
You two have One way Left, yourselves to' intwine, 55
Besides thys Bishops knott, or Bishop Valentine.

5. But Oh, what ayles the Sunne, that here he stayes
    Longer to-day than other Dayes?
    Stayes he new light, from these to gett?
And, finding here such store, is loth to sett? 60
    And why doe you two walke
So slowly pac'd in thys Processiön?
Is all your Care but to be Look'd upon,
And be to others, Spectacle and Talke?
    The Feast with glotonous delayes 65

Is eaten, and too Long theyre meate they prayse.
The Maskers come too Late and, I thincke, 'will stay,
Like Fayeries, till the Cocke crowe them awaye.
Alas, did not Antiquitye assigne
A Night, as well as Day, to Thee, O Valentine?   70

6. They did, and Night is come; And yett wee see
    Formalityes retarding Thee.
    What meane these Ladyes which, as though
They were to take a Clocke in peeces, goe
    So nicely' about the Bride?   75

[132v]   A Bride, before a Good Night could be sayd,
Should vanish from her Clothes, into her bed,
As soules from Bodyes steale, and are not spyed.
    But now Shee' ys layd; What though shee bee?
Yett there are more delayes, for where ys Hee?   80
He comes, and passes through Spheare after Spheare:
First her Sheetes, then her Armes, then Any where.
Lett not then thys Day, but thys Night bee thyne;
Thy Day was but thy Eve to thys, O Valentyne.

7. Here lyes a Shee Sunne, and a Hee Moone here.   85
    She gives the best Light to hys Spheare,
    Or Each is both And All; and So
They unto One Another, Nothing owe.
    And yett they doe, but are
So just and ritch in that Coyne which they pay,   90
That neyther would nor needes forbeare, nor stay.
Neyther [desires] to be spar'd, nor to spare;
    They quickly pay theyre debt, and then
Take no Acquittance[s], but pay agen.
They Pay, they Give, they Lend, and soe Lett fall   95
    No such occasion to be Liberall.
More Truith, more Corage in these two doe shyne
Than All thy Turtles have, and Sparrowes, Valentine.

8. And by thys Act of these two Phenixes,
    Nature agayne restorëd ys   100
[133r]   For since these two are two no more,
There 'ys but one Phenix still, as was before.
    Rest nowe at Last, and wee,
    As Satyrs watch the Sunnes Uprise, will stay,
Wayting when your Eyes, opened, let out day,   105
Only desir'd, because your face wee see.

Others nere you shall whispering speake,
And wagers Lay, at which side Day will breake,
And win by' Observing then, whose hand it is,
That opens first a Curtayne: Hers, or His.   110
Thys wilbe tryed to morrowe after Nine:
Tyll which houre wee thy Day enlardge, O Valentyne. /

Eclogue. 1613. December 26.

*Allophanes finding Idios in the Country thys Christmas,
reprehendes his Absence from the Court, at the Maryage of the
Earle of Sommersett; Idios gives [an] Account of his Purpose
therein, And of hys Absence there.*

Allophanes.
Unseasonable Man, Statue of Ice,
    What could to Countreys Solitude entice
Thee, in thys yeares cold and decrepitt time?
    Natures Instinct drawes to the warmer clime
Even small Birdes who, by that Courage, dare   5   [133v]
    In numerous fleetes sayle through theyre Sea, the Ayre.
What delicacy can in fields appeare
    Whylst Flora herselfe doth a frieze Jerkin weare;
Whylst windes doe all the Trees, and Hedges strip
    Of Leafes, to furnish rodds enough, to whip   10
Thy madnesse from Thee; And all Springs by frost
    Have taken Cold, and theyre sweete Murmure lost?
If Thou thy faltes, or Fortunes wouldst lament
    With Just Solemnitye, doe it in Lent.
At Court the Springe already' avancëd ys;   15
    The Sunne stayes longer up. And yett, not hys
The Glory is: farr other, other fyres.
    First, Zeale to Prince, and State; Then, Loves Desyres
Burne in One brest and, like Heav'ns two greate lights,
    The first doth governe dayes, the Other, Nights;   20
And then that earlye light, which did appeare
    Before the Sunne and Moone created were,
The Princes favor is diffus'd o'er All,
    From which all fortunes, Names, and Natures fall.
Then from those wombes of Starrs, the Brides bright Eyes,   25
    At every Glance, a Constellation flyes

And sowes the Court with Starrs, and doth prevent
    In Light and Power, the All-Ey'd firmament.
First her Eyes kindle other Ladyes Eyes;
[134r]   Then from theyre beames theyre Jewells Lustres rise.   30
And from theyre Jewells, Torches doe take fyre,
    And all ys warmth, and light, and Good Desire.
Most other Courts, Alas, are like to Hell,
    Where in darke Plotts, fire without Light doth dwell,
Or but like Stoves: For Lust, and Envy gett   35
    Continuall, but artificiall heate.
Here, Zeale and Love, grown One, All Cloudes disgest,
    And make One Court an Everlasting East.
And Canst Thou bee from Thence?

Idios.   No: I ame there.
    As Heavn, to men dispos'd, is ev'ry where,   40
So are those Courts whose Princes animate
    Not only all theyre house, but all theyre state.
Let no Man thincke because he 'ys full, he 'hath All,
    Kings (as theyre Patterne, God) are liberall
Not only' in fullnes, but Capacitee,   45
    Enlardging narrow men, to feele and see,
And comprehend the blessings they bestowe.
    So, reclus'd Hermites often Times doe knowe
More of heavens Glory than a Wor[l]dling can.
    As Man is, of the worlde, the Hart of Man   50
Is an Epitome of Gods greate booke
    Of Creatures, and Man neede no farther looke:
So ys the Country,' of Courts, where sweete Peace doth
[134v]   As theyre One Common soule, give Life to both.
I am not, then, from Court.

Allophanes.   Dreamer, Thou art.   55
    Thinckst thou, Fantastique, that thou hast a Part
In the East-Indian fleete, because thou hast
    A litle Spice or Amber in thy tast?
Because thou art not frozen, art Thou warme?
    Seest thou all Good, because thou seest no harme?   60
The Earth doth in her inward Bowells holde
    Stuffe well dispos'd; and which woulde fayne be Golde,
But never shall, except it chance to lye
    So upward that Heav'n gild yt with his Eye.

As for devine thinges, Fayth comes from above,   65
   So for best Civill Use, All Tinctures move
From higher Powers: From God Religion springs;
   Wisdome and Honor from the Use of Kinges.
Then Unbeguile Thyselfe; And know, with mee,
   That Angells, though on Earth employd they bee,   70
Are still in Heavn: So ys he still at home
   That doth abroad to honest actions come.
Chide thyselfe then, O foole, which yesterday
   Mightst have read more than all thy bookes bewray.
Hadst thou a Historee, which doth present   75
   A Court where all Affections doe assent
Unto the Kings? and that, that Kings are Just?   [135r]
   And where it is no Levitye to trust?
Where there is no Ambition, but to obaye?
   Where Men neede whisper nothing, and yett may?   80
Where the Kings favors are so plac'd, that All
   Finde that the King therein is liberall
To them, in Him, because hys favors bend
   To Vertue, to the which they all pretend?
Thou hast no Such: Yett here was thys, and more.   85
   An Earnest Lover, wise then and before,
Our Litle Cupid hath sued Lyverye,
   And is no more in hys Mynorytye.
He is admitted now into that brest,
   Where the Kings Counsayls, and hys Secretts rest.   90
What hast thou Lost, O Ignorant Man?

Idios.   I knew
   All thys, and only therefore I withdrewe.
To know and feele all thys, and not to have
   Wordes to expresse yt, makes a Man a Grave
Of hys owne Thoughts. I would not therefore stay   95
   At a Greate Feast, having no Grace to say;
And yett I scapt not here; for beeing come
   Full of the Common Joy, I utterd some.
Read then thys Nuptiall Song, which was not made
   Eyther the Court, or Mens harts to invade: 100
But since I 'am dead, and Buryed, I could frame   [135v]
   No Epitaph which might advance my fame
So much as thys Poore Songe, which testifyes
   I did unto that Day, some Sacrifice.

Epithalamion.

1. The Time of the Mariadge.

Thou art repriev'd, Old yeare; Thou shalt not Dye,   105
    Though thou upon thy death-bed lye,
    And shouldst within five dayes expire;
Yett thou art rescued by a Mightyer fire
    Than thy Olde Soule, the Sunne,
When he doth in this Largest Circle runne.   110
The Passage of the West or East would thawe
And open wide theyre easy liquid Jawe
To all our Ships, could a Promethean Art
Eyther unto the Northern Pole impart
The fyre of these inflaming Eys, or of thys Loving hart.   115

2. Equalitye of Persons.

But, Undiscerning Muse, which Hart, which Eyes
    In thys new Couple dost thou prize
    When hys Eye as Inflaming is
[136r]   As Hers, and her Hart loves as well as hys?
    Bee tryed by beauty,'and then   120
The Bridegroome is a Mayd, and not a Man.
If by that Manlye Courage they bee tryed
Which scornes unjust Opinion, then the Bride
Becomes a Man. Shoulde Chance or Envies Art
Devide these two, whom Nature scarce did part?   125
Since both have both th' Inflaming Eyes, and both the
    Loving Hart.

3. Raysing of the Bridegroome.

Though it bee some Divorce to thinck of you
    Singly, so much One are you two,
    Lett mee here contemplate Thee
First, cheerfull Bridegroome, and first lett mee see   130
    How thou preventst the Sunne,
And hys red foming horses dost outrunne.
How having Layd downe in thy Soveraignes brest

All Businesses, from thence to reinvest
Them when these Tryumphs cease, thou forward art   135
To showe to her, who doth the like impart
The fyre of thy inflaming Eyes, and of thy Loving Hart.

4. *Raysing of the Bride.*

But now, to Thee, Fayre Bride, it is some wronge
    To thincke Thou wert in Bed so Long,
        Since soone Thou lyest downe first, 't is fitt   140
Thou, in first rising, shouldst allowe for ytt.
        Powder thy radyant hayre   [136v]
Which, if without such Ashes thou wouldst weare,
Thou which, to all which come to Looke upon,
Art ment for Phoebus, wouldst bee Phaëthon.   145
For our Ease, give thyne Eyes th' Unusuall part
Of Joy, a Teare: So, quench'd, thou mayst impart
To Us, that come, thy' inflaming Eyes, to him, thy
        Loving Hart.

5. *Her Apparrelling.*

Thus Thou descend'st to our Infirmitee,
    Who can the Sunne in water see: 150
        So dost thou, when in Silke and Golde
Thou cloudst thyselfe; Since wee which doe beholde
        Are dust, and wormes, 't is Just
Our Objects bee the fruites of wormes, and Dust.
Lett every Jewell bee a glorious Starr,   155
Yett Starrs are not so pure as theyre Spheares are.
And though Thou stoope to' appeare to Us in Part,
Still, in that Picture thou intirelye art,
Which thy inflaming Eyes have made within hys loving hart.

6. *Going to the Chappell.*

Now from your Easts you yssue forth, and wee,   160
    As men which through a Cypres see

The rising Sunne, doe thincke it two,
So, as you goe to church, doe thincke of you.
    But that Vayle beeing gone
By the Church rites, you are from thence forth One.   165
The Church Tryumphant made thys match before;
And now the Militant doth strive noe more.
Then, Reverend Priest, who Gods Recorder art,
Do, from his Dictates, to these two impart
All Blessings which are Seene, or thought, by Angells
    Eye or Hart.   170

[137r]

7. *The Benediction.*

Blest payre of Swanns; Oh may you interbringe
    Daily new Joyes, and never singe.
    Live, tyll all Groundes of Wishes fayle,
Tyll honor, yea, till Wisedome growe so stale
    That, new greate heights to trye,   175
It must serve your Ambitiön to dye.
Rayse Heires; And may here, to the worlds End live,
Heires for thys King, to take thankes; you, to give.
Nature and Grace doe All; and Nothing, Art.
May never Age or Error overthwart   180
With any West these radyant Eyes, with any North,
    thys Hart.

8. *Feasts and Revells.*

But you are Overblest: Plenty, thys Day
    Injures; It causes Tyme to stay.
    The Tables grone, as though thys Feast
Would, as the Flood, destroy all Fowle, and Beast.   185
    And were the Doctrine newe,
That the Earth movd, this Day would make yt true.
For every Part to dance and revell goes;
They tred the Ayre and fall not where they rose;
Though Sixe houres since, the Sunne to bed did part,   190
The Masks and banquetts will not yett Impart
A Sunsett to these weary Eyes, a Center to thys Hart.

[137v]

9. *The Brides Goeinge to Bed.*

What meanst Thou, Bride, thys Company to keepe?
  To sitt up tyll thou fayne wouldst sleepe?
  Thou mayst not, when Thou 'art layd, doe soe.   195
Thyselfe must to him, a new banquett growe;
  And you must entertayne,
And doe all thys Dayes dances o'er againe.
Know that if Sunne and Moone togeather doe
Rise in One Pointe, they doe not sett so too.   200
Therefore thou mayst, fayre Bride, to bed depart.
Thou art not gone, being gone; where e'er thou art;
Thou leavst in hym thy watchfull Eyes, in him thy
  loving Hart.

10. *The Bride Groomes Comming.*

As he that sees a Starr fall, runns apace,
  And findes a Gelly in the Place,   205
  So doth the Bride Groome haste as much,
Being told thys Starr is falne, and findes her such.
  And as frindes may Looke strange
By a newe fashion, or Apparrells change,
Theyre Soules though Long acquainted, they had beene, 210
These Clothes, theyre bodyes never yett had seene.
Therfore at first, She modestly might start,   [138r]
But must fort[h]with surrender every Part
As freely' as Each to Each before, gave eyther Eye or Hart.

11. *The Good Night.*

Now, as in Tullias Tombe, one Lampe burnt cleare,   215
  Unchang'd for fiveteene hundred yeare,
  May these Love-Lampes wee here enshrine,
In warmth, light, lasting, equall the Divine.
  Fyre ever doth aspire
And makes all like ytselfe, turnes all to fyre,   220
But ends in Ashes, which these cannot doe;
For none of them is Fuell, but fyre too.

Thys is Joyes Bonfire then, where Loves strong Arts
Make of so noble Individuall Parts
One fyre of foure Inflaming Eyes, and of two loving Harts. /   225

Idios.   As I have brought thys Song, that I may doe
                  A perfect sacrifice, Ile burne ytt too.

Allophanes.   No, Sir, Thys Paper I have justlye gott,
                  For in burnt Incense, the Perfume is not
                  Hys only that presents yt, but of All.   230
                  Whatever celebrates thys Festivall
                  Is Common, since the Joy thereof is soe.
                  Nor may Yourselfe be Priest; But lett mee goe
[138v]   Back to the Court, and I will Lay yt 'upon
                  Such Altars, as prize your Devotiön. /   235

Obsequies to the Lord Harrington, Brother to the Countesse of Bedford.

Fayre Soule, which was[t] not only,' as all Soules bee
Then, when thou wast infusëd, Harmonie,
But didst continue so, and now dost beare
A Part, in Gods greate Organ, thys whole Spheare:
If, Looking up to God or downe to us,   5
Thou find that any way is pervious
Twixt Heavn and Earth, and that Mans Actions doe
Come to your knowledge and Affections too,
See, and with Joy, Mee, to that good Degree
Of Goodnesse grown, that I can study Thee;   10
And by those Meditatiöns refind,
Can unaparrell and Enlardge my Mind,
And so can Make, by thys soft Extasye,
Thys Place a Map of Heavn, myselfe of Thee.
Thou seest mee here at Midnight. Now all rest,   15
Times dead-lowe water, when all minds divest
To morrowes busines; when the Laborers have
Such rest in bed that theyre Last Churchyard Grave
(Subject to Change) will scarce be a Type of thys.
Now, when the Clyent, whose Last hearing is   20
To morrowe, sleepes; when the Condemnëd Man
[139r] (Who when he opes hys Eyes, must shutt them then
Agayne, by Death) although sad watch he keepe,

Doth Practize Dyinge by a litle Sleepe,
Thou, at thys Midnight seest mee; and as soone   25
As that Sunne rises to Mee, Midnights noone;
All the world growes transparent, and I see
Through All, both Church and State, in seeing Thee.
And I discerne, by favor of thys Light,
My Selfe, the hardest Object of the sight.   30
God is the Glasse; As thou, when thou dost see
Him who sees all, seest all concerning Thee,
So yett unglorifyed, I comprehend
All, in these Mirrors of thy wayes and End.
Though God be truly' our Glasse, through which wee see   35
All, since the beeing of all thinges is Hee,
Yett are the Trunckes which doe to us derive
Thinges, in Proportion fitt, by Perspective,
Deedes of Good men, for by theyre living here,
Virtues indeed remote, seeme to be nere.   40
But where can I affirme, or where Arrest
My Thoughts on hys Deedes? Which shall I call Best?
For fluid Vertue cannot bee Looked on,
Nor can endure a Contemplatiön.
As Bodies change, and as I doe not weare   45
Those Spiritts, Humors, Blood, I did Last yeare;
And, as if on a Streame, I fixe myne Eye,
That dropp which I Look'd on is presently
Pusht with more waters from my sight, and gone.
So in thys Sea of Vertues, Can no One   50
Be' insisted on; Vertues as Rivers passe,   [139v]
Yett still remaynes that Vertuous Man there was.
And, as if Man feed on Mans flesh, and so
Part of hys body to an other owe,
Yett at the Last, two perfect bodyes rise,   55
Because God knowes where everye Atome lyes:
So if One knowledge were made of all those
Who knewe hys Minute[s] well, he might dispose
Hys Vertues into Names and Ranckes; but I
Should Injure Nature, Vertue,' and Destinee   60
Should I devide, and discontinue soe,
Vertue, which did in One entirenes growe.
For, as he that would say Spiritts are framd
Of all the Purest parts that can be namd,
Honors not Spiritts halfe so much as Hee   65
Which says they have no Parts, but simple bee:

So is't of Vertue; for a Pointe and One
Are much intirer than a Millione.
And had Fate ment to have hys Vertues told,
It would have lett him Live, to have bin old.   70
So then, that Vertue' in Season, and then thys
Wee might have seene, and sayd, that now he is
Witty, now wise, now temperate, now just;
In Good short lives Vertues are faine to thrust,
And, to be sure, betymes to gett a Place,   75
When they woulde [exercise], Lacke Time and Space.
So was it in thys Person; forc'd to bee,
For Lacke of Time, hys owne Epitomee;
So to exhibitt in fewe yeares as much
As all the Long-breath'd Chronicles can touch.   80

[140r]   As when an Angell down from Heav'n doth flye,
Our quicke thought cannot keepe him Companye,
Wee cannott thincke, nowe he is at the Sunne,
Now through the Moone, nowe he through th' Ayre doth
     runne;
Yett, when he' is come, wee know, he did repayre   85
To All twixt Heavn, and Earth, Sunne, Moone, and Ayre,
And, as thys Angell, in an instant knowes.
And yett wee knowe thys sodayne knowledge growes
By quicke amassing severall formes of thinges,
Which he successively to Order brings,   90
When they, whose slowe-pac'd Lame thoughts cannot goe
So fast as hee, thincke that he doth not soe:
Just as a Perfect reader doth not dwell
On ev'ry Sillable, nor stay to spell,
Yett, without doubt, he doth distinctlye see   95
And lay togeather every A and B:
So in short liv'd Good men 'is nott understood
Each severall Vertue, but the Compound, Good.
For they all Vertues Paths in that pace tread
As angells goe and knowe, and as men, read.   100
Ô why should then these men, these Lumps of Balme
Sent hither thys worlds tempests to becalme,
Before by Deedes they are diffus'd and spredd,
And so make us Alive, themselves be dead?
Ô Soule, Ô Circle, why soe quicklye be   105
Thy Ends, thy Birth, and Death clos'd up in Thee?
Since One Foote of thy Compas still was plac'd
In Heav'n, the' other might securely have pac'd

In the most Large Extent, through ev'ry path
Which the whole world, or Man, th' Abridgment hath?   110
Thou knewst, that though the Tropique Circles have   [140v]
(Yea, and those small Ones, which the Poles engrave)
All the same roundnes, Evennes, and All
The Endlessnes of the' Equinoctiall:
Yett, when wee come to measure distancys,   115
How here, how there, the Sunne affected ys,
When he doth faintly worke, and when prevayle,
Only great Circles then can be our scale.
So though thy Circle to Thy Selfe expresse
All, tending to [thy] Endles happines,   120
And wee, by our Good use of that, may trye
Both how to live well yonge, and how to dye:
Yett since wee must bee Olde, and Age endures
Hys Torrid Zone at Court, and Calentures
Of hott Ambitions, Irreligions Ice,   125
Zeales Agues, and Hydroptique Avarice,
Infirmityes which neede the Scale of Truith
As well as Lust, and Ignorance of youth:
Why didst thou not, for those, give Medicines too,
And by thy doeing, tell Us what to doe?   130
Though as small pockett Clocks, whose ev'ry wheele
Doth each Mismotion and distemper feele,
Whose hand getts shaking Palsyes, and whose stringe,
Hys Synewes, Slackens; And whose Soule, the Springe,
Expires or Languishes; whose Pulse the Flye   135
Eyther beates not or beates unevenly;
Whose Voice, the Bell, doth ratle or growe dumbe,
Or Idle, 'as men which to theyre Last houres come:
If theyse Clocks be not wound, or be wound still,
Or be not sett, or sett at ev'ry will,   140
So youth is Easyest to Destructiön,
Yf then wee follow all, or followe none:
Yett as in Greate Clocks which in Steeples chyme,   [144r]
Plac'd to informe whole townes, to' employ theyre Tyme,
An Error doth more harme, beeing Generall;   145
When small clockes falts, onely' on the wearer fall:
So worke the faltes of Age, on which the Eye
Of Children, Servants, or the State relye.
Why wouldst not Thou then, which hadst such a Soule,
A Clocke so true as might the Sunne controule,   150
And daily hadst from him who gave it Thee

Instructions, such as yt could never bee
Disorderd, Stay here, as a Generall
And Greate Sun-Dyall, to have sett us All?
O why wouldst Thou bee any Instrument 155
To thys Unnaturall Course, or why consent
To thys not Miracle, but Prodigee,
That where the Ebbs, longer than flowings bee,
Vertue, whose flood [did with thy youth begin,
Should so much faster ebb out, than flow in? 160
Though her flood] were blowen in by thy first breath,
All ys at once suncke in the Whirlpoole, Death,
Which word I would not name, but that I see
Death, Else a Desert, is a Court by Thee.
Now I grow sure, that if a Man would have 165
Good Companee, hys Entry is a Grave.
Methinckes all Cityes now but Anthills bee
Where, when the severall Laborers I see
For Children, House, Provision, taking Payne,
They 'are all but Ants carying Eggs, Strawe, and Graine; 170
And Churchyards are our Cityes, unto which
The Most repayre that are in Goodnes riche.
There is the best Concourse and Confluence;
There are the holy Suburbs, and from thence
[144v] Begins Gods City, new Jerusalem, 175
Which doth extend her utmost Gates to them.
At that Gate then, Tryumphant Soule, dost Thou
Begin thy Tryumph. But, since Lawes allowe
That at the Tryumph day, the People may
All that they will, gaynst the Tryumpher say, 180
Lett mee here use that freedome, and Expresse
My Griefe, though not to make thy Tryumphe lesse.
By Law, to Tryumphs none admitted bee,
Till they as Magistrates gott Victoree;
Though then to thy force, all youths foes did yielde, 185
Yett till fitt tyme had brought Thee to that fielde
To which thy Rancke in thys State destin'd Thee,
That there thy Counsayle might gett Victoree,
And so in that Capacitye remove
All Jelosyes, twixt Prince, and Subjects Love, 190
Thou couldst no Title to thys Tryumph have:
Thou didst intrude on Death, usurpdst a Grave.
Then (though victoriously) thou' hadst fought as yett
But with thyne owne Affections, with the heate

Of youths desires and Colds of Ignorance,   195
But tyll thou shouldst succesfully advance
Thyne Armes gaynst forayne Enimyes, which are
Both Envy 'and Acclamations populare
(For both these Engines equallye defeate,
Though by a diverse Mine, those which are greate)   200
Tyll then, thy Warr was butt a Civill Warr,
For which to Tryumphes, none admitted are;
No more are they who, though with Good Successe   [145r]
In a defensive Warr theyre Power expresse:
Before Men Tryumphe, the Dominiöne   205
Must be enlarged, and not preserv'd alone.
Why shouldst Thou then, whose Battayles were to win
Thyselfe from those strayts Nature put Thee in,
And to deliver up to God that State
Of which he gave thee the Vicariate   210
(Which is thy Soule and Body) as intire
As he, who takes Endevors, doth require,
But didst not stay t' enlardge hys kingdome too,
By making Others, what thou didst, to doe?
Why shouldst Thou Tryumphe now, when Heavn no more   215
Hath gott, by getting Thee, than 't had before?
For Heavn and Thou, even when thou livedst here,
Of One Another in Possession were.
But thys from Tryumphe most disables Thee
That that Place which is conquerëd must bee   220
Left safe from present Warr and likelye doubt
Of imminent Commotions to breake out.
And hath he left Us so? Or can it bee
Hys Territorye was noe more but Hee?
No, wee were all hys Charge; The Diocese   225
Of ev'ry 'Exemplar Man, the whole worlde ys.
And he was joynëd in Commissiöne
With Tutelar Angells, sent to ev'ry One.
But though thys freedome to upbrayd and chyde
Him who Tryumphd, were lawfull, yt was tyde   230
With thys, that yt might never reference have
Unto the Senate, who thys Tryumph gave.
Men might at Pompey jest, but they might not   [145v]
At that Autoritye, by which he gott
Leave to tryumph, before by Age he might.   235
So though, Tryumphant Soule, I dare to write,
Movd with a reverentiall Anger thus,

That Thou so early wouldst abandon us;
Yett am I farr from daring to dispute
With that greate Soverayntye whose absolute   240
Prerogative hath thus dispens'd for Thee
Gainst Natures lawes, which just impugners bee,
Of Earlye Tryumphs. And I, though with paine,
Lessen our Losse, to magnifye thy gayne
Of Tryumph, when I say, it was more fitt   245
That all men should Lacke Thee, than thou Lack ytt.
Though then, in our Time, be not sufferëd
That testimonye' of Love unto the dead
To dye with them, and in theyre Graves be hid,
As Saxon wives and french Soldurii did;   250
And though in no Degree I can expresse
Greife, in Greate Alexanders greate Excesse,
Who, at hys frendes death, made whole townes devest
Theyre Walls and Bullwarkes which became them best;
Doe not, Fayre Soule, thys Sacrifice refuse,   255
That in thy Grave, I doe enterr my Muse:
Who by my Greife, Greate as thy worth, beeing Cast
Behind hand, yett hath spoke, and spoke her Last. /

FROM THE WESTMORELAND MANUSCRIPT, RELIGIOUS LYRICS, 1607–1620

Holy Sonnets.

1.

Thou hast made me, and shall thy worke decay?
   Repaire me now, for now myne end doth hast.
   I run to death, and death meets me as fast,
And all my pleasures are like yesterday.
I dare not move my dimme eyes any way.   5
   Dispaire behind, and death before doth cast
   Such terror, and my febled fleshe doth wast
By sin in it, which towards hell doth weigh.
Only thou art above; and when towards thee
   By thy leave I can looke, I rise agayne.   10
But our old subtile foe so tempteth mee,
   That not one hower I can my selfe sustayne.
Thy grace may winge me to prevent his art;
And thou like Adamant, draw myne Iron hart. /

2.

As due by many titles I resigne
   My selfe to thee (o God) first I was made
   By thee and for thee 'and when I was decayde
Thy blood bought that, the which before was thyne.
I ame thy sonne made with thy selfe to shyne;   5
   Thy servant, whose paines thou hast still repayde;
   Thy sheepe, thyne Image; and (till I betrayde
My selfe) a Temple of thy Spirit divine.
Why doth the devill then usurpe in mee?
   Why doth he steale, nay ravish that's thy right?   10
Except thou rise, and for thyne owne worke fight,
   O I shall soone dispayre, when I do see
That thou lovs't Mankind well, yet wilt not choose mee,
And Satan hates me yet is loth to loose mee. /

3.

O might those sighes and teares returne againe
   Into my brest and eyes, which I have spent,
   That I might in this holy discontent
Mourne with some fruite, as I have mournd in vaine.
In my Idolatry what showrs of raine   5
   Myne eyes did wast? what griefes my hart did rent:
   That sufferance was my sin, now I repent;
Because I did suffer,' I must suffer paine.
Th' Hydroptique dronkerd, and night-scowting theefe,
   The itchy Lecher, and selfe-tickling proud,   10
Have the remembrance 'of past joyes, for reliefe
   Of comming ills; to poore me is allowd
No ease; for long yet vehement griefe hath beene
The' effect and cause, the punishment and sinne. /

4.

Father, part of his double interest
   Unto thy kingdome thy Sonne gives to mee;
   His joynture in the knotty trinitee
He keepes, and gives me his deaths conquest.
This lambe whose death with life the world hath blest   5
   Was from the worlds beginning slayne, and hee
   Hath made two Wills, which with the legacee
Of his, 'and thy kingdome, doth thy sonnes invest.
Yet such are thy laws, that men argue yett
   Whether a man those statutes can fulfill.   10
None doth; but all-healing grace and spiritt
   Revive and quicken what law and letter kill.
Thy lawes abridgment, and thy last command
Is all but love; Oh let that last Will stand. /

[69]

5.

Oh my black soule, now thou art summonèd
   By sicknes, Deaths Herald and Champion:
   Thou 'art a Pilgrim, which abroad had don
Treason, and durst not turne to whence he 'is fled.

Or as a thiefe which till deaths doome be read 5
   Wisheth himselfe deliverd from prison
   But damn'd and haled to executiön
Wisheth that still he might be 'imprisonëd.
Yet grace, if thou repent thou canst not lacke.
   But who shall give thee that grace to begin? 10
Oh make thy selfe with holy mourning blacke,
   And red with blushinge as thou art with sin.
Or washe thee in Christs blood, which hath this might
That beeing red, it dyes red soules to whight. /

6.

This is my Playes last scene, here heavens appoint
   My Pilgrimages last mile, and my race
   Idely, yet quickly run, hath this last pace
My spanns last inche, my minutes last pointe.
And gluttonous death will instantly unjoynt 5
   My body 'and soule, and I shall sleepe a space,
   Or presently, I know not, see that face
Whose feare allredy shakes my every joynt.
Then as my soule, to' heaven her first seat takes flight
   And earthborn body in the earth shall dwell; 10
So fall my sins, that all may have their right,
   To where they 'are bred, and would press me, to hell;
Impute me rightëous thus purgd of evill,
For thus I leave the world, the fleshe, and devill. /

7. [70]

I ame a litle world, made cunningly
   Of Elements and an Angelique spright,
   But blacke sin hath betrayd to endles night
My worlds both parts, and oh both parts must dy.
You, which beyond that heaven, which was most high 5
   Have found new sphears, and of new lands can wright
   Poure new seas in myne eyes, that so I might
Drowne my world, with my weeping ernestly.
Or washe it: if it must be drown'd no more.
   But oh it must be burn'd; alas the fyer 10

Of lust and envy 'have burnt it hertofore
  And made it fouler; let theyr flames retyre,
And burne me O God with a fiery zeale
Of thee, 'and thy house, which doth in eating heale. /

8.

At the round Earths imagind corners blow
  Your trumpets Angels, and Arise, Arise
  From Death you numberles infinities
Of Soules and to your scattered bodyes go.
All whom the flood did and fyre shall o'erthrow   5
  All whom warr, dearth, age, agues, tyrannyes,
  Dispayre, law, chance, hath slayne, and you whose eyes
Shal behold God, and never tast deaths wo.
But let them sleep, Lord, and me mourne a space,
  For if above all these my sins abound   10
'T is late to aske abundance of thy grace
  When we are there: Here on this lowly ground
Teach me how to repent, for that's as good
As 'if thou hadst seald my pardon with thy blood. /

9.

[71]

If poysonous Minerals, and if that tree
  Whose fruite threw death on els immortall us,
  If lecherous gotes, if serpents envious
Cannot be damn'd, alas why should I bee?
Why should intent, or reason, born in me   5
  Make sins els equall, in me more hainous?
  And mercy beeing easy, 'and glorious
To God in his sterne wrath, why threatens hee?
But who am I that dare dispute with thee
  O God? O of thyne only worthy blood   10
  And my teares make a heavenly Lethean flood
And drowne in it, my sins blacke memoree.
  That thou remember them, some clayme as debt
  I thinke it mercy if thou wilt forgett. /

10.

If faythfull soules be alike glorified
   As Angels, then my fathers soule doth see
   And ads this even to full felicitee
That valiantly I hels wide mouth o'erstride.
But if our minds to these soules be descride   5
   By circumstances, and by signes that bee
   Apparant in us, not immediatelee
How shall my minds whight trouthe to them be tride?
They see Idolatrous lovers weepe and mourne
   And vile blasphemous conjurers to call   10
   On Jesus' name, and pharasaicall
Dissemblers feigne devotiön. Then turne
   O pensive soule to God, for he knowes best
   Thy true griefe, for he put it in my brest. /

11.

Death be not proud, though some have called thee
   Mighty 'and dreadfull, for thou art not so.
   For those whom thou thinkst thou dost overthrow
Dy not, poore death, nor yet canst thou kill mee.
From rest and sleepe which but thy pictures bee   5
   Much pleasure; then from thee much more must flow,
   And soonest our best men with thee do go,
Rest of ther bones, and soules deliveree.
Thou 'art slave to Fate, chance, kings, and desperat men,
   And dost with poyson, warr, and sicknesse dwell;   10
   And Poppy' or charmes can make us sleepe as well,
And easier than thy stroke, why swellst thou then?
   One short sleep past, we live eternally
   And Death shalbe no more, Death thou shallt dy. /

12.

Wilt thou love God, as he, thee? then digest
   My soule, this holsome meditatiön:

How God the Spirit, by Angels wayted on
In heaven, doth make his temple in thy brest.
The father' having begott a Sonne most blest,   5
    And still begetting; (for he nere begonne)
    Hath daign'd to chuse thee by adoptiön
Coheir to' his glory 'and Saboths endles rest.
And as a robbd man, which by search doth find
    His stolne stuffe sold, must lose or buy 'it againe;   10
    The Sonne of glory came downe and was slaine
Us, whom he 'had made, and Satan stole, to' unbind.
    'T was much that man was made like God before,
    But that God should be made like man, much more. /

[73]

13.

Spitt in my face ye Jewes, and pierce my side;
    Buffet, and scoffe, scourge, and crucify mee:
For I have sin'd, and sin'd: and humbly hee
    Which could do no iniquity hath dyde.
But by my death cannot be satisfyde   5
    My sins, which passe the Jewes impietee.
They killd once an inglorious, but I
    Crucify him dayly, beeing now glorifyde.
Oh let me then his strange love still admyre:
    Kings pardon, but he bore our punishment.   10
And Jacob came clothd in vile harsh attyre
    But to supplant and with gainfull intent:
God cloth'd himself in vile mans flesh, that so
He might be weake inough to suffer wo. /

14.

Why ame I by all creatures wayted on?
    Why do the prodigall elements supply
    Life and foode to mee, beeing more pure then I,
Simple, and farther from corruptiön?
Why brookst thou, ignorant horse, subjectiön?   5
    Why dost thou Bull, and boar, so selily
    Dissemble weaknes, 'and by one mans stroke dy

Whose whole kind you might swallow and feed upon?
Alas I' ame weaker, wo 'is me, and worse than you,
   You have not sin'd, nor neede be timorous.   10
   But wonder at a greater wonder; for to 'us
Created nature doth these things subdue,
   But their Creator, whom sin nor nature tyed,
   For us, his creatures and his foes, hath dyed. /

15. [74]

What yf this present were the worlds laste night?
   Looke in my Hart, O Soule, where thou dost dwell,
   The picture of Christ crucifyde and tell
Whether that countenance can thee affright?
Teares in his eyes quench the amazing light;   5
   Blood fills his frowns which from his pierc'd head fell.
   And can that tongue adjudge thee unto hell
Which prayed forgivenes for his foes ranck spight?
   No, No; but as in myne idolatree
   I sayd to all my prophane mistressis   10
   Bewty of pity, foulnes only is
A sign of rigor; so I say to thee
   To wicked sprights are horrid shapes assignd,
   This bewteous forme assures a piteous mind. /

16.

Batter my hart, three-person'd God, for you
   As yet but knock, breathe, shine, and seeke to mend;
   That I may rise, and stand, o'erthrow me; 'and bend
Your force to breake, blow, burne, and make me new.
I like an usurp'd towne to' another due   5
   Labor to' admit you, but oh to no end.
   Reason your viceroy in' me, me should defend,
But is captiv'd and proves weake or untrew.
Yet dearly' I love you, and would be loved faine:
   But ame betroth'd unto your enemy: 10
Divorce me, unty or breake that knott agayne,
   Take me to you, emprison me, for I

Except you enthrall me never shalbe free,
Nor ever chast except you ravishe mee. /

17.

Since she whom I lovd, hath payd her last debt
   To nature, and to' hers, and my good is dead
   And her soule early' into heaven ravishëd,
Wholy in heavenly things my mind is sett.
Here the admyring her my mind did whett   5
   To seeke thee, God; so streames do shew the head,
   But though I 'have found thee; 'and thou my thirst
       hath fed,
A holy thirsty dropsy melts mee yett.
But why should I begg more love, when as thou
   Dost wooe my soule, for hers offring all thine,   10
And dost not only feare lest I allow
   My love to saints and Angels, things divine,
But in thy tender jealosy dost doubt
Lest the world, fleshe, yea Devill putt thee out. /

18.

Show me deare Christ, thy spouse, so bright and cleare.
   What, is it she, which on the other shore
   Goes richly painted? or which robb'd and tore
Laments and mournes in Germany and here?
Sleeps she a thousand, then peepes up one yeare?   5
   Is she selfe truth 'and errs? now new, now outwore?
   Doth she, and did shee, and shall she evermore
On one, on seaven, or on no hill appeare?
Dwells she with us, or like adventuring knights
   First travaile we to seeke, and then make love?   10
Betray kind husband thy spouse to our sights,
   And let myne amorous soule court thy mild Dove,
Who is most trew, and pleasing to thee, then
When she 's embrac'd and open to most men. /

19.

Oh, to vex me, contraryes meete in one:
   Inconstancy unnat'rally hath begott
   A constant habit; that when I would not
I change in vowes, and in devotiöne.
As humorous is my contritiöne   5
   As my prophane love, and as soone forgott:
   As ridlingly distemperd, cold and hott,
As praying, as mute; as infinite, as none.
I durst not view heaven yesterday, 'and to day
   In prayers, and flatter'ing speeches I court God: 10
   To morrow I quake with true feare of his rod.
So my devout fitts come and go away
   Like a fantastique Ague: save that here
Those are my best dayes, when I shake with feare. /

DEVOTIONS
VPON
Emergent Occasions, and se-
uerall steps in my Sicknes.

Digested into

1. MEDITATIONS *vpon our Hu-*
mane Condition.

2. EXPOSTVLATIONS, *and De-*
batements with God.

3. PRAYERS, *vpon the seuerall Oc-*
casions, to him.

By IOHN DONNE, Deane of
S. Pauls, London.

LONDON,
Printed by *A. M.* for THOMAS
IONES. 1 6 2 4.

10. Title-page of *Devotions upon Emergent Occasions*, 1st edn, 1624.
Bodleian Library, STC 7033, sig. A1.

DEVOTIONS

UPON

Emergent Occasions, and severall steps in my Sicknes:

Digested into

1. MEDITATIONS *upon our Humane Condition.*
2. EXPOSTULATIONS, *and Debatements with God.*
3. PRAYERS, *upon the severall Occasions, to him.*

By JOHN DONNE, Deane of S[aint] *Pauls*, London.

LONDON,
Printed by A[ugustin] M[atthewes] for THOMAS JONES.
1624.

TO THE
MOST EXCELLENT
Prince, Prince
CHARLES.

Most Excellent Prince,

[A2v] *I have had three* Births; *One,* Naturall, *when I came into the* World; *One,* Supernatural, *when I entred into the* Ministery; *and now, a* preter-naturall Birth, *in returning to* Life, *from this* Sicknes. *In my* second Birth, *your* Highnesse Royall Father *vouchsafed mee his Hand, not onely to sustaine mee*

[A3r] in it, *but to lead mee* to it. *In this* last Birth, *I my selfe am born a* Father: *This* Child *of mine, this* Booke, *comes into the world,* from *mee, and* with *mee. And therefore, I presume (as I did the* Father *to the* Father*) to present the* Sonne *to the*

[A3v] Sonne; *This* Image *of my* Humiliation, *to the lively* Image *of his* Majesty, *your* Highnesse. *It might bee enough, that* God *hath seene my* Devotions: *But* Examples *of* Good Kings *are* Commandements; *And* Hezekiah *writt the* Meditations *of his* Sickness, *after his* Sicknesse. *Besides, as I have liv'd to see,*

[A4r] *(not as a* Witnesse *onely, but as a* Partaker*) the happiness of a part of your* Royal Fathers *time, so shall I live,* (in my way) *to see the happinesses of the times of your* Highnesse *too, if this* Child *of mine, inanimated by your gracious*

[A4v] *Acceptation, may so long preserve alive the* Memory *of*

Your Highnesse
Humblest and Devotedst
JOHN DONNE.

7 Socios *sibi jungier instat;*

8 *Et* Rex *ipse suum mittit;*

9 Medicamina scribunt;

10 Lentè *et Serpenti satagunt occurrere Morbo.*

11 *Nobilibusque trahunt, a cincto corde, venenum,*   [A5v]
   Succis, et Gemmis; *et quae Generosa, ministrant*
   Ars, et Natura, *instillant;*

12 *Spirante* Columbâ, *Suppositâ pedibus, revocantur*
   ad ima vapores;

13 *Atque* Malum Genium, *numeroso* stigmate, *fassus,*
   Pellitur ad pectus, Morbique Suburbia, Morbus:

14 *Idque notant* Criticis, *Medici, evenisse* diebus.

15 *Interea* insomnes *Noctes ego duco, Diesque*:

16 *Et properare* meum, *clamant, e turre propinqua*
   Obstreperae Campanae, aliorum *in funere, funus.*

17 *Nunc* lento sonitu *dicunt,*
   Morieris; 18 *At inde,*
   Mortuus *es, sonitu* celeri,   [A6r]
   pulsusque agitato.

19 Oceano *tandem emenso,*
   aspicienda resurgit
   Terra; *vident, justis,* Medici,
    iam cocta *mederi*
   Se posse, indiciis; 20 Id agunt;

21 *Atque annuit* Ille,
   Qui per eos *clamat, linquas*
    iam Lazare *lectum;*

22 *Sit* Morbi Fomes *tibi*
   Cura; 23 Metusque Relabi.

Errata.   [A6v]

Pag. 40. pro 2. 3. Meditat.

Pag. 43. ult. pasture, posture.

Pag. 96. lin, penult. flesh, God,

Pag. 152. in marg. Buxdor.

Pag. 173. lin. 13. add, hast.

Pag. 184. in marg. Augustin.

Pag. 185. lin. 17. blow, flow.

DEVOTIONS.

1. Insultus Morbi Primus;
The first alteration, The first grudging of the sicknesse.

1. Meditation.

Variable, and therfore miserable condition of Man; this minute
[2] I was well, and am ill, this minute. I am surpriz'd with a sodaine change, and alteration to worse, and can impute it to no cause, nor call it by any name. We study *Health,* and we deliberate upon our *meats,* and *drink,* and *Ayre,* and *exercises,* and we hew, and wee polish every stone, that goes to that building; and so our *Health* is a long and a regular work; But in a minute a Cannon batters all,
[3] overthrowes all, demolishes all; a *Sicknes* unprevented for all our diligence, unsuspected for all our curiositie; nay, undeserved, if we consider only *disorder,* summons us, seizes us, possesses us, destroyes us in an instant. O miserable condition of Man, which was not imprinted by *God;* who as hee is *immortall* himselfe, had put a *coale,* a *beame* of *Immortalitie* into us, which we might have blowen into a *flame,* but blew it out, by our first sinne; wee beggard
[4] our selves by hearkning after false riches, and infatuated our selves by hearkning after false knowledge. So that now, we doe not onely die, but die upon the Rack, die by the torment of sicknesse; nor that onely, but are pre-afflicted, super-afflicted with these jealousies and suspitions, and apprehensions of *Sicknes,* before we can cal it a sicknes; we are not sure we are ill; one hand askes the other by the
[5] pulse, and our eye askes our own urine, how we do. O multiplied misery! we die, and cannot enjoy death, because wee die in this torment of sicknes; we are tormented with sicknes, and cannot stay till the torment come, but pre-apprehensions and presages, prophesy those torments, which induce that *death* before either come; and our *dissolution* is conceived in these *first changes, quickned* in the *sicknes* it selfe, and *born* in *death,* which beares date from
[6] these first changes. Is this the honour which Man hath, by being a *litle world,* That he hath these *earthquakes* in him selfe, sodaine shakings; these *lightnings,* sodaine flashes; these *thunders,* sodaine noises; these *Eclypses,* sodain obfuscations, and darknings of his

senses; these *blazing stars*, sodaine fiery exhalations; these *rivers of blood*, sodaine red waters? Is he a *world* to himselfe onely therefore, that he hath inough in himself, not only to destroy, and to execute [7] himselfe, but to presage that execution upon himselfe; to assist the sicknes, to antedate the sicknes, to make the sicknes the more irremediable, by sad apprehensions, and as if he would make a fire the more vehement, by sprinkling water upon the coales, so to wrap a hote fever in cold Melancholy, lest the fever alone shold not destroy fast enough, without this contribution, nor perfect the work (which is *destruction*), except we joynd an artificiall sicknes, of [8] our owne *melancholy*, to our natural, our unnaturall fever. O perplex'd discomposition, O ridling distemper, O miserable condition of Man.

1. Expostulation.

If I were but meere *dust and ashes*, I might speak unto the *Lord*, for the *Lordes* hand made me of this *dust*, and the *Lords* hand shall recollect these *ashes;* the *Lords* hand was the wheele, upon which [9] this vessell of clay was framed, and the *Lordes* hand is the *Urne*, in which these *ashes* shall be preserv'd. I am the *dust*, and the *ashes* of the *Temple* of the *Holy Ghost;* and what Marble is so precious? But I am more than *dust and ashes;* I am my best part, I am my *soule*. And being so, the *breath* of God, I may breathe back these pious *expostulations* to my *God. My God, my God*, why is not my *soule*, as [10] sensible as my *body?* Why hath not my *soule* these apprehensions, these presages, these changes, those antedates, those jealousies, those suspitions of a *sinne*, as well as my body of a *sicknes?* why is there not alwayes a *pulse* in my *Soule*, to beat at the approch of a tentation to sinne? why are there not alwayes *waters* in mine eyes, to testifie my spiritual sicknes? I stand in the way of tentations, (naturally, necessarily, all men doe so: for there is a *Snake in every* [11] *path*, tentations in every vocation) but I go, I run, I flie into the wayes of tentation, which I might shun; nay, I breake into houses, wher the plague is; I press into places of tentation, and tempt the *devill* himselfe, and solicite and importune them, who had rather be left unsolicited by me. I fall sick of *Sin*, and am bedded and bedrid, buried and putrified in the practise of *Sin*, and all this [12] while have no presage, no pulse, no sense of my *sicknesse;* O heighth, O depth of misery, where the first *Symptome* of the sicknes is Hell, and where I never see the fever of lust, of envy, of ambition, by any other light, than the darknesse and horror of *Hell* it selfe;

and where the first Messenger that speaks to me doth not say, *Thou*
[13] *mayst die,* no, nor *Thou must die,* but *Thou art dead:* and where the
first notice, that my *Soule* hath of her sicknes, is *irrecoverablenes,*
irremediablenes: but, O *my God, Job did not charge thee foolishly,* in
his temporall afflictions, nor may I in my spirituall. Thou hast
imprinted a *pulse* in our *Soule,* but we do not examine it; a voice in
our conscience, but wee doe not hearken unto it. We talk it out, we
jest it out, we drinke it out, we sleepe it out; and when we wake, we
Gen. 28.16 [14] doe not say with *Jacob, Surely the Lord is in this place, and I knew it*
not: but though we might know it, we do not, we wil not. But will
God pretend to make a *Watch,* and leave out the *springe?* to make so
many various wheels in the faculties of the Soule, and in the organs
of the body, and leave out *Grace,* that should move them? or wil
God make a *springe,* and not *wind* it up? Infuse his first *grace,* and
[15] not second it with more, without which, we can no more use his
first *grace,* when we have it, than wee could dispose our selves by
Nature, to have it? But alas, that is not our case; we are all *prodigall*
sonnes, and *not disinherited;* wee have received our portion, and
misspent it, not bin denied it. We are *Gods tenants* heere, and yet
here, he, our *Land-lord* payes us *Rents;* not yearely, nor quarterly,
but hourely, and quarterly; *Every minute he renewes his mercy,* but
Mat. 13.15 [16] wee *will not understand, lest that we should be converted, and he*
should heale us.

1. Prayer.

O eternall, and most gracious *God,* who considered in thy selfe, art
a *Circle,* first and last, and altogether; but considered in thy working
upon us, art a *direct line,* and leadest us from our *beginning,* through
[17] all our wayes, to our *end,* enable me by thy *grace,* to looke forward
to mine end, and to looke backward too, to the considerations of
thy mercies afforded mee from the beginning; that so by that
practise of considering thy mercy, in my beginning in this world,
when thou plantedst me in the *Christian Church,* and thy mercy in
the beginning in the other world, when thou writest me in the
[18] *Booke of life,* in my *Election,* I may come to a holy consideration of
thy *mercy,* in the beginning of all my actions here: That in all the
beginnings, in all the accesses, and approches of spirituall
2. Kings 4.40 sicknesses of *Sinn,* I may heare and hearken to that voice, *O thou*
Man of God, there is death in the pot, and so refraine from that,
Prov. 13.17 which I was so hungerly, so greedily flying to. *A faithfull Ambassador*

is health, says thy wise servant *Solomon.* Thy voice received, in the beginning of a sicknesse, of a sinne, is true health. If I can see that [19] light betimes, and heare that voyce early, *Then shall my light breake forth as the morning, and my health shall spring foorth speedily.* Isa. 58.8 Deliver me therefore, O my God, from these vaine imaginations; that it is an overcurious thing, a dangerous thing, to come to that tendernesse, that rawnesse, that scrupulousnesse, to feare every *concupiscence,* every offer of *Sin,* that this suspicious, and jealous [20] diligence will turn to an inordinate dejection of spirit, and a diffidence in thy care and providence; but keep me still establish'd, both in a constant assurance, that thou wilt speake to me at the beginning of every such sicknes, at the approach of every such *Sinne;* and that, if I take knowledg of that voice then, and flye to thee, thou wilt preserve mee from falling, or raise me againe, when by naturall infirmitie I am fallen: doe this, *O Lord,* for his sake, [21] who knowes our naturall infirmities, for he had them; and knowes the weight of our sinns, for he paid a deare price for them, *Thy Sonne, our Saviour, Christ Jesus, Amen.*   Gen. 3.19

2. Actio Laesa.

The strength, and the function of the Senses, and other faculties change and faile.

2. Meditation.

The *Heavens* are not the less constant, because they move [22] continually, because they move continually one and the same way. The *Earth* is not the more constant, because it lyes stil continually, because continually it changes, and melts in al the parts thereof. *Man,* who is the noblest part of the *Earth,* melts so away, as if he were a *statue,* not of *Earth,* but of *Snowe.* We see his owne *Envie* melts him, hee growes leane with that; he will say, anothers *beautie* [23] melts him; but he feeles that a *Fever* doth not melt him like *snow,* but pour him out like lead, like yron, like brasse melted in a furnace: It doth not only *melt* him, but *Calcine* him, reduce him to *Atomes,* and to *ashes;* not to *water,* but to *lime.* And how quickly? Sooner than thou canst receive an answer, sooner than thou canst

[24] conceive the question; *Earth* is the *center* of my *body, Heaven* is the *center* of my *Soule;* these two are the naturall places of those two; but those goe not to these two, in an equall place; My *body* falls downe without pushing, my *Soule* does not go up without pulling: *Ascension* is my *Soules* pace and measure, but *precipitation* my *bodyes:* And, even *Angells* whose home is *Heaven,* and who are winged too, yet had a *Ladder* to goe to *Heaven,* by steps. The *Sunne*

[25] who goes so many miles in a minut, The *Starres* of the *Firmament,* which go so very many more, goe not so fast, as my *body* to the *earth.* In the same instant that I feele the first attempt of the disease, I feele the victory; In the twinckling of an eye, I can scarce see; instantly the tast is insipid, and fatuous; instantly the appetite is dull and desirelesse; instantly the knees are sinking and

[26] strengthlesse; and in an instant, sleepe, which is the picture, the copy of death, is taken away, that the *Originall, Death* it selfe may succeed, and that so I might have death to the life. It was part of *Adams* punishment, *In the sweat of thy browes thou shalt eate thy bread:* it is multiplied to me, I have earned bread in the sweat of my browes, in the labor of my calling, and I have it; and I sweat againe, and againe, from the brow, to the sole of the foot, but I eat no

[27] bread, I tast no sustenance: Miserable distribution of *Mankind,* where one halfe lacks meat, and the other stomacke.

2. *Expostulation.*

1 Sam. 24.15   *David* professes himself a *dead dog,* to his *king Saul,* and so doth
2 Sam. 9.8   *Mephibosheth* to his king *David:* and yet *David* speaks to *Saul,* and *Mephibosheth* to *David.* No man is so little, in respect of the greatest man, as the greatest in respect of *God;* for here, in that, wee have

[28] not so much as a *measure* to try it by; *proportion* is no measure for *infinitie.* He that hath no more of this world but a grave, hee that hath his grave but lent him, til a better man, or another man, must bee buried in the same *grave,* he that hath no *grave,* but a *dung-hill,* hee that hath no more *earth,* but that which he carries, but that which hee is, hee that hath not that *earth,* which hee is, but even in

[29] that, is anothers salve, hath as much proportion to *God,* as if all *Davids Worthies,* and all the *worlds Monarchs,* and all *imaginations Gyants* were kneaded and incorporated into one, and as though that one were the survivor of all the sonnes of men, to whom *God* had given the world. And therefore how little soever I bee, as *God calls things that are not, as though they were,* I, who am as though I were not, may call upon *God,* and say, *My God, my God,* why

comes thine anger so fast upon me? Why dost thou melt me, scatter [30]
me, poure me like water upon the ground so instantly? Thou
staidst for the first world, in *Noahs* time 120 yeres; thou staidst for
a rebellious generation in the wildernesse 40 yeares, wilt thou stay
no minute for me? Wilt thou make thy *Processe,* and thy *Decree,* thy
Citation, and thy *Judgement* but one act? Thy *Summons,* thy *Battell,* [31]
thy *Victorie,* thy *Triumph,* all but one act; and lead me captive, nay
deliver me captive to death, as soon as thou declarest mee to be
enemy, and so cut me off even with the drawing of thy sword out of
the scabberd, and for that question, *How long was he sicke?* leave no
other answere, but that the hand of death pressed upon him from
the first minute? *My God, my God,* thou wast not wont to come in
Whirlwinds, but in soft and gentle ayre. Thy first breath breathed a [32]
Soule into mee, and shall thy breath blow it out? Thy breath in the
Congregation, thy *Word* in the *Church,* breathes *communion,* and
consolation here, and *consummation* heereafter; shall thy breath in
this Chamber breathe *dissolution,* and *destruction, divorce,* and
separation? Surely it is not thou; it is not thy hand. The devouring
sword, the consuming fire, the winds from the wildernes, the [33]
diseases of the body, all that afflicted *Job,* were from the hand of
Satan; it is not thou. It is thou, Thou *my God,* who hast led mee so
continually with thy hand, from the hand of my Nurce, as that I
know, thou wilt not correct mee, but with thine own hand. My
parents would not give mee over to a *Servants* correction, nor my
God, to *Satans.* I am *fallen into the handes of God* with *David,* and 2 Sam. 24.14
with *David* I see that his *Mercies are great.* For by that mercy, I [34]
consider in my present state, not the haste, and the dispatch of the
disease, in dissolving this body, so much, as the much more hast,
and dispatch, which my *God* shal use, in recollecting, and reuniting
this *dust* againe at the *Resurrection.* Then I shall heare his *Angels*
proclaime the *Surgite Mortui, Rise yee dead.* Though I be dead, I
shall heare the voice; the sounding of the voice, and the working of [35]
the voice shall be all one; and all shall rise there in a lesse *Minute,*
than any one dies here.

2. *Prayer.*

O most gracious *God,* who pursuest and perfitest thine own purposes,
and dost not only remember mee by the first accesses of this sicknes,
that I must die, but informe me by this further proceeding therin,
that I may die now, who hast not only waked mee with the first, but [36]
calld me up, by casting me further downe, and clothd me with thy

selfe, by stripping me of my selfe, and by dulling my bodily senses, to the meats, and eases of this world, hast whet, and sharpned my spirituall senses, to the apprehension of thee; by what steps and degrees soever it shal please thee to go, in the dissolution of this body, [37] hasten *O Lord* that pace, and multiply *O my God* those degrees, in the Psal. 34.8 exaltation of my *Soule,* toward thee now, and to thee then. My tast is not gone away, but gone up to sit at *Davids* table, *To tast, and see, that the Lord is good:* My stomach is not gone, but gone up, so far upwards toward the *Supper of the Lamb,* with thy *Saints* in *heaven,* as to the *Table,* to the *Communion* of thy *Saints* heere in *earth:* my knees are weak, but weak therfore that I should easily fall to, and fix my selfe Prov. 14.30 [38] long upon my devotions to thee. *A sound heart is the life of the flesh;* and a heart visited by thee, and directed to thee, by that visitation is a Psal. 38.3 sound hart. *There is no soundnesse in my flesh, because of thine anger.* Interpret thine own worke, and call this sicknes, correction, and not Ibid. anger, and there is soundnes in my flesh. *There is no rest in my bones,* [39] *because of my sinne;* transferre my sinnes, with which thou art so displeased, upon him, with whom thou art so well pleased, *Christ Jesus,* and there will be rest in my bones: And, *O my God,* who madest thy selfe a *Light* in a *Bush,* in the middest of these *brambles,* and *thornes* of a sharpe sicknesse, appeare unto me so, that I may see thee, and know thee to be my *God,* applying thy self to me, even in these [40] sharp, and thorny passages. Doe this, *O Lord,* for his sake, who was not the lesse the *King of Heaven,* for thy suffering him to be *crowned* with *thornes,* in this world.

3. Decubitus sequitur tandem.
The Patient takes his bed.

3. Meditation.

Wee attribute but one priviledge, and advantage to Mans body, above other moving creatures, that he is not as others, groveling, [41] but of an erect, of an upright form, naturally built, and disposed to the contemplation of *Heaven.* Indeed it is a thankfull forme, and recompences that *soule,* which gives it, with carrying that *soule* so many foot higher, towards *heaven.* Other creatures look to the *earth;* and even that is no unfit object, no unfit contemplation [42] for *Man;* for thither hee must come; but because *Man* is not to stay there, as other creatures are, *Man* in his naturall forme, is carried to the contemplation of that place, which is his *home, Heaven.* This is *Mans* prerogative; but what state hath he in this *dignitie?* A fever can fillip him downe, a fever can depose him; a fever can bring that head, which yesterday caried a *crown* of gold, five foot towards a *crown* of glory, as low as his own foot, today. When *God* came to breathe into *Man* the breath of life, he found [43] him flat upon the ground; when hee comes to withdraw that breath from him againe, hee prepares him to it, by laying him flat upon his bed. Scarse any prison so close, that affords not the prisoner two, or three steps. The *Anchorites* that barqu'd themselves up in hollowe trees, and immur'd themselves in hollow walls; That perverse man, that barrell'd himselfe in a Tubb, all could stand, or sit, and enjoy some change of posture. A sicke bed, [44] is a grave; and all that the patient saies there, is but a varying of his owne *Epitaph.* Every nights bed is a *Type* of the *grave:* At night wee tell our servants at what houre wee will rise; here we cannot tell our selves, at what day, what week, what moneth. Here the head lies as low as the foot; the *Head* of the people, as lowe as they, whom those feet trod upon; And that hande that signed Pardons is too weake to begge his owne, if hee might have it for lifting up [45] that hand: Strange fetters to the feete, strange Manacles to the hands, when the feete, and hands are bound so much the faster, by how much the cords are slacker; So much the lesse able to doe their Offices, by how much more the Sinewes and Ligaments are the looser. In the *Grave* I may speak through the stones, in the [46] voice of my friends, and in the accents of those wordes, which their love may afford my memory; Here I am mine owne *Ghost,* and rather affright my beholders, than instruct them; they conceive the worst of me now, and yet feare worse; they give me for dead now, and yet wonder how I doe, when they wake at [47] midnight, and aske how I doe, to morrow. Miserable, and, (though common to all) inhuman *posture,* where I must practise my lying in the *grave,* by lying still, and not practise my *Resurrection,* by rising any more.

3. *Expostulation*

My God, and *my Jesus, my Lord,* and *my Christ, my Strength,* and *my Salvation,* I heare thee, and I hearken to thee, when thou rebukest thy *Disciples,* for rebuking them, who brought children to [48] Mat. 19.14 thee; *Suffer little children to come to mee,* saiest thou. Is there a verier

Jer. 1.6 child than I am now? I cannot say with thy servant *Jeremy, Lord, I am a child, and cannot speake;* but, *O Lord,* I am a sucking childe, and cannot eat, a creeping childe, and cannot goe; how shall I come to thee? Whither shall I come to thee? To this bed? I have this
[49] weake, and childish frowardnes too, I cannot sit up, and yet am loth to go to bed; shall I find thee in bed? Oh, have I alwaies done so? The bed is not ordinarily thy *Scene,* thy *Climate: Lord,* dost thou not accuse me, dost thou not reproach to mee my former sinns, when thou layest mee upon this bed? Is not this to hang a man at his owne dore, to lay him sicke in his owne bed of wantonnesse?
Amos 6.4 When thou chidest us by thy *Prophet* for lying in *beds of Ivory,* is
[50] not thine anger vented; not till thou changest our *bedds of Ivory,*
Psal. 132.3 into beds of *Ebony? David* sweares unto thee, *that hee will not goe up into his bed, till he had built thee a House.* To go up into the bed,
Rev. 2.22 denotes strength, and promises ease; but when thou saiest, *That thou wilt cast Jezebel into a bed,* thou mak'st thine own comment upon that, Thou callest the bed *Tribulation,* great *Tribulation:* How
[51] shal they come to thee, whom thou hast nayled to their bed? Thou
Mat. 8.6 art in the *Congregation,* and I in a solitude: when the *Centurions*
Mar. 2.3 servant lay sicke at home, his *Master* was faine to come to *Christ;* the sicke man could not. Their friend lay sicke of the *Palsey,* and
Mat. 8.14 the four charitable men were faine to bring him to *Christ;* he could not come. *Peters* wifes mother lay sicke of a fever, and *Christ* came to her; shee could not come to him. My friends may carrie mee
[52] home to thee, in their prayers in the *Congregation;* Thou must come home to me in the visitation of thy *Spirit,* and in the seale of thy *Sacrament:* But when I am cast into this bedd, my slacke
Psal. 26.8 sinewes are yron fetters, and those thin sheets, yron dores upon me; And, *Lord, I have loved the habitation of thy house, and the place*
Psal. 84.4 *where thine honour dwelleth;* I lye here, and say, *Blessed are they, that*
Psal. 5.8 [53] *dwell in thy house;* but I cannot say, *I will come into thy house;* I may
Psal. 69.9 say, *In thy feare will I worship towards thy holy Temple,* but I cannot say in thy holy *Temple;* And, *Lord, the zeale of thy House, eats me up,* as fast as my fever; It is not a *Recusancie,* for I would come, but it is an *Excommunication,* I must not. But *Lord,* thou art *Lord of Hosts,*
Psal. 6.5 and lovest *Action;* Why callest thou me from my calling? *In the grave no man shall praise thee;* In the doore of the grave, this sicke
[54] bed, no Man shal heare mee praise thee: Thou hast not opened my lips, that my mouth might shew *thee* thy praise, but that my mouth might shew *foorth* thy praise. But thine *Apostles* feare takes hold of
1 Cor. 9.27 mee, *that when I have preached to others, I my selfe should be a cast-away;* and therefore am I *cast downe,* that I might not be *cast away;*
2 Kin. 2.11 Thou couldst take mee by the head, as thou didst *Habakkuk,* and

carrie mee so; By a *Chariot*, as thou didst *Elijah*, and carrie me so; [55]
but thou carriest me thine own private way, the way by which thou
carryedst thy *Sonne*, who first lay upon the *earth*, and praid, and
then had his *Exaltation*, as himselfe calls his *Crucifying*, and first
descended into hell, and then had his *Ascension*. There is another
Station (indeed neither are *stations* but *prostrations*) lower than this
bed; To morrow I may be laid one Story lower, upon the *Floore*, the
face of the earth, and next day another Story, in the *grave*, the [56]
wombe of the Earth: As yet God suspends mee betweene *Heaven*
and *Earth*, as a *Meteor;* and I am not in Heaven, because an earthly
bodie clogges me, and I am not in the Earth, because a heavenly
Soule sustaines mee. And it is thine owne Law, O God, that *if a* Exod. 21.18, 19
man bee smitten so by another, as that hee keepe his bed, though he dye
not, hee that hurt him, must take care of his healing, and recompence [57]
him. Thy hand strikes mee into this bed; and therefore if I rise
againe, thou wilt bee my recompence, all the dayes of my life, in
making the memory of this sicknes beneficiall to me; and if my
body fall yet lower, thou wilt take my *soule* out of this bath, and
present it to thy Father, washed againe, and againe, and again, in
thine own *teares*, in thine owne *sweat*, in thine owne *blood*.

3. Prayer [58]

O most mightie and most merciful *God*, who though thou have
taken me off my feet, hast not taken me off of my foundation,
which is *thy selfe*, who though thou have removed me from that
upright forme, in which I could stand, and see thy throne, the
Heavens, yet hast not removed from mee that light, by which I can [59]
lie and see thy selfe, who, though thou have weakened my bodily
knees, that they cannot bow to thee, hast yet left mee the knees of
my heart, which are bowed unto thee evermore; As thou hast made
this *bed*, thine *Altar*, make me thy *Sacrifice;* and as thou makest thy
Sonne Christ Jesus the *Priest*, so make me his *Deacon*, to minister to
him in a chereful surrender of my body and soule to thy pleasure,
by his hands. I come unto thee, *O God, my God*, I come unto thee, [60]
(so as I can come, I come to thee, by imbracing thy comming to
me) I come in the confidence, and in the application of thy servant Psal. 41.3
Davids promise, *That thou wilt make all my bed in my sicknesse; All*
my bedd; That which way soever I turne, I may turne to thee; And
as I feele thy hand upon all my body, so I may find it upon all my
bedde, and see all my *corrections*, and all my *refreshings* to flow from [61]
one and the same, and all, from thy hand. As thou hast made these

feathers, thornes, in the sharpnes of this sicknes, so, *Lord,* make these *thornes, feathers* againe, *feathers* of thy *Dove,* in the peace of Conscience, and in a holy recourse to thine *Arke,* to the Instruments of true comfort, in thy Institutions, and in the Ordinances of thy *Church.* Forget my bed, *O Lord,* as it hath beene a bedde of sloth,

[62] and worse than sloth; Take mee not, *O Lord,* at this advantage, to terrifie my soule, with saying, now I have met thee there, where thou hast so often departed from me; but having burnt up that bed, by these vehement heates, and washed that bed in these

Psal. 4.4 abundant sweats, make my bed againe, *O Lord,* and enable me

[63] according to thy command, *to commune with mine owne heart upon my bed, and be still.* To provide a bed for all my former sinnes, whilest I lie upon this bed, and a grave for my sins, before I come to my grave; and when I have deposed them in the wounds of thy Sonn, to rest in that assurance, that my Conscience is discharged from further *anxietie,* and my soule from farther *danger,* and my Memory from further *calumny.* Doe this, *O Lord,* for his sake, who

[64] did, and suffered so much, that thou mightest, as well in thy Justice, as in thy Mercy, doe it for me, thy *Sonne,* our *Saviour,* *Christ Jesus.*

4. Medicusque vocatur.
The Phisician is sent for.

4. *Meditation.*

It is too little to call *Man* a *little World;* Except *God,* Man is a *diminutive* to nothing. Man consistes of more pieces, more parts,

[65] than the world; than the world doth, nay than the world is. And if those pieces were extended, and stretched out in Man, as they are in the world, Man would bee the *Gyant,* and the world the *Dwarfe,* the world but the *Map,* and the man the *World.* If all the *Veines* in our bodies, were extended to *Rivers,* and all the *Sinewes,* to *vaines*

[66] *of Mines,* and all the *Muscles,* that lye upon one another, to *Hilles,* and all the *Bones* to *Quarries* of stones, and all the other pieces, to the proportion of those which correspond to them in the *world,* the *aire* would be too litle for this *Orbe* of Man to move in, the firmament would bee but enough for this *star;* for, as the whole world hath nothing, to which something in man doth not answere,

so hath man many pieces, of which the whole world hath no
representation. Inlarge this Meditation upon this *great world,*   [67]
Man, so farr, as to consider the immensity of the creatures this
world produces; our *creatures* are our *thoughts; creatures* that are
born *Gyants:* that reach from *East* to *West,* from *earth* to *Heaven,*
that doe not onely bestride all the *Sea,* and *Land,* but span the
Sunn and *Firmament* at once; My thoughts reach all, comprehend
all. Inexplicable mistery; I their *Creator* am in a close prison, in a   [68]
sicke bed, any where, and any one of my *Creatures,* my *thoughts,* is
with the *Sunne,* and beyond the *Sunne,* overtakes the *Sunne,* and
overgoes the *Sunne* in one pace, one steppe, every where. And then
as the other *world* produces *Serpents,* and *Vipers,* malignant, and
venimous creatures, and *Wormes,* and *Caterpillars,* that endeavour
to devoure that world which produces them, and *Monsters*
compiled and complicated of divers parents, and kinds, so this   [69]
world, our selves, produces all these in us, in producing *diseases,*
and *sicknesses,* of all those sorts; venimous, and infectious diseases,
feeding and consuming diseases, and manifold, and entangled
diseases, made up of many several ones. And can the other world
name so many *venimous,* so many consuming, so many monstrous
creatures, as we can diseases, of all these kindes? O miserable
abundance, O beggarly riches! how much doe wee lacke of having   [70]
remedies for everie disease, when as yet we have not *names* for them?
But wee have a *Hercules* against these *Gyants,* these *Monsters;* that
is, the *Phisician;* hee musters up al the forces of the other world, to
succour this; all Nature, to relieve Man. We *have* the Phisician, but
we *are not* the Phisician. Heere we shrinke in our proportion, sink   [71]
in our dignitie, in respect of verie meane creatures, who are
Phisicians to themselves. The *Hart* that is pursued and wounded,
they say, knowes an Herbe, which being eaten, throwes off the
arrow; A strange kind of *vomit.* The *dog* that pursues it, though hee
bee subject to sicknes, even *proverbially,* knowes his *grasse* that
recovers him. And it may be true, that the *Drugger* is as neere to
Man, as to other *creatures,* it may be that obvious and present
Simples, easie to bee had, would cure him; but the *Apothecary* is   [72]
not so neere him, nor the *Phisician* so neere him, as they two are to
other creatures; Man hath not that *innate instinct,* to apply those
naturall medicines to his present danger, as those inferiour
creatures have; he is not his owne *Apothecary,* his owne *Phisician,*
as they are. Call back therefore thy Meditations again, and bring it
downe; whats become of mans great extent and proportion, when   [73]
himselfe shrinkes himselfe, and consumes himselfe to a handfull
of dust; whats become of his soaring thoughts, his compassing

thoughts, when himselfe brings himselfe to the ignorance, to the thoughtlesnesse of the *Grave?* His *diseases* are his owne, but the *Phisician* is not; hee hath them at home, but hee must send for the Phisician.

[74]   *4. Expostulation*

Job 13.3 I have not the *righteousnesse* of *Job*, but I have the desire of *Job*, *I would speake to the Almighty, and I would reason with God.* My *God, my God,* how soone wouldest thou have me goe to the *Phisician,* and how far wouldest thou have me go with the *Phisician?*

[75] I know thou hast made the *Matter,* and the *Man,* and the *Art,* and I goe not from *thee* when I go to the *Phisician.* Thou didst not make *clothes* before ther was a shame of the nakednes of the body; but thou didst make *Phisick* before there was any grudging of any *sicknes;* for thou didst imprint a *medicinall vertue* in many *Simples,* even from the beginning; didst thou meane that we should be *sicke,* when thou didst so? when thou madest them? No more than thou

[76] didst meane, that we should *sinne,* when thou madest us: thou fore-
Ezek. 47.12 sawest both, but *causedst* neither. Thou, *Lord,* promisest heere trees, *whose fruit shall bee for meat, and their leaves for Medicine.* It
Joh. 5.6, 7 is the voyce of thy Sonn, *Wilt thou bee made whole?* That drawes from the patient a confession that hee was ill, and could not make
Jer. 8.22 himself wel. And it is thine owne voyce, *Is there no Phisician?* That
[77] inclines us, disposes us to accept thine *Ordinance.* And it is the
Ecclus. 38.4 voyce of the Wise man, both for the *matter, phisicke* it selfe, *The Lorde hath created Medicines out of the Earth, and hee that is wise, shall not abhorre them,* And for the *Arte,* and the *Person, The Phisician cutteth off a long disease.* In all these voyces, thou sendest
Ecclus. 38.15 us to those helpes, which thou hast afforded us in that. But wilt not
[78] thou avowe that voyce too, *Hee that hath sinned against his Maker, let him fall into the hands of the Phisician;* and wilt not thou affoord me an understanding of those wordes? Thou who sendest us for a blessing to the *Phisician,* doest not make it a curse to us, to go, when thou sendest. Is not the curse rather in this, that onely hee falls into the hands of the *Phisician,* that casts himself wholy,
[79] intirely upon the *Phisician,* confides in him, relies upon him, attends all from him, and neglects that *spirituall phisicke,* which thou also hast instituted in thy *Church:* so *to fall into the hands of*
2 Chro. 16.12 *the Phisician,* is a *sinne,* and a *punishment* of former sinnes; so, as *Asa fell,* who in his disease, *sought not to the Lord, but to the Phisician.* Reveale therefore to me thy *method, O Lord,* and see, whether I

have followed it; that thou mayest have glory, if I have, and I,
pardon, if I have not, and helpe that I may. Thy *Method* is, *In time*   [80] Ecclus. 38.9
of thy sicknesse, be not negligent: Wherein wilt thou have my
diligence expressed? *Pray unto the Lord, and hee will make thee*
whole. O Lord, I doe; I pray, and pray thy Servaunt *Davids* prayer,   Psal. 6.2
Have mercy upon mee, O Lord, for I am weake; Heale mee, O Lord,
for my bones are vexed: I knowe, that even my weaknesse is a reason,
a motive, to induce thy mercie, and my sicknes an occasion of thy   [81]
sending health. When art thou so readie, when is it so seasonable
to thee, to commiserate, as in miserie? But is Prayer for health in   Ecclus. 38.10
season, as soone as I am sicke? Thy *Method* goes further; *Leave off*
from sinne, and order thy handes aright, and cleanse thy heart from all
wickednesse; Have I, O *Lord,* done so? O *Lord,* I have; by thy grace,
I am come to a holy detestation of my former sin; Is there any
more? In thy *Method* there is more; *Give a sweet savor, and a*   [82] ver. 11
memoriall of fine flower, and make a fat offering, as not being. And,
Lord, by thy grace, I have done that, sacrificed a little, of that litle
which thou lentst me, to them, for whom thou lentst it: and now in
thy *method,* and by thy steps, I am come to that, *Then give place to*   ver. 12
the Phisician, for the Lord hath created him, let him not goe from thee,
for thou hast need of him, I send for the *Phisician,* but I will heare   [83] Act. 9.34
him enter with those words of *Peter, Jesus Christ maketh thee whole;*   Luk. 5.17
I long for his presence, but I look, *that the power of the Lord, should*
bee present to heale mee.

4. *Prayer*

O most mightie, and most merciful *God,* who art so the *God* of
health, and strength, as that without thee, all health is but the fuell,
and all strength, but the bellows of sinne; Behold mee under the   [84]
vehemence of two diseases, and under the necessity of two
Phisicians authorized by thee, the *bodily,* and the *spiritual Phisician.*
I come to both, as to thine *Ordinance,* and blesse, and glorifie thy
Name, that in both cases, thou hast afforded help to Man by the
Ministery of man. Even in the new *Jerusalem,* in *Heaven* it selfe, it   Rev. 22.2
hath pleased thee to discover a *Tree,* which *is a Tree of life there, but*   [85]
the leaves thereof are for the healing of the Nations; Life it selfe is
with thee there, for thou art *life;* and all kinds of *Health,* wrought
upon us here, by thine *Instruments,* descend from thence. *Thou*   Jer. 51.9
wouldest have healed Babylon, *but she is not healed;* Take from mee,
O *Lord,* her perversenesse, her wilfulnesse, her refractarinesse,
and heare thy *Spirit* saying in my *Soule,* Heale mee, O *Lord,* for I   Hos. 5.13

[86] would bee healed. *Ephraim saw his sicknesse, and Judah his wound; then went Ephraim to the Assyrian, and sent to King Jareb, yet could not hee heale you, nor cure you of your wound.* Keepe me back O *Lord,* from them who mis-professe artes of healing the *Soule,* or of the *Body,* by meanes not imprinted by thee in the *Church,* for the *soule,* or not in *nature* for the *body;* There is no *spirituall health* to [87] be had by *superstition,* nor *bodily* by *witchcraft;* thou *Lord,* and Isa. 53.5 onely thou art *Lord* of both. Thou in thy selfe art *Lord* of both, and thou in thy *Son* art the *Phisician,* the *applyer* of both. *With his stripes wee are healed,* says the *Prophet* there; there, *before* hee was scourged, wee were healed with his stripes; how much more shall I bee healed now, now, when that which he hath already suffred actually, is actually, and effectually applied to me? Is there any [88] thing incurable, upon which that *Balme* dropps? Any veine so 2 Chro. 7.14 emptie, as that that *blood* cannot fil it? Thou promisest to *heale the* Ezek. 47.11 *earth;* but it is when the inhabitants of the earth *pray that thou wouldest heale it.* Thou promisest to heale their *Waters,* but *their miry places, and standing waters,* thou sayest there, *Thou wilt not heale:* My returning to any sinne, if I should return to the abilitie [89] of sinning over all my sins againe, thou wouldest not pardon. Heale this *earth,* O my *God,* by repentant tears, and heale these *waters,* these teares, from all bitternes, from all diffidence, from all Mat. 4.23 dejection, by establishing my irremovable assurance in thee. *Thy Sonn went about healing all manner of sickenesses.* (No disease Luk. 6.19 incurable, none difficult; he healed them *in passing.*) *Vertue went* Joh. 7.23 *out of him, and he healed all,* all the multitude (no person incurable) [90] he healed them *every whit,* (as himselfe speaks) he left no relikes of the disease; and will this universall *Phisician* passe by this *Hospitall,* 2 King. 20.5 and not visit me? not heale me wholy? *Lord,* I looke not that thou shouldest say by thy Messenger to mee, as to *Hezekiah, Behold, I* Num. 12.14 *will heale thee, and on the third day thou shalt goe up to the house of the Lord.* I looke not that thou shouldst say to me, as to *Moses* in [91] *Miriams* behalfe, when *Moses* would have had her heald presently, *If her father had but spit in her face, should she not have been ashamed seven dayes? Let her be shut up seven daies, and then returne;* but if thou be pleased to multiply seven dayes, (and seven is infinite) by the number of my *sinnes,* (and that is more infinite) if this day must remove me, till *dayes shall bee no more,* seale to me my spirituall [92] health in affording me the *Seales* of thy *Church,* and for my temporall health, prosper thine *ordinance,* in their hands who shall assist in this sicknes, in that manner, and in that measure, as may most glorifie thee, and most edifie those, who observe the issues of thy servants, to their owne spirituall benefit.

5. Solus adest.
The Phisician comes.

5. Meditation.

As Sicknesse is the greatest misery, so the greatest misery of sicknes [93]
is *solitude;* when the infectiousnes of the disease deterrs them who
should assist, from comming; Even the *Phisician* dares scarse
come. *Solitude* is a torment, which is not threatned in *hell* it selfe.
Meere *vacuitie,* the first *Agent, God,* the first *instrument* of *God,
Nature,* will not admit; Nothing can be utterly *emptie,* but so neere
a degree towards *Vacuitie,* as *Solitude,* to bee but one, they love not.
When I am dead, and my body might infect, they have a remedy, [94]
they may bury me; but when I am but sick, and might infect, they
have no remedy, but their absence and my solitude. It is an *excuse*
to them that are *great,* and pretend, and yet are loth to come; it is
an *inhibition* to those who would truly come, because they may be
made instruments, and pestiducts, to the infection of others, by
their comming. And it is an *Outlawry,* an *Excommunication* upon [95]
the *patient,* and seperats him from all offices not onely of *Civilitie,*
but of *working Charitie.* A long sicknesse will weary friends at last,
but a pestilentiall sicknes averts them from the beginning. *God*
himself would admit a *figure* of *Society,* as there is a plurality of
persons in *God,* though there bee but one *God;* and all his externall
actions testifie a love of *Societie,* and *communion.* In *Heaven* there [96]
are *Orders* of *Angels,* and *Armies of Martyrs,* and *in that house, many
mansions;* in *Earth, Families, Cities, Churches, Colleges,* all *plurall
things;* and lest either of these should not be company enough
alone, there is an association of both, a *Communion of Saints,* which
makes the *Militant,* and *Triumphant Church,* one Parish; So that
Christ, was not out of his *Dioces,* when hee was upon the *Earth,* nor
out of his *Temple,* when he was in our flesh. *God,* who sawe that all [97]
that hee made, was good, came not so neer seeing a *defect* in any of
his works, as when he saw that it was not good, for man to bee
alone, therefore *hee made him a helper;* and one that should helpe   Gen. 2.18
him so, as to increase the *number,* and give him *her owne,* and *more
societie. Angels,* who do not propagate, nor multiply, were made at
first in an abundant number; and so were starres; But for the [98]
things of this world, their blessing was, *Encrease;* for I think, I
need not aske leave to think, that there is no *Phenix;* nothing
singular, nothing alone: Men that inhere upon *Nature* only, are so

far from thinking, that there is any thing *singular* in this world, as
that they will scarce thinke, that this world it selfe is *singular,* but
that every *Planet,* and every *Starre,* is another *World* like this;
[99] They finde reason to conceive, not onely a *pluralitie* in every
Species in the world, but a *pluralitie of worlds;* so that the
abhorrers of *Solitude,* are not solitary; for *God,* and *Nature,* and
Reason concurre against it. Now, a man may counterfeyt the
Plague in a *vowe,* and mistake a *Disease* for *Religion;* by such a
retiring, and recluding of himselfe from all men, as to doe good
[100] to no man, to converse with no man. *God* hath two *Testaments,*
two *Wils;* but this is a *Scedule,* and not of his, a *Codicill,* and not
of his, not in the *body* of his *Testaments,* but *interlind,* and
postscrib'd by others, that the way to the *Communion of Saints,*
should be by such a *solitude,* as excludes all doing of good here.
That is a *disease* of the *mind;* as the height of an infectious disease
of the body, is *solitude,* to be left alone: for this makes an infectious
[101] bed, equall, nay worse than a *grave,* that thogh in both I be
equally alone, in my bed I *know* it, and *feele* it, and shall not in my
grave: and this too, that in my bedd, my soule is still in an
infectious body, and shall not in my grave bee so.

5. *Expostulation*

O *God, my God,* thy *Son* tooke it not ill at *Marthas* handes, that
when he said unto her, *Thy brother Lazarus shall rise againe,* she
Joh. 11.23 [102] expostulated it so far with him, as to reply, *I know that he shal rise
againe in the Resurrection, at the last day;* for shee was miserable by
wanting him then. Take it not ill, O *my God,* from me, that thogh
Num. 23.9 thou have ordained it for a *blessing,* and for a *dignitie* to thy people,
That they should dwell alone, and not bee reckoned among the Nations,
Deut. 33.28 [103] (because they should be above them) and that *they should dwell in
Eccles. 4.9, 10 safetie alone,* (free from the infestation of enemies) yet I take thy
leave to remember thee, that thou hast said too, *Two are better than
one;* And *Woe be unto him that is alone when he falleth;* and so, when
Wisd. 1.15 he is fallen, and laid in the bedde of sicknesse too. *Righteousnesse is
immortall;* I know thy *wisdome* hath said so; but no *Man,* though
covered with the righteousnes of thy *Sonne,* is immortall so, as not
Mat. 14.23 [104] to die; for he who was *righteousnes* it selfe, did die. I know that the
Son of righteousnes, thy *Son,* refused not, nay affected *solitarinesse,*
Mat. 26.53 *lonenesse,* many, many times; but at all times, he was able to command
more than twelve legions of Angels to his service; and when he did not
Joh. 8.16 so, he was farre from being alone; for, *I am not alone,* saies he, *but I,
and the Father that sent me.* I cannot feare, but that I shall alwaies be

with thee, and him; but whether this *disease* may not alien, and   [105] Psa.l 38.11
remoove my friends, so that *they stand aloofe from my sore, and my*
kinsmen stand afar off, I cannot tel. I cannot feare, but that thou wilt
reckon with me from this minute, in which, by thy grace, I see thee:
whether this *understanding,* and this *will,* and this *memory,* may not
decay, to the *discouragement,* and the *ill interpretation* of them, that
see that heavy change in me, I cannot tell. It was for thy blessed, thy   Isa. 63.3
powerfull *Sonne* alone, *to tread the wine- presse alone, and none of the*   [106]
people with him; I am not able to passe this agony alone; not alone
without *thee;* Thou art thy spirit; not alone without *thine;* spirituall
and temporal *Phisicians,* are *thine;* not alone without *mine;* Those
whom the bands of *blood,* or *friendship,* hath made *mine,* are *mine;*
And if *thou,* or *thine,* or *mine,* abandon me, I am *alone;* and wo unto
me if I bee alone. *Elijah* himselfe fainted under that apprehension,   [107] 1 King. 19.14
Loe, I am left alone; and *Martha* murmured at that, and said to   Luk. 10.40
Christ, Lord doest not thou care, that my sister hath left me to serve
alone? Neither could *Jeremiah* enter into his *Lamentations,* from a   Lam. 1.1
higher ground, than to say, *How doth the city sit solitary, that was full*
of people. O *my God,* it is the *Leper,* that thou hast condemned *to live*   Lev. 13.46
alone; Have I such a *Leprosie* in my *Soule,* that I must die alone;
alone without thee? Shall this come to such a *Leprosie* in my *body,*   [108]
that I must die alone? Alone without them that should assist, that
should comfort me? But comes not this *Expostulation* too neere a
murmuring? Must I bee concluded with that, that *Moses was*   Exo. 24.2
commaunded to come neere the Lord alone? That solitarines, and
dereliction, and abandoning of others, disposes us best for *God,*
who accompanies us most alone? May I not remember, and apply   [109] Gen. 32.24
too; that though *God* came not to *Jacob,* till he found him *alone,* yet
when he found him alone, *hee wrestled with him, and lamed him?*
That when in the dereliction and forsaking of friends and *Phisicians,*
a man is left alone to *God, God* may so wrestle with this *Jacob,* with
this *Conscience,* as to put it out of *joynt,* and so appeare to him, as
that he dares not looke upon him face to face, when as by way of
reflection, in the consolation of his temporall or spirituall servants,   [110]
and ordinances hee durst, if they were there? But a *faithfull friend is*   Ecclus. 6.16
the phisicke of life, and they that feare the Lord, shall finde him.
Therefore hath the *Lord* afforded me both in one person, that
Phisician, who is my faithfull friend.

5. *Prayer*

O *Eternall,* and most *gracious God,* who calledst down fire from
Heaven upon the sinfull *Cities,* but *once,* and openedst the *Earth* to   [111]

swallow the *Murmurers*, but *once*, and threwst down the *Tower of Siloam* upon sinners, but *once*, but for thy workes of mercie repeatest them often, and still workest by thine owne paternes, as thou broghtest *Man* into this world, by giving him a *helper* fit for him here, so whether it bee thy will to continue mee long thus, or to dismisse me by death, be pleased to afford me the helpes fit for [112] both conditions, either for my weak stay here, or my finall transmigration from hence. And if thou mayest receive glory by that way (and, by all wayes thou maist receive glory) glorifie thy selfe in preserving this *body* from such infections, as might withhold those, who would come, or indanger them who doe come; and preserve this *soule* in the faculties thereof, from all such [113] distempers, as might shake the assurance which my selfe and others have had, that because thou hast loved me, thou wouldst love me to my *end*, and at my *end*. Open none of my *dores*, not of my *hart*, not of mine *eares*, not of my *house*, to any *supplanter* that would enter to undermine me in my *Religion* to thee, in the time of my weaknesse, or to defame me, and magnifie himselfe, with false rumors of such a victory, and surprisall of me, after I am dead; *Be* [114] my salvation, and *plead* my salvation; *work* it, and *declare* it; and as thy *triumphant* shall be, so let the *Militant Church* bee assured, that thou wast my *God*, and I thy servant, *to*, and *in* my consummation. Blesse thou the learning, and the labours of this Man, whom thou sendest to assist me; and since thou takest mee by the hand, and puttest me into his hands (for I come to him in thy name, who, in [115] thy name comes to me) since I clog not my *hopes* in him, no nor my *prayers* to thee, with any limited conditions, but inwrap all in those two petitions, *Thy kingdome come, thy will be done*, prosper him, and relieve me, in thy way, in thy time, and in thy measure. *Amen.*

6. Metuit.
The Phisician is afraid.

6. *Meditation*

I observe the *Phisician*, with the same diligence, as hee the *disease;* [116] I see hee *feares*, and I feare with him: I overtake him, I overrun him in his feare, and I go the faster, because he makes his pace slow; I feare the more, because he disguises his fear, and I see it with the more sharpnesse, because hee would not have me see it. He knowes that his *feare* shall not disorder the practise, and exercise of his *Art*, but he knows that my *fear* may disorder the effect, and working of his practise. As the ill affections of the *spleene*, complicate, and mingle themselvs with every infirmitie of the body, so doth *feare* insinuat it self in every *action*, or *passion* of the *mind:* and as *wind* in the body will counterfet any disease, and seem the *Stone*, and seem the *Gout*, so *feare* will counterfet any disease of the *Mind;* it shall seeme *love*, a love of having, and it is but a *fear*, a jealous, and suspitious feare of losing; It shall seem *valor* in despising, and undervaluing danger, and it is but *feare*, in an over-valuing of *opinion*, and *estimation*, and a feare of losing that. A man that is not afraid of a *Lion*, is afraid of a *Cat;* not afraid of *starving*, and yet is afraid of some *joynt of meat* at the table, presented to feed him; not afraid of the sound of *Drummes*, and *Trumpets*, and *Shot*, and those, which they seeke to drowne, the last cries of men, and is afraid of some particular *harmonious instrument;* so much afraid, as that with any of these the *enemy* might drive this man, otherwise valiant enough, out of the field. I know not, what fear is, nor I know not what it is that I fear now; I feare not the hastening of my *death*, and yet I do fear the increase of the *disease;* I should belie *Nature*, if I should deny that I feard this, and if I should say that I feared *death*, I should belye *God;* My weaknesse is from *Nature*, who hath but her *Measure*, my strength is from *God*, who possesses, and distributes infinitely. As then every cold ayre, is not a *dampe*, every *shivering* is not a *stupefaction*, so every *feare*, is not a *fearefulnes*, every declination is not a running away, every debating is not a resolving, every wish, that it were not thus, is not a murmuring, nor a dejection though it bee thus; but as my *Phisicians* fear puts not him from his *practise*, neither doth mine put me, from receiving from *God*, and *Man*, and *my selfe*, *spirituall*, and *civill*, and *morall* assistances, and consolations.

[117]

[118]

[119]

[120]

[121]

6. *Expostulation.*

My God, my God, I find in thy *Booke*, that *feare* is a stifling spirit, a spirit of *suffocation;* That *Ishbosheth could not speak, not reply in his own defence to Abner, because hee was afraid.* It was thy servant *Jobs* case too, who before hee could say any thing *to thee*, saies *of thee*, *Let him take his rod away from me, and let not his feare terrifie mee, then would I speake with him, and not feare him; but it is not so with mee.* Shall a feare of *thee*, take away my devotion *to thee?* Dost thou

2 Sam. 3.11

[122] Job 9.34, 35

command me to *speake* to thee, and commaund me to feare thee, and do these destroy one another? There is no perplexity in thee, *my God;* no inextricablenes in thee, my *light,* and my *clearnes,* my [123] *Sun,* and my *Moone,* that directest me as wel in the night of adversity and fear, as in my day of prosperity and confidence. I must then *speak* to thee, at all times, but when must I *feare* thee? At Luk. 18.1 all times too. When didst thou rebuke any petitioner, with the name of *Importunate?* Thou hast proposd to us a *parable* of a *Judge* that did Justice at last, *because the client was importunate, and troubled him;* But thou hast told us plainely, that thy use in that [124] *parable,* was not, that thou wast troubled with our importunities, Luk. 11.5–8 but (as thou sayest there) *That wee should alwayes pray.* And to the same purpose thou proposest another, that *If I presse my friend, when hee is in bed, at midnight, to lend mee bread, though hee will not rise because I am his friend, yet because of mine importunitie, he will.* God will do this, whensoever thou askest, and never call it *importunitie.* Pray in thy bed at midnight, and God wil not say, I [125] will heare thee to morrow upon thy knees, at thy bed side; pray upon thy knees there, then, and God will not say, I will heare thee on *Sunday,* at *Church; God* is no *dilatory God,* no froward *God;* Praier is never *unseasonable, God* is never asleep nor absent. But, *O my God,* can I doe this, and *feare* thee; come to thee, and speak to thee, in all places, at all houres, and *feare* thee? Dare I aske this [126] question? There is more boldnesse in the *question,* than in the *comming:* I may doe it, though I *feare* thee; I cannot doe it, except I feare thee. So well hast thou provided, that we should alwayes feare thee, as that thou hast provided, that we should fear no Psal. 27.1 person but thee, nothing but thee; no men? No. Whom? *The Lord is my helpe, and my salvation, whome shall I feare? Great enemies:* not *great enemies;* for no enemies are great to them that feare thee; Numb. 14.9 [127] *Feare not the people of this land, for they are Bread to you;* They shall not only not *eat* us, not *eat* our *bread,* but they shall bee our *Bread;* Why should we feare them? But for all this *Metaphoricall Bread,* victory over enemies, that thought to devoure us, may we not feare, that we may lack bread literally? And feare famine, though we feare Psal. 34.10 not enemies? *Young Lyons do lacke, and suffer Hunger, but they that* [128] *seeke the Lord, shall not want any good thing.* Never? Though it bee well with them at one time, may they not feare, that it may be Psal. 49.5 worse? *Wherfore should I feare in the dayes of evill?* saies thy servant *David.* Though his own sins had made them evill, he feared them not. No? not if this evill determin in death? Not though in a death; Ecclus. 41.3 not, though in a death inflicted by violence, by malice, by our own

desert; *feare not the sentence of death,* if thou feare God. Thou art, [129]
O my God, so far from admitting us, that feare thee, to feare others, Mar. 6.20
as that thou makest others to feare us; *As Herod feared John, because*
hee was a holy, and a just man, and observed him. How *fully* then O
my abundant God, how *gently,* O *my sweet,* my *easie God,* doest thou
unentangle mee, in any scruple arising out of the consideration of
this thy feare? Is not this that which thou intendest, when thou Psal. 25.14
sayst, *The secret of the Lord is with them, that feare him;* The secret, [130]
the mistery of the right use of feare. Dost thou not meane this, Prov. 2.5
when thou sayest, *Wee shall understand the feare of the Lord? Have*
it, and *have benefit by it;* have it, and stand under it; be directed by
it, and not bee dejected with it. And dost thou not propose that
Church for our example, when thou sayest, *The Church of Judaea,* Act. 9.31
walked in the feare of God; they had it, but did not sit down lazily, [131]
nor fall downe weakly, nor sinke under it. There is a feare which Gen. 3.10
weakens men in the service of God: *Adam was afrayde, because hee*
was naked. They who have put off *thee,* are a prey to all. They may Prov. 1.26
feare, *for thou wilt laugh, when their feare comes upon them,* as thou 10.24
hast tolde them, *more than once;* And *thou wilt make them feare,* Psal. 14.5
where no cause of feare is, as thou hast told them *more than once too.* [132] 53.6
There is a feare that is a punishment of *former* wickednesses, and Joh. 7.12, 13
induces *more: Though some said of thy Sonne, Christ Jesus, that hee*
was a good Man, yet no Man spake openly, for feare of the Jewes: Joh. 19.38
Joseph was his Disciple; but secretly, for feare of the Jewes: The 20.19
Disciples kept some meetings, but with dores shut, *for feare of the*
Jewes. O *my God,* thou givest us *feare* for ballast to cary us stedily
in all weathers. But thou wouldst *ballast* us, with such sand, as [133]
should have *gold* in it, with that feare which is *thy feare;* for *the* Isa. 33.6
feare of the Lord is his treasure. Hee that hath that, lacks nothing
that Man can have, nothing that *God* does give. Timorous men Mat. 8.26
thou rebukest; *Why are yee fearfull,* O *yee of little faith?* Such thou
dismissest from thy Service, with scorne, though of them there Judg. 7.3
went from *Gideons* Army, 22000. and remained but 10000. Such [134]
thou sendest farther than so; thither from whence they never Rev. 21.8
returne, *The fearefull and the unbeleeving, into that burning lake,*
which is the second death. There is a *feare,* and there is a *hope,* which
are equall abominations to thee: for, *they were confounded, because* Job 6.20
they hoped, saies thy servant *Job:* because they had *mis-placed, mis-*
centred their *hopes;* they hoped, and not in *thee,* and such shall
feare, and not feare *thee.* But in *thy feare, my God,* and my feare, my [135]
God, and my hope, is *hope,* and *love,* and *confidence,* and *peace,* and
every limbe, and ingredient of *Happinesse* enwrapped; for *Joy*

Mat. 28.8 includes all; and *feare,* and *joy* consist together; nay, constitute one
another; *The women departed from the sepulchre,* the women who
were made *super-numerary Apostles, Apostles* to the *Apostles;*
Mothers of the *Church, and of the Fathers, Grandfathers of the*
[136] *Church,* the *Apostles* themselves, the *women, Angels* of the
Resurrection, went from the *sepulchre,* with *feare* and *joy;* they *ran,*
sayes the text, and they ran upon those two legs, *feare,* and *joy;* and
both was the *right legg;* they *joy* in thee, O *Lord,* that *feare* thee, and
feare thee only, who feele this *joy in thee.* Nay, thy *feare* and thy *love,*
are inseperable; still we are called upon, in infinite places, to *feare*
[137] *God;* yet the *Commandement,* which is the *roote* of all, is, *Thou shalt*
love the Lord thy God; Hee doeth *neither,* that doth not *both;* hee
Psal. 111.10 omits *neither,* that does *one.* Therfore when thy servant *David had*
Prov. 1.7 *said, that the feare of the Lord is the beginning of wisedome,* And his
Ecclus. 1.20, 27 *Sonne* had *repeated* it againe; Hee that collects both, calls this *feare,*
the *root* of *wisdome;* And that it may embrace all, hee calls it
wisedome it selfe. A wise man therefore is never without it, never
Deut. 4.10 [138] without the exercise of it: Therefore thou sentest *Moses* to thy
people, *That they might learne to feare thee all the dayes of their*
lives: not in heavy, and calamitous, but in good, and cheerfull dayes
Heb. 11.7 too: for, *Noah,* who had assurance of his deliverance, yet *mooved*
Ecclus. 18.27 *with feare, prepared an Arke, for the saving of his house. A wise man*
wil feare in every thing. And therefore though I pretend, to no
other degree of wisedome, I am abundantly rich in this, that I lye
[139] heere possest with that feare, which is *thy feare,* both that this
sicknesse is thy immediate correction, and not meerely a *naturall*
Heb. 10.31 *accident,* and therefore fearefull, because *it is a fearful thing to fall*
into thy hands, and that this feare preserves me from all inordinate
feare, arising out of the infirmitie of Nature, because thy hand
being upon me, thou wilt never let me fall out of thy hand.

[140]
6. *Prayer*

O *most mightie God and mercifull God,* the *God* of all true *sorrow,*
and true *joy* too, of all *feare,* and of al *hope* too, as thou hast
given me a *Repentance,* not to be repented of, so give me, O
Lord, a *feare,* of which I may not be *afraid.* Give me tender, and
supple, and conformable affections, that as I *joy* with them that
joy, and *mourne* with them, that *mourne,* so I may *feare* with
[141] them that *feare.* And since thou hast vouchsafed to discover to
me, in his *feare* whom thou hast admitted to be my assistance,
in this sicknesse, that there is danger therein, let me not, O

Lord, go about to overcome the sense of that fear, so far, as to pretermit the fitting, and preparing of my selfe, for the worst that may be feard, the passage out of this life. Many of thy blessed *Martyrs,* have passed out of this life, without any showe [142] of *feare:* But thy *most blessed Sonne* himselfe did not so. Thy *Martyrs* were known to be but *men,* and therfore it pleased thee, to fill them with thy *Spirit,* and thy *power,* in that they did *more* than *Men;* Thy *Son* was declared by thee, and by himselfe to be *God;* and it was requisite, that he should declare himselfe to be *Man* also, in the weaknesses of man. Let mee not therefore, *O my God,* bee ashamed of these *feares,* but let me feele them to [143] determine, where his feare did, in a present submitting of all to thy will. And when thou shalt have inflamd, and thawd my former coldnesses, and indevotions, with these heats, and quenched my former heates, with these sweats, and inundations, and rectified my former presumptions, and negligences with these fears, bee pleased, *O Lord,* as one, made so by thee, to thinke me fit for thee; And whether it be thy pleasure, to dispose [144] of this body, this garment so, as to put it to a farther wearing in this world, or to lay it up in the *common wardrobe,* the grave, for the next, glorifie thy selfe in thy choyce now, and glorifie it then, with that glory, which thy *Son,* our *Saviour Christ Jesus* hath purchased for them, whome thou makest partakers of his *Resurrection. Amen.*

7. Socios sibi jungier instat. [145]
The Phisician desires to have others joyned with him.

7. Meditation

There is *more feare,* therefore *more cause.* If the *Phisician* desire help, the burden grows great: There is a growth of the *Disease* then; But there must bee an *Autumne* too; But whether an *Autumne* of the *disease* or *mee,* it is not my part to choose: but if it bee of *me,* [146] it is of *both;* My disease cannot *survive mee,* I may *overlive it.* Howsoever, his desiring of others, argues his *candor,* and his *ingenuitie;* If the danger be *great,* hee *justifies* his proceedings, and he *disguises* nothing, that calls in *witnesses;* And if the danger bee

[147] not *great*, hee is not *ambitious*, that is so readie to divide the thankes, and the honour of that work, which he begun alone, with others, It diminishes not the dignitie of a *Monarch*, that hee derive part of his care upon others; *God* hath not made many *Suns*, but he hath made many *bodies*, that *receive*, and *give* light. The *Romans* began with *one King*; they came to *two Consuls*; they returned in extremities, to *one Dictator*; whether in one, or many, the

[148] *soveraigntie* is the same, in all *States*, and the danger is not the more, and the providence is the more, wher there are more *Phisicians*; as the State is the happier, where businesses are carried by more counsels, than can be in one breast, how large soever. *Diseases* themselves hold *Consultations*, and conspire how they may multiply, and joyn with one another, and *exalt* one anothers force, so; and shal we not call *Phisicians*, to *consultations*? *Death* is in an

[149] olde mans dore, he appeares, and tels him so, and *death* is at a yong mans *backe*, and saies nothing; *Age* is a *sicknesse*, and *Youth* is an *ambush*; and we need so many *Phisicians*, as may make up a *Watch*, and spie every inconvenience. There is scarce any thing, that hath not killed some body; a *haire*, a *feather* hath done it; Nay, that which is our best *Antidote* against it, hath donn it; the best *Cordiall* hath bene *deadly poyson*; Men have dyed of *Joy*, and allmost

[150] forbidden their friends to weep for them, when they have seen them dye laughing. Even that *Tirant Dionysius* (I thinke the same, that suffered so much after) who could not die of that sorrow, of that high fal, from a *King* to a *wretched private man*, dyed of so poore a *Joy*, as to be declared by the *people* at a *Theater*, that hee was a good *Poet*. We say often that a *Man may live of a litle*, but,

[151] alas, of how much lesse may a Man *dye*? And therfore the more assistants, the better; who comes to a day of hearing, in a cause of any importance, with one *Advocate*? In our *Funerals*, we our selves have no interest; there wee cannot *advise*, we cannot *direct*: And though some *Nations*, (the *Egyptians* in particular) built themselves better *Tombs*, than *houses*, because they were to dwell *longer* in them; yet, amongst our selves, the greatest *Man of Stile*, whom we

[152] have had, *The Conqueror*, was left, as soone as his soule left him, not only without persons to assist at his *grave*, but without a *grave*. Who will keepe us then, we know not; As long as we can, let us admit as much helpe as wee can; Another, and another *Phisician*, is not another, and another *Indication*, and *Symptom* of death, but another, and another *Assistant*, and *Proctor* of *life*: Nor doe they so

[153] much feed the imagination with apprehension of *danger*, as the understanding with *comfort*; Let not one bring *Learning*, another *Diligence*, another *Religion*, but every one bring all, and, as many

Ingredients enter into a Receit, so may many men make the Receit. But why doe I exercise my Meditation so long upon this, of having plentifull helpe in time of need? Is not my Meditation rather to be enclined another way, to condole, and commiserate their distresse, who have *none*? How many are sicker (perchance) than I, and laid [154] in their wofull straw at home (if that corner be a home) and have no more hope of helpe, though they die, than of preferment, though they live? Nor doe no more expect to see a *Phisician* then, than to bee an *Officer* after; of whome, the first that takes knowledge, is the *Sexton* that buries them; who buries them in *oblivion* too? For [155] they doe but fill up the number of the dead in the Bill, but we shall never heare their *Names*, till wee reade them in the Booke of life, with our owne. How many are sicker (perchance) than I, and thrown into *Hospitals*, where, (as a fish left upon the Sand, must stay the tide) they must stay the *Phisicians* houre of visiting, and then can bee but *visited*? How many are sicker (perchaunce) than all we, and have not this *Hospitall* to cover them, not this straw, to [156] lie in, to die in, but have their *Grave-stone* under them, and breathe out their soules in the eares, and in the eies of passengers, harder than their bed, the flint of the street? That taste of no part of our *Phisick*, but a *sparing dyet;* to whom ordinary porridge would bee *Julip* enough, the refuse of our servants, *Bezar* enough, and the off-scouring of our Kitchin tables, *Cordiall* enough. O my *soule*, [157] when thou art not enough awake, to blesse thy *God* enough for his plentifull mercy, in affoording thee many *Helpers*, remember how many lacke them, and helpe them to them, or to those other things, which they lack as much as them.

7. Expostulation

My God, my God, thy blessed *Servant Augustine* begg'd of thee, [158] that *Moses* might come, and tell him what hee meant by some places of *Genesis*: May I have leave to aske of that *Spirit*, that writ that Booke, why when *David* expected newes from *Joabs* armie, 2 Sam. 18.25 and that the Watchman tolde him, that *hee sawe a man running alone*, *David* concluded out of that circumstance, *That if hee came* *So all*, but our *alone, hee brought good newes?* I see the *Grammar*, the word signifies Translation take so, and is so ever accepted, *Good newes*; but I see not the *Logique*, [159] it. Even nor the *Rhetorique*, how *David* would proove, or perswade that his *Buxdorf* and newes was *good*, because hee was *alone*, except a greater company *Schindler*. might have made great impressions of danger, by imploring, and importuning present supplies. Howsoever that bee, I am sure,

2 Tim. 4.11   that that which thy *Apostle* sayes to *Timothy, Onely Luke is with*
[160]   *me, Luke,* and no body but *Luke,* hath a taste of complaint, and
sorrow in it: Though *Luke* want no testimony of *abilitie,* or
forwardnes, of *constancie,* and *perseverance,* in assisting that great
building, which *St. Paul* laboured in, yet *St. Paul* is affected with
that, that ther was none but *Luke,* to assist. We take *St. Luke* to
have bin a *Phisician,* and it admits the application the better, that
[161]   in the presence of one good *Phisician,* we may bee glad of more. It
was not only a civill spirit of policy, or order that moved *Moses*
Exod. 18.14,   father in law, to perswade him to divide the burden of Government,
21–22   and Judicature, with others, and take others to his assistance, but
it was also thy immediat spirit *O my God,* that mov'd *Moses* to
Numb. 11.16   present unto thee *70 of the Elders of Israel,* to receive of that spirit,
which was upon *Moses* onely before, such a portion as might ease
[162]   him in the government of that people; though *Moses* alone had
indowments above all, thou gavest him other assistants. I consider
thy plentifull goodnesse, *O my God,* in employing *Angels,* more
Heb. 1.6   than one, in so many of thy remarkable workes. Of thy *Sonne,* thou
saist, *Let all the Angels of God worship him;* If that bee in *Heaven,*
Mat. 26.53   upon *Earth,* hee sayes *that hee could commaund twelve legions of*
Mat. 25.31 [163]   *Angels;* And when *Heaven,* and *Earth* shall bee all one, at the last
Luk. 2.11   day, *Thy Sonne, O God, the Son of Man, shall come in his glory, and
all the holy Angels with him.* The *Angels* that celebrated his birth to
the *Shepheards,* the *Angels* that celebrated his second birth, his
Joh. 20.12   *Resurrection* to the *Maries,* were in the *plurall, Angells* associated
Gen. 28.12   with *Angels.* In *Jacobs* ladder, they which *ascended and descended,*
and maintain'd the trade between *Heaven* and *Earth,* between
Psal. 91.11 [164]   thee and us, they who have the Commission, and charge *to guide*
Gen. 19.15   *us in all our wayes,* they who hastned *Lot,* and in him, us, from
Rev. 1.20   places of danger, and tentation, they who are *appoynted to instruct*
Rev. 8.2   *and governe us in the Church heere,* they who are sent to *punish the
disobedient and refractarie,* they that are to be the *Mowers,* and
Mat. 13.39   *harvest men,* after we are growne up in one field, *the church,* at the
Luk. 16.22   day of *Judgment,* they that are to carrie our *soules* whither they
Rev. 21.12 [165]   caried *Lazarus,* they who attend at the several gates of the new
Jerusalem, to admit us there; all these, who administer to thy
servants, from the first, to their last, are *Angels, Angels* in the
2 King. 19.35   plurall, in every service, *Angels* associated with *Angells.* The power
of a single Angell wee see in that one, who in one night destroyed
almost 200. thousand in *Sennacheribs* army, yet thou often
[166]   imployest many; as we know the power of salvation is abundantly
Luk. 4.18   in any one *Evangelist,* and yet thou hast afforded us *foure.* Thy
Sonne proclaimes of himselfe, *that thy Spirit, hath annoynted him*

to preach the Gospell, yet he hath given others *for the perfiting of the*   Eph. 4.12
Saints in the worke of the Ministery. Thou hast made him *Bishop of*   1 Pet. 2.25
our soules, but there are others, *Bishops* too. Hee gave the *holy*   Joh. 20.22
Ghost, and others gave it also. Thy way, *O my God,* (and, *O my
God,* thou lovest to walk in thine own waies, for they are large) thy
way from the beginning, is *multiplication of thy helps;* and therfore   [167]
it were a degree of *ingratitude,* not to accept this mercy of affording
me many *helpes* for my bodily health, as a *type* and *earnest* of thy
gracious purpose now, and ever, to affoord mee the same
assistances. That for thy great *Helpe,* thy *Word,* I may seeke that,
not from *corners,* nor *Conventicles,* nor *schismatical singularities,*
but from the assotiation, and communion of thy *Catholique*   [168]
Church, and those persons, whom thou hast alwayes furnished
that *Church* withall: And that I may associate thy *Word,* with thy
Sacrament, thy *Seale* with thy *Patent;* and in that *Sacrament*
associate *the signe* with the *thing signified,* the *Bread* with the *Body*
of thy *Sonne,* so, as I may be sure to have received both, and to bee
made thereby, (as thy blessed servant *Augustine* sayes) the *Arke,*
and the *Monument,* and the *Tombe* of thy most blessed *Sonne,* that   [169]
hee, and all the *merits* of his death, may, by that receiving, bee
buried in me, to my quickning in this world, and my immortall
establishing in the next.

7. *Prayer*

O *eternall,* and *most gracious God,* who gavest to thy servants in the
wildernes, thy *Manna,* bread so conditiond, qualified so, as that,
to every man, *Manna tasted like that, which that man liked best,* I   [170]
humbly beseech thee, to make this correction, which I acknowledg
to be part of my *daily bread,* to tast so to me, not as I would, but as
thou wouldest have it taste, and to conform my tast, and make it
agreeable to thy will. Thou wouldst have thy corrections tast of
humiliation, but thou wouldest have them tast of *consolation,* too;
taste of *danger,* but tast of *assurance* too. As therefore thou hast   [171]
imprinted in all thine *Elements,* of which our bodies consist, two
manifest qualities, so that, as thy fire *dries,* so it *heats* too; and as thy
water *moysts,* so it *cooles* too, so, O *Lord,* in these corrections, which
are the *elements of our regeneration,* by which our *soules* are made
thine, imprint thy two qualities, those two operations, that as they
scourge us, they may scourge us into the way to thee: that when   [172]
they have shewed us, that we are nothing in our selves, they may
also shew us, that thou art all things unto us. When therfore in this

particular circumstance, O *Lord* (but none of thy judgements are *circumstances;* they are all of the *substance* of thy good purpose upon us) when in this particular, that he, whom thou hast sent to
[173] assist me, desires *assistants* to him, thou hast let mee see, in how few houres thou canst throw me beyond the helpe of man, let me by the same light see, that no vehemence of sicknes, no tentation of Satan, no guiltines of sin, no prison of death, not this first, this *sicke bed,* not the other prison, the close and dark *grave,* can remoove me from the determined, and good purpose, which thou [hast] sealed concerning mee. Let me think no degree of this thy
[174] correction, *casuall,* or without *signification;* but yet when I have read it in that language, as it is a *correction,* let me translate it into another, and read it as a *mercy;* and which of these is the *Originall,* and which is the *Translation,* whether thy *Mercy,* or thy *Correction,* were thy primary, and original intention in this sicknes, I cannot conclude, though death conclude me; for as it must necessarily appeare to bee a *correction,* so I can have no greater argument of
[175] thy *mercy,* than to die in *thee,* and by that death, to bee united to him, who died for me.

8. Et Rex ipse suum mittit.
The King sends his owne Phisician.

8. Meditation

Stil when we return to that Meditation, that *Man is a World,* we find new *discoveries.* Let him be a *world,* and him self will be the
[176] *land,* and *misery* the *sea.* His misery, (for misery is his, his own; of the happinesses even of this world, hee is but *tenant,* but of misery the *free-holder;* of happines hee is but the *farmer,* but the *usufructuary:* but of misery the *Lord,* the *proprietary)* his misery, as the *sea,* swells above all the hilles, and reaches to the remotest parts of this earth, *Man;* who of himselfe is but *dust,* and
[177] coagulated and kneaded into earth, by *teares;* his *matter* is *earth,* his *forme, misery.* In this *world,* that is *Mankinde,* the highest ground, the eminentest *hils,* are *kings;* and have they line, and lead enough to fathome this *sea,* and say, My misery is but this deepe? Scarce any misery equal to *sicknesse;* and they are subject to that equally, with their lowest subject. A glasse is not the lesse

brittle, because a *Kings* face is represented in it; nor a King the less brittle, because *God* is represented in him. They have *Phisicians* continually about them, and therfore *sicknesses*, or the [178] worst of sicknesses, continuall feare of it. Are they *gods?* He that calld them so, cannot flatter. They are *Gods*, but *sicke gods;* and *God* is presented to us under many human affections, as far as *infirmities;* God is called *angry*, and *sorry*, and *weary*, and *heavy;* but never a *sicke God:* for then he might *die* like men, as our *gods* do. The worst that they could say in reproch, and scorne of the [179] *gods* of the *Heathen*, was, that perchance they were *asleepe;* but *Gods* that are so sicke, as that they cannot sleepe, are in an infirmer condition. A *God*, and need a *Phisician?* A *Jupiter* and need an *Aesculapius?* that must have *Rheubarbe* to purge his *Choller*, lest he be too angry, and *Agarick* to purge his *flegme*, lest he be too drowsie; that as *Tertullian* saies of the *Egyptian gods, plants* and [180] *herbes, That God was beholden to Man, for growing in his garden*, so wee must say of these *gods, Their eternity, (an eternity* of threescore and ten yeares) is in the *Apothecaryes* shop, and not in the *Metaphoricall Deity*. But their *Deitye* is better expressed in their *humility*, than in their *heighth;* when abounding and overflowing, as *God*, in means of doing good, they descend, as *God*, to a communication of their abundances with men, according to their [181] necessities, then they are *Gods*. No man is well, that understands not, that values not his being well; that hath not a cheerefulnesse, and a joy in it; and whosoever hath this *Joy*, hath a desire to communicate, to propagate that, which occasions his happinesse, and his *Joy*, to others; for every man loves witnesses of his happinesse; and the best witnesses, are experimentall witnesses; they who have tasted of that in themselves, which makes us [182] happie; It consummates therefore, it perfits the happinesse of *Kings*, to confer, to transfer, honor, and riches, and (as they can) health, upon those that need them.

8. *Expostulation*

My God, my God, I have a warning from the *Wiseman, that when a*   Ecclus. 13.23
rich man speaketh, every man holdeth his tong; and looke what hee [183]
saith, they extoll it to the clouds; but if a poore man speake, they say,
what fellowe is this? And if hee stumble, they will help to overthrow
him. Therefore may my words be undervalued, and my errors aggravated, if I offer to speak of *Kings;* but not by thee, *O my God*, because I speak of them as they are in *thee*, and of *thee*, as thou

art *in them.* Certainly those men prepare a way of speaking
[184] negligently, or irreverently of *thee,* that give themselves that liberty,
Augustine in speaking of thy *Vice-gerents, Kings:* for thou who gavest *Augustus*
the *Empire,* gavest it to *Nero* too, and as *Vespasian* had it from thee,
so had *Julian;* Though *Kings* deface in themselves thy first *image,*
in their owne *soule,* thou givest no man leave to deface thy second
Image, imprinted indelibly in their *power.* But thou knowest, O
[185] *God,* that if I should be slacke in celebrating thy mercies to mee
exhibited by that royall Instrument, my *Soveraigne,* to many other
faults, that touch upon *Allegiance,* I should add the worst of all,
Ingratitude; which constitutes an il man; and faults which are
defects in any particular function, are not so great, as those that
destroy our *humanitie;* It is not so ill, to bee an ill *subject,* as to be
[186] an ill *man;* for he hath an universall illnesse, ready to flow, and
poure out it selfe into any mold, any form, and to spend it selfe in
any function. As therfore thy *Son* did upon the *Coyne,* I look upon
the *King,* and I aske whose *image,* and whose *inscription* hee hath;
and he hath *thine;* And I give unto thee, that which is *thine,* I
recommend his happines to thee, in all my sacrifices of thanks, for
that which hee enjoyes, and in al my praiers, for the continuance
[187] and inlargement of them. But let me stop, *my God,* and consider;
will not this look like a piece of art, and cunning, to convey into the
world an opinion, that I were more particularly in his care, than
other men? And that heerein, in a shew of *humilitie,* and
thankefulnesse, I magnifie my selfe more than there is cause? But let
not that *jealousie* stopp mee, O God, but let me go forward in
celebrating thy *mercy* exhibited by *him.* This which hee doth now,
[188] in assisting so my bodily health, I know is common to me with
many; Many, many, have tasted of that expression of his graciousnes.
Where hee can give health by his owne hands, hee doth; and to
more, than any of his *predecessors* have done; Therefore hath *God*
reserved one disease for him, that hee onely might cure it, though
perchance not onely by one *Title,* and *Interest,* nor only as *one king.*
[189] To those that need it not, in that kind, and so cannot have it by his
owne hand, he sends a *donative* of *health,* in sending his *Phisician.*
The holy *King St. Louis in France,* and our *Maud* is celebrated for
that, that personally they visited *Hospitals,* and assisted in the
Cure, even of loathsome *Diseases.* And when that religious *Empress*
Placilla, the wife of *Theodosius* was told, that she diminished her
selfe too much in those personal assistances, and might doe enough
[190] in sending reliefe, shee said, *Shee would send in that capacitie, as*
Empresse, but shee would go too, in that capacitie, as a Christian, as a
fellow member of the body of thy Son, with them. So thy servant *David*

applies him selfe to his people, so he incorporates himselfe in his 2 Sam. 19.12
people, by calling them *his brethren, his bones, his flesh;* and when
they fel under thy hand, even to the pretermitting of himselfe, he
presses upon thee, by prayer for them; *I have sinned, but these sheepe* 2 Sam. 24.14
what have they donne? let thine hand I pray thee be against me and [191]
against my fathers house. It is kingly to *give;* when *Araunah* gave
that great, and free present to *David,* that place, those instruments
for sacrifice, and the *sacrifices* themselves, it is said there, by thy
Spirit, *Al these things did Araunah give, as a King, to the King.* To 2 Sam. 24.23
give is an approaching to the Condition of *Kings,* but to give *health,* [192]
an approching to the *King* of *Kings,* to *thee.* But this his assisting to
my bodily health, thou knowest, O *God,* and so doe some others of
thine *Honorable servants* know, is but the twy-light, of that day,
wherein thou, through him, hast shind upon mee before; but the
Eccho of that voyce, whereby thou, through him, hast spoke to mee
before; Then, when he first of any man conceiv'd a hope, that I [193]
might be of some use in thy *Church,* and descended to an intimation,
to a perswasion, almost to a solicitation, that I would embrace that
calling. And thou who hadst put that desire into his heart, didst
also put into mine, an obedience to it; and I who was sicke before,
of a vertiginous giddiness, and irresolution, and almost spent all
my time in consulting how I should spend it, was by this *man of*
God, and *God of men,* put into the poole, and recoverd: when I [194]
asked, perchance, a *stone,* he gave me *bread;* when I asked,
perchance, a *Scorpion,* he gave me a *fish;* when I asked a temporall
office, hee denied not, refused not that, but let mee see, that hee had
rather I tooke this. These things, thou O *God,* who forgettest
nothing, hast not forgot, though perchance, he, because they were
benefits, hath; but I am not only a *witnesse,* but an *instance,* that our 2 Chro. 19.8
Jehosophat hath a care to ordaine *Priests,* as well as *Judges:* and not [195]
only to send *Phisicians* for *temporall,* but to bee the *Phisician* for
spirituall health.

8. Prayer

O eternall and most gracious *God,* who though thou have reserved
thy tresure of perfit joy, and perfit glory, to be given by thine own
hands then, when by seeing thee, as thou art in thy selfe, and
knowing thee, as we are known, wee shall possesse in an instant,
and possesse for ever, all that can any way conduce to our [196]
happinesses, yet here also in this world, givest us such *earnests* of
that full payment, as by the value of the *earnest,* we may give some

estimat of the tresure, humbly, and thankfully I acknowledge, that thy blessed *spirit* instructs mee, to make a difference of thy blessings in this world, by that difference of the *Instruments*, by which it hath [197] pleased thee to derive them unto me. As we see thee heere in a *glasse*, so we receive from thee here by *reflexion*, and by *instruments*. Even *casual things* come from *thee*, and that which we call *Fortune* here, hath another *name* above. *Nature* reaches out her hand, and gives us corne, and wine, and oyle, and milk, but thou fillest her hand before, and thou openest her hand, that she may rain down her showres upon us. *Industry* reaches out her hand to us, and [198] gives us fruits of our labor, for our selves, and our posteritie; but thy hand guides that hand, when it *sowes*, and when it *waters*, and the *increase* is from thee. *Friends* reach out their hands, and prefer us, but thy hand supports that hand, that supports us. Of all these thy *instruments* have I received thy blessing, O *God*, but bless thy name most for the greatest; that as a member of the publike, and as [199] a partaker of private favours too, by thy right hand, thy powerfull hand set over us, I have had my portion, not only in the hearing, but in the *preaching of thy Gospel*. Humbly beseeching thee, that as thou continuest thy wonted goodnes upon the whole world, by the wonted meanes, and instruments, the same *Sun*, and *Moon*, the same *Nature*, and *Industry*, so to continue the same blessings upon [200] this *State*, and this *Church* by the same hand, so long, as that thy *Son* when he comes in the *clouds*, may find *him*, or his *Son*, or his *sonnes sonnes* ready to give an account, and able to stand in that *judgment*, for their faithfull *Stewardship*, and *dispensation* of thy *talents* so abundantly committed to them; And be to him, O *God*, in all distempers of his body, in all anxieties of *spirit*, in all holy *sadnesses of soule*, such a *Phisician* in thy proportion, who art the greatest in *heaven*, as hee hath bin in *soule, and body* to me, in his proportion, who is the greatest upon earth.

9. Medicamina scribunt.
[201]   *Upon their Consultation, they prescribe.*

9. Meditation

They have seene me, and heard mee, arraign'd mee in these fetters, and receiv'd the *evidence;* I have cut up mine own *Anatomy,*

dissected my selfe, and they are gon to *read* upon me. O how
manifold, and perplexed a thing, nay, how wanton and various a   [202]
thing is *ruine* and *destruction? God* presented to *David* three kinds,
War, Famine, and *Pestilence; Satan* left out these, and brought in,
fires from heaven, and *windes from the wildernes.* If there were no
ruine but *sicknes,* wee see, the Masters of that *Art* can scarce *number,*
not *name* all sicknesses; every thing that *disorders* a faculty, and the
function of that is a sicknesse: The names wil not serve them which
are given from the *place affected,* the *Plurisie* is so; nor from the   [203]
effect which it works, the *falling sicknes* is so; they cannot have
names ynough, from *what it does,* nor *where it is,* but they must
extort names from what *it is like,* what it *resembles,* and but in some
one thing, or els they would lack names; for the *Wolf,* and the
Canker, and the *Polypus* are so; and that question, *whether there be
more names or things,* is as perplexed in sicknesses, as in any thing
else; except it be easily resolved upon that side, that there are more   [204]
sicknesses than *names.* If *ruine* were reduc'd to that one way, that
Man could perish no way but by *sicknes,* yet his danger were infinit;
and if *sicknes* were reduc'd to that one way, that there were no
sicknes but a *fever,* yet the way were infinite still; for it would
overlode, and oppress any naturall, disorder and discompose any
artificiall *Memory,* to deliver the *names* of severall *Fevers;* how
intricate a work then have they, who are gone to *consult,* which of   [205]
these *sicknesses* mine is, and then which of these *fevers,* and then
what it would do, and then how it may be countermind. But even
in *ill,* it is a degree of *good,* when the *evil* wil admit *consultation.* In
many *diseases,* that which is but an *accident,* but a *symptom* of the
main *disease,* is so violent, that the *phisician* must attend the cure of
that, though hee pretermit (so far as to intermit) the cure of the   [206]
disease it self. Is it not so in *States* too? somtimes the insolency of
those that are *great,* put the people into *commotions;* the great
disease, and the greatest danger to the *Head,* is the *insolency of the
great ones;* and yet, they execute *Martial law,* they come to present
executions upon the *people,* whose commotion was indeed but a
symptom, but an *accident* of the maine *disease;* but this *symptom,*
grown so violent, wold allow no time for a *consultation.* Is it not so   [207]
in the accidents of the *diseases* of our *mind* too? Is it not evidently
so in our *affections,* in our *passions?* If a *cholerick* man be ready to
strike, must I goe about to purge his *choler,* or to breake the blow?
But where there is room for *consultation,* things are not desperate.
They *consult;* so there is nothing *rashly, inconsideratly* done; and
then they *prescribe,* they *write,* so there is nothing *covertly,*
disguisedly, unavowedly done. In *bodily diseases* it is not alwaies so;   [208]

sometimes, as soon as the *Phisicians* foote is in the chamber, his *knife* is in the patients arme; the *disease* would not allow a *minutes* forbearing of *blood*, nor prescribing of other remedies. In States and matter of government it is so too; they are sometimes surprizd with such *accidents*, as that the *Magistrat* asks not what may be done by *law*, but does that, which must necessarily be don in that case. But it is a degree of *good*, in *evill*, a degree that caries hope [209] and comfort in it, when we may have recourse to that which is *written*, and that the proceedings may bee apert, and ingenuous, and candid; and avowable, for that gives satisfaction, and acquiescence. They who have received my *Anatomy* of my selfe, *consult*, and end their *consultation* in *prescribing*, and in prescribing *Phisick*, proper and convenient remedy: for if they should come in [210] again, and chide mee, for some disorder, that had occasion'd, and induced, or that had hastned and exalted this *sicknes*, or if they should begin to write now rules for my *dyet*, and *exercise* when I were well, this were to *antedate*, or to *postdate* their *Consultation*, not to give *phisick*. It were rather a vexation, than a reliefe, to tell a condemnd prisoner, you might have liv'd if you had done this; and if you can get your pardon, you shal do wel, to take this, or this course hereafter. I am glad they know (I have hid nothing from [211] them) glad they consult, (they hide nothing from one another) glad they write (they hide nothing from the world) glad that they write and prescribe *Phisick*, that there are *remedies* for the present case.

9. *Expostulation*

My *God*, my *God*, allow me a just indignation, a holy detestation of the insolency of that Man, who because he was of that high ranke, [212] of whom thou hast said, *They are gods*, thought himselfe more than equall to thee; That *king* of *Aragon Alfonsus*, so perfit in the motions of the heavenly bodies, as that hee adventured to say, That *if he had bin of councell with thee, in the making of the heavens, then the heavens should have bin disposed in a better order, than they are.* The *king Amaziah* would not indure thy *prophet* to reprehend him, 2 Chro. 25.16 but asked him in anger, *Art thou made of the kings councell?* When [213] thy Prophet *Isaiah* asks that question, *who hath directed the spirit* Isa. 40.13 *of the Lord, or being his councellor hath tought him*, It is after hee had setled and determined that office, upon thy *sonne*, and him *onely*, Isa. 9.6 when he joyns with those great *Titles, The mighty God*, and the Isa. 11.2 *prince of peace*, this also, *the Councellor*; and after he had setled upon him, *the spirit of might, and of councell*. So that then, thou *O*

God, thogh thou have no *councell* from Man, yet doest nothing [214]
upon man, without *councell;* In the making of Man there was a Gen. 1.26
consultation; let us make man. In the preserving of Man, *O thou* Job 7.20
great preserver of men, thou proceedest by *councell;* for all thy
externall workes, are the workes of the whole *Trinity,* and their
hand is to every action. How much more must I apprehend, that al
you blessed, and glorious persons of the *Trinitie* are in *Consultation* [215]
now, what you wil do with this infirm *body,* with this leprous *Soule,*
that attends guiltily, but yet comfortably, your determination upon
it. I offer not to counsell them, who meet in *consultation* for my
body now, but I open my infirmities, I anatomise my *body* to them.
So I do my *soule* to thee, O my *God,* in an humble confession, That
there is no *veine* in mee, that is not full of the bloud of thy *Son,*
whom I have crucified, and Crucified againe, by multiplying many, [216]
and often repeating the same sinnes; that there is no *Artery* in me,
that hath not the *spirit of error, the spirit of lust, the spirit of giddines* 1 Tim. 4.1
n it; no *bone* in me that is not hardned with the custome of *sin,* and Hos. 4.12
nourished, and soupled with the *marrow* of *sinn;* no *sinews,* no Isa. 19.14
ligaments, that do not tie, and chain sin and sin together. Yet, *O*
blessed and glorious Trinity, O holy, and whole Colledge, and yet but
one *Phisician,* if you take this confession into a *consultation,* my [217]
case is not desperate, my destruction is not *decreed;* If your
consultation determin in *writing,* if you refer mee to that which is
written, you intend my recovery: for al the way, *O my God,* (ever
constant to thine owne wayes) thou hast proceeded *openly,*
intelligibly, manifestly, by the book. From thy first *book,* the book of
life, never shut to thee, but never thoroughly open to us; from thy
second *book,* the *booke* of *Nature,* wher though sub-obscurely, and [218]
in shadows, thou hast expressed thine own *Image;* from thy third
booke, the *Scriptures,* where thou hadst written all in the *Old,* and
then lightedst us a candle to read it by, in the *New Testament;* To
these thou hadst added the *booke* of just, and usefull *Lawes,*
established by them, to whom thou hast committed thy people; To
those, the *Manualls,* the *pocket,* the *bosome books* of our own
Consciences; To those thy particular *books* of all our particular sins; [219]
and to those, the *Booke* with *seven seales,* which only *the Lamb* Rev. 5.9
which was slaine, was found worthy to open; which, I hope, it shall
not disagree with the meaning of thy blessed *Spirit,* to interprete,
the *promulgation of their pardon, and righteousnes, who are washed in*
the blood of that Lambe; And if thou refer me to these *Bookes,* to a
new reading, a new triall by these *bookes,* this *fever* may be but a
burning in the hand, and I may be saved, thogh not by my book, [220]
mine owne *conscience,* nor by thy other *books,* yet by thy *first,* the

book of *life,* thy *decree for my election,* and by thy *last,* the book of the *Lamb,* and the shedding of his blood upon me; If I be stil under *consultation,* I am not condemned yet; if I be sent to these books I shall not be condem'd at all: for, though there be somthing written in some of those *books* (particularly in the *Scriptures)* which some men [221] turne to *poyson,* yet upon these *consultations* (these *confessions,* these takings of our particular cases, into thy consideration) thou intendest all for *phisick,* and even from those *Sentences,* from which a too-late *Repenter* will sucke *desperation,* he that seeks thee early, shall receive thy *morning dew,* thy seasonable *mercy,* thy forward *consolation.*

9. *Prayer*

[222] O eternall and most gracious *God,* who art of so pure *eyes,* as that thou canst not look upon *sinn,* and we of so unpure constitutions, as that wee can present no object but *sin,* and therfore might justly feare, that thou wouldst turn thine *eyes* for ever from us, as, though we cannot indure *afflictions* in our selves, yet in *thee* we can; so thogh thou canst not indure *sinne* in us, yet in thy *Sonn* thou canst, and he hath taken upon him selfe, and presented to thee, al those [223] *sins,* which might displease thee in us. There is an *Eye* in *Nature,* that kills, as soon as it sees, the eye of a *Serpent,* no eye in *Nature,* that *nourishes* us by looking upon us; But thine *Eye, O Lord,* does so. Looke therefore upon me, *O Lord,* in this distresse, and that will recall mee from the borders of this bodily death; Look upon me, and that wil raise me again from that *spirituall death,* in which [224] my parents buried me, when they begot mee in *sinne,* and in which I have pierced even to the jawes of *hell,* by multiplying such heaps of *actuall sins,* upon that foundation, that root of *originall sinn.* Yet take me again, into your *Consultation, O blessed* and *glorious Trinitie;* and thogh the *Father* know, that I have defaced his *Image* received in my *Creation;* though the *Son* know, I have neglected mine interest in the *Redemption,* yet, *O blessed spirit,* as thou art to my [225] *Conscience,* so be to them a witnes, that at this *minute,* I accept that which I have so often, so often, so rebelliously refused, thy blessed inspirations; be thou my witnes to them, that at more pores than this slacke body sweates teares, this sad soule weeps blood; and more for the *displeasure* of my *God,* than for the stripes of his displeasure. Take me then, *O blessed, and glorious Trinitie,* into a [226] *Reconsultation,* and prescribe me any *phisick;* If it bee a long, and painful holding of this *soule* in *sicknes,* it is *phisick,* if I may discern thy hand to give it, and it is *phisick,* if it be a speedy departing of this *Soule,* if I may discerne thy hand to receive it.

10. Lentè et Serpenti satagunt occurrere Morbo.
They find the Disease to steale on insensibly,
and endeavour to meet with it so.

10. Meditation

This is *Natures nest of Boxes;* The *Heavens* containe the *Earth;* the
Earth, Cities; Cities, Men. And all these are *Concentrique;* the [227]
common *center* to them all, is *decay, ruine;* only that is *Eccentrique,*
which was never made; only that place, or garment rather, which
we can *imagine,* but not *demonstrate,* That light, which is the very
emanation of the light of *God,* in which the *Saints* shall dwell, with
which the *Saints* shall be appareld, only that bends not to this
Center, to *Ruine;* that which was not made of *Nothing,* is not [228]
threatned with this annihilation. All other things are; even *Angels,*
even our *soules;* they move upon the same *poles,* they bend to the
same *Center;* and if they were not made immortall by *preservation,*
their *Nature* could not keepe them from sinking to this *center,*
Annihilation. In all these (the *frame of the heavens,* the *States upon
earth,* and *Men in them,* comprehend all) Those are the greatest [229]
mischifs, which are least discerned; the most insensible in their
wayes come to bee the most sensible in their *ends.* The *Heavens*
have had their *Dropsie,* they drownd the world, and they shall have
their *Fever,* and burn the world. Of the *dropsie,* the flood, the world
had a foreknowledge 120 yeares before it came; and so some made
provision against it, and were saved; the *fever* shall break out in an [230]
instant, and consume all; The *dropsie* did no harm to the *heavens,*
from whence it fell, it did not put out those *lights,* it did not quench
those *heates;* but the *fever,* the fire shall burne the *furnace* it selfe,
annihilate those *heavens,* that breathe it out; Though the *Dog-
Starre* have a pestilent breath, an infectious exhalation, yet because
we know when it wil rise, we clothe ourselves, and wee diet our
selves, and wee shadow our selves to a sufficient prevention; but
Comets and *blazing starres,* whose effects or significations, no man [231]
can interrupt or frustrat, no man foresaw: no *Almanack* tells us,
when a *blazing starre* will break out, the matter is carried up in
secret; no *Astrologer* tels us when the effects wil be accomplished,
for thats a secret of a higher spheare, than the other; and that
which is most *secret,* is most *dangerous.* It is so also here in the
societies of men, in *States,* and *Commonwealths.* Twentie *rebellious* [232]
drums make not so dangerous a noise, as a few *whisperers,* and secret
plotters in corners. The *Cannon* doth not so much hurt against a

wal, as a *Myne* under the wall; nor a thousand enemies that threaten, so much as a few that take an oath to say nothing. *God* knew many heavy sins of the people, in the wildernes and after, but still he charges them with that one, with *Murmuring, murmuring* in [233] their *hearts,* secret disobediences, secret repugnances against his declar'd wil; and these are the most deadly, the most pernicious. And it is so too, with the *diseases* of the *body;* and that is my case. The *pulse,* the *urine,* the *sweat,* all have sworn to say *nothing,* to give no *Indication* of any dangerous *sicknesse.* My forces are not enfeebled, I find no decay in my strength; my provisions are not cut off; I find no abhorring in mine appetite; my counsels are not [234] corrupted nor infatuated, I find no false apprehensions, to work upon mine understanding; and yet they see, that invisibly, and I feele, that insensibly the *disease* prevails. The *disease* hath established a *Kingdome,* an *Empire* in mee, and will have certaine *Arcana Imperii, secrets of State,* by which it will proceed, and not be bound to *declare* them. But yet against those secret conspiracies in the State, the *Magistrate* hath the *rack;* and against these insensible [235] diseases, *Phisicians* have their *examiners;* and those these imploy now.

10. *Expostulation*

My God, my God, I have bin told, and told by relation, by her own *brother,* that did it, by thy servant *Nazianzen,* that his *Sister* in the vehemency of her *prayer,* did use to *threaten thee, with a holy importunitie, with a pious impudencie.* I dare not doe so, *O God;* but [236] as thy servant *Augustine,* wisht *that Adam had not sinned, therefore that Christ might not have died,* may I not to this one purpose wish, Josephus That if the *Serpent* before the tentation of *Eve,* did *goe upright,* and *speake,* that he did so still, because I should the sooner heare him, if he *spoke,* the sooner see him, if he *went upright?* In his curse, I am cursed too; his *creeping* undoes mee: for howsoever hee begin at the Jere. 9.21 *heele,* and doe but *bruise* that; yet *he,* and *Death in him is come into* [237] *our windowes;* into our *Eyes,* and *Eares,* the entrances and inlets of our *soule.* He works upon us in secret, and we doe not discerne him; And one great work of his upon us, is to make us so like himselfe, as to sin in *secret,* that others may not see us; But his *Master-piece* is, to make us sin in secret so, as that we may not see our selves sin. For the first, the hiding of our sins from other men, Joh. 8.44 [238] hee hath induc'd that, which was his *off-spring* from the beginning, *A lye:* for man, is in Nature, yet, in possession of some such sparkes of *ingenuitie, and noblenesse,* as that, but to disguise *Evill,* hee would not *lye.* The *bodie,* the *Sinne,* is the *Serpents,* and the *garment* that covers it, *the lye,* is his too. These are *his;* but the hiding of sinne from our selves, is *Hee himselfe:* when we have the sting of the *Serpent* in us, and doe not sting our selves, the venim of sin, and no remorse for sinn, then, as thy blessed Sonne said of **[239]** *Judas, Hee is a devill,* not that he *had* one, but *was* one, so we are Joh. 6.70 become *devils* to our selves, and we have not only a *Serpent* in our bosome, but we our selves, are to our selves that *Serpent.* How farre did thy servant *David* presse upon thy pardon, in that Psal. 19.12 petition, *Clense thou me from secret sinns?* can any sin bee secret? For, a great part of our sinnes, though, says thy *Prophet, we* **[240]** *conceive them in the darke, upon our bed,* yet sayes he, *We doe them in the light;* there are many sins, which we *glorie* in doing, and would not doe, if no body should know them. Thy blessed servant *Augustine* confesses, that hee was *ashamed of his shamefastnes, and tendernesse of Conscience,* and *that he often belied himself with sinnes, which he never did, lest he should be unacceptable to his sinfull companions.* But if we would conceale them (thy *Prophet* found **[241]** such a desire, and such a practise in some, when he said, *Thou hast* Isa. 47.10 *trusted in thy wickednes, and thou hast sayd, None shall see me*) yet can we conceale them? Thou O *God,* canst heare of them by others, Gen. 4.10 *The voice of Abels blood,* will tell thee of *Cains* murder; the *Heavens* Joh. 20.27 themselves will tell thee, *Heaven shal reveale his iniquity;* a smal Eccles. 10.20 creature alone, shall doe it, *A bird of the ayre shall carry the voice, and tell the matter:* Thou wilt trouble no *Informer,* thou thy selfe **[242]** Gen. 3.8 revealedst *Adams* sin, to thy selfe; And the manifestation of sin is so ful to thee, as that *thou shalt reveale all to all, Thou shalt bring* Eccles. 12.14 *every worke to Judgement, with every secret thing, and there is nothing* Mat. 10.26 *covered, that shall not bee revealed:* But, *O my God,* there is another way of knowing my sins, which thou lovest better than any of these; To know them by my *Confession.* As *Phisicke* works so, it **[243]** draws the *peccant humour* to itselfe, that when it is gathered together, the weight of it selfe may carry that humour away, so thy *Spirit* returns to my *Memory* my former sinnes, that being so recollected, they may poure out themselves by *Confession. When I* Psal. 32.3, 4 *kept silence,* says thy servant *David, day, and night, thy hand was* ver. 8 *heavy upon mee,* But when I said, *I wil confesse my transgressions unto the Lord, thou forgavest the iniquitie of my sinne.* Thou **[244]** interpretest the very *purpose* of *Confession* so well, as that thou scarce leavest any *new Mercy* for the *action* it selfe. This *Mercy* thou leavest, that thou armest us thereupon, against *relapses* into the sinnes which wee have confessed. And that *mercy,* which thy servant *Augustine* apprehends, when he sayes to thee, *Thou hast forgiven me those sinnes which I have done, and those sinnes which only* [245] *by thy grace I have not done:* they were done in our *inclination* to them, and even that *inclination* needs thy *mercy*, and that *Mercy* he calls a *Pardon*. And these are most truly *secret* sinnes, because they were never done, and because no other man, nor I my selfe, but onely thou knowest, how many and how great sinnes I have scaped by thy grace, which without that, I should have multiplied against thee.

[246]   *10. Prayer*

O eternall, and most gracious *God*, who as thy *Sonne Christ Jesus*, though hee knew all things, yet said *hee knew not the day of Judgement*, because he knew it not so, as that he might tell it us; so though thou knowest all my sins, yet thou knowest them not to my *comfort*, except thou know them by my telling them to thee; how [247] shall I bring to thy knowledg by that way, those sinns, which I my selfe know not? If I accuse my self of *Originall sin*, wilt thou ask me if I know what *originall sin is?* I know not enough of it to satisfie others, but I know enough to condemne my self, and to solicit thee. If I confesse to thee the *sinnes* of my *youth*, wilt thou aske me, if I know what those sins were? I know them not so well, as to name [248] them all, nor am sure to live houres enough to name them al, (for I did them then, faster than I can speak them now, when every thing that I did, conduc'd to some sinne) but I know them so well, as to know, that nothing but thy mercy is so *infinite* as they. If the naming of Sinnes, of *Thought, Word,* and *Deed,* of sinns of *Omission,* and of *Action,* of sins against *thee,* against my *neighbour,* and against *my self,* of sinns *unrepented,* and sinnes *relapsed* into after [249] *Repentance,* of sinnes of *Ignorance,* and sinnes against the testimonie of my *Conscience,* of sinnes against thy *Commaundements,* sinnes against thy *Sonnes Prayer,* and sinns against our owne *Creed,* of sins against the laws of that *Church,* and sinnes against the lawes of that *State,* in which thou hast given mee my station, If the naming of these *sinnes* reach not home to all mine, I know what will; *O Lord* [250] pardon me, me, all those *sinnes,* which thy *Sonne Christ Jesus* suffered for, who suffered for all the sinnes of all the world; for there is no sinne amongst all those which had not been my sinne, if thou hadst not beene my *God,* and *antedated* me a pardon in thy *preventing grace.* And since sinne in the nature of it, retaines still so much of the author of it, that it is a *Serpent,* insensibly insinuating it selfe, into my *Soule*, let thy *brazen Serpent*, (the contemplation of thy *Sonne* crucified for me) be evermore present to me, for my recovery [251] against the sting of the first *Serpent;* That so, as I have a *Lyon* against a *Lyon, The Lyon of the Tribe of Judah*, against that *Lyon, that seekes whom hee may devoure*, so I may have a *Serpent* against a *Serpent*, the *Wisedome of the Serpent*, against the *Malice of the Serpent*, And, both against that *Lyon*, and *Serpent*, forcible, and subtill tentations, Thy [252] *Dove* with thy *Olive*, in thy *Arke, Humilitie*, and *Peace*, and *Reconciliation* to thee, by the *ordinances* of thy *Church. Amen.*

11. Nobilibusque trahunt, a cincto Corde, venenum, Succis et Gemmis, et quae generosa, Ministrant Ars, et Natura, instillant.

They use Cordials, to keep the venim and Malignitie of the disease from the Heart.

11. Meditation

Whence can wee take a better argument, a clearer demonstration, [253] that all the *Greatnes* of this world, is built upon *opinion* of others, and hath in it self no *reall being*, nor power of subsistence, than from the *heart of man?* It is alwayes in *Action*, and *motion*, still busie, still pretending to doe all, to furnish all the powers, and faculties with all that they have; But if an enemy dare rise up against it, it is the soonest endangered, the soonest defeated of any part. The *Braine* will hold out longer than it, and the *Liver* longer [254] than that; They will endure a *Siege;* but an unnatural heat, a rebellious heat, will blow up the *heart*, like a *Myne*, in a *minute*. But howsoever, since the *Heart* hath the *birth-right*, and *Primogeniture*, and that it is *Natures eldest Sonne* in us, the part which is first born to life in man, and that the other parts, as *younger brethren*, and servants in this family, have a dependance upon it, it is reason that [255] the principall care bee had of it, though it bee not the strongest part; as the *eldest* is oftentimes not the strongest of the family. And since the *Braine*, and *Liver*, and *Heart*, hold not a *Triumvirate* in *Man*, a *Soveraignitie* equallly shed upon them all, for his *well-being*, as the foure *Elements* doe, for his very *being*, but the *Heart* alone is

[256] in the *Principalitie*, and in the *Throne*, as *King*, the rest as *Subjects*, though in eminent *Place*, and *Office*, must contribute to that, as *Children* to their *Parents*, as all persons to all kindes of *Superiours*, though oftentimes, those *Parents*, or those *Superiours*, bee not of stronger parts, than themselves, that serve and obey them that are weaker. Neither doth this Obligation fall upon us, by second
[257] *Dictates* of *Nature*, by *Consequences*, and *Conclusions* arising out of *Nature*, or deriv'd from Nature, by *Discourse*, (as many things binde us, even by the Law of *Nature*, and yet not by the *primarie* Law of *Nature;* as all Lawes of *Proprietie* in that which we possesse, are of the Law of *Nature*, which law is, *To give every one his owne*, and yet in the *primarie* law of *Nature*, there was no *Proprietie*, no
[258] *Meum et Tuum*, but an universall *Communitie* over all; So the obedience of *Superiours*, is of the law of *Nature*, and yet in the *primarie* law of *Nature*, there was no *Superioritie*, no *Magistracie*;) but this contribution of assistance of all to the *Soveraigne*, of all parts to the *Heart*, is from the very *first dictates of Nature;* which is in the first place, to have care of our owne *Preservation*, to looke
[259] first to our selves; for therefore doth the *Phisician* intermit the present care of *Braine*, or *Liver*, because there is a possibilitie, that they may subsist, though there bee not a present and a particular care had of them, but there is no possibilitie that they can subsist, if the *Heart* perish: and so, when we seeme to begin with others, in such assistances, indeed wee doe beginne with our selves, and wee
[260] our selves are principally in our contemplation; and so all these officious, and mutuall assistances, are but *complements* towards others, and our true end is *our selves*. And this is the reward of the paines of *Kings;* sometimes they neede the power of law, to be obeyd; and when they seeme to be obey'd *voluntarily*, they who doe it, doe it for their owne sakes. O how little a thing is all the *greatnes of man*, and through how false glasses doth he make shift
[261] to *multiply it*, and *magnifie* it to himselfe? And yet this is also another misery of this *King of man*, the *Heart*, which is also applyable to the *Kings* of this world, *great men*, that the venime and poyson of every pestilentiall disease directs it selfe to the *heart*, affects that, (pernicious affection,) and the *malignity* of ill men, is also directed upon the *greatest*, and the *best;* and not only *greatnesse*,
[262] but *goodnesse* loses the vigour of beeing an *Antidote*, or *Cordiall* against it. And as the noblest, and most generous *Cordialls* that *Nature* or *Art* afford, or can prepare, if they be often taken, and made *familiar*, become no *Cordialls*, nor have any extraordinary operation, so the greatest *Cordiall* of the *Heart*, patience, if it bee much exercis'd, exalts the *venim* and the *malignity* of the *Enemy*,

and the more we suffer, the more wee are insulted upon. When *God* had made this *Earth* of *nothing*, it was but a little helpe, that he had, to make other things of this *Earth*: nothing can be neerer nothing, than *Earth;* and yet how little of this *Earth*, is the *greatest Man?* Hee thinkes he treads upon the *Earth*, that all is under his feete, and the *Braine* that thinkes so, is but *Earth;* his highest Region, the flesh that covers that, is but *earth;* and even the toppe of that, that wherein so many *Absolons* take so much pride, is but a bush growing upon that *Turfe of Earth.* How litle of the world is the *Earth?* And yet that is all, that *Man hath,* or *is.* How little of a *Man* is the *Heart;* and yet it is all, by which he *is:* and this continually subject, not onely to forraine poysons, conveyed by others, but to intestine poysons bred in our selves by pestilentiall sicknesses. O who, if before hee had a beeing, he could have sense of this miserie, would buy a being here upon these conditions?

[263]

[264]

[265]

11. Expostulation

My God, my *God,* all that thou askest of mee, is my *Heart, My Sonne, give mee thy heart;* Am I thy *sonne,* as long as I have but *my heart?* Wilt thou give mee an *Inheritance, a Filiation,* any thing for *my heart?* O thou, who saydst to Satan, *Hast thou considered my servant Job, that there is none like him upon earth,* shall my feare, shall my zeale, shall my jealousie have leave to say to thee, Hast thou considered *my Heart,* that there is not so perverse a *Heart* upon earth; and wouldest thou have *that;* and shall I be thy *Sonne,* thy eternall Sonnes *Coheire,* for giving that? *The Heart is deceitfull, above all things, and desperately wicked; who can know it?* Hee that askes that question, makes the answere, *I the Lord search the Heart.* When didst thou search mine? Dost thou thinke to finde it, as thou madest it in *Adam?* Thou hast searched since, and found all these gradations in the ill of our *Hearts, That every imagination, of the thoughts of our hearts, is onely evill continually.* Doest thou remember this, and wouldest thou have my *Heart?* O *God of all light,* I know thou knowest all; and it is *Thou,* that declarest unto man, what is his *Heart.* Without thee, *O Soveraigne goodnesse,* I could not know, how ill my *heart* were. Thou hast declared unto mee, in thy Word, That for all this *deluge* of evill, that hath surrounded all *Hearts,* yet thou soughtest and *foundest a man after thine owne heart,* That *thou couldest and wouldest give thy people Pastours according to thine owne heart;* And I can gather out of thy *Word,* so good testimony of the *hearts* of men, as to finde *single*

Prov. 23.26

[266] Job 1.8

Jer. 17.9
[267]

Gen. 6.5

[268] Amos 4.13

1 Sam. 13.14
Jer. 3.15
[269]

hearts, docile, and *apprehensive hearts;* Hearts that *can,* Hearts that *have* learnt; *wise hearts,* in one place, and in another, in a great degree, *wise, perfit* hearts; *straight* hearts, no perversnesse without, and *cleane* hearts, no foulenesse within; such hearts I can find in thy Word; and if my *heart* were such a *heart,* I would give thee my *Heart.* But I find *stonie* hearts too, and I have made mine such: I have found *Hearts, that are snares;* and I have conversed with such; *hearts that burne like Ovens;* and the fuell of *Lust,* and *Envie,* and *Ambition,* hath inflamed mine; *Hearts in which their Masters trust, And hee that trusteth in his owne heart, is a foole;* His confidence in his owne morall Constancie, and civill fortitude, will betray him, when thou shalt cast a spirituall dampe, a heavinesse, and dejection of spirit upon him. I have found these *Hearts,* and a worse than these, a *Heart* into which the *Devill* himselfe is entred, *Judas heart.* The first kind of heart, alas, my *God,* I have not; The last are not *Hearts* to bee given to thee; What shall I do? Without that present I cannot bee thy *Sonne,* and I have it not. To those of the first kinde, thou givest *joyfulnes of heart,* and I have not that; To those of the other kinde, thou givest *faintnesse of heart:* And blessed bee thou, *O God,* for that forbearance, I have not that yet. There is then a middle kinde of *Hearts,* not so perfit, as to bee given, but that the very giving, mends them: Not so desperate, as not to bee accepted, but that the very accepting dignifies them. This is a *melting* heart, and a *troubled* heart; and a *wounded* heart, and a *broken* heart, and a *contrite* heart; and by the powerfull working of thy piercing spirit, such a *Heart* I have; *Thy Samuel* spake unto all the house of thy *Israel,* and sayd, *If you return to the Lord with all your hearts, prepare your hearts unto the Lord.* If my heart bee *prepared,* it is a *returning* heart; And if thou see it upon the *way,* thou wilt carrie it *home;* Nay, the *preparation* is thine too; this *melting,* this *wounding,* this *breaking,* this *contrition,* which I have now, is thy *Way,* to thy *Ende;* And those *discomforts,* are for all that, *The earnest of thy Spirit in my heart;* and where thou givest *earnest,* thou wilt performe the *bargaine. Nabal* was confident upon his wine, but *in the morning his heart dyed within him;* Thou, O Lord, hast given mee *Wormewood,* and I have had some diffidence upon that; and thou hast cleared a *Morning* to mee againe, and my heart is alive. Davids *heart smote him, when hee cut off the skirt from Saul;* and *his heart smote him, when hee had numbred his people:* My heart hath strucke mee, when I come to number my sinnes; but that blowe is not to death, because those sinnes are not to death, but my heart lives in thee. But yet as long as I remaine in this great *Hospitall,* this sicke, this diseasefull world, as long as I remaine in this leprous house, this flesh of mine, this Heart, though thus prepared *for* thee, prepared *by* thee, will

Ezek. 11.19 [270]
Eccles. 7.26

Prov. 28.26

[271]

Joh. 13.2

[272]
Ecclus. 50.23
Levit. 16.36

Josh. 2.11 [273]

1 Sam. 7.3

[274]

2 Cor. 1.22

1 Sam. 25.37

[275]
1 Sam. 24.5
2 Sam. 24.10

[276]

still be subject to the invasion of maligne and pestilent vapours. 1 King. 8.38
But I have my *Cordialls* in thy promise; *when I shall know the plague of my heart, and pray unto thee, in thy house*, thou wilt preserve that
heart, from all mortall force, of that infection: And the *Peace of* [277] Philip. 4.7
God, which passeth all understanding, shall keepe my Heart and Minde through Christ Jesus.

11. Prayer

O eternall, and most gracious *God*, who in thy *upper house*, the
Heavens, though there bee many *Mansions*, yet art alike, and equally
in every *Mansion*, but heere in thy *lower house*, though thou fillest [278]
all, yet art otherwise in some roomes thereof, than in others,
otherwise in thy *Church*, than in my *Chamber*, and otherwise in thy
Sacraments, than in my *Prayers*, so though thou bee alwayes present,
and alwayes working in every roome of this thy House, my body, yet
I humbly beseech thee to manifest alwayes a more effectuall
presence in my *heart*, than in the other Offices. Into the house of [279]
thine Annoynted, disloyall persons, Traitors will come; Into thy
House, the *Church*, *Hypocrites*, and *Idolatrers* will come; Into some
Roomes of this thy House, my *Body*, *Tentations* will come, *Infections*
will come, but bee my *Heart*, thy *Bed-chamber*, O my *God*, and
thither let them not enter. *Job made a Covenant with his Eyes*, but
not his making of that *Covenant*, but thy dwelling in his heart, [280]
enabled him to keepe that *Covenant*. Thy *Sonne* himselfe had a
sadnesse in his Soule to death, and hee had a *reluctation*, a *deprecation*
of death, in the approaches thereof; but hee had his *Cordiall* too, *Yet
not my will, but thine bee done*. And as thou hast not delivered us,
thine *adopted sonnes*, from these infectious tentations, so neither
hast thou delivered us over to them, nor withheld thy *Cordialls* [281]
from us. I was baptized in thy *Cordiall water*, against *Originall sinne*,
and I have drunke of thy *Cordiall Blood*, for my recoverie, from
actual, and habituall sinne in the other *Sacrament*. Thou, *O Lord*,
who hast imprinted all medicinall vertues, which are in all creatures,
and hast made even the flesh of *Vipers*, to assist in *Cordialls*, art able
to make this present sicknesse, everlasting health; this weaknes, [282]
everlasting strength; and this very dejection, and faintnesse of
heart, a powerfull *Cordiall*. When thy blessed *Sonne* cryed out to
thee, *My God, my God, why hast thou forsaken mee*, thou diddest
reach out thy hand to him; but not to deliver his *sad soule*, but to
receive his *holy soule*; Neither did hee longer desire to hold it of
thee, but to recommend it to thee. I see thine hand upon mee now, [283]
O Lord, and I aske not why it comes, what it intends: whether thou

wilt bidde it stay still in this *Body*, for some time, or bidd it meet
thee this day in *Paradise*, I aske not, not in a *wish*, not in a *thought*:
Infirmitie of Nature, Curiositie of Minde, are tentations that offer;
but a silent, and absolute obedience, to thy will, even before I know
it, is my *Cordiall*. Preserve that to mee, O my *God*, and that will
[284] preserve mee to thee; that when thou hast *Catechised* mee with
affliction here, I may take a greater *degree*, and serve thee in a higher
place, in thy kingdome of *joy*, and *glory. Amen.*

12. Spirante Columbâ, Suppositâ pedibus, Revocantur ad ima vapores.

They apply Pidgeons, to draw the vapors from the Head.

12. Meditation

[285] What will not kill a man, if a *vapor* will? how great an *Elephant*,
how small a *Mouse* destroyes? To dye by a *bullet* is the *Souldiers
dayly bread*; but few men dye by *haile-shot*: A man is more worth,
than to bee sold for *single money*; a *life* to be valued above a *trifle*. If
this were a violent shaking of the Ayre by *Thunder*, or by *Cannon*,
in that case the *Ayre* is condensed above the thicknesse of *water*, of
[286] water baked into *Ice*, almost *petrified*, almost made stone, and no
wonder that that kills; but that that which is but a *vapor*, and a
vapor not forced, but breathed, should kill, that our *Nourse* should
overlay us, and *Ayre*, that nourishes us, should destroy us, but that
it is a *halfe Atheisme* to murmure against *Nature*, who is *Gods
immediate Commissioner*, who would not think himselfe miserable
[287] to bee put into the hands of *Nature*, who does not only set him up
for a *marke* for others to shoote at, but delights her selfe to blow
him up like a *glasse*, till shee see him breake, even with her owne
breath? Nay if this infectious *vapour* were sought for, or travel'd to,
as *Pliny* hunted after the *vapor* of *Aetna* and dar'd, and challenged
Death in the forme of a *vapor* to doe his worst, and felt the worst,
[288] he dyed; or if this *vapor* were met withall in an *ambush*, and we
surprized with it, out of a long shutt *Well*, or out of a new opened
Myne, who would lament, who would accuse, when we had nothing
to accuse, none to lament against, but *Fortune*, who is lesse than a
vapour: But when our selves are the *Well*, that breathes out this

exhalation, the *Oven* that spits out this fiery smoke, the *Myne* that spues out this suffocating, and strangling *dampe*, who can ever after this, aggravate his sorrow, by this *Circumstance*, That it was his [289] *Neighbor*, his *familiar friend*, his *brother* that destroyed him, and destroyed him with a whispering, and calumniating breath, when wee our selves doe it to our selves by the same meanes, kill our selves with our owne *vapors?* Or if these occasions of this selfe-destruction, had any contribution from our owne *wils*, any assistance from our owne *intentions*, nay from our owne *errors*, wee [290] might divide the rebuke, and chide our selves as much as them. *Fevers* upon wilful distempers of drinke, and surfeits, *Consumptions* upon intemperances, and licentiousnes, *Madnes* upon misplacing, or over-bending our naturall faculties, proceed from our selves, and so, as that our selves are in the plot, and wee are not onely *passive*, but *active* too, to our owne destruction; But what have I [291] done, either to *breed*, or to *breathe* these *vapors?* They tell me it is my *Melancholy*; Did I infuse, did I drinke in *Melancholly* into my selfe? It is my *thoughtfulness;* was I not made to *thinke?* It is my *study;* doth not my *Calling* call for that? I have don nothing, wilfully, perversly toward it, yet must suffer in it, die by it. There are too many *Examples* of men, that have bin their own *executioners*, [292] and that have made hard shift to bee so; some have alwayes had *poyson* about them, in a *hollow ring* upon their finger, and some in their *Pen* that they used to write with: some have beat out their *braines* at the wal of their prison, and some have eaten the *fire* out of their chimneys: and one is said to have come neerer our case Coma, Intro. in then so, to have strangled himself, though his hands were bound, Val. Max by crushing his throat between his knees; But I doe nothing upon [293] my selfe, and yet am mine own *Executioner*. And we have heard of *death*, upon small occasions, and by scornefull *instruments;* a *pinne*, a *combe*, a *haire* pulled, hath gangred, and killd; But when I have said, a *vapour*, if I were asked again, what is a *vapour*, I could not tell, it is so insensible a thing; so neere *nothing* is that that reduces us to *nothing*. But extend this *vapour*, rarefie it; from so narow a roome, as our *Naturall bodies*, to any *Politike body*, to a *State*. That [294] which is *fume* in us, is in a State, *Rumor*, and these *vapours* in us, which wee consider here pestilent, and infectious fumes, are in a State *infectious rumors*, detracting and dishonourable *Calumnies*, *Libels*. The *Heart* in that *body* is the *King*; and the *Braine*, his *Councell;* and the whole *Magistracie*, that ties all together, is the *Sinewes*, which proceed from thence; and the *life* of all is *Honour*, [295] and just *respect*, and due *reverence;* and therfore, when these *vapors*, these venimous *rumors*, are directed against these *Noble parts*, the whole body suffers. But yet for all their priviledges, they are not priviledged from our *misery*; that as the *vapours* most pernitious to us, arise in our owne bodies, so doe the most dishonorable *rumours*, [296] and those that wound a *State* most, arise at home. What ill *ayre*, that I could have met in the street, what *channell*, what *shambles*, what *dunghill*, what *vault*, could have hurt mee so much, as these home-bredd *vapours*? What *fugitive*, what *Almes-man of any forraine State*, can doe so much harme, as a *Detracter*, a *Libeller*, a scornefull *Jester* at home? For, as they that write of *Poysons*, and of Arduino [297] creatures naturally disposed to the ruine of Man, do as well mention the *Flea*, as the *Viper*, because the *Flea*, though hee kill none, hee does all the harme hee can, so even these libellous and licentious *Jesters*, utter the *venim* they have: though sometimes *vertue*, and alwaies *power*, be a good *Pigeon* to draw this *vapor* from the *Head*, and from doing any deadly harme there.

12. Expostulation

[298] My *God*, my *God*, as thy servant *James*, when he asks that question, Jam. 4.14 *What is your life*, provides me my answere, *It is even a vapor, that appeareth for a little time, and then vanisheth away*, so if he did aske me what is your *death*, I am provided of my answere, *It is a vapor too;* And why should it not be all one to mee, whether I live, or die, if life, and death be all one, both a *vapor*. Thou hast made *vapor* so [299] indifferent a thing, as that thy *Blessings*, and thy *Judgements* are equally expressed by it, and it is made by thee the *Hierogliphique* of both. Why should not that bee alwaies good, by which thou Gen. 2.6 hast declared thy plentifull goodnes to us? *A vapor went up from the Earth, and watred the whole face of the ground*, And that by Levit. 16.13 which thou hast imputed a goodnes to us, and wherein thou hast Ezek. 8.11 [300] accepted our service to thee, *sacrifices;* for *Sacrifices*, were vapors, And in them it is said, that a *thicke cloude of incence went up to thee*. So it is of that, wherein thou comst to us, the dew of *Heaven*, And of that wherein we come to thee, both are *vapors;* And hee, in whom we *have*, and *are* all that we *are* or *have*, temporally, or spiritually, thy blessed *Son*, in the person of *wisedome*, is called so Wisd. 7.25 too; *she is* (that is, *he is*) *the vapor of the power of God, and the pure influence from the glory of the Almighty*. Hast thou, Thou, O my [301] *God*, perfumed *vapor*, with thine own breath, with so many sweet acceptations, in thine own *Word*, and shall this *vapor* receive an ill, and infectious sense? It must; for, since we have displeased thee, with that which is but *vapor*, (for what is *sinne*, but a *vapor*, but a *smoke*, though such a smoke, as takes away our sight, and disables

us from seeing our danger) it is just, that thou punish us with *vapors* too. For so thou dost, as the *Wiseman* tels us, *Thou canst punish us by those things, wherein wee offend thee;* as he hath [302] Wisd. 11.18,19 expressed it there, *By beasts newly created, breathing vapors.* Therefore that Commination of thine, by thy *Prophet, I will shew* Joel 2.30 *wonders in the heaven, and in the Earth, bloud and fire, and pillars of smoke,* thine *Apostle,* who knewe thy meaning best, calls *vapors of* Acts 2.19 *smoke.* One *Prophet* presents thee in thy terriblenesse, so, *There* [303] Psal. 18.8 *went out out a smoke at his Nostrils,* and another, the effect of thine anger so, *The house was filled with smoake;* And hee that continues Isa. 6.4 his *Prophesie,* as long as the world can continue, describes the miseries of the latter times so, *Out of the bottomlesse pit arose a* Rev. 9.2, 3 *smoke, that darkened the Sunne, and out of that smoke came Locusts, who had the power of Scorpions.* Now all *smokes* begin in *fire,* and all these will end so too: The smoke of *sin,* and of thy *wrath,* will end in the fire of *hell.* But hast thou afforded us no means to evaporate [304] these *smokes,* to withdraw these *vapors?* When thine *Angels* fell from heaven, thou tookst into thy care, the reparation of that place, and didst it, by assuming, by drawing us thither; when we fel from thee here, in this world, thou tookst into thy care the reparation of this place too, and didst it by assuming us another way, by descending down to assume our nature, in thy *Son.* So [305] that though our last act be an ascending to glory, (we shall ascend to the place of *Angels*) yet our first act is to goe the way of thy *Sonn, descending,* and the way of thy blessed *Spirit* too, who *descended in the Dove.* Therefore hast thou bin pleased to afford us this remedy in *Nature,* by this application of a *Dove,* to our lower parts, to make these *vapors* in our *bodies,* to descend, and to make [306] that a *type* to us, that by the visitation of thy *Spirit,* the *vapors* of sin shall descend, and we tread them under our feet. At the baptisme of thy *Son,* the *Dove* descended, and at the exalting of thine *Apostles* to preach, the same Spirit descended. Let us draw down the *vapors* of our own *pride,* our own *wits,* our own *wils,* our own *inventions,* to the *simplicitie* of thy *Sacraments,* and the obedience of thy word, and these *Doves,* thus applied, shall make us live.

12. *Prayer* [307]

O eternall and most gracious *God,* who though thou have suffred us to destroy our selves, and hast not given us the power of reparation in our selves, hast yet afforded us such meanes of

2   DEVOTIONS UPON EMERGENT OCCASIONS

reparation, as may easily, and familiarly be compassed by us,
[308] prosper I humbly beseech thee this means of bodily assistance in
this thy ordinary *creature,* and prosper thy meanes of spirituall
assistance in thy holy *ordinances.* And as thou hast caried this thy
creature the *Dove,* through all thy wayes, through *Nature,* and made
it naturally proper to conduce medicinally to our *bodily health,*
through the *Law,* and made it a *sacrifice* for *sinne* there; and
through the *Gospel,* and made it, and thy Spirit in it, a witnes of
[309] thy *Sonnes baptisme* there: so carry it, and the qualities of it home
to my *soule,* and imprint there that *simplicity,* that *mildnesse,* that
harmelesnesse, which thou hast imprinted by *Nature* in this
Creature. That so all *vapours* of all disobedience to thee, being
subdued under my feete, I may in the power, and triumphe of thy
Psal. 91.13 *Sonne,* treade victoriously upon my *grave,* and trample upon the
Eze. 7.16 [310] *Lyon,* and *Dragon,* that lye under it, to devoure me. Thou *O Lord,*
by the *Prophet* callest the *Dove,* the *Dove of the Valleys,* but
promisest that *the Dove of the Valleyes shall bee upon the Mountaine:*
As thou hast layed mee low, in this *Valley* of sickenesse, so low, as
Ezek. 7.3 that I am made fit for that question, asked in the field of bones,
Sonne of man, can these bones live, so, in thy good time, carry me
up to these *Mountaynes,* of which, even in this *Valley,* thou
[311] affordest mee a prospect, the Mountain where thou dwellest, the
holy Hill, unto which none can ascend but *hee that hath cleane
hands,* which none can have, but by that one and that strong way,
of making them cleane, in the blood of thy Sonne *Christ Jesus.*
Amen.

[312] # 13. Ingeniumque malum, numeroso
stigmate, fassus Pellitur ad pectus, Morbique
Suburbia, Morbus.
The Sicknes declares the infection and
malignity therof by spots.

13. Meditation

Wee say, that the world is made of *sea,* and *land,* as though they
were equal; but we know that ther is more *sea* in the *Western,* than

in the *Eastern Hemisphere*: We say that the *Firmament* is full of
starres; as though it were equally full; but we know, that there are   [313]
more *stars* under the *Northerne*, than under the *Southern Pole*. Wee
say, the *Elements* of man are *misery*, and *happinesse*, as though he
had an equal proportion of both, and the dayes of man
vicissitudinary, as though he had as many *good* daies, as *ill*, and that
he livd under a perpetuall *Equinoctial, night* and *day* equall, good
and ill fortune in the same measure. But it is far from that; hee   [314]
drinkes misery, and he *tastes happiness*; he *mowes misery*, and hee
gleanes happinesse; hee *journies in misery*, he does but *walke in
happinesse;* and which is worst, his misery is *positive*, and
dogmaticall, his happinesse is but *disputable*, and *problematicall;* All
men call *Misery, Misery*, but *Happinesse* changes the name, by the
taste of man. In this *accident* that befalls mee now, that this
sicknesse declares it selfe by *Spots*, to be a malignant, and   [315]
pestilentiall disease, if there be a *comfort* in the declaration, that
therby the *Phisicians* see more cleerely what to doe, there may bee
as much *discomfort* in this, That the malignitie may bee so great, as
that all that they can doe, shall doe *nothing;* That an enemy *declares*
himselfe, then, when he is able to subsist, and to pursue, and to
atchive his ends, is no great comfort. In intestine Conspiracies,   [316]
voluntary Confessions doe more good, than confessions upon the
Rack; In these Infections, when *Nature* her selfe confesses, and
cries out by these outward declarations, which she is able to put
forth of her selfe, they minister *comfort;* but when all is by the
strength of *Cordials*, it is but a *Confession upon the Racke*, by which
though wee come to knowe the malice of that man, yet wee doe not   [317]
knowe, whether there bee not as much malice in his heart then, as
before his confession; we are sure of his *Treason*, but not of his
Repentance; sure of *him*, but not of his *Complices*. It is a faint
comfort to know the worst, when the worst is *remedilesse;* and a
weaker than that, to know *much ill*, and not to know, that that is the
worst. A woman is comforted with the birth of her *Son*, her body
is eased of a burden; but if shee could *prophetically* read his *History*,   [318]
how *ill a man*, perchance *how ill a sonne*, he would prove, shee
should receive a greater burden into her *Mind*. Scarce any purchase
that is not cloggd with secret *encumbrances;* scarce any *happines*,
that hath not in it so much of the *nature* of false and base money, as
that the *Alloy* is more than the *Mettall*. Nay is it not so, (at least
much towards it) even in the exercise of *Vertues?* I must bee poore,   [319]
and want, before I can exercise the vertue of *Gratitude;* miserable,
and in torment, before I can exercise the vertue of *patience;* How
deepe do we dig, and for how coarse gold? And what other

Touch-stone have we of our *gold*, but *comparison?* Whether we be as happy, as others, or as our selvs at other times; O poore stepp toward being well, when these *spots* do only tell us, that we are worse, than we were sure of before.

[320]

13. Expostulation

My God, my God, thou hast made this sick bed thine *Altar,* and I have no other *Sacrifice* to offer, but my self; and wilt thou accept *no spotted sacrifice?* Doeth thy *Son* dwel bodily in this flesh, that thou shouldst looke for an unspottednes here? Or is the *Holy* *Ghost,* the *soule* of this *body,* as he is of thy *Spouse,* who is therfore *all faire, and no spot in her?* or hath thy *Son* himself no *spots,* who hath al our stains, and deformities in him? Or hath thy *Spouse,* thy *Church,* no *spots,* when every particular limbe of that faire, and spotles body, every particular *soule* in that *Church* is full of staines, and spots? Thou bidst us *hate the garment that is spotted with the flesh.* The *flesh* it selfe is the *garment,* and it spotteth it selfe, with it self. And *if I wash my selfe with snow water, mine own clothes shall make me abominable;* and yet *no man yet ever hated his owne flesh: Lord,* if thou looke for a *spotlesnesse,* whom wilt thou looke upon? Thy mercy may goe a great way in my *soule,* and yet not leave me without *spots;* Thy corrections may go far, and burn deepe, and yet not leave me spotles: thy *children* apprehended that, when they said, *From our former iniquitie wee are not cleansed, untill this day, though there was a plague in the Congregation of the Lord;* Thou rainest upon us, and yet doest not alwaies mollifie all our hardnesse; Thou kindlest thy fires in us, and yet doest not alwayes burne up all our drosse; Thou healst our *wounds,* and yet leavest *scarres;* Thou purgest the *blood,* and yet leavest *spots.* But the *spots* that thou hatest, are the *spotts* that we hide. *The Carvers of Images cover spotts,* sayes the *Wiseman;* When we hide our *spotts,* wee became *Idolatrers* of our owne staines, of our own foulenesses. But if my *spots* come forth, by what meanes soever, whether by the strength of *Nature,* by *voluntary confession,* (for *Grace* is the *Nature* of a *Regenerate man,* and the power of *Grace* is the strength of *Nature*) or by the vertue of *Cordialls,* (for even thy *Corrections* are *Cordials*) if they come forth either way, thou receivest that *Confession* with a gracious Interpretation. When thy servant *Jacob* practised an *Invention* to procure *spotts* in his sheepe, thou diddest prosper his *Rodds;* and thou dost prosper thine owne *Rodds,* when *corrections* procure the discovery of our *spotts,* the humble

Song of Sol. 4.7
[321]

Jude ver. 23

Job 9.30, 31
Ephes. 5.29 [322]

Josh. 22.17

[323]

Wisd. 13.14
[324]

Gen. 30.37, 39 [325]

manifestation of our sinns to thee; Till then thou maist justly say, Mat. 9.12
The whole need not the Phisician; Till wee tell thee in our sicknes,
wee think our selves whole, till we shew our *spotts*, thou appliest Job 11.15
no *medicine*. But since I do that, shall I not, *Lord, lift up my face* [326]
without spot, and be stedfast, and not feare? Even my *spotts* belong to
thy *Sonnes* body, and are part of that, which he came downe to this
earth, to fetch, and challenge, and assume to himselfe. When I
open my *spotts*, I doe but present him with that which is *His*, and
till I do so, I detaine, and withhold *his right*. When therfore thou
seest them upon me, as *His*, and seest them by this way of
Confession, they shall not appear to me, as the *pinches of death*, to [327]
decline my feare to *Hell;* (for *thou hast not left thy holy one in Hell,*
thy *Sonne* is not there) but these *spotts* upon my *Breast*, and upon
my *Soule*, shal appeare to mee as the *Constellations* of the
Firmament, to direct my Contemplation to that place, where thy
Son is, thy *right hand*.

13. *Prayer*

O eternall, and most gratious *God*, who as thou givest all for [328]
nothing, if we consider any precedent Merit in us, so giv'st *Nothing*,
for *Nothing;* if we consider the *acknowledgement*, and *thankefullnesse*,
which thou lookest for, after, accept my humble thankes, both for
thy *Mercy*, and for this particular *Mercie*, that in thy *Judgement* I
can discerne thy *Mercie*, and find *comfort* in thy *corrections*. I know,
O *Lord*, the ordinary *discomfort* that accompanies that phrase, *That* [329]
the house is visited, And that, *that thy markes, and thy tokens are upon*
the patient; But what a wretched, and disconsolate *Hermitage* is
that *House*, which is not *visited* by thee, and what a *Waife*, and *Stray*
is that *Man*, that hath not thy *Markes* upon him? These heates, *O*
Lord, which thou hast broght upon this *body*, are but thy chafing of
the *wax*, that thou mightest *seale* me to thee; These *spots* are but [330]
the *letters*, in which thou hast written thine owne *Name*, and
conveyed thy selfe to mee: whether for a *present possession*, by taking
me now, or for a future *reversion*, by glorifying thy selfe in my stay
here, I limit not, I condition not, I choose not, I wish not, no more
than the house, or land, that passeth by any *Civill* conveyance.
Onely be thou ever present to me, *O my God*, and this *bed-chamber*, [331]
and thy bed-chamber shal be all one roome, and the closing of
these bodily *Eyes* here, and the opening of the *Eyes* of my *Soule*,
there, all one *Act*.

14. Idque notant Criticis, Medici, evenisse Diebus.

The Phisicians observe these accidents to have fallen upon the criticall dayes.

14. Meditation

[332] I would not make *Man* worse than hee is, Nor his Condition more miserable than it is. But could I though I would? As a Man cannot *flatter God*, nor over prayse him, so a Man cannot *injure* Man, nor undervalue him. Thus much must necessarily be presented to his remembrance, that those *false Happinesses,* which he hath in this World, have their *times,* and their *seasons,* [333] and their *Critical dayes,* and they are *Judged,* and *Denominated* according to the times, when they befall us. What poore *Elements* are our *happinesses* made of, if *Tyme, Tyme* which wee can scarce consider to be *any thing,* be an essential part of our *happines?* All things are done in some *place;* but if we consider *place* to be no more, but the next hollow *Superficies* of the *Ayre, Alas,* how thinne, and fluid a thing is *Ayre,* and how thinne a *filme* is a [334] *Superficies,* and a *Superficies* of *Ayre?* All things are done in *time* too; but if we consider *Tyme* to be but the *Measure of Motion,* and howsoever it may seeme to have three *stations, past, present,* and *future,* yet the *first* and *last* of these *are* not (one is not, now, and the other is not yet) And that which you call *present,* is not *now* the same that it was, when you began to call it so in this *Line,* [335] (before you found that word, *present,* or that *Monosyllable, now,* the present, and the *Now* is past,) if this *Imaginary halfe-nothing, Tyme,* be of the Essence of our *Happinesses,* how can they be thought *durable? Tyme* is not so; How can they bee thought to be? Tyme is not so; not so, considered in any of the *parts* thereof. If we consider *Eternity,* into that, *Tyme* never Entred; *Eternity* is not an everlasting flux of *Tyme;* but Tyme is as a short *parenthesis* [336] in a longe *period;* and *Eternity* had bin the same, as it is, though time had never beene; If we consider, not *Eternity,* but *Perpetuity,* not that which had no *tyme* to beginne in, but which shall out-live *Tyme* and be, when *Tyme shall bee no more,* what A *Minute* is the life of the Durablest *Creature,* compared to that? And what a Minute is Mans life in respect of the Sunnes, or of a tree? and yet [337] how little of our *life* is *Occasion, opportunity* to receyve good in;

and how little of that *occasion,* doe wee apprehend, and lay hold
of? How busie, and perplexed a *Cobweb,* is the *Happinesse* of Man
here? that must bee made up with a *Watchfulnesse,* to lay hold
upon *Occasion,* which is but a little peece of that, which is
Nothing, Tyme: And yet the best things are *Nothing* without that.
Honors, Pleasures, Possessions, presented to us, out of time, in our
decrepit, and distasted, and unapprehensive *Age,* lose their *office,* [338]
and lose their *Name;* They are not *Honors* to us, that shall never
appeare, nor come abroad into the Eyes of the people, to receive
Honor, from them who give it: Nor *pleasures* to us, who have lost
our sense to taste them; nor *possessions* to us, who are departing
from the possession of them. Youth is their *Criticall Day;* that
Judges them; that *Denominates* them, that *inanimates,* and *informes* [339]
them, and makes them *Honors,* and pleasures, and *possessions;*
and when they come in an unapprehensive *Age,* they come as a
Cordiall when the bell rings out, as a *Pardon* when the Head is
off. We rejoyce in the Comfort of *fire,* but does any Man cleave to
it at *Midsomer;* Wee are glad of the freshnesse, and coolenes of a
Vault, but does any Man keepe his *Christmas* there; or are the
pleasures of the *Spring* acceptable in *Autumne?* If happinesse be [340]
in the *season,* or in the *Clymate,* how much happier then are *Birds*
than *Men,* who can change the *Climate,* and accompanie, and
enjoy the same season ever.

14. Expostulation

My *God,* my *God* wouldest thou cal thy selfe the *Ancient of dayes,*   Dan. 7.9
if we were not to call our selves to an account for our *dayes?*
wouldest thou chide us for *standing idle heere all the day,* if we were   [341] Mat. 20.6
sure to have more dayes, to make up our harvest? When thou   Mat. 6.34
biddest us *take no thought for tomorrow; for sufficient unto the day* (to
every day) *is the evill thereof,* is this truely, absolutely, to put off all
that concernes the present life? When thou reprehendest the   Gal. 4.10
Galatians by thy Message to them, *That they observed dayes, and*
Moneths, and Tymes, and Yeares, when thou sendest by the same   [342] Col. 2.16
Messenger, to forbid the *Colossians* all *Criticall days, Indicatory*
dayes, Let no Man Judge you, in respect of a holy-day, or of a new
Moone, or of a Saboth, doest thou take away all Consideration, all
distinction of *dayes?* Though thou remove them from being of the
Essence of our *Salvation,* thou leavest them for *assistances,* and for
the *Exaltation* of our *Devotion,* to fix our selves, at certaine
periodicall, and *stationary times,* upon the consideration of those [343]

things, which thou hast done for us, and the *Crisis*, the *triall*, the *judgment*, how those things have wrought upon us, and disposed us to a spirituall recovery, and convalescence. For there is to every man *a day of salvation, Now is the accepted time, now is the day of salvation,* And there is *a great day of thy wrath,* which no man shal be able to stand in; And there are *evill dayes before,* and therfore thou warnest us, and armest us, *Take unto you the whole armor of God, that you may be able to stand in the evill day.* So far then our daies must be *criticall* to us, as that by consideration of them, we may make a *Judgment* of our *spiritual health;* for that is the *crisis* of our *bodily health;* Thy beloved servant St. *John* wishes to *Gaius, that he may prosper in his health, so as his soule prospers;* for if the *Soule* be leane, the marrow of the *Body* is but water; if the *Soule* wither, the verdure and the good estate of the *body,* is but an illusion, and the *goodliest man, a fearefull ghost.* Shall wee, O my *God,* determine our thoughts, and shal we never determin our disputations upon our *Climactericall yeares,* for particular men, and *periodical yeres,* for the life of *states* and *kingdoms,* and never consider these in our *long life,* and our interest in the *everlasting kingdome?* We have exercisd our *curiosity* in observing that *Adam,* the eldest of the eldest world, died in his *climactericall yere,* and *Shem* the eldest son of the next world, in his; *Abraham the father of the faithfull,* in his; and the blessed *Virgin Mary,* the garden, where the root of faith grew, in hers. But they whose *Climacteriques* wee observe, imployd their observation upon their *critical dayes,* the working of thy promise of a *Messiah* upon them. And shall we, O my *God,* make lesse use of those *dayes,* who have more of them? We, who have not only the day of the *Prophets,* the first dayes, but the last daies, in which thou hast spoken unto us, by thy *Son? We are the children of the day,* for thou hast shind in as ful a Noone, upon us, as upon the *Thessalonians;* They who were of the *night,* (a *Night,* which they had superinduc'd upon themselves) the *Pharisees,* pretended, *That if they had bin in their Fathers daies,* (those *indicatory,* and *judicatory,* those *Criticall dayes*) *they would not have been partakers of the bloud of the Prophets;* And shal we who are in the *day,* these *Daies,* not of the *Prophets,* but of the *Son,* stone those *Prophets* againe, and crucifie that *Son* againe, for all those evident *Indications,* and *critical Judicatures* which are afforded us? Those opposd adversaries of thy *Son,* the *Pharisees* with the *Herodians,* watch'd a *Critical day;* Then when the *State* was incensd against him, *they came to tempt him in the dangerous question of Tribute.* They left him; and that day was the *Critical day* to *Sadducees; The same day,* saies thy *Spirit,* in thy *Word, the Sadducees*

2 Cor. 6.2

Rev. 6.17

Eph. 6.13 [344]

3 John ver. 2

[345]

[346]

Heb. 1.2 [347]

1 Thess. 5.8

Mat. 23.30

[348]

Mat. 22.17 [349]

Mat. 22.23

came to him to question him about the Resurrection; and them hee silenc'd; They left him; and this was the *Criticall day* for the *Scribe,* expert in the *Law,* who thoght himselfe learneder than the *Herodian,* the *Pharisee* or *Sadducee;* and he tempted him *about the* *great Commandement;* and him *Christ left* without power of replying. When all was done, and that they went about to begin their *circle* of vexation, and tentation again, *Christ* silences them so, that, as they had taken their *Criticall dayes,* to come, in *That,* and in *that* day, so *Christ* imposes a *Criticall* day upon them; *From that* *day forth,* saies thy *Spirit, no man durst aske him any more questions.* This, *O my God,* my most blessed *God,* is a fearefull *Crisis,* a fearefull *Indication,* when we will study, and seeke, and finde, what *dayes* are fittest to forsake thee in; To say, Now, *Religion* is in a *Neutralitie in the world,* and this is my *day,* the day of *libertie;* Now I may make *new friends* by changing my *old religion,* and this is my *day,* the *day of advancement.* But *O my God,* with thy servant *Jacobs* holy boldnes, who *though thou lamedst him, would not let thee goe, till thou hadst given him a blessing,* Though thou have laid me upon my *hearse,* yet thou shalt not depart from mee, from this bed, till thou have given me a *Crisis,* a *Judgment* upon my selfe this *day.* Since *a* *day is as a thousand yeres with thee,* Let, *O Lord,* a *day,* be as a *weeke* to me; and in this one, let me consider *seven daies,* seven *critical daies,* and *judge my selfe, that I be not judged by thee.* First, this is the day of thy *visitation,* thy comming to me; and would I looke to be welcome to thee, and not entertaine thee in thy comming to me? We measure not the *visitations* of great persons, by their *apparel,* by their *equipage,* by the *solemnity* of their comming, but by their very comming; and therefore, howsoever thou come, it is a *Crisis* to me, that thou wouldest not lose me, who seekst me by any means. This leads me from my *first day,* thy *visitation* by sicknes, to a *second,* to the light, and testimony of my *Conscience.* There I have an *evening,* and *a morning;* a sad guiltinesse in my *soule,* but yet a cheerfull rising of thy *Son* too; Thy *Evenings* and *Mornings* made *dayes* in the *Creation,* and there is no mention of *Nights;* My sadnesses for *sins* are *evenings,* but they determin not in *night,* but deliver me over to the *day,* the day of a *Conscience* dejected, but then rectified, accused, but then acquitted, by thee, by him, who speaks thy word, and who is thy word, thy *Son.* From this *day,* the *Crisis* and examination of my *Conscience,* breakes out my *third day,* my day of preparing, and fitting my selfe for a more especial *receiving* of thy *Sonne,* in his institution of the *Sacrament:* In which *day* though there be many dark passages, and slippry steps, to them who wil entangle, and endanger themselves, in unnecessary

Mat. 22.35, 36 [350]

Mat. 22. 46 [351]

Gen. 32.26 [352]

2 Pet. 3.8

[353]

[354]

[355]

[356] disputations, yet there are light houres inough, for any man, to goe his whole *journey* intended by thee; to know that that *Bread* and *Wine*, is not more really assimilated to my *body*, and to my *blood*, than the *Body* and *blood* of thy *Sonne*, is communicated to me in that action, and participation of that *bread*, and that *wine*. And having, O *my God*, walkd with thee these *three dayes*, The day of

[357] thy *visitation*, the day of my *Conscience*, The day of *preparing* for this seale of *Reconciliation*, I am the lesse afraid of the clouds or storms of my *fourth day*, the day of my *dissolution* and *transmigration*

Ecclus. 41.1 from hence. Nothing deserves the name of *happines*, that makes the remembrance of *death* bitter; And *O death, how bitter is the remembrance of thee, to a man that lives at rest, in his possessions, the Man that hath Nothing to vexe him, yea unto him, that is able to receive meat?* Therefore hast thou, O my *God*, made this *sicknes*, in

[358] which I am not able to receive meate, my *fasting day*, my *Eve*, to this great *festival*, my *dissolution*. And this *day* of *death* shall deliver me over to my *fift day*, the day of my *Resurrection;* for how long a *day* soever thou make that *day* in the *grave*, yet there is no *day* between that, and the *Resurrection*. Then wee shall all bee invested, reapparelled in our owne *bodies;* but they who have made just use

[359] of their former *dayes*, be super-invested with *glorie*, wheras the others, condemned to their *olde clothes*, their *sinfull bodies*, shall have *Nothing* added, but *immortalitie* to *torment*. And this *day* of awaking me, and reinvesting my *Soule*, in my *body*, and my *body* in the body of *Christ*, shall present mee, *Bodie*, and *Soule*, to my *sixt day*, The day of *Judgment;* which is truely, and most literally, the

[360] *Critical*, the *Decretory day;* both because all *Judgement* shall bee manifested to *me* then, and *I* shall assist in judging the world then, and because then, that *Judgement* shall declare to me, and possesse mee of my *Seventh day*, my *Everlasting Saboth* in thy *rest*, thy *glory*, thy *joy*, thy *sight*, thy *selfe;* and where I shall live as long, without reckning any more *Dayes* after, as thy *Sonne*, and thy *Holy Spirit* lived with thee, before you three made any *Dayes* in the *Creation*.

[361] ## 14. *Prayer*

O eternall and most gracious *God*, who though thou didst permit *darknesse* to be before *light* in the *Creation*, yet in the making of *light*, didst so multiplie that *light*, as that it enlightned not the *day* only, but the *night* too, though thou have suffered some *dimnesse*, some clouds of *sadnesse* and disconsolatenesse to shed themselves

[362] upon my *soule*, I humbly blesse, and thankfully glorifie thy holy name, that thou hast afforded mee the *light* of thy *spirit*, against

which the *prince of darknesse* cannot prevaile, nor hinder his illumination of our darkest nights, of our saddest thoughts. Even the visitation of thy most blessed *Spirit*, upon the blessed *Virgin*, is called an *overshadowing*. There was the presence of the *Holy Ghost*, the fountaine of all *light*, and yet an *overshadowing;* Nay [363] except there were some *light*, there could bee no *shadow*. Let thy mercifull providence so governe all in this *sicknesse*, that I never fall into utter *darkenesse, ignorance of thee*, or *inconsideration of my selfe;* and let those *shadowes* which doe fall upon mee, *faintnesses of Spirit*, and *condemnations of my selfe*, bee overcome by the power of thine irresistible *light*, the *God* of *consolation;* that when those [364] *shadowes* have done their office upon mee, to let me see, that of my selfe I should fall into irrecoverable *darknesse*, thy *Spirit* may doe his *office* upon those *shadowes*, and disperse them, and establish mee in so bright a *day* here, as may bee a *Criticall day* to me, *a day wherein*, and *whereby* I may give thy *Judgement* upon my selfe, and that the words of thy *Sonne*, spoken to his *Apostles*, may reflect upon me, *Behold, I am with you alwaies, even to the end of the*   Mat. 28.20 *world*.

15. Intereà insomnes noctes Ego duco, Diesque. [365]
I sleepe not day nor night.

15. Meditation

Naturall Men have conceived a twofold use of *sleepe;* That it is a *refreshing* of the body in this life; That it is a *preparing* of the *soule* for the next; That is is a *feast*, and it is the *Grace* at that feast; That it is our *recreation*, and cheeres us, and it is our *Catechisme*, and [366] instructs us; wee lie downe in a hope, that wee shall rise the stronger; and we lie downe in a knowledge, that wee may rise no more. *Sleepe* is an *Opiate* which gives us *rest*, but such an *Opiate*, as perchance, being under it, we shall wake no more. But though naturall men, who have induced secondary and figurative considerations, have found out this second, this *emblematicall* use of *sleepe*, that it should be a *representation of death*, *God*, who [367] wrought and perfected his worke, before *Nature* began, (for *Nature* was but his *apprentice*, to learne in the first *seven daies*, and now is his *foreman*, and works next under him) *God*, I say, intended *sleepe* onely for the *refreshing* of man by bodily rest, and not for a *figure of*

death, for he intended not *death* it selfe then. But *Man* having
induced *death* upon himselfe, *God* hath taken *Mans Creature*,
[368] *death*, into his hand, and mended it; and whereas it hath in it selfe
a fearefull forme and aspect, so that Man is afraid of his own
Creature, *God* presents it to him, in a *familiar*, in an *assiduous*, in an
agreeable, and *acceptable* forme, in *sleepe*, that so when hee awakes
from *sleepe*, and saies to himselfe, shall I bee no otherwise when I
am dead, than I was even now, when I was asleep, hee may bee
[369] ashamed of his waking *dreames*, and of his *Melancholique* fancying
out a horrid and an affrightfull figure of that *death* which is so like
sleepe. As then wee need *sleepe* to live out our *threescore and ten
yeeres*, so we need *death*, to live that *life* which we cannot *out-live*.
And as *death* being our *enemie*, *God* allowes us to defend our selves
against it (for wee *victuall* our selves against *death*, *twice* every day,
as often as we *eat*) so *God* having so sweetned *death* unto us, as hee
[370] hath in *sleepe*, wee put our selves into our *Enemies* hands *once* every
day, so farre, as *sleepe* is *death;* and *sleepe* is as much *death*, as *meat*
is *life*. This then is the *misery* of my *sicknesse*, That death as it is
produced from mee, and is mine owne *Creature*, is now before
mine *Eies*, but in that forme, in which *God* hath mollified it to us,
and made it acceptable, in *sleepe*, I cannot see it. How many
[371] *prisoners*, who have even hollowed themselves their *graves* upon
that *Earth*, on which they have lain long under heavie fetters, yet
at this *houre* are *asleepe*, though they bee yet working upon their
owne *graves*, by their owne *waight*? Hee that hath seene his *friend*
die to *day*, or knowes hee shall see it to *morrow*, yet will sinke into
a sleepe betweene. I cannot; and oh, if I be entring now into
Eternitie, where there shall bee no more distinction of *houres*, why
[372] is it al my businesse now *to tell Clocks*? why is none of the *heavinesse*
of my *heart* dispensed into mine *Eie-lids*, that they might fall as my
heart doth? And why, since I have lost my delight in all *objects*,
cannot I discontinue the facultie of seeing them, by closing mine
Eies in *sleepe*? But why rather, being entring into that presence,
where I shall wake continually and never sleepe more, doe I not
[373] interpret my continuall waking here, to bee a *parasceve*, and a
preparation to that?

15. Expostulation

My *God*, my *God*, I know, (for thou hast said it) *That he that keepeth*
Psal. 121.4 *Israel, shall neither slumber, nor sleepe:* But shall not that *Israel*, over
whom thou watchest, sleepe? I know, (for thou hast said it) that

there are Men, *whose damnation sleepeth not;* but shall not they to
whom thou art *Salvation,* sleepe? or wilt thou take from them that
evidence, and that *testimony,* that they are thy *Israel,* or thou their
salvation? *Thou givest thy beloved sleepe.* Shall I lacke that *seale* of
thy *Love? You shall lie downe, and none shall make you afraid;* shal I
bee *outlawd* from that *protection?* Jonah *slept in one dangerous storme,*
and *thy blessed Sonne in another.* Shall I have no use, no benefit, no
application of those great *Examples? Lord, if hee sleepe, he shall do
well,* say thy *Sonnes Disciples* to him, of *Lazarus;* And shall there
bee no roome, for that *Argument* in me? or shall I bee open to the
contrary? If I sleepe not, shall I not bee well, in their sense? Let me
not, O my *God,* take this too *precisely,* too *literally: There is that
neither day nor night seeth sleep with his eies,* saies thy wise servant
Solomon; and whether hee speake that of *worldly* Men, or of Men
that *seeke wisdome,* whether in *justification* or *condemnation* of their
watchfulnesse, we can not tell: wee can tell, *That there are men, that
cannot sleepe, till they have done mischiefe,* and then they can; and
wee can tell that *the rich man cannot sleepe, because his abundance
will not let him. The tares* were *sowen when the husbandmen were
asleepe;* And the elders thought it a probable excuse, a credible lie,
that the watchmen which kept the Sepulchre, should say, *that the
bodie of thy Son was stolne away, when they were asleepe:* Since thy
blessed *Sonne* rebuked his Disciples for *sleeping,* shall I murmure
because I doe not sleepe? If *Samson* had slept any longer in *Gaza,*
he had been taken; And when he did sleepe longer with *Delilah,* he
was taken. *Sleepe* is as often taken for *naturall death* in thy *Scriptures,*
as for *naturall rest.* Nay sometimes *sleepe* hath so heavy a sense, as
to bee taken for *sinne it selfe,* as well as for the punishment of *sinne,
Death.* Much comfort is not in much sleepe, when the most
fearefull and most irrevocable Malediction is presented by thee, in
a *perpetuall sleepe. I will make their feasts, and I will make them
drunke, and they shall sleepe a perpetuall sleepe, and not wake.* I must
therefore, O my God, looke farther, than into the very act of
sleeping, before I mis-interpret my waking: for since I finde thy
whole hand light, shall any *finger* of that hand seeme heavy? since
the whole sicknesse is thy *Physicke,* shall any accident in it, bee my
poison, by my murmuring? The name of *Watchmen* belongs to our
profession; Thy *Prophets* are not onely *seers* indued with a *power* of
seeing, able to see, but *Watchmen,* evermore in the *Act* of seeing.
And therefore give me leave, O my blessed *God,* to invert the words
of thy *Sonnes Spouse;* she said, *I sleepe, but my heart waketh;* I say,
I *wake, but my heart sleepeth;* My body is in a sicke wearinesse, but
my soule in a peacefull rest with thee; and as our *eies,* in our health,

2 Pet. 2.3
[374]

Psal. 127.2
Lev. 26.6
Jon. 1.5
Mat. 8.24
[375] Joh. 11.12

Eccles. 8.16

[376]

Prov. 4.16
Eccles. 5.12
Mat. 13.25

[377] Mat. 28.13
Mat. 26.40
Judg. 16.3

ver. 19

[378] Eph. 5.14
1 Thess. 5.6

Jer. 51.39

[379]

[380] Song of
Sol. 5.2

see not the *Aire*, that is next them, nor the *fire*, nor the *spheares*, nor stop upon any thing, till they come to *starres*, so my *eies*, that are open, see nothing of this world, but passe through all that, and fix [381] themselves upon thy *peace*, and *joy*, and *glory* above. Almost as 1 Thess. 5.6 soone as thy *Apostle* had said, *Let us not sleepe*, lest we should be too ver. 10 much discomforted if we did, he saies againe, *whether we wake or sleepe, let us live together with Christ*. Though then this *absence of sleepe*, may argue the *presence of death* (the *Originall* may exclude the *Copie*, the *life*, the *picture*) yet this gentle *sleepe*, and rest of my [382] *soule* betrothes mee to thee, to whom I shall bee married *indissolubly*, though by this way of *dissolution*.

15. *Prayer*

O eternall and most gracious *God*, who art able to make, and dost make the *sicke bed* of thy servants, *Chappels of ease* to them, and the *dreames* of thy servants, *Prayers*, and *Meditations* upon thee, let not [383] this continuall watchfulnes of mine, this inabilitie to sleepe, which thou hast laid upon mee, be any *disquiet*, or *discomfort* to me, but rather an argument, that thou wouldest not have me sleepe in thy *presence*. What it may indicate or signifie, concerning the state of my *body*, let them consider to whom that consideration belongs; doe thou, who onely art the *Physitian* of my *soule*, tell her, that thou [384] wilt afford her such *defensatives* as that shee shall *wake* ever towards thee, and yet ever *sleepe* in *thee;* and that through all this sicknesse, thou wilt either preserve mine understanding, from all decaies and distractions, which these watchings might occasion, or that thou wilt reckon, and account with me, from before those violencies, and not call any peece of my *sickenesse, a sinne*. It is a heavy and indelible sinne, that I brought into the world with me; It is a heavy [385] and innumerable multitude of sins, which I have heaped up since; I have sinned *behind thy backe* (if that can be done) by wilfull abstaining from thy *Congregation*, and omitting thy *service*, and I have sinned *before thy face*, in my *hypocrisies* in Prayer, in my *ostentation*, and the mingling a respect of *my selfe*, in preaching thy Word; I have sinned in my *fasting* by repining, when a penurious [386] fortune hath kept mee low; And I have sinned even in that fulnesse, when I have been at thy table, by a negligent examination, by a wilfull prevarication, in receiving that heavenly *food* and *Physicke*. But, as I know, O my gracious *God*, that for all those sinnes committed since, yet thou wilt consider me, as I was in thy *purpose*, [387] when thou wrotest my name in the *booke of Life*, in mine *Election:* so into what deviations soever I stray, and wander, by occasion of

this sicknes, O *God,* return thou to that *Minute,* wherein thou wast
pleased with me, and consider me in that *condition.*

16. Et properare meum clamant, è Turre [388]
propinqua, Obstreperae Campanae aliorum
in funere, funus.

*From the bels of the church adjoyning, I am daily
remembred of my buriall in the funeralls
of others.*

16. Meditation

We have a *Convenient Author,* who writ a *Discourse of Bells* when   Magius
hee was Prisoner in *Turkey.* How would hee have enlarged [389]
himselfe, if he had been my *fellow Prisoner* in this *sicke bed,* so
neere to that *steeple,* which never ceases, no more than the *harmony
of the spheres,* but is more heard. When the *Turks* tooke
Constantinople, they melted the *Bells* into *Ordnance;* I have heard
both *Bells* and *Ordnance,* but never been so much affected with
those, as with these *Bells.* I have lain neere a *steeple,* in which there   Antwerp [390]
are said to be more than *thirty Bels;* And neere another, where   Rouen
there is one so bigge, as that the *Clapper* is said to weigh more
than *six hundred pound;* yet never so affected as here. Here the
Bells can scarse solemnise the funerall of any person, but that I
knew him, or knew that hee was my *Neighbour*: we dwelt in houses
neere to one another before, but now hee is gone into that house,
into which I must follow him. There is a way of correcting the [391]
Children of great persons, that other *Children* are corrected in
their *behalfe,* and in their *names,* and this workes upon them, who
indeed had more deserved it. And when these *Bells* tell me, that
now one, and now another is buried, must not I acknowledge, that
they have the *correction* due to me, and paid the *debt* that I owe?
There is a story of a *Bell* in a *Monastery,* which, when any of the [392] Rocca
house was sicke to death, rung alwaies *voluntarily,* and they knew
the inevitablenesse of the danger by that. It rung once, when no
man was sick; but the next day one of the house, fell from the
steeple, and died, and the *Bell* held the reputation of a *Prophet* still.
If these *Bells* that warne to a *Funerall* now, were appropriated

to none, may not I, by the hour of the *funerall*, supply? How many
[393] men that stand at an *execution*, if they would aske, for what dies
that Man, should heare their owne faults condemned, and see
themselves executed, by *Atturney?* We scarce heare of any man
preferred, but wee thinke of our selves, that wee might very well
have beene that *Man;* Why might not I have beene that *Man*, that
is carried to his *grave* now? Could I fit my selfe, to *stand*, or *sit* in
[394] any Mans *place*, and not to lie in any mans *grave?* I may lacke
much of the *good parts* of the meanest, but I lacke nothing of the
mortality of the weakest; They may have acquired better *abilities*
than I, but I was born to as many *infirmities* as they. To be an
incumbent by lying down in a *grave*, to be a *Doctor* by teaching
Mortification by *Example*, by *dying*, though I may have *seniors*,
others may be *elder* than I, yet I have proceeded apace in a good
[395] *University*, and gone a great way in a little time, by the furtherance
of a vehement *fever;* and whomsoever these *Bells* bring to the
ground to day, if hee and I had beene compared yesterday,
perchance I should have been thought likelier to come to this
preferment, then, than he. *God* hath kept the power of *death* in his
owne hands, lest any Man should *bribe death*. If man knew the
[396] *gaine of death*, the *ease of death*, he would solicite, he would
provoke death to assist him, by any hand, which he might use. But
as when men see many of their owne professions preferd, it
ministers a hope that that may light upon them; so when these
hourely *Bells* tell me of so many *funerals* of men like me, it
presents, if not a *desire* that it may, yet a *comfort* whensoever mine
shall come.

[397]   *16. Expostulation*

My *God*, my *God*, I doe not expostulate with *thee*, but with *them*,
who dare doe that: Who dare expostulate with *thee*, when in the
voice of thy *Church*, thou givest allowance, to this *Ceremony* of *Bells*
at *funeralls*. Is it enough to refuse it, because it was in use amongst
[398] the *Gentiles?* so were *funeralls* too. Is it because some *abuses* may have
crept in, amongst *Christians?* Is that enough, that their ringing hath
been said to drive away *evill spirits?* Truly, that is so farre true, as that
the *evill spirit* is vehemently vexed in their ringing, therefore, because
that action brings the *Congregation* together, and unites *God* and his
people, to the destruction of that *Kingdome*, which the *evill spirit*
[399] usurps. In the first *institution* of thy *Church*, in this world, in the
foundation of thy *Militant Church*, amongst the *Jews*, thou didst
Numb. 10.2   appoint the calling of the *assembly* in, to bee by *Trumpet*, and when

they were in, then thou gavest them the sound of *Bells*, in the   Exod. 28.33
garment of thy *Priest*. In the *Triumphant Church*, thou imploiest both
too, but in an inverted *Order;* we enter into the *Triumphant Church*
by the sound of Bells (for we *enter* when we *die;*) And then we receive
our further *edification*, or *consummation*, by the sound of *Trumpets*, at   [400]
the *Resurrection*. The sound of thy *Trumpets* thou didst impart to
secular and *civill* uses too, but the sound of *Bells* onely to *sacred;*
Lord, let not us breake the *Communion of Saints*, in that which was
intended for the *advancement* of it; let not that pull us asunder from
one another, which was intended for the assembling of us, in the
Militant, and associating of us to the *Triumphant Church*. But he for   [401]
whose funerall these *Bells* ring now, was at *home*, at his journies end,
yesterday; why ring they now? A *Man*, that is a world, is all the
things in the *world;* Hee is an *Army*, and when an *Army* marches, the
Vaunt may lodge to night, where the *Reare* comes not till to morrow.
A man extends to his *Act* and to his *example;* to that which he *does*,
and that which he *teaches;* so doe those things that concerne him, so   [402]
doe these *bells;* That which rung yesterday, was to convay him out of
the *world*, in his *Vaunt*, in his *soule:* that which rung to day, was to
bring him in his *Reare*, in his *body*, to the *Church;* And this continuing
of ringing after his *entring*, is to bring him to mee in the *application*.
Where I lie, I could heare the *Psalme*, and did joine with the
Congregation in it; but I could not heare the *Sermon*, and these latter
bells are a *repetition Sermon* to mee. But O my *God*, my *God*, doe I,   [403]
that have this *feaver*, need other *remembrances* of my *Mortalitie?* Is
not mine owne *hollow voice*, voice enough to pronounce that to me?
Need I looke upon a *Deaths-head* in a *Ring*, that have one in my *face?*
or goe for *death* to my *Neighbours* house, that have him in my *bosome?*
We cannot, wee cannot, O my *God*, take in too many *helps* for
religious *duties;* I know I cannot have any better *Image* of *thee*, than   [404]
thy *Sonne*, nor any better *Image* of *him*, than his *Gospell:* yet must
not I with thanks confesse to thee, that some *historicall pictures* of his,
have sometimes put mee upon better *Meditations* than otherwise I
should have fallen upon? I know thy *Church* needed not to have
taken in from *Jew* or *Gentile*, any supplies for the exaltation of thy
glory, or our *devotion;* of *absolute necessitie* I know shee needed not;   [405]
But yet wee owe thee our thanks, that thou hast given her leave to
doe so, and that as in making us *Christians*, thou diddest not destroy
that which wee were before, *naturall men*, so in the exalting of our
religious devotions now we are *Christians*, thou hast beene pleased to
continue to us those *assistances* which did worke upon the affections
of *naturall men* before: for thou lovest a *good man*, as thou lovest a   [406]
good Christian: and though *Grace* bee meerely from thee, yet thou
doest not plant Grace but in *good natures*.

16. Prayer

O eternall and most gracious *God*, who having consecrated our living *bodies*, to thine owne *Spirit*, and made us *Temples of the holy* [407] *Ghost*, doest also require a respect to bee given to these *Temples*, even when the *Priest* is gone out of them; To these *bodies*, when the *soule* is departed from them; I blesse, and glorifie thy *Name*, that as thou takest care in our life, of every haire of our head, so doest thou also of every graine of *ashes* after our death. Neither doest thou only doe good to us all, in *life* and *death*, but also wouldest have us [408] doe good to one another, as in a holy *life*, so in those things which accompanie our *death:* In that Contemplation I make account that I heare this dead brother of ours, who is now carried out to his *buriall*, to speake to mee, and to *preach* my *funerall Sermon*, in the voice of these *Bells*. In him, O *God*, thou hast accomplished to mee, even the request of *Dives* to *Abraham; Thou hast sent one from the* [409] *dead to speake unto mee.* He speakes to mee aloud from that *steeple;* Rev. 14.13 hee whispers to mee at these *Curtaines*, and hee speaks thy words; *Blessed are the dead which die in the Lord, from henceforth. Let this praier* therfore, O my *God*, be as my *last gaspe*, my *expiring*, my *dying* in *thee;* That if this bee the houre of my *transmigration*, I may die the *death* of a *sinner*, drowned in my *sinnes*, in the *bloud* of thy *Sonne;* And if I live longer, yet I may now *die* the *death* of the *righteous, die* [410] *to sinne;* which *death* is a *resurrection* to a new *life. Thou killest and thou givest life:* which soever comes, it comes from *thee;* which way soever it comes, let mee come to *thee.*

17. Nunc lento sonitu dicunt, Morieris.
Now, this Bell tolling softly for another, saies to me, Thou must die.

17. Meditation

Perchance hee for whom this *Bell* tolls, may bee so ill, as that he [411] knowes not it *tolls* for him; And perchance I may thinke my selfe so much better than I am, as that they who are about mee, and see my state, may have caused it to toll for mee, and I know not that. The *Church* is *Catholike, universall*, so are all her *Actions; All* that she does, belongs to *all*. When she *baptizes* a *child*, that action concernes mee; for that child is thereby connected to that *Head* which is my *Head* too, and engrafft into that *body*, whereof I am a *member*. And when she *buries a Man*, that action concernes me; *All mankinde* is of one *Author*, and is one *volume;* when one Man dies, one *Chapter* is not *torne* out of the *booke*, but *translated* into a better *language;* and every *Chapter* must be so *translated; God* emploies severall *translators;* some peeces are translated by *Age*, some by *sicknesse*, some by *warre*, some by *justice;* but *Gods* hand is in every *translation;* and his hand shall binde up all our scattered leaves againe, for that *Librarie* where every *booke* shall lie open to one another: As therefore the *Bell* that rings to a *Sermon*, calls not upon the *Preacher* onely, but upon the *Congregation* to come; so this *Bell* calls us all: but how much more *mee*, who am brought so neere the *doore* by this *sicknesse*. There was a *contention* as farre as a *suit*, (in which both *pietie* and *dignitie, religion,* and *estimation,* were mingled) which of the religious *Orders* should ring to *praiers* first in the *Morning;* and it was *determined,* that *they should ring first that rose earliest.* If we understand aright the *dignitie* of this *Bell*, that tolls for our *evening prayer*, wee would bee glad to make it ours, by rising early, in that *application*, that it might bee ours, as wel as his, whose indeed it is. The *Bell* doth toll for him that *thinkes* it doth; and though it *intermit* againe, yet from that *minute*, that that occasion wrought upon him, hee is united to *God*. Who casts not up his *Eie* to the *Sunne* when it rises? but who takes off his *Eie* from a *Comet*, when that breakes out? who bends not his *eare* to any *bell*, which upon any occasion rings? but who can remove it from that *bell*, which is passing a *peece of himselfe* out of this *world*? No Man is an *Iland*, intire of it selfe; every man is a peece of the *Continent*, a part of the *maine;* if a *Clod* bee washed away by the *Sea*, *Europe* is the lesse, as well as if a *Promontorie* were, as well as if a *Mannor* of thy *friends*, or of *thine owne* were; Any Mans *death* diminishes *me*, because I am involved in *Mankinde;* And therefore never send to know for whom the *bell* tolls; It tolls for *thee*. Neither can we call this a *begging* of *Miserie* or a *borrowing* of *Miserie*, as though we were not miserable enough of our selves, but must fetch in more from the next house, in taking upon us the *Miserie* of our *Neighbours*. Truly it were an excusable *covetousnesse* if wee did; for *affliction* is a *treasure*, and scarce any Man hath *enough* of it. No Man hath *affliction* enough, that is not matured, and ripened by it, and made fit for *God* by that *affliction*. If a Man carry *treasure* in *bullion*, or in a *wedge* of gold, and have none coined into *current Monies*, his *treasure* will not defray him as he travells. *Tribulation* is *Treasure* in the *nature* of it, but it is not *current money* in the use of it, except wee get nearer and nearer our *home, heaven,* by it. Another Man may be *sicke* too, and sicke to

[412]

[413]

[414]

[415]

[416]

[417]

[418]

death, and this *affliction* may lie in his *bowels*, as *gold* in a *Mine*, and
[419]   be of no use to him; but this *bell* that tels mee of his *affliction*, digs
out, and applies that *gold* to *mee*: if by this consideration of anothers
danger, I take mine owne into Contemplation, and so secure my
selfe, by making my recourse to my *God*, who is our onely securitie.

17. Expostulation

My *God*, my *God*, Is this one of thy waies, of *drawing light out of*
[420]   *darknesse*, To make *him* for whom this *bell* tolls, now in this dimnesse
of his sight, to become a *superintendent*, an *overseer*, a *Bishop*, to as
many as heare his *voice*, in this *bell*, and to give us a *confirmation* in this
action? Is this one of thy waies *to raise strength out of weaknesse*, to make
him who cannot rise *from his bed*, nor stirre *in his bed*, come *home* to *me*,
and in this sound, give mee the strength of *healthy* and vigorous
instructions? O my *God*, my *God*, what *Thunder* is not a *well-tuned*
[421]   *Cymball*, what *hoarsenesse*, what *harshnesse* is not a cleare *Organ*, if thou
bee pleased to set *thy voice* to it? and what *Organ* is not well plaied on,
if thy *hand* bee upon it? Thy *voice*, thy *hand* is in this *sound*, and in this
Gen. 49.1   one sound, I heare this *whole Consort*. I heare thy *Jacob* call unto his
sonnes, and say: *Gather your selves together, that I may tell you what shall*
[422]   *befall you in the last daies:* He saies, *That which I am now, you must bee*
Deut. 33.1   *then.* I heare thy *Moses* telling mee, and all within the *compasse* of this
sound, This is the blessing wherewith I bless you before my death; This,
2 King. 20.1   that before your death, you would consider your owne in mine. I heare
thy *Prophet* saying to *Hezekiah, Set thy house in order, for thou shalt die,*
and not live; Hee makes us of his *familie,* and calls this a setting of *his*
2 Pet. 1 [423]   house in order, to compose *us* to the *meditation* of *death.* I heare thy
13, 14   *Apostle* saying, *I thinke it meet to put you in remembrance, knowing that*
shortly I must goe out of this Tabernacle. This is the *publishing* of his *will,*
and this *bell* is our *legacie,* the applying of *his present condition* to our
Joh. 14.1   use. I heare that which makes al sounds *musique,* and all *musique* perfit;
I heare thy *Sonne* himselfe saying, *Let not your hearts be troubled;* Only
[424]   I heare this *change,* that whereas thy *Sonne* saies there, *I goe to prepare*
a place for you, this man in this *sound* saies, *I send to prepare you for a*
place, for a grave. But, O my *God*, my *God*, since *heaven* is glory and
joy, why doe not *glorious* and *joyfull* things leade us, induce us to
heaven? Thy *legacies* in thy first *will,* in thy *old Testament* were *plentie*
and *victorie; Wine* and *Oile, Milke* and *Honie, alliances of friends, ruine*
of enemies, peaceful hearts, and *cheerefull countenances,* and by these
[425]   *galleries* thou broughtest them into thy *bed-chamber,* by these *glories*
and *joies,* to the *joies* and *glories* of *heaven.* Why hast thou changed

thine old way, and carried us, by the waies of *discipline* and *mortification*, by the *waies* of *mourning* and *lamentation*, by the waies of *miserable ends*, and *miserable anticipations* of those miseries, in appropriating the *exemplary* miseries of others to our selves, and *usurping* upon their *miseries*, as our owne, to our owne *prejudice?* Is the *glory* of *heaven* no [426] perfecter in itselfe, but that it needs a *foile* of *depression* and *ingloriousnesse* in this *world*, to set it off? Is the *joy* of *heaven* no perfecter in it selfe, but that it needs the *sourenesse* of this *life* to give it a *taste?* Is that *joy* and that *glory* but a *comparative glory* and a *comparative joy?* not such in *it selfe*, but such in *comparison* of the *joylesnesse* and the *ingloriousnesse* of this *world?* I know, my *God*, it is [427] farre, farre otherwise. As thou thy selfe, who art *all*, art made of no *substances*, so the *joyes* and *glory* which are with thee, are made of none of these *circumstances; Essentiall joy*, and *glory Essentiall*. But why then, my *God*, wilt thou not *beginne* them *here?* pardon O *God*, this *unthankfull rashnesse;* I that aske why thou *doest not*, finde even now in *my selfe*, that thou *doest;* such *joy*, such *glory*, as that I conclude upon *my selfe*, upon *all*, They that finde not *joy* in their *sorrowes*, *glory* in [428] their *dejections* in this *world*, are in a fearefull *danger* of missing both in the *next*.

17. Prayer

O eternall and most gracious *God*, who hast beene pleased to *speake* to us, not onely in the *voice* of *Nature*, who speakes in our *hearts*, and of thy *Word*, which speakes to our *eares*, but in the speech of *speechlesse* [429] *Creatures*, in *Balaams Asse*, in the speech of *unbeleeving men*, in the confession of *Pilate*, in the speech of the *Devill* himselfe, in the *recognition* and *attestation* of thy *Sonne*, I humbly accept thy *voice*, in the sound of this sad and funerall *bell*. And first, I blesse thy glorious name, that in this *sound* and *voice*, I can heare thy *instructions*, in *another mans*, to consider *mine owne condition;* and to know, that this *bell* which *tolls* for another, before it come to *ring out*, may take in me [430] too. As *death is the wages of sinne*, it is *due* to mee; As death is *the end of sicknesse*, it belongs to *mee;* And though so disobedient a *servant* as I, may be afraid to *die*, yet to so mercifull a *Master* as thou, I cannot be afraid to *come;* And therefore, *into thy hands*, O my *God*, *I commend my* [431] *spirit;* A *surrender*, which I know thou wilt accept, whether I *live* or *die;* Psal. 31.5 for thy *servant David* made it, when he put himselfe into thy protection for his life; and thy blessed *Sonne* made it, when hee delivered up his *soule* at his *death;* declare thou thy will upon mee, O *Lord*, for *life* or *death*, in thy time; receive my *surrender* of my selfe now, *Into thy hands*,

O Lord, I commend my spirit. And being thus, O my *God,* prepared by
[432] thy *correction,* mellowed by thy chastisement, and conformed to thy
will, by thy *Spirit,* having received thy *pardon* for my *soule,* and asking
no *reprieve* for my *body,* I am bold, O *Lord,* to bend my *prayers* to thee,
for his *assistance,* the voice of whose *bell* hath called mee to this
devotion. Lay hold upon his *soule,* O *God,* till that *soule* have thoroughly
considered his *account,* and how few *minutes* soever it have to remaine
[433] in that *body,* let the power of thy *Spirit* recompence the shortnesse of
time, and perfect his *account,* before he passe away: present his *sinnes*
so to him, as that he may *know* what thou forgivest, and not doubt of
thy *forgivenesse;* let him *stop* upon the *infinitenesse* of those *sinnes,* but
dwell upon the *infinitenesse* of thy *Mercy:* let him discerne his owne
demerits, but wrap himselfe up in the *merits* of thy *Sonne, Christ Jesus:*
[434] Breathe inward *comforts* to his *heart,* and affoord him the power of
giving such outward *testimonies* thereof, as all that are about him may
derive comforts from thence, and have this *edification,* even in this
dissolution, that though the *body* be going the way of all *flesh,* yet that
soule is going the way of all *Saints.* When thy *Sonne* cried out upon the
Crosse, My God my God, Why hast thou forsaken me? he spake not so
much in his *owne Person,* as in the person of the *Church,* and of his
[435] afflicted *members,* who in deep distresses might feare thy *forsaking.*
This *patient,* O most blessed *God,* is one of *them;* In his behalfe, and in
his name, heare thy *Sonne* crying to thee, *My God, my God, Why hast
thou forsaken me?* and forsake him not; but with thy *left hand* lay his
body in the *grave,* (if that bee thy *determination* upon him) and with thy
right hand receive his *soule* into thy *Kingdome,* and unite *him* and *us* in
one *Communion of Saints.* Amen.

[436] 18. —At inde, Mortuus es, Sonitu celeri,
pulsuque agitato.

*The bell rings out, and tells me in him, that
I am dead.*

18. Meditation

The *Bell* rings out; the *pulse* thereof is changed; the *tolling* was a
faint, and *intermitting pulse,* upon one side; this *stronger,* and argues
[437] *more* and *better life.* His *soule* is gone out; and as a Man who had a

lease of 1000. *yeeres* after the expiration of a short one, or an *inheritance* after the *life* of a Man in a *Consumption*, he is now entred into the possession of his *better estate*. His *soule* is gone; *whither?* Who saw it *come in*, or who saw it *goe out? No body;* yet every body is sure, he *had one*, and *hath none*. If I will aske meere *Philosophers*, what the *soule* is, I shall finde amongst them, that will [438] tell me, it is nothing, but the *temperament* and *harmony*, and *just and equall composition of the Elements in the body*, which produces all those *faculties* which we ascribe to the *soule;* and so, in it selfe is *nothing*, no *seperable substance*, that over-lives the *body*. They see the *soule* is nothing else in other *Creatures*, and they affect an *impious humilitie*, to think *as low* of Man. But if my *soule* were no more than the soule of a *beast*, I could not thinke so; that *soule* that [439] can *reflect* upon it selfe, *consider* it selfe, is *more* than so. If I will aske, not meere *Philosophers*, but *mixt* Men, *Philosophicall Divines*, *how* the *soule*, being a *separate substance*, enters into *Man*, I shall finde some that will tell me, that it is by *generation*, and *procreation* from *parents*, because they thinke it hard, to charge the *soule* with the guiltinesse of *Originall* sinne, if the *soule* were infused into a [440] *body*, in which it must necessarily grow *foule*, and contract *originall sinne*, whether it *will* or *no;* and I shall finde some that will tell me, that it is by *immediate infusion from God*, because they think it hard, to maintaine an *immortality* in such a *soule*, as should be begotten, and derived with the *body* from *Mortall parents*. If I will aske, not *a few men*, but almost *whole bodies, whole Churches*, what becomes of [441] the *soules* of the *righteous*, at the *departing* thereof from the *body*, I shall bee told by some, *That they attend an expiation, a purification in a place of torment;* By some, that *they attend the fruition of the sight of God, in a place of rest; but yet, but of expectation;* By some, *that they passe to an immediate possession of the presence of God.* St. *Augustine* studied the *Nature* of the *soule*, as much as any thing, but the *salvation of the soule;* and he sent an expresse *Messenger* to St. [442] *Jerome*, to consult of some things concerning the *soule:* But he satisfies himselfe with this: *Let the departure of my soule to salvation be evident to my faith, and I care the lesse, how darke the entrance of my soule, into my body, bee to my reason.* It is the *going out*, more than the *comming in*, that concernes us. This *soule*, this *Bell* tells me, is *gone out; Whither?* Who shall tell mee that? I know not *who* it is; much lesse *what* he was; The condition of the Man, and the [443] course of his life, which should tell mee *whither* hee is gone, I know not. I was not there, in his *sicknesse*, nor at his *death;* I saw not his *way*, nor his *end*, nor can aske them who did, thereby to *conclude*, or *argue*, whither he is gone. But yet I have one neerer mee than all

these, mine owne *Charity;* I aske that; and that tels me, *He is gone*
[444] *to everlasting rest,* and *joy,* and *glory:* I owe him a good *opinion;* it is
but *thankfull charity* in mee, because I received *benefit* and
instruction from him when his *Bell* told: and I, being made the
fitter to *pray,* by that disposition, wherein I was assisted by his
occasion, did *pray* for him; and I *pray* not without *faith;* so I doe
charitably, so I do *faithfully* beleeve, that that *soule* is gone to
everlasting *rest,* and *joy,* and *glory.* But for the *body,* How poore
[445] a wretched thing is *that?* wee cannot expresse it *so fast,* as it growes
worse and *worse.* That *body* which scarce *three minutes* since was
such a *house,* as that *soule,* which made but one step from thence to
Heaven, was scarse thorowly content, to leave that for *Heaven:* that
body hath lost the *name* of a *dwelling house,* because none dwels in
it, and is making hast to lose the name of a *body,* and dissolve to
[446] *putrefaction.* Who would not bee affected, to see a cleere and sweet
River in the *Morning,* grow a *kennell* of muddy land water by *noone,*
and condemned to the saltnesse of the *Sea* by *night?* And how lame
a *Picture,* how faint a *representation,* is that, of the precipitation of
mans body to *dissolution? Now* all the parts built up, and knit by a
lovely *soule, now* but a *statue* of *clay,* and *now,* these limbs melted
[447] off, as if that *clay* were but *snow;* and now, the whole *house* is but a
handfull of sand, so much *dust,* and but *a pecke of Rubbidge,* so much
bone. If *he,* who, as this *Bell* tells mee, is gone now, were some
excellent Artificer, who comes to him for a *clocke,* or for a *garment*
now? Or for *counsaile,* if hee were a *Lawyer?* If a *Magistrate,* for
justice? Man before hee hath his *immortall soule,* hath a *soule of*
[448] *sense,* and a *soule of vegetation* before that: This *immortall soule* did
not forbid other *soules,* to be in us before, but when this *soule*
departs, it carries all with it; no more *vegetation,* no more *sense:*
such a *Mother in law* is the *Earth,* in respect of our *naturall Mother;*
in her *wombe* we *grew;* and when she was deliverd of us, wee were
planted in some *place,* in some *calling* in the *world;* In the wombe
of the Earth, wee *diminish,* and when she is *delivered* of us, our
[449] *grave* opened for another, wee are not *transplanted,* but *transported,*
our *dust* blowne away with *prophane dust,* with every wind.

18. Expostulation

My *God,* my *God,* if *Expostulation* bee too bold a word, doe thou
mollifie it with another; let it be *wonder* in my selfe; let it bee but
Levit. 21.10-12 *probleme* to others; but let me aske, why wouldest thou not suffer
[450] those, that serve thee in *holy services,* to doe any *office* about the

dead, nor *assist* at their *funerall?* Thou hadst no *Counsellor,* thou needest none; thou hast no *Controller,* thou admittest none. Why doe I aske? In *Ceremoniall things* (as that was) any *convenient reason* is enough; who can bee sure to propose that *reason,* that moved thee in the institution thereof? I satisfie my selfe with this; that in those *times,* the *Gentiles* were over-full, of an over-reverent respect to the *memory of the dead:* a great part of the *Idolatry* of the [451] *Nations,* flowed from that; an *over-amorous devotion,* an *over-zealous celebrating,* and *over-studious preserving* of the *memories,* and the *Pictures* of some *dead persons:* And by *the vaine glory of* Wisd. 14.14 *men, they entred into the world;* and their *statues,* and *pictures* contracted an opinion of *divinity,* by *age:* that which was at first, but a *picture* of a *friend,* grew a *God* in time, as the *wise man* notes, Wisd. 13.20 [452] *They called them Gods, which were the worke of an ancient hand.* And some have assigned a *certaine time,* when a *picture* should come out of *Minority,* and bee at *age,* to bee a *God,* in 60. yeeres after it is made. Those *Images* of *Men,* that had *life,* and some *Idols* of other things, which never had any *being,* are by one common name, called promiscuously, *dead;* and for that the *wise man* reprehends the *Idolatrer; for health he praies to that which is weake,* [453] Wisd. 13.18 *and for life he praies to that which is dead. Should we doe so,* saies thy Isa. 8.19 *Prophet; should we goe from the living to the dead?* So much ill then, being occasioned, by so much religious *compliment* exhibited to the *dead:* thou O *God,* (*I think*) wouldest therefore inhibit thy *principall holy servants,* from contributing any thing at all to this dangerous *intimation* of *Idolatry;* and that the people might say, [454] surely those *dead men,* are not so much to bee magnified, as men mistake, since *God* will not suffer his *holy officers,* so much as to *touch* them, not to *see* them. But those dangers being removed, thou, O my *God,* dost certainly allow, that we should doe *offices* of *piety* to the *dead,* and that we should draw *instructions* to *piety,* from the *dead.* Is not this, O my *God,* a holy kinde of *raising up* [455] *seed to my dead brother,* if I, by the meditation of *his death,* produce a better *life* in my selfe? It is the blessing upon *Reuben, Let Reuben* Deut. 33.6 *live, and not die, and let not his men be few;* let him propagate *many.* Zechar. 11.9 And it is a *Malediction, That that dieth, let it die;* let it doe no good in dying: for *Trees without fruit,* thou by thy *Apostle* callst, *twice dead.* It is a *second death,* if none live the better, by me, after my *death,* by the *manner* of my *death.* Therefore may I justly thinke, [456] that thou madest that a way to convay to the *Egyptians,* a *feare* of Exod. 12.30 *thee,* and a *feare* of *death,* that *there was not a house, where there was not one dead;* for therupon the *Egyptians* said, *we are all dead men;* the *death* of *others,* should *catechise* us to *death.* Thy *Sonne Christ* Rev. 1.5

Jesus is the *first begotten of the dead;* he rises first, the *eldest brother,* [457] and he is my *Master* in this *science* of *death:* but yet, for *mee,* I am a *younger brother* too, to this *Man,* who *died now,* and to every man whom I see, or heare to die before *mee,* and all they are *ushers* to mee in this *schoole* of *death.* I take therefore that which thy servant

1 Sam. 19.11 *Davids* wife said to *him,* to bee said to *me; If thou save not thy life to night, to morrow thou shalt bee slaine.* If the death of this man worke not upon mee now, I shall die worse, than if thou hadst not [458] afforded me this helpe: for thou hast sent *him* in this *bell* to mee,

Rev 3.2 as thou didst send to the *Angell* of *Sardis,* with *commission to strengthen the things that remaine, and that are ready to die;* that in this weaknes of *body,* I might receive spiritual strength, by these

Judg. 6.23 occasions. This is my *strength,* that whether thou say to mee, as

Numb. 20.26 thine *Angell* said to *Gideon, Peace bee unto thee, feare not, thou shalt* [459] *not die,* or whether thou say, as unto *Aaron, Thou shalt die there;*

1 King. 16.18, 19 yet thou wilt preserve that which is *ready to die,* my *soule,* from the worst *death,* that of *sinne. Zimri* died for his *sinnes,* saies thy *Spirit, which he sinned in doing evill;* and *in his sinne, which he did to make Israel sinne.* For his *sinnes,* his *many sinnes;* and then in *his sinne,* his *particular sinne:* for my *sinnes* I shall die, whensoever I die, for *death is the wages of sinne;* but I shall die in my *sinne,* in that [460] particular *sinne* of resisting thy *spirit,* if I *apply* not thy assistances. Doth it not call us to a particular consideration, That thy blessed *Sonne* varies his *forme* of Commination, and *aggravates* it in the variation, when hee saies to the *Jewes,* (because they refused the

Joh. 8.21 light offered) *you shall die in your sinne*; And then when they proceeded to farther disputations, and vexations, and tentations,

ver. 24 hee addes, *you shall die in your sinnes;* he *multiplies* the former [461] expressing, to a *plurall:* In *this sinne,* and in *all your sinnes;* doth not the resisting of thy particular *helps* at last, draw upon us the guiltinesse of all our *former* sinnes? May not the neglecting of this *sound* ministred to mee in this *mans death,* bring mee to that miserie, as that I, whom the *Lord of life* loved so, as to die for me, shall *die,* and a *Creature* of mine owne shall be *immortall;* that I

Isa. 66.14 shall die, and the *worme of mine owne conscience* shall never *die?*

[462] *18. Prayer*

O eternall and most gracious *God,* I have a new occasion of *thanks,* and a new occasion of *prayer* to *thee,* from the *ringing* of this *bell.* Thou toldst me in the other *voice,* that I was *mortall,* and approaching to *death;* In this I may heare thee say, that I am *dead,* in an *irremediable,* in an *irrecoverable* state for bodily health. If that bee thy *language* in this *voice,* how infinitely am I bound [463] to thy heavenly *Majestie,* for speaking so plainly unto mee? for even that *voice,* that I *must die now,* is not the voice of a *Judge,* that speaks by way of *condemnation,* but of a *Physitian,* that presents health in that: Thou presentest me *death* as the *cure* of my *disease,* not as the *exaltation* of it; if I mistake thy voice herein, if I over-runne thy pace, and prevent thy hand, and [464] imagine *death* more instant upon mee than thou hast bid him bee, yet the voice belongs to me; *I am dead,* I was *born dead,* and from the first laying of these *mud-walls* in my *conception,* they have *moldered* away, and the whole course of *life* is but an *active death.* Whether this *voice instruct* mee, that I am a *dead man now,* or *remember* me, that I have been a *dead man* all this while, I humbly thanke thee for speaking in this *voice* to my *soule,* and I humbly beseech thee also, to accept my prayers in his behalfe, by [465] whose occasion this *voice,* this *sound* is come to mee. For though hee bee by *death* transplanted to thee, and so in possession of inexpressible happinesse there, yet here upon earth thou hast given us such a portion of heaven, as that though men dispute, whether thy *Saints* in heaven doe *know* what we in earth in [466] particular doe stand in need of, yet without all disputation, wee upon earth doe know what thy *Saints* in heaven lacke yet, for the *consummation* of their *happinesse;* and therefore thou hast affoorded us the *dignitie,* that wee may pray for them. That therefore this *soule* now newly departed to thy *Kingdome,* may quickly returne to a joifull *reunion* to that *body* which it hath left, and that *wee* with *it,* may soone enjoy the full *consummation* of [467] all, in *body* and *soule,* I humbly beg at thy hand, O our most mercifull *God,* for thy Sonne *Christ Jesus sake;* That that blessed *Sonne* of thine, may have the *consummation* of his *dignitie,* by entring into his *last office,* the office of a *Judge,* and may have *societie* of humane *bodies* in *heaven,* as well as hee hath had ever of *soules;* And that as thou hatest *sinne* it selfe, thy *hate* to *sinne* may bee expressed in the abolishing of all *instruments of sinne,* [468] The *allurements* of this *world,* and the *world* it selfe; and all the temporarie *revenges of sinne,* the *stings of sicknesse* and of *death;* and all the *castles,* and *prisons,* and *monuments of sinne,* in the *grave;* That *time* may bee swallowed up in *Eternitie,* and *hope* swallowed in *possession,* and *ends* swallowed in *infinitenesse,* and *all men* ordained to *salvation,* in *body* and *soule,* be *one intire* and *everlasting sacrifice* to thee, where thou mayest receive *delight* [469] from them, and they *glorie* from thee, for evermore. *Amen.*

19. Oceano tandem emenso, aspicienda resurgit Terra; vident, justis, medici, iam cocta mederi se posse, indiciis.

[470] *At last, the Physitians, after a long and stormie voyage, see land; They have so good signes of the concoction of the disease, as that they may safely proceed to purge.*

19. Meditation

All this while the *Physitians* themselves have beene *patients,* patiently attending when they should see any *land* in this *Sea,* any *earth,* any *cloud,* any *indication* of *concoction* in these *waters.* Any [471] *disorder* of mine, any *pretermission* of theirs, exalts the disease, accelerates the rages of it; no *diligence* accelerates the *concoction,* the *maturitie* of the *disease;* they must stay till the *season* of the sicknesse come, and till it be ripened of it selfe, and then they may put to their hand, to *gather* it, before it *fall* off, but they cannot hasten the *ripening.* Why should wee looke for it in a *disease,* which [472] is the *disorder,* the *discord,* the *irregularitie,* the *commotion,* and *rebellion* of the *body?* It were scarce a *disease,* if it could bee *ordered,* and made obedient to our *times.* Why should wee looke for that in *disorder,* in a *disease,* when we cannot have it in *Nature,* who is so *regular,* and so *pregnant,* so forward to bring her worke to perfection, and to light? yet we cannot awake the *July-flowers* in *Januarie,* nor retard the *flowers* of the *spring* to *Autumne.* We cannot bid the *fruits* [473] come in *May,* nor the *leaves* to stick on in *December.* A *woman* that is weake, cannot put off her *ninth moneth* to a *tenth,* for her *deliverie,* and say shee will stay till shee bee *stronger;* nor a *Queene* cannot hasten it to a *seventh,* that shee may bee ready for some other pleasure. *Nature* (if we looke for *durable* and *vigorous* effects) will not admit *preventions,* nor *anticipations,* nor *obligations* upon her; for they are *precontracts,* and she will bee left to her *libertie. Nature* [474] would not be spurred, nor forced to mend her pace; nor *power,* the *power of man, greatnesse* loves not that kind of *violence* neither. There are of *them* that will *give,* that will doe *justice,* that will *pardon,* but they have their owne *seasons* for al these, and he that knowes not *them,* shall *starve* before that gift come, and *ruine,* before the Justice, and *dye* before the pardon save him: some *tree*

beares no fruit, except much *dung* be laid about it, and *Justice* [475]
comes not from some, till they be richly manured: some *trees*
require much *visiting*, much *watring*, much *labour;* and some men
give not their *fruits* but upon *importunitie;* some *trees* require
incision, and *pruning*, and *lopping;* some men must bee *intimidated*
and *syndicated* with *Commissions*, before they will deliver the fruits
of *Justice;* some *trees* require the *early* and the *often* accesse of the
Sunne; some men *open* not, but upon the *favours* and *letters* of [476]
Court mediation; some *trees* must bee *housd* and kept within doores;
some men locke up, not onely their liberalitie, but their *Justice*, and
their *compassion*, till the sollicitation of a *wife*, or a *sonne*, or a *friend*,
or a *servant* turne the *key*. *Reward* is the *season* of one man, and
importunitie of another; *feare* the *season* of one man, and *favour* of
another; *friendship* the *season* of one man, and *naturall affection* of [477]
another; and hee that knowes not their *seasons*, nor cannot *stay*
them, must lose the *fruits;* As *Nature* will not, so *power* and
greatnesse will not bee put to change their *seasons;* and shall wee
looke for this *Indulgence* in a *disease*, or thinke to shake it off before
it bee *ripe?* All this while therefore, we are but upon a *defensive*
warre, and that is but a *doubtfull state:* Especially where they who [478]
are *besieged* doe know the *best* of their *defences*, and doe not know
the *worst* of their *enemies power;* when they cannot mend their
works within, and the *enemie* can increase his *numbers without*. O
how many farre more miserable, and farre more worthy to be lesse
miserable than I, are besieged with this *sicknesse*, and lacke their
Sentinels, their *Physitians* to *watch*, and lacke their *munition*, their
cordials to *defend*, and perish before the *enemies* weaknesse might [479]
invite them to *sally*, before the *disease* shew any *declination*, or
admit any way of *working* upon it selfe? In me the *siege* is so farre
slackned, as that we may come to *fight*, and so die in the *field*, if I
die, and not in a *prison*.

19. Expostulation

My *God*, my *God*, Thou art a *direct God*, may I not say, a *literall*
God, a *God* that wouldest bee understood *literally*, and according [480]
to the *plaine sense* of all that thou saiest? But thou art also (*Lord* I
intend it to thy *glory*, and let no *prophane mis-interpreter* abuse it to
thy *diminution*) thou art a *figurative*, a *metaphoricall God* too: A *God*
in whose words there is such a height of *figures*, such *voyages*, such
peregrinations to fetch remote and precious *metaphors*, such
extentions, such *spreadings*, such *Curtaines* of *Allegories*, such *third* [481]

Heavens of *Hyperboles*, so *harmonious eloquutions*, so *retired* and so *reserved expressions*, so *commanding perswasions*, so *perswading commandements*, such *sinewes* even in thy *milke*, and such *things* in thy *words*, as all *prophane Authors* seeme of the seed of the *Serpent*, that *creepes;* thou art the *dove*, that flies. O what words but thine, [482] can expresse the inexpressible *texture*, and *composition* of thy *Word;* in which, to one Man, that *argument* that binds his faith to beleeve that to bee the Word of *God*, is *the reverent simplicity* of the Word, and to another, the *majesty* of the Word; and in which two men, equally pious, may meet, and one wonder, that all should not understand it, and the other, as much, that any man should. So, *Lord*, thou givest us the same *Earth*, to labour on, and to lie in; a [483] *house*, and a *grave*, of the same *earth;* so *Lord*, thou givest us the same *Word* for our *satisfaction*, and for our *Inquisition*, for our *instruction*, and for our *Admiration* too; for there are places, that thy servants *Jerome* and *Augustine* would scarce beleeve (when they grew warm by mutuall *letters*) of one another, that they understood them, and yet both *Jerome* and *Augustine* call upon persons, whom they knew to bee farre weaker, than they thought one another *(old* [484] *women* and *young maids)* to read thy *Scriptures*, without confining them, to these or those places. Neither art thou thus a *figurative*, a *Metaphoricall God*, in thy *Word* only, but in thy *workes* too. The *stile* of thy *works*, the *phrase* of thine *Actions*, is *Metaphoricall*. The *institution* of thy whole *worship* in the *old Law*, was a continuall *Allegory;* types and *figures* overspread all; and *figures* flowed into [485] *figures*, and poured themselves out into *farther figures; Circumcision* carried a *figure* of *Baptisme*, and *Baptisme* carries a *figure* of that *purity*, which we shall have in *perfection* in the *new Jerusalem*. Neither didst thou *speake*, and *worke* in this *language*, onely in the time of thy *Prophets;* but since thou spokest in thy *Son*, it is so too. How often, how much more often doth thy *Sonne* call himselfe a *way*, and a *light*, and a *gate*, and a *Vine*, and *bread*, than the *Sonne of God*, or of *Man?* How much oftner doth he exhibit a *Metaphoricall* [486] *Christ*, than a *reall*, a *literall?* This hath occasioned thine ancient *servants*, whose delight it was to write after thy *Copie*, to proceede the same way in their *expositions* of the *Scriptures*, and in their composing both of *publike liturgies*, and of *private prayers* to thee, to make their accesses to thee in such a kind of *language*, as thou wast pleased to speake to them, in a *figurative*, in a *Metaphoricall* [487] *language;* in which manner I am bold to call the comfort which I receive now in this *sicknesse*, in the *indication* of the *concoction* and *maturity* therof, in certaine *clouds*, and *residences*, which the *Physitians* observe, a discovering of *land* from *Sea*, after a long, and tempestuous *voyage*. But wherefore, O my *God*, hast thou presented to us, the *afflictions* and *calamities* of this life, in the name of *waters?* so often in the name of *waters*, and *deepe waters*, and *Seas* of *waters?* Must we looke to bee *drowned?* are they *bottomlesse*, are [488] they *boundles?* Thats not the *dialect* of thy *language;* thou hast given a *Remedy* against the deepest *water*, by *water;* against the *inundation* of sinne, by *Baptisme;* and the first *life*, that thou gavest to any *Creatures*, was in *waters;* therefore thou doest not threaten us, with an *irremediablenesse*, when our *affliction* is a *Sea*. It is so, if we consider *our selves;* so thou callest *Gennesaret*, which was but a lake, and not *salt*, a *Sea*, so thou callest the *Mediterranean Sea*, still [489] the *great Sea*, because the *inhabitants* saw no other *Sea;* they that dwelt there, thought a *Lake*, a *Sea*, and the others thought a *little Sea*, the *greatest*, and wee that know not the *afflictions* of others, call our owne the *heaviest*. But, O my *God*, that is *truly great*, that overflowes the *channell;* that is *really* a *great affliction*, which is [490] above my *strength*, but, thou, O *God*, art my *strength*, and then what Psal. 46.3 can bee above it? *Mountaines shake with the swelling of thy Sea*; *secular Mountaines*, men *strong in power*, *spirituall mountaines*, men Psal. 33.7 *strong in grace*, are shaked with *afflictions;* but *thou laiest up thy sea in store-houses;* even thy *corrections* are of thy *treasure*, and thou wilt not waste thy *corrections;* when they have done their *service*, to humble thy *patient*, thou wilt call them in againe; for, *thou givest the* [491] Prov. 8.29 *Sea thy decree, that the waters should not passe thy Commandement*. All our *waters* shal run into *Jordan*, and *thy servants passed Jordan* Josh. 3.17 *dry foot;* they shall run into the red Sea (the Sea of thy *Sons bloud*) and the red Sea, that red Sea, drownes none of *thine*. But, *they that* Ecclus. 43.26 *saile in the Sea, tell of the danger thereof;* I that am yet in this affliction, owe thee the *glory* of *speaking* of it; But, as the wise man ver. 29 bids me, I say, I may *speak much, and come short; wherefore in summe,* [492] *thou art all*. Since thou art so, O my *God*, and *affliction* is a *Sea*, too deepe for us, what is our *refuge?* thine *Arke*, thy *ship*. In all other *Seas*, in all other *afflictions*, those *meanes* which thou hast ordained; In this *Sea*, in *Sicknesse*, thy *Ship* is thy *Physitian*. *Thou hast made* Wisd. 14.3, 4 *a way in the Sea, and a safe path in the waters, shewing that thou canst save from all dangers; yea, though a man went to Sea without art;* yet [493] where I finde all that, I finde this added, *Nevertheless thou wouldest not, that the worke of thy wisdome should be idle*. Thou canst save without *meanes;* but thou hast told no man that thou *wilt:* Thou hast told every man, that thou *wilt not*. When the *Centurion* Act. 27.11 beleeved the *Master* of the *ship* more than St. *Paul*, they were all opened to a great danger; this was a *preferring of* thy *meanes*, before thee, the *Author* of the *meanes;* but, my *God*, though thou beest [494]

Luk. 5.3   *every where,* I have no promise of *appearing* to me, but in thy *ship:*
Thy blessed *Sonne preached out of a Ship:* The *meanes* is preaching,
Act. 27.24   he did that; and the *Ship* was a *type* of the *Church;* hee did it there.
Thou gavest St. Paul the lives of all them, that saild with him; If they
Mar. 5.2, 3   had not beene in the *Ship* with him, the gift had not extended to
[495]   them. *As soone as thy Son was come out of the ship, immediately there
met him out of the tombes, a man with an uncleane spirit, and no man
could hold him, no not with chaines.* Thy *Sonne* needed no use of
meanes; yet there wee apprehend the *danger* to us; if we leave the
ship, the *meanes;* in this case, the *Physitian.* But as they are *Ships* to
us in those *Seas,* so is there a *Ship* to them too, in which they are to
stay. Give mee leave, O my *God,* to assist my selfe with such a
[496]   *construction* of these words of thy servant *Paul,* to the *Centurion,*
Act. 27.31   when the *Mariners* would have left the *Ship: Except these abide in
the Ship, you cannot bee safe;* Except they who are our *ships,* the
Physitians, abide in that which is theirs, and our *ship,* the *truth,* and
the *sincere* and *religious worship of thee,* and thy *Gospell,* we cannot
promise our selves, so good *safety;* for though we have our *ship,* the
[497]   *Physitian,* he hath not his *ship, Religion;* And meanes are not
Jam. 3.4   meanes, but in their *concatenation,* as they *depend,* and are *chained*
together. *The ships are great,* saies thy *Apostle, but a helme turnes*
Rev. 8.9   *them;* the men are *learned,* but their *religion* turnes their *labours* to
good: And therefore it was a heavy *curse, when the third part of the
ships perished;* It is a heavy case, where either *all Religion,* or *true*
[498]   *Religion* should forsake many of these *ships,* whom thou hast sent
to convey us over these *Seas.* But, O my *God,* my *God,* since *I have
my ship,* and *they theirs,* I have *them,* and they have *thee,* why are we
yet no neerer land? As soone as thy *Sonnes Disciples* had taken *him*
Joh. 6.21   into the *ship, immediatly the ship was at the land, whither they went.*
Why have not *they* and *I* this dispatch? Every thing is *immediatly*
done, which is done when *thou* wouldst have it done. Thy purpose
[499]   *terminates* every action, and what was *done* before that, is *undone*
Lam. 3.26   yet. Shall that slacken my *hope?* Thy *Prophet* from *thee,* hath forbid
it. *It is good that a man should both hope, and quietly wait for the
salvation of the Lord.* Thou puttest off many *judgements,* till the *last*
day, many passe this life without any; and shall not I endure the
putting off thy *mercy* for a day? and yet, O my *God,* thou puttest me
[500]   not to that; for, the *assurance* of *future mercy,* is *present mercy.* But
what is my *assurance* now? What is my *seale?* It is but a *cloud;* that
which my *Physitians* call a *cloud,* is *that,* which gives them their
Indication. But a *Cloud?* Thy *great Seale* to all the world, the *raine-*
Exod. 13.21   *bow,* that secured the *world* for ever, from *drowning,* was but a
16.10   *reflexion upon a cloud.* A *cloud* it selfe was a *pillar* which guided the

church, and *the glory of God,* not only *was,* but *appeared in a cloud.*   [501]
Let me returne, O my *God,* to the consideration of thy *servant*   1 King. 18:43–45
Elijahs proceeding, in a time of *desperate drought;* he bids them
look towards the *Sea;* They looke, and see *nothing.* He bids them
againe and *againe, seven times:* and at the *seventh time,* they saw a
little *cloud* rising out of the *Sea;* and presently they had their desire
of *raine. Seven dayes,* O my *God,* have we looked for this *cloud,* and
now we have it; none of thy *Indications* are *frivolous;* thou makest
thy *signes, seales;* and thy *Seales, effects;* and thy *effects, consolation,*   [502]
and *restitution,* whersoever thou maiest receive *glory* by that way.

19. Prayer

O eternall and most gracious *God,* who though thou passedst over
infinite millions of generations, before thou camest to a *Creation* of
this *world,* yet when thou beganst, didst never intermit that *worke,*
but continuedst *day* to *day,* till thou hadst perfited all the *worke,*   [503]
and deposed it in the hands and rest of a *Sabbath,* though thou
have beene pleased to glorifie thy selfe in a long exercise of my
patience, with an *expectation* of thy *declaration* of thy selfe in this
my *sicknesse,* yet since thou hast now of thy goodnesse afforded
that, which affords us some hope, if that bee still *the way* of thy
glory, proceed in *that way,* and perfit *that worke,* and establish me   [504]
in a *Sabbath,* and *rest* in *thee,* by this thy *seale* of *bodily restitution.*
Thy *Priests* came up to thee, by steps in the *Temple;* Thy *Angels*
came *downe* to *Jacob,* by *steps* upon the *ladder;* we finde no *staire,* by
which thou *thy selfe* camest to *Adam* in *Paradise,* nor to *Sodome* in
thine *anger;* for *thou,* and *thou onely* art able to doe all at once. But,
O *Lord,* I am not *wearie* of thy *pace,* nor *wearie* of mine owne   [505]
patience. I provoke thee not with a *praier,* not with a *wish,* not with
a *hope,* to more haste than consists with thy *purpose,* nor looke that
any other thing should have entred into thy *purpose,* but thy *glory.*
To *heare* thy steps comming *towards* mee, is the same comfort, as
to see thy face present with mee; whether thou doe the worke of a
thousand yeere in a *day,* or extend the *worke of a day,* to a *thousand
yeere,* as long as *thou workest,* it is *light,* and *comfort. Heaven* it selfe   [506]
is but an *extention* of the same *joy;* and an *extention* of this *mercie,*
to proceed at thy *leisure,* in the way of *restitution,* is a *manifestation*
of *heaven* to me here upon *earth.* From that *people,* to whom thou
appearedst in *signes,* and in *Types,* the *Jews,* thou art departed,
because they trusted in *them;* but from thy *Church,* to whom thou
hast appeared in *thy selfe,* in *thy Sonne,* thou wilt never depart;   [507]

because we cannot trust *too much* in *him*. Though thou have afforded me these *signes* of *restitution*, yet if I *confide* in *them*, and beginne to say, all was but a *Naturall accident*, and *nature* begins to *discharge* her selfe, and shee will *perfit* the whole *worke*, my *hope* shall vanish because it is not in *thee*. If thou shouldest take thy *hand* utterly from me, and have nothing to doe with me, *Nature* alone were able to *destroy* mee; but if thou withdraw thy *helping hand*, alas how frivolous are the helps of *Nature*, how impotent the assistances of *Art?* As therefore the *morning dew*, is a *pawne* of the *evenings fatnesse*, so, O *Lord*, let *this daies* comfort be the *earnest* of to-*morrowes*, so farre as may *conforme* me entirely to thee, to what *end*, and by what *way* soever thy *mercie* have appointed mee.

[508]

20. Id agunt.

Upon these Indications of digested matter, they proceed to purge.

20. *Meditation*

Though *counsel* seeme rather to consist of *spirituall parts*, than *action*, yet *action* is the *spirit* and the *soule* of *counsell*. *Counsels* are not alwaies determined in *Resolutions;* Wee cannot alwaies say, *this was concluded; actions* are alwaies determined in *effects;* wee can say *this was done.* Then have *Lawes* their *reverence*, and their *majestie*, when wee see the *Judge* upon the *Bench* executing them. Then have *counsels of warre* their *impressions*, and their *operations*, when we see the *seale* of an *Armie* set to them. It was an ancient way of celebrating the *memorie* of such as deserved well of the *State*, to afford them that kinde of *statuarie representation*, which was then called *Hermes;* which was, *the head and shoulders of a man, standing upon a Cube*, but those *shoulders* without *armes* and *hands*. All together it figured a *constant supporter of the state*, by his *counsell:* But in this *Hierogliphique*, which they made without *hands*, they pass their consideration no farther, but that the *Counsellor* should bee without *hands*, so farre, as *not to reach out his hand to forraigne tentations of bribes, in matters of Counsell*, and, that it was not necessary, that the *head* should employ *his owne hand;* that *the same men* should serve in the *execution*, which assisted in the *Counsell;* but that there should not belong *hands* to

[510]

[511]

[512]

every *head, action* to every *counsell,* was never intended, so much
as in *figure,* and *representation.* For, as *matrimonie* is scarce to bee   Augustine
called *matrimonie,* where there is a *resolution* against the *fruits of*   [513]
matrimonie, against the having of *Children,* so *counsels* are not
counsels, but *illusions,* where there is from the beginning no
purpose to execute the determinations of those *counsels.* The *arts*
and *sciences* are most properly referred to the *head;* that is their
proper *Element* and *Spheare;* But yet the *art* of *proving, Logique,*
and the *Art* of *perswading, Rhetorique,* are deduced to the *hand,*
and *that* expressed by a *hand* contracted into a *fist,* and *this* by a   [514]
hand enlarged, and expanded; and evermore the *power of man,*
and the *power of God* himselfe is expressed so, *All things are in his*
hand; neither is *God* so often presented to us, by names that carry
our consideration upon *counsell,* as upon *execution of counsell;* he
is oftner called the *Lord of Hosts,* than by all other *names,* that may
be referred to the other signification. Hereby therefore wee take   [515]
into our *meditation,* the slipperie condition of *man,* whose
happinesse, in any kinde, the defect of *any one thing,* conducing to
that *happinesse,* may *ruine;* but it must have *all the peeces* to make
it up. Without *counsell,* I had not got thus farre; without *action*
and *practise,* I should goe no farther towards *health.* But what is
the present necessary *action? purging: A withdrawing,* a violating
of *Nature,* a *farther weakening:* O *deare price,* and O *strange* way of   [516]
addition, to doe it by *substraction;* of *restoring* Nature, to *violate*
Nature; of *providing strength,* by *increasing weaknesse.* Was I not
sicke before? And is it a *question* of *comfort* to be asked now, Did
your Physicke make you sicke? Was that it that my *Physicke*
promised, to make me *sicke?* This is another *step,* upon which we
may stand, and see farther into the *miserie of man,* the *time,* the   [517]
season of his *Miserie;* It must bee done now: O *over-cunning, over-*
watchfull, over-diligent, and *over-sociable misery* of *man,* that
seldome comes alone, but then when it may accompanie other
miseries, and so put one another into the higher *exaltation,* and
better *heart.* I am ground even to an *attenuation,* and must proceed
to *evacuation,* all waies to exinanition and annihilation.

20. *Expostulation*   [518]

My *God,* my *God,* the *God of Order,* but yet not of *Ambition,* who
assignest *place* to every one, but not *contention* for place, when shall
it be thy pleasure to put an *end* to all these *quarrels,* for *spirituall*
precedences? when shall men leave their uncharitable *disputations,*
which is *to take place, faith* or *repentance,* and which, when we

[519] consider *faith*, and *works?* The *head* and the *hand* too, are required to a *perfit naturall man; Counsell* and *action* too, to a *perfit civill man; faith* and *works* too, to him that is *perfitly spirituall*. But because it is easily said, I *beleeve*, and because it doth not easily *lie in proofe*, nor is easily demonstrable by any *evidence* taken from my *heart*, (for who sees that, who searches those *Rolls?*) whether I doe *beleeve*, or no, is

[520] it not therefore, O my *God*, that thou dost so *frequently*, so *earnestly*, referre us to the *hand*, to the *observation* of *actions?* There is a little *suspition*, a little *imputation* laid upon *over-tedious* and *dilatorie counsels*, Many good occasions slip away in long *consultations;* and it may be a *degree* of *sloth*, to be too long in *mending nets*, though *that*

Eccles. 11.4 must be done. *He that observeth the wind, shall not sow, and he that*

[521] *regardeth the clouds, shall not reape;* that is, he that is too *dilatorie*, too *superstitious* in these *observations*, and studies but the *excuse* of his *owne idlenesse* in *them;* But, that which the same *wise* and *royall*

Prov. 10.4 servant of thine, saies, in another place, all accept, and aske no *comment* upon it, *He becommeth poore, that dealeth with a slacke hand; but the hand of the diligent maketh rich;* All *evill* imputed to the *absence*, all *good* attributed to the *presence* of the *hand*. I know, my

[522] *God*, (and I blesse thy name for knowing it; for all good *knowledge* is from thee) that thou *considerest* the *heart;* but thou takest not off thine *eie*, till thou come to the *hand*. Nay, my *God*, doth not thy *spirit* intimate, that thou *beginnest* where wee *beginne*, (at least, that thou

Psal. 24.3, 4 allowest us to *beginne there)* when thou orderest thine owne answer to thine owne question, *Who shall ascend into the hill of the Lord?*

[523] Thus, *he that hath cleane hands, and a pure heart?* Doest thou not (at least) *send us*, first to the *hand?* And is not the worke of their *hands*,

Exod. 32.29 that declaration of their *holy zeale*, in the present execution of manifest *Idolatrers*, called a *consecration of themselves*, by thy *holy Spirit?* Their *hands* are called *all themselves:* for, even *counsell* it selfe goes under that *name*, in thy *Word*, who knowest best how to give

1 Sam. 22.17 [524] right *names:* because the *counsell of the Priests* assisted *David*, *Saul* saies, *The hand of the Priest is with David:* And that which is often

Levit. 8.36 said by *Moses*, is very often repeated by thy other *Prophets*, *These* and *these* things *the Lord spake*, and the *Lord said*, and the *Lord commanded*, not by the *counsels*, not by the *voice*, but by the *hand of Moses*, and by the *hand of the Prophets:* Evermore we are referred for

[525] our *Evidence*, of *others* and of *our selves*, to the *hand*, to *action*, to *works*. There is something *before* it, *beleeving;* and there is something *after* it, *suffering;* but in the most eminent, and obvious, and conspicuous place, stands *doing*. Why then, O my *God*, my blessed *God*, in the waies of my *spirituall strength*, come I so slow to *action?* I was whipped by thy *rod*, before I came to *consultation*, to consider my state; and shall I goe no farther? As hee that would describe a

circle in paper, if hee have brought that *circle* within one *inch* of [526]
finishing, yet if he remove his *compasse*, he cannot make it up a perfit
circle, except he fall to worke againe, to finde out the same *center*, so,
though setting that *foot* of my *compasse* upon *thee*, I have gone so
farre, as to the *consideration* of my selfe, yet if I depart from *thee*, my
center, all is unperfit. This proceeding to *action* therefore, is a
returning to *thee*, and a *working* upon *my selfe* by thy *Physicke*, by thy [527]
purgative physicke, a free and entire evacuation of my *soule* by
confession. The working of *purgative physicke*, is *violent* and contrary
to *Nature*. O *Lord*, I decline not this *potion* of *confession*, how ever it
may bee contrary to a *naturall man*. To take *physicke*, and *not according*   Galen
to the right method, is dangerous. O *Lord*, I decline not that *method* in
this *physicke*, in things that burthen my *conscience*, to make my
confession to *him*, into whose hands thou hast put the *power* of [528]
absolution. I know that *Physicke may be made so pleasant, as that it*   Galen
may easily be taken; but not so pleasant as the vertue and nature of the
medicine bee extinguished; I know, I am not submitted to such a
confession as is a *racke* and *torture* of the *Conscience;* but I know I am
not exempt from all. If it were meerely *problematicall*, left meerely
indifferent, whether we should take this *Physicke*, use this *confession*, [529]
or no, a great *Physitian* acknowledges this to have beene his *practise*,   Galen
To minister many things, which hee was not sure would doe good, but
never any other thing, but such as hee was sure would doe no harme. The
use of this spirituall *Physicke* can certainly doe no *harme;* and the
Church hath alwaies thought that it might, and doubtlesse, many
humble *soules* have found, that it hath done them *good*. I will *therefore* [530] Psa. 116.13
take the cup of Salvation, and call upon thy Name; I will fill this *Cup*
of *compunction*, as full as I have formerly filled the *Cups* of worldly
confections, that so I may scape the *cup of Malediction*, and
irrecoverable destruction that depends upon that. And since thy
blessed and glorious *Sonne*, being offered in the way to his *Execution*,   Mar. 15.23
a Cup of *Stupefaction*, to take away the sense of his *paine*, (a charity
afforded to condemned persons ordinarily in those places, and [531]
times) refused that *ease*, and embraced the whole *torment*, I take not
this *Cup*, but this *vessell* of mine owne *sinnes*, into my *contemplation*,
and I poure them out here according to the *Motions* of thy *holy*
Spirit, and *any where*, according to the ordinances of thy *holy Church*.

20. *Prayer* [532]

O eternall, and most gracious *God*, who having married *Man*, and
Woman together, and made them one *flesh*, wouldest have them
also, to become one *soule* so, as that they might maintaine a *simpathy*

in their *affections*, and have a *conformity* to one another, in the *accidents* of this *world*, good or bad, so having married this soule and this body in me, I humbly beseech thee, that my soule may looke, and make her use of thy mercifull proceedings towards my *bodily restitution*, and goe the same way to a *spirituall*. I am come by thy goodnesse, to the use of thine ordinary meanes for my *body*, to wash away those *peccant humors*, that endangered it. I have, O *Lord*, a *River* in my *body*, but a *Sea* in my *soule*, and a *Sea* swoln into the depth of a *Deluge*, above the *Sea*. Thou hast raised up certaine *hils* in *me* heretofore, by which I might have stood safe, from these *inundations* of *sin*. Even our *Naturall faculties* are a *hill*, and might preserve us from *some sinne*. *Education, study, observation, example*, are *hills* too, and might preserve us from *some*. Thy *Church*, and thy *Word*, and thy *Sacraments*, and thine *Ordinances*, are *hills*, above these; thy *Spirit* of *remorse*, and *compunction*, and *repentance* for former *sin*, are *hills* too; and to the *top* of all these *hils*, thou hast brought mee heretofore; but this *Deluge*, this *inundation*, is got above all my *Hills;* and I have sinned and sinned, and multiplied *sinne* to *sinne*, after all these thy assistances against *sinne*, and where is there *water* enough to wash away this *Deluge?* There is a *red Sea*, greater than this *Ocean;* and there is a *little spring*, through which this *Ocean*, may poure it selfe into that *red Sea*. Let thy *Spirit* of true *contrition*, and *sorrow* passe all my *sinnes* through these *eies*, into the *wounds* of thy *Sonne*, and I shall be cleane, and my *soule* so much better purged than my *body*, as it is ordained for a *better*, and a *longer* life.

21. Atque annuit Ille, Qui, per eos, clamat, Linquas iam, Lazare, lectum.

God prospers their practise, and he by them calls Lazarus out of his tombe, mee out of my bed.

21. Meditation

If man had beene left *alone* in this *world*, at first, shall I thinke, that he would not have *fallen?* If there had beene no *Woman*, would not *Man* have served, to have beene his own *Tempter?* When I see him now, subject to infinite weakenesses, fall into *infinite sinne*, without any *forraine tentations,* shall I thinke, he would have had *none,* if hee had beene *alone?* GOD saw that Man needed a *Helper,* if hee should bee well; but to make *Woman* ill, the *Devill* saw, that there needed [539] no *third.* When *God,* and *wee* were *alone,* in *Adam,* that was not enough; when the *Devill* and *wee* were *alone,* in *Eve,* it was enough. O what a *Giant* is *Man,* when hee fights against himselfe, and what a *dwarfe,* when hee *needs,* or *exercises* his own assistance for himselfe? I cannot *rise* out of my bed, till the *Physitian enable* mee, nay I cannot tel, that I am able to rise, till *hee tell* me so. I *doe* [540] nothing, I *know* nothing of my selfe: how little, and how impotent a peece of the *world,* is any *Man* alone? and how much lesse a peece of *himselfe* is *that Man?* So little, as that when it falls out, (as it falls out in some cases) that more *misery,* and more *oppression,* would bee an *ease* to a *man,* he cannot give himselfe that *miserable addition,* of *more misery;* A *man* that is *pressed to death,* and might be eased by more *weights,* cannot lay those more *weights* upon himselfe; Hee [541] can sinne *alone,* and suffer *alone,* but not *repent,* not be *absolved,* without *another. Another tels mee, I* may rise; *and I* doe *so. But is every* raising a *preferment?* or is every present *preferment* a *station?* I am readier to fall to the *Earth* now I am up, than I was when I *lay* in the bed: O *perverse way, irregular motion* of *Man;* even *rising* it selfe is the way to *Ruine.* How many *men* are raised, and then doe [542] not *fill* the place they are raised to? No *corner* of any place can bee *empty;* there can be no *vacuity;* If that *Man* doe not fill the place, *other men* will; complaints of his *insufficiency* will *fill* it; Nay, such an abhorring is there in *Nature,* of *vacuity,* that if there be but an *imagination* of *not filling,* in any *man,* that which is but *imagination,* [543] neither will *fill* it, that is, *rumor* and *voice,* and it will be *given out,* (upon no ground, but *Imagination,* and no man knowes, *whose imagination*) that hee is *corrupt* in his place, or *insufficient* in his place, and another prepared to *succeed* him in his place. A man *rises,* sometimes, and *stands* not, because hee doth not, or is not beleeved to *fill* his place; and sometimes he *stands* not, because hee *over-fills* his place: Hee may bring so much *vertue,* so much *Justice,* [544] so much *integrity* to the place, as shall *spoile* the place, *burden* the place; his *integrity* may bee a *Libell* upon his *Predecessor,* and cast an *infamy* upon him, and a *burden* upon his *successor,* to proceede by *example,* and to bring the place it selfe, to an *under-value,* and the *market* to an *uncertainty.* I am *up,* and I seeme to *stand,* and I goe *round;* and I am a *new Argument* of the *new Philosophie,* That [545] the *Earth* moves round; why may I not beleeve, that the *whole earth* moves in a *round motion,* though that seeme to mee to *stand,* when as I seeme to *stand* to my *Company,* and yet am carried, in a giddy, and *circular motion,* as I *stand?* Man hath no *center,* but *misery; there* and onely *there,* hee is *fixt,* and sure to finde himselfe. How little [546] soever he bee *raised,* he *moves,* and moves in a *circle,* giddily; and as in the *Heavens,* there are but a few *Circles,* that goe about the whole world, but many *Epicicles,* and other lesser *Circles,* but yet *Circles,* so of those men, which are *raised,* and put into *Circles;* few of them move from *place* to *place,* and pass through many and beneficial places, but fall into little *Circles,* and within a step or two, are at [547] their *end,* and not so well, as they were in the *Center,* from which they were *raised.* Every thing serves to *exemplifie,* to *illustrate* mans *misery;* But I need goe no farther, than *my selfe;* for a long time, I was not able to *rise;* At last, I must be *raised* by others; and now I am *up,* I am ready to sinke *lower* than before.

21. *Expostulation*

[548] My *God,* my *God,* how large a *glasse* of the next *World is this?* As wee have an *Art,* to cast from one *glasse* to another, and so to carry the *Species* a great way off, so hast thou, that way, much more; wee shall have a *Resurrection* in *Heaven;* the knowledge of that thou castest by another *glasse* upon us here; we *feele* that wee have a *Resurrection* from *sinne;* and that by another *glasse* too; wee see wee [549] have a *Resurrection* of the *body,* from the *miseries* and *calamities* of this life. This *Resurrection* of my *body* shewes me the *Resurrection* of my *soule;* and both *here* severally, of both together hereafter. Since thy *Martyrs* under the *Altar,* presse thee with their solicitation for the *Resurrection* of the *body* to *glory,* thou wouldest pardon mee, if I should presse thee by *Prayer,* for the acomplishing [550] of this *Resurrection,* which thou hast begunne in me to *health.* But, O my *God,* I doe not *aske,* where I might aske amisse, nor begge that which perchance might bee worse for mee. I have a *Bed* of *sinne; delight* in *Sinne,* is a *Bed;* I have a *grave* of *sinne; senselesnesse* in *sinne,* is a *grave;* and where *Lazarus* had been *foure daies,* I have beene *fifty yeeres,* in this *putrifaction;* Why dost thou not call mee, Joh. 11.43 [551] as thou diddest him, *with a loud voice,* since my *Soule* is as dead as his *Body* was? I need thy *thunder,* O my *God;* thy *musicke* will not serve me. Thou hast called thy *servants,* who are to worke upon us, in thine *Ordinance,* by all these loud *Names, Winds,* and *Chariots,* and *falls of waters;* where thou wouldest be heard, thou *wilt* bee heard. When thy *Sonne* concurred with thee, to the making of [552] Man, there is but a *speaking,* but a *saying;* There, *O blessed and glorious Trinity,* was none to *heare,* but you *three,* and you easily

heare *one another,* because you say the *same things.* But when thy
Sonne came to the worke of *Redemption, thou spokest,* and they that
heard it, tooke it for *Thunder;* and thy *Sonne* himselfe *cried with a
loud voice,* upon the *Crosse,* twice, as hee, who was to prepare his
comming, *John Baptist,* was the *voice of a cryer,* and not of a
Whisperer. Still if it be *thy voice,* it is a *loud voice; These words,* saies
thy *Moses, Thou spokest with a great voice,* and *thou addest no more,*
saies hee there; That which thou hast said, is *evident,* and it is
evident, that none can speake so *loud;* none can binde us to heare
him, as wee must *thee. The most high uttered his voice:* what was *his
voice? The Lord thundred from heaven,* it might bee heard; But this
voice, *thy voice,* is also a *mightie voice;* not onely *mightie in power,* it
may be heard, nor *mightie in obligation,* it *should* be heard, but
mightie in *operation,* it *will* bee heard; and therefore hast thou
bestowed a whole *Psalme* upon us, to leade us to the consideration
of thy *voice.* It is such a *voice,* as that thy *Sonne* saies, *the dead shall
heare it;* and thats *my state;* And why, O *God,* doest thou not speake
to me, in that *effectuall loudnesse?* St. *John* heard a voice, and hee
turned about to see the voice: sometimes we are too curious of the
instrument, by what man *God* speakes; but thou speakest loudest,
when thou speakest to the *heart. There was silence, and I heard a
voice,* saies one, to thy *servant Job.* I hearken after *thy voice, in thine
Ordinances,* and I seeke not a *whispering* in *Conventicles;* but yet, O
my God, speake *louder,* that so, though I doe heare thee now, then
I may heare *nothing but thee. My sinnes* crie aloud; *Cains murder* did
so; my *afflictions* crie aloud; *The flouds have lifted up their voice,* (and
waters are *afflictions*) but thou, O *Lord, art mightier than the voice of
many waters;* than many *temporall,* many *spirituall afflictions;* than
any of *either* kinde; and why doest thou not speak to me in *that
voice? What is man, and whereto serveth he? what is his good, and
what is his evill?* My *bed* of *sinne* is not *evill,* not desperatly evill, for
thou doest call mee out of it; but my rising out of it is not *good,* (not
perfitly good) if thou call not *louder,* and hold me now I am *up.* O
my *God,* I am afraid of a fearefull application of those words, *when
a man hath done, then hee beginneth;* when his *body* is unable to
sinne, his *sinfull memory* sinnes over his old sinnes againe; and that
which thou wouldest have us to remember for *compunction,* we
remember with *delight. Bring him to me in his bed, that I may kill
him,* saies *Saul* of *David;* Thou hast not said so, that is not *thy*
voice. *Joash his owne servants slew him, when hee was sicke in his bed;*
Thou hast not suffered that, that my *servants* should so much as
neglect mee, or be *wearie* of mee, in my *sicknesse.* Thou threatnest,
that as a shepheard takes out of the mouth of the Lion, two legs, or a

Joh. 12.28
Mat. 27.46, 50
[553]
Deut. 5.22

2 Sam. 22.14
[554] Psal. 68.33

Psal. 29

Joh. 5.25
Rev. 1.12
[555]

Job 4.16

[556]
Psal. 93.3, 4

Ecclus. 18.8

[557]

Ecclus. 18.7

[558] 1 Sam. 19.15

2 Chro. 24.25

Amos 3.12
[559]

*peece of an eare, so shall the children of Israel, that dwell in Samaria,
in the corner of a bed, and in Damascus, in a couch, bee taken away:*
That even they that are *secure* from danger, shall perish; How
much more might I, who was in the *bed* of *death, die?* But thou hast

Act. 5.15 not dealt so with mee. As *they brought out sicke persons in beds, that
thy servant Peters shadow might over-shadow them;* Thou hast, O my

[560] God, over-shadowed mee, refreshed mee: But when wilt thou doe
more? when wilt thou doe *all?* when wilt thou speake in thy *loud*

Mat. 9.5, 6 *voice?* when wilt thou bid mee *take up my bed and walke?* As my *bed*
is my *affections*, when shall I beare them so as to *subdue* them? As
my *bed* is my *afflictions*, when shall I beare them so, as not to
murmure at them? When shall *I take up my bed and walke?* not *lie*

[561] *downe* upon it, as it is my *pleasure*, not *sinke under* it, as it is my
correction? But, O my *God*, my *God*, the *God* of all *flesh*, and of all
spirit too, let me bee content with that in my *fainting spirit*, which
thou declarest in this *decaied flesh*, that as this body is content to *sit
still*, that it may learne to *stand*, and to learne by *standing* to *walke*,
and *by walking* to *travell*, so my *soule* by obeying this *thy voice* of

[562] *rising*, may by a farther and farther growth of thy *grace*, proceed so,
and bee so established, as may remove all *suspitions*, all *jealousies*
between *thee* and *mee*, and may *speake* and *heare* in such a *voice*, as
that still I may bee acceptable *to thee*, and satisfied *from thee*.

21. Prayer

O eternall and most gracious *God*, who hast made little things to
signifie *great*, and convayd the *infinite merits of thy Sonne* in the

[563] *water* of *Baptisme*, and in the *Bread* and *Wine* of thy other
Sacrament, unto us, receive the *sacrifice* of my humble thanks,
that thou hast not onely afforded mee, the abilitie to rise out of
this *bed* of *wearinesse* and *discomfort*, but hast also made this *bodily
rising*, by thy *grace*, an *earnest* of a *second resurrection* from *sinne*,
and of a *third*, to *everlasting glory*. Thy *Sonne* himselfe, alwaies
infinite in *himselfe*, and incapable of *addition*, was yet pleased to

[564] grow in the *Virgins* wombe, and to grow in *stature*, in the sight of
men. Thy good purposes upon mee, I know, have their
determination and *perfection*, in thy holy *will* upon mee; there thy
grace is, and there I am *altogether;* but manifest them so unto me
in thy *seasons*, and in thy *measures* and *degrees*, that I may not
onely have that *comfort* of knowing *thee* to be *infinitely good*, but

[565] that also of finding thee to bee every day *better* and *better* to mee:
and that as thou gavest *St. Paul*, the *Messenger of Satan*, to *humble*

him, so for my *humiliation,* thou maiest give me *thy selfe,* in this knowledge, that what *grace* soever thou afford me *to day,* yet I should perish *to morrow,* if I had not *to morrowes grace too.* Therefore I begge of thee, *my daily bread;* and as thou gavest mee the *bread* of *sorrow* for many daies, and since, the *bread* of *hope* for some, and this day, the *bread* of *possessing,* in *rising* by that [566] strength, which thou, the *God* of all strength, hast infused into me: so, O *Lord,* continue to mee the *bread of life;* the *spirituall bread of life,* in a faithfull assurance in *thee;* the *sacramentall bread of life,* in a worthy receiving of *thee;* and the *more reall bread of life,* in an everlasting *union to thee.* I know, O *Lord,* that when thou hadst created *Angels,* and they saw thee produce *fowle,* and *fish,* and *beasts,* and *wormes,* they did not importune thee, and say, [567] shall wee have no better *Creatures* than these, no better *companions* than these; but staid thy *leisure,* and then had *man* delivered over to them, not much inferiour in *nature* to themselves. No more doe I, O *God,* now that by thy *first mercie,* I am able to *rise,* importune thee for present confirmation of *health;*nor now, that [568] by thy *mercie,* I am brought to see, that thy *correction* hath wrought *medicinally* upon mee, presume I upon that *spirituall strength* I have; but as I acknowledge, that my *bodily strength* is subject to every *puffe of wind,* so is my *spirituall strength* to every *blast of vanitie.* Keepe me therefore still, O my gracious *God,* in such a *proportion* of both *strengths,* as I may still have something to thanke thee for, which I *have received,* and still something to *pray for,* and aske at thy hand.

22. Sit morbi fomes tibi cura; [569]
The Physitians consider the root and occasion, the embers, and coales, and fuell of the disease, and seeke to purge or correct that.

22. *Meditation*

How *ruinous* a *farme* hath *man* taken, in taking *himselfe?* how ready is the *house* every day to fall downe, and how is all the *ground* over- [570] spread with *weeds,* all the *body* with *diseases?* where not onely every *turfe,* but every *stone,* beares *weeds;* not onely every *muscle* of

the *flesh*, but every *bone* of the *body*, hath some *infirmitie;* every little *flint* upon the *face* of this *soile*, hath some *infectious weede*, every *tooth* in our *head*, such a paine, as a *constant man* is afraid of,
[571] and yet *ashamed* of that *feare*, of that sense of the paine. How *deare*, and how *often* a *rent* doth Man pay for this *farme?* hee paies *twice a day*, in double *meales*, and how little time he hath to *raise his rent?* How many *holy daies* to call him from his labour? Every day is *halfe-holy day*, halfe spent in *sleepe*. What *reparations*, and *subsidies*, and *contributions* he is put to, besides his *rent?* What
[572] *medicines*, besides his *diet?* and what *Inmates* he is faine to take in, besides his owne *familie*, what *infectious diseases, from other* men? *Adam* might have had *Paradise* for *dressing* and *keeping* it; and *then* his *rent* was not *improved* to such a *labour*, as would have made his *brow sweat;* and yet he gave it over; how farre greater a *rent* doe wee pay for this *farme*, this *body*, who pay *our selves*, who pay the *farme it selfe*, and cannot *live* upon it? Neither is our *labour* at an
[573] end, when wee have cut downe some *weed*, as soone as it sprung up, corrected some *violent* and dangerous *accident* of a *disease*, which would have destroied *speedily;* nor when wee have pulled up that *weed*, from the very *root*, recovered *entirely* and *soundly*, from that *particular disease;* but the whole *ground* is of an *ill nature*, the whole soile *ill disposed;* there are inclinations, there is a propensnesse to *diseases* in the *body*, out of which without any
[574] other *disorder, diseases* will grow, and so wee are put to a continuall labour upon this *farme*, to a continuall studie of the whole *complexion* and *constitution* of our *body*. In the *distempers* and *diseases* of *soiles, sourenesse, driness, weeping*, any kinde of *barrennesse*, the *remedy* and the *physicke*, is, for a great part, sometimes in *themselves;* sometimes the very *situation* releeves them, the *hanger* of a *hill*, will purge and vent his owne *malignant*
[575] *moisture;* and the burning of the upper *turfe* of some ground (as *health* from *cauterizing*) puts a *new* and a *vigorous youth* into that *soile*, and there rises a kind of *Phoenix* out of the *ashes*, a *fruitfulnesse* out of that which was *barren* before, and *by that*, which is the barrennest of all, *ashes*. And where the *ground* cannot give it selfe
[576] *physicke*, yet it receives *Physicke* from other grounds, from other soiles, which are not the worse, for having contributed that helpe to them, from *Marle* in other *hils*, or from *slimie sand* in other *shoares: grounds* help *themselves*, or hurt not other *grounds*, from whence they receive *helpe*. But I have taken a *farme* at this *hard rent*, and upon those *heavie covenants*, that it can afford it selfe no *helpe;* (no part of my *body*, if it were cut off, would *cure* another

part; in some cases it might *preserve* a sound part, but in no case [577]
recover an infected) and, if my *body* may have any *Physicke,* any
Medicine from another *body,* one *Man* from the flesh of another
Man (as by *Mummy,* or any such *composition,*) it must bee from a
man that is dead, and not, as in other *soiles,* which are never the
worse for contributing their *Marle,* or their fat slime to my *ground.*
There is nothing in the same *man,* to helpe *man,* nothing in
mankind to helpe *one another,* (in this sort, by way of *Physicke*) but [578]
that hee who *ministers* the *helpe,* is in as ill case, as he that *receives*
it would have beene, if he had not had it; for hee, from whose *body*
the *Physicke* comes, is *dead.* When therefore I tooke this *farme,*
undertooke this body, I undertooke to *draine,* not a *marsh,* but a
moat, where there was, not water *mingled* to offend, but all was
water; I undertooke to *perfume dung,* where no one part, but all [579]
was equally *unsavory;* I undertooke to make such a thing *wholsome,*
as was not *poison* by any manifest quality, *intense heat,* or *cold,* but
poison in the *whole substance,* and in the *specifique forme* of it. To
cure the *sharpe accidents* of *diseases,* is a great worke; to cure the
disease it selfe, is a greater; but to cure the *body,* the *root,* the
occasion of *diseases,* is a worke reserved for the great *Physitian,* [580]
which he doth never any other way, but by *glorifying* these *bodies*
in the next world.

22. *Expostulation*

My *God,* my *God,* what am I put to, when I am put to *consider,*
and *put off,* the *root,* the *fuell,* the *occasion* of my *sicknesse?* What
Hippocrates, what *Galen,* could shew mee that in my *body?* It lies
deeper than so; it lies in my *soule:* And deeper than so; for we
may wel consider the *body,* before the *soule* came, before [581]
inanimation, to bee *without sinne;* and the *soule* before it come to
the *body,* before that *infection,* to be *without sinne; sinne* is the
root, and the *fuell* of all *sickenesse,* and yet that which destroies
body and *soule,* is in *neither,* but in *both together;* It is in the *union*
of the *body* and *soule;* and, O my *God,* could I *prevent* that, or can
I *dissolve* that? The *root,* and the *fuell* of my *sicknesse,* is my *sinne,*
my *actuall sinne;* but even that *sinne* hath another *root,* another [582]
fuell, originall sinne; and can I *divest* that? Wilt thou bid me to
separate the *leaven,* that a lumpe of Dough hath received, or the
salt, that the water hath contracted, from the *Sea?* Dost thou
looke, that I should so looke to the *fuell,* or *embers* of *sinne,* that I

never take fire? The whole world is *a pile of fagots*, upon which wee are laid, and (as though there were no other) *we are the bellowes. Ignorance* blowes the *fire, He that touched any uncleane thing, though he knew it not, became uncleane,* and *a sacrifice was required,* (therefore a *sin* imputed) *though it were done in ignorance. Ignorance* blowes this *Coale;* but then *knowledge* much more; for, *there are that know thy judgements, and yet not onely doe, but have pleasure in others, that doe against them. Nature* blowes this Coale; *By nature wee are the children of wrath:* And the *Law* blowes it, thy *Apostle,* St. *Paul,* found, *That sinne tooke occasion by the Law,* that therefore because it is forbidden, we do some things. If wee breake the *Law,* wee sinne; *Sinne is the transgression of the Law;* And *sinne it selfe becomes a Law in our members.* Our *fathers* have imprinted the *seed,* infused a *spring of sinne* in us; *As a fountaine casteth out her waters, wee cast out our wickednesse; but we have done worse than our fathers.* We are open to infinite *tentations,* and yet, as though we lacked, *we are tempted of our owne lusts.* And not satisfied with that, as though we were not *powerfull* enough, or *cunning* enough, to demolish, or undermine our selves, when wee our selves have no pleasure in the *sinne,* we *sinne* for others sakes. When *Adam* sinned for *Eves* sake, and *Solomon* to gratifie his wives, it was an *uxorious* sinne: When the *Judges* sinned for *Jezabels* sake, and *Joab* to obey *David,* it was an *ambitious* sinne: When *Pilate* sinned to *humor the people,* and *Herod* to *give farther contentment to the Jewes,* it was a *popular* sinne: Any thing serves, to *occasion* sin, at *home,* in my bosome, or *abroad,* in my *Marke,* and *aime;* that which *I am,* and that which *I am not,* that which I *would* be, proves *coales,* and *embers,* and *fuell,* and *bellowes* to sin; and dost thou put me, O my *God,* to discharge my selfe, of *my selfe,* before I can be *well?* When thou bidst me *to put off the old Man,* doest thou meane, not onely my old *habits* of *actuall* sin, but the *oldest of all, originall sinne?* When thou biddest me *purge out the leaven,* dost thou meane, not only the sourenesse of mine owne ill contracted *customes,* but the innate *tincture* of sin, imprinted by *Nature?* How shall I doe that which thou requirest, and not *falsifie* that which thou hast *said, that sin is gone over all?* But, O my *God,* I presse thee not, with *thine owne text,* without *thine owne comment;* I know that in the state of my *body,* which is more *discernible,* than that of my *soule,* thou dost *effigiate* my *Soule* to me. And though no *Anatomist* can say, in dissecting a *body,* here lay the *coale,* the *fuell,* the *occasion* of all *bodily diseases,* but yet *a man* may have such a knowledge of his owne constitution, and bodily inclination to *diseases,* as that he may *prevent* his

Levit. 5.2 [583]
Numb. 15.24
Rom. 1.32
Eph. 2.3 [584]
1 Joh. 3.4
Rom. 7.23
Jer. 6.7
Jer. 7.26 [585]
Jam. 1.14
Gen 3.6
1 King.11.3
21.11 [586]
2 Sam. 11.6
Luk. 23.23
Act. 12.3
[587]
Eph. 4.22
1 Cor. 5.7
[588]
[589]

danger in a great part: so though wee cannot assigne the *place* of *originall sinne*, nor the *Nature* of it, so *exactly*, as of *actuall*, or by any diligence *divest* it, yet having *washed it* in the water of thy *Baptisme*, wee have not onely so cleansed it, that wee may the better look upon it, and *discerne* it, but so *weakned* it, that [590] howsoever it may retaine the *former nature*, it doth not retaine the *former force*, and though it may have the *same name*, it hath not the same *venome*.

22. *Prayer*

O eternall and most gracious *God*, the *God* of *securitie*, and the *enemie* of *securitie* too, who wouldest have us alwaies *sure* of thy *love*, and yet wouldest have us alwaies *doing something* for it, let mee [591] alwaies so apprehend *thee*, as *present* with me, and yet so *follow* after thee, as though I had not apprehended thee. Thou enlargedst *Hezekiahs* lease for *fifteene yeeres;* Thou renewedst *Lazarus* his lease, for a time, which we know not: But thou didst never so put out any of these *fires*, as that thou didst not rake up the *embers*, and wrap up a *future mortalitie*, in that *body*, which thou hadst then so [592] *reprieved*. Thou proceedest no otherwise in our *soules*, O our *good*, but *fearefull God:* Thou pardonest no *sinne* so, as that that *sinner* can sinne no more; thou makest no *man* so *acceptable*, as that thou makest him *impeccable*. Though therefore it were a *diminution* of the *largenesse*, and *derogatorie* to the *fulnesse* of thy *mercie*, to looke backe upon those sinnes which in a true *repentance*, I have buried [593] in the wounds of thy *Sonne*, with a *jealous* or *suspicious eie*, as though they were now *my sinnes*, when I had so transferred them upon thy *Sonne*, as though they could now bee *raised* to life againe, to *condemne* mee to death, when they are dead in *him*, who is the *fountaine of life;* yet were it an *irregular anticipation*, and an *insolent presumption*, to thinke that thy *present mercie* extended to all my *future sinnes*, or that there were no *embers*, no *coales* of *future sinnes* [594] left in mee. Temper therefore thy *mercie* so to my *soule*, O my *God*, that I may neither *decline* to any faintnesse of spirit, in suspecting thy *mercie* now, to bee lesse *hearty*, lesse *sincere*, than it uses to be, to those who are perfitly reconciled to thee, nor *presume* so of it, as either to thinke this *present mercie* an *antidote* against *all poisons*, and so *expose* my selfe to *tentations*, upon confidence that this thy [595] *mercie* shall *preserve* mee, or that when I doe cast my selfe into *new sinnes*, I may have *new mercie* at *any time*, because thou didst *so* easily afford mee *this*.

[596]   ## 23. —Metusque, Relabi.
*They warne mee of the feareful danger
of relapsing.*

23. Meditation

It is not in *mans body*, as it is in the *Citie*, that when *the Bell* hath rung, to cover your *fire*, and rake up the *embers*, you may lie downe,
[597] and sleepe without feare. Though you have by *physicke* and *diet*, raked up the *embers* of your *disease*, stil there is a feare of a *relapse;* and the greater *danger* is in that. Even in *pleasures*, and in *paines*, there is a *propriety*, a *Meum et Tuum;* and a man is most affected with that *pleasure* which is *his*, *his* by former enjoying and experience, and most intimidated with those *paines* which are *his*,
[598] *his* by a wofull sense of them, in former afflictions. A *covetous* person, who hath preoccupated all his senses, filled all his capacities, with the *delight* of *gathering*, wonders how any man can have *any taste* of *any pleasure* in *any opennesse*, or *liberalitie;* So also in *bodily paines*, in a fit of the *stone*, the patient wonders why any man should call the *Gout* a *paine:* And hee that hath felt neither, but the *tooth-ach*, is as much afraid of a fit of that, as either of the
[599] other, of either of the other. *Diseases*, which we never *felt* in our selves, come but to a *compassion* of others that have endured them; Nay, *compassion* it selfe, comes to no great *degree*, if wee have not *felt*, in some *proportion*, in *our selves*, that which wee lament and condole in another. But when wee have had those torments in their *exaltation*, *our selves*, wee tremble at a *relapse*. When wee must *pant*
[600] through all those *fierie heats*, and *saile* through all those *overflowing sweats*, when wee must *watch* through all those long *nights*, and *mourne* through all those long *daies*, *(daies* and *nights*, so *long*, as that *Nature* her selfe shall seeme to be *perverted*, and to have put the *longest day*, and the *longest night*, which should bee *six moneths* asunder, into one *naturall*, *unnaturall day)* when wee must stand at the same *barre*, expect the returne of *Physitians* from their
[601] *consultations*, and not bee sure of the same *verdict*, in any good *Indications*, when we must goe the same *way* over againe, and not see the same *issue*, this is a *state*, a *condition*, a *calamitie*, in respect of which, any other *sickenesse* were a *convalescence*, and any *greater*, *lesse*. It addes to the *affliction*, that *relapses* are, (and for the most part justly) imputed to *our selves*, as occasioned by some *disorder* in
[602] us; and so we are not onely *passive*, but *active*, in our owne *ruine;* we doe not onely stand under a *falling house*, but *pull it* downe upon

us; and wee are not onely *executed*, (that implies *guiltinesse*) but wee are *executioners*, (that implies *dishonor*,) and *executioners of our selves*, (and that implies *impietie*.) And wee fall from that *comfort* which wee might have in our first *sicknesse*, from that *meditation*, *Alas, how generally miserable is Man, and how subject to diseases*, (for [603] in that, it is some degree of *comfort*, that wee are but in the state *common* to all) we fall, I say, to this *discomfort*, and *selfe accusing*, and *selfe condemning; Alas, how unprovident, and in that, how unthankfull to God and his instruments am I, in making so ill use of so great benefits, in destroying so soone, so long a worke, in relapsing, by my disorder, to that from which they had delivered mee;* and so my *meditation* is fearefully transferred from the *body* to the *minde*, and [604] from the consideration of the *sickenesse*, to *that sinne*, that sinfull *carelesnesse*, by which I have occasioned my *relapse*. And amongst the many *weights* that aggravate a *relapse*, this also is one, that a *relapse* proceeds with a more violent dispatch, and more *irremediably*, because it finds the *Countrie weakned*, and *depopulated* before. Upon a *sicknesse*, which as yet appeares not, wee can scarce [605] fix a *feare*, because wee know not what to feare; but as *feare* is the *busiest* and *irksomest affection*, so is a *relapse* (which is still *ready to come*) into that, which is but newly gone, the *nearest object*, the *most immediate* exercise of that *affection* of *feare*.

23. *Expostulation*   [606]

My *God*, my *God*, my *God*, thou mightie *Father*, who hast been my *Physitian;* Thou glorious *Sonne*, who hast beene my *physicke;* Thou blessed *Spirit*, who hast *prepared* and *applied* all to mee, shall *I alone* bee able to overthrow the worke of *all you*, and *relapse* into those *spirituall sicknesses*, from which your infinite *mercies* have withdrawne me? Though thou, O my *God*, have filled my *measure* [607] with *mercie*, yet my *measure* was not so *large*, as that of thy *whole people*, the *Nation*, the *numerous* and *glorious nation of Israel;* and yet how often, how often did they fall into *relapses*? And then, where is my *assurance*? how easily thou passedst over many other sinnes in them, and how vehemently thou insistedst in those, into which they so often *relapsed;* Those were their *murmurings* against [608] thee, in thine *Instruments*, and *Ministers*, and their turnings upon other *gods*, and embracing the *Idolatries* of their *neighbours*. O my *God*, how *slipperie* a way, to how *irrecoverable* a bottome, is *murmuring?* and how neere *thy selfe* hee comes, that *murmures* at him, who comes from *thee?* The *Magistrate* is the *garment* in which [609] thou apparellest *thy selfe;* and hee that shoots at the *cloathes*, cannot say, hee meant no ill to the *man:* Thy *people* were feareful *examples* of that; for, how often did their *murmuring* against thy *Ministers,* end in a *departing* from *thee?* when they would have *other officers,* they would have *other gods;* and still *to daies murmuring,* was *to morrowes Idolatrie;* As their *murmuring* induced *Idolatrie,* and they [610] *relapsed* often into *both,* I have found in my selfe, O my *God,* (O my *God,* thou hast found it in me, and thy finding it, hath shewed it to me) such a *transmigration* of *sinne,* as makes mee afraid of *relapsing too.* The *soule* of *sinne,* (for wee have made *sinne immortall,* and it must have a *soule*) The *soule* of *sinne,* is *disobedience* to thee; and when one *sinne* hath beene *dead* in mee, that *soule* hath passed into [611] another *sinne.* Our *youth* dies, and the *sinnes* of our *youth* with it; some *sinnes* die a *violent death,* and some a *naturall; povertie, penurie, imprisonment, banishment,* kill some sinnes in us, and some die of *age;* many waies wee become *unable* to doe that *sinne;* but still the *soule* lives, and passes into another *sinne;* and that, that was *licentiousnesse,* growes *ambition,* and that comes to *indevotion,* and [612] *spirituall coldnesse;* wee have *three lives,* in our *state* of *sinne;* and where the *sinnes* of *youth* expire, those of our *middle yeeres* enter; and those of our *age* after them. This *transmigration* of *sinne,* found in my selfe, makes me afraid, O my *God,* of a *Relapse:* but the *occasion* of my *feare,* is more *pregnant* than so; for, I have *had,* I have *multiplied Relapses* already. Why, O my *God,* is a *relapse* so odious to thee? Not so much their *murmuring,* and their *Idolatry,* as their [613] *relapsing* into those *sinnes,* seemes to affect thee, in thy disobedient Psal. 78.41 people. *They limited the holy one of Israel,* as thou complainest of them: That was a *murmuring;* but before thou chargest them with the *fault it selfe,* in the same place, thou chargest them, with the Psal. 78.40 *iterating,* the *redoubling* of that *fault,* before the *fault* was named; *How oft did they provoke mee in the Wildernesse; and grieve me in the* Numb. 14 [614] *Desart?* That which brings thee to that exasperation against them, 22, 23 as to say, that *thou wouldest breake thine owne oath,* rather than leave them *unpunished, (They shall not see the land, which I sware unto their fathers)* was because *they had tempted thee ten times,* infinitely; Josh. 23.12, 13 upon that, thou threatnest with that *vehemencie, if ye do in any wise goe backe, know for a certainty, God will no more drive out any of* [615] *these Nations from before you; but they shall be snares, and traps unto you, and scourges in your sides, and thornes in your eies, till ye perish.* No *tongue,* but *thine owne,* O my GOD, can expresse thine indignation, against a *Nation relapsing to Idolatry. Idolatry* in any *Nation* is *deadly;* but when the *disease* is *complicated* with a *relapse* (a *knowledge* and a *profession* of a *former recoverie*) it is *desperate:* And thine *anger* workes, not onely where the *evidence* is *pregnant,*

and without *exception*, (so thou saiest, *when it is said, That certaine* [616]
men in a Citie, have withdrawne others to Idolatrie, and that inquirie   Deut. 13.13-15
is made, and it is found true, the Citie, and the inhabitants, and the
Cattell are to bee destroied) but where there is but a *suspicion*, a
rumor, of such a *relapse* to *Idolatrie*, thine *anger* is awakened, and
thine *indignation* stirred. In the government of thy servant *Joshua*,   Josh. 22.11
there was a voice, that Reuben and Gad, with those of Manasseh, had   [617]
built a new altar. Israel doth not *send* one to enquire; but *the whole*   ver. 12
congregation gathered to goe up to warre against them; and *there went*
a Prince of every Tribe: And they *object* to them, not so much their
present declination to *Idolatry*, as their *Relapse; Is the iniquity of*   Josh. 22.17
Peor too little for us? An *idolatry* formerly committed, and punished
with the slaughter of *twenty foure thousand delinquents*. At last   [618]
Reuben, and *Gad* satisfie them, *That that Altar was not built for*
Idolatry, but built as *a patterne of theirs*, that they might thereby
professe themselves to bee of the *same profession*, that they were; and
so the *Army* returned without bloud. Even where it comes not so
farre, as to an *actuall Relapse* into *Idolatry*, Thou, O my GOD,
becommest sensible of it; though thou, who seest the heart all the   [619]
way, preventest all *dangerous effects*, where there was no *ill meaning*,
how ever there were *occasion* of *suspicious rumours*, given to thine
Israel, of *relapsing*. So *odious* to thee, and so *aggravating* a weight
upon *sinne*, is a *relapse*. But, O my *God*, why is it so? so *odious*? It
must bee so, because hee that hath *sinned*, and then *repented*, hath
weighed God and the *Devill* in a *ballance;* hee hath *heard God* and
the *Devill plead;* and after *hearing*, given *Judgement* on that *side*, to   [620]
which he *adheres*, by his *subsequent practise;* if he returne to his   Tertullian
sinne, he *decrees* for *Satan;* he prefers *sinne* before *grace*, and *Satan*
before *God;* and in *contempt* of God, declares the *precedency* for his
adversary: And a contempt wounds deeper than an injury; a *relapse*
deeper, than a *blasphemy*. And when thou hast told me, that a
relapse is more *odious* to *thee*, neede I ask why it is more *dangerous*,   [621]
more *pernitious* to *me*? Is there any other *measure* of the greatnesse
of my *danger*, than the greatnesse of thy *displeasure*? How *fitly*, and
how *fearefully* hast thou expressed my *case*, in a *storm at Sea*, if I   Psal. 107.26
relapse? (*They mount up to Heaven, and they goe downe againe to the*
depth:) My *sicknesse* brought mee to *thee* in *repentance*, and my
relapse hath cast mee farther from thee: *The end of that man shall be*   Mat. 12.45
worse than the beginning, saies thy *Word*, thy *Sonne;* My *beginning*   [622]
was *sicknesse, punishment* for *sin;* but *a worse thing may follow*, saies   Joh. 5.14
he also, if I *sin* againe: not only *death*, which is an *end* worse than
sicknesse, which was the *beginning*, but *Hell*, which is a *beginning*
worse than that *end*. Thy *great servant* denied thy *Sonne*, and he   Mar. 14.70

denied him againe; but all before *Repentance;* here was no *relapse.*
[623] O, if thou haddest ever re-admitted *Adam* into *Paradise,* how *abstinently* would hee have walked by that *tree?* and would not the *Angels,* that *fell,* have *fixed* themselves upon thee, if thou hadst
Ecclus. 2.18 once *re-admitted* them to thy *sight?* They never *relapsed;* If I doe, must not my case be as desperate? Not so desperate, for, *as thy*
[624] *Majestie, so is thy Mercie,* both *infinite:* and thou who hast commanded me *to pardon my brother seventy times seven,* hast limited thy selfe to no *Number.* If *death* were ill in it *selfe,* thou wouldest never have *raised* any *dead Man,* to life againe, because that man must necessarily *die againe.* If thy *Mercy,* in *pardoning,* did so farre *aggravate a Relapse,* as that there were no more *mercy* after it, our case were the worse for that *former Mercy;* for who is not under, even a *necessity of sinning,* whilst hee is here, if wee place
[625] this *necessity* in our own *infirmity,* and not in thy *Decree?* But I speak not this, O my *God,* as preparing a way to my *Relapse* out of *presumption,* but to *preclude* all accesses of *desperation,* though out of *infirmity,* I should *Relapse.*

23. *Prayer*

O eternall and most gracious *God,* who though thou beest *ever*
[626] *infinite,* yet *enlargest* thy selfe, by the *Number* of our prayers, and takest our *often petitions* to thee, to be an *addition* to thy *glory,* and thy *greatnesse,* as *ever* upon all occasions, so now, O my *God,* I come to thy *Majestie* with *two Prayers, two Supplications.* I have *Meditated* upon the *Jelousie,* which thou hast of thine owne *honour;* and considered, that Nothing can come neerer a *violating* of that *honor,*
[627] neerer to the *Nature* of a *scorne* to thee, than to sue out thy *Pardon,* and receive the *Seales* of *Reconciliation* to thee, and then *returne* to that *sinne,* for which I *needed,* and *had* thy pardon before. I know that this comes too neare, to a making thy holy *Ordinances,* thy *Word,* thy *Sacraments,* thy *Seales,* thy *Grace,* instruments of my *Spirituall Fornications.* Since therefore thy *Correction* hath brought mee to such a *participation of thy selfe (thy selfe,* O my *God,* cannot
[628] bee *parted*), to such an *intire possession* of thee, as that I durst deliver my selfe over to thee this *Minute, If this Minute* thou wouldest accept my *dissolution, preserve* me, O my *God,* the *God* of *constancie,* and *perseverance,* in this state, from all *relapses* into those *sinnes,* which have induc'd thy *former Judgements* upon me. But because, by too lamentable *Experience,* I know how slippery my *customs* of *sinne,* have made my *wayes* of *sinne,* I presume to adde

this *petition* too, That if my *infirmitie* overtake mee, thou *forsake* [629]
mee not. Say to my *Soule, My Sonne, thou hast sinned, doe so no*   Ecclus. 21.1
more; but say also, that though I doe, thy *Spirit* of *Remorce,* and
Compunction shall never *depart* from mee. Thy holy *Apostle, Saint* 2 Cor. 11.25
Paul, was shipwrackd *thrice;* and yet *stil saved.* Though the *rockes,*
and the *sands,* the *heights,* and the *shallowes,* the *prosperitie,* and the
adversitie of this *world* do diversly threaten mee, though mine own [630]
leakes endanger mee, yet, O *God,* let mee never put my selfe *aboard* 1 Tim. 1.20
with Hymenaeus, nor *make shipwracke of faith, and a good Conscience;*
and then thy *long-livd,* thy *everlasting Mercy,* will visit me, though
that, which I most earnestly pray against, should fall upon mee, a
relapse into those *sinnes,* which I have *truely repented,* and thou hast
fully pardoned.

FINIS.

NOTES

FROM THE WESTMORELAND MANUSCRIPT, PRE-1600 COMPOSITIONS

The Westmoreland Manuscript is held in the Henry W. and Albert A. Berg Collection of the New York Public Library; its contents are electronically accessible on the NYPL website as Digital Gallery, Detail IDs 1695866-1695972. Bound in vellum, this manuscript is written in the fluent, compact italic handwriting of Rowland Woodward. Westmoreland is uniquely important as the closest known source to Donne's originals for the two categories of material it contains. One is the unparalleled assemblage of early verse and prose entrusted by Donne to a limited circle of male friends; none of these compositions appear to date later than 1599. The other is the fullest extant set of Donne's Holy Sonnets, to which his other religious sonnet sequence, 'La Corona', is conjoined. The first four pages of the manuscript contain various notations in modern hands, including the signature of Edmund Gosse, author of *The Life and Letters of John Donne* (1899) and a former owner of the Westmoreland MS.

VERSE SATIRE: THE GENRE

Verse satire became popular in England in the 1590s. Besides Donne, prominent satirists included Joseph Hall and John Marston. These poets looked to Roman predecessors, especially Juvenal and Persius and to some extent Horace, for guidance in a genre broad in its abuse, obscure in its references, crude in its vocabulary, and colloquial to rough in its rhythms. A false etymology underlay the conception of satire, which Elizabethans derived from satyr, the mythological half-goat, half-man, and the rude tunes he played on his reed-pipes, rather than from Latin satura, a mixture. For the Romans the mixture that defined satire had a set framing device: an encounter between a speaker and an opposite or opposites whose extremes of vice or folly provoked the speaker to attack. The materials and modes of attack constituted the defining mixture: wide freedom regarding subject materials (dramatic incidents, fictional experiences, anecdotes, proverbs) and tonalities (sarcasm, mockery, invective, irony). A satirist could employ anything to expose his object(s) as ridiculous or despicable.

English verse satire of the 1590s focused on concerns of politics and religion, both domestic and foreign, and on the seekers of influence and personal gain in various venues—law-courts, the royal court, society at large. But the vogue of this genre was brief, attesting to the disruptive impact of its unbridled expression and its fomenting of dissent. In June 1599 the Court of High Commission prohibited the printing and circulation of verse satires without permission, to be sought presumably from the bishop of London. Satiric energy consequently migrated to another venue: the theatres of London. See Gregory Kneidel, 'The Formal Verse Satire', in Shami, Flynn, and Hester, eds, *The Oxford Handbook of John Donne*, 122–33.

Satire 1 (MS p. 5)

Cued by the Latin titles of the satires (*Satyra 1ᵃ* or *Prima*, etc.), the reader observes
Donne domesticate the tonalities and techniques of classical Roman satire in a con-
temporary London setting. Horace, *Satires*, 1.9, may have suggested the idea of a walk
through city streets with an annoying companion. Satire 1 was evidently written *c.*1593-4,
judging from Thomas Nashe's references to the performing horse and ape, and the
shared references in Sir John Davies's epigrams to the horse and the ape, the elephant,
the new water-work, and the tomb of the lord chancellor (Sir Christopher Hatton died
in 1591) as current curiosities of the city. Everard Guilpin's satirical *Skialetheia* (1598)
contains an imitation of Donne's opening lines: 'Let me alone I prethee in thys Cell,
| Entice me not into the Citties hell; | ... | I had rather be encoffin'd in this chest
| Amongst these books and papers'.

ll. 1-9.   *changeling*: inconstant. *motley*: variable in character or mood. *humorist*: fad-
dist. *this... chest*: the half-chamber with a wooden partition dividing the
sleeping and study areas, occupied by individual members of Lincoln's Inn.
Natures...Philosopher: Aristotle. *joly*: excessively self-confident. *Sinews...
mystique body*: connections that sustain a commonwealth, a 'body politic'.
gathering Chroniclers: compilers of historical material; cf. Satire 4, ll. 97-8.

ll. 15-31.   *in the middle street*: a literal rendering of Latin 'in media via'. *Bright...pay*:
Army captains would keep the names of dead men in their company on the
muster roll so as to collect their pay; some might be spent on such finery as
partly gilded (*parcel-gilt*) armor. *blewcotes*: livery worn by servants of lower
status. A dozen or more such servants trailing their master in the streets
would make an extravagant display. *monster, superstitious Puritane... ceremo-
nial man*: The *humorist* companion is monstrous in his excessive concern with
refind manners and, even more, with ceremony, which Puritans were known to
abhor. *broker*: pawnbroker. *prize*: appraise. *vaile*: lower. The vailing (lowering)
of a vessel's topsails signified courtesy or submission to another vessel.

ll. 36-46.   *Joyntures*: joint holdings of property by spouses, which Donne's metaphor
generalizes as greediness for another's possessions. *Mans first... beasts skin*:
God clothed Adam and Eve in 'coats of skins' (Genesis 3:21).

ll. 54-68.   *Worne*: used. *black feathers*: a fashion accessory worn by gallants. *muske
color*: the reddish brown of the male musk-deer's secretion, used in perfumes,
making its colour fashionable, perhaps, by association with an agreeable
smell. *infant*: a young person of noble or gentle birth—more particularly, a
Spanish or Portuguese prince or princess. *an India*: vast wealth. *gulling
weather spy*: deceptive observer of the weather. *heavens Scheame*: a diagram
of the relative positions of the heavenly bodies. *supple-witted*: easily influ-
enced or persuaded. *antiek* (antic): fantastic. *Improvidently... the wall*: The
companion edges into the preferred inside position for walking in the city,
closer to the walls of buildings and better protected from the filth of the
streets and the chamber pots emptied from windows. But his move is
short-sighted, for, on the inside, he sees approaching passers-by less well,
and his access to them is restricted.

ll. 80–8.   *wise politique horse*: The bay gelding Morocco owned by the trainer Banks
could bow his head at the name of Queen Elizabeth, and gnash his teeth
when the king of Spain was named. Thomas Nashe refers to the 'jugling
horse' of 'our Brother *Bankes*' in *The Unfortunate Traveller* (1594; *Works*,
ed. R. B. McKerrow, rev. F. P. Wilson (1958), 2:230; 3:21; 4.266). *Elephant
or Ape*: Joseph Hall mentions 'some tricke | Of... the young Elephant'
in *Virgidemiarum* (1597–8), 4.2.93–5. Nashe refers to the teaching of
'trickes... like an ape over the chaine' in *Have with You to Saffron Walden*
(1596; *Works*, ed. McKerrow, rev. edn, 3:37). *drinking... Tabacco*: The
OED records only two references earlier than Donne's to smoking tobacco
(1588, 1589). 'Drink' was the then usual verb for smoking.

ll. 97–109. *pink*: a hole or eyelet in a garment, which, in multiples, produced a deco-
rative pattern. *panes*: long incisions in sleeves and doublets, opening to
show a fine lining or undergarment. *cutt*: in general, fashionable contour;
in particular, an ornamental series of incisions along the edge of a gar-
ment. *print*: crimping or creasing of a neck-ruff or other pleated garment.
pleight: lace or braid made of plaited metal threads or flat metal strips of
gold or silver. See Janet Arnold, *Queen Elizabeth's Wardrobe Unlock'd*
(1988), 359–76. *Our dull Comedians want him*: This fashionable clothes
horse would be a prime resource for actors needing costumes; cf. Satire 4,
ll. 180–5. *Which understand none*: Editors of Donne have enclosed this
clause in parentheses, marking it off as an aside inserted by the narrator
in his flighty companion's stream of prattle. It is equally possible that the
flighty companion attempts self-deprecating modesty but merely achieves
self-exposure. *Many were... no more*: The companion's mistress was
entertaining other suitors, and he was far from being in control of the
situation.

Satire 2 (MS p. 8)

The figure of Coscus, the bad poet and bad lawyer, may have been suggested to Donne
by the publication of the anonymous sonnet sequence, *Zepheria* (1594); three of its
poems (nos 20, 37, 38) make absurd use of legal terminology to woo a lady, and others
are sprinkled with it. The affinities with Coscus's language as a wooer (ll. 49–57) and
the mention that he has been a poet 'of late' (l. 43) support the connection with
Zepheria and a date in or after 1594 for Satire 2. The allusion to *dearths and Spaniards*
(l. 6) would have been most timely in the last quarter of 1595. Donne's likely intended
readership would have been his fellow law-students.

  The ultimate concern in Satire 2, however, is not the debased state of much poetic
practice, but the evils that result from subverting the rule of law. Coscus personifies
this range of focus, which opens out from a generalization: An evil will take some one
form so vicious that hatred of this enables pity for lesser forms of the evil (ll. 1–4).
Poetry is a manifest evil, but hapless poets are pitiful, not hated (ll. 5–10), whether
they are playwrights (ll. 11–16), wooers (ll. 16–20), paid flatterers (ll. 21–2), trendy
scribblers (ll. 23–4), or plagiarists (ll. 25–30). Other evil-doers can be pitied too, for
they punish themselves (ll. 31–9). When Coscus wrote poetry, he was the worst of the

lot for verbal affectation, but not beyond all hope (ll. 39–62). When, however, he began to practise law only for gain, using every dirty trick, he exceeded all pity and hope as he attained the *excellently best* or most extreme form of evil. The remainder of Satire 2 addresses the proliferating effects of this extremity of evil, for which only hatred can be felt.

ll. 1–3.   *Sir*: Christopher Brooke may have been Donne's addressee. *I do hate |*
Perfectly: Voicing righteous indignation with an echo of Psalm 138:22 (Vulgate), 'With a perfect hatred I hate them; they have become my enemies', the speaker sets the terms of the paradox to follow. *ther is … excellently best*: Everything, including evil, has a state of perfection in being what it is.

ll. 5–10.   *dearths and Spaniards*: England experienced crop failures and food shortages in 1586 and 1594–8, both times in conjunction with fears of a Spanish invasion. *ridlingly*: puzzlingly. *like Papists not worth hate*: The remark runs counter to the letter and the spirit of the Act against Jesuits and Seminarists, 27° Eliz. c. 2 (1585), which specified that Jesuits and seminary priests who refused to take the oath of supremacy (acknowledging the queen, not the pope, as 'supreme governor' of the Church of England) were to be banished from the realm. Anyone who failed to disclose the presence of a priest in the kingdom to a justice of the peace or other such officer was to be fined or imprisoned (*Statutes of the Realm*, 4.1:706 ff., excerpted as no. 299 in Geoffrey R. Elton, *The Tudor Constitution: Documents and Commentary*, 2nd edn (1982), 433–7).

ll. 11–13.   *One like … his life*: A person charged with a capital offence could avoid the death penalty by claiming 'benefit of clergy', clemency because he could read. The ability to read and thus to save one's neck was tested by the 'neck verse', usually Psalm 50:2 (Vulgate), 'Have pity on me O God, according to thy great mercy'. Donne imagines a capital offender who prompts a fellow capital offender to recite the neck verse and saves the fellow's life. This, Donne continues, is like what playwrights do in writing plays that are performed by actors as mindless as the puppets set in motion by the bellows of contemporary organs.

ll. 19–20.   *Ramms … best Artillerie*: Outmoded contrivances like battering rams and slingshots (or the *witchcrafts charmes* of ll. 17–18) are foolish weapons now. *Pistolets*—punning on the double meaning, a small pistol, and a Spanish gold coin—are the most effective. Cf. Elegy 1 ('The Bracelet'), ll. 31–2.

ll. 29–33.   *For if … his owne*: This contemptuous pronouncement on plagiarists is adapted by John Marston, *The Scourge of Villainy* (1598), 3.11.90–1: 'O … this Eccho … doth speake, spit, write | Naught but the excrements of others spright'. *outswive dildos*: out-copulate artificial phalluses; cf. Elegy 10 ('The Anagram'), l. 53. *out sweare the Letanee*: An audacious characterization of the repeated addresses to God in the Elizabethan litany (*The Book of Common Prayer* (1559), ed. John E. Booty (1976), 68). This half-line was omitted from earlier editions of Donne's *Poems*, and first printed in the fifth edition (1669).

ll. 35–8.   *for whose . . . must make*: It was traditionally believed (and memorably imaged in Dante's *Inferno*) that all souls damned for a particular sin were assigned to the same region of hell. But it is scholastic theologians, not God, who presumptuously undertake to add rooms to hell for new kinds of sinners and their *strange sins*. *Canonists*: scholars of canon (church) law. *large receite*: broad scope.

ll. 41–8.   *botches*: boils or sores. *poxe*: a general name for several diseases characterized by 'pocks' or pustules on the skin. *Jolyer*: more self-confident. *new-benefic'd*: newly appointed to an ecclesiastical office with an endowment. [*Like nets . . . he goes*]: Woodward omits this line—a clear case of eyeskip; the missing end rhyme is the sole clue. *Language . . . Benche*: terminology of the Court of Common Pleas and the Queen's Bench. All of Coscus's legal terms pertain to action by which a litigant could claim possession of a contested piece of land; the effect is to objectify the lady.

ll. 50–60. *tricesimo . . . Queene*: thirtieth year of Elizabeth's reign, 1588. *Hilary terme*: at Westminster, 23 January to 12 February. *Sise* (assize): sitting of the courts. *in remitter of*: have a prior claim to. *afidavits*: sworn statements. *tender Labyrinth*: spiral-like formation. *Sclavonians scolding*: The Slavs of eastern Europe, figured as barbaric peoples who speak harsh-sounding languages. *ruynd Abbeys rore*: Monastic houses and abbeys were officially dissolved under Henry VIII; see G. W. Bernard, *The King's Reformation* (2005), chap. 5.

ll. 61–4.   A key transition focuses on the shameless Coscus. *When sick . . . with Muse*, he was at worst *mad*. Now that he practises *Law . . . for meere gayne*, his *bold Soule* should *repute* (consider, reckon) that he has become *Worse than* women who sell their bodies. Coscus is in the process of selling his soul by selling out justice and a whole way of life in England.

ll. 66–75. *bill*: a pun on two of the word's senses—the halberd that is the watchman's weapon, and the legal term for a written statement of a case. *Suretiship*: responsibility taken by one person on behalf of another, as for payment of a debt. This is a good self-serving pretext to offer for being found in a bad place (in prison or in court). It is also a good lie to cloak Coscus's actual, venal motives for being in court. *And to every . . . a king*: This couplet was omitted from Donne's *Poems*, 1st edn (1633). *Like a wedge . . . Asses*: As a wedge is worked through a block of wood, so Coscus struggles to make his way through a crowded courtroom to the bar at the front. He exhibits both the obstinate stupidity of an ass and his own shamelessness in lying to the judge. *carted whores*: Convicted prostitutes were taken in a cart to a public place where they were stripped naked and whipped. *Simony*: sale of church livings, prohibited but not ended by a 1589 statute, 31° Eliz., cap. 6, secs. 4–5. *Sodomy*: a principal charge against the monastic orders during the dissolution of the monasteries (and a recurrent allegation in Reformation polemics thereafter); see Bernard, *The King's Reformation*, chap. 3.

ll. 77–90. *compasse*: encompass. *all our land*: Coscus will gain possession of the whole of Britain, from Scotland to the Isle of Wight, from Mount St. Michael to the Dover coast. *snuffe…candels*: butt-ends of nearly burnt-out candles. *Wringing*: wresting from the *heires*. *men pulling Prime*: Primero, a kind of poker, was fashionable among courtiers. To 'pull for prime' was to draw for a card or cards that would make a winning hand; with no more effort than that, Coscus extracts profit from land. *Assurances*: legal documents securing the title to property, which when drawn up to Coscus's specifications become as large as the whole corpus of *civil Lawes* and the commentary on it. *fathers…Church*: Voluminous authors included Basil the Great and John Chrysostom among the Greek fathers, and Jerome, Augustine, and Gregory the Great among the Latin fathers.

ll. 93–6. *When Luther…power and glory clause*: When Martin Luther was an Augustinian friar, he prayed the Lord's Prayer in the Latin Vulgate version, which lacks the closing ascription, 'For Thine is the kingdom, the power, and the glory forever'. When Desiderius Erasmus found this ascription in the Greek codices he was using to prepare his Greek–Latin version of the New Testament (1516), he incorporated it in his text. After Luther repudiated papal authority and renounced his vows, he included in his German translation of the New Testament (1521) the closing ascription from Erasmus. Donne's association of a breach of faith with an incursion on something sacred (the Scripture, the law) may hint at his religious outlook in the mid-1590s when he was still a Roman Catholic.

ll. 97–102. *But when he…cleare the doubt*: Coscus omits any reference to his heirs in documents of sale or exchange of lands, thereby assuring his sole interest and control. Likewise pursuing their controlling interests, commentators on difficult texts pass over difficult *words or sense*, and controversialists in divinity ignore *Shrewd Words* that could tell against the evidence *vouch'd* by them to confirm their argument. *Shrewd*: hard to deal with.

ll. 104–12. *Where are…wardrobes*: Coscus's ruthless pursuit of property includes *bought lands*. One such acquisition has despoiled *th' old landlord* of his *troops* (his extended household of family, servants, and guests) and *almes* (his hospitality to the poor and needy), bringing to an end a whole way of life and its associated *Good workes*. Neither *Carthusian fasts* (severe asceticism) nor *fulsome Bacchanalls* (lavish drinking and feasting) characterized this life. Moderation was its virtue and the source of its contentment. *Means blesse*: The poetic speaker declares in favour of this life of moderation: *I bid kill some…not Hecatomes* (literally, 'hundreds of sacrificial animals'). On the centrality of moderation in the thought of this period, see Joshua Scodel, *Excess and the Mean in Early Modern English Literature* (2002). *But my words…Lawes*: The truths disclosed in Satire 2 about criminal legal practices and the injustices they cause have no power to arrest, indict, try, convict, or punish any offender, even one as brazen as Coscus.

Satire 3 (MS p. 11)

More than any other of Donne's satires, his incisive survey of the contested state of religion at the close of the sixteenth century has drawn admiration. 'If you would teach a scholar in the highest forms to *read*', enthused Samuel Taylor Coleridge, 'take Donne, and of Donne this satire' (*Coleridge's Miscellaneous Criticism*, ed. T. M. Raynor (1936), 134). Even when allowance is made for complexities in the speaker's persona, it does not seem that Donne could have written as a believing Roman Catholic, for Satire 3 denies that church's assertion of its own authority to validate belief. The question then arises: When did Donne undertake the personal quest for the religious assurance that results from discovering Truth? Topical allusions in Satire 3 offer little help in dating the poem. In general, it can be noted that Donne committed himself to the service of his Protestant queen against her Roman Catholic enemies by taking part in the Cadiz expedition in June 1596. Moreover, if Drummond of Hawthornden was correct in the note he added to his manuscript copy of Satire 4, that it 'was indeed the Authors fourth in nomber and order; he having wreten five in all' (National Library of Scotland, MS 2062), then Satire 3 was written after Satire 2 with its probable date of 1594–5 and before Satire 4, which belongs to 1597.

Satire 3 has affinities with the Renaissance 'problem', a genre with medieval origins in the pseudo-Aristotelian *Problemata*. Among the Scholastics the problem saw wide educational use in the form of the disputed question, a tool for sharpening skill in dialectical reasoning. Donne himself composed nineteen Problems, thought to date between 1603 and 1609–10 (*Donne: Paradoxes and Problems*, ed. Helen Peters (1980), v, xvi–xvii). One of these, Problem 6, 'Why doe young Laymen so much study Divinity?', crisply reprises the main line of development in Satire 3, suggesting that the urgency of its questions stayed with Donne for years. Problem 6 asks 'Had the church of *Rome* shutt up all our wayes till the Lutherans broke downe theyr uttermost stubborne dores and the Calvinists pick'd theyr inwardest and subtillest locks? Surely the Devill cannot bee such a foole to hope that he shall make this study [of the true way to God] contemptible by making it common...Hee cannot hope for better...than...a dull and stupid security in which many grosse things are swallowed' (*Paradoxes and Problems*, ed. Peters, 27–8).

Satire 3 has a threefold progression. First, since satirical pity and scorn cancel themselves out, railing may provide a cure for weakness and cowardice in religion. Donne's harsh scolding aims to shame supposed Christians for living less virtuously than pagans in antiquity, for misdirecting their courage while yielding to the devil's wiles, and for valuing bodily pleasures above spiritual joys (ll. 1–43). Next comes a survey of the trivial reasons why men adopt one or another form of religion (ll. 43–69). This modulates into a final section in which Donne gravely exhorts his reader (in the tones of address characteristic of his verse letters to male friends) to the active pursuit of a personal faith, setting aside worldly motives and considerations.

ll. 1–7. *Kind pity...spleene*: Natural sympathy suppresses my ill will and bad temper. The spleen was thought to be the seat of both positive and negative feelings; satirists predictably focused on the latter. *brave*: a fine display of (as befits a satirist). *worne*: over-used. *blind*: deprived of the light of divine revelation.

ll. 12–13.   *whose meritt…fayth*: An inversion of the Lutheran tenet of justification by faith alone (*sola fides*), which attributed salvation solely to Christ, without any cooperating act or affection on the part of sinful humans. While retaining the core of the Lutheran tenet, Thomas Cranmer's 'Homily of Salvation' (1547) carefully made a place for good works in the doctrine of the Church of England. His formulations leave open the possibility that God might save pagan (pre-Christian) philosophers of virtuous life, as Donne imagines.

ll. 17–23.   *mutinous Dutch*: The States-General of Holland had been in revolt against Spanish rule since 1568; Elizabeth had been providing troops and aid since 1586. Critics of her policy claimed that it put England in danger of Spanish invasion. *Shipps wooden Sepulchers*: Cf. 'The Storme', l. 45. The phrasing could allude to Donne's experiences during the Cadiz expedition of 1596. *dungeons*: underground regions. *frozen…discoveryes*: Attempts at finding a northwest passage from the Atlantic to the Pacific had been undertaken by various English explorers between 1497 and 1587, but the three attempts by the Dutchman Willem Barents (1594–7) supply the closest referent in time to Satire 3. *Colder…Salamanders*: These lizard-like creatures were thought to have so cold a nature that they could extinguish fire (Aristotle, *Historia animalium* [History of Animals], 5.19.552b; Pliny, *Historia naturalis* [Natural History], 10:86).

ll. 23–6.   Donne's train of thought regarding occasions for courage moves rapidly through associations of human bodies braving heat or flame. *divine…oven*: Shadrach, Meshach, and Abednego, steadfast servants of the Hebrew God, refused to worship a golden image as commanded by Nebuchadnezzar, king of Babylon. They miraculously emerged alive from the fiery furnace into which the king ordered them to be cast (Daniel 3:11–30). This allusion recurs in 'The Calme', l. 28, which describes an experience of Donne's on the Islands expedition of 1597. *fires…the Line*: Literally, the intense heats of the Spanish Main and the equatorial line; perhaps figuratively, the fires of the Inquisition, a danger that faced English soldiers captured by the Spanish during the hostilities of 1596–7. *Cuntryes…bodies bee*: These regions are alembics, or vessels of distillation; they make our bodies sweat profusely. *Canst thou…beare?*: Can you endure such hardships for mere worldly rewards?

ll. 26–32.   *must every hee…poysonous words?*: The speaker's modicum of respect for exploration and warfare gives way to contempt for love rivalry and duelling, which manifest *Courage of straw*. *O desperate…appointed field*: A recapitulation and clarification of the essential issue: such contestations with fellow humans engage the wrong set of *foes* and are contrary to God's purposes (*forbid warrs*). To *stand | Soldier in his worlds garrison* is God's *appointed field* for the spiritual warfare that solely matters.

ll. 33–42.   *Know thy foes*: The world, the flesh, and the devil of Christian tradition. The sequencing of this trio as the devil, the world, and the flesh sharpens the antithesis of the last, in particular, with *thy fayre goodly soule* and prepares the transition in l. 43. *allow…be ridd*: permit you to be removed by violence from his kingdom (the world). A soul dying with its sins unrepented and unforgiven would become the devil's permanent possession. *decrepit wayne*: ruinous deficiency.

ll. 43–9. *Myrius*: In Woodward's spelling, presumably close to Donne's own, the name is a Latin transliteration of Greek *murios*, meaning 'numberless, countless' or, as a definite numeral, 'ten thousand'. Like Donne's subsequent names for adherents of various strains of Christianity, *Myrius* seems broadly generic. It may allude to the numbers of Roman Catholics or to their veneration of historical continuity (*a thousand yeares ago*). The image of the cloth of state—a canopy and backdrop enclosing a monarch's throne—suggests the emptiness of such veneration: the monarch is elsewhere. *Crantz*: Kranz in German is 'a victor's wreath' or 'a garland of flowers'. Although the Calvinist *Crantz* rather oddly has a German (not a French) name, its associations are satiric enough: Crantz fancies himself to have triumphed in embracing Calvinism as his religion; Calvinism as a religion is so bereft of ornament that it could benefit from a garland of flowers.

ll. 55–65. *Graius*: Latin for 'a Greek'. *Phrygas*: Latin for 'a Phrygian' or 'a Trojan'. The antithesis of Greek and Trojan points the contrast between these two type figures. The acquiescent *Graius* takes the word of others for the perfection of the Church of England, accepting it as readily as he does the wife his guardian chooses for him. The suspicious *Phrygas* thinks the worst of all religion and will espouse none. *Ambitious bawds*: Preachers who prostitute their calling by claiming that the Church of England is *only perfect* in order to gain advancement within it. *Tender...tender*: Offer while he is immature in years and judgement—punning on the godfathers' manipulations. *Pay values*: A 'value' was a fine that a ward who refused an advantageous arranged marriage had to pay to his guardian. The implicit allegory tracks *Graius*, who accepts the Church of England because his godfathers (his sponsors at baptism; the statutory bodies, Parliament and Convocation) have so determined. If Graius were to decide otherwise for himself, he would have to pay a fine for not attending his parish church (according to the 1559 Act of Uniformity), just like a ward who would have to pay his guardian. *Graccus*: The name of a Roman family whose most notable members were Tiberius and Caius Sempronius Gracchus, advocates of the redistribution of patrician landholdings and other reforms to benefit the plebian classes in the second century BCE. *Graccus* may bear the name of these champions of the people because he *loves all as one* and thinks them *still one kind*.

ll. 68–70. *blind- | nes*: Line divisions that break up word units are a graphic and prosodic device for highlighting satiric roughness; cf. Satire 4, ll. 13–14; 104–5. *breeds*: causes. *Too much light* (seeing the truth everywhere, in every sect) causes blindness to true *Religion* (whenever or wherever it is encountered). *unmoved*: unswayed. *Of force...allow*: Woodward in copying registered the difficulty of the line, first writing 'Must one, and forc'd but one allow;' and then adding 'Of force' in the left margin. *Of force*: With binding power, validly—a phrase no longer current. The extremely compressed line seems to mean 'You are (validly) bound to admit and approve a religion, and being (validly) bound, you must admit and approve one religion, and one only'.

ll. 71–5.   *aske thy father… Lett him aske his*: The speaker projects a stepwise retracing back to the primitive purity of the church, which all parties in the religious controversies of the day purported to do. The gist of the image is therefore the imperative of inquiring strenuously after truth itself, not the certainty of some one given claim to the truth. The point is made more explicitly in *Bee busy to seeke her. Though Truth… elder is*: This image evidently derives from the church father Tertullian's sharp reproach to a heretic: 'Let this be a judgment in advance against all heresies: that to be true, whatever is first; that to be false, whatever is later' (*Adversus Praxeam* 2, in *Patrologia Latina Cursus Completus*, gen. ed. J.-P. Migne (1878), 2:180A).

ll. 77–8.   *doubt wisely*: Donne the preacher would return to this theme: 'To come to a doubt, and to a debatement in any religious duty, is the voyce of God in our conscience: Would you know the truth? Doubt, and then you will inquire' (*Sermons of John Donne*, ed. George Potter and Evelyn M. Simpson (1962), 5:38). *In strange way*: on an unfamiliar path. *To stand… stray*: Again, Donne the preacher would reprise this key assertion: 'a man may stand upon the way, and inquire, and then proceed in the way, if he be right, or to the way if he be wrong; But when he is fallen, and lies still, he proceeds no farther, inquires no farther' (*Sermons*, 6:69).

ll. 79–81. *On a high hill… Truthe dwels*: In Greek antiquity Hesiod, Xenophon, and Kebes had employed the image of toiling up a rough, steep ascent to Virtue or to True Learning. Donne's religiously inflected variant, the hill of Truth, finds its closest known verbal analogue in Thomas Drant's preface to his translation of *Horace His Art of Poetry* (1567): '[If I] would come to the upmost top of an highe hill, not beinge able directly to go foreward for the steapnes thereof, if [I] step a foot… or more out of the way,… so to cum to… the top… [I] must learn… not to… lose my way, but to fynde my waye more apparaunte reddie before me'. The closest known visual analogue is Hans Holbein's engraving of a zigzag path up a hill leading to Truth; this engraving adorned the title page of the 1521 edition of Erasmus's Greek New Testament. See Donne, *The Satires, Epigrams and Verse Letters*, ed. Milgate, 290–2. *Ragged*: having a rough, jagged outline or surface. *To reach it… [must] go*: Woodward's omission of the line's second *must* is a feature shared by all but three of the major manuscript witnesses of Donne's poetry; the clue to the omission is the defective rhythm of the line. The 1st edn of Donne's *Poems* (1633) has the second *must*—an emendation presumably made in preparing the text to print.

ll. 86–8.   The body's pains arrive at hard deeds; the mind's endeavors arrive at hard knowledge. The double inversion of subject phrases and object phrases mimics the extreme exertion to which the speaker exhorts the reader. *dazeling… playne*: overpowering with excess of brightness, yet open and manifest—qualities traditionally associated with religious illumination.

ll. 91–2.   *blanc charters*: written promises of payment (the space for the amount left
blank) which wealthy gentry and nobility were forced to sign; the amount
was filled in at the pleasure of the king's officers. God has signed no com-
parable warrant for kings to kill whomever they designate. *Nor are ... fate*:
Kings who do *kill whom they hate* for differing from them in religion are not
agents appointed by destiny to act for her, but mere *hangmen*. The thought
is strikingly close to Martin Luther's in *Temporal Authority: to what extent
it should be obeyed* (1523): 'Where the temporal authority presumes to pre-
scribe laws for the soul, it encroaches upon God's government and only
misleads souls and destroys them. Worldly princes ... are God's execution-
ers and hangmen ... to punish the wicked and to maintain outward peace'
(*Luther's Works*, gen. ed. Helmut T. Lehmann; vol. 45, ed. Walther I.
Brandt (1962), 105, 113).

ll. 96–7.   *Philipp*: Philip II, king of Spain, under whose auspices the Spanish Inquisition
continued its course. *Gregorie*: Probably Pope Gregory XIII (1572–8), who
undertook to reform the Roman Catholic Church by enforcing the stricter
regulation and oversight advocated by the Council of Trent. He greatly
increased papal power; he also approved the Babington plot to assassinate
Queen Elizabeth. *Harry*: Henry VIII, instigator of England's break with
papal jurisdiction and authorizer of *A necessary doctrine and erudition for
any crysten man set furthe by the kinges majesty of Englande* (1543). *Martin*:
Martin Luther, whose *Ninety-Five Theses* or *Disputation on the Power and
Efficacy of Indulgences* (1517) sparked the Reformation. Both Henry VIII
and Philip II numbered 'Defender of the Faith' among their royal titles, in
both cases bestowed by a pope.

ll. 103–6.   *As streames ... power is*: Donne's simile envisages flowers thriving where they
are rooted *At the rough streames calm head* but nonetheless uprooting and
abandoning themselves *To the streames tyrannous rage*, to be lost finally in
the sea. These self-destructive flowers are unnatural in uprooting them-
selves, that is, failing to trust where God has placed them and instead con-
signing themselves to the operation of some merely worldly power; the
application to human souls is clear. In preparing himself for ordination in
January 1615, Donne would hail his own providential placement and affirm
the groundedness of his own soul: 'In my poor opinion, the form of Gods
worship, established in the Church of *England* be more convenient, and
advantageous than of any other Kingdome, both to provoke and kindle
devotion, and also to fix it ... [In] all my thanksgivings to God, I ever hum-
bly acknowledg, as one of his greatest Mercies to me, that he gave me my
Pasture in this Park, and my milk from the brests of this Church' (*Essays in
Divinity*, 51).

Satire 4 (MS p. 14)

This satire can be dated by its reference in l. 114 to the *losse of Amiens* to the Spanish
in March 1597; the French retook the city in September 1597. Donne composed
Satire 4 at some point in this six-month interval, probably before embarking on the

Islands expedition in July. Since it is likely that Donne made his first appearance at court between the Cadiz expedition (1596) and the Islands expedition, Satire 4 can be taken to refract his first-hand observations of courtiers through a satiric lens. A general indebtedness to Horace, *Satires* 1.9, has been seen in the obsessive self-reference of the bore whose company cannot be shaken off and in the heavy reliance on conversational address and exchange. Donne's bore, however, is a mix of character types found in the comedy and satire of his day: part malcontent, part traveller, part politician, part informer, part Jesuit in disguise. This complexity enables Donne to satirize a range of follies and evils and gradate into a comprehensive critique of life at court, where the bore is a hanger-on.

ll. 1–8.   *Well, I...went to Court*: The satiric speaker is ready to make his confession before receiving last rites (Roman Catholic extreme unction or Church of England communion of the sick). His visit to the court has been such that *feard hell* itself seems a *recreation* (diversion) and a *scant mapp* (inadequate image) of the *Purgatory* he experienced. *love to see, or to bee seene*: Ovid describes female playgoers in *Ars Amatoria* 1.99: 'They come to see; they come that they may be seen themselves'. *suite...sute*: The pun exposes the courtier's mentality, in which a petition to the queen and a new set of clothes have equal significance.

ll. 8–16.   *Glaze*: The name bespeaks the nature: an overlay of slippery sheen. *The hundred Marks...curse*: A parliamentary act to retain the queen's majesty's subjects in their due obedience was passed in 1581; it prescribed a fine of 100 marks and a year in prison for hearing mass (*Statutes of the Realm*, 4:657–8; Elton, *The Tudor Constitution*, 2nd edn, 431–3). *dwell*: are continually present at. The satirical speaker suffers the same damage to his reputation and character that habitual attenders at court do, even though (like Glaze at mass) he made just one casual visit.

ll. 18–20. *A thing...bredd*: An example of 'spontaneous generation', the belief that living things could originate from inanimate matter and that the occurrence was commonplace. Aristotle lent his prestige to this belief (*Historia animalium*, 3.5, 5.1), first questioned in the seventeenth century by Francesco Redi, and disproven in the nineteenth century by Louis Pasteur. Cf. 'To L. of D.', ll. 1–2. *Noahs Arke*. God instructed Noah to take male and female pairs of 'every living thing' into the ark 'to keep them alive' during the destructiveness of the flood (Genesis 6:17, 18–19). *pos'd*: puzzled. *Adam to name*: God entrusted to Adam the naming of 'every living creature' (Genesis 2:19–20).

ll. 21–6.   *Antiquaries studyes*: On the association of study with collecting old objects, see Donne's epigram 'Antiquary'. *Africks Monsters*: Africa was believed to teem with monstrous beasts. *Guyanas rarityes*: Sir Walter Raleigh's *The Discovery of Guiana* (1596) recorded his 1595 voyage, with descriptions of armadillos, Amazons, and cannibals. *Danes Massacre*: King Ethelred II ordered a massacre of the insurgent Danes of England on St Brice's day, 13 November 1002. *next the Prentises...rise*: Riots by London apprentices against the competition of foreign merchants and traders were a recurrent feature of sixteenth-century London life; see Susan Brigden, *London and the Reformation* (1989).

l. 28. *th' examining Justice*: A series of acts and proclamations declared Jesuits and seminary priests to be traitors subject to the death penalty if they entered the queen's dominions; see *Tudor Royal Proclamations*, ed. Paul L. Hughes and James F. Larkin, 3 vols (1964–9), nos 660, 739. For the parliamentary act against Jesuits and seminarists, see Elton, *The Tudor Constitution*, 2nd edn, 433–7. Donne's sensitivity in these matters could not have been more acute. His younger brother Henry had died of the plague in Newgate prison in 1593 where he was being held on a charge of harbouring a Catholic priest (Bald, *Donne: A Life*, 58–9).

ll. 31-4. *Jerkin*: a waist-length, fitted jacket, with or without sleeves. *Velvett*: a closely woven silk fabric with a short pile or nap. *ground*: underlying part of a textile. *tufftaffeta*: a glossy silk with tufts of velvet. *rash*: a twilled material, either silk or wool. See Arnold, *Queen Elizabeth's Wardrobe Unlock'd*, Index 2. This vocabulary images the dilapidation of an evermore-worn garment.

ll. 38-48. *one Language*: The courtier-bore's concoction of bits of various languages picked up in his travels, not the idealized original language that all peoples spoke before God confounded it in the many tongues of Babel (Genesis 11:1–9). *Pedants...tong*: learned jargon that imports Latin and Greek terms into English. *soldiers bumbast*: bigmouthed talk comprised of jokes, obscenities, and other camp slang. *Bumbast* was a quantity of fabric scraps used to pad clothing. *Montebancks drugg tong*: sales pitch of quack-medicine sellers. *Complement*: No longer current senses include 'accomplishment' and 'fullness', both relevant to the bore's self-vaunting. As an alternative spelling of 'compliment', the term can refer equally well to a courteous expression that implies or bestows praise. *outly...Jovius, or Surius*: Paulus Jovius, an Italian bishop, published a Latin history of his own times (1550–2); Laurentius Surius, a German monk, published several Latin works: a commentary on world events after 1550 (1568), four volumes on church councils, and six volumes of saints' lives (1570–5). Both of these churchmen-authors acquired reputations for inaccuracy or untruthfulness.

ll. 51-9. *He sayth....And I...Sayd*: These speech markers introduce a series of exchanges between the courtier-bore and the satirist-speaker that generate humour by way of offbeat uptakes (Tom Stoppard's Rosencrantz and Guildenstern are a present-day analogue). *selely*: innocently or triflingly. The pun signals the sort of exchanges that follow. *Calepines Dictionary*: The Italian friar, Ambrosius Calepino, published a Latin dictionary in 1502 which continuators expanded into a dictionary (1590) of eleven languages. *Beza*: The Calvinist theologian Theodore Beza translated the Greek New Testament into Latin (1556) and published a Latin–Greek New Testament (1565). *our two Academyes*: Oxford and Cambridge. *Apostles*: After the Holy Spirit descended on the gathered apostles, 'every man heard them speak in his own language' (Acts 2:4, 6). *Panurge*: A cunning, talkative buffoon and a major character in François Rabelais's *Gargantua and Pantagruel* (1532–4), who demonstrates his skill in a dozen languages. *pas*: surpass.

ll. 67–70. *not alone | My loneness is*: The speaker appropriates to himself a phrase from Scipio the Younger's description of the statesman Cato writing: 'He was never less alone than when he was alone' (Cicero, *De Officiis* [On Responsibilities], 3.1.1). This is the *holesome solitarines* of l. 155. *Spartanes fashione*: According to Plutarch, Spartan army officers would make slave-soldiers drunk, then display them to young soldiers of higher rank to arouse their disgust (*Life of Lycurgus*, 28.4). Donne envisages using pictures of drunkards for the same purpose. *Aretines Pictures*: Pietro Aretino wrote a set of obscene sonnets (*Sonnetti lussuriosi* (1524)) to accompany drawings by Giulio Romano illustrating various postures in sexual intercourse.

ll. 74–91. *talke of kings*: Donne adapts to an English setting satiric notes struck from talk of Roman rulers in Horace, *Satires*, 1.3.12; 1.7. *Kings Street*: The sole means of access to the royal palace at Westminster from Charing Cross. *smackd*: made a sound of disgust with his mouth. *mechanique*: lower class (cf. 'manual' worker). *I have . . . he followes mee*: A letter from Donne to Goodyere refers to 'my promise to distribute your other Letters . . . as fast as my Monsieur can do it' (*Letters*, 201). At that date (*c*.1613), and possibly much earlier, Donne had a French servant. *Your only . . . I have more*: The courtier-bore makes a fashion statement: '*Grogerame* [French ribbed silk twill] is your only wearable fabric'. The satirist deliberately mistakes: 'No; I have other things to wear'. *Under this pitche . . . not fly. pitche*: the height to which a trained hawk flew. The courtier-bore will not fly lower again lest the satirist, as hawk, catch him again as prey. *Crossing*: contradicting.

ll. 94–7. *He takes my hand*: An echo of Horace, *Satire*, 1.9.4. *a Still*: The image likens very slow, halting speech to drop-by-drop distillation. *A Sembriefe*: the duration of the longest musical note then in use. *Holinsheds, and Halls, and Stowes*: Raphael Holinshed published his *Chronicles* in 1577; he personally authored its *Historie of England*. Edward Hall published *The Union of the Noble and Illustre Families of Lancastre and York* in 1542. John Stow published his *Summarie of Englyshe Chronicles* in 1565 and the first of several editions of *The Annales of England* in 1580. Thomas Nashe shared Donne's scorn for this popular genre: 'your lay Chronigraphers . . . write of nothing but of Mayors and Sheriefs, and the deare yeere, and the great Frost' (*Pierce Peniless His Supplication to the Divell* (1592), in *Works*, ed. McKerrow, rev. edn, 1:194).

ll. 102–6. *reversiön*: The Crown sold the rights to succeed to state offices. *transport*: import or export. *blowpoynt*: A game in which the severed metal tips ('points') of garment laces were piled up inside a circle drawn on the ground. Players used rods or sticks to strike 'blows' at the points; the winner would be the one who knocked the most points outside the circle. *span counter*: A game in which a player tried to throw his 'counters' (balls of

wood or metal) so close to his opponent's counters that the distance
between them could be spanned with the hand.

ll. 112–17. *Gallobelgicus*: In 1588 Michael von Isselt began *Mercurius Gallo-Belgicus*,
a register of news and gossip. Donne's epigram, 'Like Aesops fellow
slaves, O Mercury', attacks this periodical's untrustworthy reporting.
The Spanyards came: the Armada in 1588. *Like a bigg Wife... travayle*:
Like a woman in late pregnancy ready to go into labour at the sight of
food she loathes. *Maccaron talke*: Loutish talk or foppish talk or an out-
landish mixture, depending on whether *Maccaron* is construed as mac-
aroni (humble fare) or as macaroon (a delicate pastry) or as macaronic (a
burlesque style that mixed words and phrases from several
languages).

ll. 123–7. *offices are entayld*: The next bestowals of court appointments have been
predetermined to pass by inheritance. *Perpetuityes*: inalienable future
rights. *the Pyrats... and Dunkirkers*: In Donne's time Dunkirk was a noto-
rious haven for pirates preying on ships of all nations, but there is no
known evidence for the courtier-bore's assertion that *great officers* take
shares of the loot. *wasts in*: spends his inheritance on. *meat*: food.

ll. 129–36. *Circes Prisoners... turn beasts*: A powerful enchantress's feat in Homer,
Odyssey, 10:235–40. *felt myselfe... Becomming traytor*: Registering the
negative fascination of the courtier-bore's slanders, the speaker fears
that he himself might say something that could be judged treasonous. *mee
thought... suck me in*: He next imagines that one of the broad treason stat-
utes might indict him for merely listening to the courtier-bore. *I might
grow | Guilty and he free*: The speaker's mounting fear of dangerous con-
tamination activates in his mind the superstition that persons with vene-
real disease (*burnt venomd Lechers*) could rid themselves of it by infecting
someone else.

ll. 137–50. *in*: involved. *myne, and my forefathers sin*: The satirist's own sins cannot
deserve such extreme punishment; he must be paying for his forefathers'
sins too. The Old Testament God claims as one of his attributes the visit-
ing of retribution on successive generations (Exodus 34:7; Numbers
14:18; Deuteronomy 5:9). *to my power... I beare this crosse*: This passing
suggestion of a likeness to Christ skirts blasphemy as it exposes the speaker's
wild desperation. *spare me?... Willingly*: The speaker deliberately misin-
terprets the courtier-bore by interrupting him, but the bore triumphs
in both getting what he asks and being further annoying. *Prerogative...
Crowne*: A punning use of a set phrase for royal sovereignty. The bore
behaves as if empowered like a king by the gift of a silver coin worth five
shillings.

ll. 155–68. *a traunce... he saw hell*: An allusion to Dante's *Inferno* and the onset of the
poet's dream-vision there ushers in a scathing panorama of life at court,
composed safely *At home in holesome solitarines*. *bladder*: hollow, inflated
receptacle.

ll. 169–79.   *yon waxen garden…flouts our Court here…Just such gay paynted things…*
ours are: Like Madame Tussaud's in today's London, this Italian wax-
work garden became a sightseeing attraction. Michael Drayton mentions
it in *England's Heroical Epistles (Poems*, ed. J. W. Hebel (1932), 2: 248). In
the speaker's eyes the garden's artificiality rivals that of the court. *Mues*:
mews, a set of stables serving as riding-schools. *Balon*: a game in which a
leather ball filled with air was batted with the hand or fist. *Dyett*: Either
the eating of aphrodisiac foods to prepare for sexual activity or the inges-
tion of antidotes for sexually transmitted diseases. *Stewes*: brothels.
Joseph Hall offers a sidelight on places that courtiers frequented: 'as
neere, as by report, | The stewes had wont to be to the Tenis-court'
(*Virgidemiarum*, 4.1.94–5). *the Presence*: the presence chamber, hung
with rich tapestries, where Queen Elizabeth appeared to her courtiers.
Here, *flocks* of courtiers have assembled to await her arrival.

ll. 184–95.   *Wants reach all states*: Every rank of courtier feels the financial pinch of
maintaining an extravagant wardrobe. *Cheapside bookes*: Accounts kept
of courtiers' debts in the clothiers' shops along Cheapside. *Cuchianel*
(cochineal): A brilliant scarlet dye produced from the dried bodies of the
insect *Coccus cacti*, found in Mexico and elsewhere. It was valued like
gold and spices—hence, its interest to *Pyrats*. *boord*: accost. With cinched
waists and billowing boned petticoats, women's courtly fashions of the
day evoked the silhouettes of ships coming into view on the horizon. The
image of male–female court encounters as pirates boarding weakly
defended ships adds satirical bite. *both are bought*: The ladies' beauty, the
men's wit. The speaker elaborates: courtiers never *weare scarlett gownes*
(achieve distinction as doctors of divinity or law or as judges) because the
gentlemen spend their money on ingenious speeches to pass off as their
own, while the court ladies buy up all the scarlet dye to use as cosmetics.
He calld her bewty Lymetwiggs, her haire nett: Lime twigs and nets were
used to catch small birds; the images are trite commonplaces for the ensnar-
ing of a heart.

ll. 197–205.   *Heraclitus*: The pre-Socratic Greek philosopher would laugh, departing
from the melancholic character ascribed to him by Diogenes Laertius in
Lives of the Eminent Philosophers, 9.1.4. *Macrine*: The friend and fellow
student of the Roman poet Persius who receives a birthday greeting in
his Satire 2.1. Perhaps by the same principle of inversion that transforms
Heraclitus from mourning to laughing, Macrine undergoes alteration
from Persius's admirable youth to a finicky one obsessed with every
detail of his appearance. *As…a Meschite*: As if the presence chamber
were a mosque that required ritual purification of one's body before
entering. *call…to shrift*: summon to confession of *mortal* and *venial*
(deadly and pardonable) sins. *fornicate*: intermingle. *by Durers rules*:
Albrecht Dürer methodized his art of engraving in *Four Books of Human
Proportion* (1528) where diagrams of male and female figures were marked

to show proportions of parts of the body to other parts, and to the whole. Measuring with pieces of string, Macrine tests these *odds* (proportions) on his own body.

ll. 212–18. *protests, protests, protests…whisperd by Jhesu so often*: Macrine draws indiscriminately on Protestant and Roman Catholic vocabulary in frantically trying to catch a lady's attention. Such utterances would endanger him equally with an agent of the Inquisition in Rome and with a *Pursevant*—an agent of the English Crown paid to detect Roman Catholics. *But t'is fitt*: But at the court Macrine's punishment (*plague*) is merely to suffer the lady's indifference, hers is to suffer the garbled mouthings of his affected fervency.

ll. 219–26. *Glorius…will plague them both*: As his name suggests, this personage is patterned on the type figure of the 'miles gloriosus' (braggart soldier) in Roman comedy. The *spurs* Glorius wears were prohibited not only at court but also in London, unless the wearer was riding out of the city. *old hangings*: medieval tapestries.

ll. 231–6. *the great Chamber…flagons of wine*: The great chamber lay between the presence chamber and the guard chamber. Tapestries representing *the 7 deadly sins* were hung by Cardinal Thomas Wolsey, the builder of Hampton Court, in 1522; they remained a conspicuous furnishing after Henry VIII made the palace a principal royal residence (Simon Thurley, *The Royal Palaces of Tudor England* (1993), 133). The queen is guarded by *Ascaparts*— an allusion to the thirty-foot-tall giant vanquished by Sir Bevis of Hampton in the popular medieval verse romance of that name. These guards are *bigg inough to throw | Charing Crosse for a barr*, that is, to hurl a monumental Gothic stone cross as if it were an ordinary wooden or iron bar. The yeomen of the guard, who had guarded the royal residences and the Tower of London since the accession of the Tudors in 1485 were already known as 'beefeaters' for their *Fine | Living, barrells of beefe, flagons of wine*.

ll. 242–4. *Maccabees Modesty*: An allusion to 2 Maccabees 15:38: 'If I have done well, and as becomes the story, it is that which I desired: but if slenderly and meanly, it is that which I could attain unto.' The speaker of Satire 4 professes a *Modesty* befitting an author of an apocryphal book of the Bible. He then ventures to voice the hope that persons wise enough to recognize the truth of his negative portrayal of the court will judge it *canonicall*, that is, truthful and authoritative.

Satire 5 (MS p. 21)

The allusion to Queen Elizabeth (l. 28) dates this satire before March 1603; its evident address to Sir Thomas Egerton (ll. 31–2) further dates it after his appointment as Lord Keeper of the Great Seal in 1596 and after Donne entered Egerton's service. Satire 5 may also be presumed to follow Satire 4, which would date it after March 1597. The assertion that Egerton was 'authorizd' (by the queen) 'To know and weede out this enormous sin' (ll. 33–4) has been convincingly identified with the Lord Keeper's efforts, begun in 1597, to curb the excessive fees charged by the clerk of the Star Chamber for the trying of cases in that court. The probable date of composition is 1599.

The speaker of Satire 5 sounds the notes of an eager—even an overeager—assistant, enthused about his employer's clean-up reformist initiatives. The poem has features of an occasional piece, somewhat hastily assembled. Donne recycles to lesser effect (ll. 13–16) his earlier contrast between the elemental force of a brook or spring and the sea (Satire 4, ll. 238–40) while the image of the Thames as a symbol of royal authority (ll. 29–30) lacks the uncanny power of the river image that concludes Satire 3. Satire 5, moreover, deals in commonplaces rare or absent in Donne's other satires: *man is a world* (l. 13); *All men are dust* (l. 19); *All things follow their likes* (l. 56). Finally, bursts of dismissive contempt (ll. 20–7, 88–91) detract from what the poem as a whole seems to intend: a cumulative satiric indictment of the late Elizabethan court. Yet Satire 5 can gain from being read in conjunction with Satire 2. The depiction of the suitor and the harsh judgement passed on him in Satire 5 have clear affinities with the earlier handling of Coscus the lawyer. In portraying first a lawyer, then a suitor, both venal beyond redemption, Donne mounts a strong implicit argument on behalf of Egerton's efforts to restore probity to the courts of England.

ll. 1–8.   *Thou shalt not laugh...nor...pity*: Satire 3 also opens with the speaker's rejection of laughter and pity. *He which did lay | Rules to make Courtiers... Frees from the stings of jeasts all...wretched or wicked*: An allusion to the great contemporary authority of Castiglione's dialogue on the arts of courtiership: 'it provoketh no laughter to mocke and skorne a seelye soule in miserie and calamitie, nor yet a naughtie knave' (*The Book of the Courtier from the Italian of Count Baldessare Castiglione, done into English by Sir Thomas Hoby, Anno 1561* (1900; rpt. 1967), 138). The *wretched* are those involved in lawsuits (*Suters miseree*); the *wicked* are the unscrupulous *Officers* of the courts. *a theame...give me*: compassion for suitors and freedom to criticize injustice furnish me with my subject.

ll. 9–12.   *If all things be in all...Each thing, each thing implyes*: The classical doctrine of one originary substance for all things in nature became a Renaissance commonplace. Here and in subsequent references (*Letters*, 96; *Sermons*, 9.173), Donne forefronts the four elements posited by the pre-Socratic philosopher, Empedocles.

ll. 13–21.   *man is a world...the world a man*: The speaker satirically offers proofs that are patently invalid, equivocating on disparate senses of *man* (mankind, a human body) and committing the logical fallacy of affirming the consequent (what is to be proved): *These selfe* (selfsame) *reasons* that prove *man is a world* also *Prove the world a man*. *excrement*: Suitors are transmuted to waste by the officials who drain all their substance from them. *wormes meat*: A widely current phrase for human mortality in sixteenth-century England.

ll. 26–7.   *Adulterate...wittols...issue*: The suitors' tame submission to the injuries done them by predatory officers is like that of husbands who acquiesce in their wives' adultery (*wittols*), and accept the bastard *issue* of such infidelity even though it is their *owne ruine*.

ll. 28–9. *Greatest... Empresse, know you this?*: Queen Elizabeth is uninformed (and blameless) regarding the outrages committed by officials far distant from her as the source of sovereign power. *calme head*: serene source. Their lawlessness is like a natural disaster: the flooding of meadows and wheatfields in the Thames' lower reaches. This image of destructiveness is reinforced by the later ones of the hapless suitor in a lawsuit as a swimmer endangered by a sink hole (ll. 45–6) or enfeebled by trying to swim against the current (ll. 49–51).

l. 31. *You, Sir*: Sir Thomas Egerton (1540–1617) benefited from the favour of the queen, who appointed him attorney general (1592), master of the rolls (1594), and Lord Keeper of the Great Seal (1596). Exercising the latter two offices concurrently, Egerton applied his characteristic energy to reforming the court of Chancery, achieving efficiencies in its practices and establishing a set scale of fees. Satire 5 heralds these initiatives. Egerton was less successful in seeking to monitor the keeping of public records at the Tower of London and to regularize the jurisdiction of the court of Star Chamber (*Oxford Dictionary of National Biography* online).

ll. 35–44. *O age of rusty Iron... The Iron Age that was... now | Injustice is sold deerer farr*: The point of departure for this sequence of images is another Renaissance commonplace originating in antiquity: the four ages of the world, golden, silver, iron, and lead. Juvenal invoked the four ages in his *Satires* (6.23; 13.28). Donne's innovation is to have two Iron Ages. In the earlier of these, justice is bought and sold, but in the latter Iron Age, the present, *Injustice is sold deerer farr* because suitors get nothing at all for the *fees and dutyes* they pay to corrupt court officials. Suitors are like *Gamesters* (gamblers) taking a chance on regaining the *mony* and *controverted lands* for which they have brought suit. But they stand no chance: the *mony... is gone | Into' other hands* and the lands *scape the strivers hands*. The witty substitution of rusty iron for lead as the fourth and final age intensifies the account of moral corrosion in Satire 5; cf. the reuse of this image in *First Anniversary*, ll. 425–6. *Like Angelica*: A famously evasive heroine in Ariosto's epic, *Orlando Furioso* (1572), who escapes from Rinaldo and Ferrau as they fight over her, and does the same when Rinaldo and Sacripante fight over her (1.14–23; 2.2–12). *letter or fee*: letter from a person of influence or a bribe, either of which might corrupt the judge.

ll. 53–5. *Become great seas... make golden bridges*: The speaker's outrage transmutes the water imagery into a moral allegory. Officers who have extorted money from the suitors but done nothing to advance their lawsuits now reveal the depth and extent of their depravity. If these officers (*great seas*) seek to extort even more money from the suitors as the cost of advancing their suits (*make golden bridges*), the suitors will discover how futile it was to imagine that they could successfully bribe corrupt and greedy men (*all thy gold was drownd in them before). only who have, may have more*: A sardonic turn on the commonplace 'like to like'.

ll. 57–61. *Judges are Gods...all heavens Courts*: The imagery shifts into a religious register, signalling a higher outrage. The point of departure is the reproach God delivers in Psalm 82:2, 6: 'How long will ye judge unjustly?...I have said, Ye are gods'. *By meanes of Angells*: The pun is enabled by the existence of an English gold coin, the 'angel', worth about ten shillings and stamped with the device of the archangel Michael killing the dragon. Donne's fondness for this pun becomes a structuring principle in Elegy 1 ('The Bracelet'). *Dominatïons...and all heavens Courts*: The orders of angels were first systematized for Christians by the fourth- or fifth-century author known as 'pseudo-Dionysius the Areopagite' in his work *The Celestial Hierarchy*, based on passages from the New Testament, especially Ephesians 1:21 and Colossians 1:16.

ll. 65–70. *a Pursevant*: This official detector of Roman Catholics employs forcible entry of dwellings to confiscate religious vestments (*Copes*), missals (*Primmers*), and utensils (*Chalices*). *mistake*: mis-take, take wrongly although permissibly by law. The following exclamation makes the outrage explicit: *Oh ne'er may | Fayre laws...be strumpeted | To warrant thefts.*

ll. 71–7. *Recorder to Destiny on Earth...Speakes fates words*: A *Recorder* in Donne's day was a judge or magistrate who exercised civil and criminal jurisdiction over a borough or shire. The formulation ascribing to positive (man-made) law the exercise of such powers with respect to *Destiny* or Fate appears to be original, but the underlying notion that human law should accord with natural law was commonplace. *foule long nayles...are th' extremityes*: Law's unclean and untrimmed fingernails are the one blemish on her beauty. The hurt they cause can obviously be addressed; a basic manicure is in order. *Officers* who *stretch to more than law can do* must be pared away.

ll. 79–83. *Why bar'st thou...?*: Why do you take off your hat? *Thou' hast bought wrong, and now...Begst right*: The speaker intensifies his haranguing of the suitor about the magnitude of his mental and moral mistake: he has paid dearly for injustice (the action or inaction of bribed officials) and has thus reduced himself to begging for justice (which he has no prospect of obtaining) *till these* (officials) *dy. laws Urim and Thummin*: the names of the jewels set into the 'breastplate of judgement' worn by the high priest Aaron (Exodus 28:30); they symbolize the clarity and integrity of the law.

ll. 84–7. *Thou...hast paper | Inough...Sell that, and...thou much more shalt leese*: The haranguing of the suitor becomes more intense and more obscure. The speaker taunts him with having *paper* (legal documents) enough to wrap all of the cargo of pepper carried by the Spanish *Carrique* (carrack or merchant vessel), the Madre de Dios, when it was captured by the English in August 1592. Yet if pepper was a precious commodity, the suitor's *paper* (whether legal documents or wrapping paper) is implied to be of little or no worth. Selling his paper would *leese* (lose) the suitor more than the antiquary *Hamman* would lose by selling his antiquities—by implication, a worthless collection.

ll. 88–91. *O wretch...AEsops fables...Thou art that swimming dogg...And div'dst...for what vanishëd*: Donne embellishes a Latin version of a fable ascribed to the legendary Aesop. The first-century writer Gaius Julius Phaedrus composed five books of fables in verse; in one of these (I.4) a dog with a piece of meat in its mouth catches sight of its image reflected in a river. When it snaps at the reflection of the meat, the dog loses the real meat. Phaedrus's moral is that one who seeks what belongs to another loses what is properly one's own. Donne's moral, however, is far more severe: the suitor has been *cosend* (deceived) by *shadows* (illusions of justice) and is close to being utterly lost (*div'dst neere drowning*) because he is pursuing *what vanishëd* (the justice that he helped to make of no effect).

ELEGY: THE GENRE

In Greek literature where it originated, *elegeia* referred both to a specific verse form and to the emotions associated with it. The verse took the form of sequential couplets consisting of a hexameter (six-foot) line and a pentameter (five-foot) line; the range of associated emotions included lament for the dead, summons to war, political satire, and love complaint. Later Greek elegists used the form mainly for erotic verse. In Latin literature the elegy (elegia) was distinguished from other genres by its two-line compositional units, the theme of love, and the tone of complaint. In making love his dominant theme, Ovid sparked it with sensual directness, colloquial address, and impudent wit. He also restored the broader emotional range associated with elegy in its Greek origins, charting personal experiences as diverse as the life-threatening illness of his mistress Corinna and the death of Tibullus, a fellow poet.

From their grouping in Westmoreland and other authoritative manuscripts, Donne's elegies appear to have circulated together, as his satires did. Topical references in the amatory elegies indicate likely dates of composition between 1593 and 1596, while the funeral elegy that concludes this group has been convincingly linked with the death of Donne's friend and son of his employer, the younger Thomas Egerton, in August 1599. But the presence of topical references is an insufficient warrant for a broader autobiographical reading of Donne's elegies. These poems are artful contrivances by an ingenious, verbally gifted student of the law who while honing his ability to argue difficult cases is also testing the limits of what he can think to say in verse, delighting himself and some fellow students, no doubt, with the exuberance of the enterprise.

Donne's elegies inventively adapt some prototypes in Ovid's *Amores*. One of his signature touches is to turn the tables on his self-confident speaker at the poem's end. Like Ovid's, Donne's first-person speaker dramatizes amatory intrigue, lustfulness and its interruptions and frustrations, as well as varied experiences of loss—an expensive gold chain gone missing, a mistress's rejection, an admired friend's premature death. The shock quotient in both poets' verse drew official censure: as the emperor Augustus had banished Ovid from Rome for his notoriously frank treatment of love-making, so too London censors excluded from the first editions of *Poems, by J.D.*

(1633, 1635) the elegies that came to be known as 'The Comparison', 'Love's War', 'On Love's Progress', and 'To His Mistress, Going to Bed', even as these poems circulated in manuscript.

Besides Ovid and another Roman elegist, Propertius, who inspired some thematic elements, contemporary poetic developments show their influence on Donne: the clash between Petrarchan idealization and anti-Petrarchan denigration of a female love object (Elegies 2 and 5) and the bravado of Italian verse paradox in mounting an elaborate argument to affirm the perfect beauty of an ugly woman (Elegy 10). See further, R. V. Young, 'The Elegy', in Shami, Flynn, and Hester, eds, *The Oxford Handbook of John Donne*, 134–48.

Elegy 1 (MS p. 25), titled 'Armilla' [Latin for 'The Bracelet'] in Poems, by J.D. *(1635), its first appearance in print*

ll. 1–8.   *Not that . . . Nor that . . . Nor for that . . . Nor for the lucke sake but the bitter cost*: The speaker's address to his mistress states the problem while setting a satiric tone unusual in elegy. He regrets losing her gold chain, not so much for its associations with their intimacy, but for what it will cost to replace it. By contrast, in Thomas Kyd's *Soliman and Perseda* (acted *c*.1592), the lover's loss of his mistress's gold chain brings despair, duelling, and death in its wake. *silly old moralitee*: foolish, worn-out proverb.

ll. 9–22.   The speaker deplores the loss of twelve innocent *Angels* (gold coins valued at ten shillings) that will compound the loss of the chain. While wordplay on 'good and bad angels' was commonplace in London drama of the 1590s, Donne's ingenuity in multiplying analogies sets his performance apart. *vile sodder . . . taint . . . first state of ther creation*: Theology undergirds the first analogy. As these angel coins have not been adulterated with any base metal, so their creation is free of any original sin. *Angels . . . To comfort my soul*: Guardian angels in Scripture perform various supportive roles; Raphael in the apocryphal book of Tobit is the prime example. *Shall these twelve innocents . . . my sins great burden beare?*: The analogy risks blasphemy as it skirts the central Christian doctrine of Christ's atonement for human sin. *thy severe | Sentence, dread Judge*: Likening his mistress to God at the Last Judgement, the speaker goes further still in imploring her to be forgiving like God and not exercise her right to demand restitution.

ll. 23–8.   *crownes of France . . . circumcis'd most Jewishly*: A fresh line of analogy opens by alluding to the gold coin stamped with a large crown (also known as the écu), first issued by the French monarchy in the fourteenth century, and emulated by Henry VIII with his gold 'crown of the Rose' (1526). Associations with the French 'crown' shift to another meaning of the word, 'the head', as the speaker deplores the appearance of sufferers from syphilis, *their naturall cuntry rott* (a disease also called 'the French pox'). *howsoe'er french kings most Christian bee*: In 1464 the pope gave the king of France the title of 'rex Christianissimus'. *Their crownes*: The line of analogy shifts back to the French écu or crown issued by *most Christian* kings. This honorific title does not protect the edges of these gold coins from being clipped in the course of circulation—*circumcis'd most Jewishly*, alluding to sharp practice by a stock figure of the time, the Jewish money-lender, e.g., Shylock in Shakespeare's *The Merchant of Venice*.

ll. 29–36. *Spanish stamps...justice from her course*: Another line of analogy picks up with Spain and its gold coinage, found abundantly in Europe. *as Catholique as their king*: In 1492 the pope gave Ferdinand of Aragon the title of 'His Most Catholic Majesty'. *Those unlick'd beare whelps, unfild pistolets... left unrounded*: The *pistolet* was the Spanish écu, faulted for its careless minting by way of another analogy: the belief that bear cubs were born shapeless and licked by their mother into their familiar form (Pliny, *Historia Naturalis*, 8.54). Like *many angled figures... | Of some great Conjuror*: The irregular Spanish écus are likened to the pentagrams (five-pointed stars) employed by conjurors to cast spells in attempts to alter the course of nature. But the coins have a more sinister effect as bribes; they pervert the *course* of *justice to* advance the political and military objectives of Spain.

ll. 39–41. *have slily made | Gorgious France ragged,... and decayd | Scotland*: These allusions enable Elegy 1 to be dated to the first half of 1593. Spanish activity in France and Scotland was a major concern of the Parliament convened that year. The lord keeper, Sir John Puckering, detailed Philip IV's efforts to revenge the defeat of the Armada by fomenting religious warfare in France, providing support to the Catholic factions then opposing by force of arms the (still Protestant and uncrowned, but lawful) king, Henri IV. Puckering also charged Spain with bribery and corruption in faction-ridden Scotland. William Cecil, Lord Burghley, further fed anti-Spanish fears by describing an intrigue being conducted personally by Philip. He had offered to send money and an army to consolidate a pro-Spanish party in Scotland that would join forces with a Spanish invasion (Scotland made, in Donne's scornful phrase, *proud in one day*). Donne's representation in ll. 39–40 would have had little point after July 1593, when Henri IV made his politic conversion to Catholicism.

l. 42. *And mangled seventene-headed Belgia*: Religious warfare begun in the 1560s and complicated by resistance to Spanish domination precipitated division of the seventeen provinces of the Netherlands in 1579. The Southern Union was predominantly Catholic; the Northern Union predominantly Protestant. *mangled*: An image as applicable to political-religious dismemberment as to the carnage of war. *Belgia*: The Roman name for a territory that later comprised the Netherlands and parts of southern Germany.

ll. 43–6. *Or were it such gold... gulled*: The practice of alchemy was based on the supposition that the 'soul' of mercury was intrinsic to all minerals. It could be extracted (*outpulled*) by fiery heat, then purportedly transmuted to gold by applying the so-called 'philosopher's stone'. Donne is dismissive about alchemy. He ironizes its trial-and-error practitioners as *Almighty Chimicks* deluded (*gulld*) in persisting with their efforts *durtely and desperatly*. Cf. Elegy 2, ll. 35–7.

ll. 55–63.　*Oh be content... if they meet*: In Kyd's *Soliman and Perseda*, 1. 4, a Crier is sent through the streets to announce the loss of a chain. *groat*: an English coin valued at four pence. *some dread Conjurer... mouthe of destiny*: In early modern England, people commonly resorted to conjurers, astrologers, and fortune-tellers for advice or instructions on recovering items they had lost or had stolen from them. Donne's *Conjurer* uses astrological charts (*fantastique schemes*) that apportion the heavens among the signs of the zodiac (*tenements*) and specify the trades and occupations ruled by each sign. The whores, theves, and murderers may be disreputable examples of such occupations on an astrological chart or they may be customers whom the conjurer has overcharged (*stuffd his rents*).

ll. 71–9.　*in those first falne Angels... gone*: According to Aquinas, *Summa Theologica*, 1a.64.1–2, of the three kinds of knowledge—natural, speculative, and affective (leading to the love of God)—the fallen angels retained the first and, in part, the second, but altogether lacked the third. Against this implicit conceptual backdrop, the speaker reflects on his twelve gold coins that are to be made into a replacement chain for his mistress. They are not *bad Angels*, even though they will now *nource... pride* rather than *provide | Necessities*. Melting down will relieve these coins of any badness that might be imputed to them, *For forme gives beeing, and their forme is gone*. *Vertues, Powers, and Principalityes*: the angelic orders. *thy will be donne*: The speaker again skirts blasphemy by applying to his mistress a phrase from the Lord's Prayer.

ll. 91–2.　*thou wretched finder... thy estate*: The speaker modulates from a declaration of hatred to a drawn-out curse, a subgenre introduced into elegy by Ovid (*Amores*, 1.12). Anticipating the violence of what he is about to say, the speaker *allmost* pities the chain's hapless finder. *Gold... heaviest metall*: This was true until platinum was discovered in the eighteenth century.

ll. 100–6.　*nimble fume*: fast-acting vapor. *Or libells... thy ruyne bring*: This may be an allusion to Thomas Kyd's arrest and examination in May 1593, during which he was tortured. Kyd gave this account of himself: 'When I was first suspected for that libell that concern'd the state,... unaskt I did deliver up... waste and idle papers... amongst those... were found some fragments of a disputation toching that opinion [atheism], affirmed by Marlowe... and shufled with some of myne (unknowne to me)'. *interdicted*: forbidden. *no abilitee*: impotence. [*All mischiefes which all devills ever thought*]: In copying Donne's text Rowland Woodward accidentally omitted this line. The omission does not affect the syntax; its only sign is the missing rhyme for *wrought*.

ll. 112–14.　*Gold is restorative*: There is testimony to Donne's later punning on *restorative*: 'At one time when Bishop Morton gave him a good quantity of Gold (then a useful token) saying, *Here Mr. Donne take this, Gold is restorative:* He presently answered *Sir I doubt I shall never restore it back again*: and I am assured that he never did' (Richard Baddeley, *Life of Morton* (1669), 103–4). *Because... at thy hart*: The root sense of *cordiall* in Latin was 'of or belonging to the heart'. In wishing the gold to press upon or obstruct the finder's heart the speaker sustains the force of his curse while rendering his own words *cordiall* in yet another sense: 'heartfelt'.

Elegy 2 (MS p. 29), titled 'The Comparison' in Poems, by J.D. *(1635), its first appearance in print*

Elegy 2 alternates between the opposing poetic traditions of Petrarchanism and anti-Petrarchanism, where catalogues of mistresses' beauties were countered by parodic catalogues of female deformities. The clustered allusions to classical mythology are untypical of Donne. The comparison of the two mistresses' vaginas (*best lovd part*) surely accounts for the omission of this poem from the first edition of Donne's *Poems* (1633), even as it circulated to an unknown extent in manuscript.

ll. 1–6.   The speaker compares the drops of his mistress's sweat to three substances from which perfume was produced: attar of roses, musk oil, and balm of Gilead (*allmighty balme of the' early East*). *chafd muscatts pores*: abdominal sacs of male musk-deer, heated or rubbed to release their aromatic contents. *carcanetts*: collars or necklaces, usually set with jewels.

ll. 8–14.   The speaker likens the sweat of his opponent's mistress to repulsive secretions (*ripe menstrous biles* or boils), food substitutes concocted by *starvëd men*, lumps of tin painted yellow to counterfeit gold (*vile lying stones in saffrond tinne*), and disfiguring skin eruptions (*warts, wheales*, or itchy swellings). *Sancerres starvëd men*: Beseiged for nine months by Catholic forces in 1573, the Protestants of Sancerre resorted to boiling cattle hides, harnesses, leather belts, old books, and parchments for broth in attempting to compensate for the absence of meat in the city (Jean de Léry, *Histoire memorable de la ville de Sancerre* (1574)). *soveraigne*: supreme.

ll. 15–22.   *Round... is her head*: The perfect spherical form of the head of the speaker's mistress is likened to two famous mythical objects: the golden apple awarded to Aphrodite by the shepherd Paris when he judged her the most beautiful goddess, and the apple that Adam and Eve disobediently ate. *raveshing*: plucking. *Thy head*: Thy mistress's head. This condensed form of reference recurs throughout the poem. *like a roughewen statue of jeat...* | *Like the first Chaos, or...face* | *Of Cinthia*: Darkness without light and connotations of formlessness are the unifying features of this trio of images. *Cinthia* (or Diana): the Roman moon-goddess.

ll. 23–8.   *Like Proserpines... chest*: The bosom of the speaker's mistress is like the alabaster box that Psyche took to the underworld to beg from Proserpina a little beauty for Venus (Apuleius, *Metamorphoses* [*The Golden Ass*], 6.16.20–1) or *Joves* (Zeus's) *urne* of good fortune (Homer, *Iliad*, 24.527). The bosom of the opponent's mistress is like *worme eaten truncks*—boxes or coffers—which in turn prompt associations with the *durt* and *stinck* of a grave. *Celes skin*: sealskin. *woodbine*: This term, applied to a range of vines including ivy and honeysuckle, evokes the slender sinuosity of the mistress's arms and fingers.

ll. 35–42. The vaginal passage to the speaker's mistress's *warme wombe* emits a *chea-rishing heate* like that of an alchemical vessel—*limbeck* (alembic)—that transmutes *durt* into *a soule of gold*. By contrast, cf. Elegy 1, ll. 43–6. The extreme heat of the opponent's mistress's vaginal opening is compounded by its sootiness (*like…a fired gun*), its shapelessness (*like hott liquid metals newly run*), and its tendency to scorching eruptions (*like…Etna*, the Sicilian volcano). *drad*: dread.

ll. 43–52. Inverted ordering in this culminating comparison works to the speaker's rhetorical advantage. He can proceed directly to apply his earlier associa-tions of sores and wormy putrefaction to the opponent's and his mis-tress's *kissings*. He can intensify the image of his opponent's *fearfull hand in feeling* the body of his mistress with a proverbial reference to a snake in hiding. And he can disparage their act of intercourse by likening it to the ploughing of *a stony ground*. By contrast, the acts of intimacy in which the speaker and his mistress engage are like the billing and cooing of turtle doves; their treatment of each other's bodies is as respectful as that of *priests…handling…sacrifice* and as careful as *the surgeon…searching wounds*.

ll. 53–4. *Comparisons are odious*: Reaching the utmost extreme of his exercise, the speaker ends dismissively with another proverb (M. P. Tilley, *A Dictionary of the Proverbs in England in the Sixteenth and Seventeenth Centuries* (1950), C576).

Elegy 3 *(MS p. 31), first titled 'The Perfume' in* Poems, by J.D. *(1635)*

In Elegy 3, a dandified young man-about-town addresses his co-conspirator in erotic intrigue. Donne's sexually responsive young woman closely watched by her suspicious parents is a late Elizabethan counterpart of such figures in Roman elegy as the wife with a jealous husband or the courtesan with rival lovers.

ll. 2–11. *escapes* (or *scapes*): breaking free from restraint. *at barr*: arraigned in court. *this trayterous meanes*: An anticipatory reference to the speaker's perfume. *Hydroptique* (hydroptic): bloated from accumulated fluid, dropsical. The word is a favourite with Donne. *catechiz'd*: questioned. *glazèd*: covered with a film, bleary. *cocatrice*: A mythical serpent identified with the basilisk, said to hatch from a cock's egg and to kill with a look (Pliny, *Natural History*, 29.66). *Thy bewtyes bewty…* | *Hope of his goods*: The cynical phrasing may be the young man's but could equally well be that of the girl's suspicious father.

ll. 20–9. *lest thou 'art swolne*: that you might be pregnant. *to try yf thou long…strange meates*: to see if you crave odd foods—a symptom of pregnancy in popular lore. *gull*: deceive. The figure of the *gull* in the 'rogue' pamphlets of the 1590s was a credulous countryman preyed on by London pickpockets and shysters of both sexes. *ingled*: fondled.

ll. 31–3. *grimm…Iron-bound serving man*: This sharply sketched human obstacle may have been suggested by a formidable gate-keeper in Ovid, *Amores*, 1.6.

Rhodian Colossus: The gigantic statue of Apollo at Rhodes was one of the seven wonders of the ancient world; its feet reportedly rested on piers forming the entrance to the harbor, and ships passed between its legs.

ll. 41–52. *A loud perfume*: An instance of catachresis: the use of a word in a sense radically different from its normal one, yielding a mixed metaphor. The young man's perfume sounds an alarm throughout the house. *as we... none at all*: As we English, who inhabit an island whose only native animal species are cattle and dogs, consider *pretious Unicornes strange Monsters*, so your father, having no good smell about his own body, thought my *good* perfume alien (*strange*). *my opprest shoes...speachles were*: In so-called 'peine forte et dure', crushing weights were laid on the bodies of accused felons who remained mute in court, refusing to plead. The speaker has inverted the judicial procedure; he has forcibly kept his shoes from making any noise.

ll. 53–70. *Only thou bitter sweet... that takes the good away*: These lines exemplify the sort of proficiency that Donne was acquiring as a law student in 1592–4. The extended attack on perfume is an instance of epideictic or demonstrative rhetoric, the purpose of which is either to praise or to blame (Aristotle, *Rhetoric*, 1.1358b). To generate blame, the speaker employs Aristotle's 'topics' of rhetoric. For example, he argues from origins: perfume is bad because it is derived from *Base excrement* (e.g., musk oil glands). He argues from context and associations: perfume is bad because *leprous* (scabby) *harlots* and their foolish customers (*the seely amorous*) who use it infect each other with deadly diseases; it is also bad because men who wear it are considered *effeminate*. He argues from shallow or misperceived motives: perfume is *much lov'd in the Princes hall* because courtiers are concerned only with appearances; the gods loved the burning of incense as a sign of the worship paid to them, *not that they likd the smell*. The speaker clinches his attack with a pair of syllogisms: If perfume is *lothsome* in each of its specifics, how can *we love ill things joyned* (perfume as a whole)? If the *good* of perfume *doth soon decay* (the fragrance vanishes), it cannot have the true nature of *the good*, which is uniform and unchanging. The final thrust: You, perfume, are *rare* (exceptional) in not only not being good but in actually detracting from what is good. The reader is left wondering why the speaker wears perfume; his attack redounds on himself.

Elegy 4 (MS p. 33), first titled 'Jealosie' in Poems, by J.D., 2nd edn (1635)

This elegy is markedly more Ovidian than Elizabethan in its characters, setting, and implied narrative. In *Amores*, 1.4 Ovid's speaker instructs his mistress in tactics for conducting their lovemaking in her husband's presence. One tactic is to ply him with wine until he falls asleep. Even Donne's passing references to the faked grief of legacy-hunters and the eagerness of a slave about to be freed are more suggestive of Rome than London. Again, the workings of satire emerge in Elegy 4, particularly in the last

two lines, where the speaker seems unaware that he is deflating the sense of adventure
in this love affair and undermining his pretensions to being in charge.

ll. 1–9.   *Fond*: foolish. *sere barke*: dry crust. *crocheting*: trilling half-minims (modern
              quarter-notes). *pure kindreds howling cryes…few faignd teares*: *Pure* is
              ironic, as *faignd* (pretended) immediately indicates.

ll. 19–22.   *boord*: table. *adulterate*: make less pure—with submerged wordplay on
              'adultery'. *swolne…great fare*: Donne's hoodwinked husband is put to
              sleep with a big meal, not wine, as in Ovid. *snorts*: snores. *basket*: wicker.

ll. 24–30.   *his house… his Diocis* (diocese): Elaborating rather pompously on the prov-
              erb 'A man's home is his castle', the speaker drives an obvious point about
              the risks he and his mistress have been taking. *But if… what should we
              feare?*: The speaker's character assumes darker overtones as he imagines a
              more clandestine location for his and his mistress's adultery. This change
              of venue will free them to commit major transgressions, like those who exile
              themselves to perform treasonous acts: *revile | Their Prince, or coyne* (coun-
              terfeit) *his gold*.

ll. 31–4.   *There we will skorn*: The final comparisons reduce the speaker's bravado to
              anticlimax. The safety of *an other house* will merely allow him and his mis-
              tress to evade the reach of her husband's authority. Those who live on
              Thames right side (outside the lord mayor of London's jurisdiction) have
              acted similarly, as have the Protestant *Germans* by making papal authority
              of no effect in their localities.

Elegy 5 (MS p. 34), untitled in Poems, by J.D. *(1635) and elsewhere;
title 'Love's Recusant' proposed by Robbins,* Complete Poems of Donne

This self-accounting by a disillusioned lover begins with a critique of basic compo-
nents of Petrarchanism: love worship, a sovereign mistress, sexual attraction imaged as
a moth's immolation in a candle flame. The Ovidian extravagance of the speaker's
rhetoric (repeated declarations of hate, evocations of nature as violent and destruc-
tive) intensifies the anti-Petrarchan critique. But the ecclesiastical and judicial terms
that operate as pivots in Elegy 5—*in Ordinary, a Recusant*—are purely Elizabethan.
They indicate that this disillusioned lover's dilemma and identity are those of a con-
temporary (or fictive alter ego) of Donne.

ll. 1–10.   *Oh let not me serve so*: As potential models for his own conduct, the speaker
              disdains seekers of *honors smokes* (insubstantial titles) and patronage from
              great men and *idolaterous flatterers* of *Princes*, whose efforts and attentions
              go unrewarded, making them *dead Names. in Ordinary*: exercising jurisdic-
              tion in ecclesiastical or civil cases as one's own right and not by special
              deputation. The speaker asks his mistress for the right to exercise jurisdic-
              tion over her as her favourite.

ll. 11–14.   The speaker discloses his rationale for invoking ecclesiastical or civil ana-
              logues. He has wooed a seemingly honorable and receptive mistress (*Thy
              hart seemd waxe, and steele thy constancee*) in full good faith (*my soule… by*

   Othes betrothd). Yet her infidelity has caused him suffering (*my Purgatory,*
   faythles thee).

ll. 15–34. *So careles flowers…So the tapers beamy ey…beckens the giddy fly*: The
   speaker's train of thought shifts to the realm of nature, where contact and
   interaction among various phenomena end in destruction and violence.
   These images figure the destructiveness and violence inherent in human
   sexuality, as the speaker flatly declares: *Then say I That* (the rampaging
   stream) *is shee, and this* (the dry, abandoned channel) *ame I*.

ll. 35–46. *Yet let not thy deepe bitternes begett* | *Careles despayre in me*: The speaker
   attempts to control his disillusionment with his mistress, whose favourite
   he no longer seeks to become. He struggles to resist *despayre*, which will
   only breed *skorne*, and to arm himself with *disdayne*, by which, he predicts,
   utterly | *I will renounce thy dallyance*. He recognizes, though, the difficulty
   of rejecting his mistress, to whom his gaze is still drawn (*with new eyes I
   shall survay thee*) and with whom he recalls an earlier good relationship
   (*hope bred Fayth and love*). But is the speaker in a position to reject his
   mistress? Hasn't she already rejected him? He implies as much in *My
   hate shall outgrow thine* and *What hurts it me to be excommunicate?* (in this
   context, cut off from his mistress's favour). In a final effort to salvage his
   independence from his mistress's sway, he declares himself a *Recusant*:
   a Catholic who refuses to attend Church of England services. But recu-
   sants in the 1590s were liable to arrest, arraignment, and severe fines for
   repeated non-attendance. Not even his hatred and defiance can release
   this speaker from subservience to this mistress.

Elegy 6 (MS p. 35), untitled in Poems, by J.D. *(1635) and elsewhere;
title 'Love's Pupil' proposed by Robbins,* Complete Poems of Donne

In tone and attitude, Elegy 6 resembles Elegy 3 ('Once and but once') and Elegy 4
('Fond woman'), but the enacted situation is quite different: the obstacle to the speak-
er's lust is not a father or a husband, rather, it is the partner herself. He has educated
her in the subtleties of a love affair. She has profited to the extent of graduating from
his attentions and taking another lover. The speaker's self-righteous anger and injured
self-worth know no limits as he loads her with reproaches.

ll. 1–12. *Natures lay Ideott*: Naturally ignorant no-brain. *Sophistry*: trickery—a
   sense no longer current. *by th' eyes water…a malady*: On analogy with the
   medical use of urine analysis, the mistress was taught to diagnose the gen-
   uineness of a lover's passion by his tears. *the Alphabett* | *Of flowers*: The
   arrangement of blossoms in a nosegay could express various sentiments
   like those engraved on rings. *devisefully*: symbolically. *arrands* (errands):
   messages—a sense no longer current.

ll. 13–16. *Remember since*: Remember when. *Aye, yf my frinds agree*: The 1590s equiv-
   alent of 'Yeah, I guess so'. *houshold charmes…to teach*: There were various
   traditional ways of guessing at a future husband's identity—for example,
   tossing an apple peel on the floor to see whose first initial it seemed to spell.

ll. 20–7.   *Thou art not...oh, shall strangers tast?*: The speaker gets at the heart of his anger: he has lost possession of the woman to a rival. Images of communal and private ownership and differing uses of land objectify her as valuable property. The rival has enclosed (*inlayd*) the mistress like an open pasture no longer to be grazed by cattle but reserved for the growing of crops. *neyther to bee seene nor see*: An inversion of Ovid's famous line about fashionable ladies at the theatre (*Art of Love*, 1.99). It enrages the speaker that a fertile, now cultivated woman should be so confined after he had *Refined* her *into a blisfull paradise,* and he focuses his rage in an image both Edenic and phallic—*lifes tree.*

ll. 28–30.   *Frame...drinke in glas?*: Shape and decorate a golden cup, and drink out of glass myself? *Chafe*: soften by rubbing or warming. *seals*: phallic impressings (a then current obscene sense); cf. Elegy 8, l.32. *redy*: fit for riding (with a sexual innuendo).

Elegy 7 (MS p. 36), first published in 1804; title 'Love's War' proposed by Grierson, The Poems of John Donne (1912)

The contrast between the wars of Mars and the wars of Venus is a stock theme of Roman elegists (Ovid, *Amores*, 1.9; Tibullus, 1.10). But Donne's intermingling of references to actual warfare most closely resembles two elegies of Propertius (3.4, 5). In the one, Propertius wishes success to the Roman campaign against Parthia, imagining how he will watch the returning army's triumphal procession while reclining on his beloved's breast, and pledging that the soldiers can keep the booty they won as far as he is concerned. In the other elegy, Propertius repudiates war, replacing it with love. Donne's treatment of erotic manoeuvring does not seem to warrant the poem's history of censorship. Perhaps the explicitness about the on-top male position (l. 36) caused offence.

   The allusion to Henri IV's conversion *of late* (l. 10) suggests a date of 1594. After Henri embraced Catholicism in July 1593, popular support in England for the expedition to France turned to war-weariness. By February 1595 all English troops had been withdrawn. The idea of fighting in France would not have occurred to Donne's speaker after the close of 1594.

ll. 3–6.   *scrupulous*: hedged with conditions that impose restraints. War has laws, but love does not. *free City*: one that exercises autonomy in opening its gates and ports. *In Flanders, who can tell...?*: In the 1590s, fighting in *Flanders*—here a general term for the Netherlands—involved mutinies of unpaid Spanish soldiers, disputes between the Spanish authorities and the Southern Provinces, and open revolt in the Northern Provinces. This confused situation makes it impossible to determine whether *the Maister* is a tyrant oppressing his subjects or whether the subjects *rebell* against lawful authority. *Ideots*: those who concern themselves only with private affairs.

ll. 9–12.   *France...giddiness*: A traditional English view of the French as flighty gained strength in the 1590s from the treatment of English troops fighting in France, from factionalism and shifts in policy after Henri III's death, from Henri IV's conversion, and from his large indebtedness to England. *our Angels...ne'er returne*: Elizabeth's loans to Henri IV totalled more than 400,000 pounds; the first modest repayment on this debt was not made until 1603, the year of the queen's death. *no more...fell*: While the primary reference of *Angels* is to coins lost as surely as the rebel angels, there may be a sub-reference to the English soldiers fallen in France.

ll. 13–16. *Sick Ireland...let blood*: The rebellion against the English crown spear-headed by Hugh O'Neill, 2nd earl of Tyrone, between 1594 and 1596 was viewed as a serious threat requiring harsh repressive measures. The purging and bloodletting in Donne's extended metaphor tallies with the official English outlook.

ll. 17–24. *Midas...no food to live*: Granted the power of turning everything he touched to gold, this mythical king nearly starved to death (Ovid, *Metamorphoses*, 11.100–45). Donne's analogy requires taking *we touch all gold* to refer to the spectacular successes of professional English privateers like Sir Francis Drake and Sir John Hawkins, who had Crown commissions authorizing them to attack and confiscate foreign ships and their cargoes. The *we* of *find no food to live* are presumably English gentlemen-venturers without such commissions. *mew*: confine. *swaggering*: lurching.

ll. 30–7. *parley*: negotiate. *bleed*: Sperm was thought to be a concentration of the blood. *dy*: experience orgasm (period slang). *under*: subordinate to a commanding officer, or in submission to an enemy. *Engines*: A general term for all offensive weapons.

Elegy 8 (MS p. 37), first printed in the 5th edn of Poems, by J.D. *(1669), and there titled 'To his Mistris Going to Bed'*

In *Amores*, 1.5, the Ovidian speaker relates how Corinna came to visit him as he lay in bed in the heat of the day, how he stripped off her garments and admired her naked beauty, then took her to bed. Donne transposes this past-tense narrative into an immediate present, adding topical references to the woman's fashionable Elizabethan clothing and accessories as well as an imperious tone. Avoiding crudity, his speaker's monologue traces a course from eager anticipation through mutual arousal to the near prospect of mutual gratification. The sexual energy and loving desire that impel this course ensure poetic as well as erotic completion. On the political constructions that later seventeenth-century readers overlaid on Elegy 8, see Joshua Eckhardt, *Manuscript Verse-Collectors and the Politics of Anti-Courtly Love Poetry* (2009).

l. 2. *labor*: work hard. *in labor*: The *OED*'s first example of a woman 'in labor' is dated 1799, but cf. Elegy 10, l. 49.

ll. 5–17. *heavens zones*: In ancient cosmography the tropics of Cancer and Capricorn and the Arctic and Antarctic polar circles divided the celestial sphere into torrid, temperate, and frigid zones. To a speaker in the heat of desire, the woman's *girdle* (belt) encircling her waist correlates with the torrid zone lying between the tropics. There may be a latent pun: Greek zónê means 'girdle'. *glistering*: glittering. *spangled brestplate*: ornamental covering for the bosom. *harmonious chime*: watch that strikes the hours. *buske*: dress. Its bodice has sewn-in stays of wood or bone *That... still can stand* when the dress is taken off. *Off with... doth grow*: Remove your wire hairnet and display the crowning glory of your hair.

l. 21–4.   *A heaven... Paradise*: Beautiful female companions are a defining feature of the blessed afterlife in the Qu'ran. *And though...flesh upright*: While both evil and good spirits may wear white garments, they can be distinguished by their effects: evil spirits make the spectator's hair stand on end, good spirits elicit sexual arousal.

ll. 32–6.   *seale*: phallic impression. *Full Nakedness, all joyes*: Propertius's rapturous theme in *Elegiae* 2.15. *As soules...whole joyes*: This analogy takes its cue from Aquinas, *Summa Theologica*, 1a2ae.69.2, who concludes that the blessed have their full reward after death, and only a foretaste of it in this life. *Gems... mens views*: Donne's speaker inverts Ovid's myth in which Hippomenes cast golden balls in Atalanta's path to divert her from the race she was running (*Metamorphoses*, 10:650–80). The inversion serves to cast male and female as equal participants and beneficiaries in this sexual encounter.

ll. 41–6.   *mistique*: containing sacred mysteries. *imputed grace*: In the Reformation dispute over justification, Catholics held that Christ's saving grace was infused into the souls of repentant sinners; Protestants held that it was merely ascribed (*imputed*), since no sinful human soul was capable of directly receiving Christ's saving grace. By aligning with the Protestant position, Donne's speaker pays women the daring compliment of likening their *grace* or favour (here, their revealing of themselves to chosen lovers) to Christ's grace in saving humankind. *There is no penance, much lesse innocence*: The woman's *imputed grace* remains fully operative. *Penance* has no place, on her part or on his: neither she nor he will be sorry for what she grants him willingly. *Innocence* has even less place, for both know exactly what they are doing. The two concluding lines urge that they get on with it.

Elegy 9 (MS p. 39), first titled 'Change' in Poems, by J.D. (1635)

As a strain of thought persisting from classical antiquity through the early modern period, naturalism—or, as later termed, libertinism—holds that humans are free to follow their natural promptings without regard to the strictures of conventional law and morality. Major literary prototypes for the naturalism expressed in Elegy 9 and elsewhere in Donne's verse include Myrrha's monologue debating and defending her incestuous desire for her father in Ovid, *Metamorphoses*, 10:319–55, and Michel de Montaigne's reflections on female sexual appetite in 'Upon some verses of Virgil' (*Essais*, 3.5).

ll. 3–9.   *fall back*: 'Relapse to a former love' seems to be the principal sense, with a
pun on a posture in lovemaking. *that Apostasee | Confirme thy love*: A para-
doxical formulation, perhaps with this sense: If you forsake your commit-
ment to me and return to another lover, you thereby confirm that you have
experienced love. *Women are ... Open to all*: Erasmus's *Adagia*, a frequently
reprinted collection of Latin proverbs, includes 'The Muses' doors are
open wide', 1629 edn, 221. *as these things bee*: in the same way.

ll. 14–16.   *apter ... than men*: A woman's desire may outlast a man's sexual potency.
They are ... their owne: They are our shackles, and they are (mistresses) of
themselves. The contrast is between men fastened to women like galley
slaves, and women not fastened to men, who may go as they please.

ll. 23–30.   *Likenes glues love*: A variant of the proverb 'Like will to like' (Tilley,
Dictionary of Proverbs, L294). *yf so thou do*: if you change. *And so not
teache ... nor every one*: The speaker will not teach promiscuity, as the
woman does, by example. Instead he will urge (a no longer current sense of
force) his belief that neither one single woman nor every woman is to be
loved. He then promotes his belief into a general principle.

ll. 35–6.   *Change is ... Eternity*: To close, the speaker makes specious use of the rhe-
torical topic of association. As things dependent on *Change* (variation,
movement) for their existence, *Musick, Joye, Life* comprise a well-formed
set of associations. But *Eternity* cannot belong; it is the contrary of the set.
Undercutting his universal affirmation of *Change* by invoking *Eternity*, the
speaker's monologue collapses in upon itself.

Elegy 10 (MS p. 40), first titled 'The Anagram' in Poems, *by J.D. (1635)*

Among mid-seventeenth-century collectors of verse in manuscript miscellanies,
Donne's Elegy 10 was a favourite. Drummond of Hawthornden remarked on its
resemblance to Torquato Tasso's *Rime 37*: 'Compare Song: *Marry and Love*, &c. with
Tasso's stanzas against beauty; one shall hardly know who hath the best' (*Works* (1711),
226). Tasso had elaborated in detail his wish for an ugly mistress:

> Let her have a huge nose which casts a shadow as far as her chin; let her mouth
> be large enough to hold anything, her teeth be few and far between, and her eyes
> set crooked—the teeth of ebony and the eyes silvery ... I shall have no fear of her
> being loved by anyone else, or followed, or admired; I shall not be alarmed if
> she looks at anyone else or if she sighs and seems sad ... She will be wholly mine
> and I wholly hers (*The Monarch of Wit*, trans. J. B. Leishman, 7th edn (1967),
> 81–2).

Donne additionally draws on another aspect of the mode of paradoxical praise: the
right qualities in the wrong places—a yellow face rather than yellow hair, pearly eyes
rather than pearly teeth, and so on. Derived from Francesco Berni's mocking Sonnet
23, this aspect had been brought into English by Sir Philip Sidney in verses praising
Mopsa in his *Arcadia*, composed in the 1580s. What Donne contributes to this mode
are flashes of argument by analogy or enthymeme (compressed syllogism), so rapid

and compressed that their fallaciousness may slip by the reader unnoticed. Although it is found in all manuscripts containing Elegy 10, the couplet (ll. 53–4) listing devices for female sexual stimulation was omitted from early editions of *Poems, by J.D.* and first printed in 1669.

ll. 1–10.   *Flavia...beuteous bee*: The speaker defines beauty loosely in terms of an aggregate of elements rather than their integration in, e.g., proportion, order, or symmetry. By his definition, Flavia is a beauty—a perfect beauty. *Jeat* (jet): black. *they*: her eyes. *light*: sexually available. *rough*: hairy.

ll. 11–16. Voiced by others or imagined by the speaker, objections have been raised to the quick conclusion that Flavia is a perfect beauty. The speaker moves to counter-argue.

ll. 19–22. *the gamut*: The musical ground note added in medieval times to a previously existing series of six notes (the classical hexachord). Later *the gamut* referred to the whole series of notes, or 'scale', recognized by musicians. *Things simply good...unfitt*: A generalization reached by way of an example. *A perfect song* composed in one *gamut* or scale is not superseded or nullified when changes are made in that *gamut* to allow for new compositions that might *equall* the earlier *perfect song*. *unfitt*: useless or substandard.

ll. 25–6.   *All love...lovely too?*: The speaker's enthymeme has two formal flaws. First, the terms *lovely* and *wonderful* are not synonymous although they are treated as if they were. The second can be shown by syllogistic expansion of the enthymeme: All that is lovely is wonderful; Your mistress is wonderful; Therefore your mistress is lovely. The speaker commits the fallacy of affirming the consequent, or asserting what is to be proved. A valid syllogism requires the middle premise 'Your mistress is lovely' and yields the conclusion 'Your mistress is wonderful'.

ll. 35–42. *husbands*: men married to women; men who till and cultivate the soil. The images of *best land* and *foulest way* sustain the double sense. *plaister*: a bandage applied with adhesive. *spyes...eunuchs*: guardians of her sexuality. *Marmositt* (marmoset): an ape or small monkey; figuratively, a male darling. *When Belgiaes citties...towne*: Dikes were opened at Alkmaar in 1573 and at Leiden in 1574 to break the sieges of these cities by inundating the would-be invaders with *durty foulnes*.

ll. 47–54. *the stews*: brothels. *timpany* (tympany): abdominal distension caused by gas. *dildoes...velvett glas*: Stimuli for a woman's self-induced orgasm. *dildoes*: artificial penises. *bedstaves*: spindles from a bed-frame. *velvett glas*: glass receptacle covered with fabric having a short, soft, dense pile. *as Joseph was*: Joseph fled from Potiphar's wife, who tried to lure him into sleeping with her (Genesis 39:7–12).

ll. 55–6.   *One...fittest were*: The speaker's closing equivocation on *like none* (comparable to none) and *likd of none* reprises the subject of the entire poem: Flavia's physical repulsiveness as a guarantee of her faithfulness. How strong is a case built on specious logical moves? Donne the law student has been conducting just such a test.

Elegy 11 (MS p. 41), titled 'On his Mistress desire to be disguised and to goe like a Page with him' in Poems, by J.D. *(1635), its first appearance in print*

A woman in disguise accompanying her lover is a stock romantic plot device. In Arthur Brook's verse translation of Bandello's *The tragicall historie of Romeus and Juliet* (1562), Juliet pleads to be allowed to disguise herself and follow Romeus into exile. Although Shakespeare's Juliet makes no such plea, she is almost inevitably brought to mind by ll. 50–3, where the young woman's outcries awaken her nurse. In the Bridgewater manuscript, an early but rather slipshod collection of Donne's verse once owned by his former employer's son, John Egerton, first earl of Bridgewater, this poem is prefaced by a note: 'His wife would have gone as his Page'. While lacking factual validity, the note is a tribute to the realism of Elegy 11; it also attests to the knowledge some contemporaries had of Donne's clandestine marriage to Anne More. The poem's omission from the first edition of *Poems, by J.D.* is probably to be accounted for by the evocations of gallantly clad French syphilitics and bisexual Italian predators (ll. 33–41).

ll. 1–16. *fatal interview*: all-determining sight of one another. *remorce*: pity, compassion—senses no longer current. *spyes . . . rivalls*: Stock opponents in Ovidian love elegy. *Divorcement*: A secondary sense, 'enforced separation', seems to be primary here, while the primary sense, 'dissolution of the marriage tie', suggests the intensity of the bond between the speaker and his mistress. *conjure*: beseech, entreat. *only*: solely.

ll. 21–5. *wild Boreas . . . Fayr Orithia*: The source for this variant of the classical myth in which Orithyia, daughter of the king of Athens, is abducted and raped by Boreas, the north wind, appears to be the demythologized version proposed by Socrates: 'I might have a rational explanation that Orithyia was playing . . . when a northern gust carried her over the neighboring rocks; and this being the manner of her death, she was said to have been carried away by Boreas' (Plato, *Phaedrus*, 229). *provd*: made trial of. *unurg'd*: not thrust or pressed upon one. *flatteree*: coaxing sweet talk.

ll. 34–42. *Spittles*: hospitals. *shops of fashions*: wearers who show off trendy clothes. *fuellers*: stokers. *quickly know thee, and know thee*: instantly recognize you for a young woman, and have intercourse with you. *indifferent*: undifferentiating—here, with regard to sex. This Italian would pose a sexual danger whether the mistress dressed in her own clothing or disguised herself as a boy. *Lots fayre guests were vext*: The men of Sodom demanded that Lot turn over his two angel guests to them for homosexual purposes, but the angels thwarted the Sodomites (Genesis 19:4–11). *spungy Hydroptique Dutche*: German soaked (with beer)—an ethnic stereotype.

ll. 44–6. *England is . . . walke in*: Donne's consistent esteem for his native country contrasts with much else in his often satiric earlier verse; cf. 'The Storme', l. 9. *Our great king . . . his presence*: Donne the preacher would elaborate: 'The Heaven of Heavens [is] the Presence Chamber of God himselfe . . . Let this Kingdome, where God hath blessed thee with a being, be the Gallery' (*Sermons*, 4.47, 49).

l. 55.   *Augur...chance*: Foresee better luck for me than this. Cf. 'Sweetest love I doe not goe', ll. 33–6, and 'A Valediction: of Weeping', ll. 19–25.

Elegy 12 (MS p. 43), first titled 'His Picture' in Poems, by J.D. *(1635)*

The Bridgewater manuscript also supplied this poem with a note: 'Traveling he leaves his Picture with his mystris'. While it is equally lacking in factual validity, scholars have tended to credit Elegy 12 with autobiographical resonance. Gardner remarks: 'One need not believe that Donne actually handed a miniature [portrait of himself] to a mistress before sailing to connect this poem with his participation in the attack on Cadiz in 1596' (*The Elegies and Songs and Sonnets*, 143). The immediacy of the speaker's projected self-description (ll. 5–10) does make a source in first-hand experience seem attractive, but it is important also to credit Donne's artistry.

ll. 1–8.   *Here...picture*: Miniature portraits were popular at this period in England as love-tokens and mementos. Nicholas Hilliard and Isaac Oliver were the ranking masters in this genre. Oliver's miniature of Donne, dated 1616 (when Donne was forty-four), is at Windsor Castle. *shadows*: Several senses of the word are in play: its rhetorical use, to contrast portraits with their human subjects; slight or faint appearances, traces; and spectral forms, phantoms. *My face...hayrecloth*: His face will be shaggy (because he has let his beard grow), and the hair on his chest will be matted (from sweat and infrequent bathing). *hoarines*: gray or white (hairs).

ll. 13–20. *This shall say... thou shalt say*: The speaker imagines what he hopes his mistress will say about how their mutual love has developed during their separation. She is represented as speaking from l. 14 onward. *Do his hurts... my worthe decay?*: Do his hardships affect me negatively? Does he value me less? 'Not in the least' is her implicit answer. To express her tried and true love, the mistress adapts the contrast between milk for babies and meat for strong adults that figures the soul's progression from spiritual and moral beginnings to full maturation as a Christian in 1 Corinthians 3:1–2 and Hebrews 5:13–14. *disusd*: unaccustomed.

Elegy 13 (MS p. 43), printed without title in Poems, by J.D. *(1633); printed among Donne's later funeral elegies and titled 'Elegie on the L. C.' in* Poems, by J.D. *(1635)*

I. A. Shapiro argued convincingly (*English Remaissance Studies Presented to Dame Helen Gardner* (1980), 141–50) that the subject of Elegy 13 is Sir Thomas Egerton, son of the elder Sir Thomas. The friendship between Donne and the younger Sir Thomas may trace to the summer of 1597 when both took part in the Islands expedition, but it could have begun even earlier when both were students at Lincoln's Inn.

It was the son's idea that his friend should become his father's secretary, an appointment that brought Donne to reside in the Egerton household. Donne noted in a 1602 letter to the father: 'By the favour which your good son's love to me obtained, I was four years your Lordship's secretary'. By the time this letter was written, however, the son had been dead for over two and a half years. When Essex gathered an army to quash Tyrone's rebellion in 1599, the younger Sir Thomas embarked for Ireland, as captain of a company, in April. Wounded in action, he died on 23 August. When his son's death was confirmed on 5 September, the Lord Keeper had the body brought back to England to receive a solemn funeral in Chester cathedral on 27 September. Donne carried a sword in the funeral procession (Bald, *Donne: A Life*, 105–6). These facts and circumstances make it highly likely that Elegy 13 is the verse tribute that Donne composed to this dead friend.

Internal allusions strengthen the identification. *Sorrow, who to this house, scarse knew the way* (l. 1) accords with the happiness that the Lord Keeper was enjoying with his second wife, Elizabeth, sister of Sir George More of Loseley, and aunt of his daughter Anne, whom Donne would marry two years later. The speaker refers familiarly to *this house*; Donne the secretary was residing with the Egertons. *This strange chance claymes strange wonder* (l. 3)—the death in question was untimely and unexpected. *His lifes loud speaking works deserve | And give prayse too* (ll. 5–6)—the younger Sir Thomas died in action against Irish rebels. *His Children are his pictures* (l. 23)—his three daughters, Elizabeth, Mary, and Vere, were all very young at the time of his death.

This wealth of textual confirmation, however, did not suffice to preserve the identity of the subject of Elegy 13, which circulated in manuscript without a title. The eventual title 'Elegie on the L.C.' seems to be a misplaced reference to the father, who was appointed Lord Chancellor ('L. C.') in 1603, and died in 1617. The memory of the younger Sir Thomas, dying in his late twenties, was evidently eclipsed by that of his far more illustrious father, who survived him by eighteen years.

Further implications emerge from assigning a date of September 1599 to Elegy 13. Both the satires and the elegies are numbered sequences of poems that appear, from the evidence of the earlier manuscripts (like Westmoreland, the copy-text here), to have circulated in generic groupings. It is reasonable to assume that the numbers given the satires and elegies in the earlier manuscripts indicate the order in which Donne composed them, and scholars have worked on that assumption. Topical references in the satires provide useful further clues for dating. But topical references in the elegies are fewer, and there is more variation in their ordering in the earlier manuscripts. Westmoreland's placement of its funeral elegy at the end of its sequence appears to reflect (someone's) generic subdivision: grouping all the love elegies together, then appending the funeral elegy. In addition, the final positioning of Elegy 13 may materially imply that Donne had written all of the elegies preceding it by September 1599.

ll. 10–13. *yf a sweete bryer…for him dead*: The dead man is invested with a sacred, transcendent status, that of a tree destined for transplanting *to Paradise* or felling and burning *for holy sacrifice*. By contrast, his surviving friends and family are left with an earthbound life utterly dependent on him; they *must wither* like a climbing rose (*sweete bryer*) bereft of its source of nourishment. This mode of radical inversion—the dead seen as alive and superior, the living as perishing and inferior—would become an integral feature of

Donne's compositional strategy in commemorative verse. It reaches its apogee in his figurations of Elizabeth Drury in the *Anniversaries*.

ll. 13–18.   *no family... more venturers*: Egerton's leadership abilities and conspicuous piety are figured as a ship with such potential for attaining the objective of *heavens discovery* that it emboldens others to *Venter* (venture)... *with him. he gaines... life by Deathe*: Radical inversion reveals its basis in the Christian belief in an (eternal) afterlife.

ll. 23–6.   *His Children... turnd to stone*: Inversion persists in the closing metaphors of inert forms, painted canvas and carved stone, that figure the surviving family and friends.

EPITHALAMIA (WEDDING SONGS): THE GENRE

In early Greek antiquity, the epithalamion was a sexually explicit song sung outside the door of the bridal chamber. It equated wedding with bedding, urging the newly-weds to get on with their primary business of producing offspring. Later classical culture introduced various refinements such as linking the epithalamion with pastoral personages and settings (e.g., shepherds singing in idealized landscapes), personifying the bride and groom as heroes of myth and epic (for example, Helen marrying Menelaus), and making poetic artistry (composition in intricate stanzas) a generic requisite. The epithalamion was enthusiastically revived in Renaissance Italy and France and subsequently in England by Sir Philip Sidney in *Arcadia* and Edmund Spenser in his *Epithalamion* (entered for publication in the Stationers' Register on 19 November 1594).

Epithalamium (MS p. 45), titled 'Epithalamion made at Lincolnes Inne' in Poems, *by J.D. (1633)*

Similarities in phrasing and verse-form (stanzas with varying line lengths and inter-linking rhymes anchored by a twelve-syllable final line) strongly suggest that Spenser's *Epithalamion* provided Donne with the rival incentive to compose a wedding song in his own vein and style. Information regarding the place and date of composition survives in the fuller title, 'Epithalamium made at Lincoln's Inn', found in Group 2 manuscripts of Donne's poetry. (For characterizations of the contents and editorial significance of manuscript Groups 1, 2, and 3 of Donne's verse, see *The Divine Poems*, ed. Helen Gardner, rev. edn (1978), lvii–lxviii; and *The Satires, Epigrams and Verse Letters*, ed. Wesley Milgate (1967), xli–liv. *The Poems of John Donne*, ed. Herbert J. C. Grierson (1912), 2:cxi–cxii, originated these manuscript groupings.)

The last entry on Donne the law student in the records of Lincoln's Inn, on 26 November 1594, notes his election to serve jointly as master of the revels for the upcoming Christmas season. Since Donne did not eventually serve in this capacity, that fact has been speculatively taken to indicate the pressure he was under to compose his 'Epithalamium' for inclusion in the Inn's Christmas celebrations (Bald, *Donne: A Life*, 57). There is, however, the further complication that Spenser's *Epithalamion* did not appear in print until 1595. Perhaps Donne wrote his 'Epithalamium' for midsummer festivities in the latter year. Whatever the merits of these speculations, their linkage of this poem with the free-spirited holiday revels of law students prepares the reader for a range of discordant elements (satire, parody, sexual explicitness, physical violence, and death) that protrude like outcroppings in the enveloping lyric loveliness of this wedding song.

ll. 1–12. *The sun beames...spred*: Cf. 'His golden beame upon the hils doth spred' (Spenser, *Epithalamion*, l. 20). *your bodyes print...doth dint*: In Donne's day, corpses might be wrapped in wool and buried without a coffin. Multiple images of death characterize this epithalamium. *You...other you*: the bride and bridegroom; in friendship and marriage theory, love makes two persons one, and one person two. *an other...more nigh*: An oblique gesture toward the virginity that the bride brings to the marriage bed. *perfection and a womans name*: That a woman was incomplete as a woman until she joined with a man in sexual union was an early modern commonplace. It was rooted in the Aristotelian doctrine that the male contributed the form (soul) and the female the matter (flesh and blood) in the conception of an infant. This one-sided conclusion regarding female imperfection (for why not male imperfection also, since conception requires both male and female?) evidently turns on the further presumption of the superiority of soul to body and the idea that motherhood is a woman's destiny.

ll. 13–22. *Daughters of London... These rites*: An apparent parody of Spenser's address to 'merchants daughters' to confirm with their admiration the beauty and virtue of the bride, Elizabeth Boyle, who became Spenser's wife (*Epithalamion*, ll. 167–79). *You which are Angels... Thousands of Angels*: With this now familiar wordplay on 'angel' as well as the sardonic idea that the gold coins might have superior attraction for a man, cf. Elegy 1, ll. 9–90. *Conceitedly dres...fitt fuell*: Clothe her in such a fashion that the symbolism of *every flower and Jewell* kindles the bridegroom's desire. *Flora*: the ancient Roman goddess of flowers and spring. *Inde*: India, land of precious gems.

ll. 25–34. *frolique Patriciäns*: revelling young nobles accompanying the bridegroom. *Sonnes of these Senators*: Donne the preacher would refer to the wealthy aldermen, officials, and merchants of the City as 'Senators of London' and warn them of spendthrift sons (*Sermons*, 1.208). *Barrells*: receptacles. *Yee Cuntrymen... love none*: 'Every man as he loveth, quoth the goodman [yeoman farmer], when that he kissed his cow' (John Heywood, *Dialogue of Proverbs* (1546; rpt. 1963), 138). *those fellowships*: A possible reference to attendees from Inns of Court other than Lincoln's Inn or to the attendees' former affiliations with Oxford and Cambridge colleges. *Of study...Hermaphroditts*: Conjoined legal studies and revelry, possibly with a submerged allusion to young men playing the parts of the bride and her attendants. These circumstantial references strengthen the plausibility of a Lincoln's Inn setting for a performative recital of this poem. *the Temple*: Spenser's term for the church in which the pair will be wedded

(*Epithalamion*, l. 204); and a possible punning reference to the chapel of the Inner and Middle Temples, two of the Inns of Court. *strawd*: strewn. *no other thing*: It is surprising that a *sober virgin* can be found in the City and that the bridegroom is marrying such a one in preference to, say, a woman who brings with her *Thousands of Angels*.

ll. 39–45.　*mistically joyned*: The Church of England's 'Form or Solemnization of Matrimony' characterizes marriage as 'signifying unto us the mystical union that is betwixt Christ and his Church' (*Book of Common Prayer* (1559), 290). *thy leane and hunger starvëd wombe ... ther tombe*: The church's undercroft or burial chapel is figured as a belly craving to be filled with dead bodies. Donne may be playing on the etymology of sarcophagus, a term for a stone coffin, which literally means 'flesh-eater' in Greek. *elder claymes*: involvements with previous lovers. *Which might ... dissever*: 'What therefore God hath joined together, let not man put asunder' (Matthew 19:6; Mark 10:9).

ll. 54–8.　*the Sun still ... stands still*: Cf. Spenser, 'Ah when will this long weary day have end, ... Hast thee O fayrest Planet to thy home ... Thy tyred steedes long since have need of rest' (*Epithalamion*, ll. 278–84). Spenser may furnish Donne with a precedent for the summer solstice as the occasion of a wedding, or Donne may be signalling that his occasion is the midsummer revels at Lincoln's Inn. *the worlds half frame*: the dome-like appearance of the sky overhead.

ll. 61–71.　*amorous evening star*: Venus as Hesperus, condensing Spenser's 'bright evening star ... glorious lampe of love' (*Epithalamion*, ll. 286–8). *lest ... the same*: lest she return as a virgin still.

ll. 73–82.　*in thy nuptiall bed ... pleasing sacrifice*: The bride's purity and passivity are likened to the young, unblemished sacrificial animals of classical Greek and Roman ritual and the Old Testament. Donne assigns the bridegroom the place of the deity for whom animal sacrifice was performed. *now disposses ... best in nakednes*: Cf. Elegy 8, ll. 5–11, 33–5. *a better state*: motherhood. Paradoxically, the *grave* precedes the *cradle*. *No more ... I may be, but I ame*: The contrasting moods of the verbs convey the shift from potentiality to actuality in the bride's womanhood, signalling that the action is about to reach (poetic and mimetic) completion. The bride will shortly *put on perfection and a womans name*.

ll. 85–94.　*Ev'n like ... doth ly | Like an appointed lambe*: Serial similes intensify the earlier associations of sacred sacrifice with the sexual consummation reached by the bride and the groom. Donne skirts blasphemy in comparing the bride with the Lamb of God, Christ, as figured in the New Testament (John 1:29, 36; 1 Peter 1:19; Revelation 5:6) and in the 'Agnus Dei' of Christian liturgy. *embowell*: stick his knife into. This bold touch of erotic sadism draws on the unbridled revelry of a mock wedding, enacted by fellow law students—all of whom would have been men, and familiar associates to one degree or another. There is no woman to be penetrated and 'perfected'. This wedding song of Donne's celebrates a fictive, not a real-life union, as Spenser's was.

VERSE LETTERS TO MALE FRIENDS: THE GENRE

Throughout its history the genre of the verse letter (*epistula*) has attracted comparatively little critical attention, even though its preeminent classical practitioner was Horace, who made it a vehicle for one of his major moral and poetic themes: the superiority of country retirement to city life. One recurrent problem is the difficulty of fixing the genre's boundaries: if an address to some person is inserted into a lyric, a satire, an extended description, or a sequence of reflections in verse, the whole composition can be termed a verse letter. This indeterminacy is well exemplified by the first poem in the series contained in the Westmoreland manuscript—Donne's evocation of a prodigious storm at sea.

Thomas Lodge, a contemporary of Donne's, recognized that the verse letter was something of an innovation in his time. He carefully staked his own claim to priority in the preface to *A Fig for Momus* (1595): 'For my *Epistles*, they are in that kind, wherein no Englishman of our time hath publiquely written' (A3–A4). 'Publiquely' is the key word here. Conceived as free-standing compositions rather than commendatory or dedicatory verses prefixed to works of other kinds, verse letters had certainly been circulated in manuscript by Donne and others before Lodge's appeared in print.

Donne's earliest verse letters—also, evidently, his earliest surviving poems—seem to have evolved out of short commendations of his friends' writings into expanded discussions of his and their writings and other pursuits. In these tentative expressions that apparently begin around 1592, Donne, like many young poets, preoccupies himself with the writing of poetry, extolling his friends' productions while downplaying his own. Some uncertainty about the direction he should take and his place in the world clings to these early poetic efforts. As he strains for striking effects to convey the warmth of his personal attachments, Donne experiments with verse form and with imagery, sometimes even resorting to blasphemous or erotically sensational images. In particular, Donne and the Woodward brothers, Thomas and Rowland, figure their mutual poetic passions as lesbian lovemaking by their personal Muses. In view of this precedent, it is curious that authorship of the Ovidian heroic verse epistle, 'Sappho to Philaenis', ascribed to Donne in the first edition of his poems (1633) and in the otherwise highly regarded Group 2 manuscripts of his poetry, should still be so consistently doubted by editors.

Around 1597–8 Donne's maturing mode of composition makes its appearance in such reflectively charged verse letters as 'Sir, more than kisses', written to Sir Henry Wotton, and 'Like one who 'in her third widdowhed', written to Rowland Woodward. His newly assured handling of the genre reveals its potential for conceptual originality and formal mastery. Another outstanding example is the searching personal advice given to Sir Henry Goodyere in 'Who makes the Past a Patterne for next yeare', found in the Dowden manuscript, and probably dated 1608–9. Donne subsumes his earlier concerns in broadened and deepened considerations of personal and public morality, often in the mordant observations on court and city life that his verse letters share with his satires. He takes stock of his priorities and cultivates his relations with others in complex articulations of what he termed 'my second religion, friendship'.

As in his satires, Donne's chief subject in his verse letters to male friends is the dichotomy between surface appearances and underlying realities. He writes of integrity in mind and spirit and the imperative to cultivate (frequently with agricultural metaphors) one's moral and spiritual capacities so as to direct them virtuously under God's guidance. Donne also writes about making the virtue thus cultivated perceptible in one's conduct. The conduct to be striven towards will display a knowledge of right action while exposing the self to others' judgement. Self-examination, application of the will to control what is base and to foster what is right and honorable in oneself—these are the concerns of Donne's verse letters to male friends. Their thematic intensity and their management of stanzaic form situate Donne's achievements above even Ben Jonson's in rivalling the frankness, seriousness, and manliness of expression that Horace had introduced to this genre.

To Mr C. B. (MS p. 49), titled 'The Storme' in Poems, by J.D. *(1633), its first appearance in print, as well as in one Group 1 manuscript and one Group 2 manuscript*

Mr C. B. Christopher Brooke was one of Donne's closest friends; see the Introduction. From 1610 onwards, Brooke was a bencher and treasurer of Lincoln's Inn (1623–4); he also served six terms in Parliament (1604–26).

The precision and immediacy of Donne's meteorological description in 'The Storme' are unequalled in the poetry of his age. He innovates even more decisively, however, in his psychologically acute portrayal of the storm as experienced by the sailors. This poem's survival in an unusually large number of manuscripts attests the recognition of Donne's originality by seventeenth-century readers. This may account for the pride of place assigned to this poem in the sequence of verse letters that Rowland Woodward copied into the Westmoreland manuscript.

Westmoreland lacks Donne's 'The Calme', a companion piece to 'The Storme' and (presumably) also addressed to Christopher Brooke. The Dowden manuscript, however, does contain 'The Calme'. For its text, see pp. 181–2 above.

ll. 1–8. *Thou . . . by these shalt know . . . our passage*: Donne writes as a participant in an English naval action against Spain ('the Islands expedition'). Sixty ships set sail on 3 June 1597 under the command of Robert Devereux, earl of Essex, and sixty more on 9 July with Lord Thomas Howard as vice admiral and Sir Walter Raleigh as rear admiral. However, the objectives of attacking the Spanish war fleet in Ferrol, capturing Spanish treasure ships returning from the West Indies, and taking the Spanish stronghold in the Azores were brought to nothing within a few days at sea by a cataclysmic storm. When the heavily damaged English fleet returned to Plymouth for repairs in mid-July, Donne remained with the expedition. He probably sent his lines to Brooke from Plymouth before the fleet undertook to sail again on 17 August. *Thou, which art I*: In early modern friendship theory, the friend is another self, an 'alter ego'. See Laurie Shannon, *Sovereign Amity: Figures of Friendship in Shakespearean Contexts* (2002). *Hilliard*: Nicholas Hilliard (1547–1619) was the foremost miniaturist of the reigns of Elizabeth I and James I. *dignifyde*: honored, exalted.

ll. 9–23.   *England... sigh'd a wind | Which... did find | Such strong resistance, that it selfe it threw | Downward agayne*: The personification is that of England and her patriotic *sonnes*, who acknowledge her motherhood fully (*to' whom we owe, what we be and have*) and seek to advance her *Honor*. Mother England, however, can view her sons' naval expedition only as impending *Misery* from unpredictable *Fates or Fortunes drifts*. Her sigh on her sons' behalf, emitting from her *pregnant intrails* (the bowels of the earth, where winds were believed to originate) is *a wind* that the cold middle region of the air (believed to be the source of snow, hail, and meteors) deflects back upon the earth. There it encounters the becalmed ships *in the Port*, likened to *prisoners which ly but for fees*: persons who have served their time but remain in detention because they cannot pay the jailer's charges. *leese*: lose. *Sara' her swelling joyd to see*: Sarah, Abraham's formerly barren wife, bore him a son, Isaac, when both parents were in old age (Genesis 21:6–7). *swole*: swelled.

ll. 25–34.   Mother England's sighing is felt benevolently by sailors but ironically precipitates a war of winds, turbulence, and an increasingly violent weather system on the open seas. *Jonah, I... curse those men | Who... did wake thee then*: Jonah 1:4–6.

ll. 37–50.   *when I wakd... I saw not*: Blindness figures the absence of morning light. *Thousands our noyses were, yet we... Could none by his right name, but Thunder call*: As with sight, so with sound: the thunderclaps drown out the sailors' cries and groans. *Like jealous husbands what they would not know*: Donne adapts Ovid's wry observation: 'to no husband are accusations of misdeeds welcome | nor, even though he hears, do they please him' (*Amores*, 2.2.51–2).

ll. 52–74.   *feare away*: frighten away. *Wast* (waist): the midsection of the ship, where the curve of the deck was lowest, and water was prone to collect—hence, *With a salt dropsy cloy'd*. *one hang'd in chaines*: a contemporary method of executing condemned murderers. *our Ordnance... Strive to breake loose*. In 'A larger Relation of the... Iland Voyage' Sir Arthur Gorges, captain of Raleigh's ship, noted of the storm's violence that 'we looked hourely when the Orlope [lowest deck] would fall, and the ordnance sinke downe to the keele' (*Purchas His Pilgrimage, or Relations of the World* (1613; facs. 1907), 20:25). *the Bermuda calme*: Raleigh termed 'the *Bermudas* a hellish sea for thunder, lightning, and stormes' (*Discoverie of Bermuda* (1596), 96). *All things are one... Doth cover*: In this impenetrable darkness everything has been reduced to one thing; yet that one thing cannot be anything, because a universal formlessness obscures all. The primordial chaos out of which God created the world has come again, *except God say | Another Fiat* ('Let there be'—the Creator's command in Genesis 1) we *shall have no more Day*. John Manningham echoed Donne in his retrospective account of this storm: 'It was soe darke a storme, that a man could never looke for day, unles God would have said againe *Fiat Lux*' (*Diary*, ed. John Bruce (1868), 154).

To Mr H.W. ('Here' is no more news') (MS p. 51)

Mr H. W. Henry Wotton (1568–1639) went from Winchester College to New College, Oxford, in 1584, subsequently transferring to Hart Hall, where Donne enrolled in October of that year. The two became friends. After taking his B.A. from Queen's College, Oxford, in 1588, Wotton travelled and studied in Germany, Italy, France, and Switzerland for several years, acquiring fluency in German and French while strengthening his Protestantism and patriotism through exposure to politics and diplomacy in which religious antagonisms loomed large. On returning home, Wotton was appointed as a secretary to Essex in late 1594. In the spring of 1596 Wotton and Donne joined the naval expedition against Cadiz, and they sailed together again in the summer of 1597 on the fruitless expedition to the Azores (the setting for 'To C. B.' ('The Storme').

20 July 1598. At Court. The specific date and place for this verse letter enables the context of this verse letter to be identified. On 1 July the court that Donne was attending, probably at Greenwich, witnessed a gross insult to Queen Elizabeth. During a fierce disagreement over who should be appointed to lead a force to suppress insurrection in Ireland, the earl of Essex turned his back on his sovereign, whereupon she struck him on the ear, bidding him go and be hanged. Retiring from court in a fury, Essex did not seek reinstatement in the royal favour until September. Meanwhile, the hostilities between England and Spain remained a source of acute anxiety. Donne's dismissive tone in this verse letter may be compared with his scathing observations on the corruption and venality of the court in Satire 4.

ll. 2–6.   *Tell you...for newes*: Tell you about the Cadiz or Islands expeditions. The 'Islands of St. Michael' was an alternative name for the Azores. Since Donne and Wotton had participated in both expeditions, for Donne to tell Wotton such a *tale* would be no *newes* whatever. / The upward sloping lines marking the start of each stanza in triple rhyme were very probably a feature of the original text in Donne's own handwriting, as they are in his autograph text of another verse letter in triple-rhymed stanzas, 'To the Lady Carey and Mrs Essex Riche, from Amiens'. Because of their likely authorial origins, these markings are reproduced just as Rowland Woodward inserted them. *stomacks*: appetites. *so may God frowne*: God might disapprove (of Donne's paradoxical behaviour in frequenting the court or London to intensify his loathing for these venues).

ll. 10–15.   *Commissary*: deputy or representative, especially one in the service of a religious official. *Fate as Gods Commissary* registers the speaker's Christian perspective. *seely*: simple. *wishing prayers*: pious desires. *neat*: pure. *Indians 'gainst Spanish hostes*: Bartolomé de las Casas authored the period's starkest account of atrocities committed by Spanish troops against natives of Mexico, Peru, and the West Indies; an English translation, *The Spanish Colonie, or Briefe Chronicle of the Acts of the Spaniardes*, appeared in 1583.

ll. 16–25.   *Suspicious boldnes...belongs*: In the Elizabethan court of the 1590s, the factions gathered around the Cecils and Essex spied and counter-spied on one another as they jockeyed for the queen's favor and control of policy and patronage. *Mimick Antiques*: posturing, laughable figures. *egregious*

gests: significant doings. *Chests*, a variant form of the noun 'chess', supplies a
needed rhyme. The author of *Ludus Scacchiae: Chess-play…Translated…by
G. B.* (1597) declares that chess 'breedeth in the players, a certaine
study,…wherein both Counsellers at home and Captaines abroade may
picke out of these wooden peeces some pretty pollicy, both how to governe
their subjects in peace, and howe to leade or conduct lively men in…warre'
(Preface). *'tis incongruity to smile*: the thought of court politics is unlikely to
bring a smile to anyone's face.

To Mr H. W. ('Sir, more than kisses, letters mingle soules') (MS p. 52)

Mr H. W. On Henry Wotton, see the headnote to the preceding poem. The present
poem seems to date between the late spring and early fall of 1598, when Wotton and
Donne were seeking employment at court.

'Sir, more than kisses' participates in a literary debate among some of the young
men associated with the earl of Essex, on Horace's question: Which life is best—that
at court, in the city, or in the country? A copy of Francis Bacon's poetic contribution
to the debate, 'The world's a bubble', was preserved among Wotton's papers; Donne
echoes Bacon's lines in ll. 19–20. Wotton's poetic contribution, headed in several
manuscripts 'To J.D. from Mr H.W.', began, 'Worthie Sir: | 'Tis not a coate of gray
or Shepheards life.' An allusion to this debate by another contemporary bears a date
of April 1598, which helps to situate these exchanges that would remain timely until
(at least) September 1598, when Essex was reinstated in Elizabeth's favour.

ll. 1–5.   *letters mingle soules*: The church father Ambrose reflected on this genre 'in
which we intermingle our soul with our friend, and pour out our mind to
him' (*Epistulae, Patrologia Latina*, 16:1151). *This ease controules*: This easing
(of the soul in letter-writing) holds in check. *these*: either 'friends' or 'letters
to friends'. *Ideate*: conceive of. *I should wither in one day*: Psalm 102:11: 'I am
withered like grass'. *bottle*: bundle. *locke*: tuft. Donne imagines his vital
energies as having the wispiness of grass, which can dry quickly into hay.

ll. 7–13.   *Life is a voyage*: The commonplace is apt; Donne and Wotton had recently
returned from the Islands expedition. *Remoraes*: sucking-fish (*Echeneis rem-
ora*) capable, according to Pliny, of stopping a ship's course (*Historia natu-
ralis*, 32.1.2–6). *than pitche they staine worse*: Ecclesiasticus 13:1: 'he that
toucheth pitch shall be defiled'. *even line*: the equator, equidistant from *th'
adverse Icy Poles* (North and South). *two temperate regions*: the tropic of
Cancer in the northern hemisphere, and the tropic of Capricorn in the
southern.

l. 15.   *Parch'd in the Court, and in the Cuntry frozen*: A letter written to Goodyere in
late 1609 from Mitcham, where the Donnes were living in retirement after
their marriage, would probe this contrast more deeply: 'they which dwell far-
thest from the Sun,…have longer daies, better appetites, better digestion,
better growth, and longer life: And all these advantages have their mindes
who are well removed from the scorchings…of the worlds glory: but nei-
ther of our lives are in such extremes; for you living at Court without

ambition, which would burn you,...live in the Sun, not in the fire: And
I which live in the Country without stupefying, am not in darknesse, but
in shadow...subject to the barbarousnesse and insipid dulnesse of the
Country' (*Letters*, 62–3).

ll. 17–22. *Dung and Garlick*: Smelly substances associated with opposite ends of
the alimentary tract. *Scorpion and Torpedo*: Pliny asserted that the *Scorpion*
could cure its own sting if its ashes were ingested in a drink, while the
Torpedo, or electric ray, could deliver only a numbing shock (*Historia natu-
ralis*, 11.30.90; 32.2.7). *Cityes are worst of all three*: In the poem titled 'The
world's a bubble' mentioned in the headnote earlier, Bacon had written:
'And where's a city from all vice so free | But may be termed the worst of
all three?' *Of all three | (O knotty riddle) each is worst equally*: Donne
would later apply the phrase 'O knotty riddle' to the Trinity in his holy
sonnet beginning 'Father, as part of his double interest', l. 3. *Carcases as if
no such ther were*: dead bodies in the form of the walking dead.

ll. 25–8. *no Good | Gaind, as Habitts, not borne*: Donne works off a pair of Thomistic
definitions: human virtues are habits, that is, behaviours attributable to
understanding or reason; and original sin is an inborn condition stemming
from our corrupt nature after the Fall (Aquinas, *Summa Theologica*,
1a2.55.3; 1a2.82.1). *become Beasts, and prone to more Evills*: In the country,
men become as beasts, but more liable to sin, because while beasts lack the
understanding required to develop virtue, they are also devoid of original
sin. *blocks*: blockheads.

ll. 29–36. *in the first Chaos, confusedlie | Each Elements qualityes were in th' other three*:
Aristotle asserted that fire, air, water, and earth originate from one another,
and each of them exists potentially in each (*Meterologica*, 1.3.339a–b). *So
Pride, Lust, Covetise...all are in all*: The three named deadly sins are ele-
mental in the moral universe and typical of country, court, and city, respec-
tively. Since the contemporary moral universe is in a state of chaos, each of
these three sins is equally in all three places. *And mingled thus, ther issue'
incestuous*: Even more monstrous sins result from the mingling of the three
closely related deadly sins. *denizend*: naturalized as a resident and citizen.
barbarous: classed as an outsider and alien, as the so-called 'barbarians'
were by the ancient Greeks. *lock*: confine, restrain.

ll. 39–42. *in best understandings, sinne began*: Donne the preacher would reflect: 'God
made this whole world...as...an instrument, perfectly in tune:...; the best
understandings, Angels and Men, put this instrument out of tune' (*Sermons*,
2:170). *Only perchance Beasts...whight integritee*: Donne the preacher
would elaborate: 'Ever since' he fell, 'man...expresses more of the nature
of the Beast than of his own...no creature but man...degenerates will-
ingly from his naturall Dignity. Those degrees of goodnesse, which
God imprinted in them at first, they preserve still' (*Sermons*, 9:372).
Utopian: ideally raised and trained, as in Sir Thomas More's *Utopia*
(1516); Donne's use of the adjective is unusually modern. *old Italian*:
A stereotype of Italians as degenerate and corrupt was current in later
sixteenth-century England.

ll. 47–8. *Bee then…in thy selfe dwell*: 'Reside in yourself,' exhorted the Roman satirist Persius (*Satires*, 4.52). *Inne*: lodge temporarily. *Continuance maketh Hell*: Staying in any one place—country, court, or city—will infect one with damnable evils.

ll. 59–62. *Galenist*: Adherent of the method of the ancient Greek physician Claudius Galen, who theorized health as the harmonious balance of hot, cold, moist, and dry humours in the body and accordingly administered medicines to correct excess or deficiency. Donne is saying that where a deficiency is good, *do not add | Correctives, but…purge the badd*. *Chimicks*: Physicians such as Paracelsus (Philipp von Hohenheim, 1493–1541) who relied on chemical preparations to induce diarrhea or vomiting.

ll. 65–70. *German Schismes*: The divided geopolitical situation of Germany (duke-doms, princedoms, free cities) continually generated local conflicts of a secular as well as religious nature. *lightnes | Of France*: The French were proverbial for changefulness in their moods, opinions, and tastes. *Italyes faythlesnes*: *Faythlesnes* is a pun with several senses—sexual infidelity, per-sonal disloyalty, irreligion or false religion, all viewed from an English perspective. *that Faythe, which you caryed forthe*: the post-Reformation 'settlement' of the Church of England under Elizabeth. *Donne*: This pun was evidently irresistible. When Donne resigned as reader in divinity at Lincoln's Inn to become dean of St Paul's Cathedral, the benchers offi-cially noted the effect of the new appointment: 'he cannot conveniently supply the place of public Preacher of God's Word in this House, as for-merly he hath Donne' (*The Records of the Honorable Society of Lincoln's Inn: The Black Books*, ed. W. P. Baildon (1898), 2:229).

To Mr. R.W. ('Like one who' in her third widowhed doth profes') (MS p. 54)

Mr. R. W. On the personal relations of Rowland Woodward and Donne, see the Introduction. This verse letter is apparently a response to a request by Woodward for copies of other poems that Donne had written. It is found in a number of manuscript collections grouped with 'Thou which art I' ('The Storme'), 'Here's no more newes', and 'Sir, more than kisses'—verse letters all dating to around 1597–9. The triple-rhymed stanzas of this verse letter are demarcated with the upward sloping lines that evidently originated with Donne himself.

ll. 1–6. *widowhed*: Only a few words in present-day English (Godhead, maiden-head) retain the archaic suffix that is Donne's preferred form of this word. *tir'd to a retirednes*: attired in a veil and habit like an avowed recluse. *Since she to few…thornes are growne*: Donne charges himself not only with hav-ing written his elegies and his satires, but also with having circulated them. *weedes…thornes*: In his *A Hundredth Sundrie Flowres* (1573), revised as *Posies* (1575), George Gascoigne had used such labels to differentiate among specimens of his verse that had no perceptible moral or didactic purpose ('weeds'), had perceptible moral or didactic purpose ('herbs'), or celebrated beauty and virtue ('posies').

ll. 7–12.   *use…love…Betroth'd to no one…no adulteree*: Donne's image defends the exercise of his poetic talent and his love of poetry. Since he has no vocation (perhaps indicating that he is not yet employed as Egerton's secretary), he can and does play the field. *Omissions of good, ill, as ill deedes be*: Self-defence gives way to self-reproach with religious overtones. The general confession in the Order for Morning Prayer contains the admission, 'We have left undone those things which we ought to have done' (*Book of Common Prayer* (1559), 50). *vanity weighs…as sin*: God accounts the *vanity* of *poetry* as reprehensible as *sin* because time, energy, and opportunities for doing good are frittered away.

ll. 13–15.   *their first whight*: Donne implies that newborn infants are sinless. According to the Church of England, however, the most that could be claimed was that newborn infants had not yet committed sin. *yet wee | May clothe them*: Donne endows human initiative with greater efficacy than the Church of England explicitly allowed. It held that public baptism is the only means of remitting the soul's accountability for original sin (*Book of Common Prayer* (1559), 270). *deare honestee*: precious virtue. *imputes*: treats as equivalent to.

ll. 17–19.   *Wise, valiant, sober, just*: Wisdom, courage, temperance, justice are the cardinal virtues of classical antiquity (Plato, *Republic*, 442c.58). *names… discretione*: These can be used as names for questionable actions by anyone discreet enough to cover up their vices. *Seeke we…in our selves*: Let us then seek to know ourselves as we really are, and not as we appear. 'I had rather understand my selfe well in my selfe, than in Cicero' (Montaigne, *Essays*, trans. John Florio, Tudor Translations (1893), 3:338–9).

ll. 20–4.   *Men force the Sun…with a christall glas*: A so-called 'burning glass' was a large convex lens—or, in its earlier form, an assemblage of polygonal mirrors—that concentrated the sun's rays onto a small area, causing the exposed surface to ignite. The most notable use was credited to the Greek mathematician Archimedes, who incinerated Roman ships besieging the port of Syracuse in 212 BCE. *if we into our selves will turne*: Augustine exhorted, 'Do not go outside, return into yourself; truth resides in the inner man' (*De vera Religione* [On true Religion], 39.72; *PL*, 34:154). *outburne*: burn out. *straw*: trifling stuff.

ll. 25–8.   *Phisitians*: Here, alchemists. *oyle*: the liquid form of any substance. *the soule of simples*: the spiritual or purest element in a substance having a single ingredient. *Places…still warme*: Infusion typically involved heating to liquefy or soften the substances being combined. *So works retirednesse in us*: In retirement, virtue can be infused into our inner selves as a liquid is infused into the heart of a single substance.

ll. 31–3.   *but Farmers*: only cultivators of land we do not own. God is in possession, as clarified by the subsequent allusions to Jesus's admonition in Matthew 6:20 (*uplay | Much, much dear treasure*) and to the last judgment (*the great rent day*) as figured in Jesus's parable of the talents in Matthew 19:19. The day of one's death was a lesser rent day, as Donne the preacher would declare: 'We know, O Lord, that our Rent due to thee is our Soule, and the day of our death is the day, and our Death-bed the place, where this rent is to be paid' (*Sermons*, 8:61).

l. 34. *Manure*: Cultivate—from French manoeuvrer (work by hand, handle, manage). This sense of this verb declined in English from the sixteenth century onwards as the noun 'manure' became a euphuism for dung. *to thy selfe be' aprov'd*: 'Desire finally to satisfy your own self' (Epictetus, *Discourses*, 2.18.19).

To Mr. T. W. ('All haile sweet Poet, more full of more strong fyre') (MS p. 56)

Mr. T. W. The addressee has been plausibly identified as Thomas Woodward, a younger brother of Rowland, and four years younger than Donne. A Thomas Woodward matriculated as a pensioner from Clare College, Cambridge, in 1593, and Thomas Woodward 'of Buckinghamshire' was admitted to Lincoln's Inn on 8 October 1597. These may or may not be the same person. Overall, the likelihood is that Donne came to know Thomas through his familiarity with Rowland.

This verse letter praises T. W.'s merit as a poet and openly declares erotic attraction. The latter caused offence to a later reader of Westmoreland who, with a different pen and ink, heavily overwrote l. 12 and half of ll. 13 and 15. Assuming that Rowland's younger brother would not have written poetry worthy of commendation before about the age of sixteen, when adolescent charms would also be manifest, a date of *c.*1592 seems plausible for 'All haile sweet Poet'. Donne's subject, the writing of poetry, adds credence to an early date.

ll. 4–8. *witt and art*: native ability and acquired skill—a frequent pairing in the literature of the age. *mans firm stay . . . midday*: T. W.'s poetic mastery is an assured achievement, compared with which all other poets' *works* will seem either merely promising or in decline.

ll. 9–20. *better . . . envied than pitied*: Proverbial. *But care not for mee*: But thou dost not care for me. *a foole*: In aspiring to T. W.'s love. *suspect* (a noun stressed on its second syllable): suspicion. *surquedry*: arrogance, presumption.

ll. 26–32. *The Painters bad god made a good devill*: The source of this allusion has not been traced, but its gist is clear: a bad example of one thing can be a good example of its opposite. *foyle*: to set off T. W.'s brilliance. *Zanee* (zany): imitative clown, close in sense to *Ape* (l. 32).

[To Mr. J. D. ('Thou sendst me prose and rimes; I send, for those') (MS p. 57)]

This verse letter is evidently addressed to Donne and presumably authored by Thomas Woodward as part of an exchange that revels in poetic licence taken to extremes: facetious exploitation of religious terminology and lesbian erotics (two Muses' reciprocal stimulation) figuring the impetus to write verse.

ll. 2–20. *or . . . or*: either . . . or. *fyre of heaven*: the sun. *conferr*: bring together—a no longer current sense. *pithe*: vigor. *tribadree* (tribadry, from Greek *tribeín*, to rub): lesbian lovemaking. *Bassaes adultery*: In Martial's epigram, Bassa had the reputation of a Lucretia for chastity because she was never seen with men, only with women. But since Bassa had sexual relations with these women, she inspired the composition of a riddle: 'There, where no man is, may be adultery' (*Epigrams*, 1. 90). *lecheree*: lustful abandon. *gott*: begot.

To Mr. T. W. ('Hast thee, harsh verse, as fast 'as thy lame measure') (MS p. 57)

The reference to plague conditions in ll. 11–12 suggests a date for this verse letter between August 1592 and sometime in 1594, a period when London witnessed a fresh outbreak and the danger of contagion persisted for over a year and a half. An early reader again took offence at portions of this poem, heavily overwriting the last half of l. 2 as well as ll. 5–6 and ll. 9–10.

ll. 1–14.   *harsh verse . . . lame measure*: Donne echoes 'harsh and lame' in l. 3 of 'To J. D.'. *payne and pleasure*: a major cliché of Petrarchan love poetry, conjoining opposites to convey the lover's extreme changes of mood and feeling. *I ame thy creator, thou my saviour*: Donne has created the verse, which pleads for mercy and favor, on the expectation that T. W. will grant Donne his love. *all questions . . . / Both of the place and paynes of hell*. Cf. Satire 2, l. 36, and *First Anniversary*, ll. 295–8. *hell is but privation*. Donne the preacher offers the formulation, 'Privation of the presence of God, is Hell' (*Sermons*, 1:186). *this earths habitation*: this life. *by you my love is sent*: Donne's verses convey his love to T. W., who is not in London, perhaps because of the plague. *you' are my [pawnes] or els my testament*: If Donne escapes the plague and lives, his verses will serve as pledges of his love. If he dies of the plague, his verses will serve as his *testament*, implying that he has only these movable assets to bequeath and no property, which would necessitate a will. *[pawnes]*: objects of some worth, on the basis of which credit is secured. The consistent reading of other manuscripts supplies the blank at this point in Westmoreland.

To L. of D. ('See, Sir, how as the suns hott masculine flame') (MS p. 58)

Rowland Woodward's caption for this sonnet of Donne's seemingly gestures towards Ferdinando Stanley (1559–1594), 5th earl of Derby, as its recipient. Peers with place-name titles were often referred to as 'my Lord of X'. Ferdinando, whose previous title was Lord Strange, succeeded to his earldom on 25 September 1593 but held it less than a year, dying on 16 April 1594. A date for Donne's sonnet within this interval fits well with the earl's service as a member of Parliament during this period, when he would have resided in London.

  Stanley's taste for erotic verse can be inferred from Nashe's dedication of his 'Choice of Valentines' to the earl; the subject of this pornographic verse narrative was a visit to a London brothel. Donne writes more suavely but with similar suggestiveness. The earl's poetic creativity has fathered seven *songs* on Donne, of which he is sending six. Donne terms these offspring *strange creatures*—possibly punning on the name 'Strange'. The placement of the sonnet 'See, Sir' in the manuscript context of erotically explicit lyrics to and from T. W. intensifies the associations of sexually uninhibited conduct with the libertine poetic expression shared by this group of verse letters as a whole. Such associations are worth pursuing for their possible relevance to the identity of the seven songs to which Donne refers.

Eight of Donne's lyrics carry the designation 'Song' in earlier seventeenth-century manuscripts. These include 'Goe, and catch a falling Starr', 'Sweetest Love I doe not goe', 'Send home my long strayd eyes to mee' (elsewhere titled 'The Message'), 'Come live with mee, and be my Love' (elsewhere titled 'The Baite'), 'Hee is starke madd, who ever sayes' (elsewhere titled 'The Broken Heart'), 'I can love both fayre and browne' (elsewhere titled 'The Indifferent'), 'I am two fooles, I knowe' (elsewhere titled 'The Triple Foole'), and 'When I dyed last, and Deare, I dye' (elsewhere titled 'The Legacie'). The label 'Song', however, does not exhaust the category of Donne's lyrics that were actually sung. In addition to musical settings for 'Goe, and catch', 'Sweetest Love', and 'Send home', whole or partial settings survive for 'Tis true, 'tis day, what though it bee?' (elsewhere titled 'Breake of Day'), and 'When by thy scorne, O murdresse' (elsewhere titled 'The Apparition'), 'Good we must love, and must hate ill' (elsewhere titled 'Communitie'), and 'Some man unworthy to be possessor' (elsewhere titled 'Confined Love').

Although a number of the lyrics designated 'Song' and the lyrics with musical settings are likely to postdate 1592–4, it is noteworthy that seven of them feature themes of sexual freedom and promiscuity or their obverse, sexual disillusion. They include 'Goe, and catch', 'Send home', 'I can love both fayre and browne', 'Tis true, 'tis day', 'When by thy scorne', 'Good we must love', and 'Some man unworthy to be possessor'. These may with some plausibility be taken as the *songs* that Donne ascribed to the literary paternity of the earl of Derby. There seems to be no way of guessing which song was held back for the amending of *some maime*. For the backstory of the vexed critical history of 'To E. of D.', see Robbins, *Complete Poems of Donne*, 42–3; for an alternative interpretation, see Starza Smith, *Donne and the Conway Papers*, 184–5.

ll. 1–10. *the suns…flame…Nile's durty slime*: Ovid evokes the Nile's polymorphous fecundity which generates creatures under the influence of the sun's heat (*Metamorphoses*, 1.422–37). *your judgment…your invention, hold*: L. of D. has self-sufficient poetic powers, comparable to those of an *Alchimist* in their capacity to purify what is base and transform bad to good.

To Mr T.W. (*'Pregnant again with th'old twins Hope and Feare'*) (MS p. 58)

This poem and the next work a variation on sonnet form: four units of triple rhymes with a concluding rhymed couplet. Both display the extreme ingenuity of language that typifies the 'religion' of male friendship. T. W.'s failure to write has killed the poet, portrayed as a street beggar, but a *letter* in which T. W. conveys his *love*, imaged as *alms* that provide a meal, has restored him to life. The effect of T. W.'s expressions of love is like what gluttons say about their favorite food: what T. W. offers as sustenance is devouring Donne.

To Mr T.W. ('At once from hence my lines and I depart') (MS p. 59)

A later reader of Westmoreland who took offence at this poem's erotics heavily overwrote with a different pen and ink the latter half of l. 2 , l. 9, and l. 14. This poem is the earliest instance of a genre in which Donne would distinguish himself: the valediction (saying goodbye while offering consolation).

l. 12.   *picture or bare sacrament*: These verse lines may simply convey a likeness of Donne, the sender. Or they may serve as a pledge (*sacrament* in the legal sense) deposited as a bond by parties to a suit. Either way, they will serve as love tokens.

To Mr R.W. ('Zealously my Muse doth salute all thee') (MS p. 59)

Following the sequence of verse letters addressed to his younger brother, Rowland Woodward copies a pair of verse letters that Donne had addressed to him in a loosely sonnet-like form (12 lines in couplets).

ll. 2–11.   *that mistique trinitee*: Subsequently identified as *Thy body, mind, and Muse*. After saluting R. W.'s exalted nature, Donne assimilates what is particular about R. W. to the lofty Renaissance conception of male friendship. *devout*: devoted. *joyne then*: The closing appeal that the two meet again resorts to sex-speak about the Muses—the private language in which Donne and the Woodward brothers articulated their mutual literary passions.

To Mr R.W. ('Muse not that by thy mind thy body 'is led') (MS p. 60)

In this companion poem Donne works with three instances of how human bodies and souls interrelate. The most basic is the *lay mans Genius* (l. 7), an ordinary individual's interdependence of *Body and mind* (l. 8). *The Muse* that is *the Soules Soule | Of Poets* (ll. 8–9) is more complex in her severe effects on sensitive natures like Donne's and R. W.'s (l. 10). But the knowledge that *the Muse*, the capacity for poetic creativity, resides in them *should ease* their *anguish* (l. 9). Most complex and powerful of all are the reciprocities of sensibility that hold between two poets who are close friends. These can be restorative as well as painful.

To Mr C.B. ('Thy friend whom thy deserts to thee enchaine') (MS p. 60)

On Christopher Brooke, see the Introduction. The present context is *this inexcusable occasion* (compulsory set of circumstances) requiring Donne to travel to the north *wher sterne winter ay doth wonne* (reside) (l. 9) and to leave behind in London his *friend* C. B. (l. 1) and the woman he loves (l. 3). A date in the early 1590s is consistent with the thoroughly conventional character of this sonnet: its Petrarchan verse form and equally Petrarchan tone and imagery combine a lover's complaint with hyperbole idealizing the woman. The dual expression of love and longing—for his friend and for his beloved—and the even apportionment of lines between the friend and the beloved are the only poetic features to suggest Donne's individuating touch.

l. 6.   [*this*]. Rowland Woodward accidentally omitted the pronoun, which is found in Group 2 and Group 3 manuscripts of the poems and in the first two printed editions.

To Mr E.G. ('Even as lame things thirst their perfection, so') (MS p. 61)

E. G. has been identified as Everard Guilpin (*c*.1572/3–?), a native of Suffolk (see l. 19). In April 1591 Guilpin matriculated at Gray's Inn, adjacent to Lincoln's Inn. Guilpin modelled a passage in one of his satires published in 1598 (*Skialetheia*, 5.1–36) on Donne's Satire 1, indicating some acquaintance between the two men. The familiar address and the allusions to shared London pastimes also suggest a friendship. A probable date of summer 1592 for this poem can be inferred from the allusions to the deserted streets and empty theatres of plague-ridden London (ll. 7–12). E. G. has already left the city, and the poetic speaker is about to do so.

ll. 1–6.   *Even as... their perfection, so*: Sir Henry Goodyere would echo this line in a poem he addressed to Prince Charles in May 1623, defending the wooing of the Spanish Infanta. Goodyere's couplet reads: 'As lame things thirst for their perfection, soe | These raw conceptions towards our Sunn doe goe' (*Calendar of State Papers Domestic*, 145:585). The underlying conception is from Aquinas, *Summa contra Gentiles*, 3.19–20: 'All things desire...to be like God...The divine being contains the whole fulness of perfection'. *lame*: defective, incomplete. *slimy rimes*: An allusion to the creatures supposedly engendered from the mud of the Nile. *Parnassus*: Donne compliments E.G. as a fellow poet by alluding to the mountain range above Delphi in Greece, where a temple and spring had been dedicated to the Muses. *o'erseest... overseene*: A punning differentiation: E. G. can survey the expanse of London (presumably from Highgate, where his father owned property), while Donne's doings in London have been too closely surveyed (or, perhaps, have not been noticed).

ll. 7–12.   *pleasures dearth...filld with emptines*: Theatres were closed to control the spread of plague in London in the summer of 1592. But other public gatherings were allowed—*bearbaitings* and *law exercise* (mock legal proceedings, vacation activities required of Inns of Court students). An official order of January 1593, however, suspended all public gatherings, 'preaching and divine service at churches excepted' (*Acts of the Privy Council*, 24:31). *spleene*: scorn.

ll. 14–19. *retrive*: retrieve. The variant word-form supplies the rhyme. *a Bee...honey*: A commonplace image of industriousness, applied especially in this period to students eager for learning. *Russian Merchants...retaile it here*: Members of the Muscovy Company traded in Russian ports during the navigable summer months. They sold their imports in England during the winter months when ice blocked Russian ports. *Suffolks Sweets*: the poems that E.G. will compose at his family's country house during the summer vacation. *make thy hive and warehouse this*: E. G. is invited to entrust his compositions to Donne's keeping, as Donne himself entrusted his compositions to Goodyere's keeping.

To Mr R.W. ('If as myne is, thy life a slumber bee') (MS p. 62)

Several topical references enable identification of the date and circumstances of this verse letter to Rowland Woodward. Away from London, the centre of *news* (l. 15), Donne writes to R. W. there. The allusions to *Havens, ships… which both Gospel and sterne threatnings bringe*, and *Guyanaes harvest* (ll. 16–18) indicate that Donne is in Plymouth and that it is early August 1597.

Plymouth was the port to which the English fleet returned in July 1597 after the severe storm evoked in 'The Storme'. On 1 August the commanders Essex and Raleigh went to London to try to persuade Queen Elizabeth to change their fleet's directive and to authorize an attack on Spanish colonies in the Americas, citing evangelization of the natives as a prime motive. This is the gist of Donne's allusions to *ships* as *wing'd Angels* that would *bring Gospel* (to the Indians) and *sterne threatnings* (to the Spanish conquistadors). But the queen rejected the change of mission, insisting that the fleet proceed with the original plan of attacking island possessions of peninsular Spain.

Writing frankly to his close friend, Donne reflects negatively on Elizabeth's decision: *Guiana's harvest* (the plunder anticipated from an attack on this Spanish possession, the reputed site of El Dorado) *is nipt in the spring* (l. 18); Essex and Raleigh have been put in the position of *the Jewes Guide*, Moses, and his brother Aaron, whom God *did show* the promised land *but barr'd the entry in* (ll. 20–1, alluding to Numbers 20:12). Revealing the strength of his support for Essex, Donne even reflects negatively on Elizabeth herself and her penchant for postponement and delay: *Ah slownes is our punishment and sin* (l. 22). He consoles himself and R. W. by taking a longer view than that of the immediate moment: *Perchance these Spanish busnesses beeing donne,… Our discontinued hopes we shall retrive* (ll. 23, 26). It may prove possible to do both: attack Spain and her American colonies as well.

The verse letter turns away, however, from such earthbound prospects. It ends with another shift of perspective, setting its sights on the timeless realm of *allmighty Vertu* and reflecting on the ultimate rewards of self-cultivation in *Vertu* (ll. 28, 32). These surpassing rewards—*an India* (l. 28)—are within the reach of all at some level (ll. 29–31).

ll. 3–27.   *Never did Morpheus…weare* | *Shapes so like*: Ovid describes the shapes assumed by Morpheus, the god of sleep, and his kindred in *Metamorphoses*, 11. 613–15, 633–45. *feete*: A pun on bodily and metrical components. *retyrings*: withdrawals from public life. *Patiënt*: sufferer. *all th' All*: the entire world.

To Mr R. W. ('Kindly I envy thy songs perfection') (MS p. 63)

The Petrarchan sonnet form, the metrical ambiguities of ll. 1–2 and 12–14, the imagery of *garden* and *sweetes* (shared with 'To Mr E. G.', MS p. 61), and the admiration of R. W.'s poetic capacities played off against an admitted impulsion to write satire all suggest a relatively early date of *c*.1593–4 for this verse letter.

ll. 1–9.   In a balance that enlivens every aspect of his verse, R. W. integrates the elements of *earth*, *fyer*, and *Ayre*, and by implication, nourishing moisture (*a faire | Delicious garden*). *Kindly*: in my nature. Donne contrasts with R. W.'s creativity the instability and extremism that have beset his own poetic compositions and promptings: *Griefe...did drowne me*; *Satirique fyres...urg'd me to have writt | In skorne of all*. *Griefe*: A possible allusion to the death of Donne's younger brother Henry in Newgate prison in May 1593.

ll. 10–14. Donne has *tost and movd* about in his mind's *emptiness* the lines sent by R. W. There they have reverberated as in an echo chamber, infusing Donne with *new life*.

To Mr S. B. ('O thou which to search out the secret parts') (MS p. 63)

S. B. is almost certainly Samuel Brooke (*c*.1575–1631), younger brother of Christopher. After taking his M.A. at Cambridge in 1598, he was ordained in 1599, and served as chaplain of Trinity College, Cambridge, from 1600 to 1615. Subsequently he served as chaplain to Henry, Prince of Wales, James I, and Charles I. Samuel, his brother Christopher, and Donne were made readers of Lincoln's Inn in 1618. Donne's will referred to Samuel Brooke as 'my ancient friend' (Bald, *Donne: A Life*, 563).

The indicated occasion of the poem is Samuel's matriculation at Cambridge: *thou... Lately launched into the vast sea of Arts*. This would suggest a date of 1592 or 1593, when Samuel would have been about seventeen. Donne fashions a graceful compliment to the poetic promise of a friend's younger brother.

ll. 2–9.   *India*: Donne's recurrent image for the source of great riches. *advise*: counsel. *travailing*: Period spelling enables a pun on academic work (travail) and the discoveries afforded by travel. *Heliconian Spring*: the water that flowed in the grove of the Muses (Ovid, *Metamorphoses*, 5.254–63)—the source of poetic inspiration. *Syren-like to tempt*: seductively, with fatal intent, like the mermaids' singing.

ll. 10–14. *those Scismatiques with you*: Evidently an allusion to the mounting influence of such figures as William Perkins, William Ames, and Thomas Cartwright at Cambridge University in the 1590s. Addressing a range of issues from doctrine to forms of worship to modes of governance, these prominent early Puritans called for further reformation of the English church. Donne's term *Scismatiques* reveals the perspective of the Roman Catholicism in which he had been reared. Word accent falls on the first syllable of *Scismatiques*. *seene*: This reading is possibly, though not necessarily, a miswriting of 'seeing'.

To Mr J.L. ('Of that short roll of frinds, writt in my hart') (MS p. 64)

Persistent mystery has shrouded the identity of J. L. or I. L. (capital I and J are indistinguishable in most period handwriting). Robbins staked what he termed the unique claim of Ingram Lister (*c*.1578?–1628) to fit the description of 'someone of northern, rural origin, with no known subsequent profession and of a possible date' among names recorded in 'the Oxford, Cambridge, and Inns of Courts records' (*Complete Poems of Donne*, 35). Nothing is known of Donne's and Lister's possible acquaintance. Scholars including Robbins, however, agree that the references to the Po, Seine, and Danube rivers in l. 4 allude to the continental travels of Donne's friend Wotton in 1591–5, years when Ingram Lister would have been between thirteen and seventeen years old. Such a young age disqualifies him from being, as this verse letter declares, both one of Donne's closest *frinds* (l. 1) and a married man currently enjoying himself with his wife on a rich familial estate beyond the Trent river (ll. 6–11).

A more plausible addressee is Sir John Leveson (1555–1613) who married his second wife, Christian, daughter of Sir Walter Mildmay, in 1587. Appointed deputy lieutenant for Kent in 1590, Leveson distinguished himself as a military commander, a collector of royal subsidies, and a recruiter for several naval expeditions including that of the attack on Cadiz (1596).

Like Leveson, Wotton's father, Sir Thomas (*c*.1521–87) was prominent among the Kentish gentry. Leveson and Wotton senior came into repeated contact as members of their class were called upon to show leadership in matters of public importance (Peter Clark, *English Provincial Society from the Reformation to the* Revolution (1977), 129, 131–2, 137). Donne, Henry Wotton, and Leveson could have become acquainted through Wotton's father; this verse letter implies some prior connection. The three men's participation in the Cadiz expedition increases the likelihood of mutual acquaintance.

While Kent was the base of Leveson's personal property and professional and political activities, it was his father who had taken up residence there. There was a family estate of over 30,000 acres in Staffordshire and Shropshire (portions of which could have lain north of the meandering Trent river). Sir John's young son Richard inherited these vast landholdings in 1605.

Known biographical facts thus establish Sir John Leveson in the mid-1590s as a married man, a leading figure in organizing the Cadiz expedition in which Donne and Wotton served, and a close blood relative of the current owner of extensive properties in the vicinity of the Trent. Nothing, however, seems to be known about Leveson's possible residence there for a time or his poetic interests. See the biographies of Wotton and Leveson in the online *Oxford Dictionary of National Biography*.

ll. 4–9. *drinke of Po, Sequane, or Danubee*: Uniquely among Donne's close friends, Henry Wotton made a lengthy sojourn in Europe between September 1591 and December 1595. Since the clear implication is that Wotton is abroad, this verse letter must date before the end of the latter year. *Sequane*: the Seine—Latin 'Sequana'. Padua is situated on the Po river, Paris on the Seine, and Vienna and Prague on the Danube. *Lethe*: In classical mythology, the river of the underworld that caused forgetfulness in anyone who drank its water. Metrical contraction makes the name a single syllable. *fatt beasts…labord fields*: Donne's emphasis on the abundant prosperity of this country estate strikes a rare echo of Horace's praise of the retired country life.

To Mr B.B. ('Is not thy sacred hunger' and 'If thou unto thy Muse')
(MS pp. 64–5)

The identification of B. B. with Beaupré Bell, son of Sir Robert Bell, has gained general acceptance; the circumstances alluded to by Donne fit neatly with what is known of the historical person. Bell was admitted to Emmanuel College, Cambridge, in 1587, taking his B.A. in 1591, whereupon he proceeded to an M.A. at Queen's College, Cambridge, in 1594. Bell next went to Lincoln's Inn, where he joined Donne in May 1594. Nothing else is known of him except that his burial took place on 27 August 1638.

This verse letter is comprised of two Petrarchan sonnets. Their internal rhyme patterns distinguish the one from the other, although the text as copied by Woodward runs continuously without an intervening vertical space. 'Is not thy sacred hunger of science' was clearly written while B. B. was still at Cambridge but was expected at Lincoln's Inn to begin his new course of study. 'If thou unto thy Muse' gives no indication of its date. But the second sonnet seems close in date to the first because it emphasizes the poetic affinities shared by B. B. and Donne, not their study of English common law.

ll. 1–14.   *sacred hunger of science*: Donne transposes to a positive register Virgil's negative formulation 'auri sacra fames' (*Aeneid*, 3.57), standardly translated 'impious hunger for gold' because incited by greed. *science*: knowledge, cognate with Latin *scientia*. *Arts... Quintessence*: The alchemist distills the essential *spirits* of substances; their *Quintessence* is an ultimate essence purged of all impurity and perishability. B. B.'s course in *arts* would have included rhetoric, logic, natural and moral philosophy, and metaphysics. *digest*: The technical term for systematically condensing a body of law. *the rest*: your other friends. *giddy*: foolish, imprudent. *ride post*: gallop non-stop.

ll.16–28.   *Be farr from me... To tempt thee and procure her widowhed* raises only to reject the prospect of Donne's seducing B. B., causing him to forsake his Muse and cease the writing of poetry. The situation is shown to be exactly the opposite: Donne's Muse has divorced him for being poetically unmotivated and incapable. Since he is the *cause* of the divorce, he cannot remarry and take a new Muse, an impossibility termed *bigamee*. As the *prophane* (unhallowed by a Muse) issue of an all but impotent father, *these rimes* that Donne now produces are *imperfect*. His only hope for them is that B. B. may legitimate them as *children of Poetree* with a favourable reception (on analogy with a bishop's power of confirmation).

To Mr J.L. ('Blest are your North parts') (MS p. 65)

On the addressee's possible identity, see the headnote of the preceding poem to Mr J. L. Bald's argument (*Huntington Library Quarterly* (1952), 15:286) for dating this verse letter to the summer of 1594 has won general acceptance. Bald quotes John Stowe's account of that summer's extraordinary weather: excessive rains in May, June,

July, and September; sunshine and 'a faire harvest' in August (*The Annales of England* (1601), 1278). Donne remarks on the prolonged absence of the sun (l. 3) followed by a spell of hot weather that raised fears of another outbreak of plague in London (l. 6). The latter would correlate with August in Stowe's account.

This verse letter provides a graceful and unusual twist by again conjoining the subjects of Donne's absent beloved and absent friend. The beloved has been making an extended visit to the absent friend's country estate, but Donne mutes the notes of Petrarchan convention. Instead, the emphasis falls on an appeal to the friend to perform the offices of friendship in his Edenic surroundings, which activates some Horatian themes: the natural abundance of his friend's estate, the prospect of continuing domestic bliss with his *sonne* and *fair wife* (l. 18).

ll. 11–14.   *And since thou' art in Paradise, and needst crave | No joyes addition, helpe thy frind to save*: Since these lines are found only in the Westmoreland manuscript, copyists other than Rowland Woodward must have considered them blasphemous. Heaven is the *Paradise* where joy is complete; thus *save* has a religious resonance.

ll. 15–16.   *may thy woods... a golden haire*: Donne whimsically suggests that J. L. can decide when the leaves of his trees will be green and when they will turn to autumnal gold. *polld*: lopped off (referring to tops or branches of a plant).

ll. 19–20.   *courage*: vigor, vital energy—no longer current senses. *ward*: orphan, with an inheritance that would be held in trust (and, to one extent or another, enjoyed) by a powerful court official, the Master of the Court of Wards.

RENAISSANCE LITERARY PARADOX: THE GENRE

The Renaissance prose genre of the literary paradox flourished in two forms: the mock encomium, or praise lavished on an unworthy subject; and the argument against received opinion (Greek 'paradoxé' means 'contrary judgement'). While both forms trace their origins to classical antiquity, the practice of the genre by earlier Renaissance authors exercised the greatest influence on later ones.

Desiderius Erasmus's *Moriae Encomium* (1509), translated from Latin by Sir Thomas Chaloner as *The Praise of Folly* (1549), set a prominent and complex precedent for the mock encomium. For the argument against received opinion, the trend-setter was the Italian writer Ortensio Lando. The first of many editions was published in 1543 as *Paradossi cioè, sententie fuori del comun parere, novellamente venute in luce* (Paradoxes, that is, opinions beyond ordinary reach, newly come to light). Lando's paradoxes included arguments that it is better to be ugly than beautiful, ignorant than wise, and drunk than sober, that it is not an evil to have an unfaithful wife, that it is better to die than to live a long life, that it is better to be at war than at peace, and that woman is more excellent than man. Anthony Munday published the first of several English translations of Lando as *The Defence of Contraries: Paradoxes against common opinion* (1593).

More broadly conceived as witty exercises that yielded striking thoughts in striking formulations, paradoxes became a fashionable feature of revels at the Inns of Court in the late sixteenth and early seventeenth centuries. In 1618 a character named Paradox had a leading role in the revels at Gray's Inn (Philip J. Finkelpearl, *John Marston of the Middle Temple* (1969), 228). But while paradoxes were well received at the Inns of Court, their university status seems to have been dubious. In 1573 Gabriel Harvey defended himself in a letter to Dr. John Young of Pembroke College, Cambridge, against accusations made by Thomas Nevil, a fellow of Pembroke. Nevil, says Harvey, offered as a 'reason...against me...that I was a great and continual patron of paradoxis and a main defender of straung opinions, and that communly against Aristotle too' (Harvey, *Letter-Book*, ed. E. J. L. Scott (1884), 10). Harvey protested that he never invented paradoxes but only made use of ones proposed by others.

As in Donne's elegies where the crafting of an ingenious argument is frequently observable, so too in his paradoxes—another congenial genre for a student of the law. While he mainly wrote the form that argued against received opinion, false praise (the function of the mock encomium) could also figure, as seen in Paradoxes 6 and 7. Donne generally opens a paradox with a vigorous assertion that bears either directly or indirectly on the topic at issue. The sequence of arguments moves quickly; some are developed, some not. The sequence, moreover, is not always easy to track through complications introduced by wordplay (on 'paint' in Paradox 2), contradiction (Paradox 1), and false logic (Paradox 6). Donne typically ends a paradox with a witty twist that does issue from the foregoing arguments but so audaciously that it takes the reader aback.

In a letter to Goodyere written in 1599, Donne gave vent to his mixed feelings about writing paradoxes; see the Introduction. On the one hand he admits his unserious motives: 'they were made rather to deceave tyme than her daughter truth'. On the other hand he asserts that paradoxes can serve serious purposes: 'If they make you to find better reasons against them, they do their office...They are rather alarums to truth, to arme her, than enemies.' See further Michael W. Price, 'The Paradox', in Shami, Flynn, and Hester, eds, *The Oxford Handbook of John Donne*, 149–52.

Not the least significant feature of this letter is the linkage Donne draws between his satires, his elegies, and his paradoxes as being, each in their way, problematic. This linkage, compounded with the thematic and tonal resemblances found in Donne's paradoxes, satires, and elegies, suggests a dating of all three to the same period, 1593–8.

Paradox 1 'That all things kill themselves' (MS p. 81)

Here Donne argues that self-destruction, not self-preservation, is the law governing all living beings. He bases his examples on the triad of vegetative, sensitive, and rational souls that Aristotle ascribed to humans. Humans share the vegetative soul with all living beings, and the sensitive soul with animals, but humans alone have a rational soul. For Aristotle the soul meant the form of a living being—that is, what endows a living being with the characteristics and nature specific to it. Paradox 1 offers a preliminary sketch of an argument that Donne would later develop in *Biathanatos*, characterized by its subtitle as 'A Declaration of that Paradoxe, or Thesis, that *Selfe-homicide* is not so Naturally Sinne, that it may never be otherwise.'

affect: aim at, aspire to—senses no longer current. *effect*: bring about. Wordplay on *affect* | *effect* highlights the near identity (in sound) of the two verbs. Establishing this identity figures centrally in the argument of Paradox 1. *importun'd*: impelled, urged—senses no longer current.

perfects... perfects: Wordplay on two senses of this verb: first, 'brings to completion, finishes' and second, 'instructs and informs completely'—a sense no longer current.

the most unworthy soule: the vegetative, with capacities for growth and nutrition. *neyther will, nor worke*: The vegetative soul is incapable of willing or performing an action. *perfection*: completed state—a sense no longer current.

spirits: that which enlivens physical organisms, in contrast to their purely material components; animating or vital principles.

by mans industry... pampered: An ironic perspective on agriculture, the whole purpose of which is to cultivate plants for food (at which point, their life ends).

yf between men, not to defend, be to kill, what a heinous selfe murder is it: Donne would revert to this idea in *Biathanatos*, 2.6.2. *galantest*: finest, most excellent.

Or how shall man... taught us this?: Donne would elaborate on the bringing of death into the world as a consequence of the fall of Adam and Eve in *Biathanatos*, 2.6.3. *surfeits*: excessive intakes of food or drink.

And if these things kill themselves... not the same things: The reasoning is as follows: Things are in their finished state when they kill themselves. For after they reach this state, they are no longer themselves. At any later point, then, they cannot kill themselves.

Yea the frame of the whole world... nothing is?: If God were merely passive and did not actively sustain the world, the world would end (die). In such a case, the world's end (death) would be self-induced, for there would be nothing outside the world to kill it.

Paradox 2 'That women ought to paint themselves' (MS p. 82)

Donne defends women's use of cosmetics by exposing the inconsistencies in what men consider to be beauty in women and what they judge beautiful in nature and art. While Lando's Paradosso 2 argues a different proposition, that it is better to be ugly than beautiful, one sharply worded sentence on cosmetics may have caught Donne's attention: 'Given by God a grace so beautiful as to be ugly, they [women] seek with... applications of white lead, softeners and smoothers, oils... to appear beautiful' (*Paradossi* (1544), 13).

Donne elsewhere displays ambivalence about women's use of cosmetics. He can accept them as a lesser evil: 'I could more abide | She were by art, than Nature falsify'd' ('The Primrose', ll. 19–20). At one point Donne the preacher would reflect tolerantly: 'Certainly the limits of adorning and beautifying the body are not so narrow, so strict, as by some sowre men they are sometimes conceived to be' (*Sermons*, 5:302). But at another point his judgement is negative: 'It is ill... when it is not our own blood, that appeares in our cheekes; It may doe some ill offices of blood, it may tempt, but it gives over when it should doe a good office of blood, it cannot blush' (*Sermons*, 6: 269).

concernes more: matters more. *too nice a jealousy*: too fastidious a feeling of suspicion.
kissing, the strange and misticall union of soules: Cf. 'To Mr. H. W.' ('Sir, more than
kisses, letters mingle soules').

to betray her body to Ruine and Deformity ... what a hainous adultery is it?: Ingenuity
complicates the argument by analogy. Donne first claims that a woman's adultery,
even with a worthy partner, is a just cause for her man's complaint. He then asserts
that a woman who would *betray her body to* personified *Ruine and Deformity*, for lack
of *easy repayring* by means of cosmetics, would commit adultery even more
reprehensible.

Are we not more delighted ... whom trew we durst not regard?: Aristotle, *Poetics*, 4.1448b
is the source of these famous reflections: 'Everyone enjoys mimetic objects. We
enjoy contemplating the most precise images of things whose actual sight is painful
to us, such as the forms of the vilest animals and corpses.'

*We repayre ... we mend ... and wash ... our apparell ... But by the providence of women
this is prevented*: The argument from analogy runs as follows to its contrary conclu-
sion: We repair our houses because of negative effects on us (we feel the biting
cold). We mend and wash our clothes because of negative effects on us (the clothes
look and feel bad). But when women take the initiative of applying cosmetics, there
are no negative effects (they look good and we feel good).

if thou begins't to hate her then ... thou didst hate and love together: The condensed argu-
ment delivers a refutation by exposing a contradiction. This is its fuller form: You
loved her when she was painted, although you did not realize that she was painted.
If you begin to hate her when her paint comes off, you are hating her because she is
not painted. If you now say that you hated her before because she was painted, then
you hated her and loved her at the same time.

Paradox 3 'That old Men are more fantastique than younge' (MS p. 83)

Donne builds an argument that old men are more 'fantastic' (enthralled by fancy or
imagination) than young men by giving more examples of 'fantastic' old men than
of young. The force of the examples, however, derives from a crucial distinction
drawn in the third sentence: *To be fantastique in young men, is a conceitfull distemper-
ature ...: but in old men ... it becomes naturall, therfore more full and perfect.* In other
words, fancy in the young disrupts the balance of the senses and temporarily dis-
places reason, but fancy in the old becomes the predominant faculty, their very
nature, as senses and reason decline. This distinction yields opposing definitions of
'fantastic' which, in turn, predetermine a conclusion ostensibly reached by arguing
from examples.

taxe us: accuse us. *busied in conceiting apparrell*: occupied in devising and prescribing
styles of dress. Sumptuary laws issued periodically during Elizabeth's reign prohib-
ited persons of specified ranks and incomes from wearing certain fabrics and fash-
ions reserved for those higher on the social scale. *we when we are melancolique, weare
black; when lusty, greene; when forsaken, tawny*: Colour symbolism was a matter
taken seriously in the theatre of Donne's day.

The old men of our time have chang'd...their Religion. patience: constancy in labour or effort. Fundamental aspects of English life underwent alteration in the course of the sixteenth century. *their own bodyes* alludes to the vogue, in Elizabeth's reign, of cropped jackets and form-fitting legwear for men that newly revealed their lower anatomy, and of ruffs, which newly concealed the neck. *much of their laws* is probably to be taken in conjunction with *their religion*. Henry VIII (1509–47) withdrew England from papal jurisdiction; Mary I (1553–8) returned England to papal jurisdiction; Elizabeth's Act of Supremacy (1559) reinstated the English monarch's headship of the English church. *much of their language*: A likely reference to the sixteenth-century literary vogue for interspersing English with loanwords from other modern languages, especially Italian, Spanish, and French, or so-called 'inkhorn terms' (scholars' vocabulary drawn from Latin and Greek).

weare long haire...weare none: A jibe from a fashionably long-haired youth at the prevalence of baldness in aging men. *the Dogmatique which affirmes*: Dogmatic philosophy or medicine reasoned from first principles accepted as true rather than by induction. *Academique*: belonging to the Academy, the school or philosophy of Plato, associated with dialectical inquiry.

Paradox 4 'That Nature is our worst Guide' (MS p. 84)

Paradox 4 opposes the venerable Stoic principle: Follow Nature. To develop his contrary argument, Donne activates a range of meanings and associations attaching to the terms 'nature' and 'natural', exploiting their differences, even their incompatibilities.

Shall she be guide to all creatures which is herself one?: Here 'nature' means 'everything, everyone, all creation'. *Or if she allso have a guide, shall any creature have a better guide than us?*: God is Nature's guide as well as ours. Donne's contemporary, Richard Hooker, reflects: 'it cannot be but nature hath some director of infinite knowledge to guide her in all her ways. Who is the guide of nature, but only the God of nature?' (*Of the Laws of Ecclesiastical Polity* (1593), 1.3.4).

Can she be a good guide to us which hath corrupted not us only but her selfe?: Here 'nature' is what medieval theologians termed 'natura naturans' (literally, 'Nature naturing'), 'Nature doing what Nature does'. According to Aquinas, natura naturans was created innocent, what Donne terms *whight integrity*, yet had the capacity for original sin (*Summa Theologica*, 1a2ae.81–5). This Thomistic conception underlies the question Donne poses regarding Adam: *did not Nature...infuse in him this desyre of knowledge, and so this corruption...?*

If by nature we shall understand...our reasonablenes,....why shall not all men having one nature, follow one course?: If we define human nature as rational, why then should all humans act diversely? The contrary-to-fact insertion (*the ideot and wisard beeing equally reasonable*) makes a calculated mockery of this question.

Alas, how unable...our slimy bodyes?: Here 'nature' means the physical constitution and vital functions of human bodies, sustained by nourishment, digestion, and excretion. *temperature*: temperament. *slimy*: characterized by emission of some viscous substance (mucus, semen, menstrual flow). *unable*: unfit for the purpose—a sense no longer current. A definition of human nature that reduces it to our bodies and to sexual reproduction is inadequate; it fails to account for other, non-physical components of who we are: *we cannot say that we derive our inclinations, our minds, our soules, from our parents by any way*.

Donne reduces to logical absurdity the identification of human nature with bodies and sexual reproduction. This reduction proceeds in three stages:

(1) *To say it, as All from All, is error in reason, for then with the first, nothing remaynes.* If *All* that a child's nature is derives from *All* of its parents' nature, this would result in transmitting all the constituents of their natures to their first child, so that *nothing remaynes* for any children born later.

(2) *Or as part from all, is error*... This argument is a gradualist variant of (1), and the parenthetical reference to *Gavelkind lands* clarifies the point. *Gavelkind* is the technical legal term for the custom of dividing a deceased man's property equally among his heirs; such equal division of ever-smaller shares of land *would*... *in few generations become nothing*.

(3) *Or to say it by communication, is error in Divinity.* The belief that a child's soul, like its body, was transmitted to it by its parents became known as 'traducianism' and branded as heresy for its denial that God infuses the soul into the body. *communication, communicating*: conveying, transmitting.

And if thou hast thy fathers nature and inclination, he allso had his fathers, and so... all have one nature: For good measure, Donne reiterates the reductive reasoning applied to the body in (1) and (2), now applying it to *nature* defined as our souls, *our inclinations and minds*, as in (3). He arrives at the absurd conclusion that nature is one and the same in all humans. *complexions*: combinations of the four bodily humours in various proportions, or the bodily habits associated with these combinations.

Nature though we chase it away will returne: A loose adaptation from Horace, *Epistles*, 1.10.14: 'You may drive out nature with a fork, yet it will still return'. *And that old Tu nihil invita etc. must not be sayd, thou shalt, but thou wilt do nothing against nature*: Horace, *Ars poetica* (Art of Poetry), 1.385: 'You will say or do nothing beyond your ability' (Tu nihil invitâ dices facieve Minerva). In Horace the goddess Minerva personifies natural talent. Beyond echoing Horace's line, Donne sharpens a point in Horace's grammar: not *thou shalt, but thou wilt do nothing against nature*. Not speaking or acting beyond one's own ability is a fact of one's nature, not a moral injunction.

We call our bastards allways our naturall issue, and we designe a foole... by the name of naturall: Both of these usages date to sixteenth-century English, although *naturall issue* as a term for illegitimately conceived offspring has a source in Roman law. *designe*: designate—a sense no longer current. *we call Metaphisique, supernaturall*: In antiquity, 'Metaphysica' was the title given to the thirteen books of Aristotle that were listed as 'following his *Physics*' (*meta ta physica*). In later times, *Metaphysica* came to designate 'the science of things transcending what is physical, or natural'.

by following her, ... akornes and roots: Here 'nature' is equated with 'the state of nature', the condition of man before the emergence of organized society—hence, a pre-agricultural phase. This meaning reflects Epicurean and Cynic views that the earliest humans foraged for their food at a level of existence close to that of the animals. That acorns were the oldest food of humans was a classical commonplace.

no deathe is naturall: Here, as the argument makes clear, 'natural' is taken to refer to the vital powers of human beings manifested in their healthy constitutions, *that which nature made perfect and would preserve*.

Paradox 5 'That only Cowards dare dy' (MS p. 85)

Paradox 5 is logically inconsistent with Paradox 1, *That all things kill themselves*. The inconsistency is evidently deliberate. Formal exercises to hone students' skills in arguing a question 'on the one side or on the other' (Latin 'in utrumque partem') were staples of university and legal education in Donne's day. The argument of Paradox 5 apparently originated in Aristotle's *Eudemian Ethics*, 3.6, 7, which Donne would later summarize as follows: '*Aristotle* insinuates . . . that this kinde of death [suicide] caught men by two baits, *Ease* and *Honour*. Against them who would dy to avoide Miserie, (a) Hee teaches *Death to be the greatest misery which can fall upon us* . . . And then, that Honour and Fame might draw none, (b) he sayes, *It is Cowardlinesse, and Dejection, and an argument of an unsufferable and impatient minde*' (*Biathanatos*, 2.5.2.114). Here, however, Donne merely gestures at one of Aristotle's most characteristic formulations, the doctrine of the mean, in his opening sentence: *Extreames are equally removed from the meane*.

headlong desperatnes . . . backward cowardise: Aristotle, *Nicomachean Ethics*, 2.2 addresses just such a case: 'The man who flees from and fears everything and does not stand his ground against anything becomes a coward, and the man who fears nothing at all but goes to meet every danger becomes rash . . . temperance and courage, then, are destroyed by excess and defect, and preserved by the mean'.

necessited: necessitated, i.e., compelled, forced.

Fortiter ille facit qui miser esse potest: 'He acts courageously who is miserable and can endure' (Martial, *Epigrams*, 11.56.16).

[*climbing*]: Rowland Woodward's transcription has a blank at this point, which may indicate puzzlement over the probable reading, 'clyming', in Donne's original. Other manuscripts read 'climbing' at this point while varying in other specifics of phrasing. [*climbing*]: ascending, mounting up. *Spiritt*: tendency, inclination. *prest to the warrs*: compelled to do military service.

I have seene one . . . stop his breathe: Coma, a brother of Cleon, the fifth-century BCE Athenian demagogue, resorted to this ploy at the prospect of being examined under torture (Valerius Maximus, *Memorable Doings and Sayings*, 9.12.1, external series). Donne would later allude to Coma in *Biathanatos*, 1.2.3.51–2, and in Meditation 12 of *Devotions*. The phrasing *I have seene one* may imitate Latin *vidi* or *vidimus* (I have seen, we have seen) which does not always literally signify first-person eyewitness. *And we knew another, . . . to have outlivd his disgrace*: Donne's 'we knew' seems to point to some (unidentified) contemporary, but instead refers to another personage in Valerius Maximus. Herennius Siculus was a friend of Caius Gracchus, who was prosecuted for fomenting resistance to the Roman state. On the sole basis of this personal association, not for any political offence of his own, Herennius was about to be committed to prison when he bashed his head against a doorpost, 'resigning his life at the very entrance of ignominy' (*Memorable Doings and Sayings*, 9.12.1, external series).

that Allegorical death: the taking of monastic vows so as to 'die to the world'. Donne would reuse this disparaging phrase in *Pseudo-Martyr* (1610): 'that drawes them from their Office of society, by a civill and Allegorical Death, in departing from the world into a Cloyster' (Preface, D3).

Paradox 6 'That the gifts of the body are better than those of the mind or of fortune' (MS pp. 86–7)

Donne exploits some Renaissance adaptations of Platonic doctrines to reach a most un-Platonic conclusion: that the gifts of the body in every way surpass those of the mind or soul (which he equates) and those of fortune (which he treats briefly at the close). The adaptations of Platonic doctrine include (1) the complementary relation of soul and body; (2) their necessary interdependence; and (3) the refusal to honour the soul at the body's expense. Elsewhere Donne's handling of such propositions is serious and nuanced; cf. 'The Extasye', ll. 49–56; 'Ayre and Angels', ll. 11–14; 'The Litanye', ll. 143–4; *Second Anniversary*, ll. 157–68. But here, in the genre of the prose paradox, he constructs a sweeping case that admits of no exceptions: the body and its capacities and functions are superior to any benefits that the soul, mind, or fortune can provide.

I say agayne that the body makes the mind: An inversion of the Platonic doctrine that the soul is the form of the body. *And this mind... Reason or Philosophy*: The reasoning runs as follows: If the body is of primary importance and the non-bodily faculties are of secondary importance as well as dependent on the body as primary, then there is no harm in identifying the mind and the soul. *confounded*: run together so as to be difficult to separate or distinguish.

My body licenceth my soule to see... to see or heare: That the soul perceives the beauties of the world by means of the senses is a Platonic commonplace. The Platonic argument continues by affirming that the soul's contemplation of earthly beauty enables it to rise by degrees to contemplate the immaterial Idea of beauty. Donne, however, argues the total dependence of the soul on the body, not the soul's use of the body to attain to higher things. *licenceth*: permits (to do something). *though... she be as able and as willing to see behind as before*: Play on the literal and figurative meanings of 'looking before and behind': though the soul is both willing and able to look before and behind, it cannot make the backs of our heads able to see.

Now yf my soule would say... which through myne eares she heares: Donne instances the actualities of the soul's delight in sensory pleasures, dismissing as mere pretence any claim by the soul to delight *only* in *sweetnesses which her inward ey and senses apprehend*. In fact, the real issue is not pretence but something more problematic still. This is the comparative *perfection... my body hath, that it can impart to my mind all her pleasures*, while *my mind hath this maime* [grave defect], that she can *neyther teache my indisposed parts her faculties* [the 'no eyes in the back of the head' problem] nor *to the parts best disposd shew that bewty of Angels or Musicke of Spheares, whereof she boasts the contemplation* [the problem that angels are invisible, and the music of the spheres inaudible].

Chastity, Temperance, or fortitude . . . I appeale . . . whether the cause of these be not in the body: Aristotle's authority lends support to an anti-Platonic line of argument: 'Temperance and profligacy have to do with . . . those two senses whose objects are alone felt, . . . taste and touch' (*Eudemian Ethics*, 3.2); 'Temperance must be concerned with bodily pleasures' (*Nicomachean Ethics*, 3.8). Donne's inclusion of *fortitude* in this grouping of bodily virtues probably stems from the materiality of its Latin root meaning 'strength' and its specific associations with the physical strength of males.

who will say . . . patience is as good a happiness as health, when we must be extreamly miserable to have this happines?: Donne 'proves' that a virtue of the body (health) is both superior and primary in a loaded comparison with a virtue of the mind (patience). He then exalts sense perception in a most un-Platonic fashion to extend this 'proof' of the superiority and primacy of bodily virtues from the individual to the *nourishing of civil Societies and mutual love amongst men*. Because it is immediate, accessible, and common to all humans, sensory experience is superior to inward intuition. The argument may seem to be complete at this point, but it turns out not to be so.

to know these vertues . . . assure our selves that these vertues are not counterfayted?: A sudden tonal shift marks the final turn of the argument. Donne acknowledges for the first time that what the senses present to the mind—appearances—can be deceptive in themselves and can be used by other human beings to deceive. A man who is merely *flexible* (adaptable, agreeable) can be mistaken for the *Elixar of all vertue* (essence of goodness itself). How, then, *to assure our selves that these vertues are not counterfayted?* Having cast this potentially fatal doubt on his line of argument, Donne drops the subject.

But in things seene ther is not this danger: Donne denies the danger of deception *in things seene* by adding what remains an undemonstrated assumption: that an outward-to-inward correspondence exists *in a faire body* or *a goodly house* as well as in *ruinous wythered buildings* housing *varlets* (menial servants). The existence of such correspondences would ensure that appearances match realities. He concludes by extending this correspondence to *the gifts of fortune*, first characterized equivocally as *handmayds, yea pandars* (procurers of means for others to gratify their lusts). But on balance Donne considers *the gifts of fortune* positive outward means for attaining positive inward objectives that would otherwise come to nothing because they would remain imperceptible: *with ther service . . . is indeed nothing*.

Paradox 7 'That a wise man is knowne by much Laughinge' (MS pp. 87–8)

The incentive to compose this paradox seems to have arisen from two assertions in Lando's Paradosso 12, 'That it is better to weep than to laugh'. The first is 'Laughter always abounds in the mouths of madmen and those without sense'. The second is 'Heraclitus was always much more esteemed for his tears than Democritus for his laughing'. These assertions are found on the same page in Lando (*Paradossi* (1544), 46ᵛ). Donne argues to the contrary in both instances.

Ride si sapis o puella ride: 'Laugh if you are wise, girl, laugh' (Martial, *Epigrams*, 2.41.1). *the powers... only man*: Aristotle treats laughter as a uniquely human capability in *On the Parts of Animals*, 3.10.

that Adage, per risum multum possis cognoscere stultum: Tilley, *Dictionary of Proverbs*, F462m records the Italian equivalent, 'Dal riso molto, conosci lo stulto' (By much laughter, thou knowest a fool). *Which mov'd Erasmus... made beholders laughe*: 'As soone as I came forth to saie my mynd afore this your so notable assemblie, by and by all your lokes began to clere up: unbendyng the frounyng of your browes, and laughing upon me' (Erasmus, *Praise of Folie*, trans. Chaloner (1549), 7).

therfore the poet... Quid facit Canius tuus? ridet: A free rendering of Martial's line (*Epigrams*, 3.20.21), on the otherwise unknown Canius Rufus: 'Do you want to know what your Canius is doing? He is laughing'.

Democritus and Heraclitus... lovers of wisdome: Heraclitus and Democritus were respectively cast as the weeping and the laughing philosopher by Juvenal, *Satires*, 10.30–5, and by Seneca, *On the Tranquillity of the Soul*, 15.2. The pairing became a favourite subject in later literature and art. *lovers of wisdome*: A play on the etymology of 'philosopher' in Greek. *Now amongst our wise men... Democritus laughing*: Donne's view is the opposite of Lando's.

a gay man... broad gold laces: Cf. Satire 4, ll. 166–8, 180–4. *the Arras hangings*: Arras (named after the northern French city of its manufacture) was a tapestry fabric interwoven with richly coloured figures and scenes; it made sumptuous wall hangings. Some such tapestry figures in in Satire 4, ll. 231–2. These similarities may indicate that Paradox 7, like Satire 4, was written in 1597.

as cold as the Salamander: In classical antiquity the salamander, a lizard-like reptile, was thought to have a body temperature so cold that it could extinguish fire (Aristotle, *History of Animals*, 5.19; Pliny, *Natural History*, 10.86). Cf. Donne's Satire 3, ll. 22–3.

now when our superstitious civility... show themselves wise: *superstitious*: over-scrupulous, excessive—senses no longer current. The social practice described by Donne, playing the fool to make one's companions laugh and look wise by contrast, appears to have been a recent development. The customary means of provoking laughter was to make fools of one's opponents by ridiculing them, as exemplified by John Lyly: 'Now have at you my gaffers... 'tis I that must take you a peg lower... Ile make such a splinter run into your wittes, as shal ranckle till you become fooles' (Preface, *Pappe with a Hatchet* (1589), opening sentence).

Paradox 8 'That good is more common than evill' (MS pp. 88–9)

As in Paradox 4, where Donne equivocates among various meanings of 'nature', here he equivocates among various meanings of 'common'. These meanings include 'of a general or public nature', 'of general application', 'most widely occurring', 'attributable to all human beings', 'possessed or shared alike by a plurality of persons', 'ordinary', and 'sexually promiscuous'.

silly old mens exclayming...extolling ther owne: An allusion to Horace's description of an old man who is 'hard to please, complaining, a praiser of the time when he was a boy, a chastiser and critic of the young' (*Art of Poetry*, ll. 173–4).

good...must...be more common than evill...be common: Aquinas held that 'good spreads itself more widely than evil does' (*Summa Theologica*, 1a2ae.81.2). *perfection*: completed state, completeness. *common*: The operative meanings must be 'most widely occurring' and 'possessed or shared alike by all' because Donne proceeds to specify the immediate context: *the worlds early infancy, a tyme when nothing was evill*—that is, the originary creation of an all-good God.

but if this world...nothing shalbe good: Even if the world in its old age (*dotage*) suffers decay and dissolution as effects of evil (*the extremest crookedness*), there must be good as long as the world lasts. Donne is applying the definition of evil as privation, the absence of good, not something that exists in itself, as good does. *glister*: sparkle, glitter.

And as...Lapidaryes (gem-cutters)...*adorne ther works,...So good...refuseth no ayd,...yf she may be more common to us*: The reasoning runs thus: Good does not merely triumph over evil; it can actually use evil to produce a comprehensive design whose final perfection incorporates evil. This inclusiveness of which good is capable has an obvious bearing on the meaning of 'common' in Paradox 8. Donne now activates the meaning of 'sexually promiscuous': *So good doth...prostitute her owne* [*amiablenes*] *to all*. [*amiablenes*]: the quality of being lovable—a sense no longer current. Westmoreland has a blank at this point; two other manuscripts of relatively early date and good quality have the reading adopted here.

evill manners are parents of good lawes: 'Ill manners produce good laws' (Tilley, *Dictionary*, M625).

All faire, all profitable, all vertuous...embrace all things but their utter contraryes...foule may be riche and vertuous, poore may be vertuous and faire, vicious may be faire and riche: Donne's point is that the contraries of the three categories of the good (the fair, the profitable, the virtuous) can each coexist with the goodness of the other two.

So that good hath this good meanes...to accompany the evill: Again personifying goodness as a sociable and available female, Donne works a variation on an earlier point. Good can be *common* (inclusive, all-embracing) with regard to evil, either by assimilating evil to her superior power (*some subjects she can possesse intirely*) or by associating herself with evil and thereby neutralizing its effects (*she can humbly stoope to accompany the evill*). *accompany*: add or conjoin to; cohabit with—senses no longer current. *indifferent*: neither good nor bad.

I remember nothing...that occupation which they profes: The final play on *common* offers a mock-logical justification for figuring goodness as a promiscuous female: *of that occupation, the most common are the best*. The operative sense of 'good' here is 'good at' (lovemaking) or 'good for' (sex). By activating these senses, *the most common* and *the best* can be equated.

Paradox 9 'That by Discord things increase' (MS pp. 89–90)

Nullos esse Deos... videt beatum: The quotation is from Martial, *Epigrams*, 4.21.1–3: 'There are no gods, heaven is empty | Declares Selius, and he proves it, because he | Finds that he prospers, while he denies these things'. The atheist Selius thinks he has made an argument by contradiction. This arises when two propositions, taken together, yield two conclusions that are the logical, usually opposite inversions of each other. One pair of propositions in this case would be 'Selius is in a state of prosperity', 'The gods bestow prosperity', leading to the conclusion 'Therefore, the gods exist.' But Selius has previously concluded that the gods do not exist. His contradictory conclusion, however, has no logical force; it is a unilateral, unreasoning denial.

When Donne the preacher would reflect on Martial's epigram, he would conclude that self-absorption is Selius's mortal failing. 'It is... dangerous... to consider no man but himself, to make himself the measure of all... The Epigrammatist describes the Atheist so, That he desires no better argument to prove that there is no God, but that he sees himself, *Dum negat ista beatum*, prosper well enough, though he do not believe this prosperity to proceed from God' (*Sermons*, 1:228–9).

I assever this the more boldly... my body increaseth: According to the theory of the humours, health in the human body resulted from a balance among four vital fluids (blood, phlegm, choler, and black choler or melancholy); ill health resulted from the predominance of one or another of them. *assever*: assert emphatically. *increaseth*: grows in prosperity or well-being—a sense no longer current. The wit of the argument turns importantly on seeing that Donne has cast himself in the self-absorbed role of Selius and, like him, is prospering—at least as a composer of paradoxes. *feign*: represent, conjure up. *member*: component, constituent.

it is as impossible... as corruption without generation: 'The corruption of one is the generation of another'—an axiom attributed to Aristotle (Tilley, *Dictionary*, C667). *discommodity*: disadvantage.

Emperyes: sovereign dominions. *And who can deny that Controversies in religion... Religion it selfe*: Cf. Satire 3, ll. 43, 70–84, where Donne reflects on the religious disputes of his day and on the heightened imperative to 'Seek true religïon. Oh where?'

acertaind: assured—a sense no longer current.

I ow a devotion... to Discord... for all that busines of Troy: Cast by the divinity Eris (*Discord*), the apple inscribed 'For the fairest' was entrusted to the youth Paris to bestow on one of three goddesses: Hera, Aphrodite, or Athena. The 'judgement of Paris' awarded the apple to Aphrodite, who had offered Helen to Paris as a bribe. This ensured the other two goddesses' perpetual enmity (Apollodorus, *The Library*, 3.12.5). *Quinzay*: 'Quinsai', as the name was spelled in Marco Polo's *Travels*, 2.64, was then the capital of the southern Sung dynasty in China. *removed corners*: distant places.

Uxor pessima, pessimus maritus, Miror tam malè convenire vobis: 'The worst wife, the worst husband, I wonder that you get along so badly' (Martial, *Epigrams*, 8.35.2–3).

malè: Donne seems to quote from memory; Martial actually reads 'non benè' (not at all well). *perchance ther was ne'er the lesse increase*: perhaps there were none the fewer children born to this couple. The closing pun on *increase* jokingly returns to the proposition with which Paradox 9 began.

Paradox 10 'That it is possible to find some vertue in some women' *(MS pp. 90–1)*

Perhaps the most delightful feature of Donne's final paradox is its strongly registered voice—that of a self-possessed, outrageously witty young man-about-town. His ostensibly positive agenda is to argue that three of the four cardinal virtues—justice, wisdom, and fortitude, in that order—are to be found in *some* (even many) *women*. While women altogether lack the fourth cardinal virtue, temperance, this is no liability in an argument that the speaker deliberately did not cast as a universal proposition.

sear'd impudency: unfeeling shamelessness. *phisitians allow some vertue in every poyson*: 'Poisons afford Antipoisons: nothing is totally, or altogether uselessly bad' (Sir Thomas Browne, *Christian Morals*,1.28, in *Works*, ed. Geoffrey Keynes (1964), 1, 255). *wine is good for fever*: 'Men in olde tyme...found that wyne...keleth [cooleth] hot bodyes, and moisteth drye bodies' (Bartholome, *De proprietatibus rerum* [On the Properties of Things], trans. John Trevisa (1535), 17.134).

if Suum cuique dare...all civil justice: *Suum cuique dare*: To give to each his own. 'Justice is to render to each his due' (Plato, *Republic*, 1.6). *they are most just...no man*: Women are more just than justice itself, for they give what is theirs to every man. *Tanquam...negat*: 'As if it were not permitted [to say no], no girl says no' (Martial, *Epigrams*, 4.71.4). *dehort*: exhort in an effort to dissuade (someone from something)—a no longer current sense.

we must say...good Scourges for bad men: 'Law is the scourge of sin' (Tilley, *Dictionary*, L107). *These or none must serve...the World affords not one Example*: The speaker emphasizes that his argument has proceeded by giving particular examples and reasoning from them. He professes his *great happiness* that argument from particular examples proceeds independently from argument to establish a universal proposition. Hence he incurs no logical difficulty that no altogether virtuous woman is to be found in the world.

RENAISSANCE EPIGRAM: THE GENRE

There were two principal collections by which knowledge of classical antecedents in the genre of the epigram descended to the Renaissance. One was the fourteen books of *Epigrams* composed by the Latin poet Martial (*c*.40–*c*.104 CE). The other was the so-called *Planudean Anthology*, a medieval Christian selection from a compilation of fifteen centuries of Greek epigrams known as the *Palatine* (or *Greek*) *Anthology*. The Planudean epigrams achieved their widest currency by way of various selections in Latin translation, including Fausto Sabeo's *Epigrammatum libri quinque* (Five Books of Epigrams) (1556), which Donne appears to have known. There were a number of other selections in Latin translation; the epigram became a frequently practised genre, both in England and on the Continent.

While the Greek epigrammatist Cyrillus had limited the genre to two or three lines, Martial claimed the freedom to write longer epigrams, in lines of five or six feet or eleven syllables (*Epigrams*, 6.65, 10.9). Features shared by Greek and Latin epigrams included a satirical tone and an amusing surprise ending. In his influential treatise, Julius Caesar Scaliger described the epigram as brief, sharp, and clever, comprising a statement and a definition (*Poetices libri septem* [Seven Books of Poetics], 1561). Grammar school pupils were often exercised in Latin verse composition using Martial as a model, and the habit thus acquired persisted at university and into later life.

Setting a prolific precedent, Donne's grandfather, John Heywood, expanded his *Humdred Epigrammes* (1550) through intervening editions to reach a total of 1100 in his *Woorkes* (1562). Among Donne's contemporaries and acquaintances, the popularity of this genre in English and Latin is attested in epigrams by Sir John Davies, Everard Guilpin, Sir John Harington, and others. Donne's own epigrams in the Westmoreland manuscript fall into three subject categories: classical legends; military observations; and quick takes on single figures, whether typecast or individualized or some of both. William Drummond of Hawthornden said that Donne 'might easily be the best Epigrammatist we have found in *English*'. The comment was entered in a manscript written *c*.1612–16 and printed in Drummond, *Works* (1711), 226.

Epigram: 'Hero and Leander' (MS p. 93)

One of Donne's most distinctive characteristics as a poet is his usual avoidance of the classical subjects that abound in his contemporaries' writings. Since this epigram and the two following are on classical subjects and lead off the entire series, they may be the earliest extant verse from Donne's pen—perhaps dating to the late 1580s or early 1590s.

This story of a pair of tragically thwarted lovers, first narrated by Musaeus in the late fifth century CE, was well known by the late sixteenth century. In the original version, it is Leander only who drowns in attempting to swim the Hellespont and unite with Hero, who is confined in a tower on the opposite shore; Hero throws herself from her tower to the ground where Leander's corpse lies. Donne requires the lovers' double drowning (Hero throwing herself from her tower into the Hellespont) because he chose to superimpose the idea of their subjection to the four elements. *one ground*: a shared grave. *one fyer*: their mutual passion.

Epigram: 'Pyramus and Thisbe' (MS p. 93)

Donne distills to its bare essentials the tale of these two lovers, familiar from Ovid, *Metamorphoses*, 4.55–160. Pyramus and Thisbe live in neighbouring houses, separated by a common wall, in the city of Babylon. Although their rivalrous parents have forbidden them to marry, they whisper their love to each other through a crack in the wall. When they arrange to meet outside the city near Ninus's tomb, Thisbe arrives first, then flees from a lioness whose mouth is bloody from a recent kill. The frightened Thisbe leaves her veil behind, which the lioness mutilates. When Pyramus arrives, he assumes from the sight of Thisbe's veil that a fierce beast has killed her; he then kills himself, falling upon his sword. When Thisbe returns to find Pyramus dead, she grieves over him and then kills herself with the same sword. *cruell frinds, by parting*: Donne contrives to make his phrasing equally applicable to the parents who have separated the two lovers and to Pyramus and Thisbe, in their ill-fated actions at their intended meeting place.

Epigram: 'Niobe' (MS p. 93)

The myth of Niobe was first told by Homer, *Iliad*, 24.603–10, and retold in several later sources; it also became an important subject in painting and sculpture. Niobe proudly boasted of the seven boys and seven girls whom she had borne to the hero Amphion. She then disparaged the goddess Leto (or Latona), who had given birth only to Apollo and Artemis. At their enraged mother's command, using poisoned arrows, Artemis killed Niobe's daughters and Apollo killed Niobe's sons. The bereft Niobe grieved so exceedingly that her body turned to stone. Donne's Niobe finds a paradox in her condition: in her grief, she is *dry* (presumably because she cannot weep any further tears or because she cannot bear any more children).

Epigram: 'Naue arsa' (A Burned Ship) (MS p. 93)

Naue arsa: Italian for 'a ship set on fire'. It is generally accepted that the subject is the destruction of the Spanish flagship *San Felipe* on 21 June 1596 during the siege of Cadiz, at which Donne was present. According to Raleigh's account, two Spanish ships, 'the Philip [San Felipe] and the St Thomas burnt themselves: many drowned themselves; many, half burnt, leapt into the water,... many swimming with grievous wounds, stricken under water, and put out of their pain; and withal so huge a fire, ... as if any man had a desire to see Hell itself, it was there most lively figured' (cited in Bald, *Donne: A Life*, 82–3). Donne's perspective focuses on the paradoxical conjunctions with which the epigram ends. *by their shott decay*: suffer fatal gunshot wounds.

Epigram: 'Caso d'un muro' (Fall of a Wall) (MS p. 93)

The subject of this epigram has been disputed. The likeliest incident is the fall of a wall of the citadel at Corunna during the English expedition against Lisbon in 1589. During this engagement a number of English soldiers were killed, including a Captain Sydenham (John Stow, *Annals* (1615), 752–3). Although Donne was not a participant in the Lisbon expedition, he could have learned of the fall of the wall at Corunna at any time after the event. *envyde*: envied.

Epigram: 'Zoppo' (A Lame Beggar) (MS p. 93)

Attempts have been made to link the figure of Zoppo with the plight of disabled English veterans of the Armada and other campaigns, discharged without pay, who took to begging on the streets of London. But Donne's characterization is abstractly generic as well as coolly paradoxical: the beggar's plea, if true, is false, for how, if not on his own initiative, did he get into the street? John Manningham attributed a version of this epigram to Donne (entry for March 1603 in *Diary*, ed. Robert P. Sorlien (1976), 219).

Epigram: 'Cadiz and Guyana' (MS p. 93)

This epigram can be dated to late July–early August 1597. The circumstances are the same as those described in the note to ll. 1–8 of 'To Mr C.B.' ('Thou, which art I').

you: the earl of Essex and Sir Walter Raleigh. *th' old worlds farthest end*: Cadiz, west of the Pillars of Hercules, themselves the westernmost limit of classical geography. *the new world*: the West Indies and, more specifically here, Guiana. *one things end...a new*: A traditional Aristotelian doctrine.

Epigram: 'Il Cavaliere Giovanni Wingefield' (Sir John Wingfield) (MS p. 93)

The subject is the sack of Cadiz by the English in 1596. On this expedition Sir John Wingfield served as quartermaster, attached to Essex. He was the only Englishman of rank to be killed in this action, and all accounts mention him. One source records that 'that worthy famous knight Sir John Winkfield, ... sore wounded before on the thigh at the very entry of the town, ...yet for all that... to encourage and direct his company, was with the shot of a musket in the head most unfortunately slain' (Samuel Purchas, *Purchas His Pilgrimes* (1625–6, 1907 edn), 20–2).

Epigram: 'Your Mistres, that you follow whores', titled 'A Self-Accuser' in Poems (1633) (MS p. 93)

There is no need to assume a real-life target. Donne's wry wit rivals Martial.

Epigram: 'Thy sins and haires', titled 'A Licentious Person' in Poems (1633) (MS p. 93)

This epigram found favour with later wits; Francis Quarles published a wordy imitation in his *Argalus and Parthenia* (1629), 162. *Thy sins and haires*: Donne cheekily takes his point of departure from Psalm 40:12: 'Mine iniquities have taken hold upon me...: they are more than the hairs of mine head'. *thy haires do fall*: Syphilis accelerated baldness.

Epigram: 'Antiquary' (MS p. 94)

In the absence of a convincing identification of a real-life *Hammon*, an old satirical anecdote is worthy of note. Henri Estienne tells of a certain man 'who going about to catch a sottish Antiquary foolishly fond of such toyes, ...courted him a long time, [and] in the end for a goodly ancient monument shewed him his wife, who was foure score yeares of age' (*L'Introduction au traité de la conformité des merveilles anciennes avec les modernes* (1566), 11, trans. R[ichard] C[arew] as *A World of Wonders* (1607), 22). Martial, *Epigrams*, 8.6, satirizes a gullible, pretentious collector of antiquities who may well be the prototype of the figure in the anecdote.

Hammon: Donne's Satire 5, l. 87 refers to 'Hamman if he sold his antiquitees'. Other references to a similar figure include Sir John Davies, *Epigrams*, 20, and Everard Guilpin, *Skialetheia*, Satyre 1, 136–42. Either the old satirical anecdote or some contemporary who brought it to mind provided a butt for Inns of Court wits in the 1590s.

Epigram: 'Thou call'st me effeminate' (MS p. 94)

Robbins, *Complete Poems of Donne*, 17, notes that pederasty seems to have been a particularly live topic in the 1590s.

Epigram: 'Thy father all from thee' (MS p. 94)

The legal references—'last Will', 'good title'—suggest a Lincoln's Inn context and hence a date of *c.*1592–4 for this epigram. Sir John Harington, *Epigrams* (1618), 1.65, expanded Donne's distillation into a narrative:

> *Of one that vow'd to dis-inherit his sonne, and give his*
> *goods to the poore.*
>
> A Citizen that dwelt near Temple-barre,
> By hap one day fell with his Sonne at Jarre;
> Whom for his evill life, and lewd demerit,
> He oft affirm'd, he would quite dis-inherit,
> And vow'd his goods, and lands, all to the poore.
> His sonne what with his play, what with his whore,
> Was so consum'd at last, as he did lacke
> Meate for his mouth, and clothing for his backe.
> O craftie poverty! His father now
> May give him all he hath, yet keepe his vow.

Epigram: 'Thou in the fields' (MS p. 94)

Donne may have taken a cue from Martial's Philo, who swears he never eats dinner at home because he is invited to dine out all the time (*Epigrams*, 5.47). *Nebuchadnezzar*: A king of Babylon who went mad, 'was driven from men, and did eat grass as oxen' (Daniel 5:33). *A salad . . . dyeting*: The Spanish were proverbially moderate eaters.

Epigram: 'Mercurius Gallo-Belgicus' (MS p. 94)

On the popular news-sheet, *Mercurius Gallo-Belgicus*, see the note to Satire 4, ll. 112–17. Donne's *Mercury* represents the compiler as being both a gullible reporter and a fast-and-loose plagiarist. *Like Aesops fellow slaves . . . Like Aesops selfe, which nothing*: In the traditional 'Life of Aesop' familiar to most schoolboys in this era, a certain Xanthus was considering the purchase of three slaves, the ugly Aesop and two handsome youths—Liguris, a musician, and Philocalus, a teacher. Xanthus put the same question to all three: 'What do you know how to do?' Liguris and Philocalus responded, 'Everything'; Aesop, 'Nothing at all'. 'Why', asked Xanthus, 'do you say, Nothing?' Aesop replied, 'Because the other two boys know everything there is' (*Aesopica*, ed. B. E. Perry (1952), 84–5).

Thy credit lost thy credit: Your credulity forfeited your crediblity. *to doo…as thou wouldst be done unto*: A submerged allusion to Matthew 7:12. *like Mercury in stealing*. The messenger god of classical myth, Greek Hermes (Roman Mercury), acquired a reputation as a thief (*Iliad*, 5.88–91; 24.22–4); he also fathered Autolycus, the human master thief (*Odyssey*, 19.195–6). *lyest like a Greeke*: A proverbial attribute (Tilly, *Dictionary*, F11).

Epigram: 'Thy flattering picture, Phryne' (MS p. 94)

A courtesan famed for her beauty in the age of Alexander the Great, Phryne was a subject favoured by epigrammatists of the *Greek Anthology* (16, 203–5). She reportedly served as the model for two of the greatest art works in antiquity: Apelles's painting of Aphrodite rising from the sea, and Praxiteles's sculpture of Aphrodite at Cnidos. Donne treats her as a type figure: women's 'painted faces' were frequent targets of satire and epigram at this period in England. In 1619 William Drummond of Hawthornden noted that Ben Jonson 'oft' quoted this epigram (*Ben Jonson*, ed. Hereford, Simpson, and Simpson, 1.150).

Epigram: 'Philo with twelve yeares study' (MS p. 94)

What is known of the scholarly subject of this epigram is what Donne says in it; no contemporary figure who fits such a profile has yet been identified with certainty. The name suggests the prototype of Philo of Alexandria (20 BCE–50 CE), the Hellenized Jew who undertook to harmonize ideas of God, the Creation, and ethics in Greek philosophy and in Hebrew tradition by means of allegorical interpretation and number symbolism. Donne's *Philo* may be the Church of England divine George Gifford (1548–1600), who demonstrated his interest in apocalypticism by translating William Fulke's Latin commentary on the subject in 1573. In 1596 Gifford published fifty sermons on the book of Revelation, an often abstruse allegory figuring the end of the world and the last judgement.

Epigram: 'Klokius so deeply' hath vowd' (MS p. 94)

The germ of this epigram traces to an anecdote in Diogenes Laertius's 'Life of Aristippus': 'One day as he entered the house of a courtesan, one of the young men with him blushed, whereupon he remarked, "It is not going in that is dangerous, but being unable to go out"' (*Lives of Ancient Philosophers*, 2.79). Donne's snapshot of the *deeply* self-amending Klockius is enhanced by endowing him with a consistency so rigorous that it prevents him from going home to his own (implicitly promiscuous) wife. His name is a puzzle; it may derive from earlier English *clok* or 'cloak', suggesting the covert amours that Klokius now renounces, or from the German slang word *Glocke* (testicles).

Epigram: 'Martial castrato' (MS p. 94)

this man gelded Martiäl: This epigram is titled 'Raderus' in other seventeenth-century sources, thus pointing to the German Jesuit, Matthew Rader (1561–1634), who published an expurgated Latin version of Martial's epigrams (1602) for use in schools. *himselfe alone his tricks would use*: What Donne briefly proposes here about Rader's motives would be elaborated in *Ignatius His Conclave* (1610): '*Raderus*, and others of his *Order*, did use to gelde *Poets*, and other *Authors*... yet...not geld them to that purpose that the memory thereof should bee abolished' but to 'reserve to themselves...the secrets and mysteries...which they finde in the *Authors* whom they geld' (Donne, *Complete Poetry and Selected Prose*, ed. John Hayward (1936), 391–2). *As Katherine...put downe stews*: William Camden's chronicle history relates how along the Thames-side in Southwark 'little roomes or secret chambers of harlots wherein they filthily prostituted their bodies...were prohibited by King Henrie the Eighth...which in other nations are continued for gaine, under a specious shew of helping mans infirmity' (*Britain*, trans. Philemon Holland, 436). Henry issued this prohibition in 1546; Katherine Parr was then his sixth and last wife. Donne saucily imputes to this virtuous queen the hypocritical motives that Camden ascribes to 'other countries': closing the brothels of Southwark could increase the supply of whores at court. *stews*: brothels.

Epigram: 'Compassion in the world' (MS p. 94)

The irony of both the situation and the commentary is extremely compressed. What seems to be the broker's fellow-feeling (*Compassion*) stems from distress at the prospect of losing the money that *Ralphius* owes him if Ralphius dies. But the *sick* Ralphius cannot even take to *his bedd* because he has pawned it to the *Broker. Compassion* in this case proves not to be fellow-feeling at all, but joint suffering (an alternative etymology for the word). Donne's pun on *keepes his bedd* highlights the pawnbroker's unrelenting meanness.

TO A JET RING SENT TO ME (MS P. 95)

This sole exemplar of a love lyric in the Westmoreland manuscript begins a new leaf, only to be followed by ten blank leaves that end the bound volume. Why did Rowland Woodward copy just this one love lyric, and no more? Did he lack access to the texts of others? (The ten blank leaves, pp. 96–105, suggest that more material to copy was expected.) Did Donne intervene to prevent even so close a friend from copying any more of his love lyrics? The enigma remains just that.

Ovid, *Amores*, 2.15, addresses twenty-eight lines of verse to a ring being sent to a mistress. In Jonson's *Every Man in his Humor* (1598), 2.4, Stephen the gull is distressed at losing his purse because it contained 'the jet ring mistris Mary sent me'. Jet, a form of lignite, was found in great quantities on the shore at Whitby in north Yorkshire. Cheap but brittle, it was frequently carved into such ornaments as rings and buttons.

a Jet ring sent to me [title]: The phrasing suggests that the title is authorial.
ll. 1–12. *Thou art not... halfe so britle... Shee... would... breake thee*: The poem moves
antithetically and circularly from beginning to end. *black*: The proverbial colour of
jet (Tilley, *Dictionary*, B436)—also the colour associated with melancholy. *both our
properties*: his as lover, his mistress's as faithless. *Nothing more endless* than his love;
nothing sooner broke than her vow to be constant to him.

FROM THE LOSELEY PAPERS, LETTERS CONCERNING
DONNE'S SECRET MARRIAGE TO ANNE MORE,
FEBRUARY–MARCH 1602

A group of seven letters in Donne's evenly proportioned, italic hand, on his marriage
with Anne More, written to his (now) father-in-law, Sir George More, and his (sud-
denly former) employer, Sir Thomas Egerton, Lord Keeper of the Great Seal. These
letters are part of a group of eighteen belonging to a larger collection, the Loseley
Papers, acquired by the Folger Shakespeare Library, Washington, DC, between 1938
and 1954. See the facsmile, *John Donne's Marriage Letters in the Folger Shakespeare
Library*, ed. and intro. M. Thomas Hester, Robert Parker Sorlien, and Dennis Flynn,
with an afterword by Heather Wolfe (2005).

LETTER I. FOLGER MS L.B.526. JOHN DONNE
TO SIR GEORGE MORE, 2 FEBRUARY 1602.

This is the first letter Donne wrote to his father-in-law after secretly marrying Anne
More *about three weeks before Christmas* 1601 (l. 12). Donne's powerful friend, Henry
Percy, 9th earl of Northumberland, delivered the letter to Sir George. While profess-
ing the couple's honourable intentions and conduct at every stage of their courtship
and disclaiming the use of any underhanded means, this letter also declares that both
had resolved to act in secrecy because if they sought Sir George's consent or gave any
knowledge of their intention of marrying, that *had been to impossibilitate the whole mat-
ter*, in Donne's striking phrase (l. 20).

In defying not merely custom but patriarchal authority, Donne and Anne seriously
underestimated the magnitude of their offence and its negative implications for their
future. These they would learn the hard way, by experience, during the difficult years
that lay ahead. At this early point, however, six weeks after their secret marriage,
Donne's letter breaks the news with confidence that his and Anne's frankness and
deference will allay their breach of conduct and secure Sir George's goodwill. In aim-
ing at this positive outcome, however, Donne repeatedly characterizes his father-in-
law's attitudes and conduct in negative terms.

The second of three reasons Donne gives for secretly marrying Anne is made to
sound like Sir George's fault: *I knew... your opinion* (ll. 18–19). The most important
reason of all for acting unilaterally was the certainty of Sir George's unrelenting oppo-
sition, and this should exonerate him and Anne: *Me thinks... torment* (ll. 22–3). Next,

after some deferential gestures, Donne presumes to admonish his father-in-law to control his rage: *I humbly beg...you full of passion* (ll. 27–9). He tells Sir George to accept the marriage as fact, to do nothing irreversible, and to act constructively (ll. 31–2).

Although garnished fore and aft with expressions of respect and humility, Donne's first appeals to his father-in-law produced exactly the results he wanted to prevent. Sir George persuaded Egerton to terminate Donne's secretaryship; he sought and obtained a writ for Donne's arrest and imprisonment; and he filed a petition in the Court of High Commission seeking annulment of the marriage. The frequent bravado of the speaker in Donne's satires, elegies, verse letters to male friends, paradoxes, and epigrams had yielded frequent triumphs of rhetoric and wit. But one crucial triumph would elude the youthful Donne in the late Elizabethan milieu where he sought to regularize his marriage. Literature and life do speak to each other, but they do not reduce to the same thing.

ll. 1–2, 31. *my Lord*: Sir Thomas Egerton, Lord Keeper of the Great Seal. After Donne took part in the Islands expedition of 1597 together with the younger Thomas Egerton, who, like Donne, was a member of Lincoln's Inn. The Lord Keeper appointed Donne as his secretary at some point between early 1598 and early 1599. The appointment was the son's idea; cf. Letter 7, ll. 13–14. *respective*: heedful, attentive—senses no longer current.

ll. 5–8.   *wayting upon*: paying a respectful visit to. *her...York House*: Anne More first visited Egerton's London residence after he married her widowed aunt, Elizabeth Wolley, in late October 1597.

ll. 10–20.   *her...parliament*: Parliament had been in session from 27 October to 19 December 1601. Sir George had served in every Parliament since 1584; this time Anne accompanied her father to London (Bald, *Donne: A Life*, 128–9). *fyve persons*: Two of these were Christopher Brooke and his younger brother Samuel, who performed the ceremony. See the verse-letters to C.B. and S.B. Who the other three persons were remains unknown. *impossibilitate*: render impossible.

ll. 33–41.   *If any...ill thoughts of me*: A probable reference to Edmond Neville, mentioned by Donne in a letter written to Anne in late 1600 as someone who may have informed Sir George about rumours linking the two of them. See Dennis Flynn, 'Anne More, John Donne, and Edmond Neville', in M. Thomas Hester, ed., *John Donne's 'Desire of More': The Subject of Anne More Donne in His Poetry* (1996), 143–4. *fayth and...do good*: Sir George should distrust those who spread bad reports and trust only those who spread good ones. *rayse or scatter*: prop up or break into pieces.

LETTER 2. FOLGER MS L.B.527. JOHN DONNE TO SIR GEORGE MORE, 11 FEBRUARY 1602.

Nine days after sending his first letter to Sir George, Donne writes from the Fleet prison in London. He now acknowledges that he has committed a great offence, incurring the displeasure of God and Egerton as well as Sir George, but he denies acting with *a contemptuous and despightfull purpose* (l. 11). Sick, dejected, and fearful, Donne begs Sir George not to let *yll reports* (l. 15) compound his offence. He pleads not only for himself but also for Anne (ll. 25–6).

ll. 2–26. *my Lords heavy displeasure*: Egerton has dismissed Donne. *ungracious*: unac-
ceptable, disliked. *Entertainment*: consideration. *disculpe*: clear from blame.
my late lady: Elizabeth, lady Egerton, Anne's aunt, had assumed some
responsibility for Anne's upbringing after her mother died in 1590. Lady
Egerton suffered a severe case of smallpox in 1598–9 and died in January
1600 (Bald, *Donne: A Life*, 109). *my Religion*: Sir George considered Donne
a Roman Catholic, but he was likely to have taken the Oath of Supremacy
(acknowledging Elizabeth as supreme governor of the Church of England)
when he was appointed Egerton's secretary (Bald, *Donne: A Life*, 94). *vio-
lenced*: violated.

LETTER 3. FOLGER MS L.B.528. JOHN DONNE TO LORD KEEPER THOMAS EGERTON. 12 FEBRUARY 1602.

A day after writing Sir George a letter of apology, Donne addressed a pleading appeal to his former employer, requesting him *to lessen that Correction...destind for me* (ll. 16–17). Donne informs Egerton that any future course of action will be deter-mined by him since *Sir George More...referrs all to your Lordship* (ll. 14–16). This letter elicited some leniency; Donne was almost immediately released from prison and allowed to return to his lodgings.

ll. 8–12. *My services...were payd*: Since Donne's name does not appear on any extant
list of Egerton's paid employees, *favors* of association and contacts may have
been his recompense. The speaker of Satire 5, addressing Egerton, says that
he is 'By having leave to serve,...most richly | For service paid' (ll. 31–3).
yt hath much profited...dejected: This seems to be the earliest example of
paradoxically translating a bad experience into a good outcome—a turn of
thought and expression that became a signature feature of Donne's religious
outlook in the *Devotions*.

LETTER 4. FOLGER MS L.B.529. JOHN DONNE TO SIR GEORGE MORE. 13 FEBRUARY 1602.

From his rented *Chamber* (l. 30) in a house near the Savoy, Donne writes to thank his father-in-law for consenting to his release from prison. He does not deny *that fault which was layd to me...of having deceived some gentlewomen before, and...of loving a corrupt Religion* (ll. 4–6), but he assures Sir George that both are things of the past.

Next acknowledging *this Offence committed to you* (ll. 11–12), he entreats Sir George *to soften your hart...to pardon us* (l. 16). Donne further ventures to ask his father-in-law to help him gain reinstatement with Egerton (ll. 16–19). Finally he entreats Sir George to give Anne *some kind and Comfortable message* (l. 22) and permit him to *write to her* (ll. 24–5). *I ame unchangeably resolvd*, declares Donne, *to make me fitt for her* (ll. 26–7).

ll. 7–14. *Article of our Death*: very moment at which we die. *some uncharitable Malice…doble at least*: Donne again suspects someone (perhaps Edmond Neville) of exaggerating his indebtedness to Sir George. *of Evyll Manners good lawes growe*: A proverbial expression.

LETTER 5. FOLGER MS L.B.530. JOHN DONNE TO LORD KEEPER THOMAS EGERTON. 13 FEBRUARY 1602.

Opening with a graceful compliment, Donne thanks Egerton for his release from prison, which has improved his health. He seconds this compliment with another, appealing to Egerton for *pardon* that *may gaine my Mind her Chiefe Comfort* (ll. 6–7). As if to give concrete form to his self-abasement, Donne places his signature at the farthest possible distance from the body of his letter, in the right-hand bottom corner of the page. He will do this again in subsequent letters to Egerton and Sir George (see Figures 2–5).

LETTER 6. FOLGER MS L.B.532. JOHN DONNE TO SIR GEORGE MORE. 1 MARCH 1602.

In this forthright letter to his father-in-law, Donne begs for pardon, for help in regaining his position as Egerton's secretary, and for permission to write to Anne. His survey of his possible professional options and resources is of interest. His *love* for Anne and his *Conscience* as a subject loyal to the Crown and Church of England *restrain* him *from seeking* employment abroad (ll. 12–13). Yet, he recognizes, *My Lords disgracings cut me off* (l. 13) from preferments here at home. *My Emprisonments, and theyrs whose love to me brought them to yt*—both Brooke brothers were imprisoned for their roles in the marriage—have further depleted his resources (ll. 13–15). Donne senses, moreover, that the *love of my frinds* (l. 15) and their readiness to help him *suffers somewhat, in these long and uncertain disgraces of myne* (l. 15–16). Finally of interest is the allusion to the decision of the Court of High Commission—affirming the validity of the marriage—on which occasion Donne had spoken with Sir George about writing to Anne: *I understood therupon that…you were not displeased…yet I have not nor wyll not without your knowledge do yt* (ll. 21–2).

ll. 6–9. *those yll reports…of me*: Another possible reference to Edmond Neville. *my suit to my Lord*: Donne's letter of 12 February to Egerton.

ll. 22–4. *was bold…letter to you*: Donne's letter of 13 February. More than two weeks later Donne had still not been permitted to write to Anne. *the Thursday*: On Thursday, 18 February 1602, the Court of High Commission rendered positive judgement on the validity of Donne's and Anne's marriage, after which he and Sir George evidently reached some mutual understanding (Bald, *Donne: A Life*, 137).

LETTER 7. FOLGER MS L.B.533. JOHN DONNE
TO LORD KEEPER THOMAS EGERTON. I MARCH 1602.

ll. 2–5. *The Commissioners...encline also to remitt yt*: On 25 February the Court of
High Commission convened for a 'Mitigation Day' when judgements
could be lightened or remitted. *Sir George... last going*: From London home-
ward to Loseley on 18 February, after the Court of High Commission pro-
nounced the marriage valid.

ll. 10–14. *an indifferent fortune*: a modest inheritance. *a freedom and independency*:
Donne's parents afforded him latitude to chart his own course in life. *without
marking...your Lordships servant*: Another reference to the non-monetary
basis on which Donne served Egerton. *your good Sonns love to me*: the affec-
tion of the younger Sir Thomas Egerton for Donne. *I was 4 years your
Lordships Secretary*: From some point in 1598 through 1601, by Donne's
reckoning.

ll. 17–18. *that Course...to travaile*: Donne's remark redoubles the one made to Sir
George in Letter 6, l. 12. Both men would have registered the connection
between Donne's distancing of himself from Roman Catholicism and his
disinclination to seek foreign employment. *travaile*: Two meanings are in
play: 'travel', 'work abroad'.

ll. 24–35. *disgraciously*: ungraciously, with disgrace. *entender*: make tender, soften.

THE *FIRST* AND *SECOND ANNIVERSARIES*
(1ST COMPLETE EDITION, 1612)

CIRCUMSTANCES, AUTHORSHIP, ORDER OF COMPOSITION,
THEMATIC PURPOSE

In Donne's day, publishing a work anonymously could be an appealing option for an
author, either because the work's content might incur official censure or, as evidently
in Donne's case, because his name and gentlemanly status could be shielded from the
commoner associations of print. Despite gaps in the material evidence, scholarship
on Donne's *Anniversaries* has compiled a persuasive account of the circumstances,
authorship, and order of composition of the poems contained in the complete edition
of 1612. After this volume appeared, Donne did acknowledge his authorship.
Regarding the circumstances, however, he insisted that he 'never knew the gentle-
woman', fifteen-year-old Elizabeth Drury, sole heir of Sir Thomas and Lady Drury,
whose death in December 1610 devastated her parents and ended their dynastic
ambitions. But Donne's older sister, Anne, lived near Hawstead, in Suffolk, the
Drury family seat, and had at least observed the young Elizabeth. A literary acquaint-
ance of Donne's, the poet and clergyman Joseph Hall, was vicar of Hawstead and a
spiritual adviser to Lady Drury in the years between Elizabeth's sixth and twelfth
birthdays.

Donne's first composition seems to have been 'A Funerall Elegie', although it is the third poem in the published arrangement of 1612. The ascription of priority depends partly on a situational inference: this elegy's opening gestures at Elizabeth Drury's tomb in Hawstead church, which bore an epitaph by Donne, presumably written close to the time of her burial. Further compelling suggestions of the priority of 'A Funerall Elegie' emerge from textual features: it contains, in outline, themes and images that the *First* and *Second Anniversary* elaborate and complicate.

The point of departure for 'A Funerall Elegie' is the mortal wounding of the world by the death of a girl who embodied virtue and value in their purest state. She was the world's 'soule', the essence of its meaning and purpose. But since she fell prey to 'Fate', all possibility of goodness in those who survive her is merely derivative: such was the 'force and vigor' of her precedent. 'If after her | Any shall live, which dare true good prefer, | Ev'ry such person is her delegate...For future vertuous deeds are Legacies, | Which from the gift of her example rise.' In these lines the *First Anniversary* emerges in epitome. 'A Funerall Elegie' foreshadows *The Second Anniversary* more sketchily, but some key elements are discernible. 'Sickly alas, short-liv'd, aborted', the moral efforts of others contrast starkly with the departed soul's 'Virgin white integrity'. She 'tooke...Her destiny to her selfe' as 'liberty...but for thus much, thus much to die'. Her liberation into a state 'greater, purer, firmer, than before', by which she escapes 'th' infirmities which waite upon | Woman' and overcomes 'the worlds busie noyse', occasions 'joy' in heaven. There her 'cleare body...a through-light scarfe, her minde t' enroule' receives its ultimate glorification, and there too her exemplary influence gives rise to 'spirit'uall mirth, | To see how well, the good play her, on earth'.

The First Anniversary, alternatively titled *An Anatomy of the World*, appeared in print with a subtitle not necessarily supplied by Donne: *Wherein, by Occasion of the Untimely Death of Mistris Elizabeth Drury the Frailty and the Decay of this whole World is Represented*. The subtitle serves, however, to articulate the poem's emotional logic. The death of a promising girl, which otherwise defies comprehension, figures the draining away of goodness, beauty, harmony, and vitality from the universe. The linguistic fact that feminine nouns are the 'names' of virtues intensifies the emotional logic and helps to naturalize the gender of the poem's central subject. Less immediately evident, however, is Donne's purpose in invoking scientific hypotheses and discoveries of his day to register sweepingly negative poetic effects in the *First Anniversary* (and the *Second Anniversary* as well).

The question of purpose can only be addressed by working through the dense texture and manifold allusions in the two *Anniversaries* and their accompanying poems. At the outset, however, one general observation can be offered. It consistently emerges that the 'world' whose 'frailty' and 'decay' are the findings of the 'anatomy' conducted in the *First Anniversary* and whose features and composition are elided in the soul's speedy ascent to heaven in the *Second Anniversary* is the cosmic system that had been a staple of classical and Christian thought for centuries. Supposedly impervious to destruction or alteration, this cosmos comprised seven concentric spheres in which the moon, planets, and sun moved in circular orbits around a stationary central earth. Beyond these lay the domains of the elements of fire, air, and aether (the purest form of air), enclosed and bounded by the 'primum mobile', the seat of God as Prime Mover and First Cause.

This cosmic system, whose conceptual origins lay with the Pythagoreans and pre-Socratics, was developed by Plato and systematized by Aristotle. Its diagrammatic representation by the late antique astronomer Claudius Ptolemy gave rise to the term the 'Ptolemaic universe'. By according this universe the status of a Christian doctrine, Aquinas assimilated Aristotle's authority in a synthesis that remained central to the orthodoxy of later Scholastics, Catholics and Protestants alike. Both symbol and substance of the harmonizing of theology and natural philosophy, this was the geocentric world-picture that Copernicus, Galileo, and others disrupted and finally displaced with their newly direct observations of celestial phenomena, aided by the telescope, a recent invention, and advances in understanding certain physical forces (magnetism, parallax).

THE FIRST ANNIVERSARIE, SO TITLED IN 1612
(SIG. A1R)—THE GENRE

AN ANATOMIE... is represented: Title in 1611, the first edition of 'To the Praise of the Dead, and the Anatomy', 'An Anatomy of the World', and 'A Funerall Elegie'. Donne composed 'An Anatomie of the World' (*First Anniversary*) between March and October 1611.

The custom of annually commemorating a deceased person is attested for Donne's England by Shakespeare's Claudio. He hangs an epitaph on the tomb of Hero, whom he believes dead, and vows: 'Yearly will I do this rite' (*Much Ado about Nothing*, 5.3.123). Donne's poetic commemorations of Elizabeth Drury would take shape in paired creations far more intricate and extensive than Claudio's simple gesture and epitaph.

In her book-length study of the *Anniversaries*, Barbara K. Lewalski characterizes the two poems as 'complex, mixed-genre works which weld together formal, thematic, and structural elements from various sources—the occasional poem of praise, the funeral elegy, the funeral sermon, the hymn, the anatomy, the Protestant meditation, to mention only the most important' (*Donne's 'Anniversaries' and the Poetry of Praise: The Creation of a Symbolic Mode* (1973), 6). Graham Roebuck offers further commentary on the achievement registered by Donne's handling of this hybrid poetic genre ('The Anniversary Poem', in Shami, Flynn, and Hester, eds, *The Oxford Handbook of John Donne*, 273–84).

As originally titled, the *First Anniversary* develops as a four-part assemblage or 'anatomy' headed by an introduction (ll. 1–90). The first part examines the microcosm (ll. 91–190); the second part the macrocosm (ll. 191–246); the third part the beauty of proportion and colour in the microcosm and macrocosm (ll. 247–376); and the fourth and final part projects the cosmic disruption of heaven and earth (ll. 377–414). Within each part, hyperbolic extolling of Elizabeth Drury, abstractly referred to as 'she', follows lengthy negative analysis and is itself followed by a refrain renouncing a world bereft of her presence. Such is the process of Donne's 'anatomy', the *First Anniversary*.

When the *Anniversaries* appeared in print in 1611–12, certain readers recognized Donne's unprecedented reconfiguring of the genre of funeral elegy and his extra-dimensional enlargement of its poetic range. These readers—fellow poets and others with literary aspirations—promptly paid Donne tribute in imitations and echoes of his lines: John Davies of Hereford in 'A Funeral Elegie, on the death of…Elizabeth Dutton' in his *Muses Sacrifice, or Divine Meditations* (1612); Daniel Price, *Lamentations for the death of the late illustrious Prince Henry* (1611) as well as sermons entitled *Prince Henry the first anniversary* (1613) and *Prince Henry the second anniversary* (1614), and elegies on Prince Henry by Sir Henry Goodyere and Sir Edward Herbert. Lewalski surveys this early evidence of the poems' reception history (*Donne's 'Anniversaries'*, 309–35).

TO THE PRAISE OF THE DEAD, AND THE ANATOMY (SIGS. A2R–A4V)

Joseph Hall's authorship of this commendatory poem has been inferred from other evidence of his involvement in the project of Donne's *Anniversaries*. Jonson identified Hall as the author of 'The Harbinger to the Progress', the poem that prefaces the *Second Anniversary*. He may also have been signalling Hall's authorship of 'The Praise of the Dead' prefacing the *First Anniversary*, for both poems are markedly similar in style and purpose. The publisher of both editions of the *Anniversaries* was Samuel Macham, who, like Hall, was a native of Ashby de la Zouche, and had previously published several of Hall's books.

Title: *ANATOMY*: the dissection of a corpse for medical investigation or teaching purposes; also, figuratively, a searching analysis or satiric exposé.

ll. 3–15.   *No evil…good*: Every bad thing has its good side; here, the world's death offers an occasion for enhanced understanding: *thus we gaine. state*: estate: here, of a dead father, enriching heirs who pretend to grieve for him. *blacks*: mourning clothes. *this Muse lives…this spirit lives*: Hall salutes the vitality and ingenuity that Donne has infused into 'An Anatomy of the World'. *last nephews*: descendants'.

ll. 21–34. *Enough is us*: It is enough for us. *the wise Egyptians…houses*: Already in antiquity it was commonplace to note that the Egyptians built houses of mud brick but magnificent tombs, attesting their belief in an unending afterlife. Cf. *Devotions*, Meditation 7. *for being thus*: for being thus praised. *profest*: affirmed.

ll. 43–8.   *burden*: Wordplay on two senses: chorus or refrain; heavy load. *ditty*: words to a song. *note*: melody of a song.

THE FIRST ANNIVERSARY. AN ANATOMIE OF THE WORLD, SO TITLED IN 1611 (P. 1)

ll. 1–6.   *rich*: Donne the preacher would pursue the biblical connotations: 'Gods goodnesse towards us…his Grace here, his Glory hereafter, are all represented to us in Riches' (*Sermons*, 6:304). *her heav'n*: the place prepared for her in heaven. *celebrate... praise*: 'Truly to glorifie God in his Saints,...To celebrate them, is to imitate them' (*Sermons*, 10:190). *a soule*: 'We have, in our one soul,...*three faculties*...the *Understanding*, the *Will*, and the *Memory*' (*Sermons*, 2:72–3). The memory was the storehouse of sense perceptions (*see*); the understanding was the exercise of reason (*Judge*); the will impelled action toward some end—here, *follow worthinesse*. *In-mate:* lodger, guest.

ll. 7–10. *Queene... house*: The metaphor of the soul is that of a prince in the body, embarked on a journey (*progresse*) through its domains, and arriving at its permanent residence (*standing house*). *attend*: await. *a part... Song*: both a singer of praise in heaven, and part of what is praised in the song sung by *the Saints*. Cf. 'To the Praise of the Dead, and the Anatomy', ll. 35–44.

ll. 11–18. *that great earthquake... a common Bath of teares... drew the strongest vitall spirits out*: Donne's images introduce a fundamental thematic and structural relation: the correspondences between the macrocosm (the world as a whole) and the microcosm (the little world that is a human being). The departure of Elizabeth Drury's soul in death deprived the world's body of its animating principle, causing terminal convulsions, severe prostration, and enfeeblement from a fatal *wound* (l. 27). *Whether... lose or gaine*: Is the world worse or better as a result? The loss of this soul has opened a way to all who *endeavour to be as good as shee... to see her* again in heaven.

ll. 19–32. *great consumption*: The multiple bodily disorders of the *sicke world* reveal its precarious condition: a general wasting of its strength, alternating attacks (*fits*) of *fever* and chills (*Agues*), and an overall stupefaction and insensibility (*Lethargee*), which in Donne's day was identified with the loss of sense, speech, and memory that signalled the approach of death. *thou wast | Nothing... hast o'erpast*: The world lost its identity in losing this soul; in surviving her it has lasted beyond its own death. Donne the preacher would reuse the image: 'Dissolution and putrefaction is gone over thee alive; Thou hast over liv'd thine own death' (*Sermons*, 2:83).

ll. 33–8. *For as a child... thy name*: The power of the name was popularly associated with baptism (*the Font*). Forgotten in the present lethargy, *her name* is the world's name, that which *defin'd* its *forme and frame*. The soul is the 'form' of the body (Aristotle, *De Anima*, 2.2.414a4–19; Aquinas, *Summa Theologica*, 1a.76.1). Celebration of this departed soul will somewhat revive the world's memory of its name, and hence of its nature and living identity.

ll. 39–54. She has been dead for some months, but all reckoning of time ended with her death. Although she has been away *long*, nobody *Offers to tell us* what we have lost by her going (39–42). The speaker gives some reasons why others have not spoken of her death as he is preparing to do: it arouses foreboding (43–6), the sense of justice lost and of a moral vacuum cannot be expressed (47–51), it betrays weakness to admit how devastating her loss is (52–4).

ll. 55–66. The speaker announces his intention of performing an *Anatomy* on the world's *dead, yea putrified* body, to *discover* (ascertain, reveal) its *infirmities* and *study them*. The procedure is warranted because the world's body *Can never be renew'd...never live*; the departed soul was its *intrinsique Balme, and...preservative*. Donne's understanding of *Balme* or balsamum as 'our naturall inborn preservative' (*Letters*, 97–8) derived from Paracelsus (Philipp von Hohenheim), a Swiss physician, alchemist, astrologer, and advocate of the occult arts who credited this substance with keeping the body healthy by healing wounds and counteracting poisons (*Hermetic and Alchemical Writings*, trans. A. E. Wait (1894), 2:69–74). To conclude his announcement, the speaker simply sidesteps the objection that no man would be *Alive to study this dissectiön...the world it self being dead*.

ll. 67–78. *What life...still*: The explanation of *a kind of world remaining* is based on the distinction between the instantaneous death of a human being and the gradual process by which the earth might become incapable of supporting life, or a star's light might dwindle to extinction. The speaker also draws out the ambiguity of the term *world*. The slow expiration of the *world* understood as the Earth—*a glimmering light...in this last long night*—shades into a moral universe with not only a discernible afterlife but certain generative capacities as well. *The twilight of her memory... | Creates a new world, and new creatures...The matter and the stuffe...Her vertue; and the forme our practise is*.

ll. 79–90. *thus Elemented,...These Creatures...So many weedlesse Paradises bee*: Those humans who emulate the departed soul's moral perfection are a new Eden with the purely positive characteristics of the Eden of Genesis before the Fall. *This new world...diseases of the old*: While Donne's conceptual framework of a new Eden devoid of evil has biblical authority, he chooses to employ Platonic–Aristotelian notions to represent moral aspiration in the wake of this lamented soul's departure. When rational humans acquire knowledge of good and evil, they will practise temperance and shun evils (*with due temper...forgoe*) and they will desire to possess the good (*covet things, when they their true worth know*). Having introduced this bifurcated perspective—a Christian view of the state of the world at large and a classical view of the prospect of achieving goodness within it—Donne proceeds with a detailed inventory assembled from traditional classical and Christian commonplaces regarding the decay of the world. At this period the decay of the world was becoming a prominent subject in England— e.g., Henry Cuffe's *The Differences of the Ages of Mans Life* (1607), of which Donne owned a copy; Walter Raleigh's preface to his *History of the World* (1614); and Godfrey Goodman's *The Fall of Man* (1616). See Victor Harris, *All Coherence Gone* (1949).

ll. 91–8. *no health...a neutralitee*: 'The Physicians Rule' is 'that the best state of Mans body is but a *Neutrality*, neither well nor ill' (*Sermons*, 2:80). *children...headlong come*: The French physician Fernelius (Jean François Fernel) maintained that it is normal for a child to be born head first (*Universa Medicina* (1610),

174). With wordplay on *ruinous* (root sense: rushing headlong forward) and *precipitatiön* (root sense: head-first movement), Donne transmutes the medically normal to the ethically *ominous*. 'What miserable...precipitations may we justly think our selves ordained to, if we consider, that in our coming...out of our mothers womb,...a childe comes right...with the head forward, and thereby prefigure[s] that headlong falling into calamities which it must suffer after' (*Sermons*, 6:333).

ll. 99–110. *ruine...languishment*: Eve was created as Adam's 'help meet' (Genesis 2:18), but by first sinning herself and then inducing him to disobey God, she made him vulnerable to death. *access'ory*: secondary. *principall in ill*: 'Of the woman came the beginning of sin, and through her we all die' (Ecclesiasticus 25:24). *singly...our kinde*: The idea that the ejaculation of sperm gradually depleted male vitality originated in the Aristotelian tradition (*De Longitudine et Brevitate Vitae* [On the Length and Shortness of Life], 466b).

ll. 112–20. *not now that mankinde, which was then*: Pliny ascribes the length of nine human lives to the crow, four lengths of a crow's life to the *Stag*, and three lengths of a stag's life to the *Raven* (*Historia Naturalis*, 7.48; cited by Cuffe, *Differences of the Ages of Man*, 87). *the long-liv'd tree*: Opinions differed as to whether this was the palm or the oak; Donne the preacher would specify the oak: 'the naturall man hath life more abundantly than any other creature, (howsoever Oakes...may be said to out-live him)' (*Sermons*, 9:149). *if a slow-pac'd starre...his observation plaine*: Donne invokes another commonplace, as does Cuffe (88–9), citing the ancient historian Flavius Josephus, who says of 'the first men': 'to promote the utility of their discoveries in astronomy...God would accord a longer life; for they could have predicted nothing with certainty had they not lived for six hundred years' (*Jewish Antiquities*, 1.3.9; Loeb edn (1930), 4:51). *observation plaine*: full ascertaining of a heavenly body's altitude.

ll. 122–8. *Mans growth...the meat*: The quality of the food of earlier humans was manifested in their large physiques, which grew still larger in keeping with their consumption. Josephus and Cuffe both attest the general belief that the food of the biblical patriarchs was superior; cf. *Sermons*, 7:145. *the very stature...towards Heaven direct*: Pagan and Christian commentators of antiquity agreed that the uniquely erect posture of humans was a residual sign of their first heavenly home or a present sign of their direction of thought upon heavenly things (Plato, *Timaeus*, 90a; Augustine, *Patrologia Latina*, 43.999). Donne would re-echo this idea in *Devotions*, Meditation 3. *Methuselah* lived to the age of 969 years (Genesis 5:27).

ll. 133–4. *every peasant strives...three lives*: It was a common misunderstanding that a lease on a *house, or field* for *three lives* would run for three generations. A lease for three lives, however, was made to three persons, to run for the duration of the life of the longest-lived of the three. The peasant's aspiration thus reaches no further than one all-too-brief lifetime of a latter-day man. *torn house*: rough dwelling.

ll. 139–42.   *an Elephant or Whale...so equal to him*: Pagan authors regarded large bones
found in excavations as evidence of the greater size of earlier humans (Pliny,
Historia Naturalis, 7.16). Christian commentators such as Augustine rea-
soned similarly from biblical references to giants (*On the City of God*, 15.9).
The topic figured regularly in discussions of the earth's decay. Hieronymus
Magius (cited by name in *Devotions*, Meditation 16) contains a full account
of testimonies to the decline in human body size (*Variarum Lectionum...Libri
IIII* [Four Books of Various Readings] (1564), 13–28). *The Fayries and the
Pigmies...credible*: Most later authors followed the Greek philosopher and
geographer Strabo (*Geography*, 17.2.1) in dismissing accounts of pygmies as
fables. Donne the preacher would be more cautious: 'Naturall men will
write of lands of Pygmies...But...they do not beleeve, (at least...they do
not know) that there are such' (*Sermons*, 9:100–1).

ll. 145–50.   *death addes t' our length*: The anonymous annotator of the Bodleian Library
copy of the 1621 edition of the *Anniversaries* (shelfmark: Tanner 876)
glosses this line: 'The same Person (when *layd out*) seems longer, than
alive on his legs he did'. *were light*: would be trivial. *chang'd to gold* | *Their
silver*: The primary allusion is alchemical: gold was denser than silver. The
secondary allusion is to the ages of the world; Adam lived in the golden
age, the patriarchs in the silver age. *dispos'd into lesse glas*: Another refer-
ence to alchemy, in which the proper distilling of a substance reduced its
quantity so that it could be contained in a smaller vessel while retaining its
essence at full strength (*Spirits of vertue*).

ll. 151–4.   *w' are not retir'd...bedwarfèd us*: Our littleness of mind and body does not
result from contracting and concentrating our capabilities (*not retir'd, not
close-weaving*); our littleness is like the *shrinking* of moistened wool or flax
(*dampt, crampt*). *bedwarfèd*: Donne's coinage.

ll. 156–8.   *Of nothing he made us*: God's creation of the world and all it contains *ex
nihilo* (from nothing, i.e., from no pre-existent material) became a distinc-
tive Christian doctrine. It is diametrically opposed to the views of classical
antiquity: either that the world came to be out of primordial stuff or that
the world is eternal. *do 't so soone as he*: in as short a time as God took to
create the world and its forms of life.

ll. 159–60.   *new diseases*: First and foremost, syphilis, which spread widely in fif-
teenth- and sixteenth-century Europe. Donne owned a copy of
Guillaume Rondelet's treatise on syphilis which notes that all who
treat it affirm it to be a new malady (*Le traicté de Verole* (1576), 3).
Influenza, too, reached epidemic levels in 1612; this may have been
the sickness Donne contracted in Paris shortly after finishing the
First Anniversary (Bald, *Donne: A Life*, 250). *new phisicke*: The main
target is probably the unconventional medical practice of Paracelsus.
As a character in the prose satire Donne wrote in the same year as the
First Anniversary, Paracelsus boasts that he has brought all orthodox
medicine into contempt (*Ignatius His Conclave*, ed. Timothy Healy
(1969), 21).

ll. 167–8.   *God did woo…to man descend*: Possible referents for the wooing of man
include God's descent to Eden to converse with Adam (Genesis 3:10–11)
or the visit of three mysterious strangers, traditionally allegorized as the
persons of the Trinity, who partake of Abraham's hospitality (Genesis
18:1–16). If Donne is alluding here to the incarnation of Christ, it would
be the only New Testament reference in the *First Anniversary*.

ll. 173–80.   *depart | With*: part with. *they called…name of shee*: Most abstract nouns in
Greek and Latin, including the names of virtues, have feminine gender.
poysonous tincture: In alchemy, 'tincture' figured as a purifying spiritual
substance; cf. *Second Anniversary*, ll. 163–8, 258. But the term takes a neg-
ative turn here from wordplay on another sense of 'tincture'—dye; hence,
the stayne of Eve.

ll. 187–90.   *feed (not banquet) on*: make it your daily fare, not an occasional feast.
better Growth: immortal soul. *Be more than man…an Ant*: The source is
Seneca, *Questiones Naturales* (Questions in Nature) 1, preface.

ll. 194–202.   *Corruption…seiz'd the Angels…then | The world did…take a fall*:
Genesis does not mention the creation of the angels. Aquinas reasoned
that the rebellious angels must have fallen as soon as they apprehended
(and opposed) God's intent in creating the world and man (*Summa
Theologica*, 1a.62.6). Donne wittily casts these angels as the world's
turn'd brains, addled by their fall. *That evening…the day*: Genesis 1:5,
'And the evening and the morning were the first day', was a difficult
verse to interpret because the sun and moon had not yet been created.
Donne follows Aquinas in identifying this *evening* with the angels' sin
and fall, occurring almost as soon as light (*day*) came into being (*Summa
Theologica*, 1a.63.5).

ll. 203–4.   *Springs and Sommers…Like sonnes of women after fifty bee*: Pliny notes
that a woman ordinarily does not bear a child after the age of fifty
(*Historia Naturalis*, 7.14). The variability of the growing season was a
perennial complaint.

ll. 205–6.   *new Philosophy cals all in doubt*: Developments in sixteenth- and seven-
teenth-century natural philosophy channelled a newly aroused interest
in direct observation and careful measurement of physical phenomena.
When findings disconfirmed longstanding doctrines, the result was a
frontal challenge to the Aristotelian–Christian system of cosmic spheres
into which the Ptolemaic conception of a geocentric earth had been
absorbed. Donne registers the force of this contemporary challenge.
Element of fire…put out: From antiquity onwards, it was believed that
spheres of the four elements, earth, water, air, and fire, intervened in
ascending order between the planet Earth and the Moon. Donne evi-
dently alludes to Johannes Kepler's recent treatise on optics, *Dioptrice*
(1610–11), which disproved the existence of a sphere of fire by the
absence of refraction in light rays emitted by more distant stars.
Refraction would be observable if a fiery medium intervened between
the Earth and those stars. Cf. *Second Anniversary*, ll. 193–4.

ll. 207–8. *The Sunne is lost… where to looke for it*: In *De revolutionibus orbium coeles-*
tium (On the Revolutions of the Heavenly Spheres) (1543), Copernicus
attributed three motions to the Earth: diurnal rotation, orbital motion,
and declination, the last to account for the tilt maintained by the Earth's
axis in the course of the other two motions. In attempting to 'save the
phenomena' (salvage observations made of the heavens since antiquity),
Copernicus placed the sun in the centre of the universe, making it the
focal point of the entire cosmic system. But the opportunity to verify the
physical truth of Copernican theory awaited the advent of the telescope in
1609.

ll. 210–11. *in the Planets… many new*: A major source of evidence to counter the
changeless state of perfection ascribed to the celestial heavens by Aristotle,
Ptolemy, and their Christian continuators was the identification of 'new
stars' ('novae' or 'supernovae'). In *De Nova Stella* (On the New Star)
(1573), the Danish astronomer Tycho Brahe (mentioned in *Ignatius His*
Conclave) applied precise measurements using parallax, an optical mis-
alignment registered in the viewing of distant objects. Brahe established
that the new star of 1572 was not a temporary effect of the sublunar
atmosphere. He argued similarly about comets. The cosmic system was
not immutable, as had so long been claimed. Kepler's *De Stellla Nova* (On
the New Star) (1606) mounted a similar case regarding the discovery of a
brilliant new star in the constellation Serpentarius. Galileo's *Siderius*
Nuncius (Starry Messenger) (1610) clinched the contention that these
were physical facts, not hypotheses; using evidence obtained with a tele-
scope, he claimed four new planets—the satellites of Jupiter. In this con-
text *seeke* must mean 'search out', not merely 'look for'. Donne the
preacher would sharpen the negative reaction to astronomers' findings
expressed in this passage: 'If another man see, or think he sees… by the
help of his Optick glasses, or perchance but by his imagination,… a star
or two more in any constellation than I do; yet that star… adds… no
member to the constellation, that was perfect before' (*Sermons*, 3:210).

ll. 212–19. *crumbled out againe… the worlds condition now*. Again exploiting the ambi-
guity of *world*, Donne resumes the parallel analogies of macrocosm(s)
and microcosm(s). The upsurge of scientific inquiry intensifies the sense
that the physical earth as a support for life is gradually expiring, while at
the same time its failing condition enables scientists to analyse it into its
basic elements (*Atomies* or atoms). In the *world* of politics and domestic
life, the positions of superior and subordinate have similarly *gone*, together
with the mutual ties between them. Individualism is being taken to
extremes: *every man… a Phoenix*. A phoenix was both one of a kind and
self-perpetuating: only one such bird existed at a time, so it was not a mem-
ber of any group; a new phoenix arose from the ashes of a self-immolating
old one. Significantly, the phoenix was also a mythical construct. Donne
intimates the general delusion affecting the relations of *Prince, Subject,*
Father, Sonne.

ll. 220–5.   *all parts to reunion bow... a new compasse*: The image of the departed soul
as a *Magnetique force* holding the world together indicates Donne's famil-
iarity with William Gilbert's *De Magnete* (1600), a treatise proving, by
experiments with the lodestone, that Earth is a giant magnet. Gilbert con-
cluded that it has a 'vigour' or power 'innate and diffused through all her
inward parts' that caused its diurnal rotation on its axis and produced 'a
concord without which the universe would go to pieces'. This 'concord'
consisted in 'attraction, polarity, revolution, [and] taking of positions
according to the law of the whole' (*On the Loadstone and Magnetic Bodies*,
trans. P. F. Mottelay (1893), 75–6). See further Charles Monroe Coffin,
John Donne and the New Philosophy (1937), 85–6, 94, 145. The image of
the magnetic compass directing the life voyages of *every sort of men* was a
readily available added association, for it was commonplace in Donne's
day to claim that the compass, gunpowder, and printing were the only
genuine advances in human knowledge since antiquity. *reunion*: rejoining
again.

ll. 229–34. *Steward to Fate*: She dispensed the divine will to the world. The vocabu-
lary of 'Fate', like that of 'Fellow-Commissioner with destinee' in 'A
Funerall Elegie', l. 96, points up Donne's use of a classical frame of refer-
ence for human life and action in the *First Anniversary*. *Gilt...per-
fum'd...Spice...gold...coyn'd*: In keeping with the age of exploration and
trade in which he lived, Donne repeatedly figures moral value in images of
precious and exotic commodities. *interre*: enclose in the earth. *single
money*: small change.

ll. 243–8.   *a Hectique fever...this consuming wound*: According to Fernelius, in the
third stage of 'febris hectica' (*Hectique fever*) 'the fleshly substance was
consumed' and 'this immense heat of the fever observably dries up vital
moisture' (*Universa Medicina* (1610), 260). In this stage the patient was
beyond help.

ll. 249–52. *the worlds beauty...round proportiön*: The strong connection drawn
between mathematical ratios and beauty by the ancient Pythagoreans is
the earliest source for the idea that beauty consists in symmetry and pro-
portion; colour was subsequently added as a feature. Here, however,
Donne draws on Aquinas's influential discussion of beauty in the
Christian tradition: 'Beauty includes three conditions, *integrity* or *perfec-
tion* ...; due *proportion or harmony*; and lastly, *brightness*, or *clarity*, whence
things are called beautiful which have a bright color' (*Summa Theologica*,
1a.39.8; cf. 2a2.145.2).

ll. 253–8.   *their various and perplexëd course...that pure forme*: In antiquity, the heav-
enly spheres in which the stars and planets were fixed were thought to
revolve around the same centre, Earth itself. Plato held that the fixed stars
orbited in perfect circles (*Timaeus*, 36C); Aristotle added that circular
motion alone was continuous and eternal (*De Caelo*, 269b, 286b–287a).
While retaining this general cosmic picture, the astronomer Ptolemy
sought to account for the apparently irregular movements of Mars,

Jupiter, and Saturn by postulating that their orbits did not describe perfect circles (or 'cycles') in relation to a central Earth. Instead they *disproportion that pure forme* with their *Eccentrique parts*—secondary movements in smaller circles (or 'epicycles') centred on the circumferences of their orbits. *downe-right*: straight upwards or downwards (from a continuous linear orbit). *overthwarts*: intersecting paths. *eight and forty shares*: Ptolemy's tables divided the stars into forty-eight constellations (*Almagest*, 7–8).

ll. 259–60. *there arise ... our eyes*: Both Brahe and Galileo wrote treatises on these *New starres*. In 1610 Galileo also reported finding with his telescope that the Milky Way consisted of innumerable fixed stars. *old do vanish*: Hippparchus had listed 1022 stars; Brahe's catalogue reduced the number of the stars to 777 (Coffin, *John Donne and the New Philosophy*, 135).

ll. 263–77. *a Zodiake*: a zone several degrees wide, on either side of the ecliptic, within which the apparent movements of the sun, moon, and planets were said to occur. It was divided into twelve equal parts, each with its own sign and named after a constellation, through which the sun passed once a year. *the Goat and Crabbe*: Capricorn and Cancer, in which the sun in the northern hemisphere appeared respectively at its two solstices. *Tropiques*: the maximal points of the sun's course marked by the winter and summer solstices. Donne ironically represents the zodiac in terms of multiple injustices visited upon the personified *free-borne Sunne*: he is confined (*empaled*), under surveillance (*watch his steps*), intimidated (*fright him backe*), and shackled (*these Tropiques fetter him*). The sun is characterized with equal irony. Its course is so erratic that it *might runne ... to eyther Pole* were it not controlled. The sun is stealthy (*with a cousening line | Steales by*)—an allusion to the perceptual effect of the Earth's slow movement upon its axis known as the 'precession of the equinoxes'. The sun's debility shows: it is *weary* and ready *to sleepe* by *reeling now ... nearer us*—an allusion to the belief of some of Donne's contemporaries that Ptolemy had calculated a greater distance between the sun and the Earth than the one later judged to exist.

ll. 278–85. *Meridians ... Parallels*: lines demarcating celestial longitude and latitude. *Man hath weav'd ... t' obey our pace*: The tribute paid to recent advances in human knowledge of the cosmos begins to take on darker overtones. *Loth to ... labour ... | To go to heav'n ... We spur, we rein the stars* suggests the myth of Phaethon in Ovid, *Metamorphoses*, 1.747–79; 2.1–400. Phaethon, son of Helios, the sun god, persuades his father to let him drive his fiery chariot across the sky. When Phaethon fails to control the chariot and endangers the Earth with destruction by fire, Zeus averts disaster by killing Phaethon with a thunderbolt. Like the story of Adam and Eve, the Phaethon story treats the Fall of man, but fits more closely with Donne's articulation of the (impending) Fall of Nature in the *First Anniversary*. Critias's construal of Phaethon's story apparently provided Donne with an interpretive lead: 'Now this has the form of a myth, but really signifies a declination of the bodies moving around the earth, and a great conflagration of things upon the earth' (Plato, *Timaeus*, 22D, Loeb edn, trans. R. E. Bury (1929), 7:33–5).

ll. 286–99. A rehearsal of examples of the Earth's irregularities of shape found in treatises of Donne's day. *a Teneriffe*: The mountain Pico de Teide on the island of Teneriffe has an altitude of 12,172 feet, but it impressed viewers from sea level as being higher still. *Seas...so deepe that Whales, being strooke...at...the bottom, dye*: Ulisses Aldrovandus describes the enormous plunges of a wounded whale in *De Piscibus* (Of Fishes) (1613), 673. *one of th' Antipodes*: one of the inhabitants of the diametrically opposite side of the earth. *a Vault infernall*: Donne the preacher would cite 'one Author, who is afraid of admitting too great a hollownesse in the Earth' lest there be insufficient allowance for hell and its torments (*Sermons*, 7:137). A marginal reference identifies this 'Author' as Sebastian Münster, *Cosmographia Universalis* (1572), 11–12.

l. 300.   *warts and pock-holes*: Donne would later elaborate his image of 'the face of the earth': 'hills...are but as warts upon her face: And her vaults, and caverns...are but as so many wrinkles, and pock-holes' (*Essays in Divinity*, 36).

ll. 311–16. *that Ancient*: A probable echo of Kepler's comments on Pythagoras, for whom 'Soul, the bond between Mind and Body, was in its essence nothing but Harmony, and made up of harmonies' (*The Harmony of the World by Johannes Kepler*, trans. and ed. E. J. Alton, Alistair M. Duncan, and Judith Veronica Field (1997), 133). The Pythagorean doctrine of the harmonious relation of *soules* to *bodies* was taken up widely in later antiquity; Aquinas, however, would dispute the belief that the soul is a harmony of the contraries composing an animate body (*Summa contra Gentiles*, 2.64). *Resultances*: entities issuing or emanating from another entity. She is the harmony from which the harmony of our bodies, our souls, proceeds. *to our eyes...from objects flow*: In Donne's time the standard account of vision was that of Aristotle. He asserted that objects emitted fine material impressions of themselves; these moved through the air, impacting the surface of the eyeball, from which the mind took them in (*De Sensu et Sensibilibus* [On Sense and Objects of Sense], 437a–438b).

ll. 317–22. *great Doctors...to mans proportiöns was made*: Augustine, a *Doctor* of the church, describes Noah's ark as a prefiguration of the church, constructed in the proportions of the human body that Christ assumed to rescue humankind from the flood of their sins (*De Civitate Dei*, 15.26). Another *Doctor*, Ambrose, treats the ark as symbolizing the body of the just man surrounded by an ocean of sin (*De Noe et Arca* [On Noah and the Ark], 9). *A type...that...* | *Both Elements, and Passions liv'd at peace*: Ambrose also says that the just man achieves inner harmony and peace by controlling his irrational passions and his senses (*Patrologia Latina*, 14:374). Cf. 'To Sir Edward Herbert, at Juliers', ll. 1–2.

ll. 337–8.   *good, and well*: virtue and propriety. *Wicked…indiscreet*: Discretion is the
             ability to discriminate between good and evil in our actions. Being *wicked*
             is only somewhat worse than failing to enact the good of which we are
             capable.

ll. 343–5.   *a compassionate Turcoyse*: Learned opinion of the time held that a tur-
             quoise would brighten or dull its lustre in keeping with its wearer's state
             of health (Anselmus de Boot, *Gemmarum et Lapidum Historia* [History of
             Gems and Stones] (1609), 135–6). *Gold fals sicke…Mercury*: When mer-
             cury is injected into gold, it produces a paler and less valuable alloy. Pliny
             notes that gold is the only metal with which mercury interacts (*Natural
             History*, 33.32).

ll. 347–52. *the first weeke…Rainbow did allow*: Most theologians in Donne's day held
             that God had created the rainbow before the Flood. He employed it there-
             after as the sign of his covenant with Noah never again to destroy the
             Earth (Benedict Pererius, *Commentarii et Desputationes in Genesim*
             [Commentaries and Disputations on Genesis] (1601), 525). *inow*: enough.

ll. 353–65. *Sight…noblest sense*: A commonplace. *sight…colour to feed on*: 'Whatever
             is visible is color' (Aristotle, *De Anima*, 418a). *Our blushing…soules are
             redde*: This image progression from blushing cheeks to red souls has an
             etymological grounding in the close similarity of the Hebrew for 'Adam',
             'blush', and 'red'. Like other biblical elements in the *First Anniversary*,
             the associative logic is submerged here. Donne the preacher would make
             it explicit: 'He made us all of earth…Our earth was red, even when it was
             in Gods hands…a blushing at our own infirmities, is imprinted in us, by
             Gods hand…But that redness, which we have contracted from…the
             bloud of our own souls, by sinne,…is from our selves' (*Sermons*, 9:64–6).
             Whose composition was miraculous. The miracle consists in her ensouled
             body having *color—all white, and red, and blew*—and yet being transparent
             (*Diaphanous*). In the Aristotelian thought tradition, colour and transpar-
             ency were opposites. *verdure*: greenness.

ll. 376–82. *illude*: deceive. *forbeares*: suffers the lack of. *The father, or the mother barren
             is*: In ancient Mediterranean creation myths, the sky is the father, the
             earth the mother. All living things proceed from their union, and their
             growth and vitality depend upon it. Donne's evocation of unseasonable
             occurrences intensifies the myth; it does not describe actual weather in
             England or Europe in 1610–12. *balmy showre*: fructifying spring rain.

ll. 387–90. *such Meteörs*: In Donne's time 'meteor' remained a general term for wind,
             rain, snow, lightning, dew, and other phenomena in the 'sphere' of the air
             or atmosphere. 'Meteorological' is still current as a synonym for 'weather':
             e.g., the 'Meteorological Services' of various governments. *new wormes*:
             maggots breeding in the world's decaying carcass, or possibly new species
             of snakes lately discovered in Africa and the Americas. Snakes could be
             referred to colloquially as worms. *troubled much…more such*: In Exodus
             7:10–12 Aaron casts down his rod before Pharaoh and it becomes a ser-
             pent. The Egyptian court magicians also cast down their rods, on which

they have cast spells, and their rods also become serpents. Then Aaron's serpent swallows up the others.

ll. 391–5. *Artist:* a practitioner of occult arts, or an astrologer. *constellate:* work out the favourable position of the stars for some purpose. *the influence...may...doe...all which those starres could doe:* An allusion to medical cures that purported to tap into astrological forces.

ll. 396–405. *correspondence:* interchange between earth and heaven. cf. *traffique. Embarr'd:* stopped, prohibited. *Ashes...are med'cinall:* Ancient and later writers advocated the medical use of ashes, reasoning that substances consumed by fire retained their efficacy in a purified form (Don Cameron Allen, 'John Donne and Renaissance Medicine', *Journal of English and Germanic Philology* (1943), 42:340). *vertue:* her innate goodness and her power to influence.

ll. 407–10. *one dying Swan:* Swans were traditionally thought to sing only once, on the verge of death. *some Serpents poison...live Serpent shot:* Pliny makes this assertion about the asp, the most poisonous snake known to him (*Natural History,* 29.18). Donne generalized regarding both negative and positive effects in a letter dated *c.*1608–9: 'some poisons, and some medicines, hurt not, nor profit, except the creature in which they reside, contribute their lively activitie, and vigor' (*Letters,* 107).

ll. 417–26. *not transubstantiate...yet gilded:* Transforming a substance into gold (the objective of the 'philosopher's stone' in alchemy) is contrasted to covering an object with a gold overlay. *All states* (estates): persons of all stations in life. *some people...to crave:* Some people have some restraint and ask no more than it is appropriate for kings to give to them. The satiric sideswipes here remain safely general. *Iron, and rusty too:* From the pre-classical time of Hesiod's *Theogony* to Donne's own, it was commonplace to lament that the world had decayed from a golden age through silver and brass ages to the present iron age, its last. The rust is Donne's addition; cf. Satire 5, l. 35.

ll. 436–47. *read:* reached an exact determination (as in 'reading' a thermometer). *Were punctuall:* were to proceed point by point. *thy feast:* Elizabeth Drury's name-day, 5 November, in the church calendar. *concoctiön:* refining, purifying—an alchemical term. *first yeeres rent:* this poem commemorating the first anniversary of this *blessëd maid*'s death.

ll. 460–74. *Chronicle, not verse:* An expository historical account in prose, not poetry (where literal meaning is not always required, and poetic license may be taken). *God... a song:* Donne invokes divine precedent for his composition of the *First Anniversary* and with it, implied permission for this undertaking. He alludes to Deuteronomy 21.19, 22.1–43, where God speaks to Moses and Joshua just before Moses dies and the Israelites enter the promised land. Ordering it to be put in writing, God gives them a song of his dealings with his people, *because he knew they would let fall | The Law, the Prophets, and the History* out of their minds and memories. Moses teaches the people God's song so that it will be remembered. The emphasis on the special memorability of verse suits Donne's subject and approach. He has 'represented' (the word in his title) 'by occasion of the untimely death of Mistress Elizaeth Drury' the loss of vitality, goodness, and value in the world. In terming his representation *a song*, he clarifies some of its features: the heightened emotion conveyed in exclamations, the use of a refrain to forefront his main subject. Most significant, perhaps, is Donne's affirmation of the special capacity of verse to *keepe the song* of this incomparable soul *still in... memory*. The theme of immortalizing a person in poetry, common in Latin literature, had only recently been sounded in English: in Spenser's *Amoretti* (1595) and Shakespeare's *Sonnets* (1609). *Verse hath... Fame enroules*: Donne takes the exaltation of poetry further still. He ascribes to verse a metaphysical capacity to sustain the integrity of a human subject by giving it existence as a representation, thus mediating the otherwise unbridgeable divide between death and living on in the memories of others.

A FUNERALL ELEGIE (P. 45)

ll. 1–11. *'Tis lost*: It is futile. *Tombe... Marble chest... workes... of men... these memorials, ragges of paper*: These specifics evoke a set of verses fastened to a grave monument, prompting the now general supposition that 'A Funerall Elegie' was Donne's initial tribute to Elizabeth Drury. *Priz'd*: Compared with. *Chrysolite*: This stone, the topaz of antiquity, was valued for its unsurpassed lustre (Jerome Cardan, *De Subtilitate* (1560), 200). *Joyne... 'tis glas*: The precious stones and minerals of India and the Americas are mere simulations compared with the value of what lies in Elizabeth Drury's grave. *ten Escorials*: The magnificent complex of the Escorial was completed by Philip II of Spain in 1584. Donne had previously addressed Lady Bedford as 'you, th' Escorial' (To the Countesse of Bedford: 'Madame, You have refind mee', l. 48).

ll. 16–18. *Tabernacle... house*: The body is called 'the tabernacle of the Holy Ghost' in 2 Corinthians 5:4, 6:16, and 2 Peter 1:13–14. *house*: body.

ll. 21–6. *The world containes*: One outgrowth of the macrocosm–microcosm analogy was the conception of the 'body politic', in which ranks and occupations of society corresponded to parts of the human body.

ll. 27–9. *Fine spirits*, like her, who *tune and set* (in tune) *This Organ* (the social organism) resemble the 'spirits' (*peeces* or elements) in the blood that enable the soul to produce harmony throughout the body. *Wonder and love*: Cf. 'Valediction of the Booke', ll. 28–9.

ll. 38–44. *sundred*: disassembled. *then*: when reassembled. *Afrique Niger streame*: upper waters of the Nile. *enwombs... farre greater than it was*: Pliny says the Nile begins in western Mauritania and flows eastward, twice disappearing underground; it is called the Niger (black) because of the intervals of darkness in its course (*Natural History*, 5.10).

ll. 50–6. *An Angel... Cherubin*: Angels are the lowest of the nine heavenly orders; only the seraphim are superior to cherubim and thrones. *We lose by't*: Only angels are involved with human affairs (Aquinas, *Summa Theologica*, 1a.112.2; 113.3). Cherubim and thrones serve or contemplate God. When an angel is promoted, there is one less protecting and guiding presence for humans. *last fires*: the ones that will end the world.

ll. 61–5. *a through-light scarfe*: a translucent wrapping. *enroule*: encase, enclose; cf. *Second Anniversary*, ll. 244–6. *emulate*: compete with one another.

ll. 67–70. *new starrs... starres go out*: The new star of 1572 was invisible by the end of March 1574; that of 1600 soon disappeared; that of 1604 went out by March 1606. Astronomers (*ev'ry Artist*) could not agree whether the *place* of the new stars in the traditional cosmic system was in the atmosphere below the moon, or in the rarefied air (ether) above it, or in the eighth sphere, that of the 'fixed' stars (Coffin, *Donne and the New Philosophy*, 124–30).

ll. 72–82. *So the world... nor shee*: Because of her incomparable purity, her place as a *peece* (exemplary being) in the world was questioned. The answer was that she could be no one's daughter or wife, not even herself—an inhabitant of Earth. *a Lampe... Rather t' adorne than last*: Balsam, an aromatic resin, was a costly substance in antiquity. Constantine the Great ordered its use in the lamps of certain churches, particularly at Christmas and Easter (*Patrologia Latina*, 8.804). *mariage... doth dye*: Had she married, she would have forfeited *her Virgin white integrity*. *Dye* may allude to the breaking of the hymen. *serv'd for opium*: put her to sleep (in death). *Shee' hath yeelded... Extasie*: Her thoughts, fixed on God, drew her soul out of her body and eased its departure. Donne the preacher would reflect: 'The contemplation of God, and heaven, is a kinde of... Sepulchre,... and in this death of rapture, and extasie,... I shall finde myself and all my sins enterred' (*Sermons*, 2:210–11).

ll. 91–104. 'A Funerall Elegie' concludes with vocabulary drawn from classical rather than Christian thought. *Fate did... her selfe*: Fate conferred her destiny upon her by placing it in her own hands. *which liberty... to die*: She used the liberty Fate gave her only to the extent of dying, insofar as she has died (out of earthly life). *Her modesty... no more but die*: Destiny is personified as an executor of the divine will. Though she might have exercised such powers more fully, she modestly used them only to die. *if after her... her delegate*: Donne states in embryonic form what he elaborates in *First Anniversary*, ll. 67–90: the afterlife of this soul's virtue, sustained by those who embrace and emulate her example. There his controlling metaphor is that of the expiring world. Here it is that of an orderly transfer of valuable assets: the *Legacies... from the gift of her example* that will yield the *future vertuous deeds* of those survivors who *dare true good prefer*. *that booke*: 'the booke of Destinie' (l. 83). The classical vocabulary of 'A Funerall Elegie' evokes two realms—one of cosmic law, the other of probate and inheritance law—both of which operate in a rule-bound fashion. By contrast, the classical vocabulary of the *First Anniversary* tracks the cosmic and human worlds on their erratic but inexorable course toward extinction.

ll. 105–6.   *'tis in heaven . . . on earth*: Like the differing uses of classical vocabulary, the tonal contrast between this glimpse of *spir'tuall mirth* and the solemn ending of the *First Anniversary* is marked. It strengthens the supposition that 'A Funerall Elegie' was the earlier poem, serving as a sort of first draft or trial run for the deepened notes and complexities of the later one.

THE SECOND ANNIVERSARIE (SIG. EIR)

As in the *First Anniversary*, so too in the *Second Anniversary*, the *Occasion* is the *Death of Mistris Elizabeth Drury*. But there are significant differences between the two poems. Absent from the title of the *First Anniversary* and absent or muted in the text as well, Christian vocabulary explicitly appears in the subtitle of the *Second Anniversary*: *Religious Death, this Life, the Next*. Representation by way of analogizing between the world's decay and this soul's departure is the governing poetic mode of the *First Anniversary*. Contemplation of opposites—*incommodities . . . in this life and . . . exaltation in the next*—is the governing poetic mode of the *Second Anniversary*. These modal differences, however, make their effects felt gradually. Like the *First Anniversary*, the *Second Anniversary* begins with a series of analogies to physical phenomena in this world that figure the afterlife of the departed soul.

THE HARBINGER TO THE PROGRES (SIG. E2R)

For evidence that Joseph Hall authored this poem, see the earlier discussion about his authorship of 'The Praise of the Dead' prefacing the *First Anniversary*. Hall must have written 'The Harbinger to the Progres' in early 1612 after receiving a manuscript text of Donne's *Second Anniversary*. *HARBINGER:* a herald who announces a dignitary's impending approach. *HARBINGER to the Progres*: Hall puns on Donne's subtitle, 'THE PROGRES of the Soule', activating a more specialized sense of *harbinger*: a court officer who precedes the monarch on a royal progress to ensure that lodging and entertainment will be ready. In addition, Hall's phrasing reactivates Donne's pun on 'Queene' and 'progresse time' in *First Anniversary*, l. 7, while his intertextual play pays tribute to Donne's poetic virtuosity. Little is known about the relations between the two men, both satirists in their youth, both prominent clergymen in their maturity.

ll. 1–9.   *Two soules move here*: Elizabeth Drury's, in her heavenward flight; Donne's in his flights of imagination. The *worlds . . . full degree*: In the general resurrection at the last judgement, the bodies as well as the souls of the saved will be glorified as they enter into eternal blessedness. *thou o'er-lookest*: The soul looks down from her exalted place in heaven, above the stars. *in their place . . . movëd are*: Unlike the rotating planets, the stars in the traditional cosmic system are fixed to their encompassing spheres, which rotate around the Earth. *luggage of this clay*: impediment of a body.

ll. 16–26. *Journals*: records of daily doings or journeyings. (*Great spirit*): Donne. *raught*: reached. *less'ned*: diminished by distance.

ll 36–42. *thy Laura*: The beloved in Francesco Petrarch's *Rime sparse* (Scattered Verses), object of the poet's exalted praise and rarefied love, whose death he mourned for ten years. *if those . . . sing below*: Church fathers debated whether the souls of the dead had knowledge of actions on Earth. Augustine thought they did not (*Patrologia Latina*, 40:604–5); Gregory the Great thought they did (*PL*, 75:999). Aquinas came to agree with Gregory (*Summa Theologica*, 1a.89.8). *Those acts . . . them blest*: Hall's final couplet works a variation on the final couplet in Donne's 'A Funerall Elegie', ll. 105–6. *those awfull powers*: the awe-inspiring Trinity.

THE SECOND ANNIVERSARIE—CONTEXT AND RECEPTION

Donne is thought to have composed the *Second Anniversary* between November 1611 and January 1612, probably in Amiens in northern France, where the Drurys' travelling party made a stay of several months before going on to Paris in early March. Line 3 declares that *a yeare is runne* since Elizabeth Drury departed from the world; this reckoning could have been made either from her name-day or from her date of death. The conclusion of the *Second Anniversary* locates the poetic speaker in a Roman Catholic country *where misdevotion frames | A thousand prayers to saints whose very names | The ancient church knew not* (ll. 511–13). This critical perspective is echoed in the opening lines of 'To the Lady Carey, and Mistris Essex Riche, from Amiens', a verse letter written in early 1612. Whatever its exact date of composition, Donne's commemorative tribute was offered well in advance of the second anniversary of Elizabeth Drury's death in December 1612.

The *Second Anniversary* was published in the early months of 1612 with a reprint of the *First Anniversary* and with Hall's two prefatory poems. By 14 April 1612, the date of a letter written to Goodyere from Paris, Donne had learned of negative reactions to the volume—chiefly, it seems, from noble ladies whom he had superlatively praised in verse. He had this to say for himself:

I hear from *England* of many censures of my book, of Mistris *Drury*; if any of those censures do but pardon me my descent in Printing any thing in verse, (which if they do, they are more charitable than my self; for I do not pardon my self, but confesse that I did it against my conscience, that is, against my own opinion, that I should not have done so) I doubt not but they will soon give over that other part of that indictment, which is, that I have said so much; for no body can imagine, that I who never saw her, could have any other purpose in that, than that when I had received so very good testimony of her worthinesse, and was gone down to print verses, it became me to say, not what I was sure was just truth, but the best that I could conceive; for that had been a new weaknesse in me, to have praised any body in printed verses, that had not been capable of the best praise that I could give (*Letters*, 74–5).

Like a body writhing in pain, Donne's convoluted phrases register his wounded self-esteem and what must have been dashed pride in his innovative poetic creations. But the same phrases testify equally to the fictive character of the *Anniversaries* as well as other eulogies—the verse letters and funeral elegies addressed to prospective patronesses with high status and considerable means at their disposal.

THE SECOND ANNIVERSARIE. OF THE PROGRES OF THE SOULE (P. 1)

ll. 2–6.   *everlastingnesse*: The eternity of the world was a fundamental doctrine of Aristotle (and other classical philosophers); its incompatibility with the creation account in Genesis became a major polemical issue between pagans and Christians in late antiquity. Donne's reference is lightly ironic. *this lower worlds... of this All*: Elizabeth Drury's soul was the source of light for the entire universe. *Blasphemy... fall*: Christian vocabulary wittily figures this soul's perfect virtue.

ll. 7–20.   *as a ship... as... a beheaded man... as Ice... as a Lute*: Analogies in simile form reprise the mode of the opening of the *First Anniversary*, ll. 70–8, where images of afterglow evoke a kind of afterlife of the world in the wake of this soul's departure. *a beheaded man*: There was a precedent for this image in Lucretius's catalogue of bodily extremities cut off in the heat of battle: 'The head shorn off from the hot and living trunk retains on the ground the look of life and its open eyes, until it has rendered up all that is left of the spirit' (*De Rerum Natura* [On the Nature of Things], 3:654–66, Loeb edn, trans. Martin F. Smith (1982), 239). Donne's grotesque elaboration had a possible origin in the execution of the earl of Essex for high treason in leading an abortive uprising against Queen Elizabeth in 1601. Having served under Essex's command in 1596–7, and as Lord Keeper Egerton's secretary in 1601, he was well positioned to know about the earl's trial and beheading, even possibly to have witnessed the latter. *eternall bed*: heaven or hell.

ll. 23–34.   *As some Daies... strive for life*: On the theological puzzle presented by verses in Genesis where references to day and night precede the creation of the sun and moon, see the note to *First Anniversary*, ll. 194–202. The speaker of the *Second Anniversary* has no difficulty with accepting the paradox, making it an inverted image of the afterlife of the soul he is praising. Then a different potential puzzle emerges: God had promised Noah that there would not be another flood upon the Earth. Yet *a new Deluge... Hath drown'd us all*. The image combines references to Genesis and to the classical river Lethe in Hades, which caused dead souls to forget their earlier life when they drank of its water. Again, the speaker is accepting of this paradoxical second flood and does not question God's purposes.

ll. 35–44.   *be... A Father*: enable my poetic powers to bring forth offspring, e.g., further 'anniversary' poems. *These Hymns... till Gods great Venite change the song*: In the *First Anniversary* Donne's exalted reflections on the capacities of lyric poetry (*Song*) to immortalize its subject and make the power of goodness memorable come at the poem's close. In the *Second Anniversary* his reflections on the capacities of lyric poetry (now called *Hymns*) come close to the beginning. Donne salutes the generative moral power of poetry, exercised through its vitalizing effects on successive generations of poets and readers. *Venite*: Latin for 'Come ye'. Christ will extend an invitation at the close of the last judgment: 'Come ye blessed of my Father, inherit the kingdom prepared for you from the foundation of the world' (Matthew 25:34).

ll. 45–8. *Thirst for that time,...be Hydropique so*: Diametrically opposing the *Lethe flood* of forgetting, the primary image here is *thirst* for the water of life in heaven (Revelation 22:17). While a soul is in this world, however, this *thirst* is served by *Gods safe-sealing Bowle*—an image that conflates the cup of wine at Holy Communion with the wassail bowl with which healths were drunk at the New Year. Both carry associations with celebratory rituals and affirmation of life. *safe-sealing*: salvation-confirming. *Hydropique*: insatiably thirsty.

ll. 49–66. *Forget this rotten world...worth*: The speaker begins to weigh the implications of a *World* that *is but a Carkas* for composing a *Hymn* in the contemplative mode. With the dismantling of the traditional classical–Christian cosmic system, theology and science become disjunct forms of knowledge. *thou art... a worm*: An Old Testament figure for human insignificance, as in Job 25:6, 'man, that is a worm'. Contemplation of the hereafter also imposes its particular priorities. *Forget this world... Looke upward... towards her, whose happy state | We... congratulate.*

ll. 70–6. *Some Figure...times*: some image of the world's golden age. In Christian terms, this was the time before the Fall; in classical terms, it was the age when Astraea, goddess of justice, dwelt on earth. Like this soul, Astraea departed because *this world was unfit | To be stayd in. shee was... live*: she was the soul that gave the world life; cf. *First Anniversary*, l. 37. *tried*: tested; the latent metaphor is that of heating metals to test their purity. *religious fires*: pious zeal.

ll. 78–82. *enspheard*: held as in a sphaere (like that of the fixed stars). *the South... Northern Pole*: She, still represented as the source of light, would have made the southern hemisphere surpass the northern in multitude of stars. Donne would reprise this bit of lore in *Devotions*, Meditation 13; its source is Benedict Pererius, *Commentarii et Disputationes in Genesim* (1601), 99. *rubbidge*: rubbish.

ll. 85–98. *Groome*: household servant. *outward roome*: 'This world and the next world, are not...two houses, but two roomes' (*Sermons*, 7:340). *thinke those... thy happiest Harmonee*: Reconceive the broken breath and last gasps of a dying person. Think of them in musical terms as *broken... Notes*, rapid notes ornamenting a melodic line, and as *Division*, a melodic run of short notes. *Anger... Thy Physicke*: Intensify your chills and fever by calling them your medicine. Paradoxical inversion (recasting something negative as something positive) would become prominent in Donne's later religious writing.

ll. 100–6.   *as Bels cal'd thee… So this… cals thee*: Cf. *Devotions*, Expostulation 16. *Triumphant Church*: the company of the saints in heaven. *Sergeants*: legal officers charged with arresting offenders. *for Legacies they thrust*: Unscrupulous inheritance-seekers who crowd around a deathbed are a stock target of Roman satire, and one that appealed to English writers with a satirical bent, like Donne and Jonson. *score*: debt.

ll. 114–26.   *reinvest*: clothe again. *Wormes… their state*: courtiers seeking to grow rich in a ruler's service; 'worms of the commonwealth' was a stock phrase. *Thinke… a saint Lucies night*: A minor instance of paradoxical inversion: think of your burial in the earth as your sleep during the longest night of the year (13 December). *Shee whose… more or lesse*: In her *Complexion* (physical makeup) the four humours were so evenly mixed that neither *Feare* (anxiety for her continuing health) nor *art* (the skill of doctors) could predict which humour would would *invade* | *The other three* (destroy the humoral balance): *So far were* all four humours from excess or deficiency in her body. It was generally believed that mixed (compound) substances were liable to dissolution when their components lacked equilibrium (Aquinas, *Summa Theologica*, 1a.75.6). Cf. 'The Good Morrow', l. 19: 'Whatever dies was not mixt equally'.

ll. 127–36.   *Mithridate*: a mixture of many ingredients traditionally reputed to ensure health, especially against poisoning (Pliny, *Historia Naturalis*, 29.8; 23.77). *as… quantities… this a point*: Quantities (geometrical figures) are composed of lines, and lines are composed of points. No one, however, can divide a line into points (because they have position but no magnitude) or break up a figure into lines (because they have length but no breadth) (Euclid, *The Elements of Geometrie*, trans. H. Billingsley (1570), 1.1–3). The geometrical simile illustrates the perfect integration of components *In her… even constitution*.

11. 137–42.   *wonne*: won over, persuaded. *the Sunne*: The sun was not liable to change or dissolution, since it was above the sphere of the moon and composed of unmixed celestial matter (Marsilio Ficino, *De Sole et Lumine* [Of the Sun and Light] (1503), 1.13). *make a spirit… subject were*: A spirit or soul was a single pure substance and therefore indivisible (Plato, *Phaedo*, 78–80; Aquinas, *Summa Theologica*, 1a.75.6). *To whose proportion… Angulare*: The geometrical images stake a hyperbolic claim: her body's proportions excelled those of perfectly regular three-dimensional figures and perfectly regular two-dimensional figures.

ll. 143–8.   *such a Chaine… enjoies*: The golden chain from which Zeus suspends a scale to weigh the fates of Greeks and Trojans on the battlefield (Homer, *Iliad*, 8.19) was later allegorized as the cosmic chain of causation. *enjoies*: experiences (not necessarily with pleasure). *Accident*: chance occurrence, mishap; or generally, any event. All three meanings are potentially in play. Since this is the chain of Fate, *one would thinke* that nothing could happen outside the fundamental relation of cause and effect. *shee embrac'd a sicknesse*: The seemingly impossible happened: how and why? The answer is postponed until l. 156: For even the *purest* of human beings, *Death* is inevitable.

ll. 150–6. *Title*: legal right to possession. *plead*: lay claim to. *pretend a conquest*: base a claim to possession on having taken something by force. *Heav'n... violence*: In Matthew 11:12 Jesus remarks on the ardent spiritual desire aroused by John the Baptist's preaching: 'the kingdom of heaven suffereth violence, and the violent take it by force'. *they're in Heav'n... Heav'ns workes do*: Donne the preacher would elaborate: 'Joy and the sense of Salvation... is not a joy severed from the Joy of Heaven, but... begins in us here, and continues, and accompanies us thither' (*Sermons*, 7:340). *right, and power, and Place*: respectively, a justified legal claim, the ability to assert claim to a title, and the right of long possession. *Yet Death... the doore*: One has to die before entering into possession of heaven. (It is life, paradoxically, that keeps us from what is supremely and truly ours.)

ll. 158–65. *a sinke*: sewer, cesspool—a formulaic phrase in a traditional vein of Christian spirituality that reviled the body to exalt the soul. *those two soules*: Aristotle in *De Anima*, 2.413b–415a, followed by Aquinas in *Summa Theologica*, 1a.76.3, distinguished three souls of living things. The vegetative soul, or power of *growth*, was shared with plants and animals; the sensible soul, or power of motion and *sense* perception, was shared with animals; the rational soul was unique to humans. Donne asserts that the rational soul *fed... upon, and drew... into* itself the *second soule of sense, and first of growth*, thus projecting the integrated human psyche as the end result of reason absorbing the other faculties within itself. *obnoxioüs*: vulnerable to harm. *a snall lump of flesh... orig'nal sinne*: The standard Christian view was that sin did not infect the body if the soul was not infected. This together with another standard Christian view—that the *original sin* of Adam and Eve was transmitted to all subsequent generations of humans—gave rise to a difficulty. Since God cannot be supposed to create something already evil, how does sin come to infect the newly created souls of new human beings? Here Donne takes the position that the sin of Adam and Eve permanently tainted all human flesh. His later position was that original sin derived not from the body or the soul alone, but from the union of the two (*Sermons*, 2:58–9; 5:172). *unlittered whelpe*: unborn puppy.

ll. 169–73. *Anchorit* (anchorite): one who had withdrawn from society to live in a solitary place. *fixt... doth sit*: Some early Christian ascetics withdrew into the wilderness, where two (Simeon the Elder and Simeon the Younger) chose to live on small platforms atop pillars, and another (Baradatos) chose to live in a hole in the ground. *Bedded and Bath'd... as our soules in their first-built Cels*: The comparison of these hermits' living conditions with that of fetuses in the womb derives from a then-current medical notion that, as soon as their relevant organs had formed, unborn babies urinated and defecated inside their mother, floating in their and her bodily wastes (Hieronymus Fabricius, *De Formato Foetu* [On the Formation of the Fetus] (1601), 128–38). *how poore a prison*: The notion of the body as the soul's prison had both classical and biblical antecedents (Plato, *Phaedo*, 82; Psalm 142:7: 'Bring my soul out of prison').

ll. 175–84. *Thinke…thy Soule hatch'd but now*: Donne assembles commonplaces from the classical genre of 'consolation' (e.g., Plutarch, *Consolatio ad Apollonium*; Seneca, *Consolatio ad Marciam*). These include the soul as a lodger in a meanly furnished body, *a poore Inne*; the body threatened with *sicknesses, or…Age*; the liberation of the soul by death. *Peece*: firearm. *his owne*: free to act on its own.

ll. 185–95. *And thinke this…soule…* | *Dispatches in a minute…* | *Twixt Heav'n and Earth*: Donne plainly declares on one side of a then-current theological issue. His position is that, at the moment of death, a saved soul goes immediately to heaven and shares in the direct apprehension of God. Cf. *Sermons*, 7:71. *Meteors*: elements of weather (rain, snow, wind, etc.). *intense*: densely compacted by extreme cold. *th' Element of fire*: Cf. *First Anniversary*, l. 206. *bates not*: does not slow down. *trie*: discover.

ll. 197–206. *Venus…Mercury…Mars*: In charting the soul's heavenward course, Donne employs Tycho Brahe's sequence of the planetary spheres, which interchanged the places of Venus and Mercury in the traditional classical–Christian system. But there is no anxiety about contested cosmologies, as in the *First Anniversary*. The soul here is rapt in its instantaneous flight to union with God. *Hesper 'and Vesper*: Two names for Venus as the evening star. In one of his prose 'problems' written *c*.1605–7 Donne asked, 'Why is Venus-star…called both *Hesperus* and *Vesper*?' (*Paradoxes and Problems*, ed. Peters, 35–6). *Argus' eies…Mercury*: Ovid tells how the messenger god Mercury used a flute and a magic wand to charm the hundred-eyed watchdog Argus to sleep, thus giving Jupiter access to his beloved, Io (*Metamorphoses*, 1.622–721). *Workes not…all Ey*: Mercury in his dual identity as pagan god and planet can exert no power over the heaven-bound soul. *in Mars…barrd*: Nor can *Mars* (the pagan god of war, who might be expected to put up armed resistance), or Jupiter (*Jove*), or Saturn (*his father*), in their dual identities as planets and supposed divinities, block the soul's trajectory. *corps of Guard*: contingent of men armed to prevent passage.

ll. 207–13. *And as these stars…string Heav'n and Earth*: The speed at which death propels the soul through the universe imposes a grand sequential ordering on the multitude of stars traversed; they appear to be *so many beades…still one thing*. This cohesive effect of death on the cosmos resembles the function of the spinal cord in human anatomy: *the Pith which…* | *Strings fast the little bones of necke, and backe*. Death paradoxically becomes a vital principle.

ll. 214–19. *our soule...grace*): The formulation is thoroughly Christian. Our first birth is our emergence from our mother's womb. A second birth is conferred by our baptism into new life as a member of Christ's body, the church. Here the notion of a third birth follows directly from the preceding figurations of death as a vital principle, uniting the soul with God in heaven. Donne the preacher would figure the 'third birth' more conventionally as the reuniting of soul and body in the general resurrection at the end of time (*Sermons*, 6:134–5). *long-short Progresse*: advancing a long distance in a short time, and reactivating the sense of *Progresse* as a monarch's journey through his or her dominions.

ll. 223–34. This soul's surpassing spiritual value is figured by pairings with precious earthly commodities; these take the form of money metaphors and metaphors of trade and exploration. Cf. 'A Funerall Elegie', ll. 1–11.

ll. 235–40. *they...who did...betrothe | The Tute'lar Angels, and assigned. they*: Medieval theologians, whom Donne considered to have multiplied to absurd lengths the idea of a guardian angel, for which Daniel 10:13 was the source. He comments to Goodyere in a letter of December 1611: 'It is...imperfect which is taught by that religion...most accommodate to sense...That all mankinde hath one protecting Angel; all Christians one other, all English one other, all of one Corporation and every civill...society one other; and every man one other' (*Letters*, 43).

ll. 241–3. *whose soule... 'twas Gold, | Her body was th' Electrum*: Further metaphorical figuring of spiritual value as earthly value. *Electrum*: an amalgam consisting of four-fifths gold and one-fifth silver. According to Paracelsus, electrum was a substance intermediate between ore and metal, neither perfect nor imperfect, but moving towards perfection (*Hermetic and Alchemical Writings*, 2:364).

ll. 244–7. *her pure and elo'quent blood... her bodie thought*: These lines were quoted or paraphrased by a number of later authors over the course of the next century and more (see *John Donne: The Critical Heritage*, ed. A. J. Smith (1975), 60, 64, 168, 173). *largely*: bountifully.

ll. 249–62. *prisons prison*: The body, itself a prison of the soul, is in turn imprisoned by its dependence on the Earth for its survival and maintenance. *what dost thou know?* In Cicero's *Prior Academics*, 2.23, Lucullus quotes from Metrodorus's *On Nature*: 'I say we do not know whether we know anything or whether we know nothing...Socrates held knowledge to be impossible. He made only one exception, that he knew himself to know nothing'. Cf. *Sermons*, 7:260. *Thou know'st thy self so little*: Donne the preacher would reiterate: 'How little we know our selves, which is the end of all knowledge' (*Sermons*, 8:107). *did'st die*: incurred the penalty of original sin (Genesis 3:3). *at first cam'st in*: received a soul by 'infusion' from God or by 'traduction' (transfer) from one's parents. This disputed question held a recurring fascination for Donne. *took'st the poyson of mans sin*: Luther termed sin 'the poison of Satan' with which we are 'infected', commenting 'we are born from unclean seed' (*On Genesis*, in *Works*, gen.

ed. Jaroslav Pelikan (1958), 1:163, 166). Donne seems to imply agreement that original sin was transmitted bodily in the procreation of a child. *By what way...made immortall*: The immortality of the soul was an article of faith, not a matter of demonstration. How the soul became immortal would be equally inaccessible to human reason. *narrow*: limited. *bend*: apply thy mind.

ll. 263–78. *To know thy body*: Cicero declared that we know nothing of our own bodies with regard to the location of each organ, the function of each part, and the structure of the nerves and veins (*Prior Academics*, 2.39, 122–4). *wrought* | *Of Ayre, and Fire, and other Elements*: Traditional medicine deriving from Galen was based on the theory that the human body was composed of the four elements; cf. *First Anniversary*, ll. 205–6. *new ingredients*: sulphur, mercury, and salt, in the theory popularized by Paracelsus. *lay*: bet. *the stone...how blood...doth flow...the putrid stuffe...spit*: Although medical explanations were lacking, the production of bladder stones and of mucus were not matters of current controversy. But the passage of blood from one ventricle of the heart to another was the subject of much discussion. In 1543 Andreas Vesalius followed Galen in asserting that blood 'sweats from the right into the left ventricle through passages that escape human vision' (*Lectures on the History of Physiology*, trans. Sir Michael Foster (1901), 14). *piercing of substances*: The ancient Stoics maintained that elements in a compound substance penetrated one another, while the Peripatetics (Aristotelians) insisted that only the mixture of elements was possible. *many' opinions...Of Nailes and Haires*: It was disputed whether nails and hair were to be classed as skin, bones, organs of the body, or waste products not properly part of the body at all. Fernelius had no doubt that they were excrements (*Universa Medicina*, 44).

ll. 281–90. *stiffe*: stubbornly opinionated. *A hundred controversies of an Ant*: Donne would remark similarly in *Essays in Divinity*: 'Man...sees all...so dimly, that there are marked an hundred differences in mens Writings concerning an *Ant*' (139). These authors have not been identified. *Catechismes and Alphabets*: basics of knowledge. *unconcerning*: irrelevant. *what Cicero said*: Cicero says that nothing is swifter than the soul's movement as it mounts through the atmosphere and reaches its natural habitation among the stars. There the eye of the mind, freed from bodily desires and limitations, can apprehend truth (*Tusculan Disputations*, 1.43–5). *why our blood is red*: One of the problems attributed to Aristotle (*The Problems of Aristotle* (1575), E5v). *low forme*: base condition.

ll. 291–9. *Pedantery*: elementary learning. *taught by sense and Fantasy*: The prevailing opinion, based on Aristotle, *De Anima* 3, and adopted by Aquinas, held that we do not have direct knowledge of the world outside us, but that our senses carry impressions to a part of the mind called the 'fantasy', which produces a 'phantasm' (synthetic image of the object perceived). 'Our intellect understands material things by abstracting from the phantasms' (*Summa Theologica*, 1a.80.15, 75.6, 74.7, 76.1). *spectacles*:

As a mediating device for seeing, an apt material analogue for the fantasy and its production of phantasms for the mind to work upon. *watch-towre*: There were classical and biblical antecedents for this metaphor of the attentive mind (Plato, *Timaeus*, 70A; *Republic*, 560B; Isaiah 22:6; Habakkuk 2:1). *despoyled of fallacies*: stripped of deceptions. *circuit, or collections*: roundabout methods, or inferences. *In Heav'n... all*: Donne the preacher would elaborate: 'we shall see all things...as they are:...We shall be no more deluded with outward appearances; for...there will be no delusory thing to be seen...I shall see nothing but God, and what is in him' (*Sermons*, 3:111–12).

ll. 302–20. *as learned... as shee... shee... our best, and worthiest booke:* Donne ingeniously extends a commonplace image: the book of the mind inscribed with the wisdom of God. He had earlier extolled Lady Bedford as an authoritative book of both history and prophecy (To the Countesse of Bedford: 'Madame,You have refind me', ll. 51–60). *aye*: always. *over-freight... Ballast*: Overload and cause to sink, as contrasted with loading a vessel just enough to keep it on an even keel.

ll. 321–38. *Returne not... To earthly thoughts... | With whom wilt thou Converse?*: The speaker's focus shifts back to earth as he considers with whom he will associate and what the nature of these associations will be. Earthly prospects appear toxic; a satiric perspective returns. *no things bee | So like as Courts*: Donne the preacher would clarify: 'No things are liker one another, than Court and Court, the same ambitions, the same underminings in one Court as in another' (*Sermons*, 3:123). *poysons affect | Chiefly the cheefest parts*: Cardan cites Galen's authority for the claim that sunlight diffuses poison through the nerves, from whence it is transmitted to the brain; he adds that some poisons first affect the liver or the heart (*De Venenis* [On Poisons], 1.15, appended to *In Septem Aphorismorum Hippocrates particulas commentaria* [Commentary on Seven Sections of Hippocrates' Aphorisms] (1564), 896). *but some effect... will show:* Cardan (*De Venenis*, 2.13) again cites Galen to the effect that, in those who die of poison, the nails will blacken and the hair will fall out.

ll. 339–56. *Up, up...where...the Angels...the blessëd Mother-maid...those Patriarckes... those Prophets...th' Apostles...those Martyrs...those Virgins...live*: Recoiling from his prospects of earthly association, the speaker exhorts his soul to make another heavenward flight and contemplate the associations to be gained there. Donne's celestial hierarchy largely reproduces the order in the Roman Catholic litany of the saints, but it corresponds most closely to Thomas Cranmer's vernacular litany for the Church of England (1544). Like Cranmer, Donne streamlines the ranks by omitting certain groups (e.g., confessors and doctors), which he had previously included in 'The Litanye'. *new eare*: newly spiritualized ear; cf. 'growne al Ey' (l. 200). *Joy in not being that, which men have said*: Some theologians, mere *men*, asserted that the Virgin Mary was unique in being free of original sin. Donne represents her as rejoicing in her uniqueness as Jesus's mother. A sermon passage would reveal his thinking more fully: Christ came 'not...into so clean a woman as had no sin at all, none contracted from her Parents, no original sin;...Christ had placed his favours and his honors ill, if he had favoured her most who had no need of him' (*Sermons*, 1:307). *did longer sit...enjoyed him yet*: The time from the creation of the world to the birth of Christ exceeded the time from the birth of Christ to Donne's own day. *did bravely runne...the Sunne*: The apostles preached the Gospel throughout the known Earth, spreading a spiritual light superior to the sun's. *did calmely bleed...dew to their seed*: An allusion to Tertullian's celebrated dictum, 'the blood of the martyrs is the seed of the church' (*Apologeticus*, 50.13). *joynt-tenants*: co-occupants. *his Temple*: the virgins' bodies. Cf. 1 Corinthians 6:19: 'Know ye not that your body is the temple of the Holy Ghost?'

ll. 357–75. *Shee...hath carried thither, new degrees...to their dignitees*: Elizabeth Drury's soul has brought to heaven new ranks and categories of sainthood by performing functions previously regarded as institutional and political, but now seen to be, in her, individual, moral, and spiritual. *Shee...being to herself a state...any state employd*: Another commonplace: the correspondences between an individual human being and a body politic. 'Every Christian is a state, a common-wealth to *himselfe*' (*Sermons*, 4:216). *royalties*: the *prerogatives* of a sovereign. Recast as spiritual functions, these include making war and concluding peace, administering justice by exercising absolute authority and by granting pardons, coining money, and extending protection against arrest and prosecution. *religiön | Made her a Church*: This identification seemed perhaps more natural in England, where Henry VIII's break with papal supremacy made state and church coextensive. 'Every man is a little *Church*'; 'every man hath a *Church* in himselfe' (*Sermons*, 4:194; 7:403).

ll. 382–8. *accidental joyes*: Scholastic theology, drawing on Aristotle, distinguished *accidental* (or non-essential) from *essential* joys. The essential joy of heaven is the sight of God. Accidental joys of heaven, which can increase (*doe grow*), include joy at the conversion of a sinner and joy in the conversation of the saints (*Sermons*, 3:339). Her presence in heaven is an accidental joy to others; she herself possesses essential joy. *before Accesso'ries...tried*: 'An accessorie' in a felony 'shal be punished...but...shal never be put to that till the principal be attaint or convict, or bee outlawed' (John Rastell, *An Exposition of...Termes of the Lawes* (1609), 7r). *And what...upon earth?*: 'In this world we enjoy nothing; enjoying presumes perpetuity; and here, all things are fluid, transitory: There I shall enjoy, and possesse for ever, God himself' (*Sermons*, 9:128).

ll. 391–400. *cous'ned cous'nor*: deceived deceiver. *You are...chang'd since yesterday*: Michel de Montaigne argued that we are not the same persons today that we were yesterday, for we have neither a permanent existence nor a fixed identity (*Essais*, 2.12, trans. John Florio (1603), 350–1). Cf. 'Obsequies to the Lord Harrington', ll. 47–9. *That saint, nor Pilgrime*: The Petrarchan beloved and her lover. *hourly in inconstancee*: Cf. 'Woman's Constancy' ('Now Thou hast Lov'd mee one whole day'), ll. 2–5.

ll. 401–12. *Honour*: esteem, reverence. *pretence unto:* claim upon. *God did live...* | *Without this honour...then...made Creatures to bestow* | *Honour on him*: Donne later clarifies: God 'is content to receive his Honour from us, (for although all cause of Honour be eternally inherent in himselfe, yet that Act proceeds from us, and of that Honour...he could have none til he had made Creatures to exhibit it)' (*Essays in Divinity*, 54). *that, to his hands...more fit*: Two meanings are in play: that man might more fittingly appear to be God's creation, and might grow fitter to carry out God's purposes. It was generally believed that Adam would have increased in goodness if he had not fallen (Aquinas, *Summa Theologica*, 1a.102.4; *Sermons*, 7:108). *since all honors...so honor'd*: Donne recycles a point from an earlier verse letter 'To the Countess of Bedford' ('Honour is so sublime perfection'), ll. 7–9. *casuall*: accidental, dependent on chance and change.

ll. 414–24. *arrest*: give rest to. *tane*: taken. *They who did labour...the Base*: Donne the preacher would elaborate, suggesting a source that has not been identified: 'Men have considered usefully the incongruity of building the towre of Babel, in this, That to have erected...that height that they intended...the whole body of the earth...would not have served...for a foundation to that Towre. If all the timber of all the forests in the world, all the quarries of stones, all the mines of Lead and Iron...would not have served...for a foundation...from whence then must they have had their materials for all the superedifications?' (*Sermons*, 8:322–3). *this Center*: the planet Earth, in the Ptolemaic system.

ll. 425–34. *as the Heathen...his Rods*: Cicero speaks of the deification of Love, Grief, Sickness, Work, Fate, Old Age, Death, and much else, remarking that 'the name of gods should not be ascribed thus to pernicious things' (*De Deorum Natura* [On the Nature of the Gods], 3.17.44; 3.25.63). *Rods*: punishments. *as the Wine...Gods unto them*: Both Juvenal (Satire 15.9–11) and Tertullian speak of the worship of the onion (*Ad Nationes* [To the Nations], 2; *PL*, 1.587–607). Donne would allude to Tertullian in this regard in *Devotions*, Meditation 8. *thrust*: throng, crowd.

ll. 435–42. *thy first pitch*: Multiple meanings appear to be in play: the height of the human soul before the Fall; the perfect harmony of the soul attuned to God; the centre point from which a compass traces (*pitches*) a circle. *all lines which circles do containe*: diameters. *be thou such*: The soul should demonstrate the spiritual analogue of circularity, the perfect form, and twice as much awareness of heaven as of Earth, figured by the diameter. Donne would reuse this image in 'Obsequies to the Lord Harrington', ll. 105–10. *All will not serve*: Even if you devote your entire earthly thoughts to the joy of heaven, that will not suffice to attain *The sight of God, in fulnesse*, only to be *enjoyd* in heaven. *both the object, and the wit*: both the *object* seen and the faculty of *understanding* that enables the soul to see it. According to Aristotle, *Metaphysics*, 12.9 1075a4, divine thought and what it thinks of are the same—that is, the thinking is one with its object of thought.

ll. 447–64.   *To fill... or more*: Aquinas says that 'by the gift of grace men can merit glory in such a degree as to be equal to the angels,... and this implies that men are taken up into the orders of angels' (*Summa Theologica*, 1.108.8). *in any natu'rall Stone, or Tree*: It was a commonplace that three 'books' contained knowledge of God's nature and purposes: the Book of the Creatures or the natural world; the Bible; and the Book of Life, in which the names of all the redeemed were inscribed (Psalm 69:28, Daniel 12:1, Revelation 3:5). *reparatiön*: good repair. *decay*: deterioration or impairment, caused by original sin. *solicited*: enticed. *his safe precontract... now is marriëd*: Betrothals (precontracts of marriage) can be broken off, but God's promises are sure (*safe*). Now she is a virgin bride of God in heaven. *Who dreamt... to pray*: Donne the preacher would clarify his meaning and reveal his sources: 'those Saints of God who have their Heaven upon earth, do praise him in the night: according to that of S. *Jerome, Sanctis ipse somnus, oratio* [The sleep of the saints is a kind of praying], and that of S. *Basil, Etiam somnia Sanctorum preces sunt* [Even the dreams of the saints are prayers];... holy men doe praise God, and pray to God in their sleep, and in their dreams' (*Sermons*, 8:53).

ll. 471–88.   *could this low world... casuall bee?*: Even if this world could give us access to essential joys, heaven's accidental joys would far surpass them (because accidental or casual joys, although subject to change, are lasting in heaven). Examples of Earth's casual joys and their problematic effects follow: ennoblement with a title makes its recipient inhumanly prideful; an untreatable abscess (*Apostem*) brings the sufferer relief when it ruptures although the resulting inflammation (*dange'rous rest*) may cause his death. *What aye was casuäll*: What was always temporary. *What should the Nature change?*: What could possibly change uncertain joys into certain ones? *it can away*: it can vanish.

ll. 496–510.   *Degrees of growth*: Donne the preacher would clarify: 'The glory of the next world, is not in the measure of that glory, but in the measure of my capacity... I shall have as much as my soule can receive... a fulnesse in myself' (*Sermons*, 6:335). *degree*: the magnitude of her goodness and blessedness. *'Tis losse... not such as the rest*: It diminishes her to be called *best* among an inferior sort of beings when she is of a sort superior to them. *Made better*: glorified, to prepare for reunion with her soul in the general resurrection. *Rolls*: rolled-up lengths of parchment on which records were kept. *Shee, who by making... keepes it so*: Already perfect in goodness and joy, she enlarges *a Circle* (a figure of perfection) while preserving its circularity. *Long'd for*: desired by the other saints in heaven. *receives, and gives additiön*: receives joy from others' goodness, and adds to others' joy with her goodness.

ll. 511–28.   *Here*: In France, where Donne was currently staying. *where mis-devotion frames…have at least the same*: Donne does not satirize the practice of praying to saints per se. He satirizes praying to ones whose holiness is unverified (unknown to the ancient church, unknown in heaven) and whose exploits and miracles are invented or imaginary (*what lawes of poetry admit*). *Could any Saint provoke that appetite*: If he could be brought to pray to any saint, it would be she. *a French convertite*: a convert to Catholicism. Irony attaches to the word here, and in 'A Letter to the Lady Carey', l. 7, since 'convertis' in French were beggars who extracted alms from passers-by by claiming to have changed from false to true religion. *my second yeeres true Rent*: In contrast to the alms dubiously obtained, Donne pledges his *true* homage in the form of an annual commemorative poem, of which the *Second Anniversary* is the second. *stampe than his*: impression (a warrant of legitimacy) other than that of God himself. *Thou art…I am | The Trumpet*: The poetic speaker is the herald announcing the public reading of a royal *Proclamation* (God's attesting of the virtue and blessedness of this *Immortal Maid*: l. 516). Donne the preacher would also image himself as a trumpet (*Sermons*, 2:166–70), as the prophet Isaiah had imaged himself in addressing the people of Israel (Isaiah 58:1).

FROM THE DOWDEN MANUSCRIPT, PRE-1615 COMPOSITIONS

The Dowden manuscript, University of Oxford, Bodleian Library, MS Eng. poet. e.99, is a quarto book of 142 leaves containing 99 poems by Donne, entirely written in the large, sloping italic hand of his friend George Garrard. No poem in Dowden was composed later than the end of 1614. On Donne's friendship with Garrard and the likely origins of the Dowden manuscript, see the Introduction.

The five Satires, continuously paginated, lead off this collection. Folio 12r begins a new gathering, made conspicuous by a different serial pagination. Twelve of the thirteen Elegies in the Westmoreland MS follow, although in a different order. The Dowden MS lacks Westmoreland's Elegy 2 ('As the sweete sweate of roses in a still'). But Dowden does have several Elegies not found in Westmoreland; their texts and titles are transcribed here. On the diverse subjects and emotions associated with this verse form, see 'Elegy: The Genre', in the textual notes to the Westmoreland MS.

Elegye: On Loves Progresse (fol. 22v)

Among manuscripts of Donne's poems judged to be earlier and and more reliable, only Dowden and two others include 'On Loves Progresse'. Licensers kept this poem out of the earliest editions of the *Poems*; it was first printed in the fifth edition of 1669. This impudent creation shows affinities with the paradox in its argument that *the right true end* in lovemaking entails moving by a direct route up the beloved's foot, legs, and thighs rather than by the obstacle course that begins with the beloved's face and hair. There may be some connection between this elegy and Thomas Nashe's *The Choice of Valentines*, set in a London brothel, where a similar trip from the foot upwards is described (ll. 99–115). Nashe's poem is conjecturally dated before 1593; it was not published until 1899. *Progresse* in Donne's title puns on two senses of the word: to make an official journey—a no-longer current use—and to advance.

ll. 1–9.   *Who ever…end of Love*: A facetious invoking of Aristotle's principle: 'Where there is an end, all the preceding steps are for the sake of that' (*Physics* 2.8.199a8–9). *Love 'ys… a Monster make*: The belief that bear cubs were born shapeless and licked into shape by their mother traces to classical antiquity (Pliny, *Natural History*, 8.54). *a Monster… Fac'd like a Man*: Two more snippets of Aristotle: the dictum 'Monstrosities will be failures in the purposive effect' and the example of a 'man-faced ox-progeny' (*Physics*, 2.8.199b3–4, a32). *Perfection is in Unitye*: This cardinal principle was formulated by Aquinas as follows: 'Since…what is first is most perfect,…it must be that the first which reduces all into one order should be only one' (*Summa Theologica*, 1.11.3).

ll. 11–25.   *I, when I value… soule of trade*: The valuable qualities of gold are intrinsic to it, but its greatest value lies in its use as a medium of exchange. *Ductillnes*: malleability. *Applicatiöne*: workability. *wholesomeness*: medicinal value. *Ingenuitye*: fineness as shown by resistance to rust, pollution, and oxidation. *All these… Love but one*: By analogy with gold, one might think of valuable qualities intrinsic to women—if, that is, women had any. But a lover can love a woman for her (sexual) use-value. The speaker continues in mock indignation at the insults paid to women by men who profess or seek to love them for their *Vertue, Beauty* or *wealth*. *barren Angells*: Love between angels was sexless because they have 'no passions of concupiscence' (Aquinas, *Summa Theologica*, 1.59.4).

ll. 28–36.   *our Cupid…is an Infernall God…wee Love the Centrique Part*: The pretended myth of a subterranean Cupid and his worship proceeds through analogies with the earth's vagina-like openings and its cultivation with tools. *Gold and Fyre abound*: To obtain sex, a man must have money and be hotly aroused.

ll. 39–70.   *But in attayning… sett out at the face*: Myth transmutes to allegory: a voyage of discovery starting from a woman's face and proceeding downwards (Cupid's direction) along the course of her naked body. *Springës*: traps. *the first Meridian*: In Ptolemaic geography, a great circle on the Earth's surface on which the so-called Fortunate (Canary) Islands lay. *Syrens Songes*: These lured sailors to their deaths (Homer, *Odyssey*, 12.39–46). *Wise Delphique oracles*: Utterances regarding fates and futures pronounced by the priestess of Apollo at Delphi. *Remora*: A sucking-fish supposedly capable of stopping ships in mid-course (Pliny, *Natural History*, 32.1.2–6). *the streight Hellespont betweene… Sestos, and Abydos*: The setting of the tragic love of

Hero and Leander; cf. Donne's epigram on the pair. *Iland Moles*: Wordplay—dark spots on the skin; piers or breakwaters. *her India*: Figurative—source of riches. *fayre Atlantique Navell*: The Azores, also located on the first meridian, were thought to have superseded the Delphic oracle as the navel of the world (Plutarch, *Moralia* 1.409E). *embayde*: at rest in a bay (said of a ship). *another Forrest*: her pubic hair.

ll. 74–80.   *Some Symmetrye... that Part*: The sense is unclear; this may be an allusion to the channel-like indentations between the toes. *Symmetrye*: similarity of shape. *the Devill... change hys*: It was popularly believed that the devil could not disguise his cloven foot. *the Embleam... Firmnes*: The foot as an image of stability occurs in a number of sources, e.g., Psalm 121:3: 'He will not suffer thy foot to be moved'.

ll. 81–6.   *Civilitye... the Kisse*: Protocols refined social practices. Equals kiss each other on the face. Kissing someone's hand acknowledges that person's superiority; kissing a ruler's knee signifies the duty of feudal service; kissing a pope's foot signifies total subservience.

ll. 87–96.   *free Spheares... Birds*: Positioned in outer space far beyond the Earth's atmosphere, the celestial spheres were thought to make a complete circuit of the heavens every twenty-four hours. Birds flew more slowly because they had to contend with resistance from air currents and winds. The celestial spheres (*this Emptye, and Ethereall way*) correlate with direct access to the genitals, and the flying birds with lingering over a woman's cheeks, breasts, and abdomen. *Two Purses*: 'Purse' originally denoted a small bag whose opening could be drawn tightly shut by 'purse-strings'; the idiom 'pursing the lips' registers the perceived likeness between purse and mouth. Donne extends the likeness to the labia of the vagina. *aversely*: at right angles. *by Clyster... meate*: put food into the belly by means of an enema. In Donne's day this procedure was applied in medical emergencies involving children, the aged, and consumptives (Ambroise Paré, *Works*, trans. T. Johnson (1634), 1051–2).

Elegye. On the Lady Marckham ('Man is the worlde, and death the' Oceän') (fol. 24v)

After the composition of Elegy 13 in Westmoreland, evidently to mourn the death of the younger Sir Thomas Egerton, this poem is Donne's next known use of the genre to praise and commemorate a deceased person. The more than seven-year interval between the elegy on the younger Egerton and this elegy on Lady Markham witnessed the stalemate of Donne's professional prospects in the wake of his marriage. His precarious situation as husband and father of a growing family impelled him to seek patrons who had both the means and the social status to be sources of support.

Bridget, daughter of Sir James Harrington, was one of the ladies of Queen Anne's bedchamber and a first cousin of Lucy, countess of Bedford, whose patronage Donne was cultivating in this period. Bridget married Sir Anthony Markham in 1598. After his death in December 1604, she formed an intimate friendship with her cousin Lucy.

Lady Markham died at Twickenham Park, Lady Bedford's estate, in May 1609 at the age of thirty.

ll. 1–6.   *Man is... invirons all*: The human microcosm is composed of the four ele-
             ments; the heavier two, earth and water, are the mortal *Lower parts*. *invi-*
             rons: surrounds. *as yett*: we are still alive. *pretend*: assert its claim. *breakes*
             our banckes: As the sea commonly did in a tidal estuary like the Thames.

ll. 7–12.   *Then our Land waters... are Sin*: Donne the preacher would emphasize the
             misguidedness of excessive grief: 'To mourne...immoderately for the
             death of any that is passed out of this world, is not the right use of
             teares....Thy first teares must be to God for sin' (*Sermons*, 4:340–2). *Land*
             waters: floods. *her Sinn*: our soul's sin. *brackish*: salty. *funerall*: final. *Wee,*
             after...worlde agayne: God's promise never to send another cataclysmic
             flood (Genesis 9:11) has the force of an injunction to us; we violate it when
             we flood ourselves with grief.

ll. 13–20. *Nothing but Man... Inborne stinges*: The capacity of humans to harm them-
             selves is a favourite topic of Donne's; cf. *Devotions*, Meditations 12 and 23.
             embroydered workes: intricate patterns.

ll. 21–8.   *As men of China... buryed Clay*: Guido Panciroli recounted as fact a story
             perhaps devised by the Chinese to conceal a valuable trade secret. Workmen
             buried a mixture of gypsum, eggshells, and lobster shells in places dis-
             closed only to their children or grandchildren, who after eighty years dug
             up the clay-like mixture and molded it into vessels (*Nova Reperta* [New
             Inventions] (1599), 2.65). [*Porcelane*]: Emending to the reading in other
             earlier manuscripts and *Poems* (1633). The *Oxford English Dictionary*
             includes 'purcelan' and 'porseland' among variants of 'porcelain', but not
             Dowden's 'Purselende'. *So at thys Grave...thys All*: Lady Markham's
             flesh, figured as precious stones and metals, in turn prefigures the materials
             of the New Jerusalem that will replace the present heaven and earth
             (Revelation 22:10–21). As alchemists work to distill from gold an essence
             with which to transmute baser metals, so God will *recompence* the destruc-
             tion of the present world by refining it into *th' Elixar of thys All*, the purest
             quintessence of everything that formerly existed. *Lymbecke* (alembic): a
             vessel used in distillation. *Mynes*: gold and silver.

ll. 29–34. *the Sea...loseth too*: A commonplace of direct observation since antiquity
             (Aristotle, *Meterology*, 1.14). *Yf Carnall Death...freed by thys*: When our
             body dies, this *yonger* (earlier occurring) death frees our soul, but remains
             in jeopardy of *th' Elder death by Sin* (God's eternal forsaking of an unre-
             pentant soul). The notion of two deaths has biblical origins (Hebrews 9:27;
             Revelation 2:11; 21:8). [*when they*]: Emending Dowden's unmetrical and
             obscure 'who'.

ll. 35–40. *unobnoxious*: invulnerable. *none to death...is loth*: According to Aquinas, a
             turning away from God by an act of the will is essential to mortal sin
             (*Summa Theologica*, 1a.72.5.1; 2ae.78.4). [*sin*]: Emending Dowden's read-
             ing 'death', probably the result of eyeskip. [*do*]: Emending the tense shift in

Dowden's reading, 'did'. *Soe hath... Virginitye*: She attests her innocence and purity by her willingness to die in the assurance of eternal life (*thys*) and by her unwillingness to sin (*that*). *Grace... repent*: The formulations trace to Augustine: God's grace gave her what capacity she had not to sin (*Enchiridion*, 30); grace also helped her to triumph over sin by repenting (*City of God*, 21.16).

ll. 41–8. *Of what... complaynes*: Proverbial; Tilley, *Dictionary*, S781. *How litle... Christall glas?*: The (fictitious) fragility of Venetian (crystal) glass was a disputed subject in Donne's day. *zeale*: religious fervor. *extreme truith... a lye*: Her moral sense was so exacting that she came close to falsifying the degree of her faults by classing her sins of omission as sins of commission (*Acts*), and accusing herself of sins that would only have been thought such in other circumstances (*thinges that sometimes may be such*).

ll. 49–62. *As Moses... wingëd too*: Winged cherubim flanked the mercy seat that surmounted the ark of the covenant (Exodus 25:18–20). According to Aquinas, *Summa Theologica*, 1a.53.3, angels can move instantly from place to place, so why do they have wings? A similar perplexity attaches to Lady Markham, already assured of life in heaven by her virtuous life on earth. Why did she seem *To Clyme* heavenward *by Teares, the Common stayres of Men?* Purely spiritual beings are an enigma. *eaven*: steady, unwavering. *her Titles*: her entitlements to a place in heaven. *meete... Heresye*: well qualified to have corrected this presumptuous false belief. *shall not be told*: Donne avoids a conventional ending, a catalogue of Lady Markham's virtues, which would mislead hearers into supposing that she was older than thirty when she died, and would give Death (personified as the Grim Reaper) an occasion to *Tryumph* over *such a Prey*.

Elegy on Mrs Boulstred (fol. 26r)

Cecilia Bulstrode, a lady of Queen Anne's bechamber, died at Lady Bedford's residence, Twickenham Park, on 4 August 1609 at the age of twenty-five. An undated letter from Donne to Goodyere refers to her fatal illness: 'I fear earnestly that Mistress Bolstrod will not escape that sicknesse in which she labours at this time... I could... impute all her sicknesse to her minde. But the History of her sicknesse, makes me justly fear, that she will scarce last so long, as that you when you receive this letter, may do her any good office, in praying for her.' Among her symptoms Donne lists vomiting, fever, hysteria, 'and an extream ill spleen' (*Letters*, 215–16). Donne also seems to refer to Cecilia Bulstrode in an undated letter to George Garrard, who had received a copy of Ben Jonson's epitaph on her. Donne says, 'I have done nothing of that kinde... in the memory of that good Gentlewoman.... You teach me what I owe her memory' (*Letters*, 39). Previous references to Mistress Bulstrode by court wits had been of a decidedly different sort. Jonson's 'Verses on the Pucelle [Courtesan] of the Court Mistriss Boulstred' depicted an unconventional young woman who composed and circulated verses, implying as well that she had broken off two engagements to marry. Sir Edward Herbert's commemorative Latin poem recorded that Cecilia

Bulstrode died 'not without unquietness of spirit and conscience'. Her presumed deathbed repentance must account for the shift from innuendo to respect in contemporary references to her.

ll. 1–10. *Death, I recant... diminish Thee*: This opening is generally read as repudiating the scorn for death expressed in Donne's 'Death bee not Proude' (Dowden's Holy Sonnet 6). *slipt*: slipped out, with a suggestion of slip-up, error. *Spirituall Treason... to say*: Because 'the keys of hell and of death' are in Christ's hands (Revelation 1:18). *rude*: uncivilized. *hys bloodye... jaws*: War, plague, and famine recur as a trio of evils in Scripture (Ezekiel 14:21; Revelation 6:8). In 1609 London saw a sharp rise in plague deaths. *Eating... first*: It was a commonplace that 'the good die young' or, more piously, 'God taketh them soonest whom he loveth best' (Tilley, *Dictionary*, G251).

ll. 11–20. *Now wantonly... peecemeale rott*: Death nibbles here and there, not ingesting but wasting, and leaving the remainder to go bad. By extension this is how we are when friends die: we lose part of ourselves and are never the same again. *sinckes*: sinks into. *fish... keepe*: 'Mute as a fish' was proverbial. *Who... by Roes... make yt Land*: If fish did not die, their prolific spawn might accumulate as sandy, spongy landforms. *roundes*: circles (like a bird of prey). *Hymnique notes*: songs of praise. *Organique*: vibrating like organ pipes. *A tenth... Hierarchye*: Pseudo-Dionysius the Areopagite's enumeration of nine orders of angels in his *Celestial Hierarchies* was commonly accepted.

ll. 21–8. *O strong... Death*: A flat contradiction of Dowden Holy Sonnet 6, ll. 1–2. *how camst thou In?*: The question ignores a number of biblical texts, e.g., Romans 5:12: 'By one man, sin entered the world, and death by sin.' *Thou hast... Antichrist*: Death, 'the last enemy that shall be destroyed' (1 Corinthians 15.26), has witnessed the fall of the four monarchies (Babylon, Persia, Greece, and Rome), and will see the great enemy of Christ and his kingdom defeated (Revelation 19:11–17; 20:1–14). *Our Birthes... Degrees of Thee*: Regarding *Vices*, Donne the preacher would clarify: 'Our sinnes are our owne, and our destruction is from our selves' (*Sermons*, 9.65). Regarding *Vertues*, he would reflect more enigmatically that mortality inheres in being alive: 'We bring all with us into the world, that which carries us out of the world, a naturall, unnaturall consuming of that... which sustaines our life' (*Sermons*, 2.81).

ll. 31–6. *And though... the Most to Thee*: An earlier seventeenth-century reader, Alexander Dyce, remarked 'A grand passage' in a note in his copy of Donne's *Poems* (1633) (Victoria and Albert Museum, D 25: D 15). *reclaym'd*: A technical term for a hawk called back in flight, applied especially to one that had been tamed. *fewe*: the redeemed. 'For many are called, but few are chosen' (Matthew 22:14). *not ours, nor thyne owne*: She is altogether in God's keeping.

ll. 37–50. *Shee was more... and fort*: Donne elaborates a standard medieval allegory of the body as a fortified castle inhabited by the soul. *offred...roome*: attempted an assault on her body, which had the stateliness of a *Court* in attendance on its *King* (her soul). *both...fort*: failed to capture both the commanding officer (her soul in another guise) and the stronghold (her body in another guise). *Both workes*: Death and sin cause. *no Divorce*: Donne would take the opposite view in *Sermons*, 6.71; 7.103–4; 9.207; 10.176. *usher up*: announce the impending arrival of. *there | Bodyes...are here*: Donne the preacher would elaborate: 'Glory...in Heaven, shall be of that exaltation, as that my body shall...be like a soule, like a spirit, like an Angel of light' (*Sermons*, 7:254). *doe so?*: do the same—kill her as if she were an old woman?

ll. 52–66. *Must the Cost...bee lost?*: The irony is heavy. Since *Beauty* and *Witt* are liable to entice others to sin and cost them dearly, must Death forgo such a prime opportunity to increase the sinners among his victims? *Oh every Age...pursueth*: Allusions to various matters of reproach that might attach to Cecilia Bulstrode continue through l. 66. First, there are aspersions that she herself might arouse: *ambitious, Covetous...such Devotiön | Might...have stray'd to Superstitiön....Abundant Vertue...might...have bred a proud delight*: Then there are aspersions that others might cast upon her: *Some...would sinne, mis-thincking She did Sin. | Such as would...feigne | To Socyablenes, a name profane*—such as the French for 'courtesan' or 'whore'. Jonson's epigram critiques Cecilia Bulstrode's showy dress and bearing as well as her bold manner of conversing, entertaining and rivalling (male) wits (*Underwood*, no. 49). Donne, however, mocks the timid, lustful wits who *Sinne... By wishing, though they never told her what*.

ll. 67–74. *crost*: acted counter to. *to Tryumph... lost*: In order to vaunt over one eminent soul as his captive and trophy, Death has forfeited a host of other victims. Donne would elaborate at length on the ancient Roman institution of the triumph in 'Obsequies to the Lord Harrington', the last poem in the Dowden manuscript. *wee are not such*: either as she was, virtuous, or as she is, dead and in heaven. *Some Teares... her death must Cost*: 'To lament a dead friend is naturall, and civill; and he is the deader of the two, the verier carcasse, that does not so' (*Sermons*, 7:269). *Chayne*: Of friendship.

An Elegye on Prince Henry (fol. 27v)

The remainder of fol. 27v and all of fol. 28r–v have been left blank, but this poem of 98 lines is lacking. Presumably Garrard could have obtained the text, which had appeared in print in the third edition (1613) of Joshua Sylvester's *Lachrymae Lachrymarum, or the Spirit of Tears distilled from the untimely Death of the Incomparable Prince Panaretus*. Donne's poem is included in a section at the back of Sylvester's volume, headed by a separate title page: *Sundry Funerall Elegies... Composed by severall Authors*.

VERSE LETTERS TO MALE FRIENDS

Several of Donne's verse letters follow in Dowden (fols 29r–31v). There is, first, a group addressed to male friends, then a group addressed to noble ladies, all written after 1608, in which Donne's soliciting of patronage through compliment is clearly in play. With one notable exception, Westmoreland contains all of the verse letters to male friends composed before 1600 that are found in Dowden, but in a different order. That exception is the companion poem to 'The Storme', titled 'The Calme'—Donne's paired verse letters recounting experiences at sea during the 'Islands' expedition of July–September 1597. It is standardly assumed that 'The Calme', like 'The Storme', was addressed to Christopher Brooke, but Dowden is not explicit about this.

Post-1600 verse letters to male friends found in Dowden but not in Westmoreland include 'To Sir Henry Goodyere' ('Who makes the Past, a Patterne for next yeare') (1608–9) and 'To Sir Edward Herbert, at Juliers' (mid-1610); these are reproduced below in the place and order in which they occur in Dowden. For general remarks on Donne's handling of this genre, see 'Verse Letters to Male Friends: The Genre', in the textual notes to Westmoreland.

The Calme (fols 31v–32v)

Westmoreland's omission of 'The Calme' is both striking and puzzling, given the overall completeness of this source for Donne's pre-1600 compositions. Fortunately Dowden supplies the lack. For the text of 'The Storme', see pp. 38–9; for notes, see the textual notes for the verse letters of the Westmoreland manuscript.

After setting out for the second time on the 'Islands' or Azores expedition against the Spanish in September 1597, the English fleet became divided. Essex reached the islands first and, finding no treasure fleet, he cruised offshore awaiting the arrival of Raleigh and his ships. Sir Arthur Gorges, a commander serving under Raleigh, recorded that after his ship had reached the Azores, between 8 and 10 September, 'we were very much becalmed for a day or two and the weather extremely hot, insomuch that the wind could not bear the sails from the masts, but were fain to hull in the sea, to our great discontentment' ('Voyage to the Iles of Azores', in Purchas, *Purchas his Pilgrims* (1907 edn), 20:65–6). The ship on which Donne was sailing must have trailed Gorges's ship in Raleigh's squadron, since he and his shipmates were still seeking the islands when they were becalmed (ll. 9–10). Donne is irked by not being able to make contact either with *left frindes* (other participants in this divided expedition) or with *sought foes* (l. 21).

ll. 2–4.   *stupid*: motionless. *Nothing…swage*: Nothing assuages the miseries of the calm (as the calm itself had assuaged the preceding storm). *The Fable is inverted*: In a fable ascribed to Aesop, when the frogs in a pond ask Zeus for a king, he sends them a log. Growing contemptuous of this *Blocke*, the frogs ask Zeus for another king. This time he sends them *a Storke* (or a water-snake in variants of the myth) that devours the frogs. The wordplay on *Blocke* (lump of wood, blockage) strengthens the myth's pertinence to the calm Donne describes.

ll. 12–18. *Lead... Spout*: The roofs of most English churches were covered with lead. When the roofbeams caught fire, the molten lead ran off in all directions, not just through the drainage spouts, which would have been dissolving as well. *Courts removing*: When the queen and court moved from one place to another, the wall hangings and furniture changed place along with the entourage. So too did the stage properties of *Ended Plays*. *fighting-place*: area between the ship's foremast and mainmast on which hand-to-hand fighting centred. During battle it was closed off by stout wooden grates to impede boarding parties. Since no enemy can approach in the calm, the area serves for drying clothes. *supplye*: fill up. *Fripperye*: resale clothes shop—figuratively, the laundry spread out on the ship's *Tackling*. *No... Lanthornes*: Pointless to light a lantern to signal the ship's nighttime position; nothing could move at all. *in One Place laye... yesterday*: In the Hawthornden manuscript (National Library of Scotland MS 2067) Drummond reported Jonson as saying that he 'esteemeth John Done the first poet in the World in some things. His verses of the Lost Chaine [Elegy 1: 'The Bracelet'] he hath by Heart and that passage of The Calme, that dust and feathers doe not stirr, all was so quiet' (*Ben Jonson*, ed. Herford, Simpson, and Simpson, 1:135).

ll. 19–22. *Earths Hollownesses... Vault of Ayre*: In traditional cosmology, winds originated in the lowest region of the air or were exhaled from hollows in the earth. By contrast, the upper region was completely calm because no movement of air could pass beyond the middle region. Cf. 'The Storme', ll. 13–16. *Meteorlike*: Like phenomena of the atmosphere between heaven and earth. *the Calenture*: a tropical fever suffered by sailors. One of its reported symptoms was delirium in which the victim, yearning to be on land, jumped or tried to jump into the sea, mistaking it for green fields.

ll. 25–8. *on the hatches... Sacrifice*: Suffering from heat prostration, sailors lie on the hatches of the deck, where the air may be less stifling than in the cabins below. Donne's image skirts blasphemy in its affinities with the depiction of Jesus in Hebrews 8:26–7 as 'an high priest... holy, harmless, undefiled... Who needeth not... to offer up sacrifice, first for his own sins, and then for the people's: for this he did once, when he offered up himself.' *that Miracle... not dye*: Three Jews, Shadrach, Meshach, and Abednego, refused to worship a golden image as commanded by Nebuchadnezzar, king of Babylon. When they were punished for disobedience and thrown bound and fully clothed into 'a burning fiery furnace', they were shortly seen to be 'loose, walking in the midst of the fire, and they have no hurt'. Summoning the three Jews out the fire, Nebuchadnezzar acknowledged the power of their God (Daniel 3:1–29).

ll. 33–8. *Like Bajazet... Shepheards scoffe*: In Part 1 of Christopher Marlowe's *Tamburlaine the Great* (1590), 4.2, the Scythian shepherd-warrior Tamburlaine commands the conquered Turkish emperor Bajazet to be caged and brought before him to be mocked. *like slack... hayre off*: The hero of Judah,

Samson, confides the secret of his prodigious strength to Delilah in Judges 16:17: 'If I be shaven, then my strength will go from me, and I shall become weak.' *as a Myriade...invade*: The Roman emperor Tiberius reportedly had a pet snake; when he found it devoured by ants, he took this as an omen to beware the power of the people (Suetonius, *Life of Tiberius*, 72). *The crawlinge...bed ridd ships*: The *Galleyes*, a type of single-deck ship used in the Mediterranean, are presented as contemptible and un-English. They *crawl* because they move by oars; they are *Sea Jayles* because the rowers are chained prisoners; they appear *finny* because their oars protrude from their sides; and they are *Chips* because they are smaller and lighter than men-of-war. Yet these galleys might challenge *our Venices*, the English tall ships rising from the sea in stately fashion like the city of Venice, for the calm has reduced them to the helplessness of bed-ridden patients.

ll. 40–50. *disuse mee from*: get me out of the habit of. *the queasye... Loving*: Ovid proposes going to war as a cure for love in *Remedia amoris* (Remedies for Love), 153–4, and compares a love 'too fat and too sweet' to unhealthful food in *Amores* (Loves) 2.19.25–6. *my End*: my purpose. *here as well... dye*: Cf. Elegy 7: 'Till I have peace with thee, warr other Men', ll. 17–28. *Desperate*: a desperado, prepared to fight against hopeless odds. *A Scourge... pray*: The Litany of the Church of England provided a prayer to be said 'in the time of war' and another for deliverance from a 'plague of rain and waters', but nothing against calms (*The Elizabethan Prayer Book* (1559), 75, 76).

ll. 51–6. *What are...he was | Nothing*: Creation *ex nihilo* (out of nothing) was a favourite doctrine of Donne's. *Chance...disproportion it*: Our circumstances or our characters put our potential out of true balance. *Wee have...noe Sense; I lye, | I should not then thus feele thys Miserye*: A final turn of a kind found elsewhere in the Satires and Elegies ironizes the authority of the poetic speaker.

Dowden's sequence of verse letters that overlap with those in Westmoreland resumes as follows (fols 33r–34r): 'To Mr Rowland Woodward' ('Like One who in her third Widowhead'); 'To Sir Henry Wotton' ('Here is no More Newes than Vertu').

To Sir Henry Goodyere ('Who makes the Past, a Patterne for next yeare') (fol. 34r)

On the close friendship between Donne and Goodyere, see the Introduction. Ben Jonson's epigrams on Goodyere (nos 85–6) note his fondness for hawking and his 'well-made choice of friends and books'. This verse letter was written between 1605 and 1610 when Donne was living with his wife and family at *Mitcham* (l. 48) in Surrey. Its first line suggests that the occasion is a New Year's Day or Goodyere's birthday. The advice *yourselfe transplant | Awhyle from hence* (ll. 21–8) additionally suggests that this verse letter was written before Goodyere went abroad in August–September 1609. A likely date of composition is 1608–9. The poem's stanzas take the form of paired 'elegiac' couplets: cross-rhymed, five-foot lines.

ll. 4–16.   *a payre of beades*: a string of beads, i.e., the same thing repeatedly. *better*: improve. *her fayre Larger Guest*: Goodyere's soul. *Wee must not…the End*: An allusion to the contrastive images of milk and meat in Hebrews 5:13–14: 'For every one that useth milk is unskilful in the word of righteousness: for he is a babe. But strong meat belongeth to them that are of full age, even those who by reason of use have their senses exercised to discern both good and evil.' *papp*: an infant's soft food.

ll. 17–20.   *Libraryes… Courts*: Providers of knowledge, which for Goodyere have been Cambridge University, military service in Ireland, and the affiliations of the Privy Chamber. *In harvests…your Sports*: Goodyere's garners are not as full as they should be because he has ridden over his fields, pursuing the pleasure of hawking rather than harvesting their crops. Donne closes an undated letter to Goodyere with the wish, 'God send you Hawks and fortunes of a high pitch' (*Letters*, 204).

ll. 22–8.   *outlandish ground*: foreign soil. *a Stranger*: a foreigner. *that benifitt… choake*: The advice amounts to urging Goodyere to go anywhere abroad to remove himself from temptation: if he can abandon his ingrained ways, all will be to his profit. *prescribe*: lay down a rule or direction to be followed.

ll. 29–36.   *Our Soule… her father*: A conventional period perspective. *all*: everything. Dowden's reading is unique; other manuscripts read *well*. *spare*: limit your spending, *lessens*: lowers in height. *toures*: circles—or, possibly, a variant spelling of 'towers'.

ll. 42–6.   *froward*: resistant (to advice). *Fables*: In versions deemed suitable for children, each of Aesop's fables was provided with an explanatory moral at the end. *fruite trenchers*: The round wooden boards that served as plates at this period were often inscribed with mottoes. *thus…promise, Sir*: Evidently Goodyere had missed a promised meeting with Donne in London. *Riding I had you*: Donne may have drafted this verse letter as he rode home to Mitcham on horseback. This was a situation in which he occasionally composed; cf. 'Goodfriday, 1613: Riding towards Wales'.

To Sir Edward Herbert, at Juliers (fol. 35r)

Edward Herbert (1583–1648) was the eldest son of Donne's friend Magdalen Herbert, and brother of George Herbert. After studies at Oxford in 1595–1600, he became a courtier (receiving a knighthood from James I in 1603), and subsequently a traveller, soldier, and ambassador as well as a poet and philosophical writer. The reference to *Juliers* in the poem's title fixes its date quite precisely. In 1610 Herbert went to join Sir Edward Cecil who, with an English army of 4000 men, was assisting the prince of Orange in the siege of Juliers (Cleves-Juliers). The town was held by Archduke Leopold as part of the territory claimed by the Hapsburg emperor; the Dutch, French, and English were fighting on behalf of the Protestant elector of Brandenburg. Herbert can be assumed to have been present when the siege of Juliers began on 17 July, and to have departed when the town was surrendered on 22 August. Donne's verse letter variously notes Herbert's philosophical interests as well as his penchant for obscurity and indirection in composing verse.

ll. 1–4.   *Man... kneaded bee*: Donne's metaphor conjoins the biblical image of God as a potter who creates man from clay (Isaiah 64:8; Romans 9:21) with the classical myth of Prometheus who molded man out of clay, endowing him with the qualities of different animals (Plato, *Protagoras*, 320d). *Wisdome... agree*: The ark of Genesis 6–9 was commonly treated as an allegory of the human soul in which the 'beasts' (appetites, instincts, etc.) were kept under control in their contained space by reason, symbolized by Noah; cf. *First Anniversary*, ll. 318–21. Donne simultaneously pays tribute to Herbert by echoing the last two lines of Herbert's poem, 'The State Progress of Ill', composed in August 1608: 'The World, as in the Ark of Noah, rests, | Compos'd as then, few Men and many Beasts.' *a-jarre*: quarrelsomely. *a Theater*: a public place where spectacles of conflict were staged, either in Roman times with beasts in the arena or in Elizabethan times with fights to the death between dogs, bulls, and bears.

ll. 10–17.   *disaforested*: A legal term applied to land that had been reduced from the status of a forest, where animals were confined and kept for hunting, and made available for cultivation. A forest lay outside the purview of common law, while cultivated land was subject to it. *Empayld*: surrounded with a fence. *Man not only... those Devills too*: An allusion to Matthew 8:28–32, in which Jesus drove devils out of two men and into a herd of swine that, in turn, rushed into the sea and drowned.

ll. 19–22.   *As Soules... Originall Sinne*: Donne would later abandon this unorthodox view and adopt Augustine's, to the effect that the infusion of a soul into a body and the corruption of that soul occur simultaneously (*Sermons*, 1.177; 5.347). *tincture*: This alchemical term had the positive sense of a purifying, immaterial substance. *fling*: inflict. *Our Apprehension*: how we receive or understand (something).

ll. 23–32.   *To Us... Hemlocke tast*: Hemlock was widely (but wrongly) believed to be harmless to birds. Galen had speculated that the fatal effect of hemlock on humans was not due to intrinsic poison but to the 'violent chill' it produced in the body (*De causis morborum* [On the Causes of Diseases], trans. Mark Grant, *Galen on Food and Diet* (2000), 51). *Chickens*: the young of any bird—a sense no longer current. The conclusion that *God no such Specifique Poyson hath | As kills... But may be Good, | At least for Physick, if not for food* accords with Galen's view in *De alimentis facultatibus* (On the Properties of Foodstuffs); see *Galen on Food and Diet*, trans. Grant, chaps. 7–9. Donne next makes a characteristic metaphorical use of Galenic physiological lore to depict the reciprocal relations of God and humankind. The negative effects of God's punishments (*Corrosivenes, or intense Cold, or heate*) are due to the perversity of human nature (*Wee doe infuse, to what he ment for meate*). Even in God's most severe dealings, there is no intrinsic malice (*Hys fiercest wrath | Hath no Antipathye*). Humans are the source of harm to themselves: *Thus Man... is hys Rod | And... Devill. hys*: The sense is 'his own' in all four occurrences here. Donne the preacher would return to this theme: 'this affliction... man himselfe inflicts... upon himselfe, our own inherent corruption being…a Devill in our owne bosome' (*Sermons*, 7:187).

ll. 33–40.   *Since then… what She was*: Although Donne is negative about human corruption, he is positive about the human capacity to make restorative use of reason and other faculties, aided by God's grace. *wee 'are led…showe*: Those who speak of man as a microcosm mislead us, for our nature is far greater than that; cf. *Devotions*, Meditation 4. Donne the preacher would reflect: 'The properties, the qualities of every Creature, are in man; the Essence, the Existence of every Creature is for man…And therefore…he [is]…a world to which all the rest of the world is but subordinate' (*Sermons*, 4:104).

ll. 42–4.   *Cordyäll*: restorative. *Calentures*: fevers and delirium; cf. 'The Calme', l. 23. *Icy Opium*: 'All the poppies are cold, as Galen testifieth' (Gerard, *Herball* (1597), 2.68, 298). Like hemlock as discussed by Galen, opium and its derivatives lower the body's temperature, sometimes fatally.

ll. 45–50.   *Profession*: open declaration. *Actions are Authors*: Donne the preacher would observe regarding himself: 'Our actions, if they be good, speak louder than our Sermons; Our preaching is our speech, our good life is our eloquence' (*Sermons*, 9:156). *every day…New*: a large, fresh stock, as in a daily market.

VERSE LETTERS TO NOBLE LADIES: THE GENRE

Under the combined weight of unequal status and protocols governing refined personal contact between the sexes, verse letters to noble ladies become, in effect, a genre of their own. In addressing noble ladies whose patronage he sought, Donne engaged with a distinctive dynamic. He was the inferior and the lady his superior, in social fact as well as in literary tradition (courtly love, Petrarchan love-worship) where the theme of virtue was ideally suited to respectful flattery. It merged easily with the usual attribution of beauty, grace, honour, and perceptiveness to the lady addressed. Her possession of virtue as well as her other superlative qualities ensured that praise of her would not be frivolous or misdirected.

Donne's verse letters to noble ladies broaden the scope of inherited conventions while basing compliment and praise in considerations of morality. He draws centrally on the idea of the unity of the virtues (Plato, *Protagoras*, 329, 349; Cicero, *De finibus*, 5.23.66–7), expatiating as follows to Goodyere: 'Vertue is even, and continuall, and the same, and can therefore break no where, nor admit ends, nor beginnings.' A person 'is not vertuous, out of whose actions you can pick an excellent one' (*Letters*, 97). To image this idea Donne employs the Platonic metaphor of gold as well as technical vocabulary—the 'balsamum', 'tincture', or 'virtue' that is the purest essence and potency of any substance—associated by Paracelsus and his followers with gold and the philosopher's stone. Above all, for Donne, virtue had to manifest itself in the conduct of one's life. It issued from the exercise of discretion, itself an aspect of the 'wisdom' that is a gift of God's Spirit (1 Corinthians 12:8). Donne's verse letters to noble ladies link every manifestation of beauty and goodness on earth with God and the divine, thus weaving a rationale for even the most extravagant praise.

Once he has laid his serious moral foundation, Donne entertains as well as flatters with scintillating wit, flights of intellectual fancy, and gentle, graceful reiterations of basically conventional thoughts and images. The lady is a sun, a star, a saint; her virtue and beauty are shining lights. But there is nothing conventional in the elaboration of thoughts and images as Donne pursues an analogy to extremes of abstraction or paradox, or lavishes intriguing minutiae on a given theme. But the prevailing seriousness of the moral and spiritual dimension of the verse letters to noble ladies does not preclude touches of humour. In the opening lines of the letter to Lady Carey and her sister, Donne remarks sardonically on the veneration of saints in France; at a later point he offers a caricature of his own 'lowness'. By lightening the imagery and conventions of his compliment, he varies his tone while maintaining a level of familiar yet respectful address. The result, at its best, is Donne's own invention: a species of complimentary verse in which the interplay of intellect and fancy conveys both esteem and affection. Working on the assumption that a lady can appreciate the complexities of his composition, Donne pays tribute to her mind just as surely as he pays tribute to her virtue and beauty in his hyperbolic praise.

To the Countesse of Bedford ('Madame, Reason ys our Soules left hand') (fol. 36r)

Lucy Harrington (b. 1581) married Edward Russell, third earl of Bedford, in 1594. She was soon enjoying Queen Anne's special favour, playing leading roles in her court masques. Beautiful, vivacious, and intelligent, endowed as well with substantial means, Lady Bedford received the homage of dedications or other tributes from a range of contemporary poets besides Donne, including Ben Jonson, Samuel Daniel, Michael Drayton, George Chapman, and others. She herself composed poetry and circulated it privately among her literary associates; her elegy on Mistress Bulstrode ('Death be not proud; thy hand gave not this blow') echoes and revises some of Donne's phrasing. For the text of Lady Bedford's poem, see Robbins, *Complete Poems of Donne*, 753–5. Her familiarity with Donne dates from *c*.1608; his verse letters to her seem to have been composed in the years 1608–12.

ll. 1–6.   *Reason ys... reach Divinitye*: The relative status of reason and faith in attaining knowledge of God was a major concern of medieval and Renaissance philosophy and a perennial subject of reflection for Donne. *Divinitye*: Wordplay on two senses—'knowledge of God' and 'a divine being'. *blessings... Sight*: An allusion to Jesus's reproach to his doubting disciple, Thomas, in John 20:29: 'Because thou hast seen me, thou hast believed: blessed are they that have not seen, and yet have believed'. *Mine... grewe*: The phrasing suggests that Donne's acquaintance with Lady Bedford is recent. *farr fayth*: faith that grasps truth from a distance. *Ungratious*: both socially awkward and unfavourable. *want*: lack.

ll. 9–16.   *I study you … Election glorifies*: This and the next two stanzas represent
            Lady Bedford's actions in theological terms, analogizing between her select
            friends and those whom God chooses to be saved. *Accesses … Restraints*:
            what and whom Lady Bedford admits to her favour, or denies. *what your-
            selfe devi[s]e*: what she herself writes or, more generally, what intentions she
            has for her life. *Implicite fayth*: unquestioning acceptance of a belief on the
            basis of authority. *Catholic voice*: universal opinion.

ll. 19–20. *Rocks*: A key biblical image, as in Psalm 18:32 ('For who … is a rock save our
            God?') and Matthew 7:24–5, Jesus's parable of the wise man who built his
            storm-proof house upon a rock. *high to Some*: The textual difficulty here
            resists resolution. Readings in other manuscripts and *Poems* (1633) include
            'high to Sonne', 'high to seeme', and 'high to sense'. The general sense,
            however, is not in doubt; the solidity of the rocks in question (a metaphor
            for Lady Bedford's virtues) is due both to their height in the air and to their
            depth in the ground. *wash*: flow over and around.

ll. 22–6.   *A Balsamum* (balm): A fluid that preserved the body, counteracting poison
            and promoting healing (Paracelsus, *Chiurgia Magna* (1573), 73). This book
            was in Donne's library (Keynes, *Bibliography of Donne*, 4th edn, 273).
            Methridate: comprehensive antidote. King Mithridates of Pontus drank
            some poison every day to build up his immunity; he also devised antidotes
            to poison, which took their name from him. When he eventually was
            defeated by the Romans in 63 BCE, he was unable to poison himself (Pliny,
            Historia Naturalis, 25.3.5–6).

ll. 29–37. *you are here … Shape appeare*: Donne the preacher would offer another
            example—the Marys who went to Jesus's tomb but, finding he had arisen,
            brought the good news to the disciples. 'Here are good women made Angels,
            that is messengers, publishers of the greatest mysteries of our Religion'
            (*Sermons*, 9:190). Greek angelos means 'messenger'. *Hys factor … our loves*:
            God's agent, eliciting love for God by her actions. *Doe as you doe*: continue
            your angelic function. *Make your retorne … make One lyfe of two*: The impli-
            cation is dual: Lady Bedford's return to Twickenham Park will grace her
            associates with her virtuous presence; her ascent to heaven after death will be
            graced by the example of virtuous living that she has set on earth. *For … doe
            me here*: A much more complex dual implication: If Lady Bedford makes a
            stay at Twickenham, Donne will not repine at this even though it will deprive
            him of her good efforts on his behalf at court. If God were to enable Donne
            to reach heaven, he would rather have Lady Bedford's company there than
            the positive influence she exerts on him in the present circumstances.

To the Countesse of Bedford ('Madame, You have refind mee') (fol. 37r)

The opening lines of this verse letter suggest a further stage in Donne's relations with
Lady Bedford. He is now visiting her at Twickenham, or else he is on sufficiently
familiar terms with her that he can imagine himself there without impropriety. The
placement of this poem immediately after 'Madame, Reason ys our Soules left hand'

in manuscripts where both appear, as here in Dowden, additionally suggests that the two verse letters are close in date, and that 'Madame, you have refind mee' is the later of the two—perhaps dating to spring 1609.

ll. 1–6.   *You have refind…they bee*: You have sharpened my judgement, and now I perceive that things of greatest worth derive their value from rarity or usefulness. Value depends on circumstances. For Aristotle, the moral and intellectual virtues (*Virtue* and *Art* or intelligence) and goods of the body and of wealth (*Beauty, Fortune*) conduced to happiness, the chief good. But Donne denies intrinsic value to any virtue. *Two ills… and chuse*: We can never justify ourselves for doing one bad thing by pointing out that we did not do another bad thing; all sin is wrong. But we can choose between doing one or another good thing, leaving one undone.

ll. 7–12.   *at Court… not showe*: Virtue is not evident at court either because it exists at a higher latitude (*Clyme*) or because its *transcendent height* makes it invisible from below. *All my Rime… rarest be*: Your *Vertues*, the rarest things at court, claim as their due all the verse I write. *darke*: difficult to understand. *Usher*: formally announce.

ll. 13–18.   *To thys Place… display*: Lady Bedford's presemce brings the springtime to Twickenham Park, releasing fragrance into the air from the earth's confines, and causing buds to blossom. *Widow'd… Brazil dines*: Were it not for her presence, the earth, now personified as feminine (*Widow'd and reclus'd*), would keep *her sweetness* and fragrance closed up tightly. The earth closed and the earth open—the difference made by Lady Bedford's presence— yields a contrast as stark as that between midnight in China and noon in Brazil, two countries located on opposite sides of the world.

ll. 19–24.   *Out from your Charyott… new reckninges goe*: The image of Lady Bedford as a cosmic force shifts to equate her with the sun (Apollo in his *Charyott*). Even if she arrives at Twickenham *at Night, Morning breakes* when she appears. *Sight*: Other manuscripts and the 1633 *Poems* read 'Light'. The letters 's' and 'l' are closely similar in some handwritings of the period; either reading can be justified from the context. *falsifyes… Computations*: One computation is based on an arithmetical constant, the twenty-four hours of the 'artificial day'; the other is based on the variable interval between sunrise and sunset at different seasons, the 'natural day'. Since it is day wherever Lady Bedford goes, she cannot be solely identified with the 'day' in either system. On balance, her presence is more compatible with *Nature* and the definition of 'day' as daylight than with *an Artificiall day* that includes night in its definition. *lothly stray*: are disinclined to deviate from. *suffer*: permit, allow.

ll. 25–34.   *In thys… Antipodes*: Lady Bedford's presence has transformed the court into its opposite: she, not the monarch, is supreme. *the vulgar Sunne*: the sun as popularly conceived. *profane Autumnal Offices*: mundane seasonal tasks such as harvesting, contrasted with the love-worship offered by her devotees, *Sacrificers,… Priestes. Wee sound… say*: Our voices resonate with your praise, attesting the force of *your Influence, and your Dictates. These are Petitions...that I may survay the Edifice*: Donne's lines are not so much *Hymns* of praise as they are a request to meet with the beautiful Lady Bedford.

ll. 39–48. *serve Discourse, and Curiositye*: look for more superficial attractions to talk about. *invest*: clothe. *Laborinths of Schooles*: complex theological discussions. *in thys Pilgrimage*: in my visit to Twickenham. *you 'are Vertues Temple...walls of tender Christall*: Guido Panciroli gave an account of a temple of Fortune rebuilt by the emperor Nero (*Rerum Memorabilium Libri Duo* [Two Books of Remarkable Things] (1599), 1.32). The material used in the rebuilding was a soft stone, and the resulting edifice was transparent— hence, Donne's *walls of tender Christall. th' Escorial*: Philip II of Spain completed his magnificent palace and mausoleum complex in 1584; this monumental achievement figures the religious and secular distinction that combine in Lady Bedford.

ll. 49–54. *Yett not... Eye. these*: the *pure Altars* of *Eyes, Hands, Bosome* (l. 46). Donne does not regard Lady Bedford's *fayre* features *as Consecrate*, for this can properly be said only of her soul. His admiration is that of a *lay* person (not one who deals in sacred things) and of a *country Eye* (not one trained in subtle perceptions). *Of past...you are it*: You embody all exemplary (*rare*) histories, past and present, as a living *Booke of Fate*. This was popularly imagined to be an account of all that had happened and would happen; cf. Shakespeare, *2 Henry IV*, 3.1.44–5.

ll. 55–60. *If Good...not One*: A Platonic commonplace, as in *Symposium* 201. *And every Peece...All*: All goodness and all loveliness are contained in every part of you. *So intyre...You cannot two*: Cf. Donne's letter to Goodyere cited earlier in the headnote to 'Verse Letters to Noble Ladies'.

ll. 61–72. *these*: these lines of mine. *nice...Devinitye*: precise, drawn-out academic theologizing. *Poetique rage*: frenzy or transport of the poet's imagination, a concept tracing to Plato, *Phaedrus*, 245. *aliens*: makes strangers of. *Leaving...Senses Decree ys true*: Donne will lay aside the dictates of reason and the witness of memory—the mind's faculties—to accept the verdict of sense perception, the only authoritative judge of beauty. *Magazin*: storehouse. *Commonweale*: public stock. *hath seene One, would both*: had seen either Lady Bedford or Twickenham would want to see both. *Cherubine*: angels full of the knowledge and contemplation of God.

A Letter to the Lady Carey, and Mrs Essex Riche, from Amiens (fol. 38v)

The sisters to whom Donne addressed this verse letter were daughters of Robert, 3rd lord Rich, and his first wife, Penelope Devereux. Lettice, the older sister, had married Sir George Casey; the younger sister, Essex, was unmarried at the date Donne wrote— January–February 1612, ascertainable from the reference to Amiens, where Donne was staying with the Drurys. There is some indication in Donne's prose letters that he knew Sir Robert Rich, a son of the family, fairly well. Nothing is known about his connection with the two sisters beyond the carefully pitched familiarity and wit that this verse letter displays.

The original text, evidently the only poem of Donne's to survive in his own handwriting, was discovered by P. J. Croft in 1970 among the Rich family papers in the (then) Public Record Office, London; it was subsequently acquired by the Bodleian Library. See Figs. 8 and 9.

ll. 1–6.   *Here...invokèd are*: Cf. *Second Anniversary*, ll. 511–13, written at about the same time as this verse letter. *Schisme*: a division in the unity of the church. *bee Singulare*: oppose general opinion or custom. *should my Humilitye...directed bee*: In courtly and Petrarchan love poetry the abjectly humble lover addressed his beloved as a saint, a heavenly being. *heresye*: belief contrary to official dogma of the church, or denial of something determined by the church to be revealed truth. Donne the preacher would remark on the closeness of schism and heresy (*Sermons*, 2.353).

ll. 7–15.   *Convertite*: convert. *not to tell yt*: not to proclaim my worship of you. *Pardons...sold*: The medieval church's practice of granting indulgences (reductions of time in purgatory) in exchange for money was a primary target of Martin Luther's reforming ire, and would also incur repeated criticism in Donne's preaching (*Sermons*, 3.128; 5.259; 7.184–7; 10.126–7). *Where...degree*: Roman Catholics (here figured as the residents of Amiens) hold that good works are necessary to salvation; Protestants hold that justification is by faith alone. *I thought...I see*: Donne lays claim to *some Apostleship* by echoing phraseology of Paul (Romans 10:8; 2 Corinthians 5:7; Galatians 2:16); *by faith* becomes a grand refrain in Hebrews 11. *firmament*: starry sphere. *spent*: depleted. *Materialls*: elements.

ll. 17–30.   *theyre Virtues...humors*: Their seeming virtues are merely effects of their dominant temperaments. A conventional survey of the four *humors* and the corresponding semblance of virtue in each follows: phlegmatic or 'low-key' (*flegme*); *Sanguine* or cheerful (*blood*); melancholic or withdrawn (black bile); and *Cholerique* or hot-tempered (*Gall*). *dough-baked*: half-baked. *unimportun'd*: not urged to do so. Cf. Paradox 5, 'That only Cowards dare die'. *So Cloysterall men...forbeare*: Donne the preacher would elaborate: 'It is not enough to shut our selves in a cloister...and...content our selves with...peace of conscience in our selves, for we cannot have that long, if we doe not some good to others' (*Sermons*, 2:227). *Contribution*: Plural in Donne's autograph text. *Gall*: bile secreted by the gall bladder—figuratively, 'bitter rancor'.

ll. 31–6.   *Parcell-gilt*: partly covered with gold leaf. Alchemical imagery points the contrast between a superficial appearance of virtue and a complete transformation into a virtuous person. *Complexiön*: complex of humours, temperament. *Who knowes...None*: He who can distinguish his virtue from other parts of himself has no virtue. *Aguish*: shaky, shivering, as from chills and fever. *severall*: separable into parts. *Circumstantiall*: dependent on

external prompting. *True Vertue 'ys…all*: On the unity of the virtues, see
the headnote to 'Verse Letters to Noble Ladies: The Genre', and 'To the
Countesse of Bedford' ('Madame, You have refind me'), ll. 59–60.

ll. 45–54. *as an Influence…imparts*: Lady Carey, whose soul is all virtue (l. 39) and
whose beauty is all virtue (l. 42), works positively upon her friends with her
Virtuous thoughts. They may *Grow Capable…to partake your Vertues*,
Donne says, but leaves the prospect uncertain (*yf*). What is certain is that
her *Noble worthy Sister* has the requisite *sympathy, and matter* (affinity of
temperament and similarity of qualities) for virtue to work upon. *Extasye*:
transport experienced by the soul in going forth from the body. *revelation*:
receiving of divine knowledge by divine means.

ll. 55–63. *as in short Galleryes…twise to your Eyes*: In the Tudor–Stuart era, a
prominent architectural feature of royal palaces and mansions of the nobility
was the 'long gallery' lined with portraits displaying the owner's prestigious
connections. Lesser gentry and wealthy merchants imitated this feature on a
smaller scale. In *short Galleryes* the *Master* architect would install *Large*
mirrors *at the* far *End* to give a viewer the illusion of a space *twise* as long as
the actual gallery. Donne's father-in-law, Sir George More, had such a gallery
in his Surrey residence, Loseley Park. Here the image of the short gallery
doubled by its mirror reflection serves to convey the idea that to describe or
imitate the virtue and beauty of one sister is to describe or imitate the virtue
and beauty of the other. Not to do *Eyther* is *to stray* both in one's writing and
in one's conduct. *Hee that beleæves himselfe, doth never lye*: The implicit
definition takes a weaker subjective form, 'not a lie if the speaker reports what
he truly believes', rather than the stronger objective form, 'not a lie if the
speaker reports what he believes, and that belief is true'.

To the Countess of Salisbury. August 1614 (fol. 40r)

Lady Catherine Howard, youngest daughter of Thomas, 1st earl of Suffolk, was mar-
ried in 1608 to William Cecil, grandson of Lord Burleigh who had been Queen
Elizabeth's chief adviser. In 1612 the younger William succeeded his father, Robert
Cecil, earl of Salisbury, who was a chief adviser to King James. Lady Catherine's sister
was the notorious Frances Howard, countess of Essex, and subsequently countess of
Somerset, by a marriage for which Donne wrote an epithalamium that is the next to
last item in the Dowden manuscript. Little is known about Donne's connection with
the earl and countess of Salisbury, but by 1614 his friend George Garrard was in their
service. He suggested to Donne that some complimentary verses would be well
received. In a letter to Garrard Donne confides his discomfiture in undertaking to
compose a verse letter to the countess after the hyperboles he had already lavished on
other noble ladies—above all, his apotheosis of Elizabeth Drury in his *Anniversaries*:

Sir, you do me double honour when my name passes through you to that Noble
Lady in whose presence you are.…I can give you nothing in recompense of that
favor, but good counsell: which is to speake sparingly of any ability in me, lest you
indanger your own reputation, by overvaluing me. If I shall at any time take

courage by your Letter, to expresse my meditations of that Lady in writing, . . . I should be loath that in any thing of mine, composed of her, she should not appear much better than some of those of whom I have written. And yet I cannot hope for better expressings than I have given of them. So you see how much I should wrong her, by making her but equall to others. . . . I must use your favour in getting her pardon, . . . for adventuring to give any estimation of her, and when I see how much she can pardon, I shall the better discern how far farther I may dare to offend in that kinde. (*Letters*, 259–61)

If Donne was uncertain about the content of this verse letter, he nonetheless demonstrates formal surehandedness in its spacious sentence units—in particular, the sentence beginning *Since now* (l. 9) and reprising with another *Since now* (l. 31) that runs continuously through l. 36.

ll. 3–12.   *now when the Sunne . . . runne*: Cf. *First Anniversary*, ll. 268, 273–4. *Tyres* (attires): apparel in general, or hair ornaments in particular. *All the world's frame beeing crumbled*: The principal theme of the *First Anniversary*. *ev'ry Man thincks . . . to stand*: Cf. *First Anniversary*, ll. 216–18.

ll. 14–24.   *Cements*: firm bonders. *vapor'd*: evaporated. *narrowe Man . . . small wares*: Since small-minded men are satisfied with meagre portions, all careers and professions offer little in exchange for self-investment. *him that's infynite*: God.

ll. 30–8.   *fantasticall*: irrational. *this Sacrifice of myne*: Cf. 'Eclogue. 1613. December 26', l. 104. *if thinges like these . . . Of others*: In previous verse letters to noble ladies and in the *Anniversaries*. *Idolatree*: worship of false divinities.

ll. 39–48.   *had God made man first*: Instead of making humans on the sixth day of creation (Genesis 1:27). *chidde*: chided, reproached. *and that you*): and that you also are worthiest.

ll. 52–66.   *Wee first have Soules . . . swallowd into yt*: Donne the preacher would closely echo the thought here, which traces back to Aristotle's doctrine of the tripartite human soul: 'Our . . . immortal soule when it comes, swallowes up the other soules of vegetation, and of sense, which were in us before' (*Sermons*, 2:358). *Nor doth he injure . . . the Last*: To extol the superiority of the rational human soul does not detract from the virtues of plants and animals. *I owe my first Soules . . . my Clay*: Nutrition and growth were functions of the vegetative soul; the sensitive soul exercised the functions of sense perception and bodily motion.

ll. 69–74.   *Thys new greate lesson . . . could doe*: Lady Salisbury's beauty, eminence, and virtue (*Fayre, Greate, and Good*) are subjects too advanced and exalted to be grasped without *first* making preparatory *study* of the characters of other worthy (implicitly less worthy) ladies. *a darke Cave*: In the myth of the cave in Plato, *Republic*, 7.514–15, prisoners who lie chained glimpse only the shadows of reality, but the one who is released comes to perceive lesser lights, and eventually to look upon the sun. Donne implies that he can register Lady Salisbury's excellence, even if her virtues are too bright to contemplate directly. *your fellow-Angells*: Donne had termed Lady Bedford a 'Cherubine' ('Madame, You have refind mee', l. 72). *Illustrate*: give light to; enlighten with knowledge.

ll. 75–82. *The first…One borne blind:* Evidemtly a reference to Homer, acknowledged from antiquity onwards as the earliest and greatest master of the highest form of poetry (epic). Accounts of Homer in antiquity, however, do not say that he was blind from birth. In fact—quite anachronistically, since Homeric culture is now thought to have been oral or pre-literate—the early 'Life of Homer' attributed to Herodotus says that he became blind from reading too much (Robbins, *Complete Poetry of Donne*, 728). Further specification of the nature of the blindness of this unnamed *first* master of *all Artes* occurs in other manuscripts as ll. 77–8, although the Dowden manuscript and others lack them. The lines read: 'He lackt those eyes beasts have as well as wee, | Not those by which Angels are seene and see'. The lack was one of physical, not intellectual sight. *without those Eyes…Which fortune…doth give*: Fortune was traditionally portrayed as blind because her gifts were distributed randomly. *And though…be learnd*: A characteristic ending in paradox.

RELIGIOUS LYRICS

The Dowden manuscript employs the section title *Holy Sonnetts* (fol. 41v) in both a general and a generic sense. *Holy* signals that the poetry to follow is religious in nature. *Sonnets* categorizes the verse form of both the linked sequence of seven poems that is the first composition, 'La Corona', and the subsequent sequence of twelve sonnets. While several other manuscripts and early printed versions restrict the title *Holy Sonnets* to the second assemblage of twelve sonnets, the Dowden manuscript applies it inclusively to religious poems in so-called Petrarchan sonnet form. A Petrarchan sonnet is a fourteen-line, five-foot stanza comprising a subgroup of eight cross-rhymed lines (octave) followed by a subgroup of six lines (sestet), the first four of which are cross-rhymed, and the last two, a rhymed couplet that provides a conclusion to the poem as a whole. For further commentary on the genre and Donne's practice, see R. V. Young, 'The Religious Sonnet', in Shami, Flynn, and Hester, eds, *The Oxford Handbook of John Donne*, 218–32.

La Corona (Italian and Spanish for 'The Crown') (fol. 41v)

In 'La Corona' Donne creates a hybrid composition. He employs the Italian poetic form 'corona di sonnetti', a series of sonnets linked by repetition of adjacent last and first lines that had been employed in the praise of secular subjects—for example, in Annibale Caro's *Corona* (1558), George Gascoigne's *Hundredth Sundrie Flowers* (1575), and George Chapman's 'Coronet for his Mistresse Philosophie' in *Ovids Banquet of Sense* (1595). Drawing as well on prose exercises for religious meditation such as the seven-part 'corona of our Lady' and the 'corona of our Lord' described in such Roman Catholic manuals as *Societie of the Rosary* (1593–4) and *Rosarie of our Ladie* (1600), Donne crafts a poetic corona or *Crowne of Prayer and Prayse* (1.1), and offers it to Christ. In exchange he entreats his Redeemer to assure him of his own redemption: *what thy thorny Crowne gayn'd, that give mee,* | *A Crowne of Glorye which doth flowre always* (1.7–8).

Although the speaker's address is personal throughout, the verse follows pre-existent trains of thought. The linked sonnets of 'La Corona' meditate on the key paradoxes by which the Christian faith figures the nature and agency of Jesus Christ, the Son of God. Thus the first sonnet images the death of the body as the means of eternal life through the salvation brought by Christ (*att our End, beginns our Endles rest*), while the incarnation, the subject of the second sonnet, prompts an address to Christ's mother, Mary, as *Thy Makers Maker, and thy fathers Mother*. The newborn babe in the manger elicits a further paradox in the third sonnet: *Seest thou, my Soule... how Hee,* | *Which fills all Place, yet none holds him, doth lye?* The fourth sonnet locates the boy Jesus in the temple at Jerusalem, reasoning with the learned Jewish elders: *The word but latelye could not speake, and loe* | *It suddenly speakes wonders*. Paradox is redoubled with the crucifixion of Jesus in the fifth sonnet. Paradox is again redoubled in the sixth sonnet through reflection on the benefits that Christ's salvation confers on the soul. And the seventh and last sonnet salutes Christ's agency in a paradox where mercy merges reflexively with severity. Various attempts to date 'La Corona' by way of external evidence have proved inconclusive. A consensus, however, favours the years 1607–9.

1.1–11. *Deigne*: Condescend (to accept). *Prayer and Prayse*: Donne the preacher would equate the two in characterizing the Psalms: 'Prayer and Praise is the same thing' (*Sermons*, 5.270). *my... Melancholye*: humble and pious state of low spirits. To Donne the preacher, *Melancholye* would come to denote a pathological state of mind (*Sermons*, 4.343; 6.152; 8.69, 87, 135). *Antiënt of Dayes*: God is thus referred to in Daniel 7:9, 13. *thy thorny Crowne*: Jesus is mocked for identifying himself as 'King of the Jews' by having a crown of thorns pressed upon his head (Matthew 27:29; Mark 15:17; John 19:2, 5). *a Vile... Bayes*: Donne's disparagement of secular verse and its rewards as inferior to sacred verse tallies with George Herbert's sentiments in his two 'Jordan' poems and strikes an emphasis new to early seventeenth-century English poetry. *The Ends... workes*: Proverbial (Tilley, *Dictionary*, E116). Repetition of the verb *crowne* cues the realization that the *workes* referred to are not good deeds in general, but this particular sonnet sequence *of Prayer and Prayse*. *The first last End*: The death of the body.

2.1–12. *Salvatiön... nighe*: 'His salvation is nigh them that fear him' (Psalm 85:9). *That all... everywhere*: Aquinas analogizes between the human soul that is in all and every part of the body and God who is all in all things and everything (*Summa Theologica*, 1a.8.2). *In Prison, in thy* [*W*]*ombe*: Dowden and other Group 1 manuscripts have the misreading *Tombe*, which perhaps originated as a subliminal response to the locally negative tenor of the phrasing. (For characterizations of the contents and editorial significance of manuscript Groups 1, 2, and 3 of Donne's verse, see *The Divine Poems*, ed. Helen Gardner, rev. edn, lvii–lxviii; and *The Satires, Epigrams and Verse Letters*, ed. Milgate, xli–liv. *The Poems of John Donne*, ed. Grierson, 2:cxi–cxii, originated these manuscript groupings.) In *Second Anniversary*, ll. 173–4, the prison is a newborn child's body. But from a Christian perspective, to characterize the Virgin Mary's womb as a *Tombe* is odd if not flatly objectionable. *trye*: put to the test. *Ere... was Created*: Plato, *Timaeus*, 38b, held that time came into being with the heavens; Aristotle, *Physics*, 4.223b, thought time was the movement of the spheres. *thy Sonne... thy fathers Mother*: Such paradoxes are frequent and familiar in medieval poetry; their probable source is Augustine, *On Holy Virginity*, 1.5 (*PL*, 40.399). The pun on *conceivst*, *Conceivd* may be Donne's own.

3.1–14. *cloystred... wombe*: Donne, like Chaucer before him, echoes the medieval service-book known as the Primer: 'Withinne the cloistre blisful of thy sydis [sides]' (Prologue to the Second Nun's Tale). *Weake enough*: 'He was crucified through weakness' (2 Corinthians 13:4). *Hath the' Inn no roome?*: 'There was no room for them [Mary, Joseph, and the newborn Jesus] in the inn' (Luke 2:7). *from the' Orient... travel*: Three Magi come from the east to ask King Herod where they could find and worship the newborn king of the Jews (Matthew 2:1–11). *to prevent... doome*: After God warns the wise men in a dream not to report where exactly in Bethlehem they had found the baby Jesus, Herod in a murderous rage orders the killing of all children in Bethlehem under the age of two (Matthew 2:12, 16–18). *Hee... fills... holds him*: Donne re-echoes Aquinas, *Summa Theologica*, 1a.8.2: 'God fills every place; not indeed, like a body... God is not in all things,... but he rather contains them'. *Kisse him*: 'Kiss the Son' (Psalm 2:12). *with him... mother*: God instructed Joseph in a dream to avoid Herod's rage by fleeing into Egypt with Mary and the baby Jesus (Matthew 2:13–14).

4.1–12. *With hys... turne backe*: Joseph, Mary, and the boy Jesus went with a group to celebrate Passover in Jerusalem. When it was time to return home, Joseph and Mary first assumed that Jesus was travelling with others in the group, but 'when they found him not, they turned back again to Jerusalem, seeking him' (Luke 2:45). *See where... bestowe*: 'After three days they found him in the temple, sitting in the midst of the doctors, both hearing them, and asking them questions. And all that heard him were astonished at his understanding and answers' (Luke 2:46–7). *Doctors*: learned men. *The word*: 'In the beginning was the Word, and the Word was with God, and the Word was God' (John 1:1). The paradox of 'the speechless Word' (*Verbum infans*) traces to Bernard of Clairvaux (*Sermons*, 6.184). The doctrine that Jesus united two natures, *Godhead* and *Manhood*, in one person also ascribed a human soul as well as a human body to him. Donne the preacher would reflect: 'Consider the dignity, that the nature of man received in that union, wherin... was thus made this *Christ*, for, the Godhead did not swallow up the manhood; but man, that nature remained still' (*Sermons*, 3.299). *to begin his busines*: When Mary and Joseph found Jesus in the temple, he asked: 'Did you not know that I must be about my Father's business?' (Luke 2:49).

5.1–14. With this sonnet, Garrard in copying begins to align rhyming lines, thus bringing the verse form to the surface of the text. *By Miracles... some begatt*: Examples are given in John 2:23; 11:47–8; 12:18–19. *the worst... most*: 'The whole multitude of them arose, and led him unto Pilate... And they were instant with loud voices, requiring that he might be crucified... And Pilate gave sentence that it should be as they required' (Luke 23:1, 23–4). *unto the' Immaculate... an Inch*: The compressed thought turns on the two natures of Christ and on two senses of *Fate*: (1) what is predestined to happen in the world at large, and (2) the duration of an individual human life. Those who agitated to crucify the sinless Jesus, to whose divine nature Fate (1) is subservient, thought they were determining his Fate (2). But their ignorant folly ends in paradoxical futility. They purported to reduce to finite measures (*span, Inch*) the *Infinitye* of *selfe-life*, the unending life of one who is life itself. *Beares... Crosse*: John 19:17. *more*: the sins of all humankind. *Liberall dole*: generous charitable relief. *Moyst... blood*: In Aquinas's hymn 'Adoro te' (I adore Thee), one drop of Christ's blood suffices to save the whole world.

6.1–12.   *Moyst*: What the preceding sonnet couched as a prayerful request here becomes a past participle functioning as an adjective; the grammatical shift signals Christ's fulfilment of the speaker's request. *Too stonye... fleshly*: In Ezekiel 36:26 God promises to reanimate and restore the Jews as his people: 'I will take away the stony heart out of your flesh, and I will give you an heart of flesh.' By contrast Donne represents his *Soule* as being stubbornly disobedient and sunk in sensuality. *starv'd*: withered. *foule*: soiled with sin. *abled*: empowered. *Death... slew*: 'Jesus Christ... hath abolished death' (2 Timothy 1:10). *last Death*: the torments of hell, termed 'the second death' in Revelation 20:14; 21:8. *If in... inroule*: The 'little book' of Revelation 10:2, 8–11 internalizes the gift of prophecy in the visionary speaker when he eats it as commanded. But 'the book of life' of Revelation 20:12–15 contains the names of all who must face Christ's judgement. Westmoreland's reading 'life-book' thus looks superior, on grounds of sense, to Dowden's *litle Booke*. This, however, is the reading of the majority of manuscripts as well as the 1633 *Poems*, and it makes for a more metrically regular line. *Flesh... glorifyed*: Donne the preacher would elucidate: '*Adam* was made to enjoy an immortality in his body; He induced death upon himselfe: And then... man having induced and created death, by sin, God takes death, and makes it a means of the glorifying of his body, in heaven' (*Sermons*, 6:72). *that [long] Sleepe*: Dowden and one other manuscript lack *long*, a seemingly accidental omission that also mars a metrically regular line. *Sinns sleepe*: Paul's metaphor in Ephesians 5:14 and 1 Thessalonians 5:6.

7.1–12.   *the Last... Day*: The heavenly Jerusalem is described as having 'no need of the sun... for the glory of God did lighten it, and... there shall be no night there' (Revelation 21:23, 25). *th' uprising of thys Sunne, and S[o]nne*: This traditional pun has a source in Malachi 4:2: 'Unto you that fear my name shall the Son of righteousness arise'. Dowden's 'Sinne' is clearly mistaken. *showe alone*: merely put on a display or military triumph—a connotation heightened by the battering ram in l. 9. *strong Ramm*: This metaphor may have been suggested by

Micah 2:13: 'The breaker is come up before them: they have...passed through the gate...and their king shall pass before them and the Lord on the head of them.' *Mild Lambe...Blood*: 'Ye were...redeemed...with the precious blood of Christ, as of a lamb without blemish and without spot' (1 Peter 1:19). *Bright Torche...see*: 'I am the light of the world' (John 8:12). *Oh with thy owne...just wrath*: The speaker urgently pits against each other the roles of victor and victim figured in the preceding lines, thus implying that Christ's agency alone determines every element and every aspect of the soul's salvation.

SONNETT (FOL. 43R), THE SEQUENCE STANDARDLY CALLED 'HOLY SONNETS'

In place of this simple title, Dowden's earlier general heading 'Holy Sonnetts' is relocated to this position in the manuscripts of two important groups and in the first printed edition of *Poems* (1633). As a result, the 'Holy Sonnets' have specifically become identified with the sequence of twelve sonnets that follow here (and with five additional ones found uniquely in the Westmoreland manuscript).

The dating, ordering, and interpreting of the so-called 'Holy Sonnets' have occasioned much critical and scholarly debate. It is generally agreed that the twelve sonnets composing the core conception of the sequence date to 1609–10, based on the intertextual echo of 'Death be not proud' in Donne's sonnet and Lady Bedford's elegy on Cecilia Bulstrode, who died in August 1609. These years fall within the obscure period of 1606–11 when Donne alternated residence between London, where he continued to seek employment by way of court connections, and Mitcham in Surrey, where a modest house owned by his brother-in-law lodged his wife and ever-increasing family. A letter to Goodyere sets the latter scene: 'I write from the fire side in my Parler, and in the noise of three gamesome children; and by the side of her, whom because I have transplanted into a wretched fortune, I must labour to disguise that from her by...giving her my company, and discourse, therefore I steal from her, all the time which I give this Letter' (*Letters*, 137–8). During this difficult period of poverty, dependency, and elusive career prospects, Donne additionally coped with illness and depression which implicitly colour the often somber tones of the 'Divine Meditations | Holy Sonnets'.

Dowden's ordering of the twelve core sonnets, found also in other Group 1 and in Group 2 manuscripts and in *Poems* (1633), must have been influential in shaping perceptions of formal progression and thematic development by Donne's earlier readers. The first six sonnets in Dowden's ordering compose a meditative sequence that addresses in sharply delineated images what were traditionally known as the 'Four Last Things': death, judgement, heaven, and hell. In Sonnet 1 the speaker offers a preparatory prayer rehearsing the extensive and multiple claims that God has on him, and implores God to free him from the devil's hold. Sonnet 2 vividly imagines extreme sickness; Sonnet 3 the very moment of death; and Sonnet 4 the judgement to which all souls must submit at the last day. Damnation is the turbulently treated subject of Sonnet 5, while Sonnet 6 exults in the victory over death to be registered when the saved are resurrected to eternal life. The latter six sonnets reflectively probe two aspects of love: Sonnets 7–9, Christ's love for humankind and the Creator's love for his creatures, both consummated in Christ's willingness to suffer death to demonstrate this divine love. Sonnets 10–12 invert the perspective and reflect on the love humans owe to God and to their neighbour. Helen Gardner, who offered this account of form and themes, argued that this ordering incorporates Donne's original conception of the twelve-sonnet sequence (*The Divine Poems*, rev. edn, xl–xli).

Present-day opinion, however, has shifted to the view that the Westmoreland manuscript contains a still earlier assemblage in which four additional sonnets are interspersed with the twelve sonnets of what would become the core sequence. As a further complication, Westmoreland's assemblage concludes with three more sonnets evidently written in 1617–20. Westmoreland titles its composite of nineteen sonnets from various dates 'Holy Sonnets' although the manuscript group most closely related to Westmoreland (Group 3) bears the heading 'Divine Meditations', which may have been Donne's initial title. Taken altogether, the looser thematic connections and the chronological gaps and range that characterize Westmoreland's nineteen sonnets have led scholars to conclude that the twelve-sonnet sequence contained in Dowden and its related sources is Donne's definitively revised ordering. This reinterpretation, argued in detail by Patrick O'Connell in *Philological Quarterly* (1981), 60:324–38, has been adopted in *The Variorum Edition of the Poetry of John Donne*, 7.1: *The Holy Sonnets* (2005), 141–2.

Sonnett 1 ('As due by many Titles, I resigne') (fol. 43r)

1.4–14. *Thy blood...that*: 'Ye are bought with a price' (1 Corinthians 6:20). *I am thy Sonne...shyne*: Cf. 'La Corona', sonnet 7. *Thy Servant*: Paul reflects on the former status of the redeemed as servants under the law in Galatians 4:1–7. *Thy Sheepe, thyne Image*: 'My sheep hear my voice' (John 10:27); 'God created man in his own image' (Genesis 1:27). *till I betrayde...thy Spiritt devine*: Paul uses this image of the body defiled to warn against extramarital sexual intercourse in 1 Corinthians 3:17 and 6:18, 19: 'He that committeth fornication sinneth against his own body. What, know ye not that your body is the temple of the Holy Ghost which is in you?' Donne remained preoccupied with this image and its admonitory charge: 'We have betrayed thy Temples to prophaness, our bodies to sensuality' (*Essays in Divinity*, 98). *Except thou... Lose me*: The speaker implores God to take action in redeeming him and thus assuring him that he is one of the elect. Without this assurance he will *despayre* that he is the Devil's prey. *workes*: The superior variant 'work' is found in Westmoreland and other manuscripts related to it.

Sonnett 2 ('O my blacke Soule, now thou art summonèd') (fol. 43v)

2.3–14. *like a Pilgrim...whence he's fled*: A sidelight on the predicament of English Catholics like Donne's friend Toby Matthew, who converted in Florence in 1606 and returned to England, admitting his Catholicism. Donne visited Matthew in prison before his deportation in April 1608 (Bald, *Donne: A Life*,

187). *Yett Grace... to beginne?*: Two lines neatly balance a mainstream (but not universally endorsed) Roman Catholic doctrine that a repentant sinner will receive redeeming grace against the Reformation doctrine, tracing to Augustine, that a sinner is incapable of receiving redeeming grace unless God's prior gift of grace (*gratia preveniens*) enables him to receive it. Aquinas had also maintained that a sinner could not acquire grace unless aided by grace (*Summa Theologica*, 2.1.109.6). *Oh make... Christs blood*: Donne the preacher would elaborate on the black, red, and white 'complexions' that variously please or displease God. 'There growes a blacknesse, a sootinesse upon the soule, by custome in sin, which overcomes all blushing, all tendernesse...Whitenesse...preserves it selfe, not onely from being dyed all over in any foule colour, from contracting the name of any habituall sin,...but from taking any spot, from comming within distance of a tentation...To avoid these spots, is that whiteness that God loves in the soule. But there is a rednesse that God loves too...an aptnesse in the soule to blush, when any of these spots doe fall upon it' (*Sermons*, 6:57). Both in this sonnet and in the later sermon Donne's emphasis on individual moral initiative aligns more closely with mainstream Catholic doctrine than with Reformed. *Christs blood... whyght*: 'Come now,...saith the Lord: though your sins be as scarlet, they shall be as white as snow' (Isaiah 1:18). 'Jesus Christ...washed us from our sins in his own blood' (Revelation 1:5).

Sonnett 3 (*'Thys is my Playes Last Sceane'*) (*fol. 44r*)

3.1–14. *Thys is... Last pointe*: A heap of commonplaces renders emphatic the final moment before imagined death. *I shall... see that face*: Donne and some contemporaries were perplexed about the state of the soul after death. Would the soul as well as the body sleep in the grave to await a universal last judgement at Christ's second coming, or would the soul after death immediately confront the *face* of Christ and undergo judgement? The latter formulation had been Roman Catholic doctrine since the fourteenth century, but biblical passages could be found to support both alternatives: universal judgement at the end of time (Job 14:12; 1 Corinthians 15:18; 1 Thessalonians 4:14) and a more immediate coming into Christ's presence after death (Luke 23:43; Philippians 1:23). Of particular interest in this connection are the two variants of l. 7 that survive: Dowden's *Or presently, I knowe not, see that face* and *But my ever-waking part shall see that face* found in Group 2 manuscripts and adopted in *Poems* (1633, 1635). It seems that Donne's expression of doubt remained comparatively private, while his assurance attained a wider circulation. *Impute Mee righteous*: 'Imputed righteousness' is a distinctively Reformed doctrine. The soul cannot be purged of its sin by penitence, as Roman Catholics maintained. Only the merits of Christ can nullify the taint of sin. God graciously condescends to treat the soul as if Christ's merits actually belonged to it. *thus... Devill*: Donne echoes phrasing employed in another circumstance where there is action by proxy in a soul's behalf. In the rite of public baptism in the Church of England, godparents vouch for the infant at the font. The priest asks: 'Dost thou forsake the devil and all his works, the vain pomp, and glory of the world, . . . the carnal desires of the flesh?' The response comes back: 'I forsake them all' (*Book of Common Prayer* (1559), 273).

Sonnett 4 ('At the round Earths Imagind Corners') (fol. 44r–v)

4.1–14. *At . . . Trumpetts, Angells*: 'I saw four angels standing on the four corners of the earth' (Revelation 7:1); 'he shall send his angels with a great sound of a trumpet' (Matthew 24:31). *Arise . . . Bodyes goe*: Here, in imagining a universal last judgement, Donne articulates the doctrine of 'soul-sleep' as well as 'body-sleep' with which Luther had countered the Roman Catholic doctrine of purgatory. *the flood*: Genesis 7:21–3. *Fyre*: Revelation 9:18. *Dea[r] th*: shortage of food. Westmoreland uniquely preserves this superior reading; Dowden, all other manuscripts, and *Poems* (1633) read 'Death'. Four successive bad harvests in 1594–7 had triggered widespread famine and rioting in England. *Agues*: chills and fever. *Law*: In particular, capital punishment. *you whose . . . Deaths Woe*: 'There be some standing here, which shall not taste of death, till they see the Son of man coming in his kingdom' (Matthew 16:28). *lett . . . mee mourne a pace*: 'Godly sorrow worketh repentance to salvation not to be repented of' (2 Corinthians 7:10). *a pace*: the space traversed by one step; hence, a vague measure of distance. *Teach mee . . . thy Blood*: Here Donne aligns with the Roman Catholic doctrine that repentance will ensure an individual's share in the general redemption effected by Christ's death. To a Reformer like Calvin, by contrast, Christ's death on the cross ratified a redemption that God had willed even before he created the world and humankind. *seald*: The wax seals on legal documents were red.

Sonnett 5 ('If Poysonous Mineralls') (fol. 44v)

5.1–13. *If Poysonous Mineralls . . . why threatens hee?*: Job is the great biblical prototype of one who questioned God's purposes and disputed his doings (Job 3:23; 8:17–21; 10:2–20). Donne the preacher would warn at length against doing as Job did: 'It is an Execrable and Damnable Monosillable, *Why*; it exasperates God . . . : For, when we come to aske a reason of his actions, either we doubt of the *goodnesse* of God, that he is not so carefull of us, as we would be; or of his *power*, that he cannot provide for us, so well as we could doe; or of his *wisdome*, that he hath not grounded his Commandements so well as we could have advised him' (*Sermons*, 6:188). *that Tree . . . immortall Us*: Genesis 2:16–17; 3:19. *Lecherous Goats*: A proverbial conception. *envious*: ill-willed, as Satan was when he tempted Eve in serpent form (Genesis 3:1–4). *But who am I . . . dispute with Thee?*: Job comes to just such a recognition: 'How should man be just with God? . . . Who will say unto him, What doest thou? . . . How much less shall I . . . choose out my words to reason with him?' (Job 9:2, 12, 14). *A heavenlye Lethean flood*: The river Lethe, whose water caused forgetting in those who drank it, was a feature of the classical underworld (Virgil,

Aeneid, 6.714–15); Donne christianizes the image. *That thou…as Debt*: Donne the preacher would instance Psalm 19 in this connection: 'As much as *David* stands in feare of this Judge, he must intreat this Judge to remember his sinnes; Remember them O Lord,…but remember them in mercy, and not in anger' (*Sermons*, 5:320–1).

Sonnett 6 ('Death bee not Proude') (fols 44v–45r)

6.1–14. *Death bee not Proude…kill mee*: A reworking of Paul's triumphant outburst in 1 Corinthians 15:55–7: 'O death, where is thy sting? O grave, where is thy victory? The sting of death is sin…But thanks be to God, which giveth us the victory through our Lord Jesus Christ.' *From Rest…more must flow*: As in the logical sleights of hand in his youthful Paradoxes, Donne argues on the basis of a flawed analogy between the states of *Rest, and Sleepe* (both temporary) and *Death* (final). *And soonest…goe*: Cf. the proverb 'The good die young.' *Thou 'art slave…why swellst thou then?*: Donne replaces the logical equivalence of death and *Fate* based on definitions of the two terms with a rhetorical figure of death as a *slave to Fate*, lacking agency and effect of its own. *Poppy*: Opium derived from poppies was used then as now to relieve pain and induce sleep. *Charmes*: Recitations resembling today's various tactics for relaxing the mind with monotonous exercise like 'counting sheep'. *One short…no more*: The conclusion is reached by faith, not reason, as in Paul's ringing affirmation (1 Corinthians 15:54).

Sonnett 7 ('Spitt in my face you Jewes') (fol. 45r)

7.1–13. *Spitt…crucifye mee*: The speaker applies to himself specifics of the Gospels' composite passion narrative (Matthew 27:26–31; Mark 15:16–20; John 19:1–3, 34). *you Jewes*: Although Caiaphas the high priest of the Jews incites some of those in his company to abuse Jesus (Matthew 26:66–8; Mark 14:63–5), those who do so are mainly identified as soldiers under the command of the Roman governor Pilate (Matthew 27:27; Mark 15:16; John 19:2). *only hee*: Westmoreland's variant 'humbly hee' may preserve Donne's original wording. *satisfied*: A technical theological term for Jesus's death as payment in full of the penalty due from humans for their sins. *Jewes Iniquitye*: Editors of Donne have uniformly opted to emend to Westmoreland's variant, 'Jewes impietie', which avoids the repetition of *Iniquitye* in l. 4 (and could signal an error in copying). But the repetition has its own expressiveness; it starkly contrasts the sinfulness of the Jews and the speaker with the sinlessness of Jesus. *I | Cruci'fye him daily*: 'They crucify to themselves the Son of God afresh, and put him to an open shame' (Hebrews 6:6, said of repentant sinners who return to their sins). Donne the preacher would intensify the traditional association of cursing and swearing with wounding the body of Christ: 'you scourge him, and scoffe him, and spit in his face, and crucifie him, and practise every day all the Jews did to him once,…by tearing and mangling his body, now glorified, by your blasphemous oaths, and execrable imprecations'

(*Sermons*, 10:122); cf. *Devotions*, Expostulation 9. *he bore our Punishment*: 'he was wounded for our transgressions, he was bruised for our iniquities' (Isaiah 53:5). *Jacob came...gainfull intent*: Jacob, the younger of Isaac's two sons, wrapped his hands and neck in goatskins to simulate the hairy skin of his older brother, Esau, and deceived the blind Isaac into bestowing on him the blessing that was Esau's birthright (Genesis 27:1–38). *Vile Mans flesh*: The inverse process is described in Philippians 3:20–1: 'The Lord Jesus Christ...shall change our vile body, that it may be fashioned like unto his glorious body'.

Sonnett 8 ('Why are wee by all Creatures wayted on?') (fol. 45r–v)

Why...wayted on?: Pico della Mirandola, a Christian neo-Platonist cited by Donne in *Biathanatos* and *Essays in Divinity*, had reflected on this question in Chapters 6 and 7 of Exposition 5 of *Heptaplus* (1489), his Latin treatise on the six days of creation. Pico's answer to the question was complex. Man uniquely has 'this privilege of being in the image of God...The difference between God and man is that God contains all things in Himself as their origin, and man contains all things in himself as their center....There is...in man the life of the plants, performing all the same functions in him as in them—nutrition, growth, and reproduction. There is the sense of the brutes, inner and outer; there is the soul, powerful in its heavenly reason....Earthly things are subject to man, and the heavenly bodies befriend him, since he is the bond and link between heaven and earth.' Pico warned, however, that the linking function entrusted to man by God depends on man's preserving both 'peace with himself' and 'peace and alliance' between himself and the other creatures. He continues: 'It is reasonable that to the same extent that we do injury not only to ourselves but also to the universe, which we encompass within us, and to almighty God,...we should also experience all things in the world as the most severe punishers and powerful avengers of injuries, with God among the foremost. Therefore let us dread the penalties and torments which await the transgressors of divine law' (*Heptaplus*, trans. Douglas Carmichael, in *Pico della Mirandola*, intro. Paul J. W. Miller (1940), 134–6).

Donne uses Pico's discussion as a springboard for launching his own thoughts in two further directions. (1) Why do plants and animals remain in subjection to humans, when humans openly manifest their corruption and sinfulness? According to Pico, this should not be happening, as Donne's speaker observes: *Weaker I am...and worse than you.* | *You have not sinn'd.* (2) It is *a greater wonder* yet that God bestows on sinful humans the supreme benefit of reinstatement in the divine order of Creation through the death of Christ. Nothing at all comparable has been bestowed on the inherently more deserving, because sinless, plants and animals. Redemption is a paradox.

8.1–6. *Why are wee*: Most editors adopt Westmoreland's variant reading, 'Why ame I', as more dramatic, but the emendation is not obligatory. *Prodigal Elements*: The earth, air, water, and sun (for fire) that provide lavish means of sustenance. *seelily*: helplessly, defencelessly.

Sonnett 9 ('What if thys Present were the worlds Last Night?') (fol. 45v)

In undertaking to transform a staple of Petrarchan love poetry, the image of the beloved incised in the lover's heart, and turn it from secular to religious ends, Donne takes poetic experimentalism to an extreme. He saddles an analogy with the function of validating a transformation from secular to sacred: *as...I sayd to all my Prophane Mistrisses...: So I say to Thee*: But, as not infrequently in Donne, the speaker's analogy is compromised (here, by inversion), and the argument proves logically invalid.

Couched in conventional terms of courtship, the speaker's address to his soul about the *Picture of Christ crucifyed* develops inversely to his address to *all my Prophane Mistrisses*, and it does so twice over. First, Christ's appearance and features are presented not as the signs of *Beautye* that the mistresses' are, but as a *Countenance* that *can Thee affright...Blood fills hys frownes*: Then the speaker argues from his assurance regarding Christ's *Piteous mind* to a positively transformed perception of his appearance and features. *Can that Tongue adjudge Thee [un]to Hell, | Which Prayed forgivenes for hys foes fierce Spight? | No, no*: This is the opposite of arguing from the mistresses' *Beautye* to *Pitty*; it is an argument from Christ's *Pitty* to his *Beautye* in the grateful eyes of a redeemed soul. Accordingly, by the sonnet's own logic, its conclusion should be: 'This Piteous mind assures a beauteous forme.'

Despite its flawed reasoning, Donne's experiment with turns of thought and imagination that can directly register something bad in worldly terms as something good in heavenly terms would develop into a major undertaking in the *Devotions*, where his near-fatal illness is reinterpreted as special spiritual favour from God.

9.7–8. *[un]to*: Dowden's 'to' has been supplemented with Westmoreland's 'unto' because the line is metrically defective otherwise. *Which Prayed...Spight?*: 'Then said Jesus, Father, forgive them; for they know not what they do' (Luke 23:33).

Sonnett 10 ('Batter my hart, three Person'd God') (fols 45v–46r)

This poem bears witness to the sixteenth- and seventeenth-century fascination with the use of erotic images and vocabulary in religious verse. It is also a further experiment in paradoxical reinterpretation. Scholars have noted a significant analogue in Pierre Ronsard's sonnet 'Foudroye moi le cors' (Strike down my body) in Book 4 of his *Odes* (1561). Like Ronsard, Donne employs a tone of intense urgency as he projects a city under siege, betrayed by Reason, and pleads to God to use overpowering force to do for a divided self what its own incapacitated will cannot do by way of rescue and restoration. Donne the preacher would strike similar notes in reflecting on the paradoxes of negative experiences that work positive effects: 'He that is well prepared...shall desire that day of the Lord, as that day signifies *affliction*...I am mended by my sicknesse, enriched by my poverty, and strengthened by my weaknesse;...O Lord be angry with me, for if thou chidest me not, thou considerest me not, if I taste no bitternesse, I have no Physick; If thou correct me not, I am not thy son' (*Sermons*, 2:362).

10.1–14.   *Batter*: The word introduces all three of what become the sonnet's main image groups: (1) interpersonal violence ranging from corporeal punishment to forcible seizure and imprisonment to rape; (2) shaping a metal vessel on a forge by means of tongs and bellows; and (3) bombardment and demolition of a town's outworks. The vocabulary of these image groups has a number of overlaps—for example, *knocke, seeke to mend, bend | Your force to…make mee newe* (interpersonal violence, metal-working); *o'er-throwe…breake, blowe, burne* (metal-working, military bombardment and demolition). *your Enemye*: Satan, whose name derives from the Hebrew for 'enemy'. *ravish*: The word's two senses in medieval and early modern English were 'rape' and 'carry off', the latter as in abducting a person or as in God's taking a soul to heaven, to remove it from sin.

Sonnett 11 ('Wilt thou Love God, as Hee Thee') (fol. 46r)

11.1–8.   As positioned in the Dowden ordering, the calm, even stately movement of Sonnets 11 and 12 conveys a sense that the speaker's plea to God has been granted, and that *Reason your Viceroy in Mee* (10.7) has regained its ascendancy over the escalating passions and tormented succession of thoughts in Sonnets 5, 7, 9, and 10. The language of Sonnets 11 and 12 resonates repeatedly with that of Scripture. For all the composure and clarity of these sonnets, the central paradoxes of Christian faith—the incarnation of Christ and his redemption of sinful humankind by his death—remain fundamental to the utterances of the speaker's rational voice. *God the Spiritt…thy brest*: 'Know ye not that your body is the temple of the Holy Ghost…?' (1 Corinthians 6:19). *the Father'…begott a Sonne most blest*: 'the only begotten of the Father, full of grace and truth' (John 1:14). *still begetting (for he ne'er begonne)*: This paradox encapsulates the theological doctrine of the eternal (not temporal) procession or begetting of the Son by the Father. *chuse Thee by Adoptiöne*: 'God sent forth his Son…To redeem them that were under the law, that we might receive the adoption of sons' (Galatians 4:4–5). *Co-heyre to' hys Glory*: 'The Spirit itself beareth witness with our spirit, that we are the children of God: And if children, then heirs; heirs of God, and joint-heirs with Christ…that we may be also glorified together' (Romans 8:16, 17). *Sabbaths endles rest*: In the Old Testament prototype, God commands Moses to institute a day among the Jews, 'to make an atonement for you before the Lord your God…It shall be unto you a sabbath of rest, and ye shall afflict your souls' (Leviticus 23:28, 31, 32). The *Sabbaths endless rest* would accordingly be that of the souls in heaven, whose sins Christ atoned for, once and for all.

11.9–14.   *a robbd man…buy' it agayne*: Repurchase or relinquishment were the only options open to one who had been robbed, according to the rule of law merchant 'that a sale of goods in market overt passes the property to a purchaser, even though the vendor had no title to them' (W. S. Holdsworth, *A History of English Law* (1922–45), 4:522). *The S[o]nne of Glory came downe*: 'the Son of man…cometh in the glory of his Father' (Mark 8:38). *S[o]nne*:

Dowden reads 'Sinne', a penslip. *Man was made like God*: 'God said, Let us make man in our image, after our likeness' (Genesis 1:26).

Sonnett 12 ('Father, Part of his doble Interest') (fol. 46r–v)

12.1–14. Donne the preacher would usefully elucidate the pervasive legal vocabulary and images in this sonnet: 'The two Volumes of the Scriptures are justly, and properly called two Testaments, for they are...The attestation...of the will and pleasure of God, how it pleased him to be served under the Law, and how in the state of the Gospell. But...the Testament, that is, The last Will of Christ Jesus, is this speech...to his Apostles, of which this text is a part...By this Wil then,...having given them so great a Legacy, as *a place in the kingdome of heaven*, yet he...gives more, he gives them the evidence by which they should maintain their right to that kingdome, that is, the testimony of the Spirit,...*the Holy Ghost*, whom he promises to send to them' (*Sermons*, 9:232). *his doble Interest*: his twofold claim. *Jointure*: the holding of an estate by two or more persons as joint tenants—a no longer current sense. *knottye*: inextricably tied together and, figuratively, full of intellectual difficulties, hard to explain. *his Deaths Conquest*: Another echo of 1 Corinthians 15:55, 57. *Thys Lambe...Was from the worlds beginning slayne*: 'And all that dwell upon the earth shall worship him,...the Lamb slain from the foundation of the world' (Revelation 13:8). *invest*: establish in an office or position, endow with authority or power. *all healing grace...letter kill*: 'God...hath made us able ministers of the new testament, not of the letter, but of the spirit; for the letter killeth, but the spirit giveth life' (2 Corinthians 3:5, 6). *Thy Lawes abridgment...Love*: 'Jesus said...Thou shalt love the Lord thy God with all thy heart, and with all thy soul, and with all thy mind. This is the first and great commandment. And the second is like unto it, Thou shalt love thy neighbour as thyself. On these two commandments hang all the law and the prophets' (Matthew 22:37–40). 'This is my commandment, That ye love one another, as I have loved you' (John 15:12).

THE CROSSE (FOLS 46V–47V)

It is generally accepted that 'The Crosse' is a relatively early composition, one with closer affinities to the sententious vein in Donne's verse letters to male friends than to the tenor of his other religious verse. A date of *c.*1604 has also been generally accepted on the plausible supposition that the poem's defence of the sign and image of the cross in Christian devotion relates to the proceedings of the Hampton Court conference in that year. Convened by King James, this series of deliberations by ranking clergy of the Church of England undertook to counter Puritan demands that the cross be eliminated from public worship and the sacraments, especially the sign of the cross in baptism. The king, an active participant in the proceedings, pointed out that crucifixes had largely been removed from English churches. The sign of the cross, however, 'was well used before popery', James said, and 'to disallow of all things which had been used at all in popery' would entail renouncing 'the Trinity and all that is holy, because it was abused in popery' (quoted in Robbins, *Complete Poems*, 468). James's position had an impact in two productions of the Hampton Court conference: an ecclesiastical canon (formal rule or decree) and a revised Book of Common Prayer. At the end of the Order of Baptism, a rubric signals the fact and purpose of the new canon: 'To take away all scruple concerning the use of the sign of the Cross in Baptism, the true explication thereof, and the just reason for the retaining of it, may be seen in the thirtieth Canon, first published in the year 1604.'

ll. 3–16.   *the Sacrifice...the chosen Altar*: 'Christ...is sacrificed for us' (1 Corinthians 5:7). 'We have an altar...Wherefore Jesus also, that he might sanctify the people with his own blood, suffered' (Hebrews 13:10, 12). *no Pulpitt...thys Crosse withdrawe*: In London the chief Puritan preachers who opposed venerating the cross had been silenced by the 1590s. *misgrounded Lawe...Scandall taken*: A probable allusion to certain iconoclasts who took prohibition of crucifixes blessed by the pope to mean prohibition of all crucifixes, including the one on the altar in Queen Elizabeth's chapel royal; see John Phillips, *The Reformation of Images: Destruction of Art in England, 1535–1660* (1973), 124–8. *No Crosse...have none*: Donne puns on the figurative sense of *Crosse*, affliction, as a later sermon passage would clarify: 'There cannot be so great a crosse as to have none...for afflictions are our spirituall nourishment' (*Sermons*, 3.166). *th' Instrument...the Sacrament*: At my baptism the officiating priest sprinkled me with holy water and signed me with the sign of the cross.

ll. 17–30.   *Who can denye mee...myne own Crosse to bee?*: The following series of likenesses to a cross was compiled from a range of church fathers by Justus Lipsius, *De Cruce* (Concerning the Cross) (1594), 1.9. *ou[t]*: Dowden reads *our*, a penslip. *Meridians...Parallells*: Lines of longitude and latitude. *Materiall Crosses...chiefe dignitye*: Donne's emphasis on the superiority of spiritual crosses to material ones leaves little substantive difference between his and the Puritan position. *extracted Chimique medicine*: drugs that draw the excess of one or more humours out of the body (a Galenic notion) or preparations that cure disease by introducing an opposite or antagonistic substance into the body in a purified form (a Paracelsian notion). *Physicke*: cure, remedy. *stilld, or purg'd*: made to emit noxious matter, by inducing vomiting or a bowel movement.

ll. 33–46.   *Carvers...doe take*: Donne the preacher would elaborate: 'A cunning Statuary [sculptor] discerns in a Marble-stone...where there will arise an Eye, and an Eare, and a Hand, and other lineaments to make it a perfect Statue' (*Sermons*, 2:276). *oft, Alchimists...prove*: Alchemists were frequently accused of counterfeiting. *gett*: beget, generate. *Pride yssued from Humilitye...Monster*: Donne the preacher would reiterate the point: 'in an over-valuation of...thy merits,...there is a pestilent pride in an imaginary humility' (*Sermons*, 6:310). *Crosse thy Senses*: 'They that are Christ's have crucified the flesh with the affections and lusts' (Galatians 5:24). *a Snake*: a temptation that fatally deceives by way of pleasing but false appearances, like Satan in serpent form in Genesis 3:1–7.

ll. 49–52. *most the Eye...come home*: Compared with the other senses, sight needs more disciplining, for the eyes can operate at a distance and move about to select their objects. The other senses are in fixed organs (ears, nose, mouth, the skin) that require direct contact with their objects. *crosse thy Hart...Palpitatiön*: According to Aristotle, man is the only animate being whose heart conveys the sensation of jumping up and down, just as man alone responds to hope and anticipation of the future (*De partibus animalium* [On the Parts of Animals], 3.6.668a). *Pants downewards*: Draws rapid, laboured breaths, during which the abdomen rises and falls. *Pants* is the reading with stronger textual warrant in manuscripts and early print editions, but most modern editors have opted for the variant *Points*, judging *Pants* to be too close in meaning to *Palpitatiön*. However, the decisive consideration in favour of *Points* is Donne's later phrasing: 'only thy heart of all others, points downwards, and onely trembles' (*Essays in Divinity*, 30). Presumably *Points* means 'indicates that the source of perturbation is located somewhere in the abdomen'.

ll. 55–64. *thy brayne...forme present*: Another formulation tracing to Aristotle, *De partibus animalium*, 2.7.653a37–b3. *A Crosses forme* refers to the X-shaped join found in certain skulls that have suffered injury where their sagittal and coronal areas meet. *Sutures*: rigid joins formed by two contiguous bones, especially the small, sawtooth-like projections that demarcate joins in the skull. *So when thy brayne...Concupiscence of Witt*: Since the brain vents itself at cross-like junctures, *Crosse* (counteract) and rectify the wanton excesses of wit that your brain emits. *crosse thyselfe in all*: Donne the preacher would take an opposing view: 'That onely is my crosse, which the hand of God hath laid upon me...that is,...tentations or tribulations in my calling; and I must not go out of my way to seeke a crosse; for, so it is not mine, nor laid for my taking up' (*Sermons*, 2:301). *when wee love...which our Crosses are*: When we love, without superstition or idolatry, the abundance of divine love imaged in the crucified Christ, and when we even more earnestly, out of the love for Christ produced in us in response to his love, endure wrongs and sufferings (*our Crosses*) for his sake.

THE ANNUNTIATION, A TITLE ELUCIDATED BY ITS VARIANT IN TWO MANUSCRIPTS, 'UPPON THE ANNUNCIATION, WHEN GOOD-FRIDAY FELL UPON THE SAME DAYE' (FOLS 47V–48V)

ll. 1–9. *Tamely...away*: The speaker admonishes himself to fast meekly when two major holy days, each celebrated with Holy Communion, coincide, thus providing his soul with double sustenance. The two days are the Annunciation, commemorating the angel Gabriel's announcement to the Virgin Mary that she would give birth to the Son of God, and Good Friday, commemorating the crucifixion and death of that same Son of God aged (as traditionally calculated) thirty-three. Within Donne's lifespan, the Annunciation and Good Friday converged in 1597 and 1608; the latter year has been thought the likelier date for this poem. *Shee*: the soul. *a Circle, Embleame ys*: In this particular year the commemoration of Christ's life on Earth, from his conception to his death, takes shape as what Donne the preacher would characterize as 'One of the most convenient Hieroglyphicks of God, . . . a Circle', noting elsewhere that 'the beginning and ending is all one' (*Sermons*, 6.173; 4.96). *doubtfull*: ambiguous (between joy and grief). *a Cedar*: The celebration of wedded love in the Song of Solomon 5:15 likens the bridegroom to 'a cedar'; when Christian commentators allegorized this book as representing the love between Christ and his church, the cedar accordingly became an image of divinity. *put to making*: created, subjected to being made.

ll. 12–23. *Reclusd*: secluded, living privately. *almost fiftye . . . fifteene*: In his widely circulated collection of saints' lives, Jacobus de Voragine stated that the Virgin Mary conceived Christ at the age of fourteen years, gave birth to him at fifteen, and lived with him for thirty-three years (*Legenda Aurea* [Golden Legend], 4.234). *Hee her to John*: From his cross, Christ entrusted his mother to the care of his disciple John (John 19:26–7). *Orbitye*: a state of bereavement from the loss of a child. *in playne Mapps . . . West is East*: One of Donne's favourite images, as exemplified in 'A Hymn to God my God', ll. 13–14, and *Sermons*, 2:199–200. *playne*: flat. *Ave*: In Luke 1:28 the angel Gabriel's words of greeting are *Ave Maria* (Hail, Mary). *Consummatum est*: 'It is finished'—Christ's last words on the cross as recorded in John 19:30, in the Latin wording of the Vulgate. *Court of Facultyes*: the archbishop of Canterbury's court that issued permits for occasional exemptions from prescribed practices.

ll. 25–34. *by the Selfe fixd Pole . . . th'other is*: With the invention of the magnetic compass and accompanying advances in astronomical observation, the oscillating course of the so-called 'pole-star' in the near vicinity of the North Pole could be determined and charted in tables. *So God, . . . wee knowe*: Donne's superlative regard for the Church of England was a constant of his religious outlook. *His Spiritt . . . to One Ende both*: God led the children of Israel out of Egypt and through the wilderness by means of 'a pillar of cloud by day, and a pillar of fire by night' (Exodus 13:21–2). *Death and Conception . . . One*: The salvation procured for humankind by Christ transmutes our death into what is effectually a second birth, an entry into eternal life (Hebrews 10:12–14).

ll. 37–46. *Creation . . . one Periöd*: Like God the Father, Christ as God the Son has made a single complete moment of the beginning and the final determination of our lives. *Hys imitating Spouse*: Another allusion to the church as the bride of Christ. *though One blood drop . . . yet shed All*: Donne the preacher would elaborate: 'Though . . . one drop of his bloud had beene enough to have redeemed infinite worlds, . . . yet he gave us a morning shower of his bloud in his Circumcision, and an evening shower at his Passion, and a shower after Sunset, in the piercing of his side' (*Sermons*, 4:296). *Shee All... every Day*: On this day when the commemoration of the Annunciation and the Passion converge, the church supplies from her own resources all that concerns Christ. Store up, my soul, this treasure in large quantities, and recount it every day of my life. *uplay*: Donne's verb choice yields an echo of Matthew 6:19–20: 'Lay up treasures for yourselves in heaven'.

THE LITANYE (FOLS 48V–54R)

In a letter from Mitcham (undated, but assignable to the autumn of 1608), Donne wrote to Goodyere:

> I have made a meditation in verse, which I call a Litany; the word you know imports no other than supplication, but all Churches have one form of supplication, by that name. Amongst ancient annals I mean some 800 years, I have met two Letanies in Latin verse, which gave me not the reason of my meditations, ... but they give me a defence, if any man, to a Lay man, and a private, impute it as a fault, to take such divine and publique names, to his own little thoughts. The first of these was made by *Ratpertus*...and the other by *S. Notker*...; they were both but Monks, and the Letanies poor and barbarous enough, yet Pope *Nicolas* the 5. valued their devotion so much, that he...commanded them for publike service in their Churches: mine is for lesser Chappels, which are my friends, and though a copy of it were due to you, now, yet I am so unable to serve my self with writing it for you at this time (being some 30 staves of 9 lines) that I must entreat you to take a promise....That by which it will deserve best acceptation, is, That neither the Roman Church need call it defective, because it abhors not the particular mention of the blessed Triumphers in heaven; nor the Reformed can discreetly accuse it, of attributing more than a rectified devotion ought to doe.   (*Letters*, 32–4)

In fact, Donne's 'Litanye' restores a considerable amount of the material that Archbishop Thomas Cranmer excised from the Roman liturgy in 1544 as he prepared a Reformed liturgy for use in the Church of England. Donne's restorations include invocations to such 'blessed Triumphers in heaven' as the Virgin Mary, the angels, the patriarchs, the prophets, the Apostles, the martyrs, the confessors (non-martyred witnesses for Christ), and the virgins (stanzas 5–12). In addition, he introduces an invocation to the doctors of the Church, theologians of great eminence (stanza 13), which was no part of the Roman litany or Cranmer's English litany, incorporated in the Book of Common Prayer beginning with its first edition (1549). A further notable feature is Donne's introduction of first-person singular pronouns into a genre previously composed for collective public use; for this he had—and probably was conscious of—the Psalms as a precedent, with their interchangeable I's and we's. The letter to Goodyere, moreover, offers an implicit rationale for the poem's first-person locutions; 'The Litanye' was written for 'lesser Chappels', Donne's friends.

ll. 4–9.   *ruinous*: likely to fall (the Latin sense). *My Hart... Vicious tinctures*: Donne synthesizes several allusions and etymologies. His heart has taken on the cold, dry, heavy properties of melancholy, the humour that corresponds to the element earth. Later sermon passages elucidate other specifics. 'Adam...signifies red earth...and therefore...ourselves, as derived from him'; we are all made 'of earth, and of red earth....But that rednesse which we have contracted from...the blood of our own souls, by sin, was not upon us when we were in the hands of God...We have dyed ourselves in sins as red as scarlet' (*Sermons*, 2:200–1; 9:64–6). *Vicious tinctures*: impurities in base metals, which alchemical processes were supposed to convert to the purity of gold. *I may rise...dead*: The paradox results from inverting the order of the 'first death', the death of the body, and the 'second death', the punishments in hell that befall great sinners (Revelation 21:8).

ll. 10–18. *Sinne...never made*: Neither sin nor death was part of God's original creation. *tryedst*: tested. *stings*: 'The sting of death is sin' (1 Corinthians 15:56). *thyne Heritage*: 'Come, ye blessed of my Father, inherit the kingdom [of heavenly glory] prepared for you' (Matthew 25:34). *O bee...agayne*: Yearning for an internalized experience of Christ's death on the cross and the salvation thus made available. *lett yt...Passion slayne*: Desire to apprehend Christ's passion so intensely as to be absorbed into it, as in Paul's figure of being 'conformed to the image of His Son' (Romans 8:29).

ll. 19–27. *O holy...Ame*: 'your body is the temple of the Holy Ghost' (1 Corinthians 6:19). *mudd walls...condensëd Dust*: Further elaboration of the etymology of 'Adam' and Genesis 2:7: 'The Lord God formed man of the dust of the ground'. *intend*: intensify. *glasse Lanterne*: A poetic synthesis of two commonplaces: the body as a glass vessel containing the breath of life, and a lantern containing the flame of the soul. *lett...Fyre, Sacrifice, Priest, Altar, be the same*: Further application of Paul's figure of being 'conformed to the image' of Christ, so that the penitent speaker has a part in his own salvation, following the precedent of Christ who combined priest and sacrifice in himself (Hebrews 6:24–7).

ll. 29–36. *Bones*: illogicalities or obscurities. Donne the preacher would characterize the resurrection of the body as 'one of the hardest bones,...in the mysteries of our Religion' (*Sermons*, 7:211). *milke*: basic nourishment. 'As newborn babes, desire the sincere milk of the word, that ye may grow thereby' (1 Peter 2:2). *wise Serpents*: Jesus exhorted his disciples, 'Be ye...wise as serpents' (Matthew 10:16). The serpent was proverbially 'more subtle than any beast of the field' (Genesis 3:1). *you Distinguish'd...Knowledge bee*: Donne's conjoint ascription of power, love, and knowledge to the Father, Son, and Holy Ghost adapts Augustine's correlation of the persons of the Trinity with the soul's functions of reason, will, and affections in *De Trinitate* (On the Trinity). *a Selfe-different Instinct*: an animating power which incorporates difference within itself while remaining one. *all mee elemented bee*: constituted in my basic capacities. *unnumbered Three*: 'these three are one' (1 John 5:7).

ll. 38–45. *Whose flesh redeem'd us*: Because Christ acquired his human nature during gestation in Mary's womb. *That shee-Cherubin*: So called because she reopened the entry to Paradise, closed after the expulsion of Adam and Eve (Genesis

3:24). Donne as preacher would downplay such extravagant glorification: 'The Virgin *Mary had not the same interest in our salvation, as* Eve had in our destruction; nothing that she did entred into that treasure, that ransom that redeemed us' (*Sermons*, 1:200). *One Clayme for Innocence*: From the time of Augustine, Mary was held to have committed no actual sin; she could not, however, make the further claim of being innocent of original sin. *disseis'd*: legally dispossessed. *clothd*: took bodily form, a metaphor tracing to Job 10:11: 'Thou hast clothed me with skin and flesh'. *Titles unto*: valid claims upon.

ll. 46–54. *Nonage*: period of being underage. *Wardship . . . Angells*. References to guardian angels include Elegy 1 ('The Bracelet'), ll. 13–14; *Second Anniversary*, ll. 236–9; 'Obsequies to the Lord Harrington', l. 228. *Denizend*: resident by permission. *study*: employ thought and effort. *blind . . . see*: The angels perceive outward actions, but not the inner motivations for them.

ll. 55–61. *thy Patriarchs*: Abraham, Isaac, and Jacob, the ancient forefathers of Israel. *greate Grandfathers . . . than Us*: Hebrews 11:13–16 says that, although they lived long before Christ, Abel, Enoch, Noah, Abraham, and Sarah died 'in faith, not having received the promises, but having seen them afar off, . . . and were persuaded of them. . . . Now they desire a better country, that is, an heavenly: wherefore God . . . hath prepared for them a city'. *in the Cloude . . . in Fyre*: The natural phenomena by which God led the Israelites out of Egypt into the promised land. *clear'd*: enlightened. *that wee | May use . . . helpes right*: 'Let us therefore come boldly unto the throne of grace, that we may obtain mercy, and find grace in time of need' (Hebrews 4:16). *Bee satisfied*: The subject of this verb is *thy Patriarchs desire* (l. 55). *fructifye*: be fruitful, a metaphor tracing to Matthew 7:17: 'Every good tree bringeth forth good fruit'.

ll. 64–72. *Eagle-sighted*: Keen in foreseeing and foretelling the coming of Christ, as the eagle was reported to be able to look directly at the sun (Pliny, *Natural History*, 10.1.10). In his letter to Goodyere describing 'The Litanye', Donne remarks: 'The eagle . . . is able to . . . pearch a whole day upon a tree, staring in contemplation of the majestie and glory of the Sun' (*Letters*, 49). *That harmonye . . . Lawe*: Christ is the *harmonye* that the prophets sounded when they foretold his role as mediator of God's two covenants with his people, reconciling the old law of works with the new law of faith (Romans 3:27–31). *Those heavenly . . . feete*: Donne the preacher would particularize the character of this admiration. 'The . . . harmony of *Poetry*, in the sweetness of composition, never met in any man, so fully as in the Prophet *Isaiah*' (*Sermons*, 4:167). 'The greatest mystery of our religion . . . is conveyed in a Song, in the third chapter of *Habakkuk*' (*Sermons*, 2:171). *seeking Secretts or Poetiquenes*: A critique of two sorts of idle curiosity: being inquisitive to know what should not or cannot be known, and getting carried away with producing rhetorically artful effects, at the expense of more essential poetic concerns.

ll. 73–81. *thy . . . Zodiacke*: Because the number of its signs corresponds to the number of apostles, but also because they, as leading lights of Christianity, resemble the zodiac in their acknowledged influence and prominence. *ingirt thys All*: encompass the universe. *throw . . . fall*: mislead others and themselves, as in Jesus's warning, 'If the blind lead the blind, both shall fall into the ditch' (Matthew 15:14). *I goe . . . Applyinge*: Donne rejects novel, obscure interpretations of the New Testament. *decline*: humble.

ll. 85–90. *thy scattered Mistique Body*: the church, an image tracing to 1 Corinthians 12:27: 'ye are the body of Christ, and members in particular.' *In Abel Die*: Abel, the son of Adam who was murdered by his twin brother Cain (Genesis 4:1–8), was interpreted as a type of Christ by Augustine in *On the City of God*, 15:18. *[of]*: Both sense and meter require the preposition, lacking in Dowden but present in other manuscripts. *oh, . . . Martyrdome*: Around the time that he composed 'The Litanye' Donne wrote of some early Christians 'growne so hungry and ravenous of it [martyrdom] that many were baptized only because they would be burned, and children taught to vexe and provoke executioners that they might be throwne into the fire' (*Biathanatos*, ed. Ernest W. Sullivan, II (1983), 1.3.3). Not long thereafter, with a view to English Catholics who refused to take the Oath of Allegiance to James I as head of the Church of England, Donne again detected and denounced 'an inordinate and corrupt affectation of martyrdom' (*Pseudo-Martyr* (1610), 2).

ll. 92–9. *A Virgin . . . Confessors*: *Confessors* are those who suffered, but were not put to death for their Christian faith. Donne allusively links them with the militancy of the *Martyrs* (*squadron*) and with the Virgins of stanza 12. The first paired cohort, martyrs and confessors, enacted steadfast adherence to Christ when facing deadly or extreme violence; the second pair, confessors and virgins, demonstrated their faith in steadfast integrity and purity of life. *Tentations . . . Diocletiän*: The comparison of temptations to persecutors is a commonplace of patristic commentators (e.g., Rabanus Maurus, *Patrologia Latina*, 111:89). Donne gives the commonplace a new twist: we tempt ourselves, and are our own worst enemies. *Diocletiän*: A Roman emperor (284–305) remembered by Christians for the severe persecution that occurred towards the end of his reign.

ll. 100–7. *Cold whyte . . . Abbesse*: Such hyperbolic language would come to characterize the extreme 'high Anglican' wing of the Church of England, as in Anthony Stafford's exhortation to those 'who have vowed Virginity': 'Kneele downe before the Grand White Immaculate *Abbesse* of your snowy *Nunneries*' (*The Femall Glory* (1635), 148–9). *obtaind*: pleaded and been granted. *Divorce*: Cf. Holy Sonnet 10 ('Batter my hart'), l. 11.

ll. 110–17. *Doctors*: Originally, 'doctors of the church' referred to Ambrose, Augustine, Jerome, and Gregory the Great; later the reference was extended to a larger number of theological authorities. *Both Bookes of lyfe*: The Bible and the register of God's elect. *wrought*: given a determinate form. *what they . . . mis-sayd*:

Donne aligns with the Reformed view that the doctors of the church were subject to human error and not infallible. *Meane wayes*: a middle course.

ll. 119–23. *That Church... warrfare*: The pairing of the Church Triumphant (redeemed souls in heaven) and the Church Militant (souls on Earth, struggling against sin) traces to early Christianity. *Pray ceaslesly*: 'Without ceasing I make mention of you always in my prayers' (Romans 1:9). *Gratiöus*: endowed with divine grace, righteous—senses no longer current.

ll. 127–35. *Secure*: over-confident—a sense no longer current. *thys Earth... fram'd*: Donne rejects the opinion of both Plato and Paul that the body is the soul's prison, which he himself would voice in *Second Anniversary*, ll. 173, 249. *Covetous*: excessively desirous. *maimd... sweet*: disabled from attaining worldly pleasures. Donne denies any incompatibility between enjoying life on Earth and seeking God intently.

ll. 136–43. *needing... Good*: being good only out of fear of hell. *trusting... Soule away*: Being over-confident that we are among the elect and assured of salvation. *light... newes*: frivolously hankering after religious innovations. Donne the preacher would level this charge against Roman Catholics: 'If it be... affectation of new things, there may be... things so new in that Religion, as that this Kingdom never saw them yet.... For we had received the Reformation before the Council of *Trent*, and before the growth of the Jesuits' (*Sermons*, 4:139). *From thinking... Soule*: 'Man is not all soul, but a body too; and... God hath married them together in thee' (*Sermons*, 4:226).

ll. 147–52. *measuring... Vitiöus*: excusing occasional sin as less bad than habitual sin. *Indiscreete*: exhibitionistic, showy. *scandalous*: offensive. *pervious*: open to the influence of.

ll. 156–61. *Of midle kinde*: between divine and human. *full of Grace*: Said of Jesus in John 1:14; said of his mother in the 'Hail Mary' of Roman Catholic liturgy. *thy poor Birth... Povertie*: 'She brought forth her firstborn son... and laid him in a manger; because there was no room for them in the inn' (Luke 2:7). *Riches... Epiphanie*: 'They saw the young child with Mary his mother, and... when they had opened their treasures, they presented unto him gifts, gold, and frankincense, and myrrh' (Matthew 2:11).

ll. 163–71. *bitter Agonie*: Jesus's torments of soul in the garden of Gethsemane: 'Being in an agony he prayed more earnestly' (Luke 22:44). *th' Agonie of pious witts*: 'To this day, thy Church... cannot see... what kind of affliction... made thy *soul heavy unto death*... in thine agony' (*Sermons*, 2:70). *thy free Confessione*: John 18:1–6 narrates how Judas betrayed Jesus into the hands of the chief priests and Pharisees by leading a band of armed men into the garden of Gethsemane. Jesus twice asks 'Whom seek ye?', twice receives the answer, 'Jesus of Nazareth', and twice responds, 'I am he.' 'As soon then as he had said unto them, I am he, they went backward, and fell to the ground.' This is the encounter, with its double round of questioning, that Donne characterizes as *they were... Made blind*. *teach us when... unjust Men*: An allusion to the heated contemporary debate on equivocation and mental reservation—misleading one's interrogator by voicing only part of a thought, as a Jesuit might say 'I am no priest' while silently adding 'of Apollo'. Donne the preacher would declare: 'Whether a man be examined before a competent Judge or no, he may not lie: we can put no case, in which it may be lawful for any man to lie to any man...And though many have put names of disguise, such as Equivocations, and Reservations, yet...they are all lies' (*Sermons*, 9:162–3).

ll. 172–8.   *To Blowes* | *Thy face*: Luke 22:64. *thy clothes to spoyle*: Matthew 27:28. *Thy fame to Scorne*: Matthew 27:37–43. *Dying...expresse*: Donne the preacher would elaborate: 'Christ died because he would die...Christ did not die naturally, nor violently, as all others doe, but only voluntarily' (*Sermons*, 2:208). *expresse*: force out, expel.

ll. 183–5.   *want*: hardship, suffering—senses no longer current. *Image:* likeness. *Seale:* promissory note stamped with a seal.

ll. 194–8.   *Plague...Angell*: When Korah, Dathan, and Abiram led a rebellion against Moses' and Aaron's authority, God sent a plague to punish the rebels and vindicate Moses and Aaron; this plague killed thousands (Numbers 16:49). *Heresye, thy second Deluge*: Donne the preacher would ascribe this figure of speech to Augustine (*Sermons*, 9:329). *Sinister way*: ill-fated path (leading to damnation).

ll. 206–7.   *Thou, who...sicke day*: 'The Lord said unto Satan, Hast thou considered my servant Job,...a perfect and an upright man, one that feareth God, and escheweth evil?...And Satan answered the Lord,...But put forth thine hand now, and touch his bone and his flesh, and he will curse thee to thy face. And the Lord said unto Satan, Behold, he is in thine hand; but save his life. So went Satan forth...and smote Job with sore boils...And he...said...What? shall we receive good at the hand of God, and shall we not receive evil? In all this did not Job sin with his lips' (Job 2:3–7, 10). *Heare Thyselfe...pray*: 'God...fills us with good and religious thoughts, and...leaves the Holy Ghost, to discharge them upon him, in prayer, for it is the Holy Ghost himself that prays in us' (*Sermons*, 3:153).

ll. 210–14.   *snatching Cramps*: sudden spasms. *Apoplexyes*: fits. *fast*: Either of two senses is applicable: 'quick' or 'firmly fastened'. *thy Promises*: 'Will the Lord...be favourable...?...Doth his promise fail...?' (Psalm 77:7–8). *threates in Thunder*: 'The voice of thy thunder was in the heaven:...the earth trembled and shook' (Psalm 77:18). *Offices*: duties.

ll. 217–24.   *our Ears...Labyrinths*: In Donne's day, a term for the cochlea or spiral cavity of the inner ear. *That wee gett not*: This is the superior reading of other manuscripts; Dowden's 'That wee may gett not' is faulty in both sense and rhythm. *Slipperines*: moral precariousness. *Senselesly*: insensibly. *From hearing...Majestye Divine*: Cf. *Devotions*, Expostulation 8.

ll. 227–33.   *to give...Physicke*: to give us medicine, and make us take it. *invenom'd*: malicious. *see...Thee decline*: perceive God to turn away.

ll. 235–43.   The reflections in stanza 27 convey much the same thought as the final line of Shakespeare's Sonnet 94, 'Lilies that fester smell far worse than weeds.' *Beauty... Physicke made*: The rose was used as a laxative. *Witt*: intelligence. *That our affections kill us not, nor Dye*: 'Walke sincerely in thy Calling, and thou shalt hear thy Saviour say... These affections... shall not destroy thee' (*Sermons*, 5:361–2). *O thou Eare, and Crye*: God both attends to our prayers and instigates them; cf. l. 207.

ll. 246–52.   *Gayne... slayne*: If we perish, neither Christ nor we have gained by his redeeming death. *free*: freed from sin. *sinne is Nothinge*: 'You know... in what sense we say... that evil is nothing;... it is but a privation, as a shadow is, as sicknesse is' (*Sermons*, 6:238).

GOODFRIDAY. 1613. RIDING TOWARDS WALES (FOL. 54R)

This poem is variously titled in the manuscripts: 'Riding to Sir Edward Herbert in wales', 'Mr J. Dun goeing from Sir H[enry] G[oodyere] on good fryday sent him back this Meditacion on the waye', and 'Goodfriday | Made as I was Rideing westward, that day'. The last title sounds like one originating with Donne himself, lending credence to the possibility that Donne's immediacy of utterance here may be more than a poetic effect.

Good Friday fell on 2 April in 1613. Donne visited Goodyere at his home, Polesworth, in Warwickshire, after the wedding of Princess Elizabeth and Elector Frederick on 14 February, for which he had written an epithalamion. On 7 April Donne wrote a letter dated from Montgomery Castle in Wales, Sir Edward Herbert's principal residence at this period (Bald, *Donne: A Life*, 270; *The Elegies and the Songs and Sonnets*, ed. Gardner, 256). This poem's sustained, intensive meditation on the crucifixion of Christ predates by less than two years Donne's ordination in the Church of England (January 1615).

ll. 1–8.   *Lett... Devotion ys*: Donne proposes to add a sphere, *Mans Soule*, to the existing cosmic set. Like them, this sphere is propelled by an angelic *Intelligence, Devotion*—characterized as 'this | Vertue, our formes forme and our soules soule is' (To Mr R. W: 'If as mine is, thy life a slumber be', l. 32). *the other... theyre owne*: While the spheres guided by their intelligences were thought to move in orbits from west to east, their natural motion was countered by the 'primum mobile' (first moving thing, of which God was the *first mover*). This was the outermost sphere, postulated to enclose the set of other spheres and to revolve around the Earth from east to west every twenty-four hours, carrying them along with it. *And beeing... forme obay*: Besides the orbital and diurnal motions, others were postulated to account for observed irregularities in the cosmic system that could not otherwise be explained.

ll. 9–22.   *I am caryed... West*: Metaphorically, towards death, on analogy with the setting sun. *There I... beget*: The speaker's *West* is offset by *the East* of eternal life (*endles day*), secured by Christ's redeeming death. *Who sees... dye*: God admonished Moses on Mt. Sinai: 'Thou canst not see my face; for there shall no man see me, and live' (Exodus 33:20). *Selfe-lyfe*: life itself.

hys foote stoolle: 'Thus saith the Lord,...the earth is my footstool' (Isaiah 66:1). *tune all Spheares*: A seeming allusion to Plato's music of the spheres in *Republic*, 10.617b; but the reading in several manuscripts, 'turn all spheres', admits uncertainty.

ll. 24–5.   Garrard accidentally omitted these two lines, a clear case of eyeskip from *which ys* at the end of l. 23 to *which ys* at the end of l. 25. The omission is made good by the Newcastle manuscript (British Library, Additional MS 4955, dated *c*.1629). *Zenith...Antipodes*: God is the highest point of all reference, to us and to those who live on the opposite side of the Earth.

ll. 25–32.   *blood...soules*: The phrasing of the Vulgate in Leviticus 17:14 underlies Donne the preacher's later reference to 'Blood being ordinarily received to be *sedes animae*, the seat and residence of the soule' (*Sermons*, 4:294). *if not of his*: It is questionable to ascribe even a contingent materiality to the soul of Christ. *Durt*: mud. *miserable*: pitiable. [*Partner*]: The reading of the Newcastle manuscript, substituted for Dowden's 'Patterne'. *Halfe*: Christ's human nature derived from Mary, his divine nature from God.

ll. 33–9.   *these thinges...towards them*: The memory was traditionally conceived as being in the back of the head, a location explained as an act of 'the great wisdom and providence of God...because it must look to the things that are past...as it were a spiritual eye' (Pierre de la Primaudaye, *Second Part of the French Academie* (1594), 162). *thou Lookst...Tree*: A phrase from Psalm 66:7, 'His eyes behold the nations', was allegorized in keeping with a tradition that Jesus was crucified facing west. *O thincke...Anger*: Donne the preacher would elaborate: 'O Lord be angry with me, for if thou chidest me not, thou considerest me not...If thou correct me not, I am not thy son' (*Sermons*, 2:87).

A striking irregularity of foliation in the Dowden manuscript suggests that George Garrard did not have in hand a determinate set of Donne's love lyrics to copy out, but instead was obliged to estimate how many of these poems might become available to him. As bound, the foliation of the Dowden manuscript skips from 55v to 100r. Folios 100r–130v contain a sizable collection of Donne's love lyrics—poems that first received the designation 'Songs and Sonnets' in the second edition of *Poems, by J. D.* (1635).

LOVE LYRICS (FOLS 100R–130R): THE GENRE

The team of scholars collaborating on *The Variorum Edition of the Poetry of John Donne* under the general editorship of Gary A. Stringer has compiled evidence that the individual love lyrics began to circulate in manuscript at different times, possibly over a span of more than two decades. Thus, Donne's earliest readers typically encountered these poems singly, and Donne himself evidently conceived of his love lyrics as stand-alone compositions. He seems, moreover, not to have taken particular care to preserve copies of his love lyrics, as he did when he entrusted his satires and elegies to Goodyere's safekeeping. Nonetheless, the manuscript evidence of the *Variorum* edition reveals that a larger number of copies, both early and later, were made of Donne's love lyrics than of any of his poems in other genres. This fact attests not only the surpassing popular appeal of the love lyrics but also the determination of readers to acquire their own copies of them.

Regarding the designation 'Songs and Sonnets', Dayton Haskin has perceptively noted that this had been the title of a heterogeneous gathering of lyrics by several poets, written on a range of subjects in varying tonalities and verse forms, otherwise known as *Tottel's Miscellany* (1557). The volume exercised a significant influence in shaping English understanding and practice of lyric form. Haskin suggests that attaching the heading 'Songs and Sonnets' to an assemblage of Donne's love lyrics alerted readers to recognize that these poems were written in 'the older tradition of the commonplace book and the miscellany', not in the newer mode of the sonnet sequence where a single poetic speaker expatiates on his love for an idealized, remote mistress. By contrast, the older tradition offers separately crafted 'poems as aesthetic performances to be read through here and there in any order that a reader wishes'. Such lyrics alert readers to recognize that these texts are not products of 'an author's self-expression' so much as 'experiments' in various verse forms and shifting perspectives, unhindered by a concern for overall consistency.

Haskin further observes that Donne's love lyrics are 'striking for the considerable resistance they mount against some frameworks' for 'contemporary love poetry'. Among these, he instances (1) not 'making one woman the fixed subject of every love poem'; (2) keeping 'the identities of the several women in the poems shadowy'; (3) refraining 'from marking the sex of the lover or the beloved'; (4) providing 'no sequence' or 'larger narrative frame for individual poems'; and (5) not identifying 'the speakers with the poet who writes the verse'. As a result, Donne's love lyrics 'prove difficult to place in relation to the dates of known events and circumstances in his own life', all the while that many of these poems 'have so distinctive a ring' that 'experienced readers feel', as Coleridge remarked, 'that none but Donne could have written them' (Dayton Haskin, 'The Love Lyric', in Shami, Flynn, and Hester, eds, *The Oxford Handbook of John John Donne*, 180–205, quotations from 183, 185).

Song ('Send home my Long stray'd Eyes to mee'), titled 'The Message' in Poems, 2nd edn (1635) (fol. 100r)

In several Group 2 manuscripts of Donne's poems, this song is grouped with two others ('Come live with mee, and be my Love', 'Sweetest love, I do not go') under the heading, 'Songs which were made to certain airs which were made before'. This phrasing and the conventionality of the song's form and content have led scholars to infer that 'Send home my Long stray'd Eyes to mee' is an early composition intended to be performed as entertainment for young men, such as those among whom Donne found himself at Lincoln's Inn in the early to mid-1590s. Hapless eyes and heart and the resentful feelings of a rejected lover are generic commonplaces of love lyric. Helen Gardner prints a modern transcription of an early seventeenth-century setting for voice and lute by Giovanni Coperario [John Cooper] (*The Elegies and the Songs and Sonnets* (1966), 241).

ll. 4–23. *forc'd*: artificial, strained. *Protestings*: solemn declarations of love. *crosse*: act
contrary to. *And may Laugh, when that Thou*: 'And may laugh and joy, when
thou' is the more metrically regular reading of the Group 2 manuscripts.
will none: wants nothing (of you).

Song ('Come live with mee, and be my Love'), titled 'The Baite' in Poems, 2nd edn (fols 100v–101r)

Christopher Marlowe's 'Come live with me, and be my love', a lyric composed in
stanzas of paired rhymed couplets, must have furnished the incentive for Donne's
variant in the same verse form. Marlowe died in 1593, and this particular lyric was first
published in *The Passionate Pilgrim* (1599) and *England's Helicon* (1600). Marlowe's
poetic precedent generated other spin-offs besides Donne's: one attributed to Sir
Walter Raleigh and another response ascribed to 'Ignoto' (By One Unknown) fol-
lowed Marlowe's text in *England's Helicon*. This circumstantial evidence of poetic
emulation among Donne's contemporaries warrants reproducing the two texts most
germane to Donne's: Marlowe's prototype of six stanzas and Ignoto's variant of two
stanzas.

Marlowe

1. Come live with me, and be my love,
   And we will all the pleasures prove
   That valleys, grovës, hills, and fields,
   Woods or steepy mountain yields.
2. And we will sit upon the rocks,
   Seeing the shepherds feed their flocks,
   By shallow rivers, to whose falls
   Melodious birds sing madrigals.
3. And I will make thee beds of roses
   And a thousand fragrant posies,
   A cap of flowers and a kirtle
   Embroidered all with leaves of myrtle.

4. A gown made of the finest wool
   Which from our pretty lambs we pull:
   Fair linëd slippers for the cold,
   With buckles of the purest gold.
5. A belt of straw and ivy-buds
   With coral clasps and amber studs,
   And if these pleasures may thee move,
   Come live with me, and be my love.
6. The shepherds' swains shall dance and sing
   For thy delight each May morning:
   If these delights thy mind may move,
   Then live with me, and be my love.

Ignoto

1. The seate for your disport shall be
   Over some River in a tree,
   Where silver sands, and pebbles sing,
   Eternall ditties with the spring.

2. There shall you see the Nimphs at play,
   And how the Satyres spend the day,
   The fishes gliding on the sands:
   Offering their bellies to your hands.

ll. 10–25. *every channel hath*: every tributary contains. *Gladder… Thou him*: Donne's
characteristic attraction to paradox extends to other aspects of the poem:
the speaker's proposals are bait for catching the woman, while she herself is

both an angler and bait. *windowy*: latticed (like windows). *Sleave-silke*: the first coarse unwinding from a silkworm's cocoon before the filaments are separated and twisted into thread. *the[e]*: Dowden reads 'these', a penslip.

The Apparition, titled 'An Apparition' in Group 2 and Group 3 manuscripts (fol. 101r)

The Petrarchan commonplace of a fatally cruel beloved, the bitter tone and implied sexual promiscuity suggest that 'The Apparition' is a relatively youthful composition. The title appears unusually in a number of manuscripts. An incomplete setting of 'The Apparition' for voice and bass by William Lawes (1602–45) has survived (*The Elegies and the Songs and Sonnets*, ed. Gardner, 243–4).

ll. 3–13.   *sollicitation*: sexual propositioning. *feign'd Vestall*: pretended virgin. *thy sick Taper... wincke*: Wax candles were believed to flicker at the approach of a ghost. *Aspen*: stirring like a poplar tree's leaves. [*Bathd*]: Dowden and other manuscripts read 'Both', but in one instance another hand corrects this to 'Bathd'—a manifestly superior reading. *Quicksilver* or mercury, which produced sweating when taken orally, was used to treat syphilis. *Veryer*: truer.

Song ('Hee is starke madd, who ever sayes'), titled 'The Broken Heart' in Poems, 1st edn (1633) (fol. 100r)

The theme of love at first sight is rare in Donne. Although a severe outbreak of plague occurred in 1593, the lighthearted reference in l. 6 offers an insufficient basis for dating. There are, however, other indications that Donne composed several poems in the song genre during the mid-1590s.

ll. 5–29.   *Who will beleæve... a yeare?*: Victims who died of bubonic plague usually did so within days or even hours after the appearance of buboes—inflamed swellings in glandular areas of the body. *flask*: a tube-like container used for storing gunpowder. *chawes*: chews. *chaynd shott*: cannonballs chained together to cause greater destruction when fired simultaneously. *Tyran*: tyrant. *Pike*: A fish noted for its fierce appetite. *frye*: young fish. *nothing... fall*: It was a philosophical commonplace that since nothing could be made of nothing (Lucretius, *De rerum natura* [On the Nature of Things], 1.155–6), nothing could be reduced to nothing. *Nor... quite*: As in the proverb, Nature abhors a vacuum. *unite*: continuously joined together. *broken glasses*: mirrors splintered into shards.

'Stand still, and I will reade to Thee', first printed in Poems, 2nd edn, and there titled 'A Lecture upon the Shadow' (fols 102r–v)

Some critics have posited a connection between Donne's relationship with Anne More, which began in or around 1599, and this poem. Donne the preacher would develop its central image very differently: 'We have brought our Sun to his *Meridional height*, to a full Noon, in which all shadows are removed: for even the *shadow of death*,

death itself, is…in the number of his Mercies. But the *Afternoon shadows* break out upon us…they grow greater and greater upon us, till they end in night, in everlasting night' (*Sermons*, 7:360).

ll. 1–12.   *I will reade…Philosophy*: The personas of teacher and student perhaps reflect the thirteen-year age difference between Donne and Anne More. *heads*: Other manuscripts read 'head', thus preserving an exact rhyme. *brave clearenes*: fine clarity. *reduc'd*: brought. *shadowes*: concealments. *Care*: caution. *Least degree*: When the sun at its zenith (greatest height) crosses the meridian, its longitude is 0 degrees; thereafter, its degrees of westward declination increase.

ll. 14–26.   *Except our Love…blind our Eyes*: The westward shadows that the lovers' bodies would cast as they continued to walk eastward are charged with ominous imaginings of acting behind one another's backs, and coming to deceive one another. *If once Love…shall disguise*: Such deception can be prevented if the lovers sustain their mutual love as *a Growinge or full constant light*; otherwise, love's *Night* will be as inevitable as night is in the natural world.

A Valediction ('As Vertuous men passe mildly away'), first printed in Poems, *1st edn, and titled 'A Valediction: forbidding Mourning' (fols 102v–103r)*

Scholars tend to associate Donne's lyrics of valediction—saying goodbye—with various journeys he made to the Continent, either to improve his diplomatic credentials or to accompany prospective or actual patrons during his long years without formal employment after his marriage in December 1601. 'As Vertuous men' may have such a connection with Donne's journey to the continent with Sir Walter Chute in early 1605 (Bald, *Donne: A Life*, 148, 241–5).

ll. 6–12.   *No teare…move*: Let us not act in the extravagant manner of Petrarchan lovers. *Prophanation*: desecration. *the Layetye* (laity): ordinary persons. *Moving…Earth*: an earthquake. *trepidations…Sphears*: oscillations of the outermost cosmic sphere that shook the other spheres enclosed within it. Such motions were predicated to account for supposed irregularities in the precession (steadily advancing earlier occurrence) of the equinoxes. *innocent*: harmless.

ll. 13–22.   *Sublunarye*: belonging to the changeable, imperfect region below the moon. *(Whose…Sense)*: who have only a sensual nature, like the animals. *admit*: allow of, accommodate. *elemented yt*: constituted its purely physical character. *Inter-assurëd*: assured about each other, by each other—Donne's coinage. *endure not yet*: still do not experience.

ll. 29–31.   *And though…roame*: Two distinct operations of the two-footed compass are visualized. In the one, the moving foot, held constant as a radius, circumscribes a circle around the fixed foot as its centre. In the other, the moving foot, beginning from a closed-up position adjacent to the fixed foot, is extended outwards to trace the arc of a circle and a single radius that

will be reinforced when the moving foot again closes up to the fixed foot.
hearkens after: sympathetically attends to.

'I wonder, by my trothe', first printed in Poems, *1st edn, and there titled*
'The Good-morrow' *(fol. 103v)*

If the lovers' waking refers to Anne More, marital cohabitation is implied, dating the
poem after March 1602.

ll. 3–5.   *suck'd... childishly*: At certain social levels it was then the practice to place
             newborn infants in the care of wet nurses. *snorted*: snored, slept soundly. *the*
             seven... den: A cave outside Ephesus, where according to tradition seven
             young Christians fell asleep and were then walled up, thus spared severe
             persecution; nearly two centuries later, after Christianity had been estab-
             lished in the Roman Empire, they awoke (Jacobus de Voragine, *Legenda*
             Aurea [Golden Legend], no. 101). *but thys*: except for this.
ll. 9–19.   *controules*: dominates. *one worlde*: 'our world' is the reading of the Group 2
             manuscripts, considered superior by some. *two... Hemispheares*: two halves
             that would make a better whole as a globe. *sharpe*: bitterly cold. *What*
             ever... equally: The soul, a homogeneous substance, could not be divided;
             thus it could not perish (Cicero, *De Senectute* [On Old Age], 21.79; Aquinas,
             Summa Theologica, 1.75.6).

Song ('Goe, and catch a falling Starr') (fols 103v–104r)

This may be one of the songs that Donne composed in the early to mid-1590s; see the
note on 'To L. of D.' under 'Verse Letters to Male Friends' of the Westmoreland
manuscript. Its appearance in 46 manuscripts attests its popularity among seven-
teenth-century readers. The list of impossibilities was a poetic device used by Ovid
and Propertius, and later by medieval poets and by Petrarch, before being taken up by
early modern wits in Europe and England. Robbins (*Complete Poetry*, 193–4) suggests
that 'Goe and catch a falling Starr' may have originated in a contest involving John
Hoskyns, a contemporary of Donne's at Oxford, a friend of their mutual friend Sir
Henry Wotton, and a student at the Middle Temple when Donne was a student at
Lincoln's Inn.

   The subject of this contest of wits is presumed to derive from cantos 27–8 of
Ariosto's epic romance *Orlando Furioso*, translated into English by Sir John Harington
in 1591. When Rodomante rails at the inconstancy of women, the poet intervenes to
express his confidence that good ones do exist although none have yet been found.
Rodomante says he will not give up his search, hoping that before more white hairs
come, he will be able to say that one woman has remained true. Giacondo and his
friend, betrayed by their wives, seek throughout Europe for a faithful woman, but
instead encounter 1001 sexually compliant ones. The two men resign themselves, con-
cluding (in Harington's rendering): 'Let us not then condemn our wives so sore, |
That are as chaste and honest as the best; | Sith they be as all other women be, | Let
us turn home, and with them well agree.'

ll. 1–13.   *Goe…Starr*: Cf. the Somerset Epithalamion, ll. 204–5. *Gett…roote*: The
mandrake's forked root, roughly resembling the human groin, was valued
in antiquity as an aphrodisiac and an enhancer of female fertility. But
impregnating a mandrake root would be an impossibility. *wind*: The noun
is ambiguous between two homonyms: 'air in motion' and 'curved or
twisted form'. Only the second completes the rhyme. Neither alternative,
however, would furnish a means of substantive or straightforward advance-
ment. [*to*] *see*: Dowden and all other manuscripts of Groups 1 and 2 read
Thinges invisible see; the infinitive marker *to* first appeared in *Poems*, 1st edn.
Till Age…thee: Ariosto's Rodomante makes this self-reference.

*'Now Thou hast Lov'd mee one whole day', titled 'Womans Constancy'
in several manuscripts and in* Poems, *1st and 2nd edns (fol. 104v)*

ll. 3–14.   *Wilt…vowe?*: Will you say that an earlier promise made to some other lover
nullifies a more recent one made to me? *Or that…forsweare?*: Promises made
under duress or coercion were deemed legally invalid. *true…untye*: Cf. 'Till
death do us part'. *Sleepe, Deaths Image*: A proverbial formulation particularly
popular in English verse of this period (Tilley, *Dictionary of Proverbs*, S527).
having purpos'd…bee true?: Another period commonplace, in the form
'Constant in nothing but inconstancy' (Tilley, F605). *fa[ls]hood*: Dowden reads
'fashhood', a penslip; the next line has the correct spelling. *Vayne*: Trifling.
Lunatique: person as changeable as the moon. *scapes*: evasions, excuses.

*'Image of her whom I love, more than Shee', untitled in the manuscripts
except for two that respectively title it 'The Dream' and 'Picture'
(fols 104v–105r)*

Helen Gardner's identification of the source of this poem has won critical acceptance
(*The Elegies and the Songs and Sonnets*, 181). In the third of Leone Ebreo's *Dialoghi
d'Amore* (Dialogues of Love) (1535), the lover Philo is reproached by his mistress
Sophia for passing by without seeing her. He replies that his mind was rapt in contem-
plating the image of her beauty. Sophia asks how that could be so strongly impressed;
Philo responds that her radiant beauty entered his faculties of perception and imagi-
nation through his eyes, penetrating the depths of his heart and mind. Sophia remains
surprised that her actual presence could go unnoticed, whereupon Philo retorts that
she would not have blamed him if he had been asleep. She admits this, and asks what
else might be able to still the senses but sleep, which is a half-death. Philo replies that
the ecstasy or distraction produced by a lover's thoughts is more than a half-death.
The two proceed to discuss the distinction between ecstasy, when the mind is rapt in
contemplating what truly is, and sleep, when the mind is occupied by dreams. Philo
then accuses Sophia of destroying him because the image of her beauty arouses insa-
tiable desire (*Dialoghi*, 197–205; 229–31). With this conception of the beloved's image
as more potent than her presence Donne combines the theme of the love-dream
(ll. 13–18), in which the state of sleep brings the lover the erotic gratification that his
mistress denies to him waking.

ll. 1–3.   *Image of her*: Presumably a portrait given as a love-token. *more than Shee*: Sophia: 'The image of my person has more sway over you than my person itself?' Philo: 'It is more potent because the image within our mind is stronger than that from without, since, being within, it has already become master over the whole of its domain' (*Dialoghi*, trans. Gardner, 229). *Medall*: love-token.

ll. 9–12.   *Reason gon…you*: The heart, the seat of reason, mediated between the brain, the seat of understanding, and the liver, the organ of sensual desires. In reason's absence, the lower faculty of *Fantasye* or fancy, activated by sensual desires, became dominant. *meaner*: less elevated. *Convenïent*: agreeable to the circumstances—a sense no longer current. *more proportionall*: in better relation.

ll. 17–26. *a Such fruition*: such a pleasurable possession. *Though you…away*: Though you as a person stay here, your youth and beauty vanish too quickly. *a Snuffe*: a mere candle-end. *Madd…none*: Ecstasy generated by contemplating her image is better than lack of reason. The lover rests his case regarding the preferable way of being 'out of his senses'.

Ad Solem ('Busy Old foole, unruly Sunne') or 'To the Sunne' is the title in most manuscripts, sometimes with the addition, 'A Song'. 'The Sunne Rising' is the title in Poems, *1st and 2nd edns (fols 105v–106r)*

Exceptionally, the allusion in l. 7 to King James's fondness for hunting enables this poem to be dated to the late summer or autumn of 1603 or 1604—probably the latter year, since there was a serious outbreak of the plague from March 1603 to May 1604. As the speaker exalts the erotic mutuality he enjoys with his beloved, his scathing dismissal of courtly honour and worldly employment bespeaks recklessness and defiance. This is a credible early reaction on Donne's part to his dismissal as secretary to Egerton and his inability to gain other secular employment after eloping with Anne More in December 1601. Beyond its possible biographical origins, however, the hyperbole reaches heights extraordinary even for Donne.

ll. 1–10.   *unruly*: out of bounds, off-limits. The sun is personified as a meddlesome old snoop. *Saucye*: disorderly. *Pedantique*: schoolmasterish. *Prentises*: apprentices. *ride*: go stag-hunting. *Countrey Ants*: agricultural labourers. *Harvest offices*: duties at harvest time. *all alike*: consistent, unchanging. *raggs:* fragments, bits. Donne the preacher would adapt this image to figure God's mercy: 'First and last are but ragges of time, and his mercy hath no relation to time, no limitation in time, it is not first, not last, but eternall, everlasting' (*Sermons*, 6:170).

ll. 17–25. *both Indies…Myne*: Spices were imported to Europe from India and the East Indies; silver was imported mainly from Mexico and Peru. The loose designations, 'Indies' and later 'West Indies', were applied to European discoveries in the Western hemisphere in the fifteenth and sixteenth centuries. *Aske…lay*: In assimilating all earthly rulers to himself, the speaker implicitly ascends to the position of lord of the universe.

The skirting of blasphemy in likening his status and power to God's is not accidental; rather, it intensifies in *She is all states... Princes doe but play us. Thou, Sunne... wee*: The sun's happiness is solitary, the happiness of one.

Song ('I can Love both fayre and browne'), titled 'The Indifferent' in Group 2 manuscripts and in Poems, 1st and 2nd edns (fols 106r–v)

Judging on the basis of genre and the theme of free love, this could well be one of the songs of the early to mid-1590s that Donne sent to 'L. of D.' The theme had important precedents in Roman love poets, especially Ovid (*Amores* 2.4.9–48), where the speaker declares that he can love women of all complexions.

ll. 2–27.   *abundance*: riches. *want*: poverty. *Loneness*: solitude. *Her who believes... tryes*: the woman who trusts a lover's promises, and the woman who tests them. *serve... turne*: suit your purpose. *Racke mee*: Put me to the torture. *came... travaile*: set to work (with a sexual implication). *your fix'd Subject*: As the ever-constant Petrarchan lover was. *Varietye*: Cf. Westmoreland's Elegy 9, ll. 35–6. *examin'd*: investigated. *were false*: A majority of manuscripts read 'are false'.

'For every houre that thou wilt spare mee nowe', titled 'Loves Usury' in two manuscripts and in Poems, 1st and 2nd edns (fols 106v–107r)

Again, the song-like stanzaic form and the theme of free love are consistent with a date in the early to mid-1590s for this lyric; the reference to *my browne... haires* also suggests a youthful speaker.

ll. 3–12.   *Usurious*: Demanding that interest be paid on a loan (of sexual prowess). *my... reigne*: my physical desire dominate. *Sojorne*: stay for a time. *Snatche*: take quick advantage of an opportunity. *Resume... mett*: Take up with a woman whom I left last year, as if we had never met before. *Rivalls letter*: letter to or from a rival. *at next... that delaye*: The speaker will anticipate his rival's midnight assignation with the woman by arriving three hours early, in ample time to make love with her maid, and then tell the woman what he has been up to when he keeps his date with her later. Ovid's speaker is less brazen, since he tries to cover up his dalliance with Corinna's maid. He resorts to frankness only to threaten the maid and secure continuation of her favours (*Amores*, 2.7–8).

ll. 13–22. *Onely Lett... Sport*: Let my sexual pleasure be free of love and lust alike. *Country Grasse*: farm girls, imaged as pastureland. *Comfitures of Court*: ladies of the court, imaged as candied fruit. *Cityes quelques choses*: showily dressed citizens' wives. *lett... transport*: The speaker will be excited by mere rumours of these women's sexual availability. *If thyne... gayne*: The god of love will extort the most by way of honour, shame, or pain from an old man in love. *Do thy will then*: At that time collect the interest I owe you. *Subject*: the speaker under the god of love's rule. *Degree*: the speaker's rank as a subordinate. *fruites*: outcomes, consequences.

The Canonization (fols 107v–108r)

Robbins, *Complete Poetry*, 147–8, weaves a tissue of allusions to propose a date for this poem in the late spring of 1604. *My five gray haires* is consonant with a speaker in his thirties, as Donne was, after 1602, while *ruind fortune* evokes his situation after his dismissal as Egerton's secretary. *Observe . . . hys Grace, And the Kings reall or hys stampëd face | Contemplate* are manifest references to James I, who acceded to the throne of England in 1603, and to the proclamations concerning various denominations of coinage stamped with the king's head issued that spring. *When did my Colds a forward Spring remove?* evidently refers to the unseasonably cold June of 1604. The *Plaguy bill* (publicly posted numbers of plague deaths) would have been a timely reference after May 1604, when the epidemic showed signs of abating.

Other scholars, by contrast, have emphasized general literary precedents and analogues for this poem's central theme. It consists in a deliberate retreat from the world of social and political ambition into the mutuality of a relationship so intense and exalted that the pair are acknowledged as saints who bear witness to heterosexual love as the supreme and encompassing value of all life.

ll. 2–9. *Palsye*: nervous tremors of the limbs. *Goute*: painful inflammation of the joints. *Take . . . a Place*: Choose a career; secure a position at court. *And the Kings . . . Contemplate*: The most successful courtier would be admitted to the inner circle of those with direct access to the king. *what you will, approve*: try anything you like. *So*: As long as.

ll. 13–26. *Colds*: episodes of love-melancholy. *forward*: early. *heates . . . fill*: accesses of sexual desire. *Call . . . by Love*: Staple images in Petrarchan love-lyric and emblem literature: the *flye* or moth that immolates itself in a candle flame and *Tapers* (love as a self-consuming passion); *the 'Eagle, and the Dove* (love as a blend of opposites—here, fierceness and gentleness respectively typifying male and female); the *Phenix* (the mythical bird, one of a kind, that regenerated itself by being consumed in fire and rising anew from its ashes). *The Phenix . . . both Sexes fitt*: The curious nature of the phoenix perfectly figures the lovers' acts of sexual consummation. [*our*]: The Dowden manuscript lacks the pronoun—an obvious penslip. *dye*: In informal English of the period, a synonym for 'reach orgasm'.

ll. 30–45. *Our Legende*: their life story as saints and martyrs of surpassing mutual love. Donne carefully differentiates between the Roman Catholic cult of the saints and the secular counterpart of canonization that he imagines for his two lovers. Their authentication will be *no Peece of Chronicle* but *pretty . . . Sonnetts*; their burial place *a well wrought Urne* (a vessel used by classical pagans), not *halfe Acre tombes* (as some shrines to major religious saints were). *Hermitage*: Here, a secluded dwelling-place for a pair of lovers, not a solitary hermit. Above all, the rarefied experience and knowledge of love ascribed to the two lovers are not imputed to the special grace conferred on religious saints as illumination or revelation from God. Instead, their experience and knowledge of love are figured as an alchemical process in which special lenses or mirrors concentrate and capture essences—here, of the whole spectrum of human life and activity (*all... Epitomize*). *A pat-terne of* [*y*]*our Love*: The Dowden manuscript reads 'Our', as do other Group 1 manuscripts and *Poems*, 1st and 2nd edns. But there are solid grounds for adopting the variant 'your' found in a substantial number of other manuscript sources. Both the grammar and the sense of the address to the lovers beginning at l. 37 require the reading 'your'. These two lovers, who discovered for themselves the paradigmatic nature of their love, are besought to bestow a favour, *A pattern of* [*y*]*our Love*, on their fellow humans generally: *Countryes... Courts*: By the end of the poem, the *pat-terne* is duly bestowed on its beseechers; it is the poem itself.

Song ('I am two fooles, I knowe'), titled 'The Triple Foole' in Poems, *1st and 2nd edns (fols 108r–v)*

This may be one of the songs that Donne composed in the mid-1590s and sent to 'L. of D.'

ll. 6–20.   *th' Earths... salt away*: A standard theory in classical antiquity from Seneca (*Naturales Questiones*, 3.5) onward. *fretfull*: wave-borne. *rimes Vexation*: the complications imposed by metre and rhyme in the writing of verse. *allaye*: lessen. *brought to numbers*: contained by the regularity of verse. *To Love and Griefe... published*: Donne makes dry situational irony of Aristotle's insight in *Poetics* 4.9–15.1448b. Pleasure is to be had even from representations of things that are unpleasant to actual sight, because contemplating the rep-resentation yields an understanding of the thing itself.

'Yf yett I have not all your Love', titled 'Mon Tout' [My All] in one manuscript and 'Lovers Infiniteness' in Poems, *1st edn (fols 108v–109r)*

The close legalistic argumentation and the terms from commerce—*Treasure, pur-chase, spent, bargayne* (ll. 5–8), *Stockes, outbid* (ll. 15–16)—group this lyric with such period exercises of wit as Shakespeare's Sonnet 87 ('Farewell, thou art too dear for my possessing') and John Dowland's song 'To ask for all thy love' in *A Pilgrim's Solace* (1612), based on Donne's last stanza. (Gardner prints Dowland's text and setting in *The Elegies and the Songs and Sonnets*, 244–5.) The copy of this poem that survives among the British Library's Conway Papers in the handwriting of Sir Henry Goodyere presents an inferior text derived from a Group 3 manuscript. Goodyere cannot have had Donne's autograph original in front of him when he made his copy. See Starza Smith, *Donne and the Conway Papers*, 281–3.

ll. 3–5.   *other... other*: more... more. *purchase Thee*: result in your being mine. The commercial vocabulary allows for an initial (false) assumption that this love relationship has a mercenary basis.

ll. 20–32.   *thy gift... General*: Phrasing ambiguous between the no longer current sense of *General* (for everybody and anybody) and the more ordinary sense of *General* (without specific exception or limitation). *Ground*: origin. *Thou... savest yt:* 'He who loseth his life for my sake shall find it'—Jesus's words in Matthew 10:39; Mark 8:35; and Luke 9:24. The echo skirts blasphemy. *liberall*: ample, open-hearted. *The*[*m*]: Dowden reads 'Thee', a penslip possibly prompted by *wee* later in l. 32.

Song ('Sweetest Love I doe not goe') (fols 109r–v)

The genre of this exquisitely tender lyric is that of the aubade: a lover's farewell to his beloved at daybreak. Its date of composition is unknown, but as a *Song*, it may be early. In other Group 1 and in Group 2 manuscripts the first, second, and fourth lines of each stanza are written as long lines—as they are here in Dowden. Group 3 manuscripts and *Poems*, 1st edm. divide these long lines into two short lines at midpoint, thereby making the rhyme scheme more evident.

ll. 13–21. *But come ... advance*: But if misfortune comes, we make it stronger by teaching it skill and persistence, so that it triumphs over us. *When thou sighst ... Soule away*: Both Greek 'psyche' and Latin 'anima' meant both 'soul' and 'breath'. Thus, in classical culture breathing one's last and the soul's departure from the body were naturally identified with each other. There was also an old popular belief that each sigh costs a drop of blood; see Shakespeare, *2 Henry VI*, 3.2.61, 63. *thy divining hart*: Juliet exclaims 'O God, I have an ill-divining soul!' (*Romeo and Juliet*, 3.5.54).

Song ('When I dyed Last, And, Deare, I dye'), titled 'The Legacie' in Poems, 1st and 2nd edns (fols 109v–110r)

This lyric reduces to absurdity Petrarchan commonplaces—lovers' parting as death, time's slow passing, exchanging of hearts—by literalizing them in images of a formal legal document drawn up by the speaker and of a surgical operation performed by the speaker on himself. If l. 14 is taken as an echo of Marlowe's *Edward II* (1591), this in combination with the *Song* genre could indicate a date of composition in the early to mid-1590s.

ll. 1–7. *When I dyed ... I goe*: The phrasing neither demands nor precludes an underlying sexual sense of *dyed*. *Though I bee dead*: One of Donne's favourite imaginings, as in 'The Computation', ll. 9–10, and 'The Expiration', l. 12. *which sent me*: i.e., he which sent me. The speaker's ghost now speaks on behalf of the speaker.

ll. 9–16. *anone* (anon): again. *that*['*s*]: Dowden and all other Group 1 manuscripts have the faulty reading *that*. *When I ... did lye*: 'Rip up this panting breast of mine, | And take my heart' (Marlowe, *Edward II*, 4.7.66–7). *rippd*: laid open. *cozen*: trick, deceive.

ll. 22–3. *for our Losse* [*is*] *sad*: The reading in Dowden and other Group 1 manuscripts, 'for our Losse, bee yee sad', obscures the sense and roughens the meter; [*is*] is the simplest emendation. *ment*: intended.

A Feaver (fols 110r–v)

The hyperbole of the destruction of the world by the death of a mistress traces to Petrarch's broodings over the death of Laura in *Rime sparse* (Scattered Verses), nos 268, 326, 338, 352. Donne's *First Anniversary* elaborates at length on the identification of the fifteen-year-old Elizabeth Drury with what here is termed *the worlds Soule* and on her premature death as reducing the world to an all but lifeless *Carkas* (ll. 9–10).

ll. 13–26.   *Schooles*: scholastic philosophers, faculties of philosophy. *what fyre... worlde*: This was a concern of Christian theologians who speculated on 2 Peter 3:10: 'the day of the Lord will come...in the which...the elements shall melt with fervent heat, the earth also and the works that are therein shall be burned up.' *much Corruption...feaver Long*: This standard doctrine originated with Galen, *De differentis febrium* (On Differences in Fevers), who explained fever as unnatural heat generated in a body by corrupt matter or putrid blood. *Meteors*: temporary atmospheric phenomena in the region above the Earth but below the moon. *Unchangeable Firmament*: the region of the universe above the moon, constituted by the heavens and the spheres containing the fixed stars. *t'was of my mind*: I thought this. *seising*: taking possession of. *it*: the fever. *persever*: last long.

Ayre and Angells (fols 111r–v)

Donne's demonstrable knowledge of Andreas Vittorelli's treatise *De Custodia Angelorum* (On the Guardianship of Angels) (1605), which he quotes explicitly in *Pseudo-Martyr* (1610), points to a date after 1605 for the composition of this poem. This in turn depends on reading ll. 22–3 as alluding to Vittorelli's assertion, on the authority of Aquinas (*Summa Theologica*, 1a.51.2), that angels take on bodies of condensed air to become visible to humans (*De Custodia*, 9r). The poem's intellectual and rhetorical intricacies are also consistent with a relatively late date.

ll. 1–14.   *Twice...or name*: Cf. 'The Good Morrow', ll. 6–7. *a shapeles flame*: an unsteady, flaring light. *Some lovely...see*: Cf. 'Negative Love', ll. 10–12. *assumes*: The reading of Dowden and other Group 1 manuscripts is inferior to the variant 'assume' found in alternative sources. 'Assume' is in parallel construction with the conditional 'fixe' in l. 14.

ll. 15–28.   *to ballast...overfraught*: The speaker's love-boat is figured as a light scouting vessel dangerously pressed into service to transport the heavy freight of the woman's physical charms. *for Love to worke upon...much too much...be sought*: The speaker's strong counter-reaction takes a turn to the opposite extreme, the purity of angelic and celestial bodies, where *Love* can *inhere*. He proposes to the woman that *thy Love...bee my Loves Spheare*, alluding to the Ptolemaic universe in which each concentric sphere is animated and ruled by a celestial intelligence. This is a cosmic analogue of Aristotle's long influential doctrine of human conception, in which the father supplied the soul of a foetus, and the mother supplied the body. Gardner notes and documents the then standard belief that a man's love for a woman was superior to a woman's love for a man because he was both the giver and the more spiritual being, she the receiver and the more material being (*The Elegies and the Songs and Sonnets*, 205–6). *Just such Disparitee...ever bee*: Donne's closing lines work to reduce male–female difference to the barest minimum—the difference between *Ayre* (the most rarefied form of matter), and *Angells Puritee* (the lowest level of spiritual being). The implication even seems to be that, if a man's love is to be realized, it requires a woman's reciprocating love.

'Tis true, tis day, what though it bee?', titled 'Breake of Day' in Group 2 manuscripts and in Poems, *1st and 2nd edns (fol. 111v)*

Another instance of the aubade genre, this lyric exists in two different versions that some scholars have interpreted as evidence of Donne's revising hand. Dowden and the other Group 1 manuscripts contain what has been considered the earlier version, because the verse is metrically rougher and the second stanza has only five lines, while the first and third have six. The presumptively later version is found in Group 2 manuscripts; its significant variants are indicated in the notes below. The supposed evidence of revision is, however, equivocal; a faulty copy-text could equally account for such variants as these. William Corkine set the Group 2 text as a song for voice and viol and published it in his *Second Book of Ayres* (1612) (*The Elegies and the Songs and Sonnets*, ed. Gardner, 243).

ll. 2–18. *Ô wilt...from mee?*: Group 1 manuscripts including Dowden lack the 'therefore' found in Group 2 manuscripts, resulting in a rhythmically defective line. *in despight of*: Group 2 reads 'in spight of'. [*Lyght hath no Tongue, but is all Eye.*]: This line is lacking in Dowden (and Group 1), but is found in Group 2 manuscripts, regularizing the stanza form. *the Foule*: the physically ugly. *the worst...goe*: Light is imagined as uttering the truth of the poetic speaker's feelings about the beloved—a *him* (l. 12). The poetic speaker seems to be a woman—an inference strengthened by the references to *the busyed man, He which hath busines, and makes Love,* and *a marryed Man* (ll. 16–18).

'Take heede of Loving Mee', titled 'The Prohibition' in Group 2 manuscripts and in Poems, *1st and 2nd edns (fol. 112r)*

The first two stanzas of this poem are cast in the logical form of a 'dilemma'—a disjunctive syllogism in which two propositions are presented as mutually exclusive alternatives, 'Either X or Y', from which the inference follows: 'Not X and Y'. But the poem's third stanza dissolves (rather than resolves) the dilemma by affirming the contradictory conclusion: 'Both X and Y'. In the Bridgewater manuscript containing a collection of Donne's poems, once owned by John Egerton, first earl of Bridgewater, a son of Donne's former employer, the initials 'J.D.' have been inserted next to the first two stanzas of this poem, and 'T.R.' next to the third. Gardner (*The Elegies and the Songs and Sonnets*, 162) and Robbins (*Complete Poems*, 238) speculate that Donne may have composed the first two stanzas and that Sir Thomas Roe, a friend, may have countered with the witty twist of the third stanza: love and hate will nullify each other and thus preserve the speaker, who is endangered by their extremes.

ll. 1–22. *Take heed*: beware. *repayre*: make up for. [*By being...wast;*]: This line is puzzlingly absent in Group 1 and Group 2 manuscripts; it was printed in *Poems*,

1st edn. *what . . . wast*: i.e., desired in vain. *so greate . . . outweares*: It was popularly believed that each act of sexual intercourse shortened a lifespan by one day. *Officer*: administrator of justice. *So shall . . . bee*: If the speaker lives, he will be the *Stage* on which the beloved can continuously display her conquest of him, not the one-time casualty of a Roman-style *Tryumph*, which ended with the victor killing his vanquished opponent. *Sta[g]e*: *Poems*, 1st edn, corrects 'Staye', the faulty reading in the manuscripts.

'All Kings, and all theyre favorites', titled *'The Anniversarie'* in Group 2 manuscripts and in Poems, *1st and 2nd edns (fols 112r–v)*

There is no critical agreement on the probable date of composition or even the occasion of this poem—what first anniversary, and whose? If the allusion is to the first meeting between Donne and Anne More, that occurred sometime in late 1598 or 1599, and would suggest a date one year later. But nothing indicates that Anne is the addressee here. Helen Gardner's observations offer perhaps the most that can be said: 'When read with "The Sun Rising" and "The Canonization", this poem seems likely to have been written, as they were, when James was on the throne. It breathes the same scorn for the Court from which Donne was an exile' (*The Elegies and the Songs and Sonnets*, 199). It may also be worth remarking that the last line of each stanza of 'All Kings, and all theyre favorites' has six feet, a metrical feature shared with 'I wonder, by my trothe, what Thou, and I' ('The Good Morrow').

ll. 1–10. *All . . . favorites*: A likely allusion to King James's well-recognized singling out of attractive young men for his personal favour and attention. *honnors*: persons of honour. *The Sunne . . . passe*: 'God said, Let there be lights in the firmament of the heaven . . . and let them be . . . for seasons, and for days, and years' (Genesis 1:14). *All . . . drawe*: Donne makes the contemporary belief that the whole universe was in terminal decay the dominant theme of his *First Anniversary*. *our Love . . . everlasting day*: Our love is eternal. Cf. 'Ad Solem' or 'The Sunne Rising', ll. 9–10.

ll. 11–20. *Two Graves . . . Corpse*: This line is regularly interpreted to imply that the lovers are not married, but the inference remains uncompelling. The line simply registers the great likelihood that the lovers will not die at the same time, and hence that their bodies will be buried separately (though possibly side by side). *Wee . . . Must leave . . . salt Teares*: The projected future of the love expressed with their bodies is contrasted with that of the lovers' souls. At the last day, their souls will *prove* that love is their whole nature or that *Love* is *encreasèd there above*. *Inmates*: temporary lodgers, as in an inn.

ll. 21–30. *throughly*: thoroughly. *wee . . . rest*: Theologians generally agreed about the equality of the joy of souls in heaven. *but wee, . . . , Subjects bee*: This remarkable formulation, in which each of the two lovers is both king and subject, contrasts with the subjection of the woman to the man in 'Ad Solem'/'The Sunne Rising', ll. 19–23. Some critics have argued that the addressee here could be of either sex. *Lett us . . . threescore*: The meaning hovers ambiguously between the prospect of a sixtieth anniversary (unimaginable in

Donne's time) and the prospect of a sixtieth birthday (Donne himself died at fifty-nine). The thematic turn, however, is unambiguous: the poem closes as it began by reckoning love and life in the time-bound terms of this world after casting an anticipatory glance at their eternal, heavenly counterparts.

A Valediction. Of my name in the window ('My name engrav'd herein') (fols 113r–114r)

The first-person reference in the poem's title, and its occurrence with variations in all manuscript groups, lend plausibility to the conjecture that it originated with Donne himself.

Elaborate efforts have been made, especially by Robbins (*Complete Poems*, 262–4), to date this poem by means of the astrological reference to the concurrent ascendancies of the planet Venus in Pisces and the planet Saturn in Libra: *When Love and Griefe theyre Exaltation had* (l. 38). The date of late August–early September 1599 that Robbins puts forward, however, rests on three debatable propositions: (1) an approximate rather than precise definition of the planetary 'exaltations' in question; (2) the identification of the beloved in the poem as Anne More, although the beloved is imagined in ll. 53, 55–6 as receptive to a rival's courtship in the speaker's absence; (3) the identification of the journey on which the speaker is departing with Donne's participation in the funeral of Sir Thomas Egerton's son—an absence unlikely to have been long enough to arouse anxiety over a beloved's possible infidelity. Charles Lauder Jr has kindly informed me (personal communication) that the astrological 'exaltations' of Venus in Pisces and Saturn in Libra did in fact occur in March 1599 and March 1600, thus providing a time-frame for dating Donne's composition of 'A Valediction: Of my name in the window'. However, there is no autobiographical correlate for the journey projected by the apprehensive speaker of this poem. Surviving letters document that Donne remained in London in Egerton's service in March 1599 and March 1600 (Bald, *Donne: A Life*, 104, 108). There is, further, the question whether Donne would have had the temerity to carve his name on a window pane in Egerton's London house.

Once again, an observation by Gardner may be the most that can be said about the circumstances of this lyric: 'This Valediction differs from all Donne's other poems of parting in that the lover is concerned to admonish rather than to console. He plainly fears his mistress will not be constant' (*The Elegies and the Songs and Sonnets*, 190).

ll. 1–6.   *My name…grav'd it was*: Period treatises on magic commonly attributed magical powers to proper names as well as to the diamond (Cornelius Agrippa, *Occult Philosophy*, trans. J. F. (1651), 153–4). *Diamonds…Rocke*: Diamonds were classified as being of old rock or new rock (Boetius de Boodt, *Gemmarum et Lapidum Historia* [History of Gems and Stones] (1609), 54–5). The diamond in question is presumably set in the speaker's ring.

ll. 8–18.   *through-shine*: transparent. *more*: Possible wordplay on Anne More's name. *all such Rules*: as that window glass has the just noted properties of transparency and reflection. *Loves Magique...ame you*: The magic worked by love extends beyond externals (the speaker whom the beloved sees) to reveal essentials (the oneness of the speaker and the beloved). *You thys Intirenes...still*: The beloved may better attain the perfect constancy of her absent lover by keeping always before her, as a *Patterne*, his unchanging name in the window.

ll. 20–4.   Alternatively, his *scratchd Name* may teach the beloved other things about her lover while he is absent: his *Mortalitye*, as a ring with an inset skull or *Deaths head* might, or *My ruinous Anatomee*. A debilitated physical state might be expected to result from the hardships of military service, such as the Cadiz and Islands expeditions of 1596–7 in which Donne took part.

ll. 25–30.   *all my Soules*: The tripartite soul of Aristotelian philosophy: rational (*I understand*), vegetative (*and Growe*), and sensitive or animal (*and see*). The speaker argues in stanza 5 that the magic of love has incorporated him in his beloved, so that she sustains his identity even in his absence. *tyle thys house*: cover this bodily frame.

ll. 31–6.   *Till my retorne...Supremacye*: When the speaker returns, his identity will be reconstituted, again by magic. This time the magic will come from the benign influence of the heavenly bodies that were in their ascendancy when he carved his name on the window pane.

ll. 37–42.   *thy[s]*: Dowden reads 'thy', a penslip. *Love...Exaltation had*: Amorous Venus and melancholy Saturn were simultaneously at their apex, infusing the force of their dominant characteristics into the name then engraved in the window. Cf. Shakespeare, *Titus Andronicus*, 2.3.30–1. *No dore...mourne*: The speaker, on the point of departure, admonishes his beloved to govern her conduct under the magically enhanced moral power of his name. *I dye daily*: Said by Paul in 1 Corinthians 15:31, and by Seneca in *Epistles*, 24.19.

ll. 43–54.   In stanzas 8–10 the speaker begins to imagine in detail his beloved's slide into unfaithfulness while he is absent. *inconsiderate*: heedless. *[on]*: lacking in Dowden. *battry to*: assault on. *frame*: devise. *Geniüs*: Originally an attendant spirit assigned to a person at birth, hence associated with that person's identity. *melted*: softened-up. The compliant *mayd* and the opportunistic *Page* are updatings of figures in Ovidian love poetry. *Disputed*: Defended. *if thys Treason...write agayne*: The speaker imagines that his beloved betrays him by writing a responsive letter to his rival. But then he fantasizes that when she addresses the letter, his own name will *flowe | Into thy fancy, from the Pane*, and that she will write to him after all, though unintentionally.

ll. 61–6.   *Glasse...keepe*: The speaker reverts to the distinction between externals and essentials with which he began to reflect on *Loves Magique* (ll. 11–12). He now disparages his *Lethargye* (low spirits) as resulting from the prospect of *Death*—another detail well suited to the departure of the speaker on a military expedition. *Idle talke*: In 1612 Donne wrote to Goodyere: 'I may die yet, if talking idly be an ill sign' (*Letters*, 57).

Elegye. Autumnall ('No Springe, nor Summer beauty hath such Grace')
(fols 114v–115r)

'The Autumnal' is not included among the set of Elegies placed to follow the Satires in Dowden and other Group 1 manuscripts, nor is it included in the comparable set of Elegies that follow the Satires in the Westmoreland manuscript. Instead, as indicated by its position here, it appears among the love lyrics in Group 1 manuscripts. Its placement may indicate that it is of later date than the Elegies taken to be youthful compositions of the 1590s.

Critical opinion regarding the date and subject of 'The Autumnal' divides over two ways of reading the poem: as a paradoxical encomium for the amusement of male readers, with precursors in classical and Renaissance epigrams, or as a sincere encomium to an actual woman (Robbins, *Complete Poems*, 355). On the one hand, analogues to several specifics of Donne's poem are found in epigrams in the *Greek Anthology*—for example, the assertion that 'your autumn excels another's spring, and your winter is warmer than another's summer' combined with praise of the woman's wrinkles and mature breasts, and the image of Love sitting in the woman's wrinkles paired with a contrast between her former flames and fire and her milder warmth now (*The Elegies and the Songs and Sonnets*, ed. Gardner, 147).

On the other hand, a number of the manuscripts that contain 'The Autumnal' bear notations connecting this poem with Magdalen Herbert, the widowed mother of Edward, George, and William, with whom she resided in Oxford at various periods from 1599 to 1608 while they pursued their studies. Donne is known to have become friendly with Magdalen Herbert around 1607, when she was thirty-nine years old and he thirty-five. He addressed two poems to her in 1607–9—a sonnet on St Mary Magdalen ('Her of your name, whose fair inheritance') and a verse epistle ('Mad paper, stay, and grudge not here to burn'). What has perplexed scholars in the present regard is the stronger affinity of 'The Autumnal'—in its classical analogues, witty paradox, and end-stopped couplets—to the Elegies Donne wrote in the 1590s than to his other verse of 1607–9. Robbins sums up: 'The date of composition, and whether Donne had a particular person in mind rather than a theme for the display of invention, remain in doubt' (*Complete Poems*, 35). It is, however, no impossibility for a poet or artist to make a deliberate return to subjects, genres, or techniques of earlier work and to do so for any of a number of reasons.

ll. 3–12.   [y]*our*: The variant reading in other sources, 'your', is superior; it sustains the poem's grammatical consistency, in which references to 'you'/'your', 'her'/'she', and 'hee' imply a male addressee (or addressees) and a heterosexual readership. *a Rape*: a violent seizure, a robbery—senses no longer current. Cf. the idioms 'steals affection' or 'steals your heart'. *scape*: avoid the attractiveness (of this mature woman). *Gold…newe*: Gold was renowned among metals for its enduring purity and integrity. *Tropique*: temperate (not 'tropical' in the current sense). The woman is in a transitional phase between torrid youth and temperate age. *Hee…Pestilence*: He wants his fever to turn into the plague.

ll. 16–28. *Anachoritt* (an alternative form of 'anchorite'): hermit confined to a fixed abode. *a Tombe*: a proper monument. *sojorne*: stay temporarily. *standing house*: permanent residence. *In all [her] wordes...sitt*: When Donne preached a sermon commemorating Magdalen Herbert Danvers's death in 1627, he remarked that 'her house was a *Court*, in the conversation of the best' (*Sermons*, 8:89). *[her]*: Dowden reads 'hys', a penslip due to inattention. *Timber*: well-seasoned lumber. *underwood*: undergrowth, brush wood. *There hee...is past*: In our youth, love, like wine, arouses passion; the best time for love is when our other appetites have lost their strength.

ll. 29–34. *Xerxes'...Barrennes*: This story draws on several classical sources. Herodotus relates that the Persian emperor Xerxes doted on the beauty of a plane tree in Lydia, which he treated like a woman by adorning it with gold ornaments and appointing a guardian for it (*Histories*, 7.31). Aelian ascribes Xerxes' passion to the tree's size (*Variae Historiae*, 2.14), while Virgil vouches for the tree's barrenness (*Georgics*, 2.70). Donne purports to identify what motivated Xerxes' attraction; his incentive is clearly to heighten paradox by dwelling on the oddity of a passion *for Age* and *Ages Glory, Barrennes*. The story is self-contained and has no perceptible bearing on Magdalen Herbert, who, as Donne would recall in 1627, gave birth to ten Herbert children after marrying at a very young age (*Sermons*, 8:87). *Yf wee Love...Compassing*: Magdalen Herbert was forty years old in 1608, one date proposed for 'The Autumnal'. Donne's *fiftye yeares* signals the general rather than specific cast of his reasoning. Generalities predominate from this point to the end of the poem, as the speaker substitutes self-reference for continuing praise of the mature woman.

ll. 38–50. *Lanke*: loose. *Unthrifts*: spendthrift's. *but a Soules Sacke*: only a limp container for a soul. *Whose Eyes...within*: A search for religious consolation is observable in some aging persons. *To vex...resurrectiön*: Souls whose body parts have been dispersed will be troubled at the difficulty of rejoining these in order to face the last judgement. *not Antiënt, but Antique*: not venerably old, just very old. *I hate Extremes*: The speaker endorses the so-called golden mean, only to align himself immediately with an extreme (*Tombes* rather than *Cradles*). *Loves Naturall Lation*: the naturally declining course of love, here figured as the downward movement of the planet Venus in the sky. *Ebb on*: slacken, fade away. *homewards*: towards the earth (death and burial).

'Blasted with Sighes and surrounded with Teares', titled 'Twicknam Garden' in Group 2 and Group 3 manuscripts and in Poems, *1st and 2nd edns (fols 115r–v)*

The house and grounds of Twickenham Park were leased to Lucy Harrington, countess of Bedford, from 1607 to 1618. There she established her principal residence, surrounding herself with cultivated companionship including that of her cousin Lady Markham and Cecilia Bulstrode. Donne wrote funeral elegies on the respective deaths of these two ladies in May and August 1609. He is thought to have written the present poem around 1608–10.

'Blasted with Sighes and surrounded with Teares' is a highly original variation on a stock theme of Petrarchan love lyric: the contrast between the pleasurable beauty of nature in springtime and the misery of the lover whose lady is unkind. In the case of social unequals such as Lady Bedford and Donne, any poetic projection of a lover–beloved relationship required nuance, indirection, and sublimated passion. During the reign of Elizabeth I, a number of prominent courtiers practised this genre of oblique poetic courtship in addresses to the queen. Robbins gives examples (*Complete Poems*, 253).

As in the other Group 1 manuscripts, Dowden's text lacks spacing between the three nine-line stanzas that comprise this poem. Line indentation provides some guidance to the verse form for ll. 1–9, but with l. 12, this patterning ceases to hold. Thereafter, the accumulating sequence of lines of different lengths becomes more random, and Dowden, together with other Group 1 manuscripts, both loses track of the rhyme scheme and omits some phrasing in ll. 14–15 (see notes for ll. 10–17). These irregularities notwithstanding, the Dowden manuscript is reliable in most of its readings and ranks high among extant witnesses to the text of this exceptionally complex poem.

ll. 1–9.   *Blasted...surrounded with*: Blighted...swimming in. *The Spyder...Gall*: The spider was popularly thought to convert its food into a potent poison. *transubstantiates*: transforms one substance into another. The root sense of this technical theological term attached to the purported transformation of consecrated bread into the actual body of Christ in the Roman Catholic Mass. Donne's sardonic usage highlights the inversion performed by his love: it turns sweetness to bitterness. *Manna*: the miraculous bread-like particles sent by God from heaven to feed the hungry Israelites wandering in the desert (Exodus 16:14–15). *the Serpent*: the guise assumed by the Devil when he tempted Eve in Eden; and, in moral emblematics more generally, a signifier of male sexual arousal.

ll. 10–17.   *wholsommer...mee*: more conducive to my well-being. *Grave*: heavy. *But that...Place bee*: This is the faulty reading unique to Group 1 manuscripts. Groups 2 and 3 and *Poems*, 2nd edn, read: *But that I may not this disgrace | Indure, nor leave this garden, Love, let mee | Some senslesse peece of this Place bee*. *grone*: Lovers at this period were supposed to groan, as in Shakespeare, *Sonnets*, 131.6; 133.1. Mandrakes (plants with forked roots resembling a human groin) were supposed to groan or shriek when they were uprooted. *stone fountayne*: A more acceptable form for a lover to assume in Lady Bedford's garden, presumably at the centre of her plantings of trees and tracing of walkways that modelled the Ptolemaic universe (Roy Strong, *The Renaissance Garden in England* (1979), 120–1).

ll. 18–26.   *Christall Vyalls*: Small vessels made of a mineral believed to have the property of detecting treachery. *trye*: test. *O Perverse...kills me*: Although she is unlike all other women in being true, she is like them in not being what she seems, because *her Truth* is her fatal cruelty to her lover.

Epitaph, so titled in all Group 1 manuscripts ('Madam, That I might make your Cabinett my Tombe') [To the Countess of Bedford] (fols 115v–116r)

This poem hinging on the conceit of the speaker's being dead and buried is conjecturally dated to the early part of 1612. It was then that Donne brought upon himself Lady Bedford's displeasure at the extravagant praise he had lavished on the deceased Elizabeth Drury in his *Anniversaries*. A letter written to Goodyere in January 1612 sheds light on Donne's chastened spirits by way of a reference to his elopement with Anne More a decade earlier: 'If at last I must confess that I died ten years ago...though I died at a blow then when my courses were diverted, yet it will please me a little to have had a long funeral, and to have kept myself so long above ground without putrefaction' (*Letters*, 122).

ll. 1–6. *Cabinett*: box for storing letters. *farewell*: Editors adopt the variant reading 'funerall', but it is not obviously superior. Both alternatives are close in meaning. 'Last funeral' is also a tautology; 'Last farewell' is not. [*Others*]: The Group 1 manuscript reading 'Ô then' is manifestly deficient in sense and grammar, and requires emendation.

ll. 7–13. *Omnibus*: This subheading, found in Dowden and one other manuscript, signals the start of the epitaph text proper. Although its reflections and morality will prove to be Christian, the form traces to pagan antiquity. It is a first-person address from one who has been entombed along the open roadside (to avert pollution of dwellings by the decomposing corpse). The deceased speaks to the passerby—here, 'To All' (Latin *Omnibus*)—offering thoughts on mortality and asking for the goodwill of those who read the words engraved on the tomb. See Joshua K. Scodel, *The English Poetic Epitaph* (1991), chap. 1. [*ch*]*oyce*: Dowden and other Group 1 manuscripts read 'Joyce', a penslip whose sound similarity enables the reading 'choice' to be retrieved. *Thou...art nowe*: Likening of the state of the living to the rotting flesh of the dead and buried was a common moral and religious motif in the arts of Jacobean England, where it functioned as a *memento mori* (reminder of the eventual fate of all humans). *ripe*: ripen.

ll. 14–24. *Parentes...Earth*: By engendering our bodies. *soules...Glasse*: Our souls are our imperceptible part, transparency here standing for what cannot be seen in itself. *Here...lye*: Alchemical transmutation into the purest of earthly substances figures ultimate redemption and union with God. *wee Ourselves...destroy*: Donne's fascination with self-destruction extended well beyond the consequences of his elopement into his later pastoral career. Meditation 12 of his *Devotions* surveys a range of negative human behaviours and drives the implication home: 'I am mine own executioner'. *miraculously*: The word choice is ironic: our self-destructiveness can subvert even the benevolent purposes of God. *Such Priviledges*: God's assurance of salvation, to be made good at the last judgement. *mend...mendest*: amend...amendest. *thincke...composd*: (1) note my mental and spiritual composure; (2) regard this verse of mine favourably as a composition. *last sick*: terminally ill.

*Valediction of the Booke, so titled in all Group 1 manuscripts; in Group 2
the title is A Valediction of the Booke ('Ile Tell thee now (Deare Love)
what thou sha[l]t doe') (fols 116 r–117v)*

On the basis of internal references, a date after 1602 has been proposed for this poem
of leave-taking—perhaps mid-1605, when Donne went abroad with Sir Walter Chute;
perhaps late 1611, when he accompanied Sir Robert and Lady Drury to France and
the Netherlands. Donne was a member of the Parliament of 1601, in which the royal
granting of monopolies, patents, and subsidies provoked outspoken discontent. The
claim that an Egyptian woman, Phantasia, composed Homer's works and deposited
them in a temple at Memphis seems to have been brought to the notice of Western
readers in Justus Lipsius's *De Bibliothecis Syntagma* (On the Arrangement of
Libraries) (1602).

ll. 1–9. *sha[l]t*: A penslip in Dowden drops a letter. *Eloyne*: send far away—a
         French loanword. *Sybills Glory*: The Cumaean Sibyl was famed for her
         prophetic powers, which she gained from possessing the books that held
         the secrets of human fate. *Her…allure:* Pindar's teacher, the Greek poet
         Corinna, bested him in a competition (Aelian, *Variae Historiae*, 13.25).
         allure: attract (notice) away. *[her]…lame*: Apollinaris Sidonius in *Epistulae*
         (Letters), 2.10.6, lists Lucan's wife, Polla Argentaria, among women who
         helped and inspired their husbands. Gardner observes that all three of the
         women here referred to—the Sibyl, Pindar's teacher, Lucan's wife—are
         explicitly lauded by François de Billon in his famous treatise on the supe-
         riority of women, *Le Fort inexpugnable de l'honneur du Sexe Feminin* (The
         Impregnable Fortress of the Honour of the Female Sex) (1555), 27–30 (*The
         Elegies and the Songs and Sonnets*, ed. Gardner, 192–3). *[her]*: Dowden lacks
         this pronoun. *her…name*: See the last sentence in this poem's headnote.
ll. 10–18. *those Myriades…Thee and Mee*: Letters between Donne and Anne More
         were likelier to have been written before marriage than after, for the pair
         were allowed to cohabit after Donne was briefly imprisoned. Of these alleg-
         edly numerous letters (*Myriades* means 'thousands'), none are known to
         survive. *Annalls*: year-by-year accounts. *Subliming*: a refining process in
         alchemy. *Scismatique* (schismatic): one who refuses to attend public wor-
         ship in the Church of England. *Grace*: divine favour.
ll. 19–27. *as Long Liv'd…forme*: Lasting for many ages, though not eternal. The
         Bible proclaimed that 'Heaven and Earth shall pass away' (Matthew 24:35);
         for Aristotle the heavens were eternal but the Earth mutable (*On the
         Heavens*, 1.9.277b27). *thys all-grævëd…Idiome*: The book of the lovers'
         love will be both a mysterious and a secret text, all of it engraved because it
         has been composed in code or symbols, not in an existing alphabet or lan-
         guage. *Wee…Instruments*: Only the lovers can interpret this book, for only
         they can read it. *Vandalls, and Goths*: Germanic tribes infamous for their
         destructive invasions of Europe in late antiquity. *Learning…Verse*: The
         speaker does not explain how others *might* come to *Learne* even more than

they already know about their own special competences from the lovers' encrypted book. He simply affirms that they would be able to do so.

ll. 28–36.   *Here Loves Devines...fygure ytt*: This stanza offers a summary of Donne's philosophy of love as dependent on both soul and body for its verification and expression. *abstract*: immaterial, ideal. *a Convenient Type*: an appropriate image.

ll. 37–45.   *Here...are Ours*: Conceivably there is a trace here of Donne's legal struggle with his father-in-law, Sir George More, to prevent annulment of his marriage in 1602; see Bald, *Donne: A Life*, 137–9. *Prerogative...Prerogative*: Male lovers' rightful possessions are consumed when Love, as sovereign, transfers these rights to women. Even as they demand sizeable amounts of affection and attention, women abandon lovers who trust them, and cite as justification their *Honor* or their *Conscience*—fabrications (*Chimeraes*) as lacking in truth or substance as they or their own claimed rights are.

ll. 46–54.   *deadly wounds*: is fatal to. *In both...dares tell*: In both love and statecraft as ordinarily understood and practised, excellence is judged by present success and by a reputation for strength—or seeming to be strong. *In this...Alchimye*: Ordinary lovers and statesmen will completely miss the fineness and rarity of these two lovers' love; instead, they will claim that the lovers' book authorizes their own dubious aims and practices.

ll. 55–63.   *vent*: express. *he removes...takes*: he who measures great altitudes positions himself at a distance to do so. *To take...brightest*: A given latitude could be determined by measuring its distance from the zenith of a star whose distance from the equator was already known. *to conclude...bee?*: Estimating longitude by noting the time intervals between successive lunar eclipses at different locations was a method that yielded imprecise results; the more reliable method was to reckon with the physical distances between occurrences of successive lunar eclipses at different locations. Donne's *marke when and where* takes both methods into account, but the reasoning is finally poetic, not scientific. *Darke Ecclipses* (periods of total invisibility) are apt images for the possible effects of absence on the durability of love.

'Good wee must Love, and m[u]st hate ill', first titled Communitie in Poems, 2nd edn (fols 117v–118r)

In one manuscript of Donne's poems, this lyric is grouped with others as 'Songs which were made to certain airs which were made before'. The implication of a date in the early to mid-1590s while Donne was a law student at Lincoln's Inn is strengthened by the cynical perspective on women developed through play with formal logic. The speaker throughout applies generalizations about women to particular women. He also posits, only to collapse them into the same conclusion, two variants of a disjunctive syllogism. The first, the simpler one, runs: We must love good, and we must hate ill, but we may make use of indifferent things; women are neither good nor ill, but indifferent; Therefore, we men must neither love nor hate women, but we may use them sexually. The second, more complicated, runs: If women were good, they would be seen to be good; if women were bad, they would be seen to cause harm to themselves and others; but women are neither perceived as good nor as causing harm to themselves or others; therefore they must be indifferent, and we men may use them sexually.

ll. 1–6.   *m[u]st*: Dowden reads 'most'—a penslip. *indifferent*: of neutral disposition or effect—a sense no longer current. *prove*: try. This first stanza develops the major premise of the first of the lyric's disjunctive syllogisms.

11. 7–12.   *rests*: remains. This second stanza develops the middle or minor premise and the conclusion of the first disjunctive syllogism.

ll. 13–18.   *[as]*: Dowden omits this conjunctive particle. *betrays*: exposes. *Bad... wast*: Aquinas (*Summa Theologica*, 2.1.85.4) maintains that sin diminishes the good aspects of natural inclination and entirely eliminates those of virtuous action. This third stanza develops the major premise and the two middle premises of the second disjunctive syllogism.

ll. 19–23.   *They... Ours*: A calculated reduction to analogy. *meate*: food. *eate*: eaten.

'Spring', so titled in Group 1 manuscripts, titled 'Loves Growth' in Group 2 manuscripts and Poems, *1st and 2nd edns ('I scarce beleave my Love to be so pure') (fols 118r–v)*

Critics inclined to find a pun on Anne More's name in l. 8 (but not in ll. 6, 21) conjecture a date of around 1600 for this poem.

ll. 1–13.   *pure*: simple and unmixed, and therefore not subject to change (especially in intensity of desire). *Vicissitude*: change. *quintessence*: substance distilled to a state of absolute purity by alchemical processes. *[else]*: Dowden's faulty reading, 'these', is not borne out by other manuscripts.

ll. 15–28.   *eminent*: prominent, lofty. *in the Firmament... showne*: Donne the preacher would elaborate: 'The Sun does not enlighten the Stars of the Firmament merely for an Ornament... but that, by the reflection of those Stars, his beams might be cast into some places to which, by a direct Emanation from himself, those beams would not have come' (*Sermons*, 8.243). *Loves awakened roote*: The image has phallic undertones. *Concentrique*: The woman is the centre and the unifying reference point of the speaker's universe, as the Earth was in the Ptolemaic system. *Princes... Peace*: At certain critical junctures—e.g., going to war—Parliament granted English monarchs the right to levy special additional taxes (subsidies) from landholders based on the valuation of their properties. *abate*: lessen.

'Love, Any Devill else but you', titled 'Loves Exchange' in Group 2 manuscripts, and in Poems, *1st and 2nd edns (fols 118v–119r)*

Critics differ over the dating of this poem. The dense legal vocabulary leads Robbins to propose the early to mid-1590s (*Complete Poems*, 215). Gardner focuses more narrowly on the references to 'A *Non Obstante*' and 'Prerogatives' (ll. 11–12) and favours a later date: 'The question was a burning one in the Parliament of 1597–8 and the struggle against patents and monopolies came to a climax in the Parliament of 1601 in which Donne sat' (*The Elegies and the Songs and Sonnets*, 168).

ll. 1–7. *Love, Any Devill…too*: The speaker appropriates Augustine's idea that devils are pagan gods (*De civitate Dei* [On the City of God], 7.13). He adds to this the idea of selling one's soul to the Devil in exchange for the granting of one's desires—the subject of Marlowe's *Doctor Faustus* (performed *c.*1588, published 1604)—and the popular belief that devils had specialties: here, *Riming, Huntsmanship and Play. I have…more*: The courtiers are represented as forfeiting their souls to gain mastery of arts; the speaker has given Love both his soul and body, but has nothing in return. *Lowly, Lower*: Wordplay heightens the speaker's paradoxical situation: by being humble (proper conduct towards his lady), he has become yet more base in her regard.

ll. 8–15. *dispensation*: special exemption from a requirement. *sue*: petition. *Non Obstante*: exemption from some law, granted by the Crown in a writ beginning with this Latin phrase meaning 'there being no hindrance'. *Prerogatives*: rights, usually those of a monarch, to override the law. *forsweare*: break a vow. *Minion*: darling, favourite. *Give…weakenes*: There may be a touch of parody: a devout Christian desired nothing more than a share in Christ's travails and sufferings.

ll. 22–7. *th*[*ou*]' *art*: Dowden reads 'th' art'. *I would…trust*: I would not take seriously your first stirrings of love in me. *Small…condition not*: Alberico Gentili, an Italian Protestant exile who became a professor of law at Oxford, stated that once artillery began to bombard a weakly defended place, the question of possible terms of surrender could no longer arise (*De Jure Belli* [On the Law of War] (1588), 2.16–17). *withstand*: stand, maintain one's position—the reading of Dowden and the other Group 1 manuscripts. Editors consistently prefer the Group 2 reading 'will stand' but the two verbs are close enough in sense to make emendation unnecessary. *Article for grace*: stipulate favourable concessions to be made.

ll. 32–5. *vow'd men*: monks under a vow of celibacy. *store*: fill up. *Mynes…before*: Love is credited with powers far superior to the sun's generative workings within the Earth in occult philosophy. Donne the preacher would elaborate: 'Precious stones are [dew drops] refined by the sun…When by long lying, they have…breathed out all their gross matter, and received another concoction from the sun, then they become precious in the eye and estimation of men' (*Sermons*, 3.372). *Mynes*: minerals.

l. 42. *Rackt…Anatomyes*: Corpses of those who had been tortured on the rack were considered unsuitable for anatomical dissection because they had lost their overall shape and proportions.

'Some man unworthy to be Possessor', first titled 'Song. Confined Love' in Poems, 2nd edn (fol. 119v)

In one manuscript of Donne's poems, this lyric is grouped with others as 'Songs which were made to certain airs which were made before'. Like 'Now Thou hast Lov'd mee one whole day' ('Woman's Constancy') and other lyrics defending sexual freedom, this one may belong to the early to mid-1590s. It distinguishes itself in one notable respect: the speaker is a self-possessed, articulate woman. There is no known musical setting for this text.

ll. 9–21.   *list*: like. *chidden*: chided, reproached. *abroad*: elsewhere than home. *did*: The reading of Dowden and other Group 1 manuscripts as well as a number of other manuscripts; editors emend to 'do'. *Jointures*: marriage settlements. *deale with All*: The reading of all manuscripts and early editions makes perfect sense in context. Editors unnecessarily emend to 'deal withall'—meaning 'use for the purpose of trade'. *Good is... possesse*: The speaker offers a colloquial counterpart to Aristotle, who maintains that the highest good must be that which is sought by all (*Nicomachean Ethics*, 7.13.1153b25; 10.2.1172b9). *doth... greedynesse*: is diminished by extreme possessiveness.

'The Dreame' ('*Deare Love, for nothing lesse than Thee*'), titled 'Dreame' in three manuscripts (fols 120r–v)

Critics differ over dating this poem. Robbins emphasizes the Ovidian origins of the theme of a dream interrupted and its purely physical projected completion (*Amores*, 1.5), suggesting that 'The Dreame' belongs to the early phase of Donne's poetic career (*Complete Poems*, 166). Gardner stresses the similarities with 'Image of her whom I love, more than Shee'—and, indeed, manuscript sources give the title 'The Dreame' to both lyrics. She highlights shared neo-Platonic elements that, in her view, would date both poems after Donne's marriage to Anne More (*The Elegies and the Songs and Sonnets*, 209).

ll. 2–8.   *thys happy Dreame... Fantasye*: Cf. 'Image of her whom I love', ll. 9–10. *so Truth*: so real because entirely composed of truth itself. *thoughts... Truth*: Cf. 'Image of her whom I love', l. 13. *Historyes*: factual accounts.

ll. 11–20. *As Lightnings... wakd me*: Donne the preacher would note, 'A sudden light brought into a room doth awaken some men, but yet a noise does it better' (*Sermons*, 9:366). *an Angell*: a member of the lowest of the three orders of celestial beings in God's service—hence, an intermediary between God and humankind. *But... Angells art*: Angels were not supposed to be able to read minds as God could; at best they might intuit thoughts from outward behaviour (Aquinas, *Summa Theologica*, 1.57.4). *yt could... but Thee*: *Profanenes* because of the divine capacities she has demonstrated in knowing the speaker's *Thoughts*.

ll. 21–30. *Thee Thee*: you to be really you. *rising*: the beloved's getting up out of bed, to depart. *pure, and brave*: perfect, and courageous (in showing itself for what it is). *goest to Come... Else will Dye*: Puns on orgasm. *will Dye*. A majority of manuscripts have the arguably superior reading 'would die', meaning 'want to have sex with his beloved'. But *will Dye* also makes sense: either the speaker *Will dreame that hope agayne* (of sexual intimacy with his beloved) *but Else will Dye* (or he will actually have that intimacy with her).

'A Valediction' ('Lett me poure forth'), so titled in all manuscripts and thus possibly authorial; titled 'A Valediction: Of Weeping' in Poems, 1st edn (fols 120v–121r)

The farewell that occasioned this poignant lyric cannot be determined. Its point of departure is the belief that an image reflected in a tear portends death by drowning. At first the lover weeps and attempts to justify indulging in grief, but when his beloved begins to weep too (l. 16), he changes his mood and course. The poem becomes a prohibition of tears, employing arguments resembling those advanced in 'Sweetest Love I doe not goe'. Robbins observes that the successive images for tears—coins, fruits, emblems, worlds, foundations, raindrops, seas—have analogues in a tradition of poems on Mary Magdalen (*Complete Poems*, 274).

ll. 3–9.   *coynes*: A frequent standard of value in Donne. *Pregnant of*: produced by—a sense no longer current. *Embleames of more*: Taken by some as a pun on Anne More's name. *that thou falls*: An obscure turn of phrase that may refer to the belief that a tear is a portent of drowning (with the beloved reflected here in the lover's tear) or it may hint at the possibility of the beloved's unfaithfulness, which would reduce their relationship to *Nothing . . . when on a diverse shore*.

ll. 10–17.   The second stanza elucidates l. 9. As a globe-maker arranges and then pastes segments of paper imprinted with the shapes of the continents *On a round Ball* of wood to make a model of the whole Earth, so the beloved's reflection in his tears models the *all* that they are to each other. The merging of her tears with his will *overflowe | This worlde* that they are to each other, and *dissolve* his *heaven*—an initially ambiguous reference—in an encompassing flood.

ll. 19–27.   The image of the beloved as the *Moone* setting tides of tears in motion confirms her as the ruling body of the lover's *heaven*, exercising the power of life or death over him in her envisaged influence on forces of nature: *Drawe not up seas, . . . forbeare | To teach the Sea . . . Lett not the Winde | Example finde. purposeth*: intends to. *Since thou . . . others death*: The two concluding lines combine the prevalent period idea that lovers are one soul in two bodies with another popular idea that a sigh consumed a drop of blood.

'Mummye', the title in the manuscripts, retitled 'Love's Alchemy' in Poems, 1st and 2nd edns ('Some that have deeper digg'd Loves Myne than I') (fols 121r–v)

There is no likelihood of determining the date of this deeply disillusioned lyric. The crude physicality of its images of the female body recalls the youthful Elegy: 'On Loves Progresse'. But the intricate stanzaic form exhibits closer affinities with the love lyrics Donne wrote after 1601, and this is where Gardner groups this poem without explanation (*The Elegies and the Songs and Sonnets*, 81, 211).

ll. 1–12.   *deeper . . . Myne*: Francis Bacon cites Democritus as saying 'that the truth of nature lieth hid in certain deep mines and caves' (*Advancement of Learning*,

2.7). Donne makes prospectors and alchemists the natural philosophers of love. *Loves Myne*... *Centrique happines*: Allusions to the vagina. *Chymique*: alchemist. *th' Elixar*: a quintessence or perfectly pure substance in alchemy. *Pregnant Pot*: the vessel used by the alchemist in his distillations and trans-mutations—with submerged connotations of the uterus. *a*... *Night*: a night both cold and short.

ll. 13–24.   *thrift*: means of thriving, occupation. *thys vaine Bubbles shadowe*: this attrac-tive but fleeting and insubstantial thing—sexual intercourse with a woman. *my Man*: my manservant. *the Short*... *Play*: the soon-ended ridiculousness of a bridegroom's role. *he in her Angelique finds*: An ambiguous phrase that seems to mean that he finds her to have an angel-like mind, but could mean that he, angel-like and thus superior, finds a mind in her, but an inferior one. *justly*: rightly, justifiably. *that dayes*... *Minstrallsey*: raucous music of a wedding celebration. *the Spheares*: the ethereal music of the cosmos. *Mummye*: Dead bodies preserved in bitumen, claimed by Paracelsus and his followers to have medicinal value. The theory was that a dead body retained its 'balsam'—an oily, softly penetrating substance natural to all organic beings, and credited with preserving health. Sick patients ingested bits of mummy to restore their vitality. The grudging conclusion of the poem may be paraphrased as follows: You will find by sexually possessing a woman that she is only a mindless lump of dead flesh; yet if she has *Sweetnes* and *Witt*, their effects can be enlivening.

'The Flea', so titled in Group *1* and Group *3* manuscripts and in Poems, *1st and 2nd edns ('Marke but thys flea, and marke in thys')* *(fols 121v–122r)*

All across Europe in the sixteenth century, the flea was a popular subject for erotic verse. The chief model was the late medieval 'Carmen de Pulice' (Song of the Flea), probably written by Ofilius Sergianus but ascribed to Ovid, in which the poet envies the liberties the flea takes with his mistress's body and desires to be transformed into one. In French especially, punning on 'puce' (flea), 'pucelle' (maiden), and 'pucelage' (virginity) yielded an abundance of versified wit. This climaxed in a published collec-tion of more than fifty poems titled *La Puce de Madame des Roches* (Madame des Roches's Flea) (1582); its point of departure was the poet Etienne Pasquier's observa-tion of a flea on the bosom of a certain Mademoiselle Catherine while visiting Madame des Roches in 1579.

Poems on fleas were of two kinds: either the poet wished to be a flea and take advantage of its liberties or he envied the flea its death at his mistress's hands and on her bosom. Donne transforms what had become a stale subject by having the flea bite both the speaker and his mistress, thus making it an image of actively desired love union rather than a vehicle of erotic yearning. Lavishly resorting to fallacious logic, he also injects a dramatic argument into what, in other poets' handling, was often no more than a flight of fancy or a display of ingenuity. The frequency of 'The Flea' in seventeenth-century man-uscript collections and its placement at the head of the 'Songs and Sonnets' section of the second edition of *Poems* suggest that it was one of Donne's most admired love lyrics.

ll. 1–7.   *Marke but*: Paltry as it is, take note of. *marke in thys...mee, ys*: The speaker
            flouts formal logic by treating the terms of his analogy—the flea's biting
            and the taking of the woman's virginity—as having equal significance and
            by treating literal and figurative references as equivalent. Tonal ambiguity
            makes for complexity: is the speaker arguing cynically, underestimating the
            woman's intelligence and judgement, or is he arguing playfully, well aware
            that they can both see through his formulations and inferences? *in thys
            flea...made of two*: Both Aristotle and Galen held that eggs and sperm con-
            sisted of the best and purest blood of the female and the male, and that the
            two bloods mingled when a foetus was conceived. *thys...would doe*: We are
            not aiming to make you pregnant.

ll. 10–18. *Oh stay...Temple ys*: That the flea has bitten both the speaker and the
            woman emerges only in the course of the ongoing argument that the flea's
            acts of mingling and union are entirely legitimate. *Cloystred*: enclosed.
            Use...kill mee: Your usual treatment of me keeps you in form to kill me
            literally (by rejection). *Sacriledge*: Violation of a sacred obligation. This
            extravagant charge hinges on the earlier assertion that the flea has served
            the speaker and the woman as a *marryage Temple*.

'The Curse', so titled in all sources ('Who ever guesses, thinckes, or dreames he knowes') (fols 122r–v)

As a free-standing poetic genre, the curse originated in classical antiquity with the
Greek poets Archilochus and Callimachus; in the love elegies of Propertius (4.5.1–4,
75–8) and Ovid (*Amores*, 1.12) particular instances are put in the mouths of thwarted
suitors. George Puttenham colourfully characterized the psychological satisfaction to
be had from the genre as 'a manner of...cursing and banning of the parties, and wish-
ing all evil to alight upon them, and though it never...happened, yet was it great
easement to the boiling stomach' (*Arte of English Poesie* (1589), 1.29).

   Donne combines the classical genre with a stock medieval theme: cursing that bane
of the lover, the loose-tongued gossiper who spreads rumour and surmise. 'The
Curse' is likely to have been composed during his student days at Lincoln's Inn. Its
tone of bravado has marked affinities with that of such elegies as 'The Bracelet', 'The
Perfume', and 'Jealousy', while its law jargon and final misogynistic stroke bolster the
sense that this poem is early work.

ll. 3–15.   *His only...Love dispose*: May his money only, and only the money he has,
            incline some unpromising woman to love him. *Forsweare...sworne*: Deny
            on oath the love he swore to her. *With feare...torne*: Torn between fear of
            losing her and shame at getting her. *fame*: his reputation. *[that]*: Dowden
            accidently omits the needed conjunction. *Scarceness*: poverty. *For Land*: for
            lack of land.

ll. 17–24. *May he dreame...dye*: In 1352 it was made capital treason in England even
            to imagine the death of a king, queen, or heir to the throne, although sup-
            porting evidence of words or actions might be required. The scope of the
            treason law was repeatedly extended in the sixteenth century. *[he]*: Omitted

in Dowden. *Parasites*: persons with self-interested motives who wangle hospitality—here, specifically, Jewish money-lenders. *at the Last...bread*: finally convert to Judaism so that he can borrow money to eat.

ll. 25–9. *The Venom...Stepdames*: It was popularly believed that later wives of husbands hated the children of earlier ones. *interwish*: wish each other— Donne's coinage. *Mynes*: minerals. *All ill...spake*: The Old Testament books of Isaiah, Jeremiah, Ezekiel, Zechariah, and Malachi all contain instances of solemn curses pronounced in God's name. *annexed...Scedules*: supplemental information appended on separate pieces of paper—a technical legal phrase.

'The Extasye', so titled in Group 1 and Group 3 manuscripts and in Poems, 1st edn ('Where like a Pillowe on a Bed') (fols 122v–124v)

It is generally agreed that 'The Extasye' is one of Donne's later love lyrics, probably written around 1610–14. His other uses of the word 'ecstasy' all occur in poems from those years: 'A Funerall Elegie', *Second Anniversary*, 'To the Honorable Lady, the Lady Carey, and Mrs Essex Riche, from Amiens', 'Elegy on Prince Henry', and 'Obsequies to the Lord Harrington'. A further verbal link occurs in one of the regular Tuesday letters Donne wrote to Goodyere, subscribed 'From *Mitcham*, my close prison ever since I saw you, 9 Octob.' (this date was a Tuesday in 1610). Donne confides to his closest friend: 'I make account that the writing of letters, when it is with any seriousness, is a kind of ecstasy, and a departure and secession and suspension of the soul, which doth then communicate itself to two bodies' (*Letters*, 11).

There is critical agreement likewise regarding the genre of 'The Extasye'. It belongs to an English tradition exemplified by the Eighth Song, 'In a grove most rich of shade', in Sir Philip Sidney's sonnet sequence, *Astrophil and Stella* (1591); by Fulke Greville's Sonnet 75 in his sequence, *Caelica*; and by Sir Edward Herbert's 'Ode upon a Question moved, Whether Love should continue for ever?' The shared features of these poems, all in simple verse forms, include a May landscape in which lovers walk, a period of silent communication, and a long, intellectually intricate exchange on love (George Williamson, 'The Convention of *The Extasie*', in *Seventeenth-Century Contexts* (1961)). Donne turns the exchange into a *Dialogue of One* that articulates the neo-Platonic philosophy of his principal source, which Helen Gardner in *The Elegies and the Songs and Sonnets*, 259–65, has shown to be Ebreo's *Dialoghi d'Amore* (1535)— also the principal source for Donne's 'Image of her whom I love'.

'The Extasye' has a three-part structure: (1) the setting of the scene and the placing of the lovers within it, spoken in the single voice of the lover to his beloved (stanzas 1–5); (2) a disquisition on the metaphysics of love, spoken by the lover on behalf of his and his beloved's souls out of a consonance so perfect (ecstasy) that no imagined over-hearer could distinguish *which Soule spake* (stanzas 6–12); (3) the lover's summons to his and his beloved's suspended souls to return to their bodies, with further reflection on the soul–body integration that defines our nature as human beings and the nature of human love. These truths the lover and his beloved can and will exemplify *So | Weake men, on Love reveald may looke* and *some Lover*, imagined as having overheard all, will recognize for what it is—love between two human beings in a perfect state of realization and equilibrium (stanzas 13–18).

The imagined presence of this third party in 'The Extasye', variously characterized as one who understands *Soules Language* and *some Lover* (ll. 22, 73), has perennially troubled readers and critics. Robbins has offered the best perspective to date—that this figure, 'a fellow-intellectual with a male point of view', may personify Donne's appreciation of Sir Edward Herbert's poetic interest and competence in the philosophy of love (*Complete Poems*, 170).

ll. 1–3. *like a Pillowe . . . reclyning head*: Specifics of the open-air setting are charged with metaphorical immediacy. *Pregnant*: fruitful, capable of producing vegetation—a no longer current sense. *Violetts . . . head*: The violet symbolized modesty and purity in English flower lore. Donne may have placed it in this context because its blossom has both a single and a double form, an apt eventual analogy (ll. 37–9) for the lovers' single and double souls.

ll. 5–8. *Our handes . . . balme*: The palms of the lovers' clasped hands are sweaty—a symptom of arousal. *Our Eyebeames . . . double string*: By contrast with the overt physicality of the lovers' hands, their eyes prompt an abstruse philosophical question in visual perception theory. Does sight proceed by extramission (beams from the eye striking the object) or by intramission (beams from the object imprinting an image on the eye)? Ebreo proposes to reconcile the two views. He says that the eye transmits beams to the object but that the representation of the object on the pupil is also necessary, and further, that the eye must direct its beam a second time to make the imprint on the pupil tally with the object of sight (*Dialoghi*, 215). Ebreo's redoubling motion of the eye may underlie Donne's formulations, *Eyebeames twisted* and *double string*.

ll. 9–12. *intergraft*: produce a living union by intertwining—Donne's coinage. *Was all the meanes . . . Propagatiön*: At this period, the image of oneself reflected in the pupils of another person was called a 'baby' from a pun on Latin *pupilla*, and the then common lovers' idiom, to 'look babies', referred to this visual phenomenon without any implication of 'making babies'.

ll. 15–27. *advance . . . state*: improve their condition; promote their interest. *like Sepulchral . . . lay*: like statues of a husband and wife entombed side by side, or unmoving like the recumbent statuary on tombs. *Soules Language*: As expressed by means of the lovers' eyes, hands, and bodily postures. *Concoction*: end-product of the alchemical refining of metals or minerals. Here the *new Concoction* would be the overhearer's refined and purified consciousness. Cf. *First Anniversary*, ll. 455–7, on the influence of Elizabeth Drury.

ll. 29–31. *Extasye*: The essential notion is the freeing of the soul from confinement in the body to obtain knowledge directly and immediately, without the use of the senses or discursive reason. Donne the preacher would offer this characterization of 'a belief of *extasie*, and *raptures*: That the body remaining upon the floore, or in the bed, the soul may be gone out to the contemplation of

heavenly things' (*Sermons*, 6:101). *what wee Love...not Sexe*: *Sexe* here is
sexual difference (male and female), not sexual intercourse; D. H. Lawrence
in 1929 is the *Oxford English Dictionary*'s earliest documented usage in the
latter sense. Ebreo's Philo teaches Sophia what is hidden from most
lovers—'what they love'. *Wee see...did move*: We recognize that we did not
perceive what impelled and attracted us. It was not sexual desire...but
'perfect love' born of reason and having for its objects the virtue, intelli-
gence, and beauty that we perceived in each other (*Dialoghi*, 56–7). Cf.
Donne's 'I have done one braver thinge' ('The Undertaking'/'Platonique
Love'), ll. 17–20. This poem immediately follows 'The Extasye' in the
Dowden manuscript.

ll. 35–40. *Love, these...and that*: Ebreo expounds the numerology of the neo-Pla-
tonic commonplace: 'Each one being transformed into the other becomes
two, at once lover, and beloved...so that each of them is twain, and both
together are one, or else four' (*Dialoghi*, 31, 260). This numerology infuses
the allegorized image of the *Violett transplant* in l. 37, which *Redobles...and
multiplyes* in *Strength, Color*, and *Size* when it is removed from a *poore and
skant* location to a more nurturing one.

ll. 41–8. *When Love...doth flowe*: Ebreo's Philo and Sophia come to see that love
has remixed their souls, uniting them to create a new, *abler Soule* that,
unlike separate and individual souls, has complete self-knowledge.
Interanimates: animates reciprocally or mutually—Donne's coinage.
Editors treat this form of the word, found in Dowden, other reliable man-
uscript sources, and *Poems*, 1st and 2nd edns, as inferior to the variant that
they print—'interinanimates'—which has the added virtue of supplying
an eighth syllable to the line. *Defectes...controules*: overcomes the short-
comings in separateness. *Wee then...and made*: The lovers, as constituted
by *thys new Soule*, recognize its and their own essential nature: they are
themselves immortal (*Soules, whom no Change can invade*) and their love
union, correspondingly, will continue forever. *Atomi* (atoms): indivisible
particles.

ll. 50–6. *Our bodyes...the Spheare*: With the recognition that their love is beyond
change, the lovers' ecstasy reaches its climax. Unless they are to pass out of
this life altogether, they must now return to their bodies. Ebreo's Philo
addresses Sophia: 'My affection and love have transformed me into
you,...in order that I, your lover, may form but a single person with you,
my beloved, and equal love may make of our two souls one, which may
likewise vivify and inform our two bodies' (*Dialoghi*, 57). Elsewhere Philo
discourses on the love that the intelligences have for the spheres that they
govern in the Ptolemaic conception of the universe (*Dialoghi*, 189–90). *con-
vay*: lead, conduct while accompanying—senses no longer current.
Yeilded...but Allay: The lovers' bodies surrendered their inferior, sensory
souls of movement and perception to a superior one, *thys new Soule* issuing
from the lovers' souls met in ecstasy. In this poem, bodies are valued less
than souls, but bodies remain necessary: *Nor are...but Allay*: The image is

that of combining a metal, such as gold, with an alloy to make it more dura-
ble and resistant to wear. *drosse*: dregs of molten metal. *Allay*: a beneficial
additive.

ll. 57–64. *On Man...the Ayre*: Paracelsus maintained that the influence of the stars was
mediated by the air as a mixture of their smell, smoke, or sweat (*Paramirum*
(1589), 1.8). *our blood...as yt can*: Donne the preacher would elaborate: 'In
our natural persons, the body and soul do not make a perfect man...except
our spirits (which are the active part of the blood) do fit this body and soul for
one anothers working' (*Sermons*, 6:128). *such fingers...makes Us man*: Donne
the preacher would again elaborate: 'In the constitution and making of a
natural man,...the union of these two [soul and body] makes up the man;
the spirits in a man, which are the thin and active part of the blood, and so
are of a kind of middle nature...doe the office, to unite and aply the facul-
ties of the soul to the organs of the body, and so there is a man' (*Sermons*,
2.261–2). *need*: are needed.

ll. 65–8. *So must... Facultyes*: Souls, for their part, must condescend to the body's
affections and faculties so that the organs of sense may be of service to
language and thought. Ebreo's Philo teaches Sophia that the mind 'con-
trols the senses and directs the voluntary movements of men...For this
purpose it must issue from within the body to its external parts and to the
organs of sense and movement in order that man may approach the objects
of sense in the world around him, and it is then that we are able to think at
the same time as we see, hear, and speak' (*Dialoghi*, 201). *Else, a Greate
Prince...lyes*: Philo teaches Sophia that a soul that fails to inform and
direct the activities of the body also fails in its divinely appointed functions
'rightly to govern the body' and to take 'intellectual life and knowledge and
the light of God down from the upper world of eternity to the lower world
of decay' and thus to realize the unity of the universe (*Dialoghi*, 189–90). If
the soul does not animate the body in all its parts, as it is appointed to do,
the soul is imprisoned in a carcass instead of reigning in its kingdom. As
Gardner observes, 'Donne is contrasting the Platonic view of the soul
imprisoned in the flesh [*Phaedo*, 82d–e] with the Aristotelian conception of
the union of the soul and body in man. A prince is no prince if he does not
rule his kingdom, and a kingdom without a prince is a chaos' (*The Elegies
and the Songs and Sonnets*, 265).

ll. 69–76. *To' our Bodyes... looke*: This newly added motive for the lovers to resume
their bodies and their lives in the world may have been suggested to Donne
by Philo's extended teaching of Sophia. As Robbins notes, 'most if not all
of Donne's matter seems to derive solely from the male speaker of Leone
Ebreo's *Dialoghi d' Amore*' (*Complete Poems*, 181). *Lett him...to Bodyes gon*:
The change will be small even if and when the lovers have sexual inter-
course, because it will issue from their fully integrated understanding and
impulsions. As Philo instructs Sophia, 'Equal love may make of our two
souls one, which may likewise vivify and inform our two bodies. The sen-
sual element in this desire excites a longing for physical union, that the

union of bodies may correspond to the unity of spirits wholly compenetrating each other' (*Dialoghi*, 57).

'I have done one braver thinge', titled 'Platonique Love' in Group 2 manuscripts, and 'The Undertaking' in Poems, *2nd edn (fols 124v–125r)*

This lyric is one of only two by Donne on the subject of Platonic love in the commonly understood sense of this phrase. The allusion to *Specular Stone* in ll. 5–8 has its source in Panciroli's *Rerum Memorabilium Libri Duo* (Two Books of Remarkable Things) (1599). The image recurs in a verse letter to Lady Bedford—'You teach, though we learn not, a thing unknown | To our late times: the use of specular stone, | Through which all things within without were shown' ('Honor is so sublime perfectiön', ll. 28–30; this poem is thought to date to 1609–11). Alternatively, the title 'Platonique Love' given to this lyric in Group 2 manuscripts and its positioning immediately after 'The Extasye' in Dowden and other Group 1 manuscripts can plausibly be construed as links with Sir Edward Herbert's poems on the same subject. Either connection, with Bedford or Herbert, comports with a date around 1611.

ll. 1–3.   *braver*: finer, more admirable. *all the Worthyes*: This group of nine figures from classical, biblical, and medieval history, distinguished for their martial prowess, became popular subjects in poetry and the visual arts. They usually included Hector, Alexander the Great, Julius Caesar, Joshua, David, Judas Maccabeus, King Arthur, Charlemagne, and Godfrey of Bouillon. Donne's point is one that Ovid had made: love is superior to war.

ll. 6–11.   *Skill*: art of cutting. *Specular Stone*: Panciroli's *Rerum Memorabilium Libri Duo*, 1.32, refers to Pliny's description of this as the material with which Nero built the temple of Fortune at Rome, adding that anyone inside the temple could be seen by those outside it, and ending by saying that specular stone is unknown today. Donne has a reference to '*Pancirollo*' and a marginal note 'De rebus nuper inventis' (On things recently found out) in the Latin version of *Ignatius His Conclave* (1611). Later he would remark in a sermon: 'The *heathen* served their Gods...where they could, in Temples made of *Specular stone*, that was transparent as glasse, or crystall, so as they which walked without in the streets, might see all that was done within' (*Sermons*, 7.397). *stuff*: material.

ll. 16–22. *theyre oldest Clothes*: what they were born with, their 'birthday suit'. *Prophane*: irreverent, unbelieving. Cf. love figured as a sacred and concealed mystery in 'A Valediction: forbidding Mourning', ll. 7–8.

'Loves Deitye', the title in a wide range of manuscripts, suggesting it may be authorial ('I Long to talke with some Old Lovers Ghost') (fols 125r–v)

The refrain that concludes each stanza is a possible formal link with Donne's *Songs* of the 1590s. Also consistent with an earlier date are the speaker's disdain for Eros/Cupid as a powerful and prescriptive god of love, and the final twist that transforms a repeated complaint about unrequited love into a spurning of the ostensible beloved. But the references to *Prerogative* and *Purlewe* (ll. 16, 18) would have had most point in the early years of James I's reign. Thus dating remains uncertain. Sir John Suckling's 'Oh! for some honest Lovers ghost' is a conventional rejoinder to 'Loves Deitye' written in the 1630s.

ll. 2–7.　　　*the God of Love*: Eros or Cupid, personifying desire, whose mother was Aphrodite/Venus in classical mythology. *Thys God . . . letts it bee*: Imitating Zeus/Jove in his exercise of supreme authority (Homer, *Iliad*, 24.527–8), the god of love boldly asserts his own authority, and *Custome*—proverbially termed 'second nature'—sanctions this.

ll. 9–26.　　*in . . . Godhead*: while his divine status was still new. *Eaven flame*: equal, reciprocal passion. *indulgently*: favourably, freely. *fitt . . . Passives*: match those initiating action with those receiving the effects of action—subjects and objects, and by implication, desiring males with their counterparts, desiring females. *Correspondenc[i]e*: Dowden has a penslip, 'Correspondence'. *Moderne God*: latter-day, self-styled authority on love. *Hys*: Eros's/Cupid's. *Prerogative*: a ruler's absolute right. Elizabeth I's claim to be able to override common and statute law in awarding monopolies was disputed in the Parliament of 1601, in which Donne sat. Under James I, disputes of this kind increased in number and intensity. *Purlewe* (purlieu): A piece or tract of land on the border of a forest, a place where one is free to range. The concept became contested when James, in his passion for hunting, tried to recover for royal use lands that had been disafforested and cultivated since the thirteenth century. *She Loves before*: she has already given her love to someone else.

'Loves Dyett', so titled in Group 1 and Group 2 manuscripts and in Poems, *1st and 2nd edns ('To what a Cumbersome unwieldines') (fols 125v–126v)*

'Loves Dyett' shares with other presumed poems of Donne's student days at Lincoln's Inn the use of legal terms, a witty argumentative structure, and a cynical perspective on female constancy. But it is the speaker's sketch of how he spends his time (ll. 28–30) that most bolsters the supposition that this is an early poem.

ll. 6–8.　　　*indu[r]es*: Dowden, like other Group 1 manuscripts and *Poems*, 1st edn, has the faulty reading 'indues'. *had part*: had a share.

ll. 12–18.　　*sound*: trustworthy. *brind*: salted. *sweate*: A symptom of sexual arousal.

ll. 21–4.　　*And that that*: And as a result that. *Title*: right of possession. *Convayde*: transmitted, transferred—senses no longer current. *Entayle*: Settlement of a landed estate on a number of persons in succession, so that it cannot be bequeathed at the pleasure of any one of them. The speaker reckons that he stands in fortieth place in the woman's favour.

ll. 25–9.　　*Bussard* (buzzard): A predatory bird considered too slow to catch anything but pigeons—hence, in a figurative sense, inept. *fawkners*: falconers. *springe*: flush out (possibly with sexual connotations). *sweare, write, sigh, weepe*: routine activities (with implications here of merely going through the motions).

'The Will', so titled in Group 1 manuscripts, in several other manuscripts, and in Poems, *1st and 2nd edns 'Before I sigh my Last gaspe, lett me breathe' (fols 126v–127v)*

Mock testaments had a long history from antiquity to the early modern era. One notable precursor of 'The Will' was the will of a pig that encouraged schoolboys to learn their Latin, mentioned by Jerome and subsequently by Erasmus in the preface to his *Moriae Encomium* (Praise of Folly) (1516), who then appended the text to his *Adagiae*, a much consulted collection of proverbs that went through many editions. Another relevant precursor was a passage (ll. 1825–44) in Thomas Nashe's *Summers Last Will and Testament* (*Works*, ed. McKerrow, 3:290–1).

A conspicuous oddity is the appearance of what is the third stanza in the often inferior texts of 'The Will' in Group 3 manuscripts, and the omission of this stanza from otherwise sound texts of the poem in Group 1 and Group 2 manuscripts. Atypically resorting to Group 3 and deviating from its usual reliance on Group 1 and Group 2, the first edition of *Poems* prints the third stanza while also introducing some local word changes to fit it into the structure of 'The Will'. Editors have variously attempted to account for the pattern of omissions and inclusions attaching to this stanza. Authorial suppression or censorship by another party has been suggested; so too has authorial revision—in which, it is supposed, what is now the second stanza of 'The Will' would have been replaced by this third stanza (*The Elegies and the Songs and Sonnets*, ed. Gardner, 175). But the oddity remains a puzzle. The Group 3 text of the third stanza reads as follows:

> My faith I give to Roman Catholiques;
> All my good works unto the Schismaticks
> Of Amsterdam; my best civility
> And Courtship, to an universitie;
> My modesty I give to souldiers bare;
>> My patiënce let gamesters share.
>> Thou Love taughtst mee, by making mee
> Love her that holds my love disparity,
> Onely to give to those that count my gifts indignity.

ll. 3–8.   *Argus*: the mythical hundred-eyed dog (Ovid, *Metamorphoses*, 1.625). *blynde*: a proverbial attribute of Cupid. *Fame*: Described as 'painted full of tongues' in Shakespeare, *2 Henry IV*, Induction. *To' Ambassadors...Eares*: Ambassadors of the period were required to memorize oral messages from and to their dispatching superiors and were also expected to gather useful information from hearsay. *twenty more*: twenty lovers in addition to the speaker.

ll. 10–18.   *Planetts*: Commonly referred to as 'wandering stars' because they moved in orbits. *My Truith...live*: My honesty to courtiers living by cunning and calculation, not unlike modern-day politicians. *Jesuits*: This Roman Catholic order was reviled in England (and by Donne in *Ignatius His Conclæve*) for devious dealings, treasonous plotting, and the practice of equivocation (giving deliberately misleading answers under oath). *Buffones* (buffoons): clowns, jesters, fools. *My Silence...been*: Returned travellers were often perceived as boastfully talkative about their experiences abroad; cf. Satire 1, ll. 100–3. *a Capuchin*: a Franciscan friar minor, who would be under a vow of poverty. *have an Incapacitye*: are incapable of making use of (the gift).

ll. 19–24.   *I give...frindes*: Former—by implication, false—friends will do just one thing with the little to no reputation the speaker has: shred it to bits. *Myne...Foes*: Implying that his enemies are already busily at work against him. *Schoolmen*: academic theologians and philosophers. *doubtfulness*: habit of asking questions and raising objections. *Physitions, or excesse*: alternative causes of feeling or being unwell. *my Companye*: my companions.

ll. 29–36.   *Phisicke bookes*: books of medicine. *Bedlam*: Bethlehem Hospital in London, where the insane were confined. *brazen Medalls*: antique Roman bronze coins (useless as present-day currency). *myne English tongue*: 'What thinke you of this English tongue?...It is a language that wyl do you good in England, but passe Dover it is worth nothing' (John Florio, *First Fruites* (1578), 50r). *Thou, Love...disproportiön*: Love, you disproportion my gifts by making me give them to those who can make no use of them, and by making me love a woman who thinks her mere friendship appropriate for a younger man (like the speaker). He implies that the woman should be consorting with older men if all she will offer is friendship.

ll. 39–41.   *all your beautyes... all your Graces*: The speaker credits the woman with considerable attractiveness as he takes what he represents as his definitive leave of her and of Love. In view of the placement of three lyrics variously thought to have Herbert family associations—'The Funerall', 'The Blossome', and 'The Primerose'—immediately after 'The Will' in the Dowden manuscript, could there be an intimation of Magdalen Herbert here?

'The Funerall', so titled in all sources. *'Who ever comes to shroude mee, doe not harme'* (fols *127v–128r*)

While agreeing that this lyric was probably written around 1607–10, critics have divided on the question whether Donne wrote it as a display piece for (as opposed to 'about') either Lady Bedford or Magdalen Herbert, both of whose patronage he was cultivating in those years. Donne was fond of imagining himself dead; besides 'The Funeral', see 'The Will', 'The Legacie', and 'The Dampe'.

ll. 3–8.   *That Subtill...Arme*: Hermia's father, Egeus, accuses Lysander of having stolen his daughter's affections 'With bracelets of thy hair...messengers | Of strong prevailment' (Shakespeare, *A Midsummer Night's Dream*, 1.1.32–5). *Subtill*: fine-textured. *Misterye...Signe*: Terminology normally applied to the bread and wine of Holy Communion in the Church of England. *Viceroy*: one who acts as governor in the name and by the authority of the supreme ruler. *Controule*: hold in place. *her Provinces*: areas ruled by the soul.

ll. 9–15.   *Sinewye thread*: system of nerves by which the brain transmitted commands. *These haires...grewe*: That hair grew in a heavenward direction was anciently taken as a sign of the soul's power over the body. The speaker credits the stronger positive influence he will receive from the hair of the woman's head—unless, he concedes, she has given him the bracelet of her hair as a painful reminder that she does not return his love.

ll. 19–24.   *Loves Martyre...Idolatree*: Conventional vocabulary in Petrarchan love worship. *humilitye*: the proper attitude of a Petrarchan lover. *braverye*: display of courage or daring. *save*: rescue from his pain by loving him. This is the reading in Dowden and the one favoured by editors. A number of other manuscripts and *Poems*, 1st and 2nd edns, read 'have'—a simpler, cruder variant.

'The Blossome', so titled in all sources ('Litle thinckst Thou, poore flowre') (fols 128r–v)

This lyric and the next three are linked both positively and negatively in manuscript tradition. They occur together in Group 1 and in *Poems*, 1st edn, but all four are missing from several otherwise reliable manuscripts that descend from different archetypes. It is intriguing to speculate that these four poems were grouped together in Donne's loose autograph papers, but there is no critical agreement regarding what the organizing principle might have been or even whether there was one.

At a basic level, these four poems display affinities in content: musings on imagery of flowers and of bodies in graves. Of greater interest is the question of the recipient or recipients for whom Donne might have intended these lyrics. While an early conjecture that Magdalen Herbert was the subject or addressee has been discredited, enlarging the focus to include both Magdalen Herbert and her son Edward as addressees has greater plausibility. The speaker of 'The Blossome' has made a visit to an unspecified country location some distance from London where he has already stayed *sixe or seven dayes* (l. 2) and will leave on the morrow. Assuming that this is a visit to Sir Edward Herbert, a fellow poet and wit superbly qualified to savour the worldly wisdom of 'The Blossome', the country-house setting would be Montgomery Castle in Wales, Herbert's principal residence after completing his studies in Oxford in 1601, and the address he gave for himself upon entering Gray's Inn in 1613 (*The Elegies and the Songs and Sonnets*, ed. Gardner, 256). Other critics have emphasized parallels of phrasing, imagery, and content found in 'The Blossome' and poems generally thought to date after 1601, including 'The Canonization', 'The Extasye', and the two Valedictions—'of the Booke' and 'forbidding Mourning'. Such fixing on particular poetic features has led interpretation and dating down divergent and finally inconclusive paths.

What can safely be said about 'The Blossome' is that a connection with Sir Edward Herbert remains plausible and that the poem's anti-Petrarchan stance is one repeatedly adopted by Donne. In particular, 'The Blossome' dismisses the obsequious worship of an inaccessible beloved by parodying the soulful address of the lover to his anguished heart exemplified in Petrarch (*Rime*, no. 242). In Donne's handling, the speaker's mind makes a lordly, condescending address to a heart so lacking in confidence that its shape wavers—first resembling a flower, then a bird seeking to nest, then the organ it is, but unrecognizable as such. In the end, the speaker's heart wordlessly capitulates to his worldly-wise mind: in twenty days the two will meet in London, where the mind will make a better disposition of the heart to a new beloved, on the mind's own terms, and these terms will be those of the beloved as well.

ll. 2–16.   *sixe...dayes*: The speaker implies that he has been on a week-long visit. *thinckst...forbidden, or forbidding Tree*: The woman whom the heart seeks is ambiguously characterized: she may belong to another lover and be off-limits, or she may be playing hard to get. Such ambiguity may indicate that the woman is a place-holder in a fiction whose real subject is the opposition between the speaker's mind and heart. *that Sunne*: a conventional Petrarchan image for the beloved.

ll. 27–37.   *A naked thincking Hart...Ghost*: Deep, sincere feeling without physical demonstration of it is simply unreal to a woman. *Practize*: sexual activity. *Fresher...fatt*: More energetic and in better physical condition. *with men*: The phrase is ambiguous between the gender-specific meaning and the general sense, 'in the presence of company'. *For Godsake*: Cf. the opening of 'The Canonization'.

'The Primerose', so titled in all sources ('Upon thys Primerose hyll') (fols 129r–v)

Gardner considers the expanded title of 'The Primerose' in *Poems*, 2nd edn (1635)— 'being at Mountgomery Castle, upon the hill, on which it is situate'—'too circumstantial not to be given credence'. She accordingly concludes that Donne wrote the poem while on a visit to Sir Edward Herbert in Wales (*The Elegies and the Songs and Sonnets*, 219). Elsewhere she remarks on the distinctive similarities between 'The Extasye' and 'The Primerose'. Both are 'exceptional among Donne's poems in setting a scene' and 'both use the structure of a flower for argument,...which connects them with Herbert's intellectual interests...The five-, four-, and six-petalled primroses and the single and double violet...are without parallel in other poems.' Taking the allusions in 'The Primerose' to *a terrestrial Galaxie* and *Small Starrs* (ll. 6–7) as references to a work of Galileo's published in 1610 which Donne cites elsewhere, and pairing these with Dowden's title, 'Goodfriday, 1613. Riding towards Wales', Gardner proposes to date 'The Primerose' to the spring of 1613 (*The Elegies and the Songs and Sonnets*, 257). Her proposal has met with general acceptance.

ll. 1–10.   *thys...hyll*: In his biography of Edward Herbert, John Aubrey located 'Primrose Hill' outside the precincts of Montgomery Castle to the south, and then cited the first line of 'The Primerose' (*Brief Lives*, ed. Andrew Clark (1898), 1.308). *Manna*: Exodus 16:14 describes the miraculous food sent by God to the Israelites as 'a small round thing...on the ground...when the dew that lay was gone up'. *a terrestrial Galaxie...Small Starrs*: Galileo's *Sidereus Nuncius* (Starry Messenger) (1610) announced that he had confirmed by telescopic observation that the Milky Way was composed of many faint stars. *a True-Love*: a primrose symbolizing true (faithful) love. True love was routinely associated with plants having either six or four petals/leaves. Since the primrose flower usually has five petals, trying to make this particular association work is problematic. *I see...woman bee*: The speaker brings to his search a prior association of women with the number five, drawn from number magic (see the note to l. 24). Now surrounded by five-petalled primroses which he takes to symbolize *woman*, he realizes that a primrose with either six or four petals, if he finds one, will prove a discrepant symbol for *woman* as the object of true love—it will be either *more, or lesse*.

ll. 18–20.   *Since there... Nature falsifyed*: The speaker turns away from his problem with faulty analogy—neither six nor four can symbolize a female *True-Love*—and instead confronts what he has observed, *Falshood in woman*. This he claims to be able to tolerate if the *Falshood* is not infidelity in her *Nature* but illusion created by her use of cosmetics (*Art*).

l. 24.   *thys Mysterious Number*: In number magic, five ranked highly: 'The number five is of no small force, for it consists of the first even, and the first odd, as of a Female, and Male; For an odd number is the Male and the even the Female...Therefore the number five is of no small perfection, or virtue...It is also the just middle of the universal number, viz. ten...and therefore it is called...the number of Wedlock, as also of justice' (Cornelius Agrippa, *Of Occult Philosophy*, trans. J. F. (1651), 188). *Ten is the furthest Number*. In number magic, ten as a 'triangular number' ($1 + 2 + 3 + 4$) was a widely acknowledged symbol of perfection. The speaker implicitly equates ten with *us men*. As in 'Ayre and Angells', ll. 26–8, so here: superiority is identified with the male, inferiority with the female.

ll. 25–30.   *if halfe Ten... halfe us men*: The meaning remains a matter of critical dispute between (a) each woman may take a man as her other half (in marriage), and thereby attain the perfection of ten; or (b) each woman may take half of the male sex as her sexual partners. The latter alternative involves an inference from a particular (*Each woman*) to a generality (*halfe us men*). *Or...since All | Numbers are odde or eaven...woemen may take Us All*: Again, the meaning is in dispute between (a) since women's number is five, which consists (in Agrippa's words) 'of the first even, and the first odd, as of a Female, and Male', women can lay claim to encompassing the whole of sexual complementarity (perhaps alluding to their capacity to give birth), or (b) having the whole within themselves, women may activate this sexual complementarity by taking all of the male sex as their sexual partners. The pairing of *woemen* in the last line with *Us All* involves the fallacy of treating a plural term and a universal term as logically equivalent.

'The Relique', so titled in all sources ('When my Grave is broke up agayne')
(fols 129v–130r)

Although connections with Magdalen and Edward Herbert have repeatedly been proposed, including the grouping of 'The Relique' in manuscripts with other poems having such connections, there is no conclusive textual evidence regarding the date or the addressee of this lyric. A link with Edward Herbert and a date *c*.1610–14 may be inferred from the closeness of wording in 'The Relique', ll. 23–5, and 'The Extasye', ll. 29–32. *You shalbe a Mary Magdalen* (l. 17) may intimate the person of Magdalen Herbert as exemplifying, together with the speaker, *What Miracles wee harmelesse Lovers wrought* (l. 22), and the ultimate inexpressibility of the relationship (ll. 32–3).

ll. 3–6.   *Graves have…bed*: During peak times of plague such as London suffered in September–November 1608 and August–October 1609, burials in certain churchyards exceeded their capacity, and the digging of new graves exposed the remains of those previously buried. *woman-head*: women collectively, womankind. The feminine gendering of this general term intimates the impropriety of multiple burials in a single grave.

ll. 12–22.   *If thys…Command*: There is strikingly similar phrasing in Donne's *Second Anniversary*, ll. 511–13. In both contexts the Reformed church is treated as normative in rejecting prayers to saints and veneration of relics. *yt*: The reading of Group 1 and Group 3 manuscripts; other sources read 'us', the variant preferred by editors. *Us* in l. 14 as well as l. 15 would seemingly have to mean 'my arm bone and the bracelet of your hair'. *a Mary Magdalen*: After Jesus healed Mary Magdalene of possession by 'seven devils' (Mark 15:40; Luke 8:2), she became one of his close followers. She was present at his crucifixion and later went to anoint his lifeless body with ointment and spices, only to find that his tomb was empty (Matthew 27:56, 28:1–9; Mark 15:40, 16:1–8; Luke 23:49, 55–6, 24:1, 10). The risen Jesus appeared to her in a garden, spoke reassuring words, and foretold his ascension 'to the Father' (John 20:1–18). In the context of 'The Relique' the bracelet of hair will be taken as a relic of a woman who loved greatly, symbolized by *Mary Magdalen*. The speaker's arm bone encircled with the bracelet of hair will be taken as the remains of an unidentified mortal recipient of the woman's great love. *since…sought*: When relics are to be authenticated as the remains of saints, corroboration will come from miracles performed by the persons in question, while still living, or from miracles attributable to their relics after they are dead. The speaker indicates that the first alternative will be pursued. *harmlesse*: causing no hurt or damage, innocuous.

ll. 24–30.   *Difference…Angells doe*: This allusion to a standard Christian doctrine may be general, or Donne may specifically have had in mind Vittorelli's *De Custodia Angelorum* (On the Guardianship of Angels) (1605), utilized in 'Ayre and Angells'. *meales*: kisses (implicitly figured as sips of nectar and bites of ambrosia). *the Seales*: that secure the bodies' 'books'; cf. 'The Extasye', l. 76. *Which Nature…free*: Monogamy and other restrictions on sexual pairing do not exist in the state of nature; cf. the arguments of the woman speaker in 'Confined Love' ('Some man, unworthy to be possessor'). The speaker here is ironic if not paradoxical in characterizing *Lawe* as injuring *Nature*.

'The Dampe', so titled in all sources ('When I am dead, and Doctors know not why') (fols 130r–v)

Three senses of a 'damp'—none of them current—are pertinent to this undatable lyric: (1) a lethal vapour or emission; (2) dazed or stupefied condition, loss of vitality; (3) state of dejection or depression. The conceits of the autopsy and the harmful image of the beloved found in the lover's heart originate in Petrarchan love poetry; that of nakedness as a woman's ultimate advantage traces to the late classical *Greek Anthology* (16.171).

ll. 5–8.   *You thincke…as mee*: This *Dampe* must be a lethal emission from the belov-ed's *Picture* in the speaker's *Hart*, because it is expected to escalate her *Murder* of him into a *Massacre* of his curious *frendes. preferre*: promote, scale up.

ll. 11–13. *braue*: admirable. *Honor*: chastity. *a Goth and Vandall*: a ravager of modes and monuments of civilized life; cf. 'A Valediction of the Booke', ll. 25, 44–5.

ll. 21–3.   *Kill mee…meere Man*: Wordplay on the colloquial sense of 'die' as 'experi-ence orgasm'. *Your Passive Valor*: your woman's capacity to be mounted by a man in intercourse. Cf. Elegy 9 (in Westmoreland numbering), 'Allthough thy hand, and fayth and good works too', l. 13, where women are said to be *apter to endure than men*; Paradox 10, 'That it is possible to find some vertue in some women' (*beeing them selves overthrowne, how much and how patiently they beare*); and 'Loves Deitye', l. 12.

'AN EPITHALAMION OR MARYAGE SONG, ON THE LADY ELISABETH, AND FREDERICK COUNT PALATINE, BEEING MARYED ON SAINT VALENTINES DAY', SO TITLED IN GROUP I MANUSCRIPTS AND IN *POEMS*, 1ST AND 2ND EDNS (FOLS 130V–133R)

James I's sixteen-year-old daughter, Princess Elizabeth, married the seven-teen-year-old German (Saxon) prince Frederick, elector Palatine, on 14 February 1613. The marriage treaty was concluded in May 1612—a highlight of Donne's visit that spring to the elector in Heidelberg with Sir Robert and Lady Drury (Bald, *Donne: A Life*, 257–8). Donne had ample time to devise a poetic tribute to the solemnizing and celebrating of this marriage. On the lavish festivities, see Robbins, *Complete Poems*, 627–8.

The genre of the epithalamion, a sexually explicit wedding song sung by a chorus of youths at the door to the couple's bedchamber, traces to Greek antiquity, while the erotic associations with Valentine's Day seem to have arisen from the Roman fertility rites of the Lupercalia on 15 February (Ovid, *Fasti*, 2.425–52). From the time of Geoffrey Chaucer's *Parliament of Fowls* (1382), believed to be the earliest articulation of the special significance of Valentine's Day for lovers (and written for the occasion of a royal match), English poets affirmed that on this day birds chose their mates: see, e.g., *A Midsummer Night's Dream*, 4.1.138–9.

ll. 1–12.   *Bishop Valentine*: This nebulous figure, one of two with that name, replaced the marriage god Hymen in Christian adaptations of the classical epithalamion. *Queristers* (choristers): Here, as Spenser's 'Epithalamion', ll. 78–84, a chorus of birds replaces the chorus of youths at the bedchamber door in Greek poetic prototypes. *The Sparrowe... Love*: The lustfulness of the sparrow was proverbial, and lustfulness was believed to shorten life. *The household... stomacher* (bodice): the robin. *speed*: attain success. *the Halcyone*: the kingfisher. *hys wife... bringes her feather bedd*: The hen mounted by the cock evokes the image of a puffy bed-covering, such as might have been found in a bride's trousseau of the time.

ll. 15–27. *multiplying*: sexually reproductive. *two Phenixes*: A wonder and a paradox, since in mythology only one phoenix was said to exist at a time. *a Taper*: mere candlelight. *Parke*: enclosure. *such fyres... give*: such heat of passion as shall produce. *Corage*: sexual vigor, desire.

ll. 29–42. *Phenix Bride*: As a traditional image of uniqueness and chastity, the phoenix figures two lovers as *one neutral thinge* in 'The Canonization', ll. 23–4. *frustrate*: render unnecessary. *thyne Eye*: rather than the sun, the eye of heaven. *by theyre blazing signifye*: Comets were believed to forewarn of the death of a prince or other major disaster; cf. Shakespeare, *Julius Caesar*, 2.2.30–1. But here the implication of *falls, but doth not Dye* is sexual consummation. *Bee Thou... those Ends*: The sector of English opinion that favoured an energetic defence of continental Protestants hoped that this marriage would alter James I's policies in the direction of greater militancy and that Elizabeth herself would play a key role. These hopes would be disappointed. *new Starr*: Cf. *First Anniversary*, ll. 259–60. *May All... Records*: Official acts and legal documents were dated from a sovereign's accession.

ll. 51–2. *Goe... to where the Bishop stayes... his way*: The marriage was performed by the Archbishop of Canterbury, George Abbot, a staunch Calvinist much admired by Elector Frederick. The *way* followed was the Order for the Solemnization of Matrimony in the Book of Common Prayer.

ll. 57–98. In stanzas 5–7 Donne avoids the bawdy jesting of classical epithalamia while generating playful humour and mock dismay at the various successive delays. He maintains decorum throughout by a tactful recourse to generalities—especially notable in the images of reciprocal financial transactions which proceed in perfect generosity and mutual trust. *passes... Spheare*: Comets were thought to do this in the traditional Ptolemaic system. This image figures the soul's flight to heaven in *Second Anniversary*, ll. 185–210, and an angel's descent to earth in 'Obsequies to the Lord Harrington', ll. 81–6. *[desires]*: Dowden has the penslip 'deserves'. *pay... debt*: Consensual sexual intercourse between husband and wife was colloquially termed 'paying one's marriage debt'. *Acquittance[s]*: receipts for payment in full. Dowden has the singular form of the noun, but the rhythm of the line requires the plural found in other sources. *Liberall*: The word encapsulates Donne's poetic tact; its overt sense is 'generosity' and its local implication is 'sexually unconstrained'. *Turtles*: turtle doves, proverbial symbols of conjugal love.

ll. 101–12. *since these two are...before*: Donne resolves by dissolving the paradox of *two Phenixes* introduced in l. 18. *wee...will stay...day*: According to Robbins (*Complete Poems*, 636–7), the morning-after greeting of the newlyweds—which as a poetic convention goes back to classical Greek sources—was an actual English custom in Donne's day. In the domestic quarters of royalty, moreover, privacy was especially minimal. *a Curtayne*: one of the hangings enclosing the bed. *tried*: tested, proved. *tomorrow after Nine*: Satire 4.175–9 implies that courtiers were admitted to the presence of Queen Elizabeth after ten o'clock in the morning. *enlardge*: extend, prolong.

'ECLOGUE. 1613. DECEMBER 26', FOLLOWED BY THE TITLE
'EPITHALAMION AT THE MARRIAGE OF THE EARL OF SOMERSET'
IN OTHER GROUP I AND IN GROUP 3 MANUSCRIPTS AND IN
POEMS, 1ST AND 2ND EDNS (1633, 1635) (FOLS 133R–138V)

James I's chief favourite, Robert Carr, came with the king from Scotland and enjoyed a heady ascent. Knighted in 1607, he was created viscount Rochester in 1611, and earl of Somerset in 1613. He formed a liaison with Frances Howard, daughter of Thomas Howard, earl of Suffolk; she and the earl of Essex (the later Parliamentary general) had married as teenagers in 1606 at the political behest of the king, but the marriage was a failure. After a long legal suit, she was granted a decree nullifying her marriage with Essex, and almost immediately thereafter, on 26 December 1613, she and Somerset were married. (In 1616 the couple would be convicted of involvement in the fatal poisoning of Sir Thomas Overbury, one of her servants who had opposed her marriage with Somerset. Although James bestowed his pardon on the pair, this conviction ended Somerset's ascendancy at court.)

Since the death of Robert Cecil, the influential earl of Salisbury, in May 1612, Donne and his patron Sir Robert Drury had been tracking the struggle for prestige and power that pitted two court factions against each other: Robert Carr, viscount Rochester (not yet earl of Somerset), was prominent in one; the countess of Bedford in the other. Donne commenced a delicate balancing act in seeking employment for himself and preferment for Drury. He attempted to stay in the countess's good graces while cultivating several courtiers who might advance him in Carr's favour. In the fall of 1612 Donne further complicated his situation by declaring a 'resolution of making divinity my profession' as 'a household servant of God' (Robbins, *Complete Poems*, 638). This intention of abandoning all prospects of secular employment and embracing ordination in the Church of England made Carr a pivotal figure for Donne's immediate future in two divergent regards. Carr continued to urge Donne to apply for various secular positions while providing him with financial support. Carr also made very clear his own special interest in the granting of ecclesiastical appointments.

In such convoluted circumstances, Donne would have been expected, at the very least, to attend the wedding of Frances Howard and Robert Carr, and further, to seize the occasion by composing an epithalamion to honour the pair. Illness kept Donne from being present at the wedding—two of his letters attest this (*Letters*, 201, 180), and the fact of his absence is registered in the prose preamble to 'Eclogue. 1613. December

26'. The public outrage that met the nullity verdict and the hasty remarriage of Frances Howard to Robert Carr left Donne deeply ambivalent about composing the anticipated epithalamion. On 19 January 1614 he conveyed his mixed feelings in a letter probably written to Goodyere, professing a greater inclination to write in defence of the nullity verdict, yet acknowledging the weight of his obligation to Somerset:

> It may prove possible, that my weak assistance may be of use in this matter, in a more serious fashion, than an Epithalamion. This made me therefore abstinent in that kinde; yet by my troth, I think I shall not scape. I deprehend in my self more than an alacrity, a vehemency to do service to that company; and so, I may find reason to make rime. (*Letters*, 180–1)

Eventually (February 1614?) Donne wrote his composite 'Eclogue'—an apology for his delay of some weeks—and 'Epithalamion'. He sent it to the eminent newly-weds by way of Sir Robert Ker, a personal friend who was a blood relative and protégé of Somerset, and even a namesake (the spellings 'Carr' and 'Ker' have been adopted by scholars to differentiate the two men). Revealingly, however, Donne had also confided his disinclination to Ker in another letter of January 1614:

> If my Muse were onely out of fashion, and but wounded and maimed, ... I should adventure to put her to an Epithalamion. But since she is dead, ... I have not so much Muse left as to lament her losse. Perchance this businesse may produce occasions, wherein I may express my opinions of it, in a more serious manner ... out of a general readinesse and alacrity to be serviceable and gratefull in any kinde. (*Letters*, 270)

Yet the poetic composite of 'Eclogue' and 'Epithalamion' did materialize after all. In the 'Eclogue' Donne impersonates himself and Ker under the Greek pseudonyms of *Idios* (the private man withdrawn from society—Donne at this juncture) and *Allophanes* (meaning 'sounds like another'—Ker, whose name when pronounced was indistinguishable from Carr's).

Synopsis. [*an*]. Dowden has the penslip 'and'.

ll. 3–16.   *decrepitt*: old and feeble. *Courage*: vigor. *Flora*: Roman goddess of blossoming plants. *a frieze Jerkin*: a coarse woolen coat (with wordplay on 'freeze'). *Springs*: water-sources. *Lent*: the forty days preceding Easter, designated a penitential season in the ecclesiastical calendar, here implicitly contrasted to Christmas festivities. *the Sunne ... up*: By 26 December, the date of the wedding, the sun would have passed the winter solstice on 13 December.

ll. 18–24.   *Zeale to Prince, and State; ... And then that earlye light ... The Princes favor is diffus'd ... From which all fortunes, Names, and Natures fall*: Allophanes's hyperbolic tribute evokes a court ardently loyal to James and his rule; its preeminent features are Somerset's combined allegiance to the king and love for his bride. This allegiance and love have sprung from the king's bestowal of special early favour, while bestowing more general favour on other courtiers, raising them to the status of nobility with titles and endowing them with wealth. James's lavish benefactions in the early years of his reign incurred disapproving notice and covert criticism from a number of contemporary observers. Here Idios (the Donne figure) discreetly maintains silence.

ll. 25–37. *wombes of Starrs*: An incoherent heightening of the Petrarchan image of the beloved's eyes as stars or suns. *prevent*: outstrip, exceed. *dark Plotts*: gloomy pieces of ground—hence, somber places—but also, deep conspiracies. *Lust, and Envy... artificiall heate*: In contrast to the warm gratitude kindled in James's courtiers by his royal favours. *disgest*: disperse, dissolve.

ll. 43–54. *full*: amply supplied.. *Kings... bestowe*: The analogy between the king in the state and God in the universe hinges on the power of both to broaden understanding of the benefits they bestow in the minds of those whom they rule. Donne the preacher would declare: 'All governments may justly represent God to me, who is...the fountain of all government, but yet I am more eased, and more accustomed to the contemplation of *Heaven* in that *notion, as Heaven is a kingdom*, by having been born, and bred in a Monarchy' (*Sermons*, 4.240–1). *reclus'd*: withdrawn. *As Man...worlde*: As man is a microcosm. *the Hart...Creatures*: 'The properties, the qualities of every Creature, are in man' (*Sermons*, 4.104). *sweete Peace*: James's most cherished self-image was that of a peacemaker. *I am...Court*: Idios sums up his train of thought. Although physically absent, he participates vicariously in the festivities at court because his understanding of what it is to be there has been enlarged by the king.

ll. 56–68. *Fantastique*: fantasizer. *Amber*: ambergris, used in perfumes and in cooking. *The Earth...Golde*: In alchemical thought, all metals were disposed to attain the perfection of gold, but this in turn required a suitable combination of their elements and sufficient proximity to the Earth's surface to absorb the influence of the sun. *Heav'n...Eye*: Besides the reference to the sun's rays, there may be a covert allusion to the king's ennobling of *well dispos'd* subjects. *Tinctures*: additives that work positive changes in the qualities of substances. *Use*: practice, function.

ll. 69–72. *Unbeguile*: undeceive. *Angells...still in Heaven*: Donne the preacher would elaborate: 'Those Angels which came from Heaven hither, bring Heaven with them, and are in Heaven here...those Angels do not divest Heaven by coming' (*Sermons*, 7.71). *So ys...actions come*: Allophanes purports to turn on its head Idios's earlier defence of his absence from court. If royal influence is like divine influence in being omnipresent, leaving no basis for distinguishing between presence at court and retirement in the country, then one not only can but ought to be present at court. Its *honest actions* (worthy public activities) will produce no estrangement in a morally grounded self (one *still at home*).

ll. 75–85. *Historee*: history book. *Affections*: desires, feelings, motives. *no Levitye to trust*: not silly or foolish to trust others. *pretend*: aspire, lay claim. *Thou hast... and more*: You have no history book that describes such a court, yet here all the while was a court like this, and more, one with *An Earnest Lover, wise then and before* (Somerset).

ll. 87–91.   *Our Little Cupid... Mynorytye*: Cupid is no longer an underage child but a young adult (like his alternate personification Eros in classical myth). He is out of wardship and can claim the right to possess and manage what is his. Cupid has done so by claiming and being *admitted now into that brest, | Where the Kings Counsayls, and hys Secretts rest*—the heart of Somerset, the king's favourite and intimate. *What hast thou Lost?*: What have you missed by being absent?

ll. 93–5.   *To know... Thoughts*: Idios puts the best face he can on his failure to be at court for the wedding and to produce a poem for the occasion: the greatness and grandeur were beyond his powers of expression.

ll. 97–104.   *And yett... Nuptiall Song*: In the end, Idios frankly acknowledges the present situation: he did compose an 'Epithalamion', but after the fact and at a distance. *since I'... Buryed*: Donne referred to his Muse as 'dead' in his January 1614 letter to Ker. Here Idios characterizes himself as *dead, and Buryed*, which seems to allude to hopes and prospects of a secular appointment as well as poetic ambition. The would-have-been courtier withdraws to the country, offering the 'Epithalamion' as an *Epitaph* on the career projections he has renounced and, more enigmatically, as *some Sacrifice*—a term repeated in l. 227 below.

'EPITHALAMION' ('THOU ART REPRIEV'D, OLD YEARE;
THOU SHALT NOT DYE') (FOLS 135V–138R)

ll. 107–13.   *five dayes*: This address to the old year is imagined as being spoken on the date of the wedding, 26 December. *Largest Circle*: The sun appears to be at the highest point of its supposed orbit at the summer solstice. *The Passage of the West or East*: Two polar routes—the Northwest Passage for ships around the northernmost reach of North America, and the presumed passage to the East Indies around the northernmost reach of Russia. Since neither had been navigated in Donne's day, nothing less than *a Promethean Art* would be required to *thawe* them and make them passable.

ll. 116–24.   *Equalitye of Persons.* (stanza 2, heading): King James elevated Robert Carr to his earldom just before the wedding, so that he would be of equal rank to Frances Howard as countess of Essex. The heading functions as a reminder of the royal power to 'create' personages of rank by bestowing titles upon them. *Bee tryed... a Mayd*: Donne daringly ascribes feminine beauty to Robert Carr (a source of his attractiveness to James). *the Bride | Becomes a Man*: Donne compounds his daring by ascribing masculine courage to Frances Howard, exhibited in her suit for the annulment of her marriage to Essex (including her charge that he was impotent)—and confirmed in 1615 when her initiative in the murder of Sir Thomas Overbury was revealed. *scornes unjust Opinion*: Frances Howard's nullity suit incurred wide popular disapproval; Donne shows himself consistent here with the willingness he expresses in his letters to write in its defence. *Envies Art*: The usual court response to criticism of it.

ll. 127–35. *some Divorce to thinck of you* | *Singly*: This is provocative phrasing on Donne's part, in view of the recent nullity suit. *preventst*: dost rise before. *reinvest* | *Them*: take up your responsibilities again. *forward*: eager, prompt.

ll. 142–7. *Powder... hayre*: A custom for brides on their wedding day. *Thou... Art ment for Phoebus, wouldst bee Phaëthon*: She is meant to play the part of the sun (*Phoebus*), but if the powdering (*Ashes*) had not tempered the radiance of her hair, she would scorch her onlookers. In Greek myth the sun god Helios granted his son Phaëthon permission to drive the chariot of the sun for one day. Phaëthon's reckless, off-course driving scorched the Earth and nearly set it on fire. *give thyne Eyes... thou mayst impart*: Like the countess's *radyant hayre*, her *inflaming Eyes* also require to be tempered for the onlookers, including Somerset, who gaze at her. For this purpose *a Teare of Joy* from her will suffice.

ll. 149–59. *Thus*: With powdered hair and tears in her eyes. *our Infirmitee*: Not being able to look at the sun without being blinded. *wee...* | *Are dust, and wormes*: Paired metaphors applied to the wretchedness of Job in Job 7:5. *Our Objects... the fruites of wormes, and Dust*: We set our sights on the *Silke and Golde* of the bride's garments. *Starrs are not so pure as theyre Spheares are*: In his commentary on Aristotle's *On the Heavens*, 2.7.289a13, Simplicius came to this conclusion, reasoning that since stars reflected light, they must be denser than the invisible spheres to which they are fixed. Donne the preacher would elaborate: 'We take a Star to be the thickest, and so the impurest, and ignoblest part of that sphear and yet, by the illustration of the Sun, it becomes a glorious star' (*Sermons*, 4.83). Compare 'Ayre and Angells', l. 27. *stoope*: condescend. *in that Picture thou intirely art... within hys loving hart*: 'The Dampe', l. 4, makes negative use of the same image.

ll. 160–8. *from your Easts you yssue forth*: The bridal pair are two suns, each rising in its own proper quarter, to be joined upon meeting at the church. *men which through a Cypres see* | *The rising Sunne, do thincke it two*: Initially the reference seems to be to an optical illusion in nature (for which no source has been identified). In the following lines, however, *that Vayle beeing gone* | *By the Church rites* refers to a black gauze fabric in folds that was used ritually for veiling. This fabric, like the tree of the same name, was called *Cypres* after its supposed origin on the island of Cyprus (Robbins, *Complete Poems*, 655). *the Church Tryumphant made thys match before*: Or, in less exalted language: marriages are made in heaven. *now the Militant doth strive no more*: A daring allusion to the eventual success of Frances Howard's protracted nullity suit. *Recorder*: officer who makes authoritative oral pronouncement of the law.

ll. 171–81. *Swanns*: Spenser had prominently employed this image of purity, beauty, and nobility in his wedding poem, *Prothalamion* (1596), ll. 37–176. *interbringe*: bring to each other—Donne's coinage. *never singe*: Swans were thought to sing only, at the point of death. *your Ambitiön*: A conspicuous trait of Somerset and Frances Howard. *may here, to the worlds End live,* | *Heires for thys King, to take thanks; you to give*: This compressed and contorted phrasing elicited many variant manuscript readings. The sense seems to be 'May there live here, till the end of the world, heirs of this king to take thanks, heirs of you both to give thanks'. *Nature and Grace doe All; and Nothing, Art*: Hyperbole to the effect of 'Your and your descendants' virtuous natures and the king's grace will bring all this to fruition; artfulness—policy and flattery—will play no part'. *overthwart*: obstruct. *West*: dimming, fading. *North*: coldness.

ll. 182–92. *you are Overblest: Plenty, thys Day | Injures*: you are celebrated to excess; lavish festivities rob the occasion (of what is love's due). *were the Doctrine newe, | That the Earth movd*: The rotation of the Earth was first hypothesized in antiquity by the Greek ship pilot Heraclides; Copernicus revived the idea. *part*: depart. *Masks* (masques): elite entertainments that emphasized spectacle, in which the costumed guests danced. *Center*: still resting point for the couple's united *Hart*.

ll. 199–211. *Know that . . . not sett so too*: The *Moone* (the bride) would set before the *Sunne* (the bridegroom). Even if they rose at the same *Pointe* in the morning, it was customary for the bride to go to the nuptial bed first. *As he that sees . . . findes her such*: As a meteorite is seen to fade in brilliance (when it enters the Earth's atmosphere) and to become a dense mass (according to popular belief) when it collides with the Earth, so the bridegroom will find his bride's palpable, quivering body after she sheds her shining robes. Again, Donne's daring is manifest in thus imaging Frances Howard, who had just won a controversial nullity verdict on her first marriage and was now marrying Somerset with whom she had openly been having an affair, as a *falne . . . Starr*, found to be *such*. Donne takes his daring to an even greater height by affirming (however implausibly) that the pair's prior relationship had been a Platonic one: *Theyre Soules though Long acquainted, . . . theyre bodyes never yett had seene.*

ll. 215–25. *In Tullias Tombe . . . fiveteene hundred yeare*: There were several period sources for the story that, during the papacy of Paul III (1534–49), an ancient tomb on the Appian Way outside Rome had been opened, disclosing the perfectly preserved body of a beautiful girl, and a lamp still burning. As air entered the tomb, the girl's body crumbled to dust, and the lamp was extinguished. The tomb was identified as that of Tullia (or Tulliola), the daughter of Marcus Tullius Cicero. In all likelihood Donne's source was Panciroli's *Rerum Memorabilium Libri Duo*, which he had identifiably used in the lyric 'I have done one braver thinge'; see the preceding note. *May these Love-Lampes . . . equall the Divine*: Taken literally, the wish is blasphemous. *Fyre ever doth aspire | And makes all like ytselfe, turnes all to fyre*: So Aristotle affirms in *On the Heavens*, 3.5, 8.304b17, 307a7, 25. *doth aspire*: tries to rise upwards. *Bonfire*: a substantial fire lit in a public space to celebrate a festive occasion. *One fyre of foure Inflaming Eyes, and of two loving Harts*: Another incoherent image.

ll. 227–35. *A perfect sacrifice*: Leviticus 22.21 enjoins that 'a sacrifice shall be perfect, to be accepted'. *of all*: shared by all. *Such Altars, as prize your Devotïon*: An explicit indication that the 'Eclogue' and 'Epithalamion' were directed to the notice of patrons, surely Somerset, who had instructed Donne to communicate with him through Sir Robert Ker, and possibly also the king himself. In the longer run, Ker would not be Donne's sole intermediary in circulating the Somerset epithalamion. The survival among the Conway Papers (British Library, Additional MS 23,229) of a mutilated copy of a later state of the poem in Sir Henry Goodyere's hand witnesses to its transmission to Edward, 1st viscount Conway, although the date and circumstances are unknown. See Starza Smith, *Donne and the Conway Papers*, 261–2.

'Obsequies to the Lord Harrington, Brother to the Countesse of Bedford',
so titled in Group 1 manuscripts and in Poems, *1st and 2nd edns*
(1633, 1635) (fols 138v–144v)

John, 2nd baron Harrington of Exton, died of smallpox at Twickenham Park, his sister's residence, in February 1614, aged twenty-one. Some weeks earlier, in a letter to Goodyere, Donne had given a hopeful report on the young Harrington's state of health: 'My Lord Harington, of whom a few days since they were doubtfull, is so well recovered that now they know all his disease to be the Pox, and Measels mingled. This I heard yesterday: for I have not been there yet' (*Letters*, 153). The young lord had enjoyed the singular advantage of being privately educated in his boyhood with James I's eldest son, Prince Henry Frederick, who himself had met an untimely death from typhoid fever in November 1613, at the age of eighteen. Harrington had continued his education at Sidney Sussex College, Cambridge, where he gained a reputation for superior talent across a wide spectrum of learning—Latin and Greek, philosophy, mathematics, military and navigational arts—and equal admiration for his religious zeal, courteous bearing, and good looks. Sir Henry Wotton, the English ambassador to Venice, projected a future for Harrington in 1609 as Prince Henry's 'right eye' when 'he will one day govern the kingdom' (Robbins, *Complete Poems*, 774–5). But only five years later, the exceptional promise that the heir to the throne and his accomplished close friend had embodied in the eyes of contemporaries was no more.

Death had left other indelible marks on the recent fortunes of the Harrington family. In August 1613 the young lord John came into his title as 2nd baron when his father, John, the 1st baron, died suddenly at Worms after escorting the recently wed Princess Elizabeth and Frederick, elector Palatine, to Heidelberg. When young John himself died six months later, he bequeathed two-thirds of his estate to his sister, Lucy Harrington, countess of Bedford, Donne's foremost patroness. Well aware of these family developments and burdened by his own low spirits, Donne resolved to compose a poem on the death of the young lord John, casting it in the time-honoured mode of the classical epicedium (funeral ode) with its threefold functions of mourning the death, praising the deceased, and consoling the survivors on their loss. Donne's chosen title for his poem, however, tacitly acknowledged that some time had elapsed since the young lord's death, for 'Obsequies', a no longer current term, meant rites to commemorate a deceased person, not ones performed at the funeral. The ultimately substantial composition, 'Obsequies to the Lord Harrington', seems to have been finished in July–August 1614. Donne sent Lady Bedford the poem and a letter rife with convolutions—she both is not and is the alter ego of her dead brother in all essentials. Far from masking Donne's expectations, the convolutions laid them bare:

To the Countesse of Bedford

Madame,

I have learn'd by those lawes wherein I am a little conversant, that hee which bestowes any cost upon the dead, obliges him which is dead, but not the heire; I do not therefore send this paper to your Ladyship, that you should thanke mee for it, or thinke that I thanke you in it; your favours and benefits to mee are so much above my merits, that they are even above my gratitude, if that were to be judged by words which must expresse it: But, Madame, since your noble brothers fortune being yours, the evidences also concerning it are yours, so his vertue being yours, the evidences concerning that belong also to you, of which by your acceptance this may be one peece, in which quality I humbly present it, and as a testimony how intirely your familie possesseth

Your Ladiships most humble, and thankfull servant
John Donne

It is not known how Lady Bedford received the 'Obsequies to the Lord Harrington'— an intricate composition that reprises notable imagery and vocabulary from several of Donne's earlier poems, especially the *Second Anniversary*, and introduces other imagery and vocabulary that would appear again in his sermons, all the while that it intersperses mordant commentary on political, social, and personal concerns of the present moment. Lady Bedford's monetary response is known, however; Donne recorded that she sent him the sum of thirty pounds. In a letter of March 1615 he unburdened himself to Goodyere:

I am almost sorry that an Elegy [Donne had previously composed elegies on the deaths of Mistress Boulstred and Lady Markham, two of the countess's intimates] should have been able to move her to so much compassion heretofore, as to offer to pay my debts; and my greater wants now, and for so good a purpose, as to come disengaged into that profession [holy orders in the Church of England], being plainly laid open to her, should work no farther but that she sent me 30 pounds, which in good faith she excused with that, which is in both parts true, that her present debts were burdensome, and that I could not doubt of her inclination, upon all future emergent occasions, to assist me. I confesse to you, her former fashion towards me, had given a better confidence. (*Letters*, 219).

ll. 1–6. *Fayre Soule...Harmonie*: Cf. *First Anniversary*, l. 312: 'Soules made of Harmony'. Donne at this period took the position that the souls of infants were infused directly into their bodies by God, not transmitted from their parents. In a letter to Goodyere of 9 October [1610] he observes that 'the opinion of infusion from God, and of a new creation...is now the more common opinion' (*Letters*, 17). *didst continue...Gods great Organ*: Harrington remained in harmony with himself and with God through the course of his life. Donne the preacher would exclaim: 'What an Organe hath that man tuned,...and what a blessed Anthem doth he sing to that Organe, that is at

peace with God' (*Sermons*, 10.131). Cf. 'The Litanye', ll. 200–1: 'A sinner
is more musique, when he prayes, | Than spheares, or Angels praises be'.
pervious: passable.

ll. 12–30. *unaparrell*: divest of clothing—here, get free of the body. *soft Extasye*: easy,
pleasant freeing of the soul from the body so as to apprehend spiritual
truth. *at Midnight*: Donne the preacher would affirm: 'Man *sees* best in the
light, but *meditates* best in the *darke*' (*Sermons*, 4.174). *Such rest... a Type of
thys*: Donne elaborates on the idiom, 'a dead sleep'. (*Subject to Change*): A
side glance at the last judgement and eventual end of time 'when the dead
shall be raised... and we shall be changed' (1 Corinthians 15:52). *although
sad watch he keepe*: despite his serious intention to stay awake. *as soone | As
that Sunne... in seeing Thee*: As he had figured Elizabeth Drury's soul as
'the Sunnes Sun' (*Second Anniversary*, l. 4), Donne figures the comprehen-
sive spiritual illumination he receives from contemplating Harrington as a
sun rising at midnight. *hardest*: hardest to see.

ll. 31–44. *Glasse*: mirror. *these Mirrors of thy wayes and End*: these mirrors of your
Christian living and your partaking of the joy of heaven. Donne the preacher
would expand upon this imagery: 'Gods light cast upon us, reflecteth upon
other men too...when God...employs those works of ours upon *other*
men...that see them done: and when we, by this light...of *Reflection*, shall
be made...such looking-glasses as *receive* Gods face upon ourselves, and
cast it upon others by a holy life, and *exemplary conversation*' (*Sermons*, 3.373–
4). *God be truly' our Glasse... the beeing of all things is Hee*: Again, Donne the
preacher would expatiate: 'Here, in this world, wee see God... by reflection,
upon a glasse... he that sees God, sees every thing else: when we shall see
God...as he is, we shall see all things...as they are' (*Sermons*, 3.111).
Trunckes: telescopes. *affirm*: place on a firm basis. *fluid Vertue cannot be
Looked on*: 'Vertue is even, and continuall, and the same...Vice and her
fruits may be seen, because they are thick bodies, but not vertue, which is all
light' (*Letters*, 97). *Contemplatiön*: fixed, focused attention.

ll. 53–69. *if Man feed... two perfect bodyes rise*: Donne the preacher would return sev-
eral times to this curious question raised by the church father Justin
Martyr: 'One man...devoured by a fish, and then another man...eats the
flesh of that fish, eats, and becomes the other man...That first man did not
become that fish that eate him, nor that fish become that second man, that
eate it;...Both that man and that fish are resolved into their owne elements
of which they were made at first' (*Sermons*, 3.96–7; cf. 4.26–7; 6.156). *God
knowes where everye Atome lyes*: Again, Donne the preacher would elabo-
rate: 'In the generall resurrection upon naturall death, God shall work
upon this dispersion of our scattered dust...God that knowes...in what
corner of the world every atome, every graine of every mans dust sleeps,
shall recollect that dust, and then recompact that body, and then re-inani-
mate that man' (*Sermons*, 7.115). *made of all those | Who knewe hys Minute[s]
well*: compiled from all the people familiar with the particulars of his life.
discontinue: disconnect. *told*: counted one by one.

ll. 67–80. *a Pointe and One | Are much intirer than a Millione*: Aristotle held that things whose essence is indivisible are 'most of all one'; he defined a unit as being indivisible and without position, a point as being indivisible but having position (*Metaphysics*, 5.6.1016b1–3, 24–7). *now wise, now temperate, now just*: Donne ascribes to Harrington three of the four cardinal virtues of classical antiquity (Plato, *Republic*, 442.c.5–8). The omission of courage is probably due to the death of the young lord before he could demonstrate his mastery of military and navigational arts. *betymes*: early in life. [*exercise*]: Dowden and the other Group 1 manuscripts read 'encrease', but the reading 'exercise' found in a range of manuscripts and adopted in *Poems*, 1st and 2nd edns, is metrically superior. While the choice between the two variants on grounds of sense is less clear-cut, *a Place* to *exercise* appears preferable to *a Place* to *encrease*. The verb *thrust* comports with either alternative. *Epitomee*: summary, abridgement. *Long-breath'd*: long-winded.

ll. 81–95. *As when an Angell . . . And as thys Angell, in a instant knowes*: Donne reworks with variations his virtuoso passage on the instantaneous ascent of Elizabeth Drury's soul through the planetary spheres to heaven in *Second Anniversary*, ll. 185–210, and even recycles some phrasing—there, 'this slow-paced soule' (185), here, 'slowe-pac'd Lame thoughts' (91). But here there is a different protagonist and a different directionality: the angel counterpart of the young Harrington descends from heaven to earth and has full and instantaneous apprehension of his virtues—which is the nature of angelic knowledge, according to Aquinas, *Summa Theologica*, 1a.58.3,4. The angel's encompassing, immediate knowledge contrasts with its laborious serial acquisition, which is how humans learn, even those who eventually become skilled readers. *repayre*: make his way, visit. *Perfect*: skilled, expert. *distinctlye*: separately.

ll. 97–101. *in short liv'd Good men . . . the Compound, Good*: As an object of his fellow humans' knowledge, the young Harrington offers an exceptional opportunity to understand virtues collectively, as goodness itself. Presumably this is because of the harmony of his soul with itself and with God (ll. 1–2) and because his early death caused his virtues to take summary form (l. 78). *in that pace*: at the same speed. *Balme* (balsam): a natural preservative. See the note on *Mummye*, ll. 13–24. In the *First Anniversary*, l. 57, Donne, addressing the 'Sicke world', had represented Elizabeth Drury as its 'intrinsique Balme, and . . . preservative'.

ll. 105–10. *Ó Soule, Ó Circle*: The circle was an emblem of eternity, unendingness, here ironized by the *End* registered in Harrington's early death. *Since One Foote of thy Compas still was plac'd | In Heav'n, the other might securely have pac'd | In the most Large Extent . . . Which the whole world . . . hath*: Analogously and at some length, Donne's 'A Valediction [Of Weeping]', ll. 25–36, had notably figured the 'One . . . Soule' of a pair of lovers as 'twin Compasses'. Other writers of the period also figured constancy and perfection as a pair of compasses; see Donne, *The Epithalamions*,

Anniversaries, and Epicedes, ed. Wesley Milgate (1978), 100–1, and Robbins, *Complete Poems*, 786. *the whole world, or Man, th' Abridgment*: Donne the preacher would specify further: 'the *Macrocosme*, and *Microcosme*, the Great and the Lesser world, man extended in the world, and the world contracted and abridged into man' (*Sermons*, 9.93).

ll. 111–30. *the Tropique Circles… Only great Circles then can be our scale*: Circles of latitude, while perfect, reduce in their circumferences from the equator to the poles. Only lines of longitude, all of the same length, and passing around the Earth in great circles through the poles, can serve to measure the height of the sun at any given point. *engrave*: mark. *the' Equinoctiall*: the equator. *So though thy Circle to Thy Selfe expresse… Why didst thou not… by thy doeing, tell Us what to doe?*: Had it completed its course, Harrington's life would have been a great circle passing through the poles of youth and age. Had he lived, he would have showed us, in every age group, how to shun vices and practise virtues at court. Through the example his actions set, he would have supplied medicines to cure every moral dysfunction there. Why did this not happen? the speaker laments, heightening pathos by addressing Harrington directly. [*thy*]: Dowden has the penslip 'theyre'. *Calentures*: tropical fevers that caused delirium. *Hydroptique*: insatiably thirsty; cf. *Second Anniversary*, l. 48. *Scale of Truth*: accurate measurement (provided by Harrington's virtue).

ll. 131–48. *Though as small pockett Clocks… So youth is Easyest to Destructiön… Yett as in Greate Clocks… So worke the faltes of Age*: The gist of this massively suspended single sentence is the following: If in the course of learning how to set the direction of our lives, we gear ourselves to the whole chaotic range of behaviour displayed by individuals (*small pockett Clocks*), we may come to personal disaster. But we are in far greater danger of coming to harm from trusting to bad decisions made on our behalf by elder statesmen and other persons in authority (*Greate Clocks… on which the Eye | Of Children, Servants, or the State relye*). *Whose hand*: The single hand indicating the hour. Until Robert Tooke's invention of the isochronous spring balance was incorporated in clock manufacture from 1665 onwards, pocket watches were too inaccurate for a minute hand to be useful. Donne the preacher would evoke the state of the art in his day: 'He that makes a Clock, bestowes all that labour upon the severall wheeles, that thereby the Bell might give a sound, and that thereby the hand might give knowledge to others how the time passes' (*Sermons*, 6.42). *stringe… Springe… Flye… Bell*: components of the watch's internal mechanism. *beates not or beates unevenly*: does not strike or strikes erratically. *be wound still*: be overwound. *Idle*: move very slowly.

ll. 149–62. *Thou… hadst such a Soule, | A Clocke… to have sett us All?*: Donne resumes his direct address to Harrington, now ratcheting hyperbole to heights not reached since he cast Elizabeth Drury as the world soul in the *Anniversaries*. Harrington is imaginatively invested with the power of God himself to *controule… the Sunne* and providentially *sett* the course of human affairs *as a Generall | And Greate Sun-Dyall*. In one seventeenth-century dictionary of emblems, the sun dial figures the just man (Robbins, *Complete Poems*, 791). *thys Unnaturall Course*: Harrington's youthful death, in the speaker's now-heightened perspective. *not Miracle, but Prodigee*: Hyperbole submits to qualification: Harrington's death was not a supernatural act of God, but a strange, abnormal occurrence in nature. *the Ebbs, longer than flowings bee*: This phenomenon had been observed on the Thames. The tide 'when it is in, and hath taken his sway, then it cannot so soone reverse backe, untyll that the water is well descended or ebbed behynde it to the Seawardes' (William Bourne, *A Booke called the Treasure for Træveilers* (1578), 5.6). *Vertue, whose flood... blowen by thy first breath*: Due to an eyeskip from one to another occurrence of 'flood' in their common source, Dowden and other Group 1 manuscripts conflate ll. 159–61. Their faulty reading runs as follows: 'Vertue, whose flood were blowen in by thy first breath, | All ys at once suncke in the Whirlepoole, Death'. *flood*: inflowing tide (here figuratively, Harrington's intake of virtue from the moment of birth). *the Whirlpoole, Death*: 'Death comes to us in the name, and notion of waters, in the Scriptures...The water of death overflows all' (*Sermons*, 9.107).

ll. 167–75. *all Cityes now but Anthills bee... They 'are all but Ants carying Eggs, Strawe, and Graine*: Donne the preacher would reuse this image in recalling the behaviour of London citizens upon receiving news of Queen Elizabeth's death: 'every one of you in the City were running up and down like Ants with their eggs bigger than themselves, every man with his bags, to seek where to hide them safely' (*Sermons*, 1.217). *Churchyards... unto which | The Most repayre that are in Goodnes riche*: A variation on the saying, 'God takes to himself early those whom he loves best'. *These are the holy Suburbs... Gods City, new Jerusalem*: Donne the preacher would reprise this image: 'this, where we are now, is the suburb of the great City, the porch of the triumphant Church... belonging to his heavenly Palace, in the heavenly Jerusalem' (*Sermons*, 3.288).

ll. 177–246. *At that Gate then, Tryumphant Soule, dost Thou | Begin thy Tryumph...I say, it was more fitt | That all men should Lacke Thee, than thou Lacke ytt*: Elaborating on the traditional ideas of the Christian as a soldier and Christian life as warfare, Donne bases this extended passage on the *jus triumphandi*: the body of ancient Roman law governing the award of a 'triumph', the greatest honour bestowed upon a victorious general. Paul had written of Christ himself in these terms in Colossians 2:15 ('having spoiled principalities and powers, he made a show of them openly, triumphing over them in it') and he extended the reference to victorious Christians generally in 2 Corinthians 2:14 ('Now thanks be unto God, which always causeth us to triumph in Christ'). Donne's application of the Roman laws of triumph to the soul differs markedly from merely conventional references to the triumph of death. He may well have drawn on Sir William Segar's summaries of ancient sources on Roman triumphs in *Honor Military, and*

Civill (1602), 3.19–21, but there were other previous treatments of the subject in Latin or Italian historical compilations; see *Epithalamions, Anniversaries, and Epicedes*, ed. Milgate, 203–4, and Robbins, *Complete Poems*, 793. *At that Gate*: The so-called *porta triumphalis*, outside of which prospective triumphers waited for the day of their honour to be appointed by the Roman senate and the people.

ll. 178–85. *since Lawes allowe | That at the Tryumph day, the People may | All that they will, gaynst the Tryumpher say*: Segar, drawing on Suetonius, notes that the soldiers often 'uttered scoffs and jests against the triumpher: such was the behaviour of Caesar's followers at his triumph' (*Honor Military, and Civill*, 3.21). *By Law, to Tryumphs none admitted bee, | Till they as Magistrates gott Victoree*: Segar observes that in the earliest age of the Roman republic 'it was unlawful for any to triumph unless he were a Dictator, a Consul, or a Praetor' (3.19). *all youths foes:* A figurative allusion reaching back to *Lust, and Ignorance of youth* (l. 12) and ahead to *thyne owne Affections, . . . the heate | Of youths desires and Colds of Ignorance* (ll. 194–5).

ll. 186–91. *Yett till fitt tyme had brought Thee to that fielde | . . . | Thou couldst no Title to thys Tryumph have*: Segar additionally notes 'Another law or custom . . . that no captain might triumph until he had . . . delivered the country of his charge quiet into the hand of his successor' (3.19). Donne manages to cast the prematurely dead Harrington as a triumpher only by speculating on what he might have become: a capable, trusted privy councillor who could *remove | All Jelosyes, twixt Prince, and Subjects Love*. In the so-called 'Addled Parliament' of 1613 in which Donne sat just prior to writing this poem, a deadlock developed between the Commons, critical of James's lavish bestowal of privileges, monopolies, and patronage of favourites, and the Lords who sided with the king. No legislation was passed, and James dissolved Parliament in June. *Jelosyes*: mistrust, resentments.

ll. 196–212. *But tyll thou shouldst succesfully advance | Thyne Armes gaynst forayne Enimyes . . . thy Warr was butt a Civill Warr, | For which to Tryumphes, none admitted are*: Segar notes, 'One other custom the Romans . . . precisely observed . . . that whosoever in any civil war had gained victory (how notable soever) he should not be admitted to triumph, because men therein slain were citizens and no strangers [foreigners]' (3.20). *Engines*: military contrivances. *a diverse Mine*: a different means of undermining or weakening. *No more are they . . . Before Men Tryumphe, the Dominiöne | Must be enlarged, and not preserv'd alone*: Segar notes, 'It was likewise by law provided, and by custom also observed, that only for recovery of dominion no man should be permitted to triumph' (3.19). *Dominiöne*: rule, jurisdiction. *Thou . . . whose Battayles were to win | Thyselfe from those strayts Nature put Thee in*: Harrington's battles were moral and internal, to overcome the susceptibility of fallen human nature to temptation and sin. *Vicariate*: responsibility as a deputy of God on Earth. *he . . . takes Endevors*: God accepts our best efforts (as achievements).

ll. 219–35. *But thys from Tryumphe most disables Thee | That that Place which is con-*
queréd must bee | Left safe from present Warr and likelye doubt | Of imminent
Commotions to breake out: See Segar's specification in the note on l. 183 that
a triumpher must have 'delivered the country of his charge quiet'. *hath he*
left Us so?: Has England been left in a state of quietness at Harrington's
departure? The negative answer to this rhetorical question is evident. *The*
Diocese | Of ev'ry 'Exemplar Man, the whole worlde ys: Exemplary persons
have a duty to care, like a bishop, for the moral condition of everyone.
joynéd in Commissiöne: jointly commissioned. *Tutelar*: guardian. *thys freed-*
ome to upbrayde and chyde … was tyde | With thys, that yt might never refer-
ence have | Unto the Senate, who thys Tryumph gave: No source has been
identified for Donne's assertion that the Roman senate was to be exempt
from criticism; he may be bolstering by analogy, on his own initiative,
James's pretensions to absolute authority based on divine right. *Men might*
at Pompey jest, but they might not | At that Autoritye, by which he gott |
Leave to triumph, before by Age he might: Segar records that 'Gnaeus
Pompeius, a gentleman Roman, before he was of age to be consul tri-
umphed twice' (3.19).

ll. 239–45. *Yet am I farr from daring to dispute | With that greate Soverayntye whose*
absolute | Prerogative hath thus dispens'd for Thee: Donne will not dispute
with God, the supreme ruler of the universe, who by an exercise of his
unconditional power determined an early death for Harington. *absolute*
Prerogative was a highly contentious term used in current attacks on
James's assertions of his monarchical right and powers. *impugners*: oppo-
nents. *I, though with paine, | Lessen our Losse to magnifye thy gayne*: Two of
the functions of funeral and commemorative poems were lament for loss
and consolation in the prospective better state of the deceased. *thy gayne*
| Of Tryumph: Here, a reference to Harrington's triumphal entry into
heaven.

ll. 248–58. *That testimonye' of Love unto the dead | To dye with them*: voluntary suicide,
a topic Donne had considered in composing *Biathanatos* (*c.*1608), which he
deemed unpublishable and allowed very few persons to read. *Saxon wives*
and french Soldurii: women of a Slavonic tribe living in the territory of
Saxony in the seventh and eighth centuries, and vassals of Roman lords sta-
tioned in French territory in Julius Caesar's time. See, further, *Epithalamions,*
Anniversaries, and Epicedes, ed. Milgate, 206–7, and Robbins, *Complete*
Poems, 798. *Greate Alexanders greate Excesse, | Who at hys frendes death,*
made whole townes devest | Theyre Walls and Bullwarkes: Plutarch relates that
the sudden illness and death of his friend Hephaestion while on a campaign
of conquest in 324 BCE rendered Alexander the Great so frenzied that he
embarked on a trail of destruction and violence including the overthrow of
the walls of cities, the crucifixion of his physician Glaucus, and the slaugh-
ter of the entire population of Cossaeians, men, women, and children alike
('Life of Alexander', 72.2, 3). *became them best*: befitted them as strongholds
of defense in the countryside. *in thy Grave, I doe enterr my Muse*: Donne

registers his solemn intention to write no more poetry upon taking holy orders; fortunately he relaxed his vow at various junctures in later life. In any case, this poem was not the success with Lady Bedford that Donne had hoped it would be. *Behind hand*: belatedly (about six months after Harrington's death).

FROM THE WESTMORELAND MANUSCRIPT, RELIGIOUS LYRICS (1607–1620) THE SEQUENCE OF 19 'HOLY SONNETS', THUS TITLED (PP. 66–76)

For a general account of the divergent features of the 'Holy Sonnets' sequences in the Westmoreland and Dowden manuscripts, and the current critical interpretation of the relation between the two, see the headnote to the Dowden texts of these poems.

The significance of the two sequences of 'Holy Sonnets'—a presumptive original order and a revised one—should not be underestimated. This is by far the most substantial evidence we have for Donne's revising of his poetry. But its significance should not be overestimated either. For the most part, the evidence of Donne's revisions is structural (the constituting and ordering of a twelve-sonnet sequence out of a matrix of sixteen sonnets), and much less importantly stylistic—a majority of the alterations could well be scribal, not authorial at all. Nonetheless, there is enough at stake interpretively to present the texts of the Westmoreland 'Holy Sonnets' in their entirety here. Annotations are not repeated for sonnets that occur in Dowden and in Westmoreland; instead, the reader is referred to the notes on the texts in the Dowden section preceding.

1. 'THOU HAST MADE ME, AND SHALL THY WORKE DECAY?' (P. 67)

ll. 1–14. *Thou...decay?*: 'Thou hast made me as the clay, and wilt thou bring me into dust again?' (Job 10:9). *I run to death*: Donne the preacher would reflect, with an allusion to Augustine, 'Before we can crawl, we run to meet death' (*Sermons*, 2:80). *my febled flesh...sin in it*: 'There is no health in my flesh...by reason of my sin...I am feeble' (Psalm 38:3, 8 in the Book of Common Prayer version of the Psalter). *when towards thee | By thy leave...I rise agayne*: The speaker is momentarily capable of acknowledging God's positive working and the uplift it produces in him. *our old subtile foe*: the devil. *prevent his art*: frustrate his wiles (which draw sinners into despair). *Adamant*: the lodestone (and its magnetic force).

2. 'AS DUE BY MANY TITLES I RESIGNE' (P. 67)

Annotated in Dowden section (fol. 43r) as Sonnet 1. Westmoreland's inclusion of both sonnets 1 and 2 makes for obvious reduplication in the tone of near despair and in the speaker's acute fear of being overcome by the Devil unless God intervenes in his behalf.

3. 'O MIGHT THOSE SIGHES AND TEARES RETURNE AGAINE' (P. 68)

ll. 1–14. *O might...in vaine*: Donne the preacher would quote Augustine in expanding on this penitential theme: 'Turn those tears which thou hast spent upon thy love, or thy losses, upon thy sins, and the displeasure of thy God' (*Sermons*, 9.384). *holy discontent*: Donne the preacher would remark on the psalmist David's 'holy scorn and indignation against his own sins' (*Sermons*, 8.206). *my Idolatry*: Presumably a reference to Donne's own youthful indulgence in Petrarchan love worship. *did rent*: did rend. *suffrance*: patient endurance, passivity—senses no longer current. *did suffer...must suffer*: Wordplay on two no longer current senses: 'permit' or 'tolerate' and 'must be subjected to'. *Hydroptique*: unquenchably thirsty. *night-scowting*: prowling about in the dark. *itchy*: constantly lustful. *vehement griefe... effect and cause*: Donne the preacher would elaborate: 'Sin makes the body of man miserable, and the remedy of sin, *mortification*, makes it miserable too' (*Sermons*, 2.63).

4. 'FATHER, PART OF HIS DOUBLE INTEREST' (P. 68)

ll. 1–14. The varied legal vocabulary in this sonnet is also frequent in the New Testament. *double interest*: dual claim of Christ to a place in God's kingdom—as co-ruler, one of the persons of the Trinity; as the Saviour who assured humankind of salvation from sin and everlasting life. *joynture*: inherited share as 'begotten of the Father' (John 1:14). *knotty*: difficult to comprehend. *This lambe...slayne*: 'all...whose names are...written in the book of life of the Lamb slain from the foundation of the world' (Revelation 13:8). *two Wills*: the Old and the New Testaments. *such are...can fulfill*: Luther, following Paul in Romans, held that only God fulfilled the law, and Calvin likewise declared it impossible for humans to fulfil the law. Contrariwise, the Roman Catholic Council of Trent (1545–63) claimed that one who was justified and in a state of grace was capable of keeping God's law. *all-healing grace...law and letter kill*: A poetic elaboration of 2 Corinthians 3:6: 'the letter killeth, but the spirit giveth life'. *Thy lawes abridgment...love*: Donne the preacher would elaborate: 'God hath manifested his will in two Testaments, and though he have abridged and contracted the doctrine of both in a narrow roome, yet he hath digested it into two Commandements: *Love God, love thy neighbor*' (*Sermons*, 2.279).

5. 'OH MY BLACK SOULE, NOW THOU ART SUMMONËD' (P. 69)

Annotated in Dowden section (fol. 43v) as Sonnet 2. The altered phrasing in line 3—from Westmoreland's *Thou' art a Pilgrim, which abroad had don* to *Thou art like a Pilgrim which abroad hath done*, the reading of Group 1 and 2 manuscripts and *Poems* (1633, 1635)—could be a revision by Donne.

6. 'THIS IS MY PLAYES LAST SCENE, HERE HEAVENS APPOINT' (P. 69)

Annotated in Dowden section (fol. 44r) as Sonnet 3. Line 7 raises a substantive stylistic question that surely involves authorial revision. The uncertainty expressed in *Or presently, I knowe not, see that face* is decisively countered in the variant of the line found in Group 2 manuscripts and in *Poems* (1633, 1635): *But my ever-waking part shall see that face*. It seems that Donne allowed himself to express doubt about the state of his soul after death in the more private and intimate genre of his 'Holy Sonnets' while making the soul's immediate enjoyment of heaven his explicit position in later, more 'public' poems addressed to patrons, and that this latter position was sustained in the texts of the printed editions of his *Poems* that appeared after his death (Robbins, *Complete Poems*, 531–2).

7. 'I AME A LITLE WORLD, MADE CUNNINGLY' (P. 70)

ll. 1–14. *I ame...Angelique spright*: To the commonplace of man as a microcosm, Donne adds a traditional notion of bodily composition in which the four elements (earth, air, fire, and water) were correlated with the four humours or fluids (blood, phlegm, choler, and melancholy or black choler). He finishes with his characteristic dual emphasis on body and soul as defining what is distinctively human; cf. 'The Litanye', ll. 143–4; 'The Extasye', ll. 61–4. *You, which... can wright*: The speaker appeals in general terms to astronomers and explorers who have registered *new* discoveries in the heavens and on Earth. In *Ignatius His Conclave* (1611) Donne characterized Galileo as having 'instructed himselfe of all the hills, woods, and Cities in the new world, the *Moone*' by means of his telescope, a reference itself hinging on the announcements made by Galileo in *Sidereus Nuncius* (1610). If the general reference here is construed as applying specifically to Galileo, this sonnet cannot have been composed before 1611. But Donne's equivocal phrasing does not compel this inference. *Drowne...weeping*: Cf. 'A Valediction: Of weeping', ll. 20–1. *it must be burn'd*: Like the heavens and earth which are 'reserved for fire' at the last judgement (2 Peter 3:7). *a fiery zeale...thy house*: 'The zeal of thine house hath eaten me up' (Psalm 69:9). Donne concludes by drawing a typically paradoxical double contrast. Unlike fire as a force in nature, the fires of *lust and envy* have not purified the speaker but *made* him *fouler*. Unlike the fire that will destroy the world, the *fiery zeale* he entreats from *God* will *in eating heale* (in consuming, restore health).

8. 'AT THE ROUND EARTHS IMAGIND CORNERS BLOW' (P. 70)

Annotated in Dowden section (fols 44r–v) as Sonnet 4. In l. 6, the Westmoreland manuscript uniquely preserves what is acknowledged to be the authorial and authoritative reading *dearth*. All other manuscripts and *Poems* (1633) read 'Death'.

9. 'IF POYSONOUS MINERALS, AND IF THAT TREE' (P. 71)

Annotated in Dowden section (fol. 44v) as Sonnet 5.

10. 'IF FAYTHFULL SOULES BE ALIKE GLORIFIED' (P. 71)

ll. 1–14. *If faythfull … o'erstride*: Donne the preacher would clarify the medieval the-
ological debate and the position taken by Duns Scotus that this sonnet
begins by adopting: 'Let *Scotus* … think, That Angels and, separate [disem-
bodied] soules have a naturall power to understand thoughts, … and let
Aquinas present his arguments to the contrary, That those spirits have no
naturall power to know thoughts' (*Sermons*, 10.82, 83). *my fathers soule*: In
Satire 3, ll. 11–15, the speaker sternly asks himself, 'shall thy fathers spiritt
| Meet blind philosophers in heavn … and heare | Thee … damn'd?' *But if
our minds … be tride?*: The speaker shifts to register the force of Aquinas's
distinction, that human souls apprehend through sense perception and rea-
son from inferences, but angels know by immediate intuition (*Summa
Theologica*, 1a.57.4, 58.6). *descride*: made known. *tride*: proved, demon-
strated. *Idolatrous lovers*: The speaker had accused himself of being one in l.
5 of Sonnet 3 ('O might those sighes and teares returne againe'). *vile blasphe-
mous conjurers … Jesus' name*: A satirical swipe at Roman Catholic priests
who claimed to transmute bread and wine into the actual body and blood of
Christ in their celebration of Mass. *pharasaicall | Dissemblers feign devotiön*:
A swipe at the more extreme Puritans of the day, who were strict hallowers
of the Sabbath and condemned such folk customs as Maypole dancing. *he
knowes best | Thy true griefe*: 'Lord … my groaning is not hid from thee'
(Psalm 38:9).

11. 'DEATH BE NOT PROUD, THOUGH SOME HAVE CALLED THEE' (P. 72)

Annotated in Dowden section (fols 44v–45r) as Sonnet 6. In Group 1 and Group 2
manuscripts and in *Poems* (1633, 1635), the reading *easier* in line 12 is replaced by
'better' and the reading *live* in line 13 is replaced by 'wake'. These substitutions could
be authorial revisions, but are not self-evidently so.

12. 'WILT THOU LOVE GOD, AS HE, THEE? THEN DIGEST' (P. 72)

Annotated in Dowden section (fol. 46r) as Sonnet 11.

13. 'SPITT IN MY FACE YE JEWES, AND PIERCE MY SIDE' (P. 73)

Annotated in Dowden section (fol. 45r) as Sonnet 7. In l. 3 Westmoreland uniquely
reads *humbly*. All other manuscripts and *Poems* (1633, 1635) read 'only', regarded as
the superior reading, and hence a likely authorial revision. In l. 6, however, editors of

Donne have uniformly opted to adopt the Westmoreland variant *Jewes impietee* in place of 'Jewes Iniquitye', the reading in Dowden and another Group 1 manuscript, thus avoiding the repetition of *Iniquitye* in l. 4 (which might signal a copyist's error). But the repetition has its own expressiveness; it starkly draws the contrast between the sinlessness of Jesus and the sinfulness of the Jews and the speaker. There is no clear choice to be made between the alternatives 'impiety' and 'iniquity' on the basis of Donne's presumed authorial preference.

14. 'WHY AME I BY ALL CREATURES WAYTED ON?' (P. 73)

Annotated in Dowden section (fols 45r–v) as Sonnet 8. Most editors adopt Westmoreland's variant reading of the opening phrase, 'Why ame I', as more dramatic, but this alteration is surely not compulsory. 'Why are wee' is the reading in the manuscripts of Groups 1, 2, and 3 as well as in *Poems* (1633, 1635). Likewise, where Westmoreland reads *Alas I'ame weaker* in l. 9, 'Weaker I am' is the reading in the manuscripts of Groups 1, 2, and 3 as well as in *Poems* (1633, 1635). Editors have allowed the latter reading to take precedence as a presumptive authorial revision.

15. 'WHAT YF THIS PRESENT WERE THE WORLDS LASTE NIGHT?' (P. 74)

Annotated in Dowden section (fol. 45v) as Sonnet 9. Two substantive variants in Westmoreland have been proposed as instances of original wording that Donne revised. (1) *Looke* in l. 2; 'Mark' is the reading in the manuscripts of Groups 1, 2, and 3 as well as in *Poems* (1633, 1635). (2) *ranck* in l. 8; 'fierce' is the reading in the manuscripts of Groups 1, 2, and 3 as well as in *Poems* (1633, 1635). 'Mark' as a revision of *Looke* is persuasive, since the grammar of the verb–object construction (*Looke... The picture*) is faulty. The superiority of 'fierce' to *ranck* is less clear, especially in light of two no longer current senses of *ranck*—'haughty' and 'stout and strong'.

16. 'BATTER MY HART, THREE-PERSON'D GOD, FOR YOU' (P. 74)

Annotated in Dowden section (fols 45v–46r) as Sonnet 10.

17. 'SINCE SHE WHOM I LOVD, HATH PAYD HER LAST DEBT' (P. 75)

Uniquely found in the Westmoreland manuscript, this sonnet is an independent creation, both thematically and chronologically, and stands outside the sequences 'Holy Sonnets' and 'Divine Meditations'. There was a select but rich tradition of male poets who claimed to gradate, as they aged, from passion for a female beloved to ardent love of God. One illustrious predecessor was Dante in his *Vita Nuova* (New Life) and *Paradiso* (Paradise), the culminating poem of his *Divine Comedy*; Petrarch was another (*Rime sparse* [Scattered Verses], no. 72; *Rime in morte di Laura* [Verses on Laura's Death], no. 75). Donne also had an English precedent in the opening lines of the last of Sir Philip Sidney's *Certain Sonnets*: 'Leave me, O love, which reachest but to dust, | And thou, my mind, aspire to higher things'.

The subject of this sonnet is widely assumed to be Donne's wife, although there are no certain textual indications to this effect. See the sensitive discussion by Achsah Guibbory, 'Fear of "loving more"': Death and the Loss of Sacramental Love', in *John Donne's 'desire of more': The Subject of Anne More Donne in His Poetry*, ed. M. Thomas Hester (1996), 204–27. Anne More Donne died in August 1617, aged thirty-two, seven days after the birth of her twelfth child. The original copy in Donne's own handwriting of the Latin epitaph that he composed for Anne's tomb (no longer extant) in the church of St Clement Danes, London, his parish of residence, has survived among the Loseley Papers. See 'John Donne's Epitaph for Anne Donne, August 15, 1617', *John Donne's Marriage Letters in the Folger Shakespeare Library*, ed. Hester, Sorlien, and Flynn, 61–3.

In view of the hardships weathered by this marriage from its beginning, it cannot seem altogether strange that it was a locus of some ambivalence. In a letter to Goodyere probably written in 1613, when he and his family were struggling with illness, Donne remarked enigmatically: 'I have now two of the best happinesses which could befall me, upon me; which are, to be a widower and my wife alive' (*Letters*, 179). His mingled acceptance and disquiet in this sonnet have led some critics to suppose that it was not written immediately after his wife's death, but after a phase of reflecting on his loss and on his still urgent yearnings, now directed upon God. The best sense that Donne can make of this turn in his life experience is to view God himself in the guise of a lover—actively wooing Donne's soul and offering himself in return, showing himself at once tender and jealously mistrustful of any rival for Donne's love. Similar images of the mutually possessive conduct of lovers pervade 'A Hymne to Christ, at the Authors last going into Germany', written before Donne accompanied Lord Doncaster's embassy in May 1619. Accordingly, this sonnet may have been written in the interval between his wife's death and his departure for Germany with Doncaster (*The Divine Poems*, ed. Gardner, rev. edn, 78).

ll. 1–6.　*debt | To nature*: In Latin, this is the phrase for dying (debitum naturae), and a staple of consolatory expressions. *debt . . . to hers*: A possible allusion to the idiom, 'to pay one's marriage debt', meaning to engage in sexual intercourse with one's spouse. *my good*: my desirable possession, my source of benefit. *ravishëd*: forcibly carried off. *Here the admyring . . . the head*: Gardner cites Thomas Twyne's translation of Petrarch's *De Remediis*: 'All earthly delyghtes, if they were governed by discretion, would styre men up to the heavenly love, and put them in minde of their first original. For . . . who ever loved a river, and hated the head thereof?' (*Phisicke against Fortune* (1579), 57v, in *The Divine Poems*, ed. Gardner, rev. edn, 79).

ll. 8–14.　*holy thirsty dropsy*: Dropsy was a condition of abnormal thirst caused by water retention in the tissues due to liver or kidney failure. Hence the necessary qualification *holy*. Compare 'holy discontent' in l. 3 of Sonnet 3, 'Oh might those sighes and teares returne againe'. *Dost wooe my soule*: The image of Christ as wooer had been sanctioned by traditional

allegorical interpretation of the biblical Song of Solomon—a series of lyr-
ical, passionate addresses to a beloved, read as figuring the love of Christ
for his Church. *love to saints and Angels*: Disallowed in Reformed devo-
tion, but Donne had made the lovers saints in 'The Canonization' and had
associated them with angels in 'Ayre and Angells' (Robbins, *Complete
Poems*, 575). *the world, fleshe, yea Devill*: A formulaic summary of the
temptations and evils besetting human life. The phrase occurs in the
Orders for Baptism and Confirmation and in the Litany in the Book of
Common Prayer.

18. 'SHOW ME DEARE CHRIST, THY SPOUSE, SO BRIGHT AND CLEARE' (P. 75)

Another sonnet found uniquely in the Westmoreland manuscript, 'Show me deare
Christ, thy spouse, so bright and cleare' has been at the centre of a sharp critical
dispute over its dating since Sir Edmund Gosse, a biographer and editor of Donne,
discovered it in the late nineteenth century. The omission of this sonnet from other
manuscripts and from early printed editions of *Poems* testifies mutely to the scandal
its circulation could have caused Donne and his reputation at any date after he was
appointed Sir Thomas Egerton's secretary in 1599, and certainly after he was
ordained a priest in the Church of England in January 1615.

Beyond these sensitive biographical concerns, Donne's casting of this sonnet in the
present tense has led to some unfortunate narrowing of the understanding of its sub-
ject, as if the desire for certainty simply reduced to which of the presently existing
churches is the true Church. But the lack of temporal specificity in the topical allu-
sions of ll. 2–6 could as well allow this sonnet to be assigned to the 1590s as to the years
around and after 1620—leaving a fraught and inconclusive situation for interpreta-
tion. Although notable affinities of tone and imagery exist between this sonnet and the
passage beginning 'Seeke true religion. Oh where?' in Satire 3, generally dated to the
mid- to late 1590s, these have not availed to resolve the ongoing critical disagreement
over dating.

There are, moreover, other considerations that might bear on interpretation. Since
this sonnet and its immediate predecessor occur only in the Westmoreland manu-
script, and since the perspective taken on the deceased Anne Donne is that of the
universal Church Triumphant (*her soule early' into heven ravishëd*), the prominent
spousal imagery of 'Show me deare Christ' could be viewed in this context as sustain-
ing emphasis on the universal Church—here, the Church Militant (the Church on
earth) as the object of Christ's love. The sonnet is a frank, impassioned series of ques-
tions about the lack of congruence between the true (by implication, universal)
Church promised in Scripture and the Church as it has appeared in manifold institu-
tional forms throughout its history.

Perhaps the most that can be said is that Donne in other writings looked both
ways: he repeatedly affirmed the comprehensiveness of one universal Church and
decried the divisiveness and antagonism that prevailed in a nominally all-Christian
Europe. On the one hand, he articulated what in his day was a rarity, an ecumenical

outlook on the various institutional forms of Christianity and an accompanying confidence that there was no single, exclusive path to salvation, expressing this memorably in a letter to Goodyere probably written in 1609: 'You know I never fettered nor imprisoned the word Religion; not...immuring it in a *Rome*, or a *Wittenberg*, or a *Geneva*; they are all virtual beams of one Sun...connaturall pieces of one circle' (*Letters*, 29). On the other hand, Donne in his sermons of the 1620s repeatedly undertook to identify and critique what he viewed as two pernicious extremes. He decried a range of Roman Catholic departures from biblical authority, which substituted tradition and human authority in its place. He equally denounced the slavish scrupulosity regarding biblical authority shown by doctrinaire Protestants ('Puritans'), especially when this manifested itself as resistance to legitimate human authority. However, it must be noted that Donne adumbrated this dual critique possibly as early as 1609 in a letter to Goodyere, seeking to stabilize his friend's doubts about what institutional form of Christianity he should embrace (*Letters*, 100–3).

l. 1.   *Show...thy spouse*: The speaker entreats fulfilment of the promise in Revelation 21:9: 'Come hither; I will shew thee the bride, the Lamb's wife'. The entreaty engages directly with a Reformation-era controversy. Roman Catholics claimed that theirs was the true Church because it had continuously existed as an institution under papal authority, asking 'Where was your church before Luther?' Protestants countered that the true 'catholic' (Greek for 'universal') Church was the invisible, spiritual one of all true believers, God's elect, and that it had been founded by Jesus Christ. *thy spouse*: The identification of the 'true' Church as the bride of Christ rested chiefly on the allegorizing of the Song of Solomon and on Revelation 19:7–8. Donne the preacher would observe, 'The union of Christ to the whole Church is not expressed by any metaphor, by any figure, so oft in the Scripture, as by this of *Mariage*' (*Sermons*, 6.82). *so bright and cleare*: The speaker's irony bespeaks his troubled frame of mind.

ll. 2–4.   *she...richly painted*: The Roman Church, with its polychrome statues, wall paintings, stained glass, embroidered vestments, and illuminated prayer books. The churches of England had been stripped of much of these during the Reformation in Edward VI's reign (1547–53). The prototype for this personification was 'the woman arrayed in purple and scarlet colour, and decked with gold and precious stones' identified as 'Babylon the Great, the Mother of Harlots and Abominations of the Earth' in Revelation 17:4–5. *which robb'd...here*: The Reformed Church, with an ambiguous reference either to the stripping of ecclesiastical regalia generally or to the specific defeat of the Protestant forces headed by James's son-in-law, Frederick, elector Palatine, newly elected king of Bohemia, and the consequent plundering of some German Protestant states in 1620. Donne the preacher would have this to say against Puritans at Christmas 1621: 'He that undervalues *outward things,* in the religious service of God, though he begin at *ceremoniall* and *rituall* things, will come quickly to call *Sacraments* but outward things, and *Sermons*, and *publique prayers*, but outward things, in contempt' (*Sermons*, 3.368).

ll. 5–14. *Sleeps…one yeare?*: The Reformers claimed that the Roman Church had been encumbered over the course of centuries during the Middle Ages with doctrines, beliefs, and practices that had no basis in Scripture or in the church fathers. The assumption of political power by the papacy was singled out as a principal deviation. *peepes up*: begins to reappear. *one yeare*: 1517, when Luther nailed his 95 theses to the church door in Wittenberg. *Is she selfe truth 'and errs?*: While the Roman Church laid claim to infallibility, it had reformulated doctrinal truths many times, conspicuously in the Council of Trent (1545–63). *Doth she…appeare?*: The *one hill* is Geneva, the site of Calvin's theocratic rule; the *seven hills* are those of Rome; Wittenberg was located on *no hill*. Donne the preacher would cast light on the first two of these images while insisting that God had provided the Church of England for the Christians of England: 'Trouble not thy selfe to know the formes and fashions of forrraine particular Churches; neither of a Church in the lake [of Geneva], nor a Church upon seven hils [of Rome]…God hath planted thee in a Church, where all things necessary for salvation are administered to thee, and where no erroneous doctrine (even in the confession of our Adversaries) is affirmed and held' (*Sermons*, 5.251). *Dwells she with us*: The Church of England. *or like adventuring knights…make love?*: The allusion to medieval romance literature has a patronizing ring, in keeping with the view of the more educated of Donne's contemporaries that this was a merely popular genre or one for children. Thus, the answer to the alternative posed in *Dwells she with us* is an implicit yes. *thy mild Dove*: A recurrent term of endearment in Song of Solomon, as in 6:9: 'My dove, my undefiled'. *most trew, and pleasing…open to most men*: The paradoxical imagery of Donne's concluding couplet forcibly highlights the universal *trew* Church *open to most men* as both the primary and the ultimate subject of this sonnet.

19. 'OH, TO VEX ME, CONTRARYES MEETE IN ONE' (P. 76)

This sonnet is the last of the group of three uniquely found in the Westmoreland manuscript. Its date is unknown and likely to remain so, unless it is independently concluded that 'Oh, to vex me' presents a subjective counterpart to the objective perplexities of 'Show me deare Christ, thy spouse'. It might then be argued that the composition of 'Oh, to vex me' pairs with that of 'Show me deare Christ', as the composition of 'Show me deare Christ' can be argued to pair with 'Since she whom I lovd' in a shared thematic of the true universal Church in its heavenly and earthly aspects.

Another feature of 'Oh, to vex me' that comports with a date around or after 1620 is its thought pattern that zigzags through a sequence of opposites to reach an unforeseen and arresting conclusion: *Those are my best dayes, when I shake with feare*. This conclusion, cast in the form of an identity relation between contraries as the distinctive hallmark of spiritual perception, exemplifies the mode of paradoxical transvaluation that comes decisively into prominence in Donne's *Devotions upon Emergent Occasions* (1624).

ll. 1–13. *contraryes meete in one*: The ostensible surface meaning, 'contraries meet in one person—me', will end by taking on a deeper paradoxical meaning: 'contraries are one and the same' in proper human perceptions of God's ways and workings. *Inconstancy . . . constant habit*: The speaker discloses his initial frame of mind grounded in a commonsensical notion of opposites: it is *unnatural* for *Inconstancy* to produce constancy. But his next turn of thought lands him in paradox, as his *constant habit* proves to be constant, involuntary changefulness: *when I would not | I change. humorous*: mood-dependent, variable. *ridlingly distempered*: perplexingly unstable. *as infinite, as none*: Donne characteristically casts his erotic and his religious attachments alike as all-or-nothing relationships. *I durst not view heaven*: Cf. 'Goodfriday. 1613', ll. 29–30. *I quake . . . his rod*: Job uses this vocabulary for the afflictions that God permits to fall on him: 'Let him take his rod away from me, and let not his fear terrify me' (Job 9:34). *fantastique Ague*: feverish imagination that alternates, like malaria, between sensations of burning and shivering. The conventional 'fire' and 'ice' extremes of the Petrarchan lover's erotic torments are here transposed in typical Donnean fashion to a religious register.

DEVOTIONS UPON EMERGENT OCCASIONS, 1ST EDN (1624) (SHORT-TITLE CATALOGUE NO. 7033; GEOFFREY KEYNES, BIBLIOGRAPHY OF DR. JOHN DONNE, 4TH EDN, NO. 34)

The title of Donne's *Devotions upon Emergent Occasions, and severall steps in my Sicknes*, identifies the genre of this prose work and the perspective to be developed on his near-fatal illness in the late fall and winter of 1623–4. The defining generic features of 'devotion' are earnest attention and self-application on the part of its practitioner(s), which find expression in addressing God in meditation and prayer.

The circumstances of the illness that suddenly lays him low but eventually allows him the tentative action of leaving his bed are the subjects probed by Donne as he broods on his experience. He activates connotations of the Latin participle 'emergens' (rising up, getting clear of) and the noun 'occasus' (downfall, ruin, death), in terming these circumstances 'emergent occasions' (Debora Shuger, 'The Title of Donne's *Devotions*', *English Language Notes* (1985), 22:39–40). Donne signals as additional subjects the 'severall steps in my Sicknes' considered in a series of twenty-three compositional units. These he terms 'Stationes, sive Periodi in Morbo' (Stages, or Cycles in the Illness) (A5r)—that is to say, junctures at which he registers a particular perception, turns it about in his mind and heart, and puts it into words.

Finally, Donne's subtitle specifies the internal structure of these twenty-three units. They are 'Digested into 1. Meditations upon our Humane Condition. 2. Expostulations, and Debatements with God. 3. Prayers, upon the severall Occasions, to him'. The tri-partite internal structure of the *Devotions* has been a focus of scholarly and critical debate; the present consensus regards the form as Donne's singular creation. On the one hand, it appears to be a hybrid adapted from systematic procedures in Catholic and Protestant devotion that in turn energize the memory as a storehouse of visual images, then the understanding and the will in setting a particular scene in the mind's eye, prob-ing its spiritual significance in direct address to God, and offering a prayer of acquies-cence and gratitude for insights gained. On the other hand, Donne supplements his appropriation of such systematic procedures with other modes of spiritual exercise including the literary tradition of *ars moriendi* (the art of dying) and the techniques of opening, expounding, and applying biblical texts used by the preacher to minister to his hearers' souls and his own. (See the overview of critical and scholarly discussion in Kate Gartner Frost, *Holy Delight* (1990), chap. 1.)

As he confronts the sufferings and uncertainties of his illness and gradually notes signs of recovery, Donne's self-scrutiny and self-reporting become intensely fraught. The *Devotions* are a gripping, accessible work despite their many complex-ities of thought, tonality, and style. Although the illness is nowhere named, perhaps because neither Donne nor his physicians were certain what to call it, he does detail his symptoms—high fever, chills, cough, blotchy rash spreading from his midsec-tion to the rest of his body, dizziness and weakness (indicators of low blood pres-sure), danger of a relapse. This specificity has enabled his illness to be identified as epidemic typhus fever caused by a strain of the *Rickettsia* bacterium, borne and transmitted by ticks or lice (Kate Frost, 'John Donne's *Devotions*: An Early Record of Epidemic Typhus', *Journal of the History of Medicine* (1976), 31:421–30; William B. Ober, MD, 'John Donne as a Patient: *Devotions upon Emergent Occasions*', *Literature & Medicine* (1990), 9:25). Yet, for all the immediacy with which Donne chronicles his bodily illness, the serial dynamic of his compositional units—medita-tion, expostulation, and prayer—drives home the recognition that the paramount concern of the *Devotions* is the state of Donne's soul in relation to God's purposes for him and to his vocation of ministering to his fellow Christians as dean of St Paul's, London.

The centrality of Donne's dual concern in the *Devotions* with God's purposes for his life personally and for his vocation as a minister to others significantly demonstrates that he had found his way to resolving the two knottiest perplexities confronted in his treatise on suicide, *Biathanatos*, composed around 1608. One major perplexity was the inaccessible subjectivity of a person who meditated or committed suicide, and hence the impossibility of another's passing judgement on the act. Deciding whether to take one's own life was, in Donne's words, a 'secret Case between the Spirit of God, and my Conscience, of which there is not certainly constituted any exteriour Judge, we are ourselves...in the same Condition as Princes are'—that is, autonomous and answer-able only to God (*Biathanatos*, ed. Sullivan (1983), 82). In the *Devotions*, especially in the Meditations and Expostulations, Donne articulates, at great length and in detail, the interworkings of God's Spirit and his own conscience, laying wide open to his read-ers what would otherwise be a closed domain. The second major perplexity confronted in *Biathanatos* was whether a 'defensative' for suicide could be produced, and on what grounds, for which cases. Donne came to the conclusion that a defence could be mounted on two grounds: 'to encorage Men to a just Contempt of this Life, and to restore them to theyr Nature, which is a desire of supreame happinesse in the next Life by the losse of this, … who religously assuring themselves, that in some cases, when we were destitute of other means, we might be to ourselves the stewards of Gods benefits, and the Ministers of his Mercyfull Justice' (*Biathanatos*, ed. Sullivan, 146). While the Donne of the *Devotions* fervently expresses his 'desire of supreame happinesse in the next Life by the losse of this', he equally fervently leaves to God the determination whether he will die or recover. Renouncing his own agency in the matter, Donne wholly accepts God's will for his future despite his severe anxieties about relapsing into the mortal sickness of sin in the sombre final sections of the *Devotions*.

Notwithstanding the differences between poetry and prose, Donne's *Anniversary* poems and the *Devotions* display an intrinsic similarity: an obsession with physical decline, decay, and death and with the spiritual imperatives that issue from these harsh, inevitable truths of our human nature. Yet what is bifurcated in the *First* and *Second Anniversary*, the 'anatomy of the world' and the 'progress of the soul', undergoes repeated integration, disintegration, and reintegration in the twenty-three units of the *Devotions*. The resulting dynamic is both cyclical and progressive. (See Barbara Kiefer Lewalski, 'Typological Symbolism and the "Progress of the Soul" in Seventeenth-Century Literature', in Earl Miner, ed., *Literary Uses of Typology from the Late Middle Ages to the Present* (1977), 81–5; Jeanne Shami, 'Anatomy and Progress: The Drama of Conversion in Donne's Men of a "Middle Nature"', *University of Toronto Quarterly* (1984), 53:221–35.)

As Donne in stages explores his symptoms and his debility as analogues of his sinful condition, illness and health initially figure as stark opposites. This opposition reaches a crux in the fourteenth Meditation, Expostulation, and Prayer where the subject is the so-called 'crisis' of Donne's illness: its 'critical days'. Now his physicians undertake to evaluate his condition and formulate a prognosis of which is likelier: life or death. Drawing on Augustine's famous reflections on time, Donne in Meditation 14 comes to equate the possibility of his recovery with the inescapability of change that accompanies re-entry into the passage of time as well as with the uncertainties that change induces. By contrast, death would afford him an entry into eternity and end his vulnerability to sin. In Expostulation 14 Donne unburdens himself: his return to the temporal order would again put at risk the fate of his soul and his present assurance about his relationship to God. Here the value of life or death appears to depend entirely on salvation as the ultimate referent. Should he, then, prefer recovery and life? The seven days of spiritual creation imaged by Donne at the end of Expostulation 14 and the profession of unconditional trust and hope in God in Prayer 14 indicate that, at this point, the answer to this question is yes.

When, however, the anxiety expressed at the onset of his sickness and in the 'crisis' of the 'critical days' returns at the end of the work to cloud the prospect of his recovery with the danger of 'relapsing', illness and health re-emerge as states whose meaning and value depend on local context and ultimate priorities. As Donne in Prayer 1 shows himself able to conceive of God simultaneously in terms of a circle and a straight line, so he comes to view his illness as at once an abject lowering and a consummate raising. Although his return to health is a worldly benefit, it is also a deferral of his heavenly union with God, so that a possible relapse figures fear and repugnance along one axis while figuring hope and anticipation along another. (See Jonathan Goldberg, 'The Understanding of Sickness in Donne's *Devotions*', *Renaissance Quarterly* (1971), 24:507–17; Sharon Cadman Seelig, 'In Sickness and in Health: Donne's *Devotions upon Emergent Occasions*', *John Donne Journal* (1989), 8:103–13.) Donne equilibrates the heavenly and the earthly within the compass of the '*Minute*' imagined in Prayer 23: 'Since therefore thy *Correction* hath brought me...to such an *intire possession* of thee, as that I durst deliver my selfe over to thee this *Minute*, If this *Minute* thou wouldest accept my *dissolution, preserve* me, O my *God* the *God* of...*perseverance*, in this state from all *relapses* into those *sinnes*, which have induc'd thy *former Judgements* upon me.' Donne's first biographer, Izaak Walton, quoted this sentence in connection with Donne's fatal illness in 1631.

Donne's evolving perception of death—less as the terminal disease that bedevils human life and more as the cure for the disease of sin that inheres in human life— becomes the thematic and structural pivot on which the *Devotions* turn. This perception bears further fruit in paradoxical transvaluations at various points in the text. Donne seeks, moreover, to foster such recognitions in his readers, his fellow Christians, of whom he makes himself a generic instance in famously reflecting that 'any mans death diminishes me, because I am involved in mankind; and therefore never send to know for whom the bell tolls; it tolls for thee'. As the *Devotions* draw to a close by locating the inevitability of death at the core of what it means to live in an ongoing awareness of God's directive purposes, they arrive at a sense of the soul's journey far removed from the *Anniversaries* and their disjunction of mortality and immortality. Now the ultimately significant aspects of life and death are recognized as being one.

[A1r]   *Emergent*: rising out of a prior or surrounding medium, issuing forth. Further connotations—unexpected, unpredicted, urgent—become germane in the course of the *Devotions*. *EXPOSTULATIONS*: questions, pleas, protest. Donne's bold, spirited addresses to God contrast markedly with the humble, reverent 'colloquy' with God that characterized the recent mode of Jesuit meditation. While there are echoes of Augustine's *Confessions* in Expostulations 7 and 10, and in Meditation 14, Donne's chief precedents appear to be Abraham, Moses, Job, and Christ, all of whom questioned God directly about the workings of his will (Genesis 18:23–32; Exodus 7:30; Job 10:2–20, 40:1–5; Matthew 26:39, 27:45; Mark 14:36, 15:34).

[A2v]   *three Births*: Donne had a liking for the typology of a person's multiple births, which in its simplest form he employed as dual: being born into the world and being born again as a Christian. He adds a 'third birth', the soul's admission to the eternal life of heaven, in his *Second Anniversary*, l. 214. Here this typology is further adjusted to compliment King James. *your Highnesse Royal Father...led mee to it*: James I's prompting was vital to Donne's decision to be ordained (Bald, *Donne: A Life*, 302–10).

[A3v]   *Examples... are Commandments*: An adaptation of Pliny the Younger's
address to the emperor Trajan: 'the life of a ruler is a judgment...we do
not so much need command as example' (*Panegyricus*, 45.6). *Hezekiah
writt... his Sicknesse*: Isaiah 38:9–20.

[A5r–A6r]   *Stationes... Relabi:* Donne's table of contents takes the form of Latin dac-
tylic hexameters; however, the lines of verse have been broken into the
discrete headings of the twenty-three units with their inserted numbers.
Readers who knew Latin had the benefit of the following synopsis (my
translation):

Stages or Cycles in the Illness, to which the following Meditations refer.

1 First, the sudden onset of the illness; 2 Thereafter, its harmful activity; 3
Confinement to bed follows at length; 4 And the physician is called in. 5 He alone is in
attendance; 6 He is fearful; 7 He urges that colleagues be joined with him; 8 And the
king himself sends his own [physician]; 9 They write out remedies; 10 They are anx-
ious to cope with the slow-moving, stealthy illness. 11 With excellent juices and buds
they draw out the poison from the congested heart, and what notable substances art
and nature instill, they administer; 12 With a dove that has breathed its last, applied
to his feet, vapours are drawn from his lowest parts; 13 And the illness, having declared
its evil nature by numerous spots, is driven into his breast, an outlying area of the
illness: 14 And this the physicians note to have befallen in the critical days. 15 In the
meanwhile, sleepless, I pass nights and days: 16 And the bells resounding from the
nearby tower proclaim and prepare my funeral in the funeral of others. 17 Now with a
heavy sound they say: Thou shalt die; 18 But then with a quick sound and a brisk
stroke: Thou art dead. 19 The ocean having been passed at length, the land rises into
view; the physicians, by good indications, see concoction now: they are able to purge.
20 They do this. 21 And He favors it, He who by them calls: Leave your bed now,
Lazarus; 22 Let the coals fueling the illness fuel serious concern in you; 23 And the
fear of relapse.

[A6v]   The errata slip suggests that Donne proofread the *Devotions* after they were set
in type.

DEVOTIONS

1. Meditation

[1–3]   *alteration*: change in the balance of the bodily humours that produces illness.
grudging: access or slight indication—senses no longer current. Donne's corre-
sponding Latin term 'Insultus' is far more vehement. *God...put a coale...into
us...a flame*: 'Take...thy faint and dimme knowledge of God, that riseth out
of this light of nature,...find out one small coale,...and blowe that coale with
thy devout *Prayers*' (*Sermons*, 3.360).

[4–5]   *one hand askes... how we do*: Self-diagnosis was standard medical practice.

[6–7]   *Man...being a little world*: Donne extends the commonplace analogy between
the macrocosm (world) and the microcosm (man). As the world is liable to

seismic upheavals and violent weather, so man's body is vulnerable to the ravages of illness. *he hath inough...to assist the sicknes*: Man, however, outdoes the world in being able to imagine and fear the worst about his illness, and thus by his own making (*artificiall sickness*) worsen his condition. Cf. Holy Sonnet 7 'I ame a little world made cunningly'.

1. Expostulation

Profuse biblical allusions and spirited commentary on them addressed to God make Donne's Expostulations an innovative contribution to systematic devotional practice. A key expostulatory prototype for Donne is Job, who more than any other biblical figure questions God's dealings with him before coming to see and accept their rightness. Cf. the opening of Expostulation 4.

[8–11] *If I were...I might speak unto the Lord*: Donne closely echoes Augustine, *Confessions*, 1.6, 7 in commenting on the same text from Genesis: 'Though I am but dust and ashes, allow me to speak, for I am addressing your mercy'. *meere dust and ashes*: Abraham's and Job's self-characterization (Genesis 18:27, Job 30:19). *the Lordes hand...this dust*: 'the Lord God formed man of the dust of the ground' (Genesis 2:7). *Temple of the Holy Ghost*: 'know ye not that your body is the temple of the Holy Ghost?' (1 Corinthians 6:19). *I am my soule...the breath of God*: 'the Lord God...breathed into his nostrils the breath of life, and man became a living soul'. *sensible*: sensitive.

[13–15] *Job did not charge thee foolishly*: 'In all this Job sinned not, nor charged God foolishly' (Job 1:22). *a Watch...the springe*. Cf. 'Obsequies to the Lord Harrington', ll. 131–54. *Infuse his first Grace...dispose ourselves by Nature, to have it?*: Donne the preacher had declared similarly: 'we are so far from being able to begin without Grace, as then where we have the first Grace, we cannot proceed to the use of that, without more' (*Sermons*, 1.293). Augustine had distinguished kinds of grace by their point of onset in the process of turning a sinner from sin: e.g., grace antecedent (going before), concomitant (accompanying), consequent (coming after). *prodigall sonnes*: Jesus's parable in Luke 15:12–39. *We are Gods tenants here*: The same phrase had occurred in *Essays in Divinity*, 70.

1. Prayer

[16–19] *God...considered in thy selfe, art a Circle*: The sphericity of God's being was a major tenet in ancient Greek philosophy, notably affirmed by Parmenides and Plato. By Donne's time it had become a prominent Christian symbol, which he would employ in his preaching: 'that Spheare, which though a Spheare, is a Center too;...that place, which, though a place, is all and every where' (*Sermons*, 9.129). *my Election*: The affirmation that he is one of the elect aligns Donne with the Calvinist theology that predominated in the Church of England in the 1620s. *Concupiscence*: craving for things of the world.

2. Meditation

[22–7] The *Heavens...move continually one and the same way*: Donne had chal-
lenged the Ptolemaic system of concentric, rotating cosmic spheres in the
*First Anniversary. a Fever doth...Calcine him, reduce him...to ashes;...to
lime*: Various alchemical processes were thought to reduce substances to their
originary elements as an effect of heating; the most drastic of these was cal-
cining or dissolving a substance to lime. *Angells...had a Ladder to goe to
Heaven*: Jacob's vision in Genesis 28:12. *fatuous*: tasteless (the sense of Latin
'fatuus'). *In the sweat...eate thy bread*: Genesis 3:19. *distribution*: division
into kinds—a sense no longer current.

2. Expostulation

[28–30] *hee...hath his grave but lent him...another...buried in the same grave*: This
practice was not uncommon in Donne's time; cf. 'The Relique', ll. 1–2.
Davids Worthies: The shorter catalogue of these battle champions is given in
2 Samuel 23:8–39, the longer one in 1 Chronicles 11:10–43. *God calls...as
though they were*: Romans 4:17; Isaiah 46:10–11. *the first world, in Noahs time
120 yeres*: This figure is not given in Genesis, which states only that 'Noah
was six hundred years old when the flood of waters was upon the earth'
(7:6). In his *Lectures on Genesis* (1536), Luther explained that Jerome had
reached an estimate of Noah's age at the time of the flood by pairing an
earlier reference to Noah as being five hundred years old (Genesis 5:32)
with God's promise (Genesis 6:3), 'My spirit shall not always strive with
man...his days shall be an hundred and twenty years.' Luther, agreeing
with Jerome, concluded: 'The text is speaking of the respite that was granted
to the world for repentance before the Flood' (*Luther's Works*, gen. ed.
Pelikan, 2:13, citing Jerome, *Book of Hebrew Questions about Genesis*,
Patrologia Latina, 23:997). *a rebellious generation...40 years*: An allusion to
Numbers 14:33.

[31–4] *My God,...not wont to come in Whirlwinds, but in soft and gentle ayre*: Elijah,
awaiting the Lord's presence, finds him not in the 'great and strong wind'
but in the 'still small voice' that follows (1 Kings 19:11–13). *Thy first breath
breathed a Soule into mee*: An allusion to Genesis 2:7. *all that afflicted
Job...hand of Satan*: Job 1:12–19; 2:6–7. *Surgite Mortui, Rise yee dead*: 'Rise
you dead, and come to judgment' summons souls to the last judgement in
the *Regula Monachorum* (Monastic Rule) formerly ascribed to Jerome
(*Patrologia Latina*, 30:417B). The phrase does not occur in the Vulgate.

2. Prayer

[37–40] *Supper of the Lamb*: Revelation 19:9. *Communion of thy Saints*: One of the
articles of belief in the so-called Apostles' Creed. *him, with whom thou art so
well pleased*: An allusion to Mark 1:11. *a Light in a Bush*: God spoke to Moses
out of a burning bush (Exodus 3:2–4). *crowned with thornes*: Jesus is thus
mocked during his trial on charges that he claimed to be a king (Matthew
27:29; Mark 15:17).

3. Meditation

[41–4] *one priviledge...to Mans body...an upright form*: This distinction between humans and animals became a commonplace in classical antiquity (Plato, *Timaeus*, 90a; Ovid, *Metamorphoses*, 1:76–86). *fillip*: flip. *When God came to breathe into Man...flat upon the ground*: An allusion to Genesis 2:7. *The Anchorites...immur'd themselves*: Early Christian and medieval recluses of both sexes withdrew from society to live and meditate in solitary confinement. *barqu'd*: enclosed in bark. *That perverse man...in a Tubb*: Diogenes the Cynic, a philosopher of the fourth century BCE, held that personal happiness consists in meeting one's natural needs and that these can be satisfied simply; accordingly, he made his lodging in a large clay jar. *Every nights bed...the grave*: Donne would speak similarly in preaching before King Charles in 1630: 'Enter into thy grave, thy metaphoricall, thy quotidian grave, thy bed' (*Sermons*, 9.217).

3. Expostulation

[48–9] *Lord, I...cannot speake*: A close paraphrase of Jeremiah 1:6. *Climate*: region.

[53–4] *Recusancie*: Refusal to attend church services, applied to English Catholics who defied Church of England requirements. *Excommunication*: Formal exclusion from the sacraments and the life of the church, pronounced by ecclesiastical authority against a determined, unrepentant offender. *Lord of hosts*: An Old Testament appellation for God, frequently used in the context of actions performed on behalf of the people of Israel. *In the grave...praise thee*: A close paraphrase of Psalm 6:5. *opened my lips,...that my mouth might shew foorth thy praise*: A close paraphrase of Psalm 51:15. *take mee by the head, as...Habakkuk*: In Daniel 13–14, two chapters added to the canonical book by the Septuagint, the first Greek translators of the Old Testament, an angel of the Lord, taking a certain Habakkuk by the hair of his head, transports him to provide relief to the prophet Daniel, captive in Babylon.

[55–6] *his Exaltation,...his Crucifying*: A paraphrase of John 12:32. *descended into hell*: A clause in the Apostles' Creed, concerning Jesus in the interval between his crucifixion and resurrection, elaborated from a passing reference in Ephesians 4:9. *betweene Heaven and Earth, as a Meteor*: In Donne's time certain luminous objects temporarily seen in the air (fireballs, shooting stars, and meteors, in their sense of the term) were thought to belong to a lower region than that of the celestial bodies; hence, the location Donne assigns. He offers this analogy with the human condition in a letter to Goodyere: 'Our nature is Meteorique...because we partake...both earth and heaven' (*Letters*, 46).

3. Prayer

[58–9] *thy throne, the Heavens*: An allusion to Isaiah 66:1. *the knees of my heart*: This expression seems to have entered English by way of the Scottish Christmas carol 'Balulalow', which runs in part: 'The knees of my heart sall I bow, | And sing that richt balulalow' (*Oxford Book of Carols*, ed. Percy Dearmer, Ralph Vaughan Williams, and Martin Shaw (1928; rpt. 1964), 384–5).

Priest…Deacon: A priest in Christian terminology is one who has been ordained by ecclesiastical superiors—standardly, bishops—to preach and administer the sacraments. A deacon—a rank subordinate to that of a priest—performs such functions as distributing alms to the poor and sick and, in some cases, assisting in the administration of Holy Communion. The role has New Testament origins (Acts 6:1–6). thy Dove…thine Arke: After the flood sent by God had covered the Earth, Noah for several days released a dove to test whether the waters were receding. When the dove no longer returned to rest in the ark, Noah judged that it would soon be safe to disembark upon the land (Genesis 8:8–13).

4. Meditation

[64–70]   call Man a little World: Cf. Meditation 1, [6–7]. Donne argues wittily for inverting the standard conception of which is the macrocosm. wee have a Hercules: In ancient Greek myth, the twelve labours imposed on the hero Hercules (Heracles) by the goddess Hera included slaying the nine-headed Hydra, stealing the cattle of the monster Geryon, and capturing and bringing back from Hades the three-headed Cerberus.

[71]   verie meane creatures…Phisicians to themselves: The observation dates to classical antiquity; see Aristotle, History of Animals, 8.5, 594a; Cicero adds the idea of physicians learning from animals (On the Nature of the Gods, 2.50.126). The Hart…knowes an Herbe, which…throwes off the arrow: The herb was dittany, a plant native to Crete. Pliny is the ultimate source for this bit of lore (Historia Naturalis, 25.53.92). A strange kind of vomit. The dog…knowes his grasse that recovers him: Pliny again is the source for the case of a dog refusing all food until he had eaten enough grass to make him vomit up what was making him sick (Historia Naturalis, 25.51.91). Simples: medicinal preparations consisting of only one substance—for instance, a single herb.

4. Expostulation

[74–9]   the Matter: the physician's practice. thou didst not make clothes…the nakednes of the body: An allusion to Genesis 3:7. The Phisician…a long disease: A loose paraphrase of the opening of Ecclesiasticus 38:7. that spirituall phisicke…instituted in thy Church: 'The Order for the Visitation of the Sick' and 'The Communion of the Sick' in The Book of Common Prayer (1559), 300–8.

[82]   as not being: as a dead man, according to the gloss on this verse in the Authorized Version (King James Bible).

4. Prayer

[85–6]   Heale mee…I would be healed: Jeremiah 17:14. King Jareb: the honorific name of a heathen idol.

[91–2]   seven is infinite: A bit of number mysticism repeated in Sermons, 10:180. Seales of thy Church: Donne's frequent term for the sacraments, implying that baptism and Holy Communion, reverently received, certify salvation.

5. Meditation

[93–5]   *when the infectiousnes…from comming*: Although canon 67 of the Church of
England directed the minister to visit sick parishioners, it made an exception
in cases where contagion was suspected (*Constititutions or Canons* (1604),
12v). *Sicknesse is the greatest misery*: So Donne had said in a Lincoln's Inn
sermon: 'put all the miseries, that man is subject to, together, *sicknesse* is
more than all' (*Sermons*, 2.79). *Nothing can be utterly emptie*: Donne recur-
rently reflected on the impossibility of a vacuum. In the traditional world
view according to which space existed to contain something, even if only air,
the law of non-contradiction bound even God not to allow empty space
(Aristotle, *Physics*, 4.8.210b; Aquinas, *Summa Theologica*, 1.104.26). *pesti-
ducts*: transmitters of the plague. *all offices not onely…Civilitie, but…Charitie*:
The civil behaviour that characterizes societies generally was conventionally
distinguished from the acts of benevolence towards the poor, sick, and needy
that were taken to characterize a specifically Christian society.

[96–7]   *in that house, many mansions*: An allusion to John 14:2. *the Militant, and
Triumphant Church*: A conventional distinction between those Christians
currently alive, who continue the fight against sin in this world, and
Christians who have passed out of this world and who, as saved souls, enjoy
their heavenly reward. Augustine made this distinction an overarching
structural principle in *On the City of God*. *not good…a helper*: Genesis 2:18.

[98]   *their blessing was, Encrease*: God repeatedly enjoins the living things of
his creation in Genesis (1:22, 28; 8:17, 9:1,7): 'Be fruitful, and multiply'. *no
Phenix; nothing singular, nothing alone*: The mythical phoenix was a sacred
firebird, the only being of its kind, reborn from its own ashes after being
consumed by fire at the end of a very long lifespan. In denying its existence,
Donne reasons from a biblical premise and from observation of Nature: the
world as created contains only pairs of beings, male and female, and they
reproduce themselves by mating. *inhere*: remain fixed or lodged in.

[99]   *a pluralitie of worlds*: In ancient Greek philosophy Anaximander and later
atomists (Democritus and Epicurus) theorized a plurality of worlds, but the
opposed opinion of Plato and Aristotle—that the Earth was unique—was
more influential. With the invention of the telescope in the early seventeenth
century, multiple worlds came to seem a much stronger possibility, which
the astronomer Johannes Kepler professed himself willing to entertain and
explore. Overall, in Donne's time, the traditional cosmic picture still weighed
strongly against the existence of multiple worlds. *recluding*: withdrawing.

[100]   *God hath two Testaments…but this is a Scedule, and not of his*: Donne main-
tains that no warrant is to be found in either the Old or the New Testament
for a vow to live a solitary life. A 'schedule' was an appendix to a will, con-
taining material that might alter or revoke the original contents. *two Wils*:
Donne refers thus to the Old and New Testaments in Holy Sonnet 12
'Father, Part of his doble interest', l. 7. He also cautions against adding a
'scedule' to God's will in a 1624 letter (*Letters*, 9). *Codicill*: in the sixteenth
and seventeenth centuries, a synonym of 'schedule'.

5. Expostulation

[103–5] *to remember thee*: to mention and thus to remind—a rare sense, no longer current. *alien*: alienate. *understanding...will, and...memory*: In Augustine's *De Trinitate*, these three faculties composed the soul created by God in his image and likeness (Genesis 1:26)—that of the Persons of the Trinity.

[110] *that Phisician...my faithfull friend*: Probably the prominent physician Simeon Foxe (1569–1642). According to the online *Oxford Dictionary of National Biography*, Foxe contributed liberally (and anonymously) towards the erection of Donne's funeral monument, still visible in the ambulatory of St Paul's cathedral, London.

5. Prayer

[110–1] *calledst down fire...sinfull Cities*: Genesis 19:32, 30:24. God would not have destroyed the cities of Sodom and Gomorrah if they had contained just ten righteous men. *openedst the Earth...Murmurers*: Numbers 16:30–3. *threwst down the Tower...sinners*: Luke 13:4. *a helper fit for him*: Genesis 2:18.

[113–15] *Open none of my dores...to any...to undermine me in my Religion..., in...my weaknesse*: A reference to attempts by disguised Catholic priests to secure secret conversions of the sick and the dying in the privacy of their beds, and to the anxiety-driven rumours of such conversions that were circulating in London at the time. *clog*: load. *thy kingdome come, thy will be done*: Two clauses of the Lord's Prayer (Matthew 6:10; Luke 11:2).

6. Meditation

[116] *As the ill affections...infirmitie of the body*: The medical thought of Donne's day held that whatever gross matter in the blood could not be refined by the spleen resulted in the production of melancholy, one of the body's four humours. The spleen in a sick person's body was also believed to be less effective in preventing melancholy in the blood from reaching the brain and the heart, where it disordered thoughts and feelings and generated fear (Timothy Bright, *A Treatise of Melancholy* (1586), 89–91). Donne noted in a 1622 letter: 'Every distemper of the body now, is complicated with the spleen, and when we were young men we scarce ever heard of the spleen...now, every accident is accompanied with heavy clouds of melancholy...It is the spleen of the minde' (*Letters*, 134–5).

[117] *wind in the body will...seem the Gout*: The discomfort produced by abdominal gas was easily confused with pain resulting from other disorders like gallstones or gout. *Wind* (flatulence) was often treated with the same herbs that were used to treat gallstones and gout. *feare...the Mind*: In the disorientation that accompanied extreme cases of melancholy; the sufferer laughed at what was sad, ridiculed what was sensible, and was negative towards what was good (Bright, 91, 95, 97–8).

[119–20] *belie*: run counter to. *a dampe*: a vapour, gas, or mist that causes noxious effects when inhaled—a sense no longer current. *a stupefaction*: a numbness that renders the mind insensible. *declination*: decline.

6. Expostulation

[123–5] *inextricablenes*: impossibility of getting free of entanglement. *dilatory*: delaying. *froward*: perverse, ill-humoured.

[133–5] *thou wouldst ballast… gold in it*: In Virgil, *Georgics*, 4.195, sailors trim their boats with sandy ballast. The Tajus and the Pactolus rivers reportedly had golden sand (Pliny, *Natural History*, 4.34; Virgil, *Aeneid*, 10.142). *Grandfathers… Church*: Donne's characterization of the patriarchs in *The Litanye*, l. 56.

[136–9] *the Commandement*: Luke 10:27. *his Sonne*: Solomon. *it is a fearful thing… thy hands*: Hebrews 10:31.

6. Prayer

[140–2] *supple*: yielding. *conformable*: compliant. *joy with them… that mourne*: Romans 12:15. *pretermit*: omit, leave out. *Thy Son was declared… to be God*: Jesus's sonship or likeness to God is affirmed in Matthew 16:17; 17:5; 27:43; Mark 1:11; 14:61, 62; Luke 3:22; 9:35; 10:22; John 1:34; 3:16; 10:36.

[143] *determine*: conclude. *where his feare… thy will*: An allusion to Matthew 26: 39, 42 and Mark 14:36 (Jesus's prayer in the garden of Gethsemane).

7. Meditation

[147] *The Romanes began… one Dictator*: Romulus (753–716 BCE), the mythic founder of Rome, divided the people into thirty parts or 'curiae' headed by a 'rex' (king). At the beginning of the republican era (509 BCE) the king was replaced by two consuls, an institution that ended when Julius Caesar assumed the dictatorship in 49 BCE. Titus Livius narrated the history of Rome from its foundations to his present, the age of Augustus Caesar, in *Ab Urbe Condita* (From the Foundations of the City). Donne alludes to subjects treated in book 1 (kingship, consulships) and book 14, section 116 (Julius Caesar).

[148] *providence*: wise or prudent arrangement—a sense no longer current. *Death… an olde mans dore… a yong mans back*: Paraphrases of two medieval proverbs, 'Mors est ante fores:… corrige mores' (Death is at the door:… mend your ways) and 'Mors est a tergo, sit cautus quilibet ergo' (Death is at one's back, so let everyone take heed). *Proverbia Sententiaque Latinitatis Medii Aevi*, comp. Hans Walther (1963–7), nos 15132, 15130.

[149] *the best Cordiall… poyson*: Donne's penchant for paradox leads him to exaggerate. In the medical practice of his day, the use of any toxic substance as a medicine for heart disease was accompanied by some antidote to counter side effects. *Men have dyed of Joy*: Cf. *Second Anniversary*, ll. 478–9, 481.

[150]   *that Tiran Dionysius... a good Poet*: Donne's aside *I thinke the same* suggests his correct sense that he may be confusing two tyrants of Syracuse, both named Dionysius. The father (ruled 407–367 BCE) did win a prize for tragedy at Athens, but it was his excessive drinking to celebrate his victory that caused his death. His son was driven from his throne by political adversaries in 357 BCE and never regained power.

[151–3] *the greatest Man of Stile... without a grave*: This remains the standing account of the treatment of William the Conqueror's corpse by his frightened and fleeing henchmen in September 1087 (John Hayward, *The Lives of Three Norman Kings* (1613), 117). *Proctor*: proxy, agent. *Receit* (receipt or recipe): list of ingredients in a medical prescription.

[156]   *breathe out... the street*: This graphic vignette reveals how some homeless and terminally ill Londoners met their deaths. *passengers*: passers-by. *Julip* (julep): a sweetened medicated drink given to soothe or to stimulate gently. *Bezar* (bezoar): an antidote against poison produced from a calcinated substance found in the intestines of some ruminant animals.

7. Expostulation

[158]   *Augustine begg'd... what hee meant*: As Augustine brooded on the difficulties of understanding Genesis 1:1, 'In the beginning God created heaven and earth', he appealed to God: 'May I... understand how in the beginning you made heaven and earth. Moses wrote this... and went his way, passing out of this world... He is not now before me, but if he were, I would... through you beg him to explain to me the creation' (*Confessions*, 11.3.5, trans. Henry Chadwick (1991), 223).

[158]   *I see the Grammar*: Donne notes the similarity of two primary roots in Hebrew: badâd (be solitary) and bâsar (good news): nos 909 and 1319 in the *Hebrew and Chaldee Dictionary* appended to James Strong, *Exhaustive Concordance of the Bible* (1890). The written forms of both (Strong, 19, 24) may be compared.

[159 mg.] *Buxdorf*: Johannes Buxtorf (1564–1629), a Protestant scholar and professor of Hebrew at the University of Basel, published his *Lexicon Hebraicum et Chaldaicum* in 1607. *Schindler*: Valentinus Schindler, another Protestant scholar and professor of Hebrew at the universities of Wittenberg and Helmsted, compiled a *Lexicon Pentaglotton* (Lexicon of Five Languages [Hebrew, Chaldee, Syriac, Talmudic-Rabbinic, and Arabic]), published in 1612.

[161–4] *Moses father in law*: Jethro. *trade*: mutual dealings—a sense no longer current. *refractarie* (refractory): stubborn, perverse.

[167–8] *earnest*: pledge of anything to be received subsequently in greater abundance. *I may seeke... not from... schismatical singularities, but from... thy Catholique Church*: Growing numbers of 'Separatists', Puritans who refused to attend Church of England services because of scruples about ceremonial worship, met instead in their own *Conventicles*. Donne's phrase *thy Catholique Church*, by contrast, employs 'catholic' in its original Greek sense of 'universal', gesturing at an inclusive body of Christian beliefs and practices. He declared his outlook in a letter to Goodyere probably written in 1609: 'You know I never fettered...the word Religion; not...immuring it in a *Rome*, or a *Wittemberg*, or a *Geneva*; they are all virtuall beams of one Sun, and...connaturall pieces of one circle. Religion is Christianity' (*Letters*, 29).

[168–9]   *Patent*: conferral of a right, privilege, or title—here, the assurance of salvation imparted to the devout recipient of Holy Communion. *associate...the Bread with the Body of thy Sonne, so...to bee made thereby, (as...Augustine sayes)*: Augustine's most explicit discussion of what is entailed in receiving Christ's body in the sacramental bread is found in his Tractate (or Sermon) 27 on the Gospel of John, chaps. 5–6 (*Patrologia Latina*, 35:1617–19), but the images of *Arke*, *Monument*, and *Tombe* do not occur there or anywhere else, it seems, in Augustine's work. Instead, Augustine develops his notable analogy (chap. 6) between the processes of ingesting and digesting bread that sustain life in the human body and the incorporating of Christians who reverently receive the Eucharist into the mystical body of Christ, the Church.

7. Prayer

[170–1]   *Manna tasted...liked best*: Exodus 16.15–18. *thou hast imprinted...two manifest qualities*: This was a standard formulation in humoral lore. 'Complexion is a combination of two dyvers qualities of the foure elements in one bodye' (Sir Thomas Elyot, *The Castel of Helth* (1541), 2).

[172–3]   *circumstance*: surrounding context or adjunct of a fact. *substance*: essential nature or subject-matter. The distinction traces to Aristotle *Metaphysics* Δ, 8.1017b. *casuall*: occurring by chance.

8. Meditation

[175 heading]   *his owne Phisician*: Sir Theodore Turquet de Mayerne (1573–1655), the son of a French Huguenot family, took his doctoral degree in medicine at Montpellier with a dissertation on chemical remedies that advocated the theories of Paracelsus. Having served as physician to Henri IV, king of France, until his assassination in 1610, de Mayerne was appointed physician to James I in 1611 and entrusted with the treatment of several members of the royal family, including Prince Henry. Charles I reappointed de Mayerne as the king's physician upon acceding to the throne in 1625.

[176]   *tenant...proprietary*: In contrast to the *free-holder*, *Lord*, and *proprietary*, who own land or goods, the *tenant*, *farmer*, and *usufructuary* merely live on or use the land or goods of another.

[178–9]   *Are they gods? He that calld them so, cannot flatter*: Psalm 82:6, a text widely regarded in Donne's time as biblical proof for the divine right of kings, reads: 'I have said, Ye are gods'. Donne's added allusion to the following verse, Psalm 82:7: 'But ye shall die like men, and fall like one of the princes', provides a most unusual twist. *God is presented... human affections*: 'God in the Scriptures is often by the Holy Ghost invested, and represented in the qualities and affections of man' (*Sermons*, 2.288). *God... angry*: Deuteronomy 9:8, 20; Psalm 7: 11. *sorry*: This word is not used of God in the English Bible. There are, however, multiple instances of the phrase 'the Lord repented': Genesis 6:6; Exodus 32:14; 1 Samuel 15:35; Jeremiah 26:19. *weary*: Isaiah 7:13; Malachi 2:17. *heavy*: This word is not used of God in the English Bible, although His hand is called 'heavy' in the sense of 'punishing, vengeful': 1 Samuel 5:6, 11; Psalm 32:4. The grieving Jesus on the Mount of Olives is characterized as 'very heavy': Mark 14:33. *The worst... they were asleepe*: 'Elijah mocked them, and said, Cry aloud: for he is a god;... peradventure he sleepeth' (1 Kings 18:27).

[179]   *Aesculapius*: the god of medicine and healing in ancient Greek religion. *Rheubarbe*: body (Gerarde, *Herball*, 318). *Agarick* (agaric): A mushroom that grew on the larch-tree in Italy, valued for purging the phlegmatic (lethargy-producing) humour.

[180]   *as Tertullian saies... growing in his garden*: Donne is subject to multiple confusions here, perhaps revealing that he was not consulting his books or notes as he composed the *Devotions* in the early stage of his recovery. A closely similar reference in *Essays in Divinity*, 15, is more accurate. It was not the Egyptian but the Roman gods of whom Tertullian remarked sarcastically in *Apologeticus*, 13.8: 'Your gods will count themselves indebted to you' for deifying Roman emperors and thereby 'making their masters their equals' (*Patrologia Latina*, 1:336c, 347a). In both of his lengthy critiques of pagan religion, Tertullian argues that all pagan gods owe their creation to human beings, and that many such gods began their existence as mortal men and women. But he consistently equates Egyptian religion with animal worship: the deification of birds, crocodiles, serpents, and even household pets such as cats (*Apologeticus*, 24; *Ad Nationes*, 3, 8). Donne's second confusion concerns *growing in his garden*. The phrase is Juvenal's: 'Who does not know what kind of monsters demented Egypt worships?... It is forbidden... to take a bite of a leek or an onion. O holy people, whose gods grow in their gardens!' (*Satires*, 15.1–2, 9–11). *their Deitye*: the authority that God confers upon kings.

8. Expostulation

[184–8]   *thou who gavest... so had Julian*: The observation is Augustine's (*On the City of God*, 5.21). *whose image... inscription*: Jesus's question when he was shown a Roman coin bearing Caesar's image (Matthew 22:20; Mark 12:16; Luke 20:24). *God reserved one disease... cure it*: In England and France until the eighteenth century, the so-called 'king's evil' or tuberculosis of the lymph nodes in the neck, traditionally known as scrofula, was believed to be curable by the 'royal touch'—a laying on of hands regarded as a prerogative of divine right.

[189–90] *donative*: A gift or present, especially one given formally as an act of bounty. *The holy King St. Lewis*: Louis IX (1215–70), canonized by Boniface VIII in 1297, was the subject of a *Life* (1309) by Jean de Joinville that related his exploits as a crusader and his conspicuous acts of charity, especially to lepers. Any of several later editions could have been available to Donne. *our Maud*: Matilda (1080–1118), first wife of Henry I of England, was notable for her hands-on care of lepers and for the hospital she built for them at St Giles in the Fields, London. Her acts are recorded in Matthew Paris's *Chronica Majora* (Greater Chronicle) (1240–53), which saw a London edition in 1571. *Empress Placilla*: Placilla or Flacilla (died 385) was notable for her visits to the sick. Donne's knowledge of her probably derived from a 1612 English translation of a patristic Greek original, *The Ecclesiastical History of Theodoret*, 362. *pretermitting*: neglecting.

[192] *when he first . . . a hope*: While King James is solely credited here, he may not have been the first to propose Donne's ordination. Thomas Morton, dean of Gloucester, reportedly broached the matter in 1607 and offered Donne a benefice (Bald, *Donne: A Life*, 205–7).

[193–4] *I . . . was by this man of God . . . recoverd*: Donne figures the king's efficacious working on him by way of an incident in which Jesus applies clay to a blind man's eyes and tells him to go and wash in the pool of Siloam, whereupon the blind man's sight is restored (John 9:1, 6–11). *when I asked . . . he gave me a fish*: Donne conveys the futility of his requests to James for secular employment by inverting (and recombining) questions put by Jesus in Luke 11:11–12: 'If a son shall ask bread of any of you that is a father, will he give him a stone? or if he ask a fish, will he for a fish give him a serpent? Or if he shall ask an egg, will he offer him a scorpion?' *when I asked a temporall office . . . rather I took this*: After reading Donne's *Pseudo-Martyr* (1610) arguing that English Catholics were unjustified in refusing to take the oath of supremacy that affirmed the king as head of the Church of England, James repeatedly prompted Donne to enter the ministry (Jeanne Shami, 'Donne's Decision to Take Orders', in Shami, Flynn, and Hester, eds, *The Oxford Handbook of John Donne*, 523–36).

8. Prayer

[197–8] *As we see . . . a glasse*: 'For now we see through a glass, darkly; but then face to face' (1 Corinthians 13:12). *Nature reaches out . . . Industry reaches out . . . but thy hand guides that hand*: Donne is evidently echoing Tertullian's claims (*Ad Nationes*, 5) that the Christian God alone is the cosmic power that rules the lesser workings of what humans call Nature, Fate, Industry, and the like. *the increase is from thee*: 1 Corinthians 3:6–7. *faithfull Stewardship . . . thy talents*: Jesus tells the parable of the talents in Matthew 25:14–30.

[200] *thy Son . . . the clouds*: Mark 13:25. *be to him, O God . . . such a Phisician*: A memoir compiled by de Mayerne, the royal physician, in December

1623—the month in which Donne probably began to compose his *Devotions*—recorded how James at the end of autumn had been struck by severe diarrhea that aggravated his chronic symptoms of bronchial congestion and 'incredible sadness'. Then the king's arthritis returned, compelling him 'to sit in a chair and be carried or be helped along by the support of others'. These excerpts from de Mayerne are reproduced in Norman Moore, *History of the Study of Medicine in the British Isles* (1908), 101–2.

9. Meditation

[201–2] *arraign'd...fetters*: examined me in the confines (of my bed). *God presented...Pestilence*: 2 Samuel 24:13. *Satan...brought in, fires from heaven, and winds from the wildernes*: This is not a biblical allusion. In John Milton's *Paradise Regained* (1673), after failing to tempt Jesus, Satan vengefully sends down upon his intended victim 'Fierce rain with lightning mixt, . . . nor slept the winds | ...but...fell | On the vext Wilderness' (4.412–16). The striking similarity between Donne's description and Milton's narration resists explanation, however, since no source or analogue for Milton's lines has yet been identified (*Variorum Commentary on the Poems of John Milton*, Vol. 4: *Paradise Regained*, ed. Walter MacKellar (1975), 230).

[202–3] *The names...the place affected*: Plurisie (pleurisy or pleuritis), an inflammation of the membrane lining the lungs and chest, is so called from Greek 'pleurîtis' (rib cage, side of body). *the falling sicknes*: epilepsy. *The Wolf*: Lupus (Latin for wolf) is a chronic disease in which the body is attacked by its own immune system, producing pain and inflammation in various body parts. *the Canker*: cancer, identified as a crawling, eating ulcer or malignant tumor, and by association given the name 'crab' (Latin 'cancer'). *the Polypus*: a tumor that grew tenaciously at its place of origin on the body, so named from the clinging tentacles of the octopus (Latin 'polypus').

[203] *that question...more names or things*: Two schools of thought in medieval philosophy, nominalism and realism, were divided on this question. Nominalism held that general, abstract, and universal terms have no objectively existing things to which they refer—hence, that there are more names than things. Realism held that universals have a real, objective existence and are the things to which general and abstract terms refer—hence, that there are as many things as names. The nominalist–realist divide continued to affect logical method in Donne's day.

[204] *to deliver the names...how intricate a work*: Contemporary medical treatises listed a great number of fevers, defined as 'unnatural heate...beginning at the heart' and spread 'by the arteries and veins into the whole body'. One authority classified fevers as either simple or compound: simple being a single fever; compound being a number of simultaneous fevers, or a fever complicated by another kind of illness (Philip Barrough, *The Method of Physick* (1583), 217).

[205] *countermind*: defeated by a counter-plot. *In many diseases,...a symptom...is so violent, that the phisician...cure of that*: Donne the preacher would make

the same point and cite 'burning Fevers' and 'Dysenteries' as examples (*Sermons*, 5:233). *accident*: non-essential feature.

[206]   *intermit*: interrupt, suspend. *Is it not so in States too?*: Extended analogies between the human body and the body politic remind the reader that the *Devotions* are dedicated to Prince Charles, the heir to the throne.

[209]   *apert*: open. *ingenuous*: straightforward. *avowable*: to be acknowledged.

[211]   *I am...glad...they write (they hide nothing from the world)*: Donne evidently refers to his physicians' posting of bulletins about his condition on the door of his residence, the deanery of St Paul's (Edmund Gosse, *Life and Letters of John Donne* (1899; rpt. 1959), 2:185).

9. Expostulation

[212]   *They are gods*: Another allusion to Psalm 82:6. On the association of this Psalm verse with kings and princes and its permutations in Donne's religious and political thought, see Debora Shuger, 'Donne's Absolutism', in Shami, Flynn, and Hester, eds, *The Oxford Handbook of John Donne*, 690–703. *That king of Aragon Alfonsus*: The monarch and astronomer who uttered this saying was Alfonso X 'el Sabio' (the Wise), king of Castille (1221–84). Its context was the difficulty of trying to make newer astronomical ideas fit with the inherited Ptolemaic system. The source is Juan de Mariana, *Historia de España* (History of Spain) (1605), 30.20. Donne would get Alfonso's title right in a later reference to this story (*Sermons*, 5.299).

[215–16] *comfortably*: with mental or spiritual contentment—a sense no longer current. *soupled* (suppled): made compliant or submissive.

[219–20] *washed...Lambe*: Revelation 7:14. *I may be saved...by...thy decree for my salvation*: Donne places notable emphasis on the doctrine of election, the salvation destined for the souls whom God has elected or chosen. This doctrine, rooted in Scripture and Augustine's theology, figured prominently in Calvinism and in the theology of the Church of England in the 1620s.

[221]   *those Sentences...desperation*: Examples include Matthew 10:33 and 25:41–6; Romans 2:5–9; Revelation 14:9–11. *thy morning dew*: In Exodus 16:13–15 the morning dew evaporated, leaving manna on the ground, the food sent by God.

9. Prayer

[223–4] *an Eye in Nature, that kills...eye of a Serpent*: The basilisk could supposedly kill its victims simply by looking at them (Pliny, *Natural History*, 8.32–3). *his Image...my Creation*: Genesis 1:27.

10. Meditation

[227]   *all these are Concentrique...only that is Eccentrique*: Donne updates the astronomical basis on which his *First Anniversary* had moralized the universe. Here he adopts the new, Copernican view in which the planets revolve around the sun as their centre, but he adds a pessimistic note by

substituting *decay, ruine* for the sun. What is outside or *Eccentrique* to this *Concentrique* universe must, by definition and in fact, lie beyond the realm of creation: it must be *never made*. This Donne identifies with the essential light emanating from the being of God.

[228]   *our soules...if...not made immortal by preservation, their Nature could not keep them from...Annihilation*: Donne articulates the position known as conditional immortality, which was gaining support in various quarters in his day. The Italian theologian Faustus Socinus (1539–1604) offered an especially clear formulation. He argued that 'since man has the power of reproducing his species, he must be naturally mortal, for an immortal being does not beget children...If man had not sinned, he might have been preserved from death by the favor of God, though naturally mortal' (*Works* (1656), 1:587). Nicholas Hill also advocated conditional immortality in *Philosophia...proposita simpliciter, non edocta* (Philosophy...set forth simply, not learnedly) (1601), 44. Donne owned a copy of Hill's work that had formerly belonged to Ben Jonson (Keynes, *Bibliography of Donne*, 4th edn, 270–1).

[229]   *The Heavens have...drownd the world*: The rain by which God brought the flood upon the earth (Genesis 7:4) lasted for forty days and forty nights. *they shall have their Fever, and burn the world*: The fire from God's altar, the flaming mountain, and the falling star will consume the world and its inhabitants in three phases (Revelation 8:5–11). *the world had a foreknowledge*: See the note on [28–30], Expostulation 2. *some made provision*: Noah and his family, obeying God's commandment (Genesis 6:18–22).

[230–1]   *the Dog-Starre...an infectious exhalation*: Sirius, the Dog-Star, in the constellation Canis Major (the Greater Dog), is the brightest star in the night sky. Due to its intense luminosity and closeness to Earth, the Dog-Star was traditionally accorded great influence in cosmic and human affairs. During the so-called 'Dog-Days' (August–September), its period of ascendancy in astrology, this star was thought to foment illness by increasing the choleric (anger-producing) humour in the body and inflicting extremes of hot weather as well as violent fevers. However, as Donne says, precautions could be taken against the effects of the Dog-Star since its period of ascendancy was fixed by calculation and therefore knowable in advance. *Comets and blazing starres...no Almanack tells us*: In Donne's day comets, shooting stars, and meteors were thought to originate as vapours solidified in the Earth and then emitted into the atmosphere rather than as heavenly phenomena. See the note on [55–6], Expostulation 3. It could not be predicted when a *blazing starre* (meteor) might occur.

[231–3]   *It is so also...in the societies of men, in States, and Commonwealths*: Again Donne may have had Prince Charles in mind when crafting this analogy. *God knew many heavy sins...murmuring in their hearts*: Exodus 16:7–12; Numbers 14:27, 29.

[234]   *infatuated*: senseless. *Arcana Imperii, secrets of State*: the prerogative,
         reserved to a monarch, of taking action without consulting his ministers or
         informing his people. In 1622 James justified its exercise in 'His Majesies
         Declaration, Touching his proceedings in the late Assemblie and Convention
         of Parliament' (King James VI and I, *Political Writings*, ed. Johann P.
         Sommerville (1994), 250). While the concept traced back to ancient Rome
         (Tacitus, *Annals*, 2.36), this presumptive royal right was an increasingly
         fraught issue for parliaments under James I and Charles I. The uncondi-
         tional secrecy that Donne attaches to *Arcana Imperii* here and elsewhere
         (*Sermons*, 5.298) bespeaks an uneasiness that remains well short of critique.
         Yet the uneasiness itself is noteworthy, given Donne's overall consistency in
         defending the royal prerogative. See Shuger, 'Donne's Absolutism', 694.

10. Expostulation

[235]   *I have bin told...by...Nazianzen, that his Sister...did use...a pious impu-*
         dencie: The incident is narrated in Gregory of Nazianzus's funeral oration
         on his sister, Gorgonia (*c*.326–*c*.372). When she suffered a mysterious and
         terrible illness, she (as the Greek says) 'was unashamed in her reverent and
         fine unashamedness'. Prostrating herself before an altar, she implored Christ
         to heal her, vowing not to remove her head from the altar until she was
         granted recovery. She then rubbed her whole body with a piece of conse-
         crated bread moistened with her tears. Gorgonia's prayer was answered; she
         was healed instantly ('In praise of his sister Gorgonia', Oration 8, sec. 18,
         Patrologia Graeca, 35:809–10). Donne would narrate this incident more cir-
         cumstantially in *Sermons*, 5.364.

[236]   *Augustine, wisht that Adam had not sinned, therefore that Christ might not have*
         died: A unique context in Augustine's copious writings against the Pelagian
         heresy is indicated by the contrast between the sinning Adam and the sin-
         less Christ. The wish that Donne alludes to takes the form of a passing
         counterfactual exclamation made by Augustine as he rejects Pelagius's
         claim regarding the necessity of sin. 'We do not say to them, what this man
         has proposed...that *sin was necessary so that there might be a cause for the*
         mercy of God. Would there had never been misery, so this mercy would not
         have been necessary': *De Natura et Gratia* (On Nature and Grace), 1.28,
         Patrologia Latina, 44:260–1. Elsewhere, however, in his anti-Pelagian writ-
         ings Augustine insists on the brute fact of Adam's sin and its universal
         effects: thus, on the necessity of Christ's death. According to the Pelagians,
         humans could escape the taint and penalty of sinfulness by exercising their
         free will in living virtuous lives or by their innate harmony with the law of
         nature; such persons saved themselves without benefit of Christ. In his
         Christmas sermon of 1624 (the same year as the *Devotions*) Donne would
         emphasize his own anti-Pelagian outlook: 'may I not say, that I had rather
         be redeemed by Christ Jesus than bee innocent? rather be beholden to
         Christs death, for my salvation, than to *Adams* standing in his innocencie?'
         (*Sermons*, 6.183).

[236 mg. Josephus] *the Serpent..., did goe upright, and speake*: God punished the serpent that deceived Adam and Eve by depriving it of the power of speech as well as its feet, compelling it to crawl and wiggle along the ground (Josephus, *Jewish Antiquities*, 1.50–1). Donne's comments on the serpent seem to have been triggered by the occurrence of *Serpenti* in his Latin heading to Meditation 10. *begin at the heele... bruise that*: Genesis 3:15.

[240]   *sayes thy Prophet, we conceive them in the darke,... We doe them in the light*: Micah 2:1. *Augustine confesses... sinnes, which he never did*: Confessions, 2.3.7.

[243]   *Physicke... draws the peccant humour to it selfe, that...the weight...may carry that humour away*: In humoral medicine, the *peccant* (unhealthy) excess of one humour needed to be purged without disturbing the balance of the other humours. To rid the body of this excess there was a process modelled on the naturally occurring crisis in an illness. Donne would detail this process in his New Year's Day sermon of 1625, a year after the illness that is the subject of the *Devotions*: 'The proper use and working of *purging Physick*' is that 'the Physick lies still, and draws the peccant humours together; and... then... Nature her selfe, and their own waight expels them out' (*Sermons*, 6.198).

[244]   *that mercy,... Augustine apprehends, when he sayes... Thou hast forgiven me those sinnes which I have done, and those sinnes which only by thy grace I have not done*: A selective and free paraphrase of Augustine's reflections on his struggle with his sexual appetites and fantasies (*Confessions*, 10.30.42).

10. Prayer

[246]   *hee knew not the day of Judgement*: Matthew 24:36. *he knew it not so, as that he might tell it us*: Donne's explanation follows that of the church fathers Jerome, Augustine, and Chrysostom. See Cornelius à Lapide, *Commentaria in Scripturam Sacram* (1614–15), 9th edn (1866–77), 15:518.

[250–1]   *preventing grace*: the grace bestowed by God even before a sinner realizes the need for it or asks for it, essential to salvation because it prepares the sinner to receive the benefits of further grace (Augustine, *De Natura et Gratia*, 1.35; *PL*, 44:264). The Easter collect in the Book of Common Prayer refers to 'Thy special grace preventing us'; preventing grace also figures in article 10 of the Thirty-Nine Articles of the Church of England. thy *brazen Serpent*: God commanded Moses to raise a serpent of brass upon a pole; the Israelites who looked on it were cured of a plague (Numbers 21:8–9); this serpent prefigured the crucified Christ (John 3:14). *Lyon... of Judah*: Hosea 5:14, and taken as a figure of Christ in Revelation 5:5. that *Lyon... may devoure*: the figure of the devil, in 1 Peter 5:8. *Wisdom... Serpent*: Jesus enjoins his disciples to be wily and wary as he sends them out into the world (Matthew 10:16). *Malice... Serpent*: Satan and his ways in Revelation 12:9. *Thy Dove... thy Arke*: The sign by which Noah knew that the flood waters had receded enough for the land to become habitable again (Genesis 8:10–12). Donne follows typological precedent in reading the dove with the olive branch as a figure for the peace with God brought by the Holy Spirit, and the ark as the Christian church.

11. Meditation

[253–4] *the heart of man…is alwayes in…motion*: Donne may be alluding to William Harvey's discovery that the contraction of the heart's right ventricle propels a charge of blood into the pulmonary artery, while the contraction of the left ventricle propels the blood through the arteries. Although this discovery was not published until 1628, in *De Motu Cordis* (On the Motion of the Heart), Harvey did make it public in lectures delivered at the College of Physicians in London in 1615. Harvey was appointed physician extraordinary to James I in 1618. Donne could have learned of the motion of the heart through one or another of these possible points of contact with Harvey's work. *still pretending…to furnish all the powers, and faculties with all that they have*: Donne expresses a view, tracing to Greek antiquity, that the heart is the seat of life and, variously, of soul, intellect, emotion, and sensation. See Plato, *Timaeus*, 69E–70D; Aristotle, *De Generatione Animalium* (On the Generation of Animals), 2.5.738B. *pretending*: claiming to have the power—a no longer current sense. *Primogeniture*: the principle, custom, or law by which the father's property or title descended to the eldest son, introduced into England at the Norman Conquest.

[255] *a Triumvirate*: a ruling body of three. Galen's conception of the heart, liver, and brain as the three 'originary' organs suggests that they function as a triumvirate (*On the Natural Faculties*, 1.6.13). *the Heart alone is…in the Throne, as King*: In what became a standard political application in medieval and early modern Europe, John of Salisbury identified the king with the head or brain in his version of the allegory of the body politic in *Policraticus* (1159), books 5 and 6. Donne by contrast articulates the metaphorical identification of the king with the heart propounded in Edward Forsett's *A Comparative Discourse of the Bodies Natural and Politic* (1606), a principal source for divine right and royalist ideas.

[256–8] *second Dictates of Nature…not…the Primarie Law of Nature*: While Donne's vocabulary is too general to trace a specific source, he is invoking a distinction basic to classical as well as Thomistic conceptions of natural law. There is a first (because prior) natural law; it is divine and universal, and it accords with human nature in being perceptible by reason. This *Primarie Law of Nature* is the eternal and immutable foundation of human law. Secondary—more often termed 'positive' from Latin 'positum' (laid down)—natural law consists in the rules enacted by civil society. It includes the rules of *Discourse* encompassed by Donne's *Consequences and Conclusions arising out of Nature, or deriv'd from Nature*. Positive or secondary natural law shares a basis in reason with primary natural law, but its formulations and applications take circumstances into account, giving it an element of variability that primary natural law does not have. Influential treatments of natural law include Aristotle, *Nicomachean Ethics*, 1134b18–1136a9; Aquinas, *Summa Theologica*, 1a2ae, 91.2.4. *no Proprietie, no Meum et Tuum, but an universall Communitie . . . there was no Superioritie, no Magistracie*: Two major examples of adaptation to circumstances in positive natural law that were not present in *the primarie Law of Nature*: (1) the institution of private property, *Meum et Tuum* (what's mine and what's yours); (2) the creation of *Magistracie*, rulers who wielded power over others by virtue of their office.

[259–60]   *when we seeme to begin with others, . . . wee ourselves are principally in our contemplation . . . And this is the reward . . . of Kings . . . when they seeme to be obey'd voluntarily, they who doe it, doe it for their owne sakes*: These remarkably frank reflections on self-interest as a motive for human actions indicate why positive or secondary natural law is necessary to sustain the bonds that hold society together against the counter-pulls of individualistic self-seeking. *officious*: active in doing one's duty—a sense no longer current.

[262–4]   *the noblest . . . Cordialls*: Donne's phrasing echoes the hitherto untranslated *Nobilibus* in the Latin heading that prefaces Meditation 11. *if they be often taken, . . . no Cordialls . . . have any extraordinary operation*: Medical experts of Donne's day warned of dire side effects if an herb mixture—such as honeysuckle or ivy—was taken for too long or in too great quantity (*The newe Jewell of Health*, trans. George Baker (1576), 50; *A New Herbal*, trans. Henry Lyte (1585), 281). *When God had made this Earth . . . it was but a little help, that he had, to make other things . . . yet how little of this Earth, is the greatest Man?*: Donne expatiates on Genesis 2:7: 'God formed man of the dust of the ground and breathed into his nostrils the breath of life; and man became a living soul.' *the toppe . . . wherein so many Absolons take so much pride, is but a bush*: King David's son Absalom, praised throughout Israel for his beauty, had an abundance of long hair. As he was riding horseback, it got caught in the branches of an oak tree, whereupon an adversary killed him (2 Samuel 14:25; 18:9, 10–14). Donne implicates the vanity of fashionable, long-haired youths of his day. *intestine*: internal, inward.

11. Expostulation

[266–70]   *thy . . . Sonnes Coheire*: Romans 8:16–17. *I the Lord search the Heart*: Jeremiah 17:10. *single hearts*: After the Holy Spirit descended on Jesus's disciples at Pentecost, they conducted themselves with 'singleness of heart' (Acts 2:46). Paul exhorts other Christian congregations to this virtue (Ephesians 6:5; Colossians 3:22). *docile*: teachable. *docile* occurs in the Vulgate Latin reading of 1 Kings 3:9. *apprehensive*: understanding. *wise hearts*: Said of the men and the women who gave gifts for the tabernacle of the Lord in Exodus 35:10, 22, 25; also of Solomon in 1 Kings 3:12; and of one who keeps the commandment in Proverbs 10:8 and Ecclesiastes 8:5; 10:2. *perfit hearts*: Ascribed to Asa in 1 Kings 15:14 and 2 Chronicles 15:17; Hezekiah in 2 Kings 20:3; those who gathered to crown David king in 1 Chronicles 12:38, and those who gathered to crown Solomon king in 1 Chronicles 29:9. *stonie hearts*: Ezekiel 11:19 and 36:26. *cleane hearts*: Psalm 51:10. *hearts . . . like Ovens*: Said of the men of the tribe of Ephraim, who debauched the king and princes in Hosea 7:6.

[273–5]   *a melting heart*: Joshua 14:8; Isaiah 13;7; 19:1; Ezekiel 21:7. *a troubled heart*:
2 Kings 6:11; John 14:1, 27. *a wounded heart*: Psalm 109:22. *a broken...a
contrite heart*: Psalm 51:17. *Thou, O Lord...Wormewood*: A complaint of the
faithful whom God has afflicted (Lamentations 3:15). The plant *artemisia
absinthium* (*Wormewood*) has an intensely bitter taste. It was used in medi-
cine. *thou hast cleared...my heart is alive*: The faithful whom God has
afflicted discover new hope (Lamentations 3:22–4).

11. Prayer

[278–83]   *many Mansions*: John 14:2. *the house...Annoynted*: the king's residence.
Job...his Eyes: Job 31:1. *Thy Sonne...a sadnesse in his Soule to death*:
Jesus's words in the garden of Gethsemane (Mark 14:34; Matthew 26:38).
reluctation: internal struggle—a common term in the seventeenth century.
deprecation: earnest desire that something be averted or removed. *Yet not
my will, but thine bee done*: Luke 22:42. *thine adopted sonnes*: Galatians 4:5.
Thou...hast made even the flesh of Vipers, to assist in Cordialls: Edward
Topsell, *Historie of Serpents* (1608), includes various recipes for preparing
the flesh of vipers to be eaten or distilled into broth or ointment (302–6).
My God...forsaken mee: Matthew 27:46; Mark 15:34. *Neither did hee...rec-
ommend it to thee*: Luke 23:46. *this day in Paradise*: Luke 23:43.

12. Meditation

[284 heading]   *They apply Pidgeons*: This curious external use of pigeon flesh had a
certain vogue in seventeenth-century England. John Hall, Shakespeare's
son-in-law, reported: 'I had...Convulsions of the Mouth and Eyes. Then
was a pigeon cut open alive, and applied to my feet, to draw down the
Vapours' (*Select Observations on English Bodies* (1657), ed. Joseph Harriet
(1964), 150).

[285–6]   *how great an Elephant...a Mouse destroyes?*: The deadly menace posed by a
mouse running up inside an elephant's trunk was noted by Garcia de Orta,
*Aromatum, et simplicium aliquot medicamentorum apud indos nascentium
Historia* (History of Spices and of Several Medicinal Simples Produced in
the Indies) (1567), 70, 388. *single money*: small change. *a violent shak-
ing...almost made stone*: In Paracelsus's synthesis of alchemy, medicine,
astrology, and occult lore, ice was the most densely compacted substance
produced by 'Coagulation...by cold.' 'Winter stars...coagulate all waters
into snows and ice' (*Hermetic and Alchemical Writings of Paracelsus*, 1:154).
our Nourse should overlay us: A caregiver who lies upon the body of a child
may smother it. The air we breathe should sustain our life, not take it away.

[287–8]   *Plinie hunted...dyed*: Pliny the Elder (23–79 CE) compiled the widely circu-
lated *Historia Naturalis* (Natural History). In 79, when Mt. Vesuvius—not
Mt. Etna, as Donne says—erupted, Pliny was a Roman naval commander
in the bay of Naples. While attempting to get closer to the volcano, perhaps
to assist in a rescue, he was fatally overcome by fumes. His nephew, Pliny
the Younger, describes the accident in his *Epistulae* (Letters), 6.16, 18–20.

a long shutt Well, or…a new opened Myne: Two man-made conduits by which lethal gases could enter the atmosphere.

[291] *But what have I done…? They tell me it is my Melancholy…It is my study: doth not my Calling call for that? I have don nothing, wilfully, perversly toward it*: Donne's physicians have advised him that he suffers from 'unnatural melancholy', 'engendered' in the brain by, so it was thought, excessive mental exercise (Bright, *Treatise of Melancholy*, 2, 24, 194). Donne refuses to accept blame.

[292–3] *Examples of men, that have bin their own executioners*: The sources are Plutarch's *Lives of the Noble Greeks and Romans* and Valerius Maximus's 'De Mortibus Non Vulgaribus' (On Extraordinary Deaths) in *Dictorum Factorum Memorabilium* (Memorable Doings and Sayings); specific references follow. *some have alwayes had poyson…in a hollow ring*: As did the eminent Carthaginian general Hannibal (247–183/2 BCE) (Plutarch, 'Life of Titus Flamininus', 20.5–6, in *Lives*, Loeb edn, 10:380–1). *some in their Pen*: Plutarch, 'Life of Demosthenes', 29.3–30.3, notes that this was reported of the famous Athenian orator and statesman (384/83–322 BCE) (*Lives*, Loeb edn, 7:72–5). *some have beat out their braines at the wal of their prison*: As did Herennius Siculus, adviser and friend of the younger of two brothers, Caius Sempronius Gracchus (d. 121). The Gracchi were prosecuted as enemies of the state when they undertook to reform Rome's social and political structures to help the lower classes. Herennius' imprisonment stemmed from his association with the Gracchi (Valerius Maximus, 9.12.6—external series; Loeb edn, 2:370–1). *some have eaten the fire out of their chimneys*: As did Porcia, daughter of Cato the Younger, wife of Brutus (Valerius Maximus, 4.6.5; Loeb edn, 1:406–7). *one is said…to have strangled himself…by crushing his throat between his knees*. Valerius Maximus (9.12.1—external series; Loeb edn, 2: 372–5) identifies the Coma who did this violence to himself as a brother of Cleon, the fifth-century BCE Athenian demagogue. *gangred*: gangrened. *insensible*: imperceptible.

[293–5] *But extend this…to any Politike body, to a State*: In the following allegory of the body politic, in which *the life of all is Honour, and just respect, and due reverence* and malicious rumours pose the most serious dangers, Donne again appears to have Prince Charles, the dedicatee of the *Devotions*, in view. The pointed references to *infectious rumors, detracting and dishonourable Calumnies, Libels…that wound a State most*, arise at home must allude to the self-appointed embassy of Prince Charles, accompanied by his close friend, George Villiers, duke of Buckingham, to seek the hand of the Spanish Infanta in marriage. The two youths' stay in Spain between March and early October 1623 aroused considerable public opposition in England. (The match did not take place.) Also noteworthy is Donne's repeated reference to the king as heart of the body politic, proposed by the royalist and divine-right apologist Edward Forsett. *gangred*: gangrened.

[296–7] *channell*: watercourse in or along a street. *shambles*: butchering place. *vault*: covered sewer—a sense no longer current. *they that write…of creatures*

naturally disposed to the ruine of Man,...mention the Flea [mg. Arduino]:
Sante Arduino, a physician active at Pisa in 1430, was the author of *De
Venenis* (On Poisons); its first edition (1562) treats the flea on 506. *a good
Pigeon...the Head*: The 'hot and moist' qualities attributed to pigeon flesh
made it an excellent antidote for the 'cold and dry' excesses of melancholy
(Thomas Coghan, *The Haven of Health* (1584), 134).

12. Expostulation

[299–300] *Hierogliphique*: A pictorial character in a writing system, specifically that of
ancient Egypt. *the dew of Heaven*: Genesis 27:28.

[301–4] *acceptations*: receivings of what is offered. *Commination*: threatening of
divine punishment or vengeance. *reparation*: spiritual restoration—a sense
no longer current. *thy blessed Spirit...the Dove*: Matthew 3:16; Mark 1:10;
Luke 3:22; John 1:32.

12. Prayer

[308–11] *through the Law...made it a sacrifice for sinne*: 'Bring...a young pigeon, or
a turtledove, for a sin offering' (Leviticus 5:7, 12:6). *a witnes of thy Sonnes
baptisme*: Matthew 3:16. *the holy Hill...cleane hands*: Psalm 24:3, 4.

13. Meditation

[312–14] *more sea in the Western, than in the Eastern Hemisphere*: This assertion that
the Pacific Ocean is larger than the Atlantic indicates the level of knowledge
that had been attained through observation, measurement, and record-keep-
ing on voyages of exploration up to Donne's day. *more stars under the
Northerne, than under the Southern Pole*: The source is evidently Benedict
Pererius, *Commentarii et Disputationes in Genesin* (1601), 99. Donne had
applied this alleged fact in the *Second Anniversary*, ll. 78–80. *vicissitudi-
nary*: marked by alteration, coming by turns—the *OED*'s earliest citation.
positive, and dogmaticall: objectively certain (a no longer current sense), and
based on first principles accepted as truths. *Happinesse changes the name*:
Donne may be reflecting on Latin, a language he knew well, where *felicitas*
is happiness in the sense of 'good fortune'; *beatus* or *beatitudo* in the sense
of 'rational contentment or blessedness'; and *commoda* in the sense of
'being to one's advantage or in one's interest'. Donne may additionally be
indebted to Augustine, who notes that while everyone pursues happiness,
whatever language they speak, the word said in Latin gives pleasure only to
the speaker of Latin, not the speaker of Greek, who takes pleasure only
from the word in Greek (*Confessions*, 10.20.29).

[315–18] *subsist*: keep on, persist—senses no longer current. *intestine*: internal to the
affairs of a country or people. *voluntary Confessions*: This theme emerges
associatively from the foregoing heading in which the *Sicknes declares* itself.
The Latin counterpart in the heading is *fassus* (confessed). *confessions...the
Rack*: In the reigns of Elizabeth I and James I, a prisoner could be sub-
jected to having his or her limbs stretched on a rack for the purpose of

gaining information, if the Privy Council so ordered, and royal permission was obtained. *Complices*: accomplices. *A woman...birth of her Son*: John 16:21. *purchase*: acquisition, gain—senses no longer current.

13. Expostulation

[320–1] *no spotted sacrifice?*: The Jewish ceremonial law specified that sacrifice to God was to be made of heifers and lambs 'without spot' (Numbers 19:2; 28:3, 9, 11; 29:17, 26). In New Testament allegorizing, the self-sacrificial death of Jesus is described as being 'without spot' (Hebrews 9:14; 1 Peter 1:19). *hath thy Spouse...no spots*: Paul affirms as much of the church redeemed by Christ (Ephesians 5:27).

[326–7] *Even my spotts...thy Sonnes body*: Paul's frequent metaphor for the church is 'the body of Christ' (Romans 7:4, 12:5; 1 Corinthians 12:27; Ephesians 5:30); Donne says in effect that as a Christian he, spots and all, remains a member of the church. *thou hast not left...in Hell*: Psalm 16:10, allegorized as a prophecy of Christ in Acts 2:27. *that place...thy right hand*: The New Testament frequently refers to Jesus as standing or sitting at God's right hand (Acts 7:56, 57; Romans 8:34; Colossians 3:1; Hebrews 10:12; 12:2; 1 Peter 3:22).

13. Prayer

[328–9] *the ordinary discomfort...That the house is visited, And that...thy tokens are upon the patient*: Donne alludes to contemporary vocabulary used to register a particular outbreak of plague. There had been a major plague epidemic in London in 1603; there would be another in 1625. Infection may have been on the rise when Donne was composing the *Devotions*. *what a wretched...House, which is not visited by thee, and what...is that Man, that hath not thy Markes upon him?*: Throughout the Bible, the expressions 'to be visited by God' or 'to be marked by God' carry mainly negative connotations of punishment or vengeance on sin. Here, however, Donne is employing paradoxical transvaluation: he asserts not just that a negative can lead to a positive outcome, but that the negative simply is the positive. Thus the likely biblical allusions in this connection are Job 10:12: 'Thy visitation hath preserved my spirit' (Job's single positive formulation in a run of bitter complaints to God), and Galatians 6:17: 'From henceforth let no man trouble me: for I bear in my body the marks of the Lord Jesus' (Paul's affirmation that the sufferings he has undergone in spreading the Christian gospel neutralize his prospective further sufferings).

[330] *reversion*: return of an estate to a donor. *Civill conveyance*: transfer of property from one person to another by means of a deed.

14. Meditation

[331 heading–332] *the criticall dayes*: 'the days wherein a man may judge, discern, or pass sentence of a Disease' according to the conjunction of its symptoms with the astrological positions of the planets (William Salmon, *Synopsis*

Medicinae (1671), 175). Hippocrates originated this notion of pathological–calendrical correlation ('Epidemics', 1.26, in *Works*, Loeb edn, 1:184–5). *their times, and their seasons*: A phrase occurring three times in Scripture (Daniel 2:21; Acts 1:7; 1 Thessalonians 5:1), each time with reference to the unknowability of when God will intervene in human life.

[333–5]   *if Tyme…be an essential part of our happines*: Augustine declares that our memory of past experiences of happiness is essential to recognizing happiness when we subsequently experience it (*Confessions*, 10.21.31). *Superficies*: outer surface as apprehended by the eye. *Tyme…the Measure of Motion*: Aristotle's definition in *Physics*, 4.11, 219B. *now, the present, and the Now is past*: Paraphrased excerpts from Augustine's meditations on time (*Confessions*, 11.24.31; 18.23; 27.34). *Eternity is not an everlasting flux of Tyme…Eternity had bin…though time had never beene*: Augustine, *Confessions*, 11.11.13.

[338–9]   *distasted*: deprived of taste—a sense no longer current. *unapprehensive*: slow to understand. *Youth is their Criticall Day; that…makes them…pleasures, and possessions*: Augustine reflects on youthful experiences that were 'times of joy': 'I experienced it in my mind when I was glad, and the knowledge of it stuck in my memory, so that I could remind myself of it, sometimes with scorn, sometimes with desire, according to the varied character of the things which I remember myself delighting in' (*Confessions*, 10.21.30, trans. Chadwick, 197–8). What Augustine emphasizes about his youthful state—his acute perceptions, his retentive memory, his ready judgement—tallies closely with Donne's characterization of *Youth* and his pun on *Criticall Day*. Greek 'kriteos' means 'to be determined', 'to be judged'; 'krísis' means 'determination', 'judgement'. *Midsomer*: in the ecclesiastical calendar, the nativity of John the Baptist (June 24); alternatively, the summer solstice (June 21). Popular celebrations through the centuries did not differentiate sharply between the two dates.

14. Expostulation

[345]   *verdure*: flourishing condition. *Climactericall yeares*: years that were multiples of seven, or nine, or both, in a person's lifespan or, by another definition, three generations. Such years were considered to be times of crisis—in particular, vulnerability to death. *Adam* lived to 930 years of age (Genesis 5:5). *Shem*, Noah's eldest son, lived 602 years (Genesis 11:10–11). *the next world*: the world after the flood. *Abraham* lived 175 years (Genesis 25:7). All three patriarchs survived for three generations of their descendants, and Shem's and Abraham's ages at death are also multiples of seven. *father of the faithful*: God named Abraham 'a father of many nations' with whom he would keep everlasting covenant if they remained faithful (Genesis 17:5–8).

[346]   *Virgin Mary…in hers*: This concern with the Virgin Mary's age at death is curious. Although the Bible does not record her death, apocryphal sources from the third century onwards reported that she was translated directly into heaven from a state of natural sleep (Dormition) or that she was resurrected and taken into heaven three days after dying a natural death

(Assumption). Both traditions, respectively those of eastern and western Christianity, held that Mary lived many years. Possibly Donne inferred that Mary lived for three generations, thus satisfying the alternative definition of *climacterical years*.

[348]   *Indications...Judicatures*: In the sequence of critical days or crisis in medical practice combined with astrology, the second phase comprised the *Indications* (a current assessment of the patient's state), and the third phase the *Judicatures* (a judgement on the patient's state, a prognosis) (Salmon, *Synopsis Medicinae*, 175, 15). Donne metaphorically extends these medical procedures to assess and judge the degree of unbelief in Christ as Saviour, in New Testament times and in his own.

[349–51]   *the Critical day to the Sadducees*: Matthew 22:36, 39. *This...is a fearefull Indication, when we will...seeke, and finde, what dayes are fittest to forsake thee in; To say...Now I may make new friends by changing my old religion*: Donne captures the fever pitch of ambition that spread among English courtiers seeking to advance themselves by associating with Spanish Catholics while the proposed marriage between Prince Charles and the Infanta remained a live possibility in 1623–4. One tireless London newshound reported to his regular correspondent, the English ambassador at The Hague: 'Priests and Jesuites swarme here extraordinarilie, and are grown so bold that yf any of qualitie, men or women,...have any frends or kindred that way affected, under that colour they will find accesse to them and use perswasion...They will finde meanes...to...give out that they were...won [converted] by them' (To Sir Dudley Carleton, 6 December 1623, in *Letters of John Chamberlain*, ed. McClure, 2:532).

[354–9]   *Evenings and Mornings...dayes in the Creation*: Genesis 1:5; 8; 13; 19; 23; 31. *determin*: come to an end. *Bread* and *Wine...action, and participation of that bread, and that wine*: Donne recasts as an affirmation a petition of the officiating minister in the post-Communion prayer: 'O merciful Father,...grant that we receiving...bread and wine, according to Thy Son our Savior Jesu Christ's holy institution, in remembrance of his death and passion, may be partakeers of his most blessed Body and Blood' (*Book of Common Prayer* (1559), 263). *the Critical, the Decretory day*: the last of the critical days, in which decisive judgement was passed on the course of an illness (Salmon, *Synopsis Medicale*, 175, 179).

14. Prayer

[362–3]   *the visitation...an overshadowing*: Luke 1:35. *God of consolation*: Romans 15:5.

15. Meditation

[366]   *sleepe...a representation of death*: Donne the preacher would reflect similarly in 1627: 'in the old Testament before Christ, I think there is no one metaphor so often used, as Sleepe for Death' (*Sermons*, 8.189).

[368–9]   *assiduous*: constant, regular—senses no longer current. *Melancholique fancying...affrightfull figure*: The fancy served as the outlet in sleep for mental images too fearsome to be coped with when one was awake (Bright, *Treatise of Melancholy*, 101). *threescore and ten yeeres*: Psalm 90:10. *victuall*: supply with food.

[370–3]   *sleepe is death*: Paul speaks of the dead as 'asleep' (1 Thessalonians 4:13–15); the Old Testament refers to death as 'sleeping with one's fathers' (Deuteronomy 31:16; 2 Samuel 7:12). *to tell Clocks*: to count the passing hours. *a parasceve*: Greek 'paraskevé' means 'preparation', 'readiness'. In the Gospels the word denotes the day of preparation of the Passover, on which Jesus was crucified (Matthew 27:62; Mark 15:42; Luke 23:54; John 19:14, 31, 42).

15. Expostulation

[374]   *they are thy Israel...thou their salvation*: Both phrases are frequent in the Old Testament. Occurrences of the possessive, in which God claims Israel as his people, include Exodus 3:10; 7:4; 18:1; 1 Samuel 9:16; 2 Samuel 3:18; 7:7, 10, 11. Occurrences of 'God of my | our salvation' include 1 Chronicles 16:35; Psalm 18:46; 25:5; 27:9; 38:22; 51:14; 65:5, 19, 20.

[379]   *The name of Watchmen... our profession*: Old Testament passages that apply this term to prophets and priests of God include Isaiah 52:8; 61:6; 62:6–7; Jeremiah 31:6; Micah 7:4.

15. Prayer

[382–3]   *Chappels of ease*: places of worship for the convenience of parishioners who lived at a distance from their parish churches. *defensatives*: medical antidotes.

16. Meditation

[388 heading]   *From the bels...funeralls of others*: Devotions 16–18 deal with church bells. From his chamber in the deanery of St Paul's to the southwest of the cathedral, Donne would have clearly heard the bells of its steeple (Bald, *Donne: A Life*, 427). The section on 'Ministers to Visit the Sick' in *Constitutions and Canons Ecclesiastical* (1604, 1612), H3, prescribes: 'When any...is dangerously sicke in any Parish, the Minister or Curate...shall resort unto him or her, (if the disease be not knowen or probably suspected to be infectious) to instruct and comfort them'. The section further directs the minister to ring the appropriate bell, one of three. 'When any is passing out of this life, a Bell shalbe tolled...And after the parties death (if it so fall out) there shall be rung no more but one short peale; and one other before buriall, and one other after the buriall.' The bell on which Donne reflects in Meditation 16 is the bell rung 'before buriall'.

[388–9] [mg. Magius]   *a Convenient Author*: Hieronymus Magius (1523–72), an engineer in the service of the Venetian republic, wrote his treatise on the sounds of bells, *De Tintinnabulis*, while a prisoner in Istanbul (*Constantinople*). *the harmony of the spheres*: The ancient Pythagoreans are reported to have held that the varying distances of the heavenly bodies from the Earth corresponded to tonal intervals in the musical scale, and that the rotation of these bodies in their spheres accorded with a numerical scheme that produced harmony. In *De Harmonice Mundi* (On the Harmony of the World) (1619), Kepler gave this idea new currency by undertaking to explain in musical terms the astronomical and astrological aspects of proportions in the natural world and to relate music to planetary motion.

[390] [mg. Antwerp] *I have lain . . . thirty Bels*: The cathedral of Notre Dame had thirty-three bells in its highest tower, as reported by Angelo Rocca in *De Campanis Commentarius* (Commentary on Church Bells) (1612), 81. Donne was likeliest to have been in Antwerp in the winter of 1611–12 while accompanying the Drurys. [mg. Rouen] *And neere another . . . six hundred pound*: This bell, cast in 1501 and named after its donor, Georges d'Ambroise, weighed more than eighteen tons and hung in the Tour de Beurre of Rouen cathedral. Donne probably encountered it too during his travels with the Drurys.

[391–3] *correcting Children of great persons*: Is this an allusion to the education of Prince Charles? In preaching before King Charles at Whitehall in 1626, Donne would observe that when schoolmasters 'find reason to forbeare . . . personal correction' of 'Children of great Persons', they resort to 'correcting other children in their *names*, and in their *sight*' and 'have wrought upon *good Natures* that way' (*Sermons*, 7:80). *a Bell in a Monastery*: Rocca narrates this incident, which allegedly occurred in a monastery for preaching friars in Salerno (*De Campanis*, 66–7). *by Atturney*: by proxy. *preferred*: advanced, promoted.

[394–5] *To be an incumbent . . . to be a Doctor by teaching Mortification*: Donne puns sardonically on the Latin roots of three English words: *incumbent*: a holder of an ecclesiastical appointment; in medieval Latin, one who has lain down or reclined; *Doctor*: a holder of the highest university degree in a given subject; in Latin, a teacher, an instructor; *Mortification*: dying—a sense no longer current; in Latin, 'mortificatio' is 'a killing', 'a destroying'. *I have proceeded apace in a good University . . . perchance I should have . . . come to this preferment . . . lest any Man should bribe death*: Ripple effects of the foregoing wordplay—*a good University* (*Doctor*); *this preferment* or promotion (*incumbent*); *bribe death* (*incumbent*, now with connotations of corruption in office). *he would provoke death*: In his treatise on suicide, Donne had reflected 'that in all ages, in all places, upon all occasions, men have affected it [suicide], and inclin'd to doe it'. This universality, he continues, 'prevails much with me, and delivers it from being against the Law of nature' (*Biathanatos*, ed. Sullivan, 49).

16. Expostulation

[398–9] *ringing . . . drive away evill spirits*: This popular belief was of great antiquity. *we enter . . . by the sound of Bells*: Cf. *Second Anniversary*, ll. 99–101.

[400–1] *Trumpets, at the Resurrection*: Matthew 24:31. *let us not breake the Communion of Saints, . . . not . . . pull us asunder from one another*: Donne was one of a modest number of churchmen in his day who made a point of lamenting divisions and expressing a desire for unity among Christians. The religious use of bells had a history of provoking disagreement within the Church of England. Edward VI forbade their use in administering Holy Communion, yet allowed the sermon bell (*Documentary Annals of the Reformed Church of England*, ed. Edward Cardwell (1839), 1:15). But John Whitgift, Archbishop of Canterbury under Elizabeth, defended the use of bells in divine service: 'They are a token of Christianity, when the people by them are gathered together' (*Works*, ed. John Ayre (1852), 2:38). *Vaunt*: vanguard—a no longer current sense.

[403]   *a repetition Sermon*: This was an exercise assigned to school and university students, to strengthen their memories and their facility in Latin. Having taken notes on a sermon delivered in English, a student then had to deliver a *repetition* of this sermon in Latin (W. Fraser Mitchell, *English Pulpit Oratory from Andrewes to Tillotson* (1932), 74–5). *a Deaths-head in a Ring*: Ivory or gems carved in the likeness of a human skull were popular insets for rings, serving as a *memento mori* (reminder of death). Cf. 'A Valediction. Of my name in the Window', ll. 13–14.

[404]   *historicall pictures of . . . thy Sonne*: depictions of events in Jesus's life. Donne's will bequeathed several pictures of biblical personages, but there is no mention of a picture of Jesus among them (Bald, *Donne: A Life*, 563–4). *I know thy Church . . . any supplies*: Whether to incorporate Jewish or pagan elements in defences of the faith was a vexed issue for the early Christian church.

16. Prayer

[406–10] *Temples of the holy Ghost*: 1 Corinthians 6:19. *thou takest care . . . of every haire of our head*: Luke 21:18; Acts 27:34. *the request of Dives to Abraham*: In Jesus's parable of the rich man (Latin Dives), the beggar Lazarus, and the patriarch Abraham in heaven (Luke 16:19–31), Abraham refuses to send Lazarus to warn Dives's five brothers of the hellfire that awaits them if they persist in their evil ways. Abraham maintains that 'Moses and the prophets' suffice as guides to a righteous life. God has dispensed with the limits set by Abraham by granting Donne a messenger, this dead parishioner, to direct him. *Thou killest and thou givest life*: 1 Samuel 2:6.

17. Meditation

[410–11] *Perchance hee for whom this Bell tolls . . . perchance . . . may . . . toll for mee*: This bell would be the first of the three specified in *Constitutions and Canons Ecclesiastical*, to be rung for one who is 'passing out of this life'. *he knowes not . . . I know not*: Donne may have taken a cue from Rocca's general remarks about the insensibility of many who are dying, as well as many who are alive, to the nearness of death. The bell tolling, as if in mourning, is a reminder of the 'human powerlessness of the living' (*De Campanis*, 133–4). *The Church is Catholike, universall . . . that Head . . . is my Head too, . . . that body, whereof I am a member*: These images of head, body, and members derive from Paul's recurrent metaphor of the church as the body of Christ. By contrast, the imagery of books, chapters, translations, and *Librarie* is evidently Donne's own.

[414]   *a contention... which... should ring to praiers first in the Morning*: Donne's reference remains untraced. Roman Catholic canon law, however, reveals how a dispute over such precedence could arise. The rector of a parish had the right to choose a fit person to ring the church bell, unless someone challenged his choice on the grounds of differing local tradition (*Traité de Droit Canonique*, ed. Charles de Clerq (1947), 3:23–4).

[415–16] *the dignitie of this Bell, ... The Bell doth toll for him that thinkes it doth*: Donne's train of thought far outpaces Rocca's in intensity and immediacy. Unlike Rocca's hearers who, at best, take from the bell a mournful message about the powerlessness of human beings, Donne's hearer, he himself, applies the bell's message to his own near-death condition. This in turn triggers his sense of intimate involvement with others in the precariousness of being human. *Any Mans death... I am involved in Mankinde*: This had not always been Donne's sense of himself in relation to others. In a letter probably written in 1611, Donne confided to Goodyere: 'I can allow my self to be *Animal sociale*, applicable to my company, but not *gregale*, to herd my self in every troup. It is not perfectly true which a very subtil, yet very deep wit *Averroes* says, that all mankinde hath but one soul, which informes and rules us all, as one Intelligence doth the firmament and all the Starres in it' (*Letters*, 43). *maine*: mainland.

[417–18] *affliction is a treasure... Tribulation is Treasure in the nature of it*: A pair of paradoxical transvaluations. Cf. Donne's non-paradoxical earlier formulation in the form of a comparative construction: 'no affliction | No Cross is so extreme, as to have none' ('The Crosse', ll. 14–15).

17. Expostulation

[419–20] *drawing light out of darknesse*: 2 Corinthians 4:6. *a superintendent, an over-seer, a Bishop*: A punning series of synonyms drawn from the word-stocks of Latin, English, and Greek. In ecclesiastical Latin, 'superintendere' meant 'to have oversight of'. In New Testament Greek, 'episcopós' means 'one who oversees'; the word was taken over in ecclesiastical Latin to refer to a bishop. *a confirmation*: Further punning: it was a bishop's duty to administer the rite of confirmation to persons being received into church membership in his diocese. *raise strength out of weaknesse*: 2 Corinthians 12:9.

[420–1]   *what Thunder... what hoarsenesse... thy voice to it?*: A pair of paradoxical transvaluations culminate in a statement of their underlying principle: this is God's way of countering human presuppositions. *That which I am now, you must bee then*: A warning from the dead that figures frequently in patristic and medieval literature (Rosemary Woolf, *The English Religious Lyric in the Middle Ages* (1968), 401–5).

[424]   *I goe to prepare a place for you*: John 14:3. *Thy legacies... in thy old Testament were plentie* (Job 22:25; Proverbs 3:10; Joel 2:26) *and victorie* (2 Samuel

23:10; Isaiah 25:8); *Wine and Oile* (Jeremiah 31:12; Joel 2:24), *Milke and Honie* (Exodus 3:5, 17; 13:5; 33:3; Leviticus 20:24; Numbers 13:27; 14:9; 16:13; Deuteronomy 6:3; 11:5; 26:9, 15; 27:3; 31:20; Jeremiah 11:5; 32:22; Ezekiel 20:6, 15),...*ruine of enemies* (Deuteronomy 28:7; Joshua 10:25; Judges 3:28; 1 Chronicles 14:11), *peaceful hearts* (Isaiah 32:14), *and cheerefull countenances* (Proverbs 15:13).

[425–7]   *Why hast thou...carried us, by the waies of discipline* (Job 36:10) *and mortification* (Romans 8:13; Colossians 3:5), *by the waies of mourning* (2 Corinthians 7:7) *and lamentation* (Amos 5:16)?: Donne sets aside a commonplace distinction between God's partial, prospective message in the Old Testament and the fulfilment of God's message with the coming of Christ in the New Testament. He finds no qualitative distinction to be drawn between the two Testaments in God's dealing of *miseries, sourenesse, joylesnesse,* and *ingloriousnesse* in life in this world. This finding reaches a climax in complex reflections addressed to God at the end of this passage. *thou thy selfe...art made of no substances*: The plural *substances* is the key to the particular sense of the word here: the materials of which physical things consist, and in virtue of which they exhibit certain properties. The uncreated being of the all-creating God works with such substances, but does not include any in the divine nature. *none of these circumstances*: no logical or physical adjuncts, such as time, place, manner, cause or occasion. *Essentiall joy,* and *glory Essentiall* would not be conditioned by *circumstances* in any way.

17. Prayer

[429–31]   *Balaams Asse*: Numbers 22:22–33. *the confession of Pilate*: Matthew 27:17, 22; Mark 15:2, 9, 12; Luke 23:3; John 19:14. *the Devill...in the recognition and attestation of thy Sonne*: Matthew 4:6; Luke 4:3–13. *death is the wages of sinne*: Romans 6:23. *death is the end of sicknesse*: 2 Kings 20:1; Isaiah 38:1. *into thy hands...my spirit*: Words of Jesus from the cross (Luke 23:46).

[432–4]   *I am bold...to bend my prayers...for his assistance, the voice of whose bell...this devotion*: Exercising his ministerial office by praying for the soul whose funeral bell he has heard, the dean of St Paul's simultaneously instructs and advises himself. This dual action is the first intimation that Donne may survive his illness. In a 1628 sermon he would reprise the experience: 'Is there any man, that in his chamber hears a bell toll for another man, and does not kneel down to pray for that dying man? and then when his charity breathes out upon another man, does he not also reflect upon himself, and dispose himself as if he were in the state of that dying man?' (*Sermons*, 8.174). *My God...forsaken me?*: Jesus's words from the cross (Matthew 27:46; Mark 15:34).

18. Meditation

[436–7]   *The Bell rings out...His soule is gone out*: Donne reflects on the death knell, the second of the three bells to be rung for the dying and the dead. As in the *Second Anniversary*, ll. 99–101, this bell is interpreted as summoning the soul to enter heaven: *the possession of his better estate*. Meditation 18, however, is less assured than the earlier poem with respect to the soul's nature and fate after death.

[437–9]   *meere Philosophers … will tell me … the soule is … nothing, no seperable substance, that over-lives the body*: Aristotle expounds but denies Empedocles' doctrine that the soul is a kind of harmony of bodily elements (*De anima*, 1.3, 408A). Pietro Pomponazzi, the author of *De immortalitate animi* (On the Immortality of the Soul) (1516), a commentary on Aristotle's *De anima*, maintained that Aristotle had clearly argued that the soul was mortal (1534 edn, 76). *But if my soule were no more than the soule of a beast, I could not thinke so; that soule that can reflect on it selfe … is more than so*: Donne reproduces both the form and the content of Aquinas's proof of the immortality of the human soul based on its capacity for self-reflection, which the soul of an animal does not have (*Summa Theologica*, 1.75.a3).

[439–40]   *If I will aske … Philosophicall Divines*: Augustine distinguishes four opinions about the union of the soul and the body in a lengthy letter written to Jerome in 415 on the origin of the human soul (no. 166 in *Epistolae* [Letters], chap. 3, secs. 10–15, *Patrologia Latina*, 33:725–6). *some … will tell me … and … some will tell me*: Donne freely appropriates Augustine's general referent, 'they who say' (dicuntur), to shape his account. In considering how the soul gets into the body to begin with, Donne draws on the first two of the four opinions in Augustine: 'whether all subsequent souls are propagated from that one given to the first man, or whether new ones are now created for each individual' (chap. 3, sec. 7; *PL*, 33:723). The latter alternative, *immediate infusion from God*, became the dominant teaching of the Church.

[440–1]   *If I will aske … what becomes of the soules of the righteous, at the departing thereof from the body, I shall bee told by some … By some … By some*: In considering what happens to the soul when it leaves the body, Donne distinguishes three opinions, one of which is found in Augustine's letter: 'if, after the natural generation that comes to it from Adam, the soul is regenerated in Christ …, it will attain rest after the death of the body, and will receive back its body for its glory' (chap. 2, sec. 5; *PL*, 33:721). Augustine did not subscribe to either of the other opinions Donne rehearses: (1) the soul's purification in purgatory; (2) the soul's immediate reception into heaven after death. Donne himself rejected the Roman Catholic doctrine of purgatory (Canon 30, Session 25, in *Canons and Decrees of the Council of Trent* (1888)); see *Sermons*, 5.260; 6.250; 7.94, 124, 176). But Donne did hold that the redeemed soul, after death, goes immediately to heaven (see Appendix A, in *Divine Poems*, ed. Gardner, rev. edn, 114–17).

[441–2]   *St. Augustine studied the Nature of the soule; and he sent … to St. Jerome, to consult of some things*: This and the two following italicized phrases occasion some interpretive difficulty. Here Donne evidently refers to Augustine's second letter to Jerome in 415 (no. 167), where in an early passage he says that the wrong question had preoccupied him in his previous letter (no. 166)—the problem of how the soul enters the body: 'How to act in the present life and how it must be spent if we are to attain eternal life, this is the question to be turned about, not what I had thought was to be sought regarding the soul'. Donne marks the stark shift in outlook with the phrase: *But he satisfies himselfe with this.* In Augustine's letter, however, what immediately follows is an anecdote illustrating his shift. A man fell into a well where the water was deep enough to break his fall, but not so deep as to cover his mouth and stifle his speech. A second man comes by, sees the first man's plight, and asks how he fell in. The first man answers, 'I pray you, think by what means you can get me out of here; do not ask how I fell in here' (*PL*, 33:733). Donne's counterpart to this anecdote is the line: *It is the going out... that concernes us.* The intervening italicized sentence, *Let the departure of my soule... my reason*, sounds like Augustine in tone and content, but no such formulation proves traceable in his works. The ostensible quotation, a distillation of the meaning of Augustine's anecdote, must be Donne's construct.

[446–7] *a kennell*: a gutter. *Rubbidge*: rubbish. *precipitation*: sudden descent.

[447–8] *Man... hath a soule of sense, and a soule of vegetation... when this... immortall soule... departs, it carries all with it*: Aquinas assimilated Aristotle's account of the 'vegetative', 'animal', and 'rational' souls unique to humans (*De anima*, 2.3) and adapted it to his theology. In the infant and the child, the vegetative and animal souls are in evidence before the rational soul is. But at death, when the rational soul leaves the body, the other two souls expire. Only the rational soul continues to exist; it alone is independent of the body (*Summa Theologica*, 1.78.21, 75.23, 26).

18. Expostulation

[450–1] *the Gentiles were over-full, of... respect to the memory of the dead... an... over-studious preserving of the memories, and the Pictures of some dead persons*: The apocryphal book, Wisdom of Solomon 14:12–17, gives two examples of how idols emerged as human inventions. A father, grief-stricken by a child's death, made an image of the child, honoring as 'a god what was once a dead human being' and transmitting 'secret rites and initiations' to his descendants. In another case, subjects who lived too far from their kings to pay them homage in person erected images of these kings, zealously honoring them as if they were the kings themselves. With time such customary practices became laws that mandated image worship.

[452] *a picture should come... to bee a God, in 60. yeeres after it is made*: The source is the *Commentarius in Librum Sapientiae* (Commentary on the Book of Wisdom) by Robert Holcot: 'Formerly there was thought to be more divine power in antique images than in new ones, on account of their age. They used to say of old images that they would share their power in the sixtieth year after their making' (*Commentarius* (1489 edn), 282). *Those Images of Men... and some Idols of other things... are... called... dead*: 'their hope is among dead things' (Wisdom of Solomon 13:10).

[454–7]   *God will not suffer his holy officers*: Leviticus 21:11–12. *raising… my dead brother*: Genesis 38:8. *Trees without fruit… twice dead*: Jude 12. *a second death*: Revelation 20:6, 14; 21:8. *the Egyptians… dead men*: Exodus 12:33. *ushers*: assistants to a schoolmaster or headmaster—a now rare term.

[459–60] *death… wages of sinne*: Romans 6:23 (phrasing inverted). *Commination*: threat of divine retribution.

18. Prayer

[463–4]   *death as the cure of my disease*: A paradoxical transvaluation. *prevent*: come before—a sense no longer current. *exaltation*: high point. *mud-walls*: Cf. 'The Litanye', ll. 19–20. Donne's image further literalizes God's creation of the first man, Adam, from 'the dust of the earth' (Genesis 2:7).

[465]   *men dispute, whether thy Saints… know what we in earth… stand in need of*: Aquinas acknowledges the matter to be disputable. He then distinguishes between the saints' knowledge of God in heaven (complete to the full capacities of their created intellects) and the saints' knowledge of what God knows (necessarily incomplete, as these intellects are creations of God). In particular, it is no part of the perfection of the created intellect in heaven, nor is it that intellect's desire in heaven, to know others' thoughts and deeds, since it is fully satisfied with its knowledge of God (*Summa Theologica*, 1.89.8). Luther concludes that 'the sleeping saints… do not know what is going on' on Earth (*Lectures on Genesis* (*c*.1541), chaps. 21–5, in *Luther's Works*, gen. ed. Lehmann, 4:316). In 1627 Donne would reduce the question to what he took to be its essentials: 'Whatsoever conduces to Gods glory, or our happinesse, we shall certainly know in heaven' (*Sermons*, 8.100).

[466]   *wee… doe know what thy Saints in heaven lacke yet*: The reunion of their souls with their bodies as part of the general reunion at the last judgement. *thou hast affoorded us… wee may pray for them*: Donne's emphasis on the Church of England's permission (not obligation) to pray for the dead is precisely calculated. The Book of Common Prayer used in his day contains three such petitions in their behalf: that 'with them we may be partakers of thy heavenly kingdom' (Prayer for the Church Militant), that 'we and all thy whole Church may obtain remission of our sins' (Holy Communion), 'that we, with all those that are departed in the true faith of thy holy name, may have our perfect consummation and bliss' (Burial of the Dead) (*Book of Common Prayer* (1559), 264, 312).

[467–8]   *his last office… a Judge*: Peter preached thus of Jesus (Acts 10:42). *time… Eternitie*: Donne appropriates Paul's verb phrase, 'swallowed up', in 1 Corinthians 15:54 and 2 Corinthians 5:4. *all men ordained to salvation… be one intire and everlasting sacrifice to thee*: Donne adapts the post-Communion prayer: 'here we offer and present unto thee, O Lord, ourselves, our souls and bodies, to be a reasonable, holy, and lively sacrifice unto thee' (*Book of Common Prayer* (1559), 264).

19. Meditation

[470: title and following text] *the concoction...in these waters*: In the medical litera-
ture of Donne's day, 'concoction' denoted the morbid matter that accumu-
lated in a patient's body before it was excreted in urine, spittle, sweat, or
pus. Physicians were directed not to purge until the morbid matter had
concocted. Such separating of 'that which is putrid and corrupt...by
meanes of the naturall heate' of the body was a sign of prospective recovery
(John Hart, *The Anatomie of Urines* (1625), 21–2). *any land in this Sea*:
Donne analogizes the *concoction* in his body to the receding waters after the
great flood sent by God (Genesis 8:3).

[471–3] *pretermission*: omission, overlooking. *pregnant*: resourceful. *July-flowers*:
gilly-flowers—clove-scented blossoms. *precontracts*: agreements entered
into prior to more binding contracts—especially, marriages.

[474–6] *There are of them...will pardon*: The extended reflections that follow may
again have Prince Charles in view. See Dave Gray and Jeanne Shami,
'Political Advice in Donne's *Devotions*', *Modern Language Quarterly* (1989),
50:337–56. *Justice...richly manured*: A swipe at officials who take bribes.
manured: cultivated—a sense no longer current. *syndicated with Commissions*:
officially censured. *of Court mediation*: serving as go-betweens from one
courtier to another. Donne's reactivated satirical vein may be taken as a
further sign of his impending recovery.

19. Expostulation

[480–1] *a direct God,...a literall God,...a figurative, a metaphoricall God too*: This
effusive tribute to the metaphors, allegories, hyperboles, and stylistic elo-
quence of the Scriptures has an influential precedent in Augustine. After
distinguishing 'words', 'things', and 'signs' as ordinary constituents of
texts, Augustine affirms the uniqueness of the literal sense of the Bible:
when its words refer to things, those things also refer to other things. This
uniqueness is due to God's use of physical reality to intimate and image
spiritual reality. Thus there is an inseparable 'parabolical' or metaphorical
sense within the literal sense of Scripture (*De doctrina Christiana* [*Of
Christian Doctrine*], 1.2–3; 2.1–6; 3.5–10). *peregrinations*: journeyings to
foreign places. *eloquutions* (elocutions): eloquent orations. *prophane
Authors...thou art the dove*: An example of how things in Scripture refer to
other things: pagan authors correlate with the creeping serpent, the form
God imposed on Satan after he deceived Adam and Eve (Genesis 3:14); the
Holy Spirit correlates with the dove sent down by God at the baptism of
Jesus, to certify his divine sonship (Matthew 3:16; Mark 1:10; Luke 3:22;
John 1:32).

[483] *Inquisition*: inquiry. *there are places, that...Jerome and Augustine...scarce
beleeve...of one another, that they understood*: Augustine initiated this dis-
pute in 394–5, criticizing Jerome for asserting that Paul in Galatians con-
doned dissimulation by Peter for the purpose of advancing the faith among

Jews as well as Gentiles: 'If this [a strategic resort to dissimulation] is once admitted,...the authority of the divine Scriptures becomes unsettled, so that everyone may believe what he likes, and reject what he does not like' (Letter 28, 1. 5). In 397, the nettled Jerome attempted to clarify what he had said, in turn accusing Augustine of dissimulation (Letter 40, 1–5). Augustine replied in 403, urging that Jerome devote himself to refining his Latin translation of the Greek version of the Old Testament (Septuagint), which had already yielded much spiritual richness, rather than dwelling on textual complexities arising from the Hebrew text of the Old Testament (Letter 71). Jerome replied in 404, defending in detail his understanding of the respective cultic practices of Jews and Christians in the early church (Letter 75). Augustine's reply to Jerome in 405 reveals that the two men were regaining a measure of mutual respect. It equally clarifies the nature of the standoff resulting from their differing priorities in the study of Scripture: Jerome sought historical and linguistic exactness; Augustine sought timeless spiritual truth (Letter 82).

[484–5]   *Neither art thou a...Metaphoricall God, in thy Word only, but...the stile of thy works...is Metaphoricall*: This extension of the figurative mode from God's verbal expressions to God's actions reveals Donne's complete alignment with Augustine's principles of Scriptural interpretation. *Circumcision...a figure of Baptisme*: Acts 10:45–8. Augustine notes the connection between circumcision and baptism (*PL*, 44:504). *that purity...in the new Jerusalem*: Revelation 21:10, 24, 27. *How often...doth thy Sonne call himself a way* (John 14:6) *and a light* (John 8:12; 9:5; 12:46) *and a gate* (John 14:6) *and a Vine* (John 15:1, 5) *and bread* (John 6:35, 41, 48, 51, 58). *Son of God, or of Man*: Matthew 16:13, 16; 22:42; 26:63, 64; 27:54.

[486]   *This hath occasioned...such a kind of language, as thou wast pleased to speake*: Donne alludes to a standard medieval practice, the fourfold interpretation of Scripture according to its literal, allegorical, moral, and anagogical senses. In his preaching, however, Donne usually stresses literal interpretation, and warns: 'though it be ever lawfull, and often times very usefull, for the raising and exaltation of our devotion...to induce the *diverse senses* that the Scriptures doe admit, yet this may not be admitted, if there may be danger thereby, to neglect or weaken the *literall sense* it selfe. For there is no necessity...of finding more than necessary senses; for, the more *lights* there are, the more *shadows* are also cast by those many lights' (*Sermons*, 3.353).

[487–93]   *residences*: residues—the 'concocted' waste matter being expelled from Donne's body. *presemted...the afflictions and calamities of this life...in the name of waters, and deepe waters, and Seas of waters*: Exodus 15:10; 2 Samuel 22:17; Job 3:24, 30:14; Psalm 69:1, 2; 124:4. 5; 144:7; Isaiah 28:2; Lamentations 3:54; Ezekiel 32:14; Amos 5:24; Jonah 2:5; Habakkuk 3:15. *the first life...was in waters*: Genesis 1:20. *Gennesaret...a Sea*: Numbers 34:11; Joshua 12:3; 13:27; Mark 6:49, 53. *the Mediterranean Sea...the great Sea*: Joshua 15:12; 23:4; Ezekiel 47:19. 20; 48:28; Daniel 7:2. *thou,*

O God, art my strength: Psalm 19:14; 27:1; 28:7; 46:1; 81:1; 118:14; 140:7; 144:1. *I finde this added*: Wisdom of Solomon 14:5.

[499–500]   *Thy Prophet from thee*: Jeremiah. *that which my Physitians call a cloud*: Cloud (clod) here means a condensed mass—a sense no longer current. Donne is using *cloud* as a synonym for *concoction*. *Thy great Seale…the raine-bow*: Genesis 9:13.

19. Prayer

[502]   *God,…thou passedst over infinite millions of generations, before…a Creation of this world*: Henry Cuffe, whose *Differences of the Ages of Mans Life* (1607) was in Donne's library, says that this was the teaching of 'learned Rabbins' who acknowledged that 'God did not rashly, nor without great deliberation make the world on this fashion rather than any other…he sawe he might have made it many other waies, and sooner,…alluding,…to *Gods* counsell-taking…touching the time and maner of the worlds creation' (*Differences*, 21–2).

[503–8]   *rest of a Sabbath*: Genesis 2:2–3. *deposed*: committed for safekeeping—a sense no longer current. *Thy Priests…steps in the Temple*: Only in Ezekiel's vision of the Temple that the Israelites are to rebuild after returning from captivity in Babylon are there stairs leading up from the four gates to the building's central portion (Ezekiel 40:22, 26, 31, 34, 37, 40; 43:17). God had prohibited any steps to the altar that he commanded Moses and the Israelites to build (Exodus 20:25). There are no stairs in the description of the Temple built by King Solomon (1 Kings 6). *Angels…ladder*: Genesis 28:12. *thy selfe…Adam in Paradise*: Genesis 3:8. *Sodome in thine anger*: Genesis 19:24–5. *a thousand yeere in a day*: Psalm 90:4. *pawne*: pledge. *fatnesse*: fullness, plenty. *earnest*: a pledge of something to be received in greater abundance in the future.

20. Meditation

[510–11]   *an ancient way…upon a Cube*: A reference to the form and purpose of the so-called herm—a type of public sculpture—in classical Rome. It took the form of a bust mounted on a rectangular pedestal. The purpose of these stylized likenesses was to commemorate citizens who had rendered notable service to the Roman state. Cicero approved of their sparing use (*De Legibus* [On Laws], 2.26.66). Donne's construal is, in his words, *Hierogliphique* (a pictorial representation of meaning): lacking hands, the herms cannot be bribed.

[512–13]   [mg. Augustine] *matrimonie is scarce…matrimonie…having of Children*: So declares Augustine in *De Bono Conjugali* (On the Good of Marriage), chap. 5 (*PL*, 40.376).

[513–14]   *the art of proving, Logique,…the Art of perswading, Rhetorique*: The double metaphor of logic (or dialectic) as a closed fist and rhetoric as an open hand was commonplace in early modern treatises on these subjects. This metaphorical contrast of the modes of proof and persuasion was attributed to Zeno of Citium (Cicero, *Orator*, 32.113; *De Finibus*, 2.6.17; Quintilian,

Institutio Oratoria, 2.20). See Wilbur Samuel Howell, *Logic and Rhetoric in England, 1500–1700* (1956; rpt. 1961). *All things... his hand*: John 3:35. *ofner called the Lord of Hosts, than... all other names*: A comprehensive biblical concordance quickly confirms this assertion.

[516–17] *substraction*: A variant of 'subtraction'—here with the meaning of withdrawing something essential. *providing strength, by increasing weakenesse*: Like letting blood, administering harsh laxatives was often observed to weaken a patient. Yet for centuries the belief that a sick body required purging (purification) remained stronger than any misgivings—such as Donne expresses here. *attenuation*: weakening of the force of a disease, by dilution. *exinanition*: exhaustion. These stages of purgation as a medical procedure are detailed in Elyot, *The Castel of Helth* (1541), 52b–53a; and Philip Moore, *The Hope of Health* (1565), 56b–57.

20. Expostulation

[518] *quarrels, for spirituall precedences*: bitter rivalries for promotions to higher ecclesiastical offices. *uncharitable disputations...faith or repentance,...faith, and works*: The Lutheran doctrine of justification by faith held that Christ did all in the act of salvation, and the saved soul nothing; the soul was saved through trust and belief in Christ as Saviour. A standard example was the thief crucified with Jesus, who appealed to him and was told, 'Today shalt thou be with me in Paradise' (Luke 23:43). Opponents objected to the example as atypical, one that could not usefully serve most Christians. Roman Catholics held that repentance (methodized in the sacrament of penance) and the performing of good works contributed to a soul's salvation. The Church of England held that repentance and good works were inseparable from a justifying faith in Christ as Saviour, and additionally served as signs that such faith was genuine. *take place*: have precedence.

[519] *a perfit naturall man...a perfit civill man...him that is perfitly spirituall*: This three-way categorization was conventional. It distinguished (1) humans in the state of nature, including the elementary social arrangements that are associated today with 'tribalism'; (2) humans in civil society, such as the various political systems of Greek and Roman antiquity; and (3) humans in a Christian polity, whatever its form of governance. Donne observes that the underlying rationale of all these modes of organization is to enable the effective taking of action.

[521–3] *dilatorie*: slow, delaying. *superstitious*: over-scrupulous—a sense no longer current. *the same wise and royall servant*: King Solomon. *Their hands are called all themselves...in thy Word*: Donne would repeat this linguistic observation in his first sermon before King Charles (3 April 1625): 'there is no *phrase* oftner in the *Scriptures*, than that *God* delivered his people, in the *hand* of *Moses*, and the *hand* of *David*, and the *hand* of the *Prophets*: all their Ministeriall office is called the *Hand*' (*Sermons*, 6.245).

[525–6] *As hee that would describe...a perfit circle*: Donne's compass images are a prominent feature of his thought; cf. 'A Valediction' ('As Vertuous men passe mildly away'), ll. 25–35; 'Obsequies to the Lord Harrington', ll. 107–10; *Sermons*, 8:97.

[527] [mg. Galen] *To take physicke, . . . not according to the right method, is dangerous*: Claudius Galen, a theorist, observer, and wide-ranging practitioner of the art of medicine in the second century CE, left a voluminous corpus of writings in Greek. Early printed editions of Galen's works abound, but even the most inclusive are not complete; the treatises, moreover, circulated most widely in Latin translations. The nugget-like phrasing of Donne's three attributions to Galen in Expostulation 20 suggests that he was doing what early modern readers and authors often did: either making use of an alphabetized collection of excerpts, often paraphrased, known as an 'epitome', or consulting an index to Galen's works that had brief phrasal additions attached to its entries. Andreas Lacuna's Latin *Epitome of Galen* offers two parallels to the foregoing pronouncement: 'Medicine is not to be a conjectural art' and 'To set the medical art in order, one must accurately know the minutiae of the human body' (*Commentarius in Hippocratem*, 1.1; *De Constitutione artis medicae*, 1, 11a, in Lacuna, *Epitome Galeni Operum* (1551)).

[527] *O Lord, I decline not . . . to make my confession to him, . . . the power of absolution*: When its supremacy as a national church was constituted under Henry VIII, the Church of England continued to insist on the importance of penance, which ordinarily included confession of one's sins to a priest and the priest's pronouncing of absolution. Yet it was recognized that a priest was not always to be had. Thus the paramount emphasis in penance fell on the sinner's wholehearted repentance in full belief that Christ's death was the sole and sufficient basis on which God forgave sins and remitted otherwise deserved damnation (*Formularies of Faith*, ed. Charles Lloyd (1856), xxiii, 97–8, 260–1). Under Edward VI and Elizabeth, penance was grouped in Church of England formularies with other non-sacramental practices as being 'partly . . . states of life alowed in the scriptures', 'partly growen of the corrupt folowing of the Apostles' (Charles Hardwick, *A History of the Articles of Religion* (1904), 322–5). However, a significant turn towards reaffirming the value of penance emerges in the *Articles of Religion agreed upon by the Archbishops and Bishops, and the rest of the Cleargie of Ireland* (1615), with the intent of 'establishing . . . consent touching true Religion' (Hardwick, *A History*, 383). Donne the preacher would emphasize the value of private confession (*Sermons*, 7.163).

[528] [mg. Galen] *Physicke may be made so pleasant . . . but not so pleasant . . . the vertue and nature of the medicine bee extinguished*: This formulation is apparently an epitome of a passage in 'De Simplicium Medicamentorum Facultatibus' (On the Properties of Simple Medicines), 1.4. Of 'simple medicines' (ones consisting of a single substance), Galen remarks that when they are administered at medium temperatures, they are 'pleasant and agreeable to us'. But, he cautions, as the medicine takes effect in our bodies, 'a very great pleasure arises'. 'If one remains too long in this state, as troublesome things are gradually evacuated, . . . these things may cause an outflowing of the soul, and at length lead to death' (*Opera Galeni* (1551), 1040).

[529] [mg. Galen] *a great Physitian…his practise*: Lacuna's *Epitome* contains this formulation drawn from Galen's *Commentarium in Epidemis* (Commentary on Epidemics), 1.2.50: 'A doctor ought above all to cure, so that he sets the illness right; if not, at least he should certainly not make it worse' (*Epitome Galeni Operum* (1551)). This formulation is recognizable as a tenet in the so-called Hippocratic Oath taken by physicians when they are certified to begin their practice.

[530] *a Cup of Stupefaction,…his paine*: The drink offered to Jesus just prior to his crucifixion is described as 'wine mingled with myrrh' in Mark 15:23 (Donne's marginal reference) and as 'vinegar mingled with gall' in Matthew 27:34. In both sources Jesus tastes the mixture and refuses it. Later, on the cross, Jesus is given drink from a sponge filled with vinegar: Matthew 27:48; Luke 23:36; John 19:29.

20. Prayer

[532] *God,…made them one flesh*: Genesis 2:24. *wouldest have them…one soule*: Cf. 'The Extasie', ll. 41–4. *accidents of this world*: chance occurrences.

[534–6] *peccant*: unhealthy, morbid. *Thou hast raised up certaine hils…safe, from these inundations of sin*: Donne reverts to his earlier analogy between his illness and the great flood sent by God upon the Earth. While the *hils* are easily understood as areas of spiritual high ground that afford a soul safety, this extension into allegory has no Scriptural basis. *Let thy Spirit…I shall be cleane*: By ascribing *true contrition, and sorrow* to the Holy Spirit's agency within him, not to his own initiative, Donne recasts a Roman Catholic belief in the efficacy of a sinner's contrition, giving it a formulation compatible with Reformed doctrine.

21. Meditation

[538–41] *Man needed a Helper*: Genesis 2:18. *A man…pressed to death*: 'Peine forte et dure' (strong and hard punishment) in English common law could be applied to an indicted person who refused to plead innocent or guilty. Heavier and heavier weights would be placed on his chest until a plea was entered or suffocation occurred. *preferment*: advancement. *station*: position in the world, vocation, office.

[542–3] *How many…they are raised to?*: The following satirical reflections on appointees to civil offices, who may be undermined by rumour and gossip or may be underqualified (or overqualified) for the appointment they hold, are perhaps offered for Prince Charles's benefit. Their origin, however, probably traces to the twelve years (1602–14) following Donne's marriage when he sought secular employment. *No corner… no vacuity*: It was long believed that a total absence of matter, a vacuum, was impossible. But empirical investigations were underway, and Evangelista Torricelli would devise the first vacuum-creating mechanism in 1643.

[544–6] *I seeme to stand...Earth moves round*: This somewhat laboured joke is in
marked contrast with the brooding on the heliocentric universe in the
*First Anniversary. as in the Heavens...many Epicicles, and other lesser
Circles*: The seven known planets in the Ptolemaic system were thought to
have circular orbits. Revisions of the Ptolemaic system that eventuated in
the radically different Copernican system made use of *Epicicles* (circles
within circles) in transitional attempts to reconcile recent planetary
observations with the pre-existing world picture. In solid geometry a
lesser circle is one whose cutting plane yields a section of a sphere smaller
than a great circle, one that passes through the diameter of a sphere.
Lesser Circles in astronomy included the tropics of Cancer and Capricorn,
and the Arctic and Antarctic parallels (Thomas Hill, *The School of Skill*
(1599), 65, 68).

21. Expostulation

[548–51] *a glasse*: mirror. *the Species*: outward appearance or aspect, visible form or
image—senses common in the seventeenth century. *Resurrection of my
body... Resurrection of my soule;...of both together hereafter*: An allusion to
the resurrection of the earthly body to heavenly glory anticipated by Paul
in 1 Corinthians 15:47, 49. The Church of England service for the Burial of
the Dead consisted largely of an extended reading of 1 Corinthians 15:20–
58 (*Book of Common Prayer* (1559), 311–12). *thy Martyrs under the Altar
presse thee*: A loose paraphrase of Revelation 6:9, 10. *Lazarus...foure daies*:
John 11:17. *Winds*: Ezekiel 37:9, 10. *Chariots*: Jeremiah 4:13. *falls of waters*:
Isaiah 19:5; Revelation 1:15. *John Baptist...a cryer*: Matthew 3:3.

[555–6] *I hearken...in Conventicles*. A declaration of fidelity to the Church of
England and its *Ordinances* of preaching and the sacraments (baptism,
Holy Communion) as well as a repudiation of so-called separatists, who
gathered for worship in *Conventicles*—places and procedures of their own
choosing. *Cains murder did so*: Genesis 4:10. *waters are afflictions*:1 Kings
22:27; 2 Chronicles 18:26.

21. Prayer

[563–7] *receive the sacrifice of my humble thanks*: A paraphrase of part of the first
sentence of the post-Communion prayer in the Order for Holy Communion:
'accept this our sacrifice of praise and thanksgiving, most humbly beseech-
ing thee' (*Book of Common Prayer* (1559), 264). *this bodily rising...an ear-
nest of a second resurrection from sinne, and of a third, to everlasting glory*: Cf.
the typology of *three Births* invoked in the dedicatory letter to Prince
Charles that prefaces the *Devotions*. *grow in stature, in the sight of men*: Luke
2:52. *the Messenger of Satan*: 2 Corinthians 12:7. *I begge...my daily bread*:
Matthew 6:11. *bread of sorrow*: Deuteronomy 16:3; 1 Kings 22:27; Hosea
9:4. *the bread of life*: John 6:35, 41, 48. *produce fowle, and fish, and beasts, and
wormes*: Genesis 1:20–5.

22. Meditation

[569–74]   *How ruinous a farme...the ground over-spread with weeds*: An ironical upending of the medieval and early modern concept of the virtuous soul as an enclosed garden (Latin 'hortus conclusus'). Although this image was applied to the Virgin Mary's sinless conception of Jesus, it also served to figure virtuous souls more generally. The garden's emblematic furnishings might include a central well or fountain (pure source of life), symmetrical beds of plantings (flowers and trees of the Bible) divided by four pathways radiating from the centre (a microcosm of the four corners of the Earth) and surrounded by a protective wall (the soul's buffer against incursions from the world). Donne by contrast depicts the human condition as that of a hard-pressed tenant farmer struggling to make ends meet for himself and his family on a weed-infested allotment of poor soil. *his brow sweat*: Genesis 3:19.

[574–6]   *sometimes the very situation releeves*: Early modern treatments of 'husbandry' (farming) included discussion of certain problems that were amenable to solution by natural means. For example, the *hanger* of a *hill* (woods and underbrush covering a hillside) might of itself reduce excessive dampness, while burning the upper *turfe* of some ground could restore fertility to soil. So could mixing in other kinds of soil such as *Marle* (a loose soil consisting of clay mixed with carbonate of lime) or *slimie* (oily) *sand* (*The Whole Art and Trade of Husbandry*, trans. Barnabe Googe (1614), 17a–b).

[576–80]   *But I have taken a farme...that...can afford it selfe no helpe*: Unlike the possibly self-ameliorating problems of poor soils, the body's ailments do not correct themselves. They often require drastic and risky interventions that only a physician can perform, such as amputating a limb or administering medicine made with mummified human flesh. Donne allegorized the latter in a letter to Goodyere (late 1607?): 'When our naturall inborn preservative is corrupted or wasted, and must be restored by a like extracted from other bodies, the chief care is that the Mummy have in it no excelling quality, but an equally digested temper: And such is true vertue' (*Letters*, 97–8). *to cure..., is...reserved for the great Physitian*: Jesus refers to his earthly mission as that of 'a physician' for sinners (Matthew 9:12; Mark 2:17; Luke 5:31).

22. Expostulation

[580]   *What Hippocrates, what Galen*: Hippocrates of Cos (*c.*460–*c.*370 BCE), known today as the 'father of Western medicine', was a Greek physician who based his medical practice in direct observation of the human body, believing that it was to be treated as a whole and not just a collection of parts. He accurately described the symptoms of epilepsy and pneumonia, and promoted a healing regimen of rest, fresh air, good diet, and good

hygiene. His writings have come down to posterity in a series of apho-
risms (quotable formulations), on which his successor Galen wrote
commentaries.

[581–8] *sinne... is in the union of the body and soule*: Donne's explicit yet enigmatic
definition accords with the wording in Article 9, 'Of Original or Birth Sin',
of the Church of England's Thirty-Nine Articles: 'it is the fault and cor-
ruption of the nature of every man, that naturally is engendered of the
offspring of Adam, whereby man is very far gone from original righteous-
ness, and is of his own nature inclined to evil'. Two heretical extremes were
to be avoided in accounting for the transmission of original sin: locating it
in the body alone (which would entail that the body was intrinsically evil)
and locating it in the soul alone (which would entail that God, the creator
of souls, was a creator of evil). *sinne tooke occasion by the Law*: Romans 7:8.
effigiate: present a likeness of.

22. Prayer

[591–3] *Thou enlargedest Hezekiahs lease for fifteene yeeres*: Isaiah 38:5. *Thou
renewedst Lazarus his lease, for a time, which we know not*: Jesus raised
Lazarus from the dead (John 11:42, 43), a miracle whose impact is recorded
(John 12:9–11), but not how long Lazarus lived thereafter. *impeccable*:
exempt from the possibility of sinning. *fountaine of life*: Revelation 21:6.

23. Meditation

[596–8] *in the Citie, ... when the Bell hath rung, to cover your fire, and rake up the
embers*: In medieval and early modern times, a bell known as the
'couvre-feu' (French 'cover-fire', which became English 'curfew') was
rung in cities at nightfall. This bell gave general notice that it was time
to place a heavy lid over the fire and coals on one's hearth, to prevent the
dwelling from catching fire while its occupants slept. *a propriety, a Meum
et Tuum*: legal terminology with the literal meaning of 'an individual
right of ownership, a mine and yours'. *preoccupated*: engrossed, to the
exclusion of other things. *fit of the stone*: acute pain brought on by kidney
stones or gall bladder stones. *he that hath felt... the tooth-ach*: Donne per-
haps alludes to the severe toothache that Augustine records in *Confessions*,
9.6.12.

[600] *put the longest day, and the longest night... into one naturall, unnatural day*:
Originally, the 'natural day' was identified with the solar day (the number
of hours of daylight in a given day); and the 24-hour period consisting of
the solar day and the following night was called the 'artificial day'. Donne's
naturall, unnaturall day is an imaginary construct. It pairs the longest con-
tinuous period of light in one day (June 21) with the longest continuous
period of darkness in one day (December 21). Conjoining these two peri-
ods of light and darkness, each lasting almost 18 hours, would yield a day
of 36 hours.

23. Expostulation

[607–9]   *how often…relapses?*: Prominent instances of the Israelites' disobeying of God include the worship of the golden calf punished by a massacre of the principal offenders (Exodus 32); the idol worship and other evil-doing punished with forced exile from their homeland (Jeremiah 12–18); and the recurrence of idol worship punished with the destruction of Jerusalem (Ezekiel 4–7). *their murmurings against…Ministers*: Leaders and prophets whom the Israelites disrespected and disregarded include Moses, Samuel, Jeremiah, Ezekiel, Hosea, and Amos. *O my God…murmuring?*: Instances are noted in Exodus 16:7–9, 12 and Numbers 14:27; 17:5, 10. *The Magistrate is the garment in which thou apparellest thy selfe*: Paul's directions to Titus for teaching new Christians 'the doctrine of God our Saviour in all things' include this precept: 'Put them in mind to be subject to principalities and powers, to obey magistrates, to be ready to every good work' (Titus 2:10; 3:1). Donne's own divine-right formulation would gratify his particular addressee, Prince Charles.

[617–23]   *An idolatry…punished with the slaughter of twenty foure thousand delinquents*: Numbers 25:9. *At last Reuben, and Gad satisfie them…and so the Army returned without bloud*: Joshua 22:26–34. *hee that hath sinned…hath weighed God and the Devill in a ballance…if he returne to his sinne, he decrees for Satan; he prefers…Satan before God…And a contempt wounds deeper, than a blasphemy* [mg. Tertullian]: Donne excerpts and recasts a passage in Tertulllian's *De Poenitentia* (On Repentance), 5: 'he does not sin lightly against the Lord who, after he had by repentance renounced His rival the devil,…raises him back up by his return to him…For he, who has known both, appears to…have pronounced judgment that he [the devil] is the better one, to whom again he prefers to belong…Thus he is shown not only to be contumacious toward the Lord, but also ungrateful' (*PL*, 1:1345–6). *pardon my brother seventy times seven*: Matthew 18:22.

23. Prayer

[626–30]   *Jelousie*: God styles himself 'a jealous God' in Exodus 20:5; Deuteronomy 5:9; Ezekiel 39:25; and Zechariah 1:14; 8:2. *Seales of Reconciliation to thee…thy Sacraments and thy Seales*: Reconciliation with God would have been effectuated in his baptism as an infant by his sponsors' pledging on his behalf to 'forsake the devil and all his works'. Reconciliation is affirmed in Holy Communion in a prayer offered by the priest after the distribution of the bread and wine. Its pertinent phrases read: 'Almighty and everliving God, we most heartily thank thee,…which have duly received these holy mysteries,…and dost assure us thereby of thy favor and goodness toward us, and that we be…heirs through hope of thy everlasting kingdom' (*Book of Common Prayer* (1559), 273, 265). *forsake mee not*: Psalm 38:21. *Compunction*: pricking of the conscience or heart, regretfulness after doing wrong. *Hymenaeus* 'made shipwreck' of 'faith, and a good conscience' by blaspheming against God (1 Timothy 1:20).

INDEX OF TITLES AND FIRST LINES

INDEX OF PROSE WORKS AND NAMES